EQUITY & TRUSTS IN AUSTRALIA

THIRD EDITION

Equity and Trusts in Australia offers an accessible introduction to the principles of Australian equity and trusts law for both undergraduate and Juris Doctor students, linking key doctrines to their wider relationship with the law. The text covers foundational topics of equity and trusts law, including the nature of equity, fiduciary relationships, the rights, powers and duties of trustees, and trust structures.

The third edition has been fully revised to include recent landmark decisions and a new chapter on termination and variation of trusts. Each chapter concludes with a guide to the online resources, which encourage students to extend their knowledge of the content through further reading, practice problems and discussion topics.

Written by a team of experienced authors, *Equity and Trusts in Australia* is an ideal text for students undertaking this area of study for the first time.

A Sourcebook on Equity and Trusts in Australia is also available and provides cases and primary legal materials to accompany *Equity and Trusts in Australia*.

M W Bryan is Professor Emeritus at the University of Melbourne.

V J Vann has over 20 years of experience teaching and writing about equity and trusts.

S Barkehall Thomas is a Senior Lecturer at Monash University.

EQUITY & TRUSTS IN AUSTRALIA

THIRD EDITION

M W Bryan
V J Vann
S Barkehall Thomas

CAMBRIDGE
UNIVERSITY PRESS

CAMBRIDGE
UNIVERSITY PRESS

Shaftesbury Road, Cambridge CB2 8EA, United Kingdom

One Liberty Plaza, 20th Floor, New York, NY 10006, USA

477 Williamstown Road, Port Melbourne, VIC 3207, Australia

314–321, 3rd Floor, Plot 3, Splendor Forum, Jasola District Centre, New Delhi – 110025, India

103 Penang Road, #05–06/07, Visioncrest Commercial, Singapore 238467

Cambridge University Press is part of Cambridge University Press & Assessment, a department of the University of Cambridge.

We share the University's mission to contribute to society through the pursuit of education, learning and research at the highest international levels of excellence.

www.cambridge.org
Information on this title: www.cambridge.org/highereducation/isbn/9781009232388

First published 2012
Second edition 2017
Third edition 2023

Cover designed by Anne-Marie Reeves
Typeset by Lumina Datamatics Ltd
Printed in China by C & C Offset Printing Co., Ltd, September 2022

A catalogue record for this publication is available from the British Library

A catalogue record for this book is available from the National Library of Australia

ISBN 978-1-009-23238-8 Paperback

Additional resources for this publication at www.cambridge.org/highereducation/isbn/9781009232388/resources.

CONTENTS

PREFACE

There are many books on equity and trusts. Ours has modest but important aims. It is unashamedly pedagogic, being designed for students enrolled in LLB and JD degrees taking semesterised and trimesterised equity and trusts units. It makes no attempt to be comprehensive but focuses only on those topics we regard as essential to a foundational understanding of equity and trusts, required for the purpose of obtaining professional qualification. The book is premised on the belief that equitable doctrine is a coherent body of doctrine which affords the student insights – for example, into the relationship between breaches of duty and remedies – that cannot be obtained from the study of other subjects in a law degree. Moreover, although legal study is not most students' idea of fun, the study of equity is intellectually interesting from a variety of perspectives. It is essential that students coming to the subject not be under the misconception that it is arcane or obscure.

The opportunity has been taken in this edition to incorporate analysis of recent decisions including *Ancient Order of Foresters in Victoria Friendly Society Ltd v Lifeplan Australia Friendly Society Ltd* (2018) 265 CLR 1; *Smethurst v Commissioner of Police* (2020) 376 ALR 575; and *Caron v Jahani (No 2)* [2020] NSWCA 117. As the last named case illustrates, intermediate appeal courts remain an important source of equity jurisprudence, and numerous State decisions, both appellate and at primary judge level, are discussed in the text. Almost every chapter has required updating, and a new chapter has been added on terminating and varying trusts.

References are made throughout the text to *A Sourcebook on Equity and Trusts in Australia*, 3rd edition published by Cambridge University Press in 2022. This book is designed to be used either as a companion to the Sourcebook or as a freestanding text. The authors' policy on gender neutrality is to vary the pronouns 'she' and 'he', and the possessive adjectives 'his' and 'hers'.

Users of the previous edition, both lecturers and students, have provided us with feedback which has assisted us in the preparation of this edition. Lucy Russell and Emily Baxter at Cambridge University Press have been patient, generous and professional, and we are grateful to them and to their colleagues at Cambridge University Press who have helped to bring this edition to fruition. Needless to say, the authors are solely responsible for any errors in this edition, notwithstanding the invaluable support and assistance they have received.

We have endeavoured to state the law as of 1 December 2021.

M W Bryan

V J Vann

S Barkehall Thomas

ACKNOWLEDGEMENTS

The authors and Cambridge University Press would like to thank the following for permission to reproduce material in this book.

Extracts from High Court of Australia (HCA): © Commonwealth of Australia.

Extract from *Bankruptcy Act 1966* (Cth): sourced from the Federal Register of Legislation and reproduced under Creative Commons Attribution 4.0 International (CC BY 4.0, https://creativecommons.org/licenses/by/4.0/). For the latest information on Australian Government law please go to https://www.legislation.gov.au.

Extracts from Victorian legislation: © State of Victoria, Australia. Copyright in all legislation of the Parliament of the State of Victoria, Australia, is owned by the Crown in right of the State of Victoria, Australia. DISCLAIMER: This product or service contains an unofficial version of the legislation of the Parliament of State of Victoria. The State of Victoria accepts no responsibility for the accuracy and completeness of any legislation contained in this product or provided through this service.

Extracts from New South Wales legislation: sourced from the New South Wales Legislation website at 1 December 2021. For the latest information on New South Wales Government legislation please go to https://www.legislation.nsw.gov.au. Reproduced under CC BY 4.0 licence: https://creativecommons.org/licenses/by/4.0/.

Every effort has been made to trace and acknowledge copyright. The publisher apologises for any accidental infringement and welcomes information that would redress this situation.

TABLE OF CASES

TABLE OF STATUTES

Australia

AUSTRALIAN CAPITAL TERRITORY

NEW SOUTH WALES

NORTHERN TERRITORY

QUEENSLAND

SOUTH AUSTRALIA

TASMANIA

VICTORIA

WESTERN AUSTRALIA

New Zealand

South Africa

United Kingdom

United States of America

International instruments

ABBREVIATIONS

F & L: HAJ Ford, WA Lee, MW Bryan, J Glover & IG Fullerton, *The Law of Trusts* (Thomson Reuters, 2019) (formerly *Principles of the Law of Trusts*).

Jacobs: JD Heydon and MJ Leeming (eds), *Jacobs' Law of Trusts in Australia* (LexisNexis Butterworths, 7th ed, 2006).

MGL: JD Heydon, MJ Leeming and PG Turner (eds), *Meagher, Gummow & Lehane's Equity: Doctrines and Remedies* (LexisNexis Butterworths, 5th ed, 2015).

References to 'the *Trustee Act*' are to the trustee legislation of each State and Territory, namely:

Trustee Act 1925 (ACT)

Trustee Act 1925 (NSW)

Trustee Act 1980 (NT)

Trusts Act 1973 (Qld)

Trustee Act 1936 (SA)

Trustee Act 1898 (Tas)

Trustee Act 1958 (Vic)

Trustees Act 1962 (WA)

For example, a reference to 'NSW s 14' is a reference to s 14 of the *Trustee Act 1925* (NSW).

PART A

INTRODUCTION

1

AN OVERVIEW OF EQUITY

What is equity?

The word 'equity' is one of the most ambiguous in the law. Its most obvious meaning is fairness and justice.[1] Many would argue that equity is the overriding goal of all law. How could the law ever justify *un*fair or *in*equitable outcomes? But a moment's thought will show that applying, without more, the criterion of 'fairness' to solve all legal problems is open to serious objections. Decisions will inevitably reflect the subjective beliefs and values of the decision-maker as to what is fair. In a pluralist democracy, disputes about what is fair or equitable are settled by elected legislators, not by unelected judges, except where legislation has explicitly authorised judges to determine cases by reference to considerations of fairness.[2] Judges do not assess what is equitable without reference to some standard or benchmark. [1.1]

Secondly, equity sometimes refers to the principles applied by judges where the law is deficient for some reason. Aristotle is the first recorded writer to define 'equity' in these terms. In *Nicomachean Ethics*, Aristotle contrasted law, which was said to be 'universal' in its application, with equity which was seen as 'a correction of law where it was defective owing to its universality'.[3] We might nowadays say that the law is only 'universal' in the sense that in a society based on the rule of law there is an expectation that like cases will be treated in a like way. The complexity of society in practice means that few legal rules, unless stated at a high level of generalisation, can be described as being of 'universal' application. Even if they can, it is doubtful whether equity should today be invoked in order to correct specific injustices caused by their over-rigid application. The preferable response in a democratic society to a legal rule that cannot do justice in an individual case is to invite the legislature to reform the law. But Aristotle anticipated the lawyer's idea of equity in two respects. First, equity corrects, or supplements, the law but does not replace it. The fact that equity modifies the application of the law in specific instances does not impair the legitimacy of the law in those cases where there is no need of equity. Secondly, some equitable doctrines can be explained in terms of the dilemma of 'universality' in the law: a soundly based legal rule of general application can, on occasions, be exploited for improper purposes. For example, where the law requires some contracts to be in writing equity can modify the writing requirement where its application would cause injustice.[4] [1.2]

Although some applications of Australian equity can be explained in Aristotelian terms, the Australian model of equity, taken as a whole, does not fit Aristotle's notion of equity. Instead, in common with equity in other common law jurisdictions, the model applied is that of *institutional* equity.

1 'I think it likely that over the years words such as unconscionable and inequitable have drawn closer to more objective concepts such as fair, reasonable and just': Somers J in *Elders Pastoral Ltd v Bank of New Zealand* [1989] 2 NZLR 180, 193.

2 An example, drawn from trusts law, is the court's statutory power to excuse a trustee from liability where 'the trustee has acted honestly and reasonably, and ought fairly to be excused for the breach of trust ...': *Trustee Act 1925* (NSW) s 85: see [20.20].

3 *The Nicomachean Ethics of Aristotle*, tr WD Ross (Oxford University Press, 1954) book 10, ch 5; *Sourcebook* 1.2.2a, p 4.

4 See [9.36]. See also Matthew Harding, 'Equity and the Rule of Law' (2016) 132(2) *Law Quarterly Review* 278.

Institutional equity

[1.3] The essence of institutional equity is the creation of a special court, distinct from the courts administering the general law, having the power to modify or correct the general law. In England, that court was the Court of Chancery until the enactment of the mid-nineteenth-century judicature legislation. In Australia, it is several courts – which include the High Court, the Federal Court, the Supreme Court of every State and Territory, and numerous inferior courts – which have inherited the jurisdiction of the Court of Chancery. Although that court no longer exists, its defining characteristics have been transmitted to other courts.

[1.4] This section provides a brief account of the history of equity. In reading this history, two points should be kept in mind.

First, the paradox of institutional equity is that it is premised on the existence of a court which no longer exists. The Court of Chancery, which administered equity doctrines developed by chancellors and other equity judges, was abolished by the judicature legislation of the mid-nineteenth century.[5] The legislation was enacted in all States except New South Wales, which retained a separate court of equity until 1972.[6] Courts applying equity today do not have to administer equity in exactly the same way as it was administered by the Court of Chancery immediately before its abolition. Equitable principles are flexible and respond to changes in social and economic conditions. For example, the law of resulting and constructive trusts has adapted to changes in patterns of family home ownership in the late twentieth century brought about by the ready availability of mortgage finance.[7]

Secondly, the Court of Chancery never had, save possibly in the earliest period of the Chancellor's jurisdiction, any *general* power to correct a common law rule when the rule caused injustice. Equitable intervention is significant in some areas of law, particularly property law, but slight in others, such as tort law. Precisely when equity modifies the law is not deducible by logical proposition. The scope of equity's jurisdiction can only be determined by reference to the history of the jurisdiction – although, as with all judge-made law, it is possible to infer that equity will modify the law on one matter from the fact that it already intervenes in another, closely-related, matter. For example, once it had been established that a contract was voidable for duress, no great extension of principle was involved in holding that a contract was also voidable for undue influence.

The emergence of institutional equity: medieval origins

[1.5] Institutional equity has its origins in the state of fourteenth-century English common law and, in particular, in the rigidity of the procedures for initiating writs to commence a common law action.[8]

5 *Supreme Court of Judicature Act 1873* (Imp) s 3.
6 *Supreme Court Act 1970* (NSW) pt 4; *Law Reform (Law and Equity) Act 1972* (NSW).
7 See chapters 22 and 23.
8 See generally JH Baker, *An Introduction to English Legal History* (Oxford University Press, 4th ed, 2002) ch 6; *Sourcebook* 1.3.1a, p 5.

Medieval common law was a highly centralised system of justice, with processes initiated by the issue of a writ by Chancery, which functioned principally as the royal secretariat. The issue of writs was the basis of the *formulary* system of law – claims could only be brought before a common law court if the facts fitted within the formula, or wording, of a writ issued by Chancery. Once a writ had been issued, the complaint would be heard by jury trial.[9]

The strictness of the formulary system meant that not all complainants could obtain a writ giving them access to the common law courts. Some litigants who could not bring their complaint within the formula of the writ petitioned the king, who retained an overriding power to administer justice. The king investigated some of these complaints himself but increasingly adopted the practice of referring petitions to the Chancellor, who was the king's first minister and the head of the Chancery. The petitions which the Chancellor investigated were varied and not confined to what we would now term equity. If there was any pattern, it was that the administration of justice had broken down and that the petitioner needed the king's assistance in enforcing his or her rights. From the late fourteenth century, the Chancellor began hearing petitions in his own right.[10] [1.6]

Most early chancellors were churchmen who had legal training in civil and canon law and, in some cases, had practised in ecclesiastical courts. They did not apply civil or canon law but their rulings were inevitably influenced by their knowledge of these systems. Although some chancellors, such as Sir Thomas More (1529–33), had a common law background, the practice of appointing legally qualified chancellors with common law experience only became settled in the late seventeenth century. [1.7]

There was no question at that time of chancellors correcting or modifying the common law – there was little common law which could meaningfully have been corrected. The common law writs did not presuppose the existence of detailed legal rules, such as we now apply in the law of tort and contract. Any doctrinal issue raised by the plaintiff's proof of the matters alleged in the writ were, in practice, settled by the jury verdict, not by judicial ruling. As Sir Thomas More remarked, [1.8]

> [the common law judges] may by the verdict of the jury cast off all quarrels from themselves upon them, which they account their chief defence.[11]

The real differences between the common law and equity in its formative stage concerned not substantive law but the procedures applied by chancellors to obtain evidence. The action was begun not by a writ but by a simple summons to appear before the Chancellor. Failure to comply with the summons would render the defendant liable for contempt of court. Evidence was taken by interrogatories (questionnaires) or written depositions. The Chancellor did not work with a jury. In practice, he collected evidence until he had obtained enough to justify taking action. [1.9]

The fifteenth century, when these procedures were developed, was the period in which uses (or trusts) of land were enforced by chancellors. Disputes typically arose when the feoffee (trustee) of land, who was bound to hold the land for the benefit of the cestui que trust (beneficiary), claimed the land for himself. The common law courts could do little to [1.10]

9 Trial by jury gradually superseded older methods of trial: Baker (n 8) 72–6.

10 See *Sourcebook* 1.3.1b, p 6, for an example of a petition.

11 EV Hitchcock (ed), *The Lyfe of Sir Thomas More* (EETS no 197, 1935) 44–5; *Sourcebook* 1.3.2a, p 6.

prevent the trustee from obtaining a personal advantage from the trust, because its methods for obtaining evidence were not suited to discovering the terms on which the trustee had agreed to hold the land. They could be ascertained, however, as a result of interrogatories administered by the Chancellor. Upon proof of the terms of the trust, the Chancellor made orders to protect the beneficiary's interest in the land. The basic features of the law of trusts therefore emerged from the orders made by chancellors to protect the interests of beneficiaries.

Chancellors enjoyed considerable discretion in making orders. Chancery was a court of conscience in which defendants could be compelled to do whatever conscience required. 'Conscience' did not, however, mean 'arbitrary justice', and chancellors generally followed the practices of their predecessors, where these were known. The Chancellor's decrees were fashioned to meet the circumstances of the case. They bound the parties to the case but no one else.[12]

Competition between common law and equity

[1.11] The period from the sixteenth century to the early seventeenth century in England was one of jurisdictional conflict and jealousy between the common law courts and Chancery. The Chancellor's court was caught up in the great constitutional struggles of that age. Chancery jurisdiction rested on the sovereign's prerogative power to administer justice, which was challenged by a parliament increasingly inclined to test the limits of the prerogative. The resolution of the dispute between the Chancellor and the common lawyers established the basis of the relationship between the common law and equity which still exists today.

[1.12] A particular grievance of common law judges was the Chancellor's power to grant an order known as a 'common injunction' to prevent the enforcement of a judgment obtained in a common law court.[13] If P obtained a common law judgment against D which the Chancellor considered had been procured by unconscionable conduct, an injunction would be granted to prevent P from enforcing the judgment. The injunction, although not formally an appeal, enabled D to avoid the consequences of the adverse judgment against him or her.

[1.13] The dispute culminated in the celebrated *Earl of Oxford's Case*[14] in which Chief Justice Coke challenged the jurisdiction of the Chancellor, Lord Ellesmere, to award common injunctions. Although Coke had the law on his side,[15] King James I ruled in favour of equity, accepting Ellesmere's argument 'that when a judgment is obtained by oppression, wrong and a bad conscience, the Chancellor will frustrate and set it aside, not for any error or defect in the judgment, but for the hard conscience of the party'.[16] The king's ruling was a landmark in the development of equity because it established for the first time the supremacy of Chancery over the common law in cases of conflict between the jurisdictions. The practical significance of the decision was, however, limited.

12 Baker (n 8) 104.

13 *Throckmorton v Finch* (1598) Co Third Instit 124.

14 (1615) 1 Ch Rep 1; 21 ER 485; *Sourcebook* 1.3.2b, p 7.

15 Common injunctions were contrary to the Statute 4 Hen IV, c 23, and had been held to be illegal in *Throckmorton v Finch* (1598) Co Third Instit 124.

16 (1615) 21 ER 485, 487.

Seventeenth-century chancellors were sparing in their award of common injunctions, which remained of doubtful legality in spite of the royal ruling.[17] The Court of Chancery might have been abolished in the course of the constitutional upheavals of that century, but the chancellors of the late seventeenth century were careful to respect the boundaries between Chancery and the common law courts.[18]

By the end of the seventeenth century, Chancery's work, particularly in enforcing uses and preventing oppression in exercising contractual rights, was recognised as being indispensable to the landholding society of the time. The political turbulence of the century was succeeded by a period of reform and consolidation undertaken by lawyer chancellors such as Lord Nottingham (1673–82), Lord Hardwicke (1736–56) and Lord Thurlow (1778–83 and 1783–92). Lord Nottingham, for example, was responsible for the development of the mortgagor's equity of redemption, the rule against perpetuities, and for formulating the principles governing relief against unconscionable bargains.[19] [1.14]

By the end of the eighteenth century, most of the basic equitable doctrines applied today had been established, although they have inevitably undergone a continual process of renewal and restatement to meet the needs of industrial and post-industrial society. In one vital respect, the constitutional battles of the seventeenth century had left their imprint on the shape of the legal system. The relationship between the common law and equity was settled. Equity was said to be a 'gloss' on the common law, modifying the common law where the enforcement of legal rights was harsh or oppressive, but not claiming to be a parallel or rival system of law.[20] [1.15]

Reform and the judicature legislation

In the early nineteenth century, the Chancery court attracted criticism, principally on account of its delays in hearing and disposing of cases. The Chancellor for most of this period, Lord Eldon, did valuable work in restating existing doctrine.[21] But he was slow to decide cases, and the caseload of Chancery was too heavy to be carried by a single judge.[22] The delays of Chancery were condemned by Charles Dickens in *Bleak House*, with its extended metaphor of the 'fog of Chancery' enveloping the Chancellor and his court.[23] [1.16]

---

17 *R v Standish* (1671) Treby MS Rep LPCL 438.

18 Chancellors began to apply the common law concept of precedent: see Selden Society, *Lord Nottingham's Chancery Cases*, DEC Yale (ed) (B Quaritch, 1955) vol 73, introduction.

19 Common law developments can rarely be ascribed to an individual judge (an exception being the concept of the duty of care ascribed to Lord Atkin in *Donoghue v Stevenson* [1932] AC 562) but it is usually not hard to identify the Chancellor responsible for the introduction of an equitable doctrine, as Jessel MR pointed out in *Re Hallett's Estate* (1880) 13 Ch D 696, 710.

20 F Maitland, *Equity: A Course of Lectures*, AH Chaytor and WJ Whittaker (eds), rev J Brunyate (Cambridge University Press, 2nd ed, 1936) 18.

21 Rose A Melikan, *John Scott, Lord Eldon, 1751–1838: The Duty of Loyalty* (Cambridge University Press, 1999).

22 'Having had doubts upon this will for twenty years, there can be no use in taking more time to consider it …': *Radnor v Shafto* (1805) 11 Ves 448; 32 ER 1160 (although Eldon had only been Chancellor for four years when he spoke these words). See also *Morgan v Lord Clarendon* (1808) in Baker (n 8) 113.

23 *Sourcebook* 1.3.3a, p 8.

[1.17] One defect of Chancery was that claimants might have to bring more than one set of proceedings in order to obtain the relief they wanted. A plaintiff who wanted to obtain an order of specific performance of a contract would have to sue in a common law court in order to establish the validity of the contract, unless its validity was conceded, and then obtain an order of specific performance in Chancery. It was not equity that was defective in such a case, but the system of civil justice that separated the administration of equity from adjudication by the common law courts. A steady flow of mid-nineteenth-century legislation patched up the system of separate equity.[24] Nonetheless, it was becoming obvious that more radical reform was needed.

[1.18] The *Judicature Acts 1873–6* enacted reforms which improved the administration of common law and equity but which, with a few exceptions,[25] did not change the substantive law of either. The *Supreme Court of Judicature Act 1873* (Imp), the principal Act, made the following major changes:

(1) The old superior common law courts were abolished and replaced by divisions of a new High Court of Justice, including common law divisions, such as the Queen's Bench, as well as the Chancery Division. The divisions reflected the conveniences of legal specialisation rather than the nature of the relief available. Every division was empowered to administer common law and equity.

(2) A unified code of procedure applied to both common law and equitable claims. Equity's discovery and interlocutory procedures were extended to the common law.

(3) Section 24 made provision for giving effect to equitable estates, interests and defences in legal proceedings in the manner that the Court of Chancery would have done. The section also provided for the recognition and enforcement of legal estates, interests and titles as they had been recognised before the enactment of the section. Section 24(5) abolished the 'common injunction', which had been the flashpoint for judicial disagreement in the *Earl of Oxford's Case*, while preserving the power to issue injunctions in cases in which the jurisdiction to do so was established.

(4) Section 25 resolved a number of conflicts between common law and equity either by providing that the equitable rule was to prevail or by enacting new law. Section 25(11) provided:

> Generally, in all matters not herein-before mentioned, in which there is any conflict or variance between the Rules of Equity and the Rules of the Common Law with reference to the same matter, the Rules of Equity shall prevail.

The subsection confirmed the supremacy of equity in the event of a conflict between common law and equity which was not otherwise resolved by the judicature legislation. At first sight, it might seem that the subsection added nothing to the *Earl of Oxford's Case*, which had established the primacy of equity more than

24 In particular, the *Common Law Procedure Act 1854* (Imp) ss 83–6, permitting equitable defences to be pleaded to common law claims. Baker (n 8) 111–13. Michael Lobban, 'Preparing for Fusion: Reforming the Nineteenth Century Court of Chancery' (2004) 22(2) *Law and History Review* 389, 565.

25 Section 25 of the *Supreme Court of Judicature Act 1873* (Imp) resolved some conflicts between common law and equity. The most significant substantive change was the introduction by s 25(6) of a statutory procedure for assigning choses in action. See [9.30].

> 250 years earlier. But s 24(5) of the 1873 Act had abolished the common injunction, which had been Chancery's means of ensuring that its principles prevailed in cases of conflict, and a statutory basis for preserving that supremacy was needed.

The enactment of the judicature legislation is a landmark in equity, but the limits of the legislation need to be kept clearly in mind. The legislation was never intended to fuse or integrate legal and equitable rights. To justify the merger of legal and equitable rights by reference to the legislation has been described as 'fusion fallacy'.[26] An example of 'fusion fallacy' is to assume that a contract to create a lease, enforceable in equity because it has been partly performed by the tenant, confers the same rights and imposes the same duties as a common law lease created by the execution of a deed.[27] Regardless of whether or not it is a fallacy, it is certainly a misreading of history. The legislation would not have been enacted in the first place if its declared purpose had been to merge the substance of common law and equity. [1.19]

Arguments about the intention of the English legislature in 1873 are irrelevant to deciding whether particular common law and equitable doctrines should be merged in twenty-first-century Australia, as proposals to fuse or merge doctrines must be considered on their merits. The history of the application of a legal or equitable doctrine is obviously relevant to the analysis, and the fact that the dual system of common law and equity has worked satisfactorily for many years supports the well-known adage 'if it ain't broke, don't fix it'; however, the reason this dual system has worked has nothing to do with the judicature legislation. Arguments about whether the common law and equity ought to be merged, and if so how complete the merger ought to be, arouse surprisingly strong emotions.[28] [1.20]

The reception of equity in Australia

The immediate need of the earliest British settlers in Australia was to establish a stable legal order. The *First Charter of Justice* in 1787 created a Court of Civil Judicature which did not distinguish between common law and equity. The *New South Wales Act 1823* conferred on the newly created Supreme Court the power to exercise locally the jurisdiction that the Chancellor exercised in England.[29] The influence of particular personalities shaped the [1.21]

26 MGL [2-125]–[2-225].

27 *Walsh v Lonsdale* (1882) 21 Ch D 9, 14, Jessel MR. Jessel had piloted the Judicature Bill 1873 through the House of Commons in the capacity of Solicitor-General, and later took a leading role in drafting procedural rules for the post-*Judicature Act* courts. Criticism of his judgments in *Walsh v Lonsdale* and in *Redgrave v Hurd* (1881) 20 Ch D 1, 12, where he suggested that damages might be available in equity for innocent misrepresentation, on the ground of 'fusion fallacy', must take into account his understanding of the judicature scheme from having been closely involved in its enactment and implementation.

28 Andrew Burrows, 'We Do This at Common Law but That in Equity' (2002) 22(1) *Oxford Journal of Legal Studies* 1; MGL [2-325]–[2-400]. For different perspectives on 'fusion fallacy', in the context of an unsuccessful claim to exemplary damages for breach of fiduciary duty, see *Harris v Digital Pulse Pty Ltd* (2003) 56 NSWLR 298, [18] (Spigelman CJ), [136]–[154] (Mason P), [353]–[393] and [444]–[445] (Heydon JA).

29 The history of the New South Wales equity legislation is traced in ML Smith, 'The Early Years of Equity in the Supreme Court of New South Wales' (1998) 72(10) *Australian Law Journal* 799; Keith Mason, 'Fusion: Fallacy, Future or Finished' in S Degeling and J Edelman (eds), *Equity in Commercial Law* (Thomson Reuters, 2005); *Sourcebook* 1.3.3d, p 10.

administration of equity within the Supreme Court framework as much as any consideration relating to the place of equity within a common law system. It was pressure exerted by the State's first equity judge, Willis J, which resulted in the provision for the appointment of a Primary Judge in Equity by the *Administration of Justice Act 1840*.[30] Thereafter, instead of steps being taken to integrate common law and equity procedures, the tendency throughout the nineteenth century was to emphasise the separation of equitable business from common law matters.[31] The identification of a judge as the Primary Judge in Equity (later the Chief Justice in Equity) encouraged the growth of an Equity Bar specialising in matters coming within the judge's jurisdiction, just as Chancery in England stimulated the creation of a Chancery Bar.

[1.22] The Supreme Court structure created by other States required judges to administer both common law and equity; however, this did not mean that the common law and equity were fused procedurally or in substance. The pre-*Judicature Act* institutional model of English equity was strictly applied. In practical terms, it meant that judges who devoted most of their time to deciding common law claims were sometimes required to hear equity suits determined by equity procedures. In the nineteenth century it was unusual for a Supreme Court to consist of more than two judges, and confining the work of a single judge to equity matters would have been considered a misallocation of judicial resources. The New South Wales experience was different both because judicial resources permitted equity specialisation, and the specialisation in turn reflected the volume of commercial and property litigation in Sydney which ensured a heavy workload for the equity judge.

The judicature legislation in Australia

[1.23] While most Australian States were content to apply the English system of equity, there were some imaginative early attempts to improve on the model. The most interesting of these was the South Australian *Supreme Court Procedure Act 1853*, enacted 20 years before the English judicature scheme was introduced.[32] It anticipated that legislation by conferring power on the Supreme Court in any proceedings to make orders of specific performance of agreements or to grant injunctions. Section 175 went even further in permitting actions at law to be brought to enforce exclusively equitable obligations, such as breach of trust.

[1.24] Another experiment in the substantive fusion of common law and equity was Queensland's *Equity Procedure Act 1873*, promoted by Sir Samuel Griffith.[33] This measure permitted common law courts to grant monetary relief in cases where an 'equitable claim or demand' had been made. Unusually, it made the monetary award dependent upon the plaintiff establishing an entitlement to a discretionary equitable remedy.

30 See Smith (n 29) 802.

31 The appointment of additional Supreme Court judges tended to emphasise the isolation of the Primary Judge in Equity who became increasingly disengaged from common law business. See Smith (n 29) 806.

32 Greg Taylor, 'South Australia's Judicature Reforms of 1853' (2001) 22(1) *Journal of Legal History* 55.

33 Peter M McDermott, 'Equitable Claims or Demands – Queensland District and Magistrates Courts and Western Australia Local Courts' (1991) 16(2) *University of Queensland Law Journal* 212.

Both experiments were soon overtaken by the rapid adoption of English-style judicature legislation in all States except New South Wales. The judicature legislation of each State and Territory is set out in the online resources for this book.

In New South Wales, legislative inertia combined with influential opposition to postpone the enactment of the judicature legislation for the best part of a century. The State legislature in the 1870s has been said to have been 'almost immune from concern for law reform.'[34] Moreover, Chief Justice Stephen pronounced the judicature legislation 'a great bungle.'[35] Even though a Select Committee had found the equity branch of the Supreme Court 'dilatory, expensive, ruinous to suitors and not in accord with the judicial process of the age', the effect of the *Equity Act 1880* (NSW) was to preserve the separate division of common law and equity administration. Other English reforms were introduced, however, such as empowering equity judges to determine questions of legal title and to award damages instead of, or in addition to, an injunction or specific performance. [1.25]

In most States, the judicature legislation has been reduced to a short common form. A typical provision is s 29 of the *Supreme Court Act 1986* (Vic). [1.26]

Law and equity to be concurrently administered

(1) Subject to the provisions of this or any other Act, every court exercising jurisdiction in Victoria in any civil proceeding must continue to administer law and equity on the basis that, if there is a conflict or variance between the rules of equity and the rules of the common law concerning the same matter, the rules of equity prevail.

(2) Every court referred to in subsection (1) must give the same effect as before the commencement of this Act–

(a) to all equitable estates, titles, rights, reliefs, defences and counter-claims, and to all equitable duties and liabilities; and

(b) subject thereto, to all legal claims and demands and all estates, titles, rights, duties, obligations and liabilities existing by the common law or created by any Act–

and, subject to the provisions of this or any other Act, must so exercise its jurisdiction in every proceeding before it as to secure that, as far as possible, all matters in dispute between the parties are completely and finally determined, and all multiplicity of proceedings concerning any of those matters is avoided.

In New South Wales, the system of separate equity, administered in a court applying special equity procedures, continued until 1972. It was made workable by the enactment of 'scissors and paste' measures which ameliorated the worst defects of a separate system of equity. Judicature legislation was eventually enacted in 1970 and 1972.[36] [1.27]

34 JM Bennett, 'Historical Trends in Australian Law Reform' (1969–70) 9 *University of Western Australia Law Review* 211, 231.

35 Ibid 232.

36 *Supreme Court Act 1970* (NSW) pt 4; *Law Reform (Law and Equity) Act 1972* (NSW) s 5.

The place of equity in the modern law

[1.28] Two related conclusions can be drawn from this brief account of the history of equity.

The first is that the subject-matter of equity can only be determined by reference to legal history. It cannot be logically deduced from general propositions.

The second is that the existence of a separate body of equitable principles means that much of Australian private law exhibits a *dual* character. Large parts of the law, including contract and property law, are drawn from both common law and equity. Whether the dual system of common law and equity should be preserved, in whole or in part, in the twenty-first century is a question that every lawyer and law student interested in the rational development of the law should consider.[37]

A map of equity

[1.29] We now turn to the task of describing the existing dual system of common law and equity. The equity student's most immediate need is an overview which identifies those areas of private law which are equitable in character. The remainder of this chapter sketches out such an overview.

Equitable remedies

[1.30] Most equity books relegate discussion of equitable remedies to the final chapters. This approach carries the risk that the significance of the remedies will be underestimated. It has been said that, in equity, 'right and remedy are indissolubly connected',[38] and equitable doctrines cannot be properly understood without a good understanding of the remedies available to the successful plaintiff. For example, a claim for breach of fiduciary obligation may be tacked onto an action for breach of contract in an attempt to compel the defendant to account for gains made, or property acquired, as a consequence of the breach.[39] Equitable claims are 'remedy driven', in the sense that attempts are sometimes made to characterise defendants as equitable wrongdoers for the purpose of obtaining a distinctive equitable remedy such as an account of profits or a constructive trust. The number and distinct remedial aims of equitable remedies, sometimes referred to as a 'smorgasbord', in contrast to the common law which only makes awards of damages, encourages attempts to fit the facts of a case to the criteria of a particular doctrine in order to achieve the remedial outcome desired by the plaintiff. If the 'remedy-driving' is successful it may result in the distortion of the fundamental ideas of equity. Generally speaking, Australian judges have not permitted basic equitable concepts to be

---

37 See JH Merryman, 'Ownership and Estate' (1974) 48(4) *Tulane Law Review* 916 for a similar argument that property law is only intelligible in terms of its history. Legal and equitable dualism is the central theme of Sarah Worthington, *Equity* (Oxford University Press, 2nd ed, 2006), especially chs 1 and 2.

38 *Chase Manhattan Bank NA v Israel-British Bank (London) Ltd* [1981] Ch 105, 124 (Goulding J).

39 The High Court decisions of *Hospital Products Ltd v United States Surgical Corporation* (1984) 156 CLR 41 and *John Alexander's Clubs Pty Ltd v White City Tennis Club Ltd* (2010) 241 CLR 1 are examples of unsuccessful attempts to establish that contractual relationships were fiduciary for the purpose of claiming profits from what was otherwise a breach of contract.

stretched or distorted solely for the purpose of enabling a plaintiff to obtain relief which is unavailable at common law. It is, however, important for the student to be aware of the remedies available for all equitable claims. An understanding of equitable relief is the key to understanding equitable doctrines and principles. For this reason, a discussion of equitable remedies is dealt with early in this book.

A fundamental distinction is made between the *exclusive* jurisdiction and the *auxiliary* [1.31] jurisdiction of equity. The *exclusive* jurisdiction of equity consists of matters which, prior to the judicature legislation, could only be adjudicated upon by Chancery, and not by common law courts. They include the enforcement of trusts and other fiduciary obligations, equitable obligations of confidence, and the rescission of contracts on equitable grounds such as misrepresentation and unconscionable conduct.

Only equitable remedies can be awarded when equity acts in its exclusive jurisdiction. Common law damages are not available, although equitable compensation – a monetary remedy compensating for financial loss caused by a breach of equitable obligation – can be ordered.[40]

Equity acts in its *auxiliary* jurisdiction when it acts in support of legal rights. This most often occurs when a tort or breach of contract has been committed and common law damages are an inadequate remedy for the plaintiff. The plaintiff's legal rights are then enforced by the award of an equitable remedy. The remedy of specific performance will be granted, for example, to enforce a contract for the sale of land because damages are, as a matter of course, considered inadequate to compensate for the breach. Similarly, an injunction will be awarded to restrain the commission of trespass to land because damages will usually be an insufficient remedy.[41]

The distinction between the exclusive and auxiliary jurisdictions of equity creates a [1.32] hierarchy of remedies. Only equitable remedies can be awarded in the exclusive jurisdiction; common law damages are never available. In the auxiliary jurisdiction, however, a court considers whether damages will adequately compensate for the plaintiff's loss, and only if that remedy is not adequate will the award of an equitable remedy be considered. Damages for breach of contract are inadequate if a monetary award will not enable the plaintiff to purchase a market substitute for the defendant's performance. The order of specific performance or an injunction compels the defendant to perform his obligations under a contract or prevents a breach of a duty owed by the defendant to the plaintiff.

Whether a hierarchy of remedies *ought* to exist is a controversial question which equity students should consider. Opponents of the hierarchy argue that the only basis on which any remedy should be awarded is its appropriateness to do justice on the facts of the case.[42]

---

40 See chapter 4.

41 Cf *Smethurst v Commissioner of Police* (2020) 376 ALR 575 where a majority of the High Court held that trespass to personal property – namely, a mobile phone taken by the Australian Federal Police pursuant to illegal search warrants – did not entitle the plaintiffs to a mandatory injunction compelling the Police to hand over data obtained from the phone. See [3.17].

42 MJ Tilbury, *Civil Remedies* (Butterworths, 1990) vol 1, [1025]; Paul Finn, 'Equitable Doctrine and Discretion in Remedies' in W Cornish et al (eds), *Restitution Past, Present & Future* (Hart Publishing, 1998) 266–73. Proponents of the appropriateness criterion point to the judicial discretion exercised under the *Competition and Consumer Act 2010* (Cth) sch 2 ss 237–8 which establish a 'menu' of remedies as the preferred model for exercising remedial discretion in private law.

[1.33] The objective of most common law claims is simple: it is to obtain compensation for the plaintiff's loss.[43] Equitable relief, on the other hand, pursues a variety of aims, which are discussed in the next chapter.[44]

[1.34] The following is a brief summary of the principal grounds of equitable intervention and the relief available.

Contract

[1.35] The common law determines the existence of a contract, and the rights and obligations of the contracting parties, but equity modifies contractual obligations and provides relief both for breach and where the plaintiff's consent to the agreement has been vitiated. The principal areas of equitable intervention are as follows:

- The creation and modification of enforceable promissory obligations. The common law rules of offer and acceptance, consideration and intention to create legal relations determine which promises are legally enforceable. In contrast, the equitable doctrine of estoppel prevents the enforcement of some promises which would otherwise give rise to legal obligations. Although not developed as a mode of promise enforcement, estoppel doctrines, particularly proprietary estoppel, sometimes have the effect of enforcing promises.
- Setting aside contracts[45] on the ground that a party's consent was vitiated by fraud, duress, unconscionable conduct, undue influence, mistake, misrepresentation, and in some cases where a guarantee is entered into without a full understanding of its nature and effect. Rescission restores the parties to their pre-contractual position.
- Rectification of the terms of a written contract where they do not conform to the agreement the parties made.
- Assigning the benefit of the performance of contractual obligations in equity. The judicature legislation introduced a procedure for assigning the benefit of contracts;[46] it did not supersede the equitable principles of assignment which continue to apply when the statutory criteria are not met.
- Preventing disproportionate relief of a plaintiff as a result of the defendant's breach of contract. Where a contractual term specifies a sum payable by the defendant upon breach of contract, and the sum exceeds the maximum loss that might be incurred on breach, equity may strike down the term on the ground that it constitutes a penalty. Similarly, equity will give relief against a contractual provision entitling the plaintiff to forfeit the defendant's property upon breach of a contractual term if forfeiture would be a disproportionate response to the breach.
- Enforcement of the contract or of its particular provisions. The remedy of specific performance compels performance of a contract according to its terms. Particular

43 Exceptions to this statement include common law claims for possession of land (which nowadays rest on a statutory basis), exemplary and restitutionary damages and rescission at common law for fraud and duress.

44 See chapter 2.

45 Gifts can also be rescinded in equity. See chapter 5.

46 See [9.30]–[9.34].

provisions of a contract can also be enforced, positively or negatively, by the award of an injunction. In contrast to the other examples of equitable intervention listed in this section, equity here acts in its auxiliary, not its exclusive, jurisdiction. The basis of equitable intervention is that common law damages would be inadequate.

Property

Equity's principal contribution to property law is the trust, which imposes obligations on a titleholder of property to manage the property for the benefit of other individuals or for legally approved purposes, such as charitable purposes. But while the trust was equity's earliest and most enduring contribution to property law, there are many others. Even legislation, such as the Torrens system of registered land titles, has not significantly modified the importance of equity in property law. Apart from the trust, equitable intervention includes: [1.36]

- The recognition and enforcement of equitable titles to property. The common law fee simple, life estate, lease and mortgage can also be created as equivalent equitable interests in property.[47]
- Equity also recognises and enforces new interests in property which have no common law counterpart. One example is the mortgagee's equity of redemption which not only entitles a mortgagor to redeem a mortgage after the legal date for repaying the mortgage debt has passed but also constitutes a marketable property interest.[48] Another is the restrictive covenant affecting land. A promise by D made to P that D and his successors in title will not undertake an activity on D's land, such as constructing more than one dwelling, will, if it benefits P's land, be enforceable not only by P against D, but also by P's successors to the land against D's successors. The characteristics of equitable property interests are considered in chapter 8.
- The creation of special rules governing the assignment of property interests. An assignment is the immediate transfer of an interest in property. Property, for this purpose, includes intangible property, such as a chose in action; for example, the right to enforce a contract. Common law and statute prescribe formalities for the transfer of most forms of property. Equity enables property to be assigned where the method of assignment does not comply with these rules. It also enables 'future property', meaning property to which the transferor does not at present have title, to be assigned. This does not mean that equity disregards form or adopts an 'anything goes' approach to the assignment of property. As chapter 9 shows, equity applies its own requirements, in some cases by requiring the assignee to provide valuable consideration for the assignment, and in other cases by requiring the assignor to have taken all the legal steps necessary for him to complete the assignment, even if other legal steps have not been taken by the assignee or by a third party.
- The recognition and enforcement of proprietary interests by application of the doctrine of equitable estoppel. Suppose that D promises P that he will grant P an

47 The doctrine of estates applies to interests in land but not to interests in personal property. Successive interests in personal property can, however, be created by settling the property on trust.

48 *Casborne v Scarfe* (1737) 26 ER 377.

interest in his (D's) property if P builds on D's land. P takes D at his word and builds a house on D's land. If D refuses to give P any interest in the property, equity will grant P equitable relief. This can include awarding P an interest in D's land.[49] The nature of P's interest will, like all equitable relief, be determined by the exercise of equitable discretion. Estoppel is discussed in chapters 7 and 8.

- The application of special rules, known as tracing rules, to identify a claimant's property. If P's property has been mixed with D's, or with the property of a third party, before being given to D, then P can only recover the property, or a share of it, if she can show that it is hers. The common law elaborated some basic rules for tracing property, but for most purposes they have been replaced by equity's identification rules. They are explained in chapter 21.
- Equitable intervention in the law of deceased estates. A number of equitable doctrines deal with the distribution of property under wills and intestacies. Several enable a deceased's intended dispositions to take effect notwithstanding her failure to comply with statutory formalities.[50] These doctrines can be rationalised as instances of equity looking to the intent of a transaction, and not to its form. A discussion of these doctrines belongs to books on succession, and accordingly they are not discussed in this text.

Civil wrongs

[1.37] Equity also relieves against the consequences of forms of wrongdoing that are only recognised in equity. These can be considered the counterparts to common law torts, but with the important qualifications that equitable bars and remedies are not comparable to common law defences, and that the grant of common law damages is not an available remedy. The principal equitable wrongs are:

- Breach of fiduciary obligation. The principles of liability for breach of fiduciary obligation are explained in chapter 10. The idea of a breach of fiduciary obligation can be explained by a simple example. Suppose that a solicitor, S, misappropriates money belonging to a client, C, and pays it into his personal bank account. Our first response is that S will be criminally liable for theft and, depending on the facts, other offences such as obtaining a financial advantage by deception. He will also have acted in breach of professional disciplinary rules.[51] The civil (ie non-criminal) wrong that S will have committed, however, is a breach of fiduciary duty. He has betrayed the trust the client placed in him. He must of course compensate C for any loss caused by the misappropriation. But in some cases, alternative equitable relief will be relevant. For example, if S has successfully invested C's money he must account

49 *Dillwyn v Llewelyn* (1862) 45 ER 1285; *Giumelli v Giumelli* (1999) 196 CLR 101; *Sourcebook* 8.5a, p 198.

50 For example, the doctrine of *donatio mortis causa*, which applies to deathbed gifts, and the rule in *Strong v Bird* (1874) LR 18 Eq 315, which validates some intended gifts where formalities have not been complied with but where the intended donee has been appointed the donor's executor. See *Cope v Keene* (1968) 118 CLR 1.

51 A breach of professional rules may independently constitute an offence, for example under State and Territory uniform legal profession laws regulating trust accounts.

to C for the profitable investment even if it is unlikely that C would have made the profit for herself. The availability of gains-based remedies is one of the characteristics of breaches of equitable obligation that distinguishes them from torts.

- Equitable relief is not limited to the fiduciary who has committed the breach of obligation. Secondary parties, such as those who receive the proceeds of fiduciary wrongdoing, or who assist in the breach, can also be held liable to make restitution of benefits received or to compensate for loss. The principles of accessory liability are discussed in chapter 11.
- Breach of confidence. Suppose that P discloses a trade secret or other confidential information to D. D then passes on the information, without authority or justification, to X. D will be liable to P in equity for breach of confidence; X will also be liable once he becomes aware that the information had initially been disclosed in confidence. In some cases, D will be subject to a contractual obligation of confidence; the unauthorised disclosure will then be a breach of contract. Equitable obligations of confidence are relevant where there is no contract; for example, where the disclosure was made in the course of negotiations which were broken off without agreement being reached between the parties. It is also a remedy for some invasions of privacy. Liability for breach of confidence is examined in chapter 12.

Civil procedure

The final category of equitable intervention is equity's regulation of civil litigation. Though not covered in this book, the topic must be mentioned for the sake of completeness. Equity's inquisitorial processes for taking accounts were superior to the common law's accounting methods in adjusting rights and liabilities, particularly where there were multiple parties to litigation. The principal applications are: [1.38]

- Contribution. Equity, operating in conjunction with the common law and statute, provides that two or more persons who are liable for a loss are rateably (in other words, proportionately) liable to compensate the plaintiff for that loss.
- Subrogation. Where legal rights are taken over by one person from another by operation of the law, the transferee is said to be subrogated to the rights of the transferor. A common example, based on common law, is that of an insurer who is entitled to have the benefit of any claim the assured has against a tortfeasor.[52] Some equitable applications of subrogation keep proprietary rights alive for the benefit of a party discharging another's debt. If P discharges a mortgage over D's property, for example, P will take over the security for her own benefit unless the evidence shows that the parties did not intend P to become D's secured creditor.[53]
- Marshalling. This doctrine regulates the enforcement of securities against a debtor where a creditor is entitled to enforce his security against more than one asset of the debtor. Where two creditors, A and B, are entitled to security over one asset of

52 Charles Mitchell and Stephen Watterson, *Subrogation: Law and Practice* (Oxford University Press, 2007).

53 *Ghana Commercial Bank v Chandiram* [1960] AC 732; *Bofinger v Kingsway Group Ltd* (2009) 239 CLR 269.

a debtor, and A has security over a second asset of the debtor to satisfy his debt, A will not be allowed to exercise his rights to the first security to the prejudice of B who only has that security available to enforce her claim. If A exercises his rights against the jointly secured asset, B will be entitled to security over the second asset in priority to the debtor's unsecured creditors.

[1.39] The purpose of this list is to give the reader an overview of the principal areas of equitable intervention. The focus has been on the contribution equity has made to private law. Equity has also made significant contributions to public law, particularly in making available declaratory relief and injunctions against the Crown. These are not covered in this book.

[1.40] A disadvantage of lists, shopping lists being a notable exception, is that they are apt to become fixed and unalterable. Some aspects of equity are not included in the list set out above. Being a list of discrete items, it fails to record examples of overlapping areas of intervention. For example, liability for breach of confidence sometimes overlaps with liability for breach of fiduciary obligation. Similarly, some contracts which are voidable as being unconscientious bargains are also voidable on the ground of undue influence. Moreover, some applications of equity belong under more than one heading. Assignments, for example, have been discussed under both the contract and property headings. The student must not only understand the subject-matter of equity; she must also understand how the different parts of equity relate to each other as well as how equity relates to rights created at common law and by statute.

The maxims of equity

[1.41] A peculiarity of equitable legal method is that some of the principles applied by courts are encapsulated in 'maxims' which are often recited in judgments applying the principles. What are these maxims, and what is their status in equity adjudication?

[1.42] To answer the second question first, the maxims are *not* equitable principles, still less rules, and equity and trust problems cannot be solved solely by reference to a maxim. In fact, maxims are apt to mislead, without knowledge of the authorities which give practical application to their content. The maxims express in concise form certain policies that inform the application of equitable doctrine. They are no substitute, however, for the precise application of equitable doctrine to the facts of the case.

While in some cases the decision and the maxim may readily align,[54] the opposite is frequently so. For example, the application of the maxim that 'equity will not assist a volunteer' (in other words, it will not assist a party who has not provided consideration) was rejected by the High Court in *Corin v Patton*.[55] The case raised the issue of when equity will give effect to a transfer of property when the transfer is not legally effective because there has not been full compliance with statutory formalities. The principle of not assisting parties who have not provided consideration was held to be irrelevant to the resolution of that issue.

54 *Milroy v Lord* (1862) 45 ER 1185.

55 (1990) 169 CLR 540; *Sourcebook* 1.4a, p 13. See [9.10].

Returning to the first question, there is no fixed list of maxims, and some are more significant than others. Commonly invoked maxims include the following: [1.43]

(a) She who seeks equity must do equity. A plaintiff claiming equitable relief must perform, or be ready to perform, her obligations arising out of the subject-matter of the dispute. For example, a purchaser of land under an instalment purchase contract will only be entitled to equitable relief from forfeiture of her interest in the land for non-payment of an instalment on condition that she pays all outstanding money due to the vendor.[56]

(b) He who comes to equity must come with clean hands. A plaintiff will be refused equitable relief if his conduct in the transaction in respect of which he is claiming relief has been improper. The maxim is discussed in chapter 6 at [6.16] and following.

(c) Equity looks to intent, rather than to form. This maxim is open to several interpretations. One is that a court of equity examines the substance of a transaction, and not its form. This meaning is not particularly 'equitable' because courts applying common law, as well as equity, will focus on the substance of a transaction, where it has been concealed by its form. All courts have the power to ignore 'sham' transactions, and focus on the true rights and duties created by the parties or imposed by law.[57] The maxim is more accurately applied to discrete areas where equity can modify strict common law rights without subverting the reality of a bargain the parties have made. One example concerns time stipulations in contracts. Under a contract for the sale of land the parties must, at common law, complete on the day fixed for completion of the contract. A court of equity, on the other hand, permits completion within a reasonable time afterwards unless time has been explicitly stated to be of the essence of the contract.[58]

(d) Equity treats as done that which ought to be done. The idea informing this maxim is that a transaction may give rise to equitable rights even though no legal rights have been created because there has not been compliance with the necessary legal formalities. For example, an oral contract for the sale of land is not enforceable at common law but it may nonetheless be enforced in equity if has been partly performed by one of the parties doing acts which are exclusively referable to the contract.[59]

(e) Equity acts *in personam*. The principal significance of the maxim is historical in that all equitable rights were once considered to be personal, rather than proprietary, just as the right to performance of a contract is personal. On this view, a court of equity makes personal orders which operated on the conscience of the legal title-holder. It is, however, now generally recognised that some equitable rights, such as the rights of a beneficiary under a fixed trust, are

56 *Stern v McArthur* (1988) 165 CLR 489. See [7.57]–[7.60].
57 See [14.13] on sham trusts.
58 *Tanwar Enterprises Pty Ltd v Cauchi* (2003) 217 CLR 315; *Sourcebook* 7.4.2a, p 182. See [7.61].
59 *Maddison v Alderson* (1883) 8 App Cas 467; *McBride v Sandland* (1918) 25 CLR 69.

proprietary.[60] The maxim is of some practical importance in private international law where equitable claims are made to land outside Australia. Courts can make personal orders affecting foreign land but cannot adjudicate directly on title to the land.[61]

(f) Equity follows the law. Courts of equity recognise legal rights, interests and estates although they will prevent the unconscientious exercise of these entitlements. Equity also sometimes applies limitation statutes by analogy to applications of the statutes at common law.[62] A more accurate proposition is, however, that 'equity follows the law, but not slavishly nor always'.[63]

(g) Equity does not assist a volunteer. The word 'volunteer' means, in this context, someone who has not provided consideration. In general terms, equitable relief is confined to those who have given value in a transaction. Consideration has a broader meaning in equity than at common law, so that, for example, in nineteenth-century marriage settlements the children of a marriage were held to be within the 'marriage consideration' even though they had not given consideration of a kind recognised by contract law. There are numerous exceptions to this maxim, and it has been suggested that it would be a mistake to set too much store by it.[64]

(h) Delay defeats an equity. The impact of a claimant's delay in bringing an equitable claim is discussed at [6.3]–[6.11].

[1.44] The maxims are discussed in greater detail where relevant to other discussion in this book and in the online resources.

WHAT'S ONLINE?

Available at www.cambridge.org/highereducation/isbn/9781009232388/resources:

- Recommended further readings
- Appendix of *Judicature* legislation
- Discussion topics

60 See [13.10].

61 *Penn v Lord Baltimore* (1750) 27 ER 1132; *Talacko v Talacko* [2009] VSC 349; *Murakami v Wiryadi* (2010) 268 ALR 377.

62 *Motor Terms Co Pty Ltd v Liberty Insurance Ltd (in liq)* (1967) 116 CLR 177.

63 *Graf v Hope Building Corporation*, 254 NY 1 (1930), 9 (Cardozo J).

64 *Corin v Patton* (1990) 169 CLR 540.

PART B

EQUITABLE REMEDIES

2

AN INTRODUCTION TO EQUITABLE REMEDIES

Introduction

Remedies evolve from the procedures courts apply. Common law courts historically divided their decision-making functions between judge and jury; the judge defined the questions for the jury to answer, which the jury then decided. This system is still generally regarded as an acceptable method of determining criminal liability; however, randomly selected ad hoc bodies such as juries cannot supervise the performance of contracts, ensure compliance with injunctions or take complex accounts. Judges, assisted by court officers, are better equipped to order these kinds of remedies, all of which require the cooperation, however reluctant, of the defendant. [2.1]

Equitable remedies grew out of the practice of chancellors, sitting without a jury but assisted by clerks and masters, exercising continuing supervision of matters that were sufficiently complex to require more than the parties having a 'day in court'. One example is the very old case of *Hewett v Hewett*,[1] where the Court had to determine which timber on a property the plaintiff would be allowed to cut down. This matter had to be decided from time to time, for the rest of his life.[2]

Because current equitable practice emerged from the Chancellor's delivery of individual justice, based on the merits of the case and the circumstances of the particular parties before it, equitable remedies are always discretionary. They are not immediately granted once a plaintiff proves her claim (as is the case with contract and tort), but may perhaps be limited or denied altogether in response to a range of factors relevant to the particular claim. It is a feature of equitable remedies that the court's discretion is exercised after consideration of the positions of *both* parties; sometimes the effect of the remedy on other parties, including the wider community, is considered too.[3] [2.2]

The array of remedies available in equity looks bewildering at first sight, but it becomes obvious in most cases that only one or two remedies will provide the kind of relief the plaintiff is looking for. At common law the plaintiff is limited to damages as a remedy; the plaintiff's question is 'How much money am I entitled to?'. In equity, however, a wide range of remedies are available; the plaintiff's question becomes 'What remedy will put me in the position I would like to be in?'. In any dispute, equity regards remedies as crucial. For this reason, we will be discussing equitable remedies *first* in this book, before discussing current equitable doctrine. [2.3]

Personal and proprietary remedies

Equitable remedies can be distinguished according to their effect, and the purpose they fulfil. In considering the effect of equitable remedies a critical distinction exists between *personal* and *proprietary* remedies. [2.4]

1 (1763–65) 2 Eden 332; 28 ER 925.

2 This degree of supervision would not be possible today; indeed, the *need* for supervision might be a reason why a particular remedy is denied: see [3.5].

3 *Giumelli v Giumelli* (1999) 196 CLR 101; *Sourcebook* 6.6a, p 138; *Miller v Jackson* [1977] QB 966; *Sourcebook* 3.3.3a, p 50; *Nelson v Nelson* (1995) 184 CLR 538; *Sourcebook* 2.2c, p 21.

Personal remedies

[2.5] Personal remedies are simply orders directed to the person of the defendant. The defendant must comply with the order, or else be in contempt of court. The award of a personal remedy has no direct impact on the defendant's property. Awards of damages for tort or breach of contract are examples of personal remedies. Equity also has personal remedies such as equitable compensation, account of profits, and injunction, all of which are discussed in following chapters.

Proprietary remedies

[2.6] A proprietary remedy is directed to property to which the defendant holds title. The order may declare that identified property belongs to the plaintiff in equity, as constructive trust orders do. Alternatively, the court can direct the sale of that property in order to satisfy the plaintiff's judgment, unless the defendant satisfies the judgment out of other resources. This is the consequence of imposing an equitable lien over the defendant's property.

Types of proprietary remedies

[2.7] There are two proprietary remedies. They are:

(1) *The constructive trust.* This is an order that the defendant hold identified property on trust for the plaintiff. The plaintiff will be entitled to the property in equity, or to a proportionate interest in that property assessed by the court. If the property appreciates in value the plaintiff will be entitled to the benefit of the appreciation. Conversely, the plaintiff carries the risk of any depreciation. A constructive trust is not a general remedy available whenever justice and fairness requires; it is imposed in carefully defined situations.[4] Those situations are explained in chapter 23.[5]

(2) *The equitable lien (or charge).* The lien is a security interest over property. Although it attaches to particular property, the plaintiff does not obtain a share of the property, as is the case with a constructive trust. Instead, the lien acts similarly to a mortgage, to secure a debt. If the defendant does not discharge the debt to the plaintiff out of other funds, the property in question will eventually be sold, and the plaintiff paid out of its proceeds.

Some liens, such as the trustee's lien over trust property to secure repayment of trust expenses,[6] arise automatically. However, liens can also be judicially imposed in support of personal remedies. For example, a lien was imposed in *Giumelli v Giumelli*[7] as security for payment of the personal remedy of equitable compensation.

4 In some cases, a resulting trust may be awarded as a proprietary remedy. The boundary between resulting and constructive trusts is not always clear. See chapter 22 for a discussion of resulting trusts.

5 See also [2.13].

6 See [19.8]. Other examples include the beneficiary's lien over property acquired by a trustee through a breach of trust: see [21.4]; *Foskett v McKeown* [2001] 1 AC 102; *Sourcebook* 21.1a, p 519.

7 (1999) 196 CLR 101.

Comparing proprietary remedies and personal remedies

Proprietary remedies enjoy important advantages over personal remedies. The principal advantage is that a plaintiff can make a claim to the property that is the subject-matter of a proprietary remedy. This is crucial if the defendant is insolvent. The property will vest in the plaintiff rather than the trustee in bankruptcy or liquidator, and therefore the defendant's unsecured creditors will not have access to it. In contrast, the award of a personal remedy entitles the plaintiff only to the status of an unsecured judgment creditor in the defendant's insolvency. If the defendant has insufficient assets to discharge its debts, the plaintiff will only recover, at best, a proportion of the debt, in common with other unsecured creditors.[8] [2.8]

Another advantage of proprietary remedies is that they are enforceable against third parties who have received the property in question from the defendant. The only limitation on the right to recover property from third parties is that they are not enforceable against a good faith purchaser of the property without notice of the plaintiff's rights. In contrast, a personal remedy is enforceable only against the party against whom the remedy was ordered. [2.9]

Further, proprietary remedies entitle the plaintiff to claim specific property to which she attaches special value, for which money cannot provide adequate compensation. This characteristic of proprietary remedies is often overlooked. A plaintiff can recover identified land or valuable chattels which have no money-substitute by obtaining an order that the property be held on constructive trust for her. A personal remedy will only entitle the plaintiff to the assessment of a sum of money representing the value of the property (including, where an account of profits is ordered, profits generated from the use of the property). [2.10]

Despite their significant advantages, there are limitations to proprietary remedies. The main limitation is that the remedy cannot be awarded if the defendant no longer has property over which it can be imposed. Suppose a fiduciary obtains $1000 from a beneficiary in breach of duty. A constructive trust (which, as we will see, is the appropriate proprietary remedy for this type of case) can be imposed over the $1000.[9] If the fiduciary has used it to buy a painting, the beneficiary can claim that;[10] but the remedy will be irrelevant if the fiduciary has spent the money on a party. A constructive trust over empty champagne bottles will not be much use to the beneficiary, who will only be entitled to a personal remedy (in this case, equitable compensation) against the delinquent fiduciary. Proprietary remedies presuppose the existence of property for the plaintiff to claim. [2.11]

The objectives of equitable remedies

Equitable remedies can be distinguished according to the function they perform. The following are the principal objectives of equitable relief.[11] [2.12]

8 This is usually referred to by percentage; for example, 'ten cents in the dollar'. Thus, if the plaintiff is owed $10, he will only recover $1.

9 See [23.36].

10 See chapter 21.

11 See generally MJ Tilbury, *Civil Remedies* (Butterworths, 1990).

Coercion

[2.13] Some equitable remedies are coercive, compelling the defendant to behave in a certain way. Specific performance, requiring the defendant to perform his contractual obligations according to the terms of the contract, is coercive. Injunctions are also coercive, either requiring the defendant to act, or cease acting, as ordered. Specific performance and injunctions are discussed in the next chapter.

Compensation

[2.14] Common law damages compensate the plaintiff for loss caused by the commission of a wrong, such as a tort or a breach of contract.[12] The equitable counterpart is equitable compensation which compensates a plaintiff for loss caused by the commission of an equitable wrong, such as a breach of trust. This is discussed in chapter 4.

Disgorgement

[2.15] Equity requires a wrongdoer who has made a profit from breach of an equitable obligation, such as a breach of confidence or fiduciary obligation, to disgorge those profits to the plaintiff. Disgorgement, or profit-stripping, can be achieved in a number of ways. The defendant can be ordered to account for the profits. This is a personal remedy, discussed in chapter 4. If the profit is identifiable – for example, as money in a bank account or land – the award of a constructive trust over the property also achieves disgorgement. Alternatively, disgorgement can be effected by the award of an account of profits secured by the imposition of an equitable lien over property purchased with the plaintiff's money.[13]

Restitution

[2.16] Restitution is an ambiguous word in the law. A trustee who has misappropriated trust moneys will be ordered to make restitution to the trust fund.[14] Unless the trustee still holds the original money, the remedy which effects restitution will be equitable compensation, discussed in chapter 4.[15]

A second, and nowadays more common, meaning of restitution is that of 'restoration'. The defendant must restore to the plaintiff property which ought to belong to her. An important equitable restitutionary remedy is rescission, discussed in chapter 5. If a fiduciary has entered into a contract with the beneficiary in breach of obligation, and has received property under the contract, the court will order rescission at the instance of the beneficiary, and will require the fiduciary to make restitution of the property as one of the terms or conditions of rescission. Where no property has to be restored under the voidable contract, rescission is a personal remedy; however, where property is returned to either or both of the contracting parties as part of the process of restoring both to their pre-contractual

12 Some common law damages are not compensatory in nature; for example, nominal and exemplary damages have other functions.

13 *Scott v Scott* (1963) 109 CLR 649; *Sourcebook* 21.7a, p 544.

14 *Re Dawson (deceased)* [1966] 2 NSWR 211; *Sourcebook* 4.3.3a, p 74.

15 See chapter 20 for remedies for breach of trust.

position, that property will be held on constructive trust for the party entitled until it has been restored.[16] When imposed over property conveyed under rescinded contracts, the constructive trust is a restitutionary remedy.

Equitable compensation is sometimes awarded as a personal restitutionary remedy. One example is where property has been conveyed under a contract which is voidable for breach of fiduciary duty, but it cannot be returned because it has been purchased by a good faith purchaser for value without notice of the equitable wrong. Usually, the plaintiff will be entitled to the purchase price paid to the wrongdoer by the honest third party.[17] But if that money has been spent, the wrongdoer will nonetheless be ordered to pay equitable compensation assessed at the value of the property received by the purchaser.[18]

Nullification

Equitable remedies will sometimes nullify the legal consequences of a transaction, without otherwise imposing obligations on the parties. Where equity orders rescission of a contract which has not been executed by either party, the contract is nullified and the parties have no further obligations to perform under the contract.[19] [2.17]

Equitable relief for breach of confidence sometimes includes directions that documents containing confidential information, and property manufactured by unauthorised use of the information, be delivered up and destroyed.[20] This is another example of equity nullifying the effects of equitable wrongdoing.

Reformation

The equitable remedy of rectification, discussed in chapter 5, reforms a legal document so that it reflects the objectively ascertained agreement of the parties. Some orders of rescission may have the incidental effect of reforming a transaction. For example, the remedy of partial rescission, whereby a part of a contract but not the whole is set aside, is in substance a reformation of the contract so that it conforms to the agreement the parties actually reached.[21] [2.18]

Vindication

Some equitable remedies serve the function of validating the plaintiff's rights. The declaration performs such a function,[22] and is discussed in chapter 5. A declaration is the court's statement [2.19]

16 *Daly v Sydney Stock Exchange Ltd* (1986) 160 CLR 371; *Sourcebook* 5.3a, p 102.

17 Sometimes adjustments need to made in recognition of improvements made by the defendant between wrongful acquisition and sale to the honest third party. See *McKenzie v McDonald* [1927] VLR 134; *Sourcebook* 2.2b, p 19.

18 *Hartigan v International Society for Krishna Consciousness Inc* [2002] NSWSC 810.

19 *Commercial Bank of Australia Ltd v Amadio* (1983) 151 CLR 447; *Sourcebook* 7.3.3b, p 158. Another view of rescission of a wholly executory contract is that it is a restitutionary remedy for unjust enrichment because each party restores to the other the right to sue for breach of contract. See Andrew Burrows, *The Law of Restitution* (Oxford University Press, 3rd ed, 2011) 16–21.

20 *Franklin v Giddins* [1978] Qd R 72.

21 *Vadasz v Pioneer Concrete (SA) Pty Ltd* (1995) 184 CLR 102; *Sourcebook* 5.2a, p 98.

22 *Lewis v Australian Capital Territory* (2020) 381 ALR 375, [119] (Gordon J).

of the respective rights of the parties before it. Injunctions, particularly final or perpetual injunctions, can serve the same purpose.

Although some remedies, such as the account of profits, fulfil only one objective, the aims of others are more various. Rescission of an executory contract nullifies the contract, but where the contract is partly or wholly executed the remedy is restitutionary. The constructive trust is chameleonic. Depending on the facts which give rise to its imposition, it can be a restitutionary remedy for unjust enrichment or a proprietary remedy for disgorgement of unauthorised gains. The scheme above is in fact insufficient to capture the varieties of constructive trust – the remedy can also, among much else, enforce a plaintiff's expectations, or entitle her to property representing her reliance expenditure. To make matters even more confusing, the constructive trust is not always a proprietary remedy – constructive trusteeship can be a formula for the imposition of personal liability.

The diversity present in equitable remedies is in sharp contrast to damages awards that are typical of the common law. The range of available equitable remedies demonstrates equity's concern with achieving justice between the parties in the most suitable way, and emphasises the discretionary nature of equitable relief.

WHAT'S ONLINE?

Available at www.cambridge.org/highereducation/isbn/9781009232388/resources:

- Recommended further readings
- Discussion topics

3

SPECIFIC PERFORMANCE, INJUNCTIONS AND EQUITABLE DAMAGES

Introduction

[3.1] The title of this chapter may look like a grab bag of remedies, but this is not the case. Specific performance and injunctions are equitable remedies. The remedy of equitable damages is a creature of statute available either *in lieu of* or *in addition to* the equitable remedies of specific performance and injunction. Thus, the three remedies are closely related. They will be discussed in turn.

Specific performance

[3.2] An order of specific performance is an order directing a party to a contract to perform the contract according to its terms. The party will be directed to perform all his obligations under the contract. The remedy of specific performance illustrates the dualist nature[1] of our legal system. It is only available in respect of the common law action of breach of contract. Specific performance exemplifies equity acting in its auxiliary jurisdiction.[2] As the remedy is usually dealt with in contract law or remedies courses our coverage will be brief.

General considerations

[3.3] There are two considerations generally relevant to an award of specific performance. These are: (a) fairness to both parties; and (b) the supervision requirement.

Fairness to both parties

[3.4] It will be unjust to hold the defendant strictly to his side of the bargain unless the plaintiff has performed her obligations under the contract, or is in a position to do so. Courts of equity have formulated tests to determine the overall fairness of an order of specific performance. One, known as 'mutuality', is that specific performance will not be ordered unless the court is satisfied that the defendant will be sufficiently protected in the event that the plaintiff does not perform her obligations.[3] This is sometimes taken to mean that the plaintiff cannot have the defendant's obligations specifically performed unless the defendant has an equivalent right to performance of the plaintiff's obligations. But mutuality does not have to take the form of 'tit for tat' specific performance – the possibility of obtaining other remedies, such as an injunction, may be sufficient in some cases. Exceptionally, a court might even consider the defendant to be protected by a damages award in the event of the plaintiff's breach.[4]

1 See [1.28]–[1.29].

2 See [1.31]. Equity's assistance may also be required to ensure performance of equitable obligations but the orders in these cases are not, strictly speaking, orders of specific performance. The enforcement of a constructive trust or an order to deliver up documents obtained in breach of confidence are examples of these mandatory orders: see *Smethurst v Commissioner of Police* (2020) 376 ALR 575, [257]–[260] (Edelman J).

3 JB Ames, *Lectures on Legal History and Miscellaneous Legal Essays* (Harvard University Press, 1913) 371; *Price v Strange* [1978] Ch 337, 367–8 (Buckley LJ); I Spry, *The Principles of Equitable Remedies: Specific Performance, Injunctions, Rectification and Equitable Damages* (Lawbook, 2001) 91; *JC Williamson Ltd v Lukey* (1931) 45 CLR 282, 298 (Dixon J).

4 *Price v Strange* [1978] Ch 337.

Fairness also explains equity's refusal to order specific performance in favour of a plaintiff who has not fully performed her contractual obligations unless she is 'ready and willing' to perform them. Indeed, a plaintiff must aver, and if necessary prove, that she is ready and willing to carry out her side of the contract. So, a plaintiff who is in substantial breach of contract will not obtain specific performance, although a plaintiff who has committed relatively minor and easily rectifiable breaches will be entitled to the remedy.[5] 'Mutuality' and 'ready and willing to perform' are both specialised applications of the broader principle that a plaintiff who comes to equity must do equity.[6]

Supervision

The court must also be satisfied that it can supervise the order of specific performance, if called upon to do so. 'Supervision' is a misleading word: it conjures up images of judges standing over a recalcitrant author to ensure that a book is completed. But supervision does not work like this. 'Supervision' means the court has to be able to determine whether its order has been broken. Failure to comply with the order, or with a ruling made to give effect to the order, is punishable as a contempt. Courts are reluctant to grant a decree of specific performance if the contract does not state what performance requires, or if the defendant is required by the terms of the contract to carry out an activity over a period of years, possibly also involving compliance with complex and detailed terms.[7] [3.5]

For example, in *Co-operative Insurance Society Ltd v Argyll Stores (Holdings) Ltd*,[8] the plaintiffs leased a supermarket to the defendant. A covenant in the lease required the defendant to maintain the premises as a supermarket, and to keep it open for retail trade during normal business hours. The defendant could not operate the supermarket profitably and closed it. The House of Lords refused to award specific performance compelling the defendant to continue carrying on the supermarket business, as specific performance would give rise to 'the possibility of the court having to give an indefinite series of … rulings in order to ensure the execution of the order'.[9] In general, specific performance is more likely to be granted where the order requires the defendant to achieve a particular result, such as to convey property to the plaintiff, rather than orders which require the defendant to carry on an activity, such as to run a business.

Particular kinds of contracts and supervision

(A) CONSTRUCTION CONTRACTS

Special principles determine whether specific performance will be ordered of a construction contract, and the practical considerations are often finely balanced. On the one hand, the costs of giving repeated rulings on how a complex construction contract is to be performed will be high. On the other hand, it is, as Lord Hoffmann remarked in the *Argyll Stores* [3.6]

5 *Bahr v Nicolay (No 2)* (1988) 164 CLR 604.

6 See [1.43].

7 *Patrick Stevedores Operations No 2 Pty Ltd v Maritime Union of Australia* (1998) 195 CLR 1; *Co-operative Insurance Society Ltd v Argyll Stores (Holdings) Ltd* [1998] AC 1; *Sourcebook* 3.2.2.1a, p 34.

8 [1998] AC 1; *Sourcebook* 3.2.2.1a, p 34.

9 *Co-operative Insurance Society Ltd v Argyll Stores (Holdings) Ltd* [1998] AC 1, 12.

case, easier to award specific performance of a contract to achieve a particular result, such as to construct a building, than to carry on a business. In *Wolverhampton Corporation v Emmons*,[10] Romer LJ stated three conditions for the award of specific performance. They are:

(1) that the contract is sufficiently precise to be enforced;

(2) that the plaintiff has a substantial interest in performance, which cannot be compensated in damages; and

(3) that the defendant has possession of the land on which the work is to be done.

(B) CONTRACTS FOR THE PERFORMANCE OF PERSONAL SERVICES

[3.7] The general rule is that contracts of employment cannot be specifically performed. The justification is partly moral – equity will not compel one person to work for another[11] – but it is also pragmatic – specific performance will not be ordered if it requires continual cooperation between the parties.[12] The prohibition on specific performance goes beyond employment contracts. It also includes contracts for services to be performed by independent contractors. In these cases, the services will often be performed, if not by the contractor, then by employees of the contractor to whom the public policy against specific performance also extends. As a general rule, courts will not order specific performance of agency contracts for similar policy reasons.[13]

There are two exceptions to the prohibition on enforcing employment contracts. The first permits enforcement where the policy and pragmatic reasons for refusing enforcement are absent. An employee can enforce the contract of employment against the employer in circumstances in which performance will not require the employer's cooperation. In *Patrick Stevedores Operations No 2 Pty Ltd v Maritime Union of Australia*,[14] the Court was asked to restrain the administrator of a company in the Patrick Stevedores group of companies from doing anything which had the effect of terminating the employment of the plaintiff employees. The High Court granted an injunction, recognising that the order was in substance one of specific performance. There were no objections in principle to making the order: the order would not reduce the employees to a condition of servitude (in fact, it would have the opposite effect); there were no problems of supervision; and employment did not require close cooperation between the employees and the employer companies.

The second exception to the principle that equity will not enforce contracts for personal services is that, in some cases, an injunction to restrain an employee from working for a rival employer will be granted even though specific performance cannot be obtained. The exception is an old one, created by the English decision of *Lumley v Wagner*,[15] in which an opera singer was restrained by injunction from singing for an opera house which was a rival to the plaintiff's theatre. Such an injunction looks like

10 [1901] 1 KB 515, 524–5. The principle has been extended to a contract for the construction of a ship: *Virtu Fast Ferries Ltd v The Ship 'Cape Leveque'* (2015) 232 FCR 9, [27].

11 *De Francesco v Barnum* (1890) 45 Ch D 430, 438 (Fry LJ).

12 *JC Williamson Ltd v Lukey* (1931) 45 CLR 282, 298 (Dixon J).

13 *Netline Pty Ltd v QAV Pty Ltd (No 2)* [2015] WASC 113, [67].

14 (1998) 195 CLR 1; *Sourcebook* 3.2.2.1b, p 38.

15 (1852) 42 ER 687. See also SM Waddams, 'Johanna Wagner and the Rival Opera Houses' (2001) 117(3) *Law Quarterly Review* 431.

an 'indirect' specific performance award in circumstances in which a direct order could not have been obtained; however, in exercising its discretion, the court considers factors which would also be relevant to an award of specific performance. For example, an injunction will not be granted if it will, in practical terms, reduce the defendant to a condition of destitution because he is unlikely to be employed by anyone except the plaintiff and the plaintiff's rival whose employment he is seeking to enter. The court will need to be satisfied that the defendant can obtain employment other than that offered by the plaintiff and the rival employer. The injunction issued will also be of short duration, its principal purpose being to bring home to the defendant the importance of performing his contractual obligations.[16]

Prerequisites to award

There are three essential prerequisites to an award of specific performance. The contract must be specifically enforceable; valuable consideration must have been given for its performance; and damages must be an inadequate remedy for non-performance. [3.8]

Specifically enforceable contracts

Decrees of specific performance are confined to the enforcement of binding contracts. Therefore, the remedy will not be granted where a contract is invalid at law (as is the case with a contract for an illegal purpose) or liable to be rescinded by the plaintiff (as is a contract obtained through duress). In addition, it may be impossible to obtain specific performance of a contract that is non-compliant with the requirements of writing that originate in the *Statute of Frauds 1677* (Imp).[17] [3.9]

Valuable consideration

Valuable consideration must have been given in return for the promise to be enforced. So, a promise executed by deed under seal is not specifically enforceable because a seal is not considered to be valuable consideration in equity – the promisee's only remedy for breach will be damages. Nominal consideration, such as a promise made in return for one dollar consideration, is also not valuable consideration in equity. [3.10]

Inadequacy of damages

As specific performance is granted in equity's auxiliary jurisdiction, the remedy will not be granted unless damages are inadequate.[18] There is no need for equity to act in support of a common law right that is already adequately protected. Damages awards for breach of [3.11]

16 *Buckenara v Hawthorn Football Club* [1988] VR 39; *Curro v Beyond Productions Pty Ltd* (1993) 30 NSWLR 337; *Sourcebook* 3.3.4a, p 53.

17 See [9.36]. Specific performance may still be an available remedy where the *Statute of Frauds 1677* (Imp) is inapplicable as being an instrument of fraud or where the contract satisfies the requirements of the doctrine of part performance: *Halloran v Minister Administering National Parks and Wildlife Act 1974* (2006) 229 CLR 545; *Pipikos v Trayans* (2018) 265 CLR 522.

18 *Loan Investment Corporation of Australasia v Bonner* [1970] NZLR 724; *Sourcebook* 3.2.1.1a, p 27. In some formulations, damages must be 'inappropriate': *Beswick v Beswick* [1968] AC 58; *Sourcebook* 3.2.1.3a, p 32.

contract assume that damages will be sufficient to make good the plaintiff's loss, so that, for example, where a defendant fails to deliver goods specified under the contract, damages will enable the plaintiff to buy substitute goods in the marketplace.

There are several approaches courts can take to determining the adequacy of damages. One is to require proof of inadequacy. Canadian courts adopt this approach in deciding whether a contract for the sale of land should be specifically enforced. The plaintiff must demonstrate why *this* property, and no other, is so important to her that money will not fully compensate her for the loss of the opportunity to buy the property.[19] Australian law, on the other hand, has adopted what might be termed a 'modified category' approach. Specific performance will routinely be ordered of certain categories of contract, unless a bar to the award of the remedy can be shown. It is also possible for a plaintiff to demonstrate that, where a contract not belonging to one of the established categories has been broken, damages would on the facts be an inadequate remedy and that specific performance should be ordered. This might be the case with a rare asset, not readily available on the market.[20]

The best-known category of specifically performable contract is the contract for the sale of land. Few nowadays agree with the traditional reason given for ordering performance; namely, that no two pieces of land are identical.[21] Many such contracts are entered into by property developers who are uninterested in any quality in the land except its profit-making capacity, yet specific performance is not denied to developers.[22] A more convincing justification is that the whole process of buying land is so lengthy and complex that it would be unfair, upon the vendor's breach, to make the purchaser take her damages and start the whole process of looking for a property again. The very fact that specific performance is the standard remedy for breach, unless it is barred by some consideration such as the plaintiff's delay in bringing proceedings, means that the vendor will know that the price he will have to pay for being allowed to withdraw from the bargain will be high.

Contracts for the sale of chattels which cannot be easily obtained on the market are also specifically enforceable. Damages are inadequate because, if awarded, they would not enable the plaintiff to purchase a satisfactory alternative chattel.[23] A plaintiff does not have to show that it is impossible to purchase an equivalent chattel. Specific performance will be granted – for example, for contracts to sell ships or lease aircraft – even though a substitute can theoretically be obtained by a damages award, because the replacement is unlikely to be procured in time to meet the commercial needs of the plaintiff.[24] It will also be ordered if a commonly available commodity becomes temporarily scarce;[25] for example, because of a strike.

Contracts to pay or lend money are not normally specifically enforceable; damages are an adequate remedy for the failure to pay money. But there are important exceptions to

19 R Chambers, 'The Importance of Specific Performance' in S Degeling and J Edelman (eds), *Equity in Commercial Law* (Lawbook, 2005) 431, 434–6; *Semelhago v Paramadevan* (1996) 136 DLR (4th) 1.

20 See, eg, a taxi licence: see *Dougan v Ley* (1946) 71 CLR 142; *Sourcebook* 3.2.1.2a, p 31.

21 *Cud v Rutter* (1719) 1 P Wms 570, 571–2.

22 *Loan Investment Corporation of Australasia v Bonner* [1970] NZLR 724, 745 (Barwick CJ dissenting).

23 *Dougan v Ley* (1946) 71 CLR 142; *Sourcebook* 3.2.1.2a, p 31.

24 *Behnke v Bede Shipping Co Ltd* [1927] 1 KB 649, 661.

25 *Sky Petroleum Ltd v VIP Petroleum Ltd* [1974] 1 All ER 954.

this principle. Mutuality requires that if a purchaser of land can obtain an order for specific performance for the sale of land, a vendor can likewise enforce the purchaser's obligation to pay the purchase price.[26] Secondly, difficulties in quantifying damages, or in ensuring that they will be paid, justify an award of specific performance in some cases. Both reasons justify the award of specific performance of a contract to pay an annuity. It will be impossible to quantify damages payable at the date of breach where the sum payable depends on the longevity of the payee. In addition, it will be unduly onerous to require the payee to sue for damages for each instalment of the annuity as it falls due.[27] Thirdly, a contract whereby P performs a service for D in return for D's promise to pay X will entitle P to obtain specific performance in favour of X in the event that D fails to keep his promise. P's damages for breach of contract will usually be nominal in this case, and specific performance will be awarded because D will, in a general sense, be unjustly enriched at the expense of P unless he is compelled to make the promised payment to X.[28]

A drawback to the method of 'specific performance by category' is that it sometimes gives rise to difficult characterisation problems of determining whether a given contract belongs to a specifically performable category (such as a contract for the sale of land) or to a class of contract which is not generally specifically performable (such as a contract to pay money). In *Loan Investment Corporation of Australasia v Bonner*,[29] for example, the Privy Council was divided as to the correct characterisation of a contract for the sale of land entered into as part of a composite loan transaction. The majority opinion analysed the arrangement as a contract of loan and denied the plaintiff specific performance. Barwick CJ, dissenting, would have granted specific performance of what, on his view, was essentially a contract for the sale of land.

Bars to specific performance

Like other equitable remedies, awards of specific performance are discretionary. The exercise of discretion is closely controlled and relief will only be withheld on well-defined grounds. Some of the grounds, such as want of mutuality, or the plaintiff's willingness and readiness to perform her own obligations, discussed above,[30] are peculiar to specific performance. Others, such as the conduct of the plaintiff or the hardship that an order will cause to the defendant, are applicable generally to equitable remedies. The bars to the award of equitable relief are discussed in chapter 6. Adverse movements in market prices does not amount to hardship justifying refusal of specific performance.[31] But the economic impact of COVID-19 has been recognised as hardship barring equitable relief.[32] If specific performance is barred for hardship, or on some other discretionary ground, the plaintiff may obtain damages for breach of contract unless the ground for refusing specific performance also provides the plaintiff with a ground for rescinding the contract.[33] [3.12]

26 *Turner v Bladin* (1951) 82 CLR 463.
27 *Beswick v Beswick* [1968] AC 58; *Sourcebook* 3.2.1.3a, p 32.
28 *Beswick v Beswick* [1968] AC 58.
29 [1970] NZLR 724; *Sourcebook* 3.2.1.1a, p 27.
30 See [3.4].
31 *Demagogue Pty Ltd v Ramensky* [1992] FCA 557, [44]
32 *NTT Australia Digital Pty Ltd v Cover Genius Services Pty Ltd* (2020) 19 BPR 40,711, [187]. Cf *Patel v Ali* [1984] 1 Ch 283; *Sourcebook* 6.5a, p 134.
33 See chapter 5.

Injunctions

[3.13] An injunction is an order enforcing legal or equitable rights,[34] either by restraining the doing of an unlawful act, or by requiring a particular act to be done, and is equity's principal coercive remedy. Injunctions are available in both the exclusive and auxiliary jurisdiction of equity. In the exclusive jurisdiction they enforce equitable rights. In the auxiliary jurisdiction they are used to support common law rights. Injunctions can be classified as follows:

(a) *Mandatory and prohibitory*. Mandatory injunctions are positive, compelling the defendant to perform an act; prohibitory injunctions are negative, requiring the defendant to refrain from carrying out an act.[35]

(b) *Perpetual, interim and interlocutory*. Perpetual injunctions are final, settling all outstanding issues between the parties. 'Perpetual' does not mean that the order is of perpetual duration; it indicates that a final order has been made following argument by both sides. Interim injunctions are temporary, effective only for a limited period of time. An interlocutory injunction preserves the rights of parties pending trial.

(c) *Ex parte*. An injunction may be required so urgently that the plaintiff does not have time to serve notice on the defendant that the application is being made. Alternatively, the plaintiff might apply for an ex parte order where there is a risk the defendant will simply take steps to avoid the court's order. An injunction granted without giving prior notice to the party who will be bound by its terms is an 'ex parte' injunction. Notice is given to the defendant once the injunction is granted so that the defendant will know precisely how he must comply with its terms, and to give him the opportunity to have the order set aside or varied.

(d) *Quia timet*. This injunction protects the plaintiff's rights where an infringement is threatened but has not yet occurred. For example, a quia timet injunction will be granted to prevent a property development if residents affected by the development prove that once completed it will constitute a nuisance.

[3.14] In addition, there are orders which were initially developed as injunctions but which have lost their specifically equitable character and are now part of the law of civil procedure. Although the orders enforce the plaintiff's legal or equitable rights, they also protect the integrity of the court's legal processes. One example is the Mareva order[36] which is an ex parte order preventing assets from being removed from the jurisdiction of the court. Another is the Anton Piller order[37] which is an ex parte interlocutory mandatory injunction compelling the defendant to allow the plaintiff or her agents to inspect the defendant's property. Its principal use is to enable the plaintiff to determine whether the defendant has infringed copyright or misused confidential information. An ex parte order is needed in these cases to prevent the defendant from disposing of evidence which might substantiate the plaintiff's claim.

34 Statutory injunctions are not covered in this book.

35 See *Smethurst v Commissioner of Police* (2020) 376 ALR 575, [248]–[260] (Edelman J); *Sourcebook* 3.3.2a, p 42.

36 Named after *Mareva Compania Naviera SA v International Bulkcarriers SA* [1975] 2 Lloyds Rep 509.

37 Named after *Anton Piller KG v Manufacturing Processes Ltd* [1976] Ch 55.

The 'anti-suit' injunction, issued to prevent a litigant from pursuing proceedings in another jurisdiction when they have already been initiated in Australia, is an example of an order which, while initiating in equity, is now regarded as part of the court's armoury to regulate its own jurisdiction.[38]

The jurisdiction to award injunctions

Injunctions were once awarded in the inherent jurisdiction of the Court of Chancery. The jurisdiction is now statutory. For example, s 37(1) of the *Supreme Court Act 1986* (Vic) provides: [3.15]

> The Court may by order, whether interlocutory or final, grant an injunction or appoint a receiver if it is just and convenient to do so.[39]

The provision appears to confer a wide-ranging and unfettered jurisdiction to grant injunctions whenever it would be 'just and convenient to do so'. However, the orthodox view is that injunctions can only be awarded in support of established legal, equitable or (in the case of statutory injunctions) statutory rights. 'Right' is, for this purpose, broadly construed. It need not be proprietary. For example, an injunction can be granted to prevent a breach of confidence, even though confidential information is not property in law.[40] The plaintiff's personal legal or equitable rights provide a recognised basis for awarding an injunction. [3.16]

In *Australian Broadcasting Corporation v Lenah Game Meats Pty Ltd*,[41] trespassers filmed the slaughter of Tasmanian brushtail possums at the plaintiff's abattoirs. The film was passed to the ABC for broadcasting. The plaintiff sought an injunction restraining broadcasting of the film. The High Court held by majority that the plaintiff was not entitled to an injunction. An award of an injunction is not at large but can only be awarded in support of a recognised legal, equitable or statutory right. While the plaintiff would be entitled to obtain an injunction against the trespasser, it had no such right exercisable against the ABC which was not a trespasser and had not committed any other legal or equitable wrong.

Even if the plaintiff can prove that the defendant has committed a recognised legal wrong, an injunction will not be granted unless the plaintiff can prove that the wrong caused injury, or is likely to cause injury, which an award of damages cannot adequately compensate. In *Smethurst v Commissioner of Police*,[42] the Australian Federal Police took a journalist's mobile [3.17]

38 *CSR Ltd v Cigna Insurance Australia Ltd* (1997) 189 CLR 345; *Australian Broadcasting Corporation v Lenah Game Meats Pty Ltd* (2001) 208 CLR 199; *Sourcebook* 3.3.1a, p 40.

39 See also *Court Procedures Act 2004* (ACT) s 62(1) ('if the court considers it appropriate to do so'); *Supreme Court Act 1970* (NSW) s 66(4); *Supreme Court Act 1979* (NT) s 69(1); *Supreme Court Act 1995* (Qld) s 246; *Supreme Court Act 1935* (SA) s 29(1); *Supreme Court Civil Procedure Act 1932* (Tas) s 11(12); *Supreme Court Act 1935* (WA) s 25(9). Many other statutes specifically allow for the remedy of injunction in cases of breach of statutory provisions; eg *Corporations Act 2001* (Cth) s 1324(1); *Competition and Consumer Act 2010* (Cth) sch 2 s 232; *Copyright Act 1968* (Cth) s 195AZA.

40 See chapter 12.

41 (2001) 208 CLR 199; *Sourcebook* 3.3.1a, p 40. See also *Glencore International AG v Commissioner of Taxation* (2019) 265 CLR 646 (professional privilege, being a legal immunity and not a legal right, cannot support grant of injunction).

42 (2020) 376 ALR 575; *Sourcebook* 3.3.2a, p 42. L Burton Crawford, 'Private Rights, Public Wrongs and the Limits of Property' 137 (2021) *Law Quarterly Review* 39.

phone pursuant to an illegal search warrant and copied data from the phone onto a USB stick. The phone was later returned. The journalist and the publisher of the newspaper employing her applied for a mandatory injunction requiring the destruction or delivery up of the information taken from her phone or, alternatively, an injunction restraining the police from making that information available to the prosecuting authority. The injunctions were sought on both public law and private law grounds. It was conceded that the illegal taking of the phone amounted to the tort of trespass. A majority of the High Court held that the plaintiffs were not entitled to the injunctions they had sought. Kiefel CJ, Bell and Keane JJ stated that 'it is not possible to regard the prospect that one may be investigated for an offence as an injury'.[43] Similarly, Nettle J stated that the possibility that the journalist might be prosecuted for a criminal offence was not compensable loss because there was a public interest in the disclosure of criminality.[44] The dissenting judges considered that common law damages for trespass would be inadequate on these facts. In the opinion of Gageler J, money could not compensate the journalist for the infringement of her rights, particularly having regard to the constitutional context of the infringements.[45] Edelman J recognised the availability of an ameliorative injunction to undo the consequences of a wrong in circumstances where the interference with the liberty of the defendant is slight and the consequences to the plaintiff of not awarding an injunction are significant.[46]

The differences between the majority and dissenting judgments reflect not only differences of opinion as to whether the plaintiffs had identified a right that had been infringed. The differences also reflect disagreement on the general question of what constitutes a compensable injury when the complaint is that a constitutional right, as well as a private law right, has been infringed.

The criteria for the award of an injunction

[3.18] The criteria for the award of an injunction are as follows:

(1) The plaintiff must show that the defendant has committed a legal, equitable or statutory wrong (or, in the case of a quia timet injunction, that there is a substantial probability that he will do so). This requirement is discussed above.[47]

(2) The plaintiff must show that the wrong is likely to continue or be repeated (or, in the case of a quia timet injunction, that a wrong causing imminent and substantial damage is likely to occur). Whereas an award of damages looks to the past, an injunction looks to the future by preventing the commission of apprehended harm. For example, in *Irving v Emu & Prospect Gravel & Road Metal Co Ltd*,[48] a stranger had removed gravel and stone from the plaintiff's land and sold it to the defendant

43 *Smethurst v Commissioner of Police* (2020) 376 ALR 575, [73].

44 Ibid [160]

45 Ibid [122]. Gordon J placed special emphasis on the availability of the injunction to support constitutional rights but also stated at [196] that 'damages would not restore Ms Smethurst to the position she was in prior to the unlawful exercise of power because the AFP would continue to have a copy of data obtained from her mobile phone'.

46 Ibid [255].

47 See [3.16]–[3.17].

48 (1909) 26 WN (NSW) 137.

company. The company did not intend to use the gravel and stone once it realised that it had been stolen, and there was no evidence that the theft would be repeated. The injunction was therefore refused.

(3) A plaintiff who wants to prevent the commission of a common law wrong must show that damages or some other common law remedy are inadequate. For example, injunctions will not usually be granted to restrain conversion of a chattel, since, unless the chattel has some special value,[49] damages will be an adequate remedy. Inadequacy need not be shown where the wrong is equitable. As equitable rights cannot be protected at common law, such an enquiry is unnecessary.

Interlocutory injunctions

Because interlocutory injunctions are ordered *during* legal proceedings, at a stage when all of the evidence has not been considered, their award is guided by different principles than those applicable to final injunctions. As in the case of specific performance, two matters are crucial. The first is whether the proposed order will be fair to *both* parties. The second is whether the court can supervise the execution of its own order, bearing in mind the resources available to the parties and to the court. [3.19]

Fairness to the parties must be considered because the plaintiff's cause of action has not yet been proved and, unless the action is undefended, may never be proved. The exercise of balancing the interests of the parties at the interlocutory stage will be more speculative than after a full trial when there has been an opportunity to evaluate all the evidence. [3.20]

In *Beecham Group Ltd v Bristol Laboratories Pty Ltd*[50] the High Court laid down two criteria for the award of an interlocutory injunction. These were affirmed in *Australian Broadcasting Corporation v O'Neill*.[51]

(1) Has the plaintiff made out a prima facie case, in the sense that if evidence remains as it is there is a probability that at the trial of the action the plaintiff will be held to be entitled to the relief sought?

(2) Will the inconvenience or injury which the plaintiff is likely to suffer if the injunction is refused outweigh the injury which the defendant will suffer if an injunction is granted?

The word 'probability' in the first criterion does not mean that the plaintiff must have better than a 50–50 chance of success. What the plaintiff has to show is 'a sufficient likelihood of success to justify in the circumstances the preservation of the status quo pending the trial'.[52]

The second criterion is often referred to as 'the balance of convenience'. Relevant matters for the court to consider include the harm the plaintiff is likely to suffer if no injunction is granted, whether damages would be an adequate remedy for the plaintiff, and the potential

49 *Dougan v Ley* (1946) 71 CLR 142; *Sourcebook* 3.2.1.2a, p 31.

50 (1968) 118 CLR 618.

51 (2006) 227 CLR 57.

52 *Australian Broadcasting Corporation v O'Neill* (2006) 227 CLR 57, [65] (Gummow and Hayne JJ). An interlocutory injunction may be refused if the plaintiff's 'success' is likely to consist of an award of nominal damages: see *Australian Broadcasting Corporation v O'Neill* (2006) 227 CLR 57, [33] (Gleeson CJ and Crennan J), [89] (Gummow and Hayne JJ).

prejudice or harm to the defendant if it is restrained.[53] If the balance favours the defendant, that may justify refusal of interlocutory relief. As an alternative to outright refusal the court can impose terms on the granting of the interlocutory injunction, designed to prevent injury to the defendant in the event of failure of the plaintiff's claim at trial. It is usual, for example, for the injunction to be conditional on the plaintiff giving an undertaking to pay damages for loss caused to the defendant by the award of an injunction which is shown at trial not to support a valid legal claim.[54]

It is unclear whether the court can take into account a public policy which is unrelated to the specific circumstances of the parties when considering where the balance of convenience lies. In *Australian Broadcasting Corporation v O'Neill*,[55] the High Court was divided on whether the protection of freedom of speech was a consideration to which a court could have regard in deciding whether to grant an interlocutory injunction to prevent publication of an alleged defamatory statement. This is discussed at [3.29].

Mandatory and prohibitory injunctions

[3.21] It is sometimes said that courts are more reluctant to award mandatory injunctions, which compel the defendant to perform acts which will rectify the consequences of his wrongdoing or prevent their occurrence, than injunctions which prohibit the defendant from carrying out an activity. Depending on its terms, a mandatory injunction will often constitute a more serious interference with the defendant's freedom of action than a prohibitory injunction. Court supervision of compliance with a mandatory injunction is also likely to be more onerous and costly.

In *Smethurst v Commissioner of Police*,[56] a majority of the High Court refused to award the plaintiff a mandatory, restorative injunction which would have compelled the police to destroy or deliver up information taken from the plaintiff's mobile phone during a search undertaken pursuant to unlawful search warrants. The plurality judgment accepted that a mandatory injunction can be granted where there is some ongoing effect from tortious conduct.[57] The prospect of being investigated for an offence did not, however, amount in law to an injury.[58] Edelman J, dissenting, noted that it was unusual for an injunction to issue in order to ameliorate the consequences of a wrong rather than to prevent its occurrence or continuation. Such an order constitutes an interference with the defendant's liberty.[59] The award of an ameliorative injunction can be justified, however, if damages would be inadequate, the terms of the injunction being crafted so as to take into account the legitimate interests of both parties.[60]

In *Smethurst v Commissioner of Police*, the criteria for the award of a mandatory injunction were considered and applied in the constitutional context of the execution of unlawful search warrants. In disputes between private parties a relevant consideration will sometimes be

53 *Samsung Electronics Co Ltd v Apple Inc* (2011) 217 FCR 238, [62]–[63].
54 *Aquatic Air Pty Ltd v Siewert (No 2)* [2016] NSWSC 10.
55 (2006) 227 CLR 57.
56 (2020) 376 ALR 575. See [3.17] for the facts.
57 Kiefel CJ, Bell and Keane JJ at [71], citing *Patrick Stevedores Operations No 2 Pty Ltd v Maritime Union of Australia* (1998) 195 CLR 1; *Sourcebook* 3.2.2.1b, p 38.
58 *Smethurst v Commissioner of Police* (2020) 376 ALR 575, [73].
59 Ibid [249]–[250].
60 Ibid [270]–[271].

whether the cost of complying with the terms of the mandatory injunction are disproportionate to the loss that the plaintiff is likely to suffer if the injunction is not awarded.[61]

Another example of the refusal of a mandatory injunction is *Wrotham Park Estate v Parkside Homes Ltd*.[62] The defendant built houses in breach of a restrictive covenant which it had thought to be unenforceable. Most of the houses had been sold and, at the time of application, were occupied. Brightman J refused to award a mandatory injunction requiring their destruction on the ground that such an order would be a waste of much-needed housing, and assessed damages in substitution for the injunction.[63] An injunction would no doubt have been granted if the breach of covenant had been deliberate, even though the social arguments against ordering the destruction of houses would have been just as strong. A practice of refusing to order the destruction of houses erected in breach of covenant would encourage developers to 'purchase' the right to break the contract by paying damages for the breach. [3.22]

A mandatory injunction will readily be granted if it can be enforced with little judicial supervision and if the defendant will not incur excessive costs, when measured against the plaintiff's loss, in complying with the order. There can therefore be no objection to granting an injunction ordering a tenant to allow the landlord onto the tenanted premises, since the only mandatory part of the order will be the simple instruction to the tenant to open the front door of the premises so that the landlord can enter.[64] [3.23]

Injunctions to restrain breach of contract: the correlation with specific performance

Breach of contract is a common law action. The equitable remedies of injunction and specific performance will only be granted where damages for breach would be an inadequate remedy. Logic might then suggest that if a plaintiff cannot obtain specific performance because damages are an adequate remedy, she should not be entitled to an injunction either. But the relationship between specific performance and injunctions is not as straightforward as this analysis might suggest, and sometimes injunctions are available where specific performance is not. [3.24]

An injunction will not be awarded if its effect would be to compel the defendant to perform obligations which could not have been specifically performed. An employee cannot be ordered by *mandatory* injunction, for example, to perform a contract of service;[65] however, negative injunctions to restrain breaches of contract are awarded more readily.[66] A well-established line of authority shows that in *some* cases a negative injunction to restrain an employee from working for a competitor of the plaintiff may in substance operate as a kind of 'indirect specific performance'. This is what occurred in *Lumley v Wagner*, discussed above at [3.7]. [3.25]

61 *Redland Bricks Ltd v Morris* [1970] AC 652.

62 [1974] 1 WLR 798.

63 Ibid 811. See [3.35] onwards.

64 *Bradto Pty Ltd v Victoria* (2006) 15 VR 65.

65 *Whitwood Chemical Co v Hardman* [1891] 2 Ch 416.

66 It has sometimes been stated that a negative injunction to restrain a breach of contract will be granted as a matter of course: *Doherty v Allman and Dowden* (1878) 3 App Cas 709, 720 (Lord Cairns); but this understates the role of equitable discretion in determining the availability of the injunction: *Dalgety Wine Estates v Rizzon* (1979) 141 CLR 552.

Despite criticism, *Lumley v Wagner* has often been applied. In *Curro v Beyond Productions Pty Ltd*,[67] the plaintiff obtained an injunction to prevent Curro from working for a rival television company in breach of her contract to present a television program exclusively for the plaintiffs. The New South Wales Court of Appeal emphasised the following factors:

(a) The injunction would not 'force her into destitution' because she had skills and intelligence which could be employed outside the television industry.

(b) The duration of the injunction, which was for the three months remaining of her contract, was short.

(c) The defendant's breach had been 'flagrant and opportunistic'.[68]

The Court of Appeal observed that *Lumley v Wagner* injunctions were only awarded in cases where the contract was one to perform 'special services', such as those performed by an entertainer or sportsperson. The Court left open the question of what constituted 'special services' for this purpose.

Injunctions to restrain the commission of a tort

Injunctions to restrain trespass to land

[3.26] Where an injunction to restrain a trespass to land is claimed, common law damages are assumed to be inadequate, and an injunction will be granted unless an equitable bar to relief applies. Equity respects the sanctity of property rights. This reflects the principles governing specific performance of contracts for the sale of land, where land is (rightly or wrongly) also considered to possess 'special value'.

In *Bendal Pty Ltd v Mirvac Project Pty Ltd*,[69] Bryson J awarded an injunction to prevent the defendants from using screens which encroached on the plaintiffs' airspace. The injunction was granted even though the plaintiffs had suffered no financial loss through the encroachment. Although compensatory damages for the trespass would have been nominal, the plaintiffs could have been awarded restitutionary damages, based on the benefit to the defendant of trespassing on the plaintiffs' land. Restitutionary damages are assessed on the *gain* made by the defendant from committing the tort. The defendant will be ordered to pay a reasonable licence fee assessed as the value of the benefit the defendant gained from trespassing on the plaintiff's land. Bryson J refused to award restitutionary damages in *Bendal v Mirvac*, partly because a licence fee for use of airspace would have been hard to assess, and partly because there was no reason why the plaintiffs should be compelled to licence a trespass to which they strenuously objected.

Injunctions to restrain loss or damage to chattels

[3.27] An injunction will usually not be granted to protect against interference with chattels, as damages are usually an appropriate remedy, unless the chattel is rare. Other reasons why damages are inadequate include difficulty of assessment[70] and doubts as to whether

67 (1993) 30 NSWLR 337.

68 For an example of refusal to grant an injunction in an employment case, see *Network Ten Pty Ltd v Seven Network (Operations) Ltd* [2014] NSWSC 692.

69 (1991) 23 NSWLR 464.

70 *Pacific Hotels Pty Ltd v Asian Pacific International Ltd* (1986) 7 IPR 239.

the defendant can pay damages.[71] The principle applied in all these cases is whether an injunction will achieve more complete justice for the parties than a damages award would have done. A leading illustration of the application of this principle is *Aristoc Industries Pty Ltd v RA Wenham (Builders) Pty Ltd*.[72] The plaintiff contracted to manufacture and install chairs adapted to the special needs of an education centre in a hospital. The chairs were delivered to the hospital site but could not be installed because the hospital was incomplete. When the defendant refused to allow the plaintiff to remove the chairs from the building site, the plaintiff sought an injunction restraining the defendant from preventing the removal of the chairs. Jacobs J identified two reasons why damages were inadequate:

(a) There was a risk that the chairs would become fixtures once they had been installed in the education centre. They would then belong to the defendant and the plaintiff could not recover them in the event of non-payment for the chairs by the defendant.

(b) The chairs were specially adapted to meet the needs of the education centre and there was no alternative market for their use.[73]

As Jacobs J observed, the defendant probably wanted to have the chairs without paying for them.[74] Accordingly, the injunction was made conditional on the plaintiff offering the chairs either to the Crown, who owned the hospital, or to the defendant at the original contract price. The conditional injunction ensured that the public interest in the prompt completion of the education centre would be satisfied while the plaintiff would receive the contract price.

Injunctions to restrain other torts

Courts have awarded injunctions to restrain the commission of an assault or battery, the criteria being not so much whether damages are inadequate but whether adequate alternative relief could be obtained under the criminal law or by exercising a statutory jurisdiction. In *Parry v Crooks*,[75] the plaintiff applied for an injunction to restrain her former partner from assaulting her and her children. A majority of the Full Court of the Supreme Court of South Australia upheld the trial judge's refusal to grant an injunction. Significantly, none of the judges denied the existence of a jurisdiction to grant injunctions to prevent the commission of any tort. The majority considered that the injunction should be refused because the processes of the criminal law, nowadays including restraint orders available under domestic violence legislation, were more appropriate. [3.28]

A much debated question is whether the award of an injunction to prevent the publication of a defamatory statement is governed by the ordinary criteria governing the award of such injunctions, set out above, or whether there are special considerations governing defamation which are not applicable to other torts. The obvious consideration is that the defendant's right to freedom of speech will be abridged by the terms of the injunction. In *Bonnard v Perryman*,[76] Lord Esher, in the English Court of Appeal, ruled that an interlocutory injunction [3.29]

71 *Patrick Stevedores Operations No 2 Pty Ltd v Maritime Union of Australia* (1998) 195 CLR 1, 32; *Sourcebook* 3.2.2.1b, p 38.
72 [1965] NSWR 581.
73 Ibid 588–9.
74 Ibid 589.
75 (1981) 27 SASR 1.
76 [1891] 2 Ch 269, 283–5.

should not be granted if the defendant intends to plead the defence of justification. An injunction granted in such a case would 'freeze' the publication of truthful matter which the public was entitled to know. In *Australian Broadcasting Corporation v O'Neill,*[77] a majority of the High Court discharged an interlocutory injunction which would have prevented the ABC from showing a program suggesting that the plaintiff, who had been convicted of a child murder in Tasmania, had also committed an unsolved murder of three Adelaide children. The majority judges rejected the notion of any 'special' principles governing the award of interlocutory injunctions in defamation cases. The ordinary principles laid down in *Beecham Group Ltd v Bristol Laboratories Pty Ltd*[78] applied to defamation cases as to other interlocutory applications. In balancing the interests of the parties, however, it was relevant to take into account the public interest in freedom of speech, as well as the fact that if the plaintiff's claim had succeeded at full trial he might have been awarded only nominal damages.

Third party interests and the role of the public interest

[3.30] An award of an injunction may have an impact on third parties not directly involved in the litigation. For example, an injunction to prevent a factory committing a nuisance by emitting noxious fumes affecting the plaintiff's land will benefit not only the plaintiff but also other landowners in the neighbourhood. Conversely, the injunction may have a detrimental impact on any employees of the factory owner who could lose their jobs if the injunction restricts the operation of the factory's processes.

The modern tendency is for the court to award an injunction in nuisance cases involving third party interests but to impose conditions on its award. So, in *Kennaway v Thompson,*[79] an injunction was granted against a defendant who organised speedboat races on a lake adjoining the plaintiff's house, but the injunction did not prohibit the races; in view of the public interest in the races, it regulated the number of races which could be held each year, the number of competitors in each race, and imposed a maximum decibel limit on all boating activities.

It is not hard to find other cases where interests additional to those of the parties to the litigation have been taken into account. A court may not, for example, grant a mandatory injunction requiring a property developer to pull down houses which have been constructed in unintentional breach of a restrictive covenant limiting the number of houses which can be built on the site.[80] The award of an injunction in such a case has been said to promote 'social waste' – the developer must instead pay damages. Possibly the most famous example of social considerations contributing to the court's refusal to grant an injunction is *Miller v Jackson.*[81] Lord Denning held that the public interest in the playing of village cricket outweighed a private individual's interest in preventing cricket balls being hit onto her property.

[3.31] In some cases, the plaintiff's interest may have to be balanced against the interests of an identified third party. This occurred in *Patrick Stevedores Operations No 2 Pty Ltd v Maritime Union of Australia,*[82] where the administrator of the defendant company argued

77 (2006) 227 CLR 57.
78 (1968) 118 CLR 618. See [3.20].
79 [1981] QB 88. Cf *Miller v Jackson* [1977] QB 966.
80 *Wrotham Park Estate v Parkside Homes Ltd* [1974] 1 WLR 798. See [3.22].
81 [1977] QB 966; *Sourcebook* 3.3.3a, p 50.
82 (1998) 195 CLR 1. See [3.7].

that the injunction sought by the plaintiff unions would adversely affect the interests of an 'alternative labour company' which had agreed to replace striking workers. The High Court agreed with the trial judge that the interests of a third party were 'relevant but not decisive' to the award of an injunction, but that the interests of the company in this case were not strong enough to justify withholding the injunction.

More difficult are the cases which involve the balancing of the plaintiff's interest in obtaining an injunction against the public interest (as opposed to the interests of identified third parties) in the continuation of the defendant's activities held to constitute a legal or equitable wrong. In *Coventry v Lawrence*,[83] the United Kingdom Supreme Court held that, although the grant of a planning permission to carry out an activity (in this case, permission to hold moto-cross events) was not a defence to an action in private nuisance, it was relevant to the exercise of discretion as to whether an injunction (see [3.33]) should be awarded. Lord Neuberger stated that the prima facie position was that an injunction should be granted, and that the legal burden rested on the defendant to show that it should not.[84] He went on to state that 'the existence of a planning permission which expressly or inherently authorizes carrying on an activity in such a way as to cause a nuisance by noise or the like, can be a factor in favour of refusing an injunction and compensating the plaintiff in damages'.[85] The argument for a damages award would be particularly strong if the planning authority considered the activity to be undertaken for the public benefit. [3.32]

Applications for an injunction to restrain a breach of confidence may also give rise to the argument that disclosure of the information should be permitted in the public interest. The position here is more complex in that, as well as arguments as to whether an injunction should be preferred to compensation in the exercise of equitable discretion, there is a defence, uncertain in scope, of disclosure in the public interest. It is unclear whether the defence is confined to disclosure of crimes, wrongs and other misdeeds, or whether it is broader, justifying disclosure of matters which would otherwise be confidential. This issue is considered at [12.17]–[12.19]. [3.33]

The exercise of discretion

Injunctions are discretionary remedies but the exercise of discretion is not arbitrary or unstructured. Even though decisions on the award of injunctions are fact-specific, and the doctrine of precedent has to be applied cautiously, with due regard to any special features of the case, there are nonetheless well-established criteria governing the exercise of discretion. [3.34]

An injunction will be denied if the defendant can establish a bar to equitable relief.[86] The bars to relief are directed to the same two matters that control an award of specific performance, although in the context of an award of an injunction they will sometimes operate differently. The first question is whether the injunction will be fair to both parties. The second is whether, as a practical matter, the court can supervise its own order.

'Fairness' in the context of injunctions is a broader notion than its equivalent in the context of specific performance because an injunction can inhibit the activities of third [3.35]

83 [2014] AC 822.
84 Ibid [121].
85 Ibid [125].
86 See chapter 6.

parties not before the court.[87] It is not an objection to the award of an injunction that it may affect the exercise of legal rights by third parties, but courts will have regard to the interests of third parties, both in deciding whether to grant the injunction and in settling its terms.[88]

Fairness between the parties can be achieved by a variety of methods. The most obvious is in fashioning the terms of the injunction so that it goes no further than is absolutely necessary to protect the plaintiff's legitimate interests. In *Lumley v Wagner*,[89] for example, the injunction obtained by the plaintiff opera house owner against the recalcitrant singer he had engaged prohibited the latter from singing for the named opera house, being the plaintiff's rival, but did not otherwise prevent the singer from taking up employment with other parties.

In some cases, the injunction will be refused on the ground that to award it will be unfair to the defendant. The 'unclean hands' defence, hardship and laches (or delay) are all equitable bars to relief which are based on considerations of fairness.[90] If fairness is to be relevant, however, it must relate to the relief the plaintiff is claiming. An injunction will not be refused just because the plaintiff has acted illegally or immorally, but it will be refused if it would be inequitable to award the injunction because of the plaintiff's illegality or immorality. The fact that a plaintiff has acted in breach of confidence in respect of one matter will not necessarily prevent her from obtaining an injunction to prevent disclosure of information relating to another matter.[91] On the other hand, it is inequitable to award a manufacturer an injunction to prevent infringement of a trademark in his goods when the manufacturer has deliberately misled the public in advertising the goods.[92]

[3.36] The other principal ground for withholding equitable relief is that the proposed order cannot be effectively enforced. Just as specific performance will not be ordered if it cannot be supervised by the court, so an injunction will not be ordered if it cannot be enforced; futility is a ground for refusing relief.[93]

Plaintiff's remedy if specific performance or injunction are denied

[3.37] The plaintiff's claim will not fail in its entirety just because the court does not grant the remedy sought. In an unsuccessful claim for specific performance, the plaintiff will be remitted to a common law claim to damages. In *Summers v Cocks*,[94] a vendor of a hotel failed to disclose to the purchaser that the hotel was subject to an application to have its licence removed on the ground that the premises had not been kept in repair. The vendor's application for specific performance was refused. However, the vendor was entitled to damages for breach of contract since non-disclosure is not a ground for rescinding a contract at law, except in special cases such as a contract entered into between parties in a fiduciary

87 *Acrow (Automation) Ltd v Rex Chainbelt Inc* [1971] 3 All ER 1175. See [3.30].
88 *Patrick Stevedores Operations No 2 Pty Ltd v Maritime Union of Australia* (1998) 195 CLR 1, [65]–[66]; *Sourcebook* 3.2.2.1b, p 38. See [3.7].
89 (1852) 42 ER 687. See [3.7].
90 See chapter 6.
91 *Duchess of Argyll v Duke of Argyll* [1967] Ch 302.
92 *Kettles & Gas Appliances Ltd v Anthony Hordern & Sons Ltd* (1934) 35 SR (NSW) 108.
93 *Humane Society International Inc v Kyodo Senpaku Kaisha Ltd* (2006) 154 FCR 425.
94 (1927) 40 CLR 321.

relationship. Where an injunction in support of a common law right is refused, such as in an action for trespass, the plaintiff will still be entitled to damages.[95] Where the injunction is sought in respect of a purely equitable right, another remedy may be appropriate, such as equitable compensation or an account of profits.[96] Finally, the unsuccessful plaintiff may be entitled to equitable damages in lieu of the specific performance or injunction sought.

Equitable damages

Damages are a common law concept. Equity has no inherent jurisdiction to award 'damages'. [3.38] Before the enactment of the judicature legislation in the nineteenth century, the separation of common law courts from the court of equity sometimes caused problems for litigants claiming the equitable remedies of specific performance or injunction. For example, an equity judge might, despite the vendor's breach of a contract to sell land, refuse to order specific performance on discretionary grounds. If the plaintiff wanted to obtain damages for breach after the application for the equitable remedy had been dismissed, he would have to start a new action in the common law courts and prove the breach of contract all over again. [3.39]

The *Chancery Amendment Act 1858* (Imp), often referred to as *Lord Cairns' Act*, was enacted to solve this problem. It empowered a judge exercising equitable jurisdiction to award damages instead of, or in addition to, specific performance or an injunction. The Act has been enacted in all Australian States and Territories.[97] The terms of the New South Wales version are set out as an example:

> **68 Damages in case for equitable relief**
>
> Where the Court has power:
>
> **(a)** to grant an injunction against the breach of any covenant, contract or agreement, or against the commission or continuance of any wrongful act, or
>
> **(b)** to order the specific performance of any covenant, contract or agreement,
>
> the Court may award damages to the party injured either in addition to or in substitution for the injunction or specific performance.[98]

The Victorian and Queensland versions of *Lord Cairns' Act* are drafted in broader terms than their counterparts. Section 38 of the *Supreme Court Act 1986* (Vic) provides that 'if the Court has jurisdiction to entertain an application for an injunction or specific performance, it may award damages in addition to, or in substitution for, an injunction or specific performance'.[99]

95 *Miller v Jackson* [1977] QB 966.

96 See chapter 4.

97 *Supreme Court Act 1933* (ACT) s 34; *Supreme Court Act 1970* (NSW) s 68; *Supreme Court Act 1979* (NT) s 14(1)(b); *Supreme Court Act 1935* (SA) s 30; *Supreme Court Civil Procedure Act 1932* (Tas) s 11(13); *Supreme Court Act 1986* (Vic) s 38; *Supreme Court Act 1935* (WA) s 25(10). The original enactments were repealed in Queensland and the ACT. In Queensland, it has been held that the jurisdiction survived the repeal: *Barbagallo v J & F Catelan Pty Ltd* [1986] 1 Qd R 245. See now *Civil Proceedings Act 2011* (Qld) s 8. This is assumed to be the case also in the ACT; however, doubts have been expressed judicially as to whether this is correct: *Financial Integrity Group Ltd v Farmer and Bravium Pty Ltd* [2009] ACTSC 143, [98]–[109].

98 *Supreme Court Act 1970* (NSW) s 68; *Sourcebook* 3.4.1, p 56.

99 *Supreme Court Act 1986* (Vic) s 38.

[3.40] An advantage of equitable damages is that, unlike common law damages, they are available where a tort such as nuisance is only threatened and damage has not yet been suffered.[100] They can also be obtained for continuing wrongs such as ongoing trespasses, so that rights can be settled between parties once and for all, without the need to regularly return to court.

Are equitable damages available for equitable wrongs?

[3.41] The statutory jurisdiction to award equitable damages was clearly intended to apply to common law wrongs arising from contract and tort. The position with regard to equitable wrongs is not so clear. On one view, the *Lord Cairns Act* should be confined to cases where the plaintiff applies (or could apply) for an injunction to prevent the commission of a tort or specific performance of a contract. On this view the Act cannot be invoked to claim damages for an equitable wrong, such as a breach of trust, fiduciary obligation or breach of confidence. There are several reasons for limiting the application of the Act to torts and breaches of contract. First, the original *Lord Cairns' Act* was enacted to deal with the problem of litigants having to run proceedings in two courts, discussed above at [3.38]. This could not have applied to purely equitable actions. Secondly, the remedy of equitable compensation discussed in chapter 4 is available to compensate victims of equitable wrongdoing. Why invoke *Lord Cairns' Act* when a perfectly good equitable remedy can be awarded?

The counter-argument is that the wording of *Lord Cairns' Act* (particularly the versions in Queensland and Victoria which make no reference to wrongs of any kind) is not limited to torts or breaches of contract. Further, there is High Court support for the availability of equitable damages for equitable wrongs.[101] In *Giller v Procopets*,[102] the Victorian Court of Appeal, following earlier Victorian authority,[103] held that damages under the Act could be awarded for an equitable breach of confidence.[104] The decision in *Giller* settled the argument for the purposes of Victorian law. The Victorian Court of Appeal would have awarded the plaintiff an identical amount by way of equitable compensation for breach of the equitable obligation of confidence.[105] Strictly speaking, therefore, the discussion of *Lord Cairns' Act* damages was unnecessary.

The jurisdiction to award *Lord Cairns' Act* damages

[3.42] Equitable damages can only be awarded where a court has jurisdiction to grant an injunction or specific performance at commencement of the suit.[106] Whether or not the court would have exercised its discretion to grant one of the equitable remedies is not important.

100 *Leeds Co-operative Society Ltd v Slack* [1924] AC 851. But damages for a threatened act cannot be awarded in Tasmania: *Supreme Court Civil Procedure Act 1932* (Tas) s 11(13)(b).
101 *Wentworth v Woollahra Municipal Council* (1982) 149 CLR 672, 676.
102 (2008) 24 VR 1; *Sourcebook* 3.4.3a, p 59.
103 *Talbot v General Television Corporation Pty Ltd* [1980] VR 224.
104 *Giller v Procopets* (2008) 24 VR 1. See [12.28].
105 *Giller v Procopets* (2008) 24 VR 1, 29–33.
106 *Mills v Ruthol Pty Ltd* (2004) 61 NSWLR 1.

There is no jurisdiction to award an injunction or specific performance, and therefore to award equitable damages, in the following situations: [3.43]

(a) Where common law damages are an adequate remedy (for example, in contracts to sell chattels for which market substitutes can be obtained);

(b) Where there is no likelihood of repetition of the alleged tort;[107]

(c) Where the plaintiff is attempting to enforce a contract of personal service;

(d) Where it was impossible to grant equitable relief at the commencement of the action, and it is still impossible at the date of judgment.

In all these cases, the plaintiff will be entitled to common law damages for tort or breach of contract.

The discretionary bars to specific performance or the award of an injunction, such as unclean hands and hardship, are not 'jurisdictional matters' and do not prevent the plaintiff from claiming equitable damages. For example, in *Patel v Ali*,[108] a purchaser of land sought specific performance of the contract. This was denied on the discretionary ground that it would cause hardship to the vendor, but the vendor remained liable to pay equitable damages.

How are equitable damages assessed?

Statutory damages are assessed on a different and more flexible basis than common law damages, because the damages award is a substitute for the equitable remedies of injunction or specific performance, or is in addition to such a remedy, rather than damages for tortious or contractual loss. [3.44]

Damages in addition to injunction or specific performance

These are awarded where grant of the specific remedy sought will not fully compensate the plaintiff. Cases often involve an order of specific performance of a contract to purchase land. Additional damages are sometimes awarded where the purchaser has been kept out of the property for a period of time, and would have earned rent in the time between the expected settlement date and actual possession.[109] [3.45]

Damages in substitution for injunction or specific performance

Equitable damages are discretionary. Factors considered when determining whether the plaintiff should have its remedy of injunction or specific performance, or instead be awarded damages in substitution, include: the magnitude of injury to the plaintiff's legal rights; whether the injury to the plaintiff can be measured in monetary terms; whether the equitable remedy [3.46]

107 *Irving v Emu & Prospect Gravel & Road Metal Co Ltd* (1909) 26 WN (NSW) 137.
108 [1984] 1 Ch 283.
109 *Oakacre Ltd v Claire Cleaners (Holdings) Ltd* [1982] 1 Ch 197.

sought would be oppressive to the defendant; and whether the plaintiff's behaviour was such that it would be unjust to award more than equitable damages.[110]

[3.47] Where damages are in substitution for one of the equitable remedies sought the court tries to place the plaintiff in the same position, as far as money can do, as she would have been if the injunction or specific performance had been granted.

Thus:

(a) Equitable damages are frequently assessed as at the date of judgment, not as at the date of breach (which is the usual but not invariable common law rule) so that they are a proper substitute for the specific performance order or injunction sought.[111] For example, if specific performance of a contract of sale of land is ordered but cannot be carried out because a mortgagee has in the meantime taken possession and sold the land, the order will be discharged and damages assessed as at the date of judgment to reflect the plaintiff's loss of the economic benefit of specific performance.[112]

(b) Damages for mental distress can be awarded. In *Giller v Procopets*,[113] the plaintiff was entitled to damages for mental distress because an injunction, if granted in time, would have prevented the mental distress caused by the defendant's behaviour. Although it was held that equitable compensation can also compensate for mental distress, the proposition is not clearly established by authority.

(c) The discretionary bars[114] to the award of specific performance or an injunction, such as hardship and unclean hands, can also be bars to the award of equitable damages. However, just because an order of (say) specific performance will be refused if it causes excessive hardship to the defendant, equitable damages will not necessarily be barred for this reason. The court must consider, independently of the consideration of whether an order of specific performance will cause hardship to the defendant, whether payment of damages will cause excessive hardship to the defendant.

WHAT'S ONLINE?

Available at www.cambridge.org/highereducation/isbn/9781009232388/resources:

- Recommended further readings
- Discussion topics
- Practice problems

110 *Break Fast Investments Pty Ltd v PCH Melbourne Pty Ltd* (2007) 20 VR 311.
111 *Wroth v Tyler* [1974] Ch 30.
112 *Johnson v Agnew* [1980] AC 367.
113 (2008) 24 VR 1.
114 See [3.34] and [3.35], and chapter 6.

4

MONETARY REMEDIES IN EQUITY

Introduction

[4.1] In certain situations, equity orders the defendant to make payments to the plaintiff as a remedy for the wrong done.[1] These are orders for the defendant to account for profits made, or pay equitable compensation to the plaintiff. These remedies impose a personal obligation on the wrongdoer to pay and do not per se attach to property.[2] This is their disadvantage compared to proprietary remedies in the case of the defendant's insolvency. The remedies perform substantially different tasks. We will now look at each remedy in turn.

Accounts of profits

[4.2] As a general rule, accounts of profits are not available at common law.[3] They are designed to strip profits made in breach of equitable obligations, preventing the wrongdoer profiting from his own wrong.[4] The remedy is awarded in response to breaches of trust, fiduciary obligations and the obligation of confidence. Third party participants in fiduciary breaches may also have to account for profits made (see chapter 11). The essence of the plaintiff's complaint is that the defendant has usurped a profit-making opportunity that should have come to the plaintiff alone (if to anyone at all[5]); justice requires the profit made be removed from the defendant and directed to the plaintiff. However, the remedy is not designed to punish the defendant.[6] As with all equitable remedies, it is designed to do corrective justice between the parties. Therefore, only net profits are stripped from the defendant. Although the defendant cannot profit from his wrong, he should not be put in a worse position than if he had not taken up the opportunity.

The remedy is said to be 'ancient'[7]; it may have been in use since the earliest days of Chancery. Its award is discretionary, and may be defeated by the traditional equitable bars such as laches and unclean hands.[8]

[4.3] The remedy focuses on *the profit made by the wrongdoer through the equitable wrong*. This results in numerous outcomes that seem strange when compared with common law remedies. For example, it is irrelevant that:

- the plaintiff has not suffered any loss, or has also suffered a loss (the focus is on profit, not loss);

---

1 This is apart from the statutory damages in addition to or in lieu of injunction or specific performance discussed in chapter 3.

2 A court can exercise discretion to make a proprietary award in support of a personal remedy, such as a lien to secure payment of compensation: see, eg, *Warman International Ltd v Dwyer* (1995) 182 CLR 544.

3 Accounts of profits are generally not ordered for breach of contract in Australia: *Hospitality Group Pty Ltd v Australian Rugby Union Ltd* (2001) 110 FCR 157. But see *Town & Country Property Management Pty Ltd v Kaltoum* [2002] NSWSC 166, [83]; *Mid-City Skin Cancer & Laser Centre v Zahedi-Anarak* (2006) 67 NSWLR 569, 625–6. The House of Lords ordered an account of profits for breach of contract in *A-G v Blake* [2001] 1 AC 268.

4 Profit-stripping is also accomplished by the constructive trust: see chapter 23.

5 In some cases, the plaintiff would not have made the profit. See [4.4].

6 *Harris v Digital Pulse Pty Ltd* (2003) 56 NSWLR 298, 369–71 (Heydon JA).

7 *Warman International Ltd v Dwyer* (1995) 182 CLR 544.

8 See chapter 6.

- the plaintiff could never have made a profit itself, or has also made a profit itself incidentally through the defendant's breach[9] (the focus is on the *defendant's* profit);
- the defendant's motives or state of mind are not dishonest[10] (the focus is not on why the profit was made);
- the plaintiff might have made more profit than the defendant from exploitation of the opportunity (the focus is on the defendant's profit).

However, because the focus is on profits made through the defendant's *wrong-doing*, allowances must sometimes be made to the defendant for aspects of the profit not referable to his wrongdoing, but instead referable to his personal inputs.[11]

How are accounts of profits calculated?

Most of the matters mentioned in the paragraph above are illustrated by *Warman International Ltd v Dwyer*.[12] Warman was a company that had an agency agreement with an Italian manufacturer of gearboxes, Bonfiglioli. Dwyer was general manager of Warman's Queensland branch. Bonfiglioli unsuccessfully approached Warman in August 1986 to set up a joint venture with it. Shortly after, Dwyer informed Bonfiglioli that he planned to leave Warman and set up his own business. Dwyer incorporated two companies, and early in 1988 began negotiating directly with Bonfiglioli. He poached Warman's staff to work in his new venture. In June 1988, Bonfiglioli terminated its agency agreement with Warman, and Dwyer resigned from Warman. Later that year, one of his new companies entered into a 20-year agreement with Bonfiglioli to assemble and distribute its gearboxes in Australia. [4.4]

The trial judge held that there was a clear breach of fiduciary duty by Dwyer, resulting in Warman losing the opportunity to retain the agency agreement. Compensation to cover the loss was assessed as well as an account of profits. The Court of Appeal denied Warman an account, holding that its remedy should be limited to equitable compensation. In reversing that decision, the High Court held that Warman was entitled to elect between equitable compensation and an account of profits.

A unanimous High Court discussed the remedy extensively, and made the following points:

- Assessment of an account of profits is 'extremely difficult in practice'.[13] As it is difficult to calculate, mathematical exactness is not called for, and a reasonable approximation is acceptable.[14]
- A fiduciary's liability to account does not depend on detriment to the plaintiff, or dishonesty or lack of bona fides on the part of the defendant.[15]

9 *Boardman v Phipps* [1967] 2 AC 46.
10 Ibid.
11 See, eg, *Bluescope Steel Ltd v Kelly* (2007) 72 IPR 289; *Sourcebook* 12.4a, p 335.
12 (1995) 182 CLR 544; *Sourcebook* 4.2a, p 64.
13 *Warman International Ltd v Dwyer* (1995) 182 CLR 544, 558.
14 Ibid.
15 Ibid.

- It is no defence that the plaintiff was unwilling, unlikely or unable to make the profit itself.[16]
- The fiduciary is usually ordered to account for the profits made within the scope and ambit of the fiduciary duty.
- If the loss suffered by the plaintiff exceeds the profit made by the fiduciary, the plaintiff may elect a compensatory remedy against the fiduciary.
- A distinction can be drawn between cases where a fiduciary acquires a specific asset within the scope of its obligations, and cases where a fiduciary establishes and operates a business to exploit an opportunity.[17] In the latter, it may be inappropriate to require the fiduciary to account for the whole of the business profits for an indefinite period of time. This is especially so where part of the profits is attributable to the fiduciary's own inputs.[18]
- The defendant bears the burden of showing that it should not account for the whole of the profits.[19]
- As a general rule, a court will not apportion the profit made between the fiduciary and the principal;[20] but if it is inequitable for the fiduciary to account for the whole of the profits, the court will make allowance for the fiduciary's skill, effort and expenses.[21]

Applying those principles to the case, the High Court held that Warman was likely to have lost its distributorship, probably within a year. This was not a case where the fiduciary had taken a specific asset that should have gone to the principal, but the new business was set up upon the foundations of the breach of fiduciary duty. An order for account of profits was appropriate, limited to an initial profits period of two years. The defendants had to account for all the net profits made in that period, less an allowance for the skill, expertise, effort and resources contributed by them.

The facts showed that Warman had also made a loss. The High Court held that Warman was entitled to elect to take either an account of profits or compensation for its loss. Further, once the account of profits was calculated, that sum would be secured by an equitable charge over the assets of the Dwyer companies to ensure payment. An important issue in practice is the length of the proposed accounting period. In *Warman*, the trial judge's award of four years' profit was reduced in the High Court to two years. The determination of the appropriate accounting period will inform the plaintiff's election of an account of profits or equitable compensation. It is clear that the plaintiff is entitled to elect whichever remedy reaps the highest return.[22]

[4.5] There must be a causative link between the wrongdoing and the profit which is to be stripped, in that the profit must have arisen by reason of the breach. The High Court had another opportunity to consider the remedy of account of profits in *Ancient Order of Foresters in Victoria Friendly Society Ltd v Lifeplan Australia Friendly Society Ltd*.[23]

16 Ibid.
17 Ibid 560.
18 Ibid 561.
19 Ibid.
20 Profits might be apportioned where antecedent profit-sharing arrangements exist: Ibid 562.
21 Ibid. See also *Grimaldi v Chameleon Mining NL (No 2)* (2012) 200 FCR 296, [523]–[536].
22 *Tang Man Sit v Capacious Investments Ltd* [1996] 1 All ER 193.
23 (2018) 265 CLR 1 ('*Lifeplan*').

The plaintiff, Lifeplan, had a profitable pre-paid funeral business. Two employees, in breach of their fiduciary duties, offered Lifeplan's competitor, Foresters, a detailed five-year business plan to establish a new business. This was 'prepared utilising valuable confidential information of their employer … that set out a detailed strategy to attack the commercial base of that employer'.[24] After the plan was implemented, Lifeplan's business was decimated, while Foresters' new business thrived. The employees were liable for breach of fiduciary duty, and Foresters was held liable as a knowing assistant under the rule in *Barnes v Addy*.[25]

At issue was calculation of the remedy of account of profits. Lifeplan sought that Foresters account for the whole value of their new funeral business. At first instance, Besanko J declined to order an account of profits against Foresters, being unconvinced that Foresters' acts of assistance in the fiduciary breaches led to the profits it ultimately earned. The Full Court of the Federal Court felt differently on appeal, holding that without its involvement in the fiduciary breaches, Foresters would not have made the profits it did.[26] However, the Full Court noted that this was not a case in which an existing business was transferred, but was instead one where a new business was set up in consequence of the breach, which would have involved Foresters in 'deployment of capital, skill and expertise, and the undertaking of business risk'.[27] These factors justified the account of profits being limited to profits made and projected to be made between February 2011 and June 2015, a period which reflected the term of the five year business plan, slightly reduced. This totalled approximately $6.5 million.

Foresters then appealed to the High Court on the grounds that there was an insufficient causal connection between the conduct in knowing assistance and the profits made, and that projected future profits should not have been included in the account order. Lifeplan cross-appealed on the grounds that the Full Court had erred in not ordering Foresters to account for the entire value of the new business. Lifeplan was successful, and the account of profits increased to approximately $14.8 million.

Causation was the key topic of discussion in the majority judgments of the High Court.[28] The plurality (Kiefel CJ, Keane and Edelman JJ) were of the view that Foresters' argument that its liability to account should be limited to the direct results of each act of assistance was incorrect. Instead, focus should have been on the overall effect of Foresters' wrongful conduct.[29] The plaintiff is entitled to profits made 'as a result' of knowing participation in a fiduciary breach, and the phrase 'as a result' was not to be read down to limit account to the result of independent acts of assistance. The plurality made the following points:

- It is sufficient to show that the profit would not have been made but for dishonest wrongdoing.
- A dishonest defendant cannot avoid liability to disgorge profits by showing that the profit might have been made honestly.

24 (2017) 250 FCR 1, 12 [32].
25 (1874) LR 9 Ch App 244. See chapter 11.
26 (2017) 250 FCR 1, 21–2 [66].
27 Ibid 26 [85].
28 Nettle J was in dissent, on application of the law to the facts at hand. His Honour was satisfied with the account ordered by the Full Court.
29 *Lifeplan* [4].

- Where causation is established, the onus is on the defendant to show that they should not account for the full value of the advantage.
- There are two ways the onus can be discharged. These are (a) by proving an entitlement to an allowance for costs incurred and efforts made in producing the advantage; or (b) by proving the benefit or advantage is beyond the scope of liability for which the wrongdoer should have to account. This might be proved by showing the profit has no reasonable connection with the wrongdoing.[30] All of the circumstances of the case, including the nature of the wrongdoing, must be considered here.

Foresters failed to discharge the onus to prove that it would be inequitable to require it to account for the whole of the advantage required. In fact, the evidence showed a 'compelling correlation'[31] between the increasing profitability of Foresters' new business and the decreasing profitability of Lifeplan's business. The decision in *Warman International Ltd v Dwyer* was distinguished on the basis that, in *Warman*, the misappropriated advantage could only be expected to continue for a short time, whereas the evidence suggested Foresters' market dominance was fully realised.

The question of anticipated future profits was swiftly dealt with. The Court held unanimously that the benefit for which a wrongdoer has to account is not limited by narrow accounting concepts, and can include unrealised profits.[32]

Gageler J, who delivered a separate judgment, agreed generally with the plurality. However, his explanation of the causal standard perhaps went further than that of the plurality. His Honour stated:

> A causal connection between a fiduciary's breach of fiduciary obligation and a benefit or gain sufficient for the fiduciary or knowing participant to be liable to the equitable remedy of account will exist if the benefit or gain to the fiduciary or knowing assistant would not have been obtained 'but for' the breach, in same way as a causal connection sufficient for the fiduciary to be liable to the equitable remedy of compensation will exist is a loss to the person to whom the fiduciary obligation is owed would not have been sustained but for the breach. Because the concern of equity is to vindicate the equitable obligation that has been breached, the 'but for' connection will be sufficient even though other contributing causes might be in play. That the fiduciary's breach of fiduciary obligation is dishonest and fraudulent is also good reason for treating a sufficient causal connection as existing if the dishonest and fraudulent breach can be concluded to have played a material part in contributing to the benefit or gain of the fiduciary or knowing participant even when it cannot be concluded that benefit or gain would not have been obtained but for the breach.[33]

30 The plurality gives the example of *Frank Music Corporation v Metro-Goldwyn-Mayer Inc*, 886 F 2d 1545 (1989). A copyright infringement in a performance at a hotel entitled the plaintiff to proportional profits earned through the performance, and a proportion of profits earned through consequential increase in hotel bookings. The plaintiff could not claim the profits from *all* the hotel bookings.

31 *Lifeplan* [17].

32 Ibid [24]; see also [75] (Gageler J), [202]–[203] (Nettle J).

33 *Lifeplan* [88].

Allowances

Calculating what should be allowed to an accounting defendant for his time, skill and effort can be a vexed question. It is occasionally said that a dishonest fiduciary will not be given an allowance at all or will be given a reduced allowance[34] but, as *Warman* shows, dishonesty may not really be the question; it can be of more relevance that, in the interests of justice between the parties, not all of the profit is attributed to the breach of fiduciary duty. Conversely, honest or well-intentioned defendants are sometimes given allowances on a liberal or generous scale.[35] Courts oscillate between explaining this as fault-based, or referrable to causation. In any event, as the High Court stressed in *Lifeplan*, the onus is on the defendant to prove an entitlement to any allowance at all.[36] [4.6]

Reported judgments concerning how liberal allowances are calculated are rare, as parties frequently settle on such figures themselves. The Victorian Supreme Court considered such a calculation in *Victoria University of Technology v Wilson*.[37] Two academics owed fiduciary obligations to their employer, a university. A former student came to them with a money-making opportunity which they exploited in breach of fiduciary duty. The trial judge appointed a special referee to determine the amount of the allowance to be made to the fiduciaries, who had put a significant amount of time, effort and money into the venture. The referee set an extremely low figure and the fiduciaries successfully appealed. Harper J held that the starting point for the calculation should have been the terms the university and the academics were most likely to have agreed on at the outset, assuming they were at arm's length, fully informed, properly advised and willing to be reasonable. The university itself had policies in place for similar situations, which allowed profits to be shared between the university and its employees, and these policies were highly relevant as indicators of what would have been agreed. The resulting figure would be reduced if the fiduciary's behaviour had in any way disadvantaged the principal. For example, neglect by the academics of their teaching duties in order to exploit the opportunity would be taken into account. [4.7]

Equitable compensation

Equitable compensation is the equitable remedy that is comparable to (but not the equivalent of) common law damages. Like common law damages, it addresses loss following breach. It is available in respect of breaches of purely equitable duties such as breaches of trust, fiduciary duty, participation in a fiduciary breach and obligations of confidence.[38] As it largely exists in equity's exclusive jurisdiction,[39] its parameters are set in equity. There is only limited cross-fertilisation between common law and equitable principles, although that may be on the increase.[40] [4.8]

34 *Green & Clara Pty Ltd v Bestobell Industries Pty Ltd (No 2)* [1984] WAR 32; *Guinness plc v Saunders* [1990] 2 AC 663; *Short v Crawley (No 30)* [2007] NSWSC 1322, [753].

35 *Boardman v Phipps* [1967] 2 AC 46.

36 *Lifeplan* [13] (Kiefel CJ, Keane and Edelman JJ), [94] (Gageler J), [186] (Nettle J).

37 (2006) 68 IPR 597; *Sourcebook* 4.2c, p 69.

38 Equitable compensation for breach of confidence is discussed at [12.35]–[12.36].

39 It is also available in equity's concurrent jurisdiction: *Nocton v Lord Ashburton* [1914] AC 932, 952 (Viscount Haldane).

40 *Giller v Procopets* (2008) 24 VR 1. See [4.13].

Emergence of the jurisdiction to award equitable compensation

[4.9] The equitable jurisdiction to award compensation appears to have arisen in cases involving breach of trust. Equity requires parties who are custodians of property to give an account of their management of that property. The process of accounting was described by Lord Millett in *Libertarian Investments v Hall*.[41] Put very simply, the accounting process allows the beneficiary to identify unauthorised disbursements from the trust fund, or losses caused by other failures to perform duties. A trustee could be ordered to give a 'common account' in the case of an unauthorised disbursement, or to account on the basis of 'wilful default' where the breach caused loss to the trust, such as in a breach of the conflicts rule. Typically, either breach would then have to be remedied in a monetary sense. In *Caffrey v Darby*,[42] the trustees sold trust property to a purchaser on installment terms. They allowed him to take possession of the property, but did not ensure that he made the agreed payments. The purchaser eventually became bankrupt without paying for the property. The trustees were liable to compensate the trust, in effect reconstituting the trust fund to the level at which it should have stood. The best known modern Australian examples of the same principle are *Re Dawson (deceased)*[43] and *Youyang Pty Ltd v Minter Ellison Morris Fletcher*.[44] The trustee's responsibility is to reconstitute the trust estate.[45] This usually requires the trustee to compensate the *trust* rather than the beneficiaries; however, in exceptional cases the beneficiary is the appropriate recipient.[46] Over time, this monetary remedy has come to be called equitable compensation.

[4.10] The jurisdiction to award equitable compensation for equitable wrongs other than breach of trust is said to be based in the early-twentieth-century decision, *Nocton v Lord Ashburton*.[47] It is, however, probably older than that, as Viscount Haldane noted in the case.[48] Certainly in the years prior to *Nocton*, courts had ordered fiduciaries to compensate principals in cases where the fiduciary had contracted with the principal, and the principal had suffered a loss.[49] In all of these cases, the contracts could no longer be rescinded, and the compensation ordered appeared to be the monetary equivalent of rescission.[50] *Nocton v Lord Ashburton* represented a major development because compensation was ordered in a situation where there was no contract to set aside between the fiduciary and the principal.

41 (2013) 16 HKCFAR 681; *Sourcebook* 4.3.1a, p 71.

42 (1801) 6 Ves 488; 31 ER 1159.

43 [1966] 2 NSWR 211; *Sourcebook* 4.3.3a, p 74. The facts of this case are discussed in greater detail at [4.16].

44 (2003) 212 CLR 484 ('*Youyang*'); *Sourcebook* 4.3.3b, p 78. See [4.17].

45 *Australian Executor Trustees (SA) Ltd v Kerr* (2021) 151 ACSR 204.

46 Where the trust is otherwise at an end, and there would be no point reconstituting it, or where the beneficiary is the sole beneficiary (as was the case in *Youyang* (n 44)), compensation can be directed to the beneficiary.

47 [1914] AC 932; *Sourcebook* 4.3.4a, p 80.

48 *Nocton v Lord Ashburton* [1914] AC 932, 946.

49 *Ballantyne v Raphael* (1889) 15 VLR 538; *Curwen v Yan Yean Land Co* (1891) 17 VLR 64; *Robinson v Abbott* (1893) 20 VLR 346; *Re Leeds and Hanley Theatres of Varieties Ltd* [1902] 2 Ch 809.

50 Birks called this 'pecuniary rescission': P Birks, 'Unjust Factors and Wrongs: Pecuniary Rescission for Undue Influence' (1997) 5 *Restitution Law Review* 72. See also [5.19]–[5.22]; D O'Sullivan, S Elliott and R Zakrzewski, *The Law of Rescission* (Oxford University Press, 2008); [15.14]–[15.22].

Nocton was Lord Ashburton's solicitor. Both of them had advanced money to a developer, secured by mortgages over land. Lord Ashburton's security was first in time, and had priority over Nocton's security. The developer wanted Lord Ashburton's security over the land removed, and Nocton, in his role as solicitor, advised Lord Ashburton to agree to its release. The developer became insolvent without repaying Lord Ashburton. Release of Lord Ashburton's security had the effect of advancing the priority of Nocton's own security. Clearly, he had been in a position of conflict when he gave advice to Lord Ashburton, and the effect of that conflict was that Lord Ashburton was in a worse position. The House of Lords held that Nocton was liable to compensate his client for the amount of the loss.[51] This was so, even though there was no contract between the solicitor and client that could be set aside.

Since *Nocton*, equitable compensation has been widely ordered for breach of fiduciary duty[52] and participation in fiduciary breaches,[53] and is routinely granted for breaches of confidence.[54] In recent times its use has extended to cases of equitable estoppel where the court is unable or unwilling to order a direct transfer of property.[55] Traditionally, it was not regarded as available for undue influence or unconscionable conduct, on the basis that an order for rescission represented the court's remedial limit. However, there are a number of instances where equitable compensation has been ordered when rescission is no longer possible (as, for example, where the property has been on-sold).[56] This closely reflects the approach in the older fiduciary cases preceding *Nocton*,[57] and this extension of the remedy seems entirely legitimate. It would be inequitable if a victim of undue influence or unconscientious conduct could be frustrated simply because the property concerned had passed out of the defendant's hands.[58] There have also been orders for compensation in respect of other equitable wrongs, such as fraud on a power.[59] [4.11]

How is equitable compensation calculated?

There has been extensive debate in recent times as to how equitable compensation should be assessed.[60] Part of the issue appears to have been whether the claim for compensation is [4.12]

51 As the parties had agreed on quantum before the appeal, the case is only indicative of calculation methods.

52 See, eg, *Stewart v Layton* (1992) 111 ALR 687; *Commonwealth Bank of Australia v Smith* (1991) 42 FCR 390; *Wan v McDonald* (1992) 33 FCR 491.

53 See *Quince v Varga* [2009] 1 Qd R 359.

54 See, eg, *Ithaca Ice Works Pty Ltd v Queensland Ice Supplies Pty Ltd* [2002] QSC 222; *Cadbury Schweppes Inc v FBI Foods Ltd* (1999) 167 DLR (4th) 577.

55 See, eg, *Donis v Donis* (2007) 19 VR 577.

56 See, eg, *Hartigan v International Society for Krishna Consciousness Inc* [2002] NSWSC 810; *Wood v Laverty* [2003] QSC 405; *Karam v Australia and New Zealand Banking Group Ltd* [2001] NSWSC 709.

57 See n 50.

58 See generally NY Nahan, 'Rescission: A Case for Rejecting the Classical Model?' (1997) 27(1) *University of Western Australia Law Review* 66.

59 *Houghton v Immer (No 155) Pty Ltd* (1997) 44 NSWLR 46.

60 See, eg, J Heydon, M Leeming and P Turner, *Meagher, Gummow & Lehane's Equity: Doctrines & Remedies* (LexisNexis Butterworths, 5th ed, 2015) ch 23; M Conaglen, 'Equitable Compensation for Breach of Fiduciary Dealing Rules' (2003) 119(2) *Law Quarterly Review* 246; C Mitchell, 'Equitable Compensation for Breach of Fiduciary Duty' (2013) 66(1) *Current Legal Problems* 307.

treated as 'substitutive' in the sense of restoring something taken from the trust or principal (or a substitute for that taken), or 'reparative' in the sense of repairing some other damage to the trust or principal.[61] These labels may reflect the accounting responsibilities of custodians of trust property, discussed above,[62] and tend to be descriptive of the facts of the cases in question.[63] However, they also serve to remind that equitable compensation is calculated in response to the duty breached. This is not to say that each equitable wrong has a different calculation method. Rather, the calculation method can only be applied in the context of the duty breached.[64]

Equitable compensation aims to put the plaintiff in the position she would have occupied had the defendant not wronged her.[65] It is not intended to be punitive in nature; instead, it is intended to effect justice between the parties. Compensation is assessed with the full benefit of hindsight, and is therefore usually judged at date of trial rather than date of breach.[66] There must be a causative link between the wrong and the claimed loss, but common law concepts such as reasonable foreseeability and *novus actus interveniens* are not applied.[67] Nor, on the whole, do other common law adjustment devices such as punitive damages[68] and contributory negligence[69] apply. However, equitable remedies are discretionary rather than automatic, and may be affected by discretionary bars to relief such as laches, hardship and unclean hands.[70]

[4.13] Traditionally, equitable compensation relieved economic losses and was not regarded as available for such personal losses as distress. In *Giller v Procopets*,[71] however, the Victorian Court of Appeal allowed equitable compensation for distress following a breach of confidence. This decision has now been followed in a similar case in Western Australia.[72]

[4.14] It is useful to have an understanding of how the remedy of equitable compensation emerged in order to understand how the quantum of compensation is calculated. Because the jurisdiction emanated from the law of trusts, the view emerged that the principles that applied in cases of misapplication of trust property applied to all calculations of equitable compensation, no matter which equitable wrong was being addressed. This view is incorrect. The aspect of calculation that has caused the greatest difficulty is the question of causation.

61 See *Agricultural Land Management Ltd v Jackson (No 2)* (2014) 48 WAR 1; *Sourcebook* 4.3.2a, p 73.

62 See [4.9].

63 The distinction between 'substitutive' and 'reparative' equitable compensation is controversial. For example, compare the approach of Edelman J in *Agricultural Land Management Ltd v Jackson (No 2)* (2014) 48 WAR 1, [333]–[353] with Heydon, Leeming and Turner (n 60) ch 23. As Gageler J commented in *Lifeplan* at [81], the accounting explanation has an air of artificiality when applied to cases where the fiduciary duty never involved holding property for the principal.

64 C Rickett, 'Equitable Compensation: Towards a Blueprint?' (2003) 25(1) *Sydney Law Review* 31. See also *Lifeplan* [84] (Gageler J).

65 *Nocton v Lord Ashburton* [1914] AC 932, 952; *O'Halloran v RT Thomas & Family Pty Ltd* (1998) 45 NSWLR 262, 272; *Schmidt v AHRKalimpa Pty Ltd* [2020] VSCA 193, [182].

66 *Youyang Pty Ltd v Minter Ellison Morris Fletcher* (2003) 212 CLR 484, 499.

67 *Re Dawson (deceased)* [1966] 2 NSWR 211; *Schmidt v AHRKalimpa Pty Ltd* [2020] VSCA 193, [183].

68 *Harris v Digital Pulse Pty Ltd* (2003) 56 NSWLR 298.

69 *Pilmer v Duke Group Ltd (in liq)* (2001) 207 CLR 165.

70 See chapter 6.

71 (2008) 24 VR 1; *Sourcebook* 12.4b, p 337. See chapter 12.

72 *Wilson v Ferguson* [2015] WASC 15.

Calculating equitable compensation for breach of trust

Trusts are primarily concerned with wealth management; what distinguishes the trust from other kinds of property-holding is that the trustee holds the property for the benefit of another – the beneficiary.[73] One of the most important responsibilities the trustee faces is to account to the beneficiaries. If the trustee cannot account to the beneficiaries because the trust fund has been misappropriated, misapplied, or distributed to someone who is not a beneficiary, the trustee is strictly responsible to reinstate the trust fund in full. Considerations of remoteness do not enter into the question. This is best illustrated by two Australian decisions: *Re Dawson (deceased)*[74] and *Youyang Pty Ltd v Minter Ellison Morris Fletcher*.[75] [4.15]

The trustee in *Re Dawson* wrongly paid away £NZ4700. At that time, the Australian and New Zealand currencies were valued equally. By the time the matter came to court, the relative value of the Australian and New Zealand currencies had altered, and the equivalent of £NZ4700 was approximately £A5829.[76] Should compensation be assessed by reference to the exchange rate at the time of breach, or at the date of judgment? Street J held that the trustee was under a duty to make restitution to the estate. The trustee had to place the trust in the same position it would have been in had no breach been committed. This was unaffected by considerations of causation, foreseeability and remoteness.[77] The estate would not be restored to its proper position unless the greater amount was paid. [4.16]

A similar outcome was reached in *Youyang*. The trust instrument required solicitors, who were acting as trustee of an investment trust at the time of its establishment, to use some of the trust funds to obtain securities before the balance could be paid over to a company for investment. The securities would have allowed the investor/beneficiary to recover all its capital at the end of ten years. The solicitor/trustee neglected to obtain the security, and paid all the funds to the investment company. Later, the investment company failed due to fraud. The High Court held that the solicitor/trustee had not performed the trust according to its terms, and had paid away trust property in breach of trust. It was therefore obliged to reconstitute the trust fund. It was irrelevant that the losses that eventuated were not reasonably foreseeable. [4.17]

The investor in *Youyang* had agreed to release the (non-existent) security after the breach had occurred. That the investor's agreement to release the security at that point would have been regarded in tort as an independent intervening act (thereby destroying the causative link between the breach of trust and the loss) was irrelevant. The breach of trust remained outstanding and had to be remedied.

It is interesting to note the effect of assessment of compensation at the date of judgment rather than the date of breach. At date of breach no funds had actually been lost, as the fraud that caused the ultimate loss had not occurred. But the loss had occurred at date of judgment, and the trust fund had to be reconstituted.

73 See chapter 13.
74 [1966] 2 NSWR 211.
75 (2003) 212 CLR 484.
76 It is unclear why the remedy was ordered in 'pounds' rather than 'dollars', given that Australia adopted decimal currency some four months prior to the decision.
77 *Re Dawson (deceased)* [1966] 2 NSWR 211, 214–15.

[4.18] Because the trust fund must be completely reinstated in order for the trustee to have performed the trust obligations, 'common law rules of damage and remoteness are out of place',[78] as the decisions discussed above show. Quantum is established by reference to the simple 'but for' test. 'But for' the trustee's breach, what would the trust fund have stood at? The trustee must then reconstitute it to that level. This includes the invested value of the trust fund, which was reflected in the award of compound interest in *Re Dawson*.

[4.19] But at which point in time should the appropriate level at which the trust fund should have stood be judged? Discussion in some cases suggests that, immediately upon a trustee misappropriating or misapplying trust funds, an equitable debt arises.[79] These cases can be read as implying that the equitable debt must be repaid to the beneficiary, regardless of the eventual fiscal outcome for the parties. A recent English decision suggests that this is not so. Equitable compensation can only be assessed when all the facts are known. 'Hindsight' may arguably work in favour of the plaintiff or the defendant.

In *AIB Group (UK) plc v Mark Redler & Co Solicitors*,[80] a firm of solicitors accepted instructions from both a lender (AIB) and borrowers (Mr and Mrs Sondhi). AIB was advancing £3.3 million, and taking security over the Sondhis' house, valued at £4.25 million. The house was subject to a mortgage in favour of Barclays Bank to secure an earlier loan. The solicitors were to discharge the debt to Barclays Bank and obtain a release of the earlier mortgage. They were to pay the balance of the amount borrowed directly to the Sondhis. It was an express term of the solicitors' instructions that they were to hold the entire amount being advanced on trust for AIB until completion of the loan arrangements. The solicitors made a mistake in calculating the amount owed to Barclays Bank. They underpaid the bank by £300 000, overpaying the borrowers the same amount. As the debt owed to Barclays Bank was not completely discharged, it refused to release its mortgage. The solicitors were unable to remedy the situation, and AIB eventually accepted a second mortgage over the property. The Sondhis refused to repay the overpayment, and eventually defaulted on the loan. By the time Barclays Bank and AIB came to enforce their mortgages, the property market had crashed. The Sondhis' house was sold for only £1.25 million.

The solicitors admitted they were in breach of trust in paying out the entire amount of £3.3 million. Did this mean they were then required to reconstitute the fund in full, as at the time of the misapplication of trust funds? A traditional 'accounting' approach[81] would suggest that outcome. Or was time of trial the correct date for assessing how much was required to reconstitute the trust fund? The UK Supreme Court held that the solicitors only had to reconstitute the trust fund to the level at which it would have stood, had they properly performed their trust. Had there been proper performance, AIB would have received a first mortgage to secure borrowings of £3.3 million. The fact that the property dropped in value from £4.25 million to £1.25 million had nothing to do with the solicitors' breach of trust. If AIB had been allowed to recover all it had claimed, the result would have placed it in a better position than it could have been in, had no breach of trust occurred.

78 P Millett, 'Equity's Place in the Law of Commerce' (1998) 114(2) *Law Quarterly Review* 214, 226.
79 See, eg, *Agricultural Land Management Ltd v Jackson (No 2)* (2014) 48 WAR 1, [336]–[337] (Edelman J).
80 [2015] AC 1503.
81 See [4.9].

The outcome in the case appears to be consistent with the aims of equitable compensation, namely, to put the plaintiff in the position as if they had not been wronged. Nevertheless, it has been divisive. Academic opinion both supports and criticises[82] the approach of the UK Supreme Court, and there are strong arguments made that it does not represent the law in Australia.[83]

Part of the problem here seems to relate back to uncertainty as to the meaning of the 'but for' test. This is discussed at [4.24] below.

Calculating equitable compensation for breach of fiduciary duty

The point was made above at [4.12] that equitable compensation can only be calculated in the context of the specific duty breached. This simple proposition has resonance in the case of breach of fiduciary duty. This is because of the twofold nature of fiduciary obligations, and the misconception that quantification principles applicable to misapplications of trust property apply equally to breaches of fiduciary duty. Taken together, these can lead to an argument that for any breach of fiduciary obligation the fiduciary must compensate the principal for all losses, unaffected by remoteness, foreseeability and causation. This argument is incorrect for two reasons: (1) equitable compensation is not available for all fiduciary breaches; and (2) it is not appropriate to unthinkingly apply the principles applied in cases of trustee misapplication to breaches of fiduciary duty. [4.20]

There are two core fiduciary obligations:[84] the profits rule and the conflicts rule. A fiduciary must not make an illicit profit from his position; nor can he place himself in a position of conflict between duties or between duty and interest. Equitable compensation is not available as a remedy for a breach of the profits rule, because it is inappropriate for such a breach. The profits rule addresses illicit profits made by the fiduciary and strips them from him. Equitable compensation addresses loss, and is not concerned with profits made by the fiduciary at all. If the principal complains that the fiduciary has made a profit that should have been made for the principal (if at all),[85] she is in effect adopting the fiduciary's wrongful act and asserting entitlement to any benefits flowing from it. Breaches of the profits rule are [4.21]

82 See, eg, R Lee, 'Substitutive Compensation for Breach of Trust: An Irrelevant Fairy Tale?' (2015) 9(1) *Journal of Equity* 94; W Gummow, 'Three Cases of Misappropriation of a Solicitor's Trust Account' (2015) 41(1) *Australian Bar Review* 5; L Ho, 'Equitable Compensation on the Road to Damascus?' (2015) 131(2) *Law Quarterly Review* 213; M Conaglen, 'Equitable Compensation for Breach of Trust: Off Target' (2016) 40(1) *Melbourne University Law Review* 126; J Edelman, 'An English Misturning with Equitable Compensation' in S Degeling and J Varuhas (eds), *Equitable Compensation and Disgorgement of Profit* (Hart Publishing, 2017).

83 Gummow (n 82); Conaglen (n 82).

84 See chapter 10.

85 If the principal claims the profit should have been made for her, she has 'lost' something in the sense that she did not gain a profit that might have come to her. But that does not comprehend the width of the profits rule. The fiduciary will be liable to account for profits made illicitly *whether or not* the principal could ever have made the profit herself. The profits rule also attacks profits that normatively have not been 'lost' by the principal. The best example here is *A-G (Hong Kong) v Reid* [1994] 1 AC 324, where a fiduciary was liable to account by way of constructive trust for a bribe received in breach of fiduciary obligation. The principal could never have validly taken that 'profit' itself, and could not be regarded as having 'lost' any tangible thing. See also chapter 10.

naturally and properly remedied only by the profit-stripping remedies, account of profits and constructive trust.[86] Conversely, profit-making is irrelevant to complaints about losses. The fiduciary is liable to compensate the principal for losses incurred by the principal due to the fiduciary's breach of the conflicts rule whether or not the fiduciary also made a profit from the breach.[87] This is naturally achieved by an order for equitable compensation which addresses loss. Thus, the remedy of equitable compensation is only called for in respect of breaches of the conflicts rule.[88]

[4.22] When considering whether the quantum methodology for misapplications of trust property applies to breaches of the conflicts rule, we can see that the field covered by the conflicts rule is much wider than that covered by misapplication. It is true that misapplications of trust property frequently breach the rule against conflicts of duty and interest, especially where there has been misappropriation. But a conflict of duty and duty[89] might not necessarily involve misapplication and may not strictly call for reconstitution of property. The fiduciary may not be holding property at all[90] and yet cause loss to the principal.

[4.23] One reason why causation has little relevance to cases involving misapplication is because causation is obvious. Say that the trustee misappropriates $100 000 and takes no step to replace it. The answer to the question 'what has caused the loss?' can only be that the misapplication caused the loss. There is no real point asking further questions at all. In rare cases like *AIB*, the answer may be more nuanced; loss in the sense of diminution of the trust fund was caused by the solicitors' incorrect payment, but loss on the overall transaction was caused by market forces. Where a breach of the conflicts rule is said to have caused a loss other than by misapplication of fiduciary property, it is important to ask causation questions, simply because we do not know what the answer will be. Otherwise, there is a grave risk of injustice to the defendant. This is illustrated by *Canson Enterprises Ltd v Boughton & Co.*[91]

In *Canson*, a solicitor owed competing duties to a client purchasing a property and to one of the vendors. A secret commission was being received on the purchase, and the solicitor should have passed that information on to the purchaser. The conflict was clearly a breach of fiduciary duty. After the contract settled, the purchasers constructed a new building on the site. Due to the negligence of engineers and contractors the new building suffered damage. The purchasers were unable to recover damages for negligence as the tortfeasors were insolvent. Instead, they sued the solicitor for equitable compensation for breach of fiduciary duty, claiming that but for the solicitor's breach they would not have suffered the loss that eventuated. It was held that the solicitor was not responsible for the losses. McLachlin J said: '(T)he plaintiff's actual loss as a consequence of the

86 The authors of *Meagher, Gummow & Lehane's Equity: Doctrines & Remedies* (n 60) disagree: [23-515]–[23-530].

87 As virtually all breaches of the profits rule are also breaches of the conflicts rule (duty and interest), the fiduciary's making of a profit only appears to require remedying via the conflicts rule.

88 This is not to suggest that the amount by which the defendant has profited is necessarily irrelevant. In some cases, it is appropriate to calculate the plaintiff's loss by reference to the profit of the defendant. Frequently, these figures will align, being flipsides of the same coin. An account of profits for breach of the profits rule would achieve the same result. See, eg, *Ferrari Investment (Townsville) Pty Ltd (in liq) v Ferrari* [2000] 2 Qd R 359, 370.

89 See [10.31].

90 See, eg, *Maguire v Makaronis* (1997) 188 CLR 449.

91 (1991) 85 DLR (4th) 129.

breach is to be assessed with the full benefit of hindsight. Foreseeability is not a concern in assessing compensation, but it is essential that the losses made good are only those which, on a common sense view of causation, were caused by the breach.'[92] Taking a common sense view, it could not be said that the fiduciary was responsible for the losses caused by the tortfeasors simply because at one point there was a breach of fiduciary duty.

The causation standard: 'but for' or 'common sense'?

Street J's dictum that causation is irrelevant to equitable compensation needs qualifying outside cases of simple misapplication of trust funds. But what should the appropriate causation standard be? The alternative test mentioned in *Canson* is the common sense standard. The 'common sense' formulation has received support in the House of Lords[93] and in the Australian High Court decision, *Maguire v Makaronis*.[94] It has been applied in Australia[95] but has also been criticised for uncertainty of meaning.[96] [4.24]

In practice, the two tests work in tandem.[97] The plaintiff must show on a common sense standard a sufficient link between the breach and the loss. In *O'Halloran v R T Thomas & Family Pty Ltd*,[98] a company director allowed a share transfer to be registered without payment of the purchase price. While the shares were out of the control of the company they declined in value. The director was liable for the whole loss as the director had disposed of property improperly. This was obviously very similar to a misapplication of trust property, and 'but for' causation was said to be appropriate.

The question is though, what does the 'but for' test mean? 'But for' can be viewed from the point of view of either the plaintiff or the defendant. Plaintiff-based 'but for' can be described as 'horse-shoe nail' causation.[99] Plaintiff-based 'but for' causation can be seen as appropriate in cases such as *Re Dawson*. But for the misappropriation of trust property, the property would not have been lost. However, an unqualified plaintiff-based 'but for' test will break down in cases of consecutive or concurrent breaches, as *Canson* demonstrates. The alternative is to view 'but for' causation from the defendant's point of view. The defendant may be permitted to show that, whether or not she had wronged the plaintiff, the plaintiff would have suffered some or all of the loss.[100] This is the correct explanation of the 'but for'

92 Ibid 163.

93 *Target Holdings Ltd v Redferns* [1996] AC 421. In England, the differentiation between equitable and common law causation standards is arguably more marked than in Australia.

94 (1997) 188 CLR 449. The causation standard at common law in Australia is also said to be 'common sense': see *March v E & MH Stramare Pty Ltd* (1991) 171 CLR 506 (negligence); *Alexander v Cambridge Credit Corporation Ltd* (1987) 9 NSWLR 310 (contract).

95 See, eg, *Gray v National Crime Authority* [2003] NSWSC 111; *Beach Petroleum NL v Abbott Tout Russell Kennedy* (1999) 48 NSWLR 1, 90.

96 See L Ho, 'Attributing Losses to a Breach of Fiduciary Duty' (1998) 12(2) *Trust Law International* 66, 69; JD Davies, 'Equitable Compensation: "Causation, Foreseeability and Remoteness"' in DWM Waters (ed), *Equity, Fiduciaries and Trusts* (Carswell, 1993) 297, 306.

97 *Mantonella v Thompson* [2009] 2 Qd R 542.

98 (1998) 45 NSWLR 262; *Sourcebook* 4.3.4b, p 82.

99 This is a reference to an old rhyme. 'For the want of a nail, the shoe was lost; for the want of a shoe, the horse was lost; for the want of a horse, the battle was lost; and all for the want of a horse-shoe nail.'

100 *Agricultural Land Management Ltd v Jackson (No 2)* (2014) 48 WAR 1, [395]–[396] (Edelman J).

test, because, in addition to explaining why the defendant in *Canson* was not responsible, it also explains why the trust in cases like *Re Dawson* must be fully reconstituted. None of the losses would have been suffered had the trustee not been in breach. In exceptional cases, the plaintiff may be able to demonstrate that the defendant's breach caused the plaintiff's exposure to the risk of loss in that, had the defendant not breached their duty, the plaintiff would never have entered into the loss-making transaction. In such cases, the plaintiff can expect to make full recovery.[101]

Plaintiffs must show a causative link between the wrong and the loss.[102] 'Common sense' serves as a reasonable description of the link to be demonstrated. Once a sufficient link is shown the plaintiff recovers the losses that it would not have incurred 'but for' the breach. While remoteness and foreseeability of the loss remain irrelevant,[103] the defendant is not responsible for those losses which (with the full benefit of hindsight) are not linked by common sense to its default.

This is demonstrated in *Stewart v Layton*.[104] A solicitor acting for both the vendor and purchaser in one transaction breached the conflicts rule through owing competing duties. The purchaser was unable to settle, and the vendor provided finance to ensure settlement. Had the solicitor properly discharged his obligations to the vendor, she would not have financed the purchase. The solicitor was liable for the losses the vendor incurred through providing vendor finance, but he was not liable for her losses on the entire transaction. The purchaser would not have been able to settle whether or not the solicitor breached the conflicts rule, a fact that exposed the vendor to some of the losses she incurred.

Quantification of equitable compensation is therefore dependent upon three matters:

(a) Identification of the duty breached;

(b) A sufficient connection between the breach and the loss; and

(c) Application of the 'but for' test to losses sufficiently connected to the breach.

Common law adjustments to quantum

[4.25] As equitable compensation is an equitable remedy, common law adjustment techniques such as mitigation, contributory negligence and punitive damages have little traction. If adjustments are made, they are usually made on equitable grounds, such as laches, hardship and unclean hands.[105]

[4.26] Contributory negligence or fault has little place in considerations of equitable compensation, largely because there is little scope for attributing blame to the plaintiff. Statutory reductions for contributory negligence are out of place because they can only be made in the context of damage caused to the plaintiff by the defendant's negligence.[106]

101 *Target Holdings Ltd v Redferns* [1996] AC 421, 441–2 (Lord Browne-Wilkinson).

102 *Maguire v Makaronis* (1997) 188 CLR 449, 473.

103 'And as with other questions of causation in equity, the inquiry into causation is not to be constrained by normative limitations imported from the common law.' (*Lifeplan* [89] (Gageler J).

104 (1992) 111 ALR 687, affirmed *Layton (t/as BM Salmon Layton & Co) v Stewart* [1994] ANZ ConvR 283.

105 See chapter 6.

106 *Perpetual Trustees Australia Ltd v Schmidt* [2010] VSC 67.

Claims that a defendant has breached an equitable obligation do not require a finding that the defendant has been negligent. In *Pilmer v Duke Group Ltd (in liq)*,[107] the High Court rejected in obiter dicta the possibility of equitable compensation for breach of fiduciary duty being reduced by reason of the principal's contributory fault. However, other jurisdictions are more receptive to the idea.[108]

Mitigation of loss is usually out of place in cases of breaches of trust. Chambers says that it is not clear whether beneficiaries can be under a duty to mitigate, but notes that in most cases they will lack the opportunity to take steps in mitigation.[109] There are Canadian authorities to the effect that a principal should mitigate following a breach of fiduciary duty[110] and some Australian support for the proposition.[111] For many purposes, however, equity achieves a similar effect to common law mitigation by use of equitable principles such as laches, acquiescence, and generally by the exercise of discretion.[112] In *Commonwealth Bank of Australia v Smith*[113] a bank manager owed fiduciary obligations to a customer. In breach of the conflicts rule he advised the client to purchase a hotel offered for sale by another customer. Von Doussa J at first instance reduced the equitable compensation payable to the plaintiffs on the grounds that they had realised that they had paid too much, but did not take steps to sell the hotel and sue for their losses until later. This can be viewed as a reduction for failure to mitigate, an example of laches or acquiescence, or an exercise of the court's remedial discretion. [4.27]

The common law adjustment which has received most attention in Australian equity is exemplary or punitive damages. Exemplary damages are awarded in tort where the defendant's behaviour has been so contemptuous of the plaintiff's rights as to deserve extra condemnation. It is frequently argued that such awards should be available in equity (particularly in cases of breach of trust and fiduciary duty) to express outrage at the fiduciary's betrayal. This was discussed at length by the New South Wales Court of Appeal in *Harris v Digital Pulse Pty Ltd*.[114] The trial judge awarded a small amount of exemplary damages for breach of fiduciary duty, but this was overturned on appeal. A majority of the Court of Appeal held that exemplary damages should not be awarded. This decision was followed by the Court of Appeal in Victoria where, in *Giller v Procopets*, Neave JA noted that there was no authority supporting punitive damages for a breach of confidence.[115] [4.28]

In *Giller*, the Victorian Court of Appeal ordered a substantial amount of aggravated damages (said to be compensatory) for breach of the equitable obligation of confidence.[116] The decision on this point can probably be regarded as being restricted to its facts in the context of a breach of highly personal confidential information. [4.29]

107 (2001) 207 CLR 165.

108 *AIB Group (UK) plc v Mark Redler & Co Solicitors* [2015] AC 1503, [136] (Lord Reed).

109 R Chambers, 'Liability' in P Birks and A Pretto (eds), *Breach of Trust* (Hart Publishing, 2002) 1, 12.

110 *Burke v Cory* (1959) 19 DLR (2d) 252; *Canson Enterprises Ltd v Boughton & Co* (1991) 85 DLR (4th) 129, 148 (La Forest J).

111 *Commonwealth Bank of Australia v Smith* (1991) 42 FCR 390; *Permanent Building Society (in liq) v Wheeler* (1994) 11 WAR 187, 249.

112 See chapter 6.

113 (1991) 42 FCR 390.

114 (2003) 56 NSWLR 298.

115 *Giller v Procopets* (2008) 24 VR 1, 103.

116 See [12.37].

WHAT'S ONLINE?

Available at www.cambridge.org/highereducation/isbn/9781009232388/resources:

- Recommended further readings
- Discussion topics
- Practice problems

5

RESCISSION, RECTIFICATION AND DECLARATIONS

Introduction

[5.1] The word 'rescission' is ambiguous, and its various meanings must be carefully distinguished. Here, we will be discussing rescission in the sense of the process for setting aside a voidable contract[1] and restoring the parties to their pre-contractual position. This is distinct from rescission (sometimes known as repudiation) for breach of contract, where the innocent party to a breach of contract exercises her right to terminate the contract and sue for damages or restitution of benefits conferred under the contract.[2] The principal difference between rescission of a voidable contract and rescission for breach of a valid contract is that the former operates retrospectively, restoring both parties to their pre-contractual position, whereas rescission for breach operates prospectively, entitling both parties to enforce their accrued rights under the contract but removing any obligation to carry out the terms of the contract in the future.

When can a voidable transaction be rescinded?

[5.2] A contract is voidable in equity for mistake, misrepresentation, duress, undue influence, unconscionable conduct, for breach of fiduciary obligation and under the rule in *Yerkey v Jones*.[3] A voidable contract is valid until the plaintiff has elected to avoid it.[4] It will then be set aside and *both* defendant *and* plaintiff must be restored to their pre-contractual position.

[5.3] Gifts may also be rescinded in equity on any of these grounds except under the rule in *Yerkey v Jones*, which only applies to contracts of guarantee.[5] It is unclear, however, whether a donor has to elect to rescind a gift that is voidable due to one of these vitiating factors, or whether a constructive trust will be automatically imposed over the property as soon as it is received by the donee, so that no election to rescind has to be made.[6]

The aim of rescission

[5.4] Rescission is a restitutionary remedy; it restores both parties to the position in which they would have been if the contract had not been entered into or the gift not made. If P buys a defective car for $10 000 as a result of D's misrepresentation as to the car's roadworthiness, P can rescind the contract. P is entitled to the return of her $10 000 (restitution) while D is entitled to the return of the car (counter-restitution).

[5.5] The contract in this example has been executed; title to the car has passed under the contract and the price has been paid. But rescission can also be ordered of an executory

1 Gifts may also be rescinded. See [5.3].
2 *McDonald v Dennys Lascelles Ltd* (1933) 48 CLR 457.
3 (1939) 63 CLR 649. See [7.36] onwards.
4 See [5.10]
5 *Elkofairi v Permanent Trustee Co Ltd* (2002) 11 BPR 20,841.
6 Cf *Allcard v Skinner* (1887) 36 Ch D 145 (where the majority required an election to rescind for undue influence, while Cotton LJ favoured a trust arising automatically at the moment of receipt) and *McCulloch v Fern* [2001] NSWSC 406 (where the trust arose at the time of receipt). See E Bant, 'Trusts, Powers and Liens: An Exercise in Ground-Clearing' 3 (2009) *Journal of Equity* 286.

contract, which neither party has taken any steps to perform. It is unclear whether rescission of a wholly executory contract is restitutionary. *Commercial Bank of Australia Ltd v Amadio*[7] is an example of rescission of an executory contract. Elderly parents, who had agreed to guarantee their son's business debts as a result of the bank's unconscionable exploitation of their position of special disadvantage,[8] were entitled to rescission of the guarantee even though they had never paid money to the bank under the guarantee. While it is possible to analyse rescission here as restitutionary, it seems simpler and less artificial to say that rescission of a wholly executory contract nullifies the contract.[9]

Rescission at common law and in equity

Rescission can be ordered at common law, as well as in equity, for fraudulent misrepresentation and for duress. The principal defect of common law rescission is that the parties have to be restored *precisely* to their pre-contract position (known as complete *restitutio in integrum*). For example, in *Clarke v Dickson*,[10] the plaintiff was induced by the defendant's fraud to buy shares in a mining company. When the fraud was discovered, the plaintiff was refused rescission at common law because the valuable shares he had received from the defendant were now worthless. The plaintiff therefore could not return equally valuable shares to the defendant. However, the plaintiff could have obtained rescission of the contract in equity, where strict *restitutio in integrum* is not required. In equity, a court can impose conditions on the award of rescission, including ordering the payment of compensation, in order to achieve practical justice for both parties. [5.6]

When a plaintiff elects to rescind a contract at law, the effect of the election is to eliminate the contract between the parties without the necessity of a court order.

Title to property which has passed under the contract revests in the transferor. The transferor may, however, have to sue in other common law actions, such as conversion or the action for money had and received, to recover the property.[11]

Summarising, the advantages of equitable rescission are: [5.7]

(a) The grounds of rescission are wider than those recognised at common law.

(b) The parties need not be restored precisely to their pre-contractual position. It is sufficient that substantial *restitutio in integrum* can be achieved. The court's aim is to achieve 'practical justice' for both parties.

(c) The court can impose terms or conditions on the award of rescission as part of the process of accomplishing 'practical justice'. For example, a defendant who is unable to return property received under the voidable contract because the property has been sold to a third party can be ordered to pay the value of the property to the plaintiff.

7 (1983) 151 CLR 447; *Sourcebook* 7.3.3b, p 158.

8 See [7.28]–[7.35].

9 See [2.17].

10 (1858) EB & E 463; 120 ER 463.

11 If revesting of legal title in property requires further acts to be performed, such as registration of title to land or to shares, common law rescission is not available and rescission in equity must be sought: *Nadinic v Drinkwater* (2017) 94 NSWLR 518, [28] (Leeming JA).

[5.8] *Alati v Kruger*[12] illustrates the operation of equitable rescission. The defendant sold a fruit business to the plaintiff for £700 after fraudulently misrepresenting the takings of the business. The plaintiff rescinded the contract. The High Court held that the plaintiff was entitled to restitution of the price on condition that he returned the fruit shop to the defendant. In addition, the High Court ordered other adjustments to be made as part of the restitutionary process. The defendant's chattels used in the business had to be returned or, if they could not be returned, the price of the chattels had to be paid to the defendant. On the other hand, the plaintiff had incurred conveyancing expenses in buying the shop. The defendant was ordered to repay the plaintiff these amounts.

Total and partial rescission

[5.9] Rescission in equity can be total or partial. Total rescission, setting aside the whole of the voidable contract, will usually be ordered. But a court will exceptionally order partial rescission, setting aside part of the contract while leaving the remainder valid and enforceable.

The leading decision on partial rescission is *Vadasz v Pioneer Concrete (SA) Pty Ltd.*[13] The plaintiffs executed a guarantee for the repayment of debts owed to the defendant by a company of which the plaintiffs were directors. The defendant represented that the guarantee only covered future debts contracted by the company, whereas the written guarantee actually covered past and future debts. The High Court held that the plaintiff was entitled to partial rescission of the guarantee. It was rescinded insofar as it related to past debts but remained enforceable against the plaintiffs in respect of future debts, contracted after the guarantee had been signed.

The decision in *Vadasz* is controversial. Its supporters argue that the remedy is a flexible response to cases of misrepresentation. Critics argue that the High Court was in effect rewriting the parties' contract. The remedy is very similar to another equitable remedy, rectification, discussed at [5.23], where the court rectifies an instrument so that it reflects the parties' actual agreement. Partial rescission is most often used in misrepresentation cases where (a) the court has clear evidence of the terms to which the plaintiff would have agreed but for the misrepresentation, and (b) the part to be rescinded can be easily severed from the rest of the contract.

The award of partial rescission in *Vadasz* can be contrasted with the order of total rescission in *Amadio.*[14] The defendant bank in *Amadio* had misrepresented to the plaintiffs that the guarantee they were signing was limited to $50 000. In fact, the parents had signed an 'all monies' agreement guaranteeing repayment of all the son's debts. Deane J stated that he had considered ordering partial rescission, limiting enforcement of the guarantee against the parents to $50 000. However, he ordered total rescission of the guarantee on the ground that, but for the defendant's unconscientious exploitation of the plaintiffs' special disadvantage, the plaintiffs would never have entered into the contract at all.

12 (1955) 94 CLR 216; *Sourcebook* 5.4a, p 107.
13 (1995) 184 CLR 102; *Sourcebook* 5.2a, p 98.
14 *Commercial Bank of Australia Ltd v Amadio* (1983) 151 CLR 447; *Sourcebook* 7.3.3b, p 158.

The election to rescind

A plaintiff must elect to rescind the voidable contract. Failure to do so means that the contract remains valid and enforceable. Rescission is sometimes described not as a remedy but as a form of self-help. The election to rescind emphasises this 'self-help' aspect. [5.10]

Daly v Sydney Stock Exchange Ltd[15] illustrates the importance of election. The plaintiff's husband sought investment advice from a firm of stockbrokers. An employee of the firm advised him not to invest his money in shares but to place it on deposit with the firm, earning a high rate of interest. However, the firm was in financial difficulty and went into liquidation after he had invested his money.

A statutory guarantee scheme protected investors who had deposited money with stockbroking firms, if the money received was held by the firm on trust for the investor, where the firm subsequently went into liquidation. The question was whether the stockbroking firm held the money deposited on trust. The plaintiff (the investor's wife, to whom the debt had been assigned) argued that the stockbrokers had acted in breach of fiduciary duty in advising investment with the firm, and claimed that the money was therefore held on constructive trust (which would have qualified for the statutory guarantee).

The High Court held the money was not held on constructive trust. It had been lent to the stockbrokers. Under a contract of loan, the borrower obtains full beneficial title to the money lent. The plaintiff could only obtain an equitable interest under a constructive trust if she first elected to rescind the contract for breach of fiduciary obligation. On election, she would have obtained an equitable interest in the money, but in this case, she had failed to elect to rescind the contract of loan. The failure to obtain an equitable interest, in turn, meant that she could not make a claim under the compensation scheme.[16]

A plaintiff elects to rescind a contract or gift when she gives notice to the other contracting party of her intention to have the contract set aside. If the defendant cannot be traced (eg he is a fraudster who has disappeared) the plaintiff must take reasonable steps to give notice, such as informing the police of her election to rescind.[17] [5.11]

The election requirement is sometimes criticised on the ground that it is a purely formal step, and that failure to elect can deprive a deserving plaintiff of justice (as possibly occurred in *Daly*). But the requirement is important for two reasons. [5.12]

First, it defines the relief that is being claimed. A plaintiff who has been induced to enter into a contract by a fraudulent misrepresentation can affirm the validity of the contract and obtain damages for breach, if the representation constitutes a term of the contract, or in the tort of deceit. Alternatively, she can rescind the contract, when the parties will be restored to their pre-contractual position. But she cannot *both* affirm the contract *and* rescind it. By electing to rescind, the plaintiff is claiming the assistance of equity to restore the parties to

15 (1986) 160 CLR 371; *Sourcebook* 5.3a, p 102. See also chapter 10.

16 No election to rescind is required where a fiduciary steals another's money and purports to lend that money to a third party. Subject to the availability of equitable defences or bars, the victim of the theft is entitled to the imposition of a constructive trust over the payment, or its traceable proceeds, without the necessity of an election: *Twigg v Twigg (No 4)* (2020) 147 ASCR 389, [197]–[205].

17 *Car & Universal Finance Co Ltd v Caldwell* [1965] 1 QB 525.

their pre-contractual position, but she is also forgoing any damages she might have obtained if she had elected to treat the contract as valid.

Secondly, election determines whether a third party who has obtained title to property which has passed under the voidable contract can retain the property. If the plaintiff has not elected to rescind the contract, the third party (whether a purchaser or a donee) takes good title to the property. If the plaintiff has elected to rescind, however, the plaintiff is entitled to the return of the property from any party except a good faith purchaser for value without notice of the ground for rescission.

Restoring the parties to their pre-contractual position

[5.13] We have seen how the parties in *Alati v Kruger*[18] were restored substantially to the position they occupied before the contract to buy the fruit shop had been entered into. The basic technique is: (1) to order the return of property transferred under the voidable contract; and (2) where property cannot be returned, or where one party has performed services for the other which have not been paid for, to order financial adjustments to be made, assessed as the value of the property transferred or of the services performed.[19] In *Alati v Kruger*, the High Court determined what had to be done in order to restore the parties to their pre-contractual position as at the date of the Court's judgment, not the date of election.

In restoring the parties to their pre-contractual position, equity is naturally more ready to protect innocent defendants than fraudsters. As Lord Wright stated in *Spence v Crawford*:

> The court will be less ready to pull a transaction to pieces where the defendant is innocent, whereas in the case of fraud the court will exercise its jurisdiction to the full in order, if possible, to prevent the defendant from enjoying the benefit of his fraud at the expense of the innocent plaintiff.[20]

[5.14] The court can impose terms on *both* parties to the rescinded transaction. If the defendant is ordered to make restitution of benefits obtained under the transaction, the plaintiff will also be required to make counter-restitution of the benefits she has obtained. If the plaintiff is unable to comply with the terms imposed by the court, or refuses to comply, the voidable contract remains valid and enforceable.

[5.15] *Maguire v Makaronis*[21] is a striking example of the court imposing terms on an innocent plaintiff. The plaintiffs, Mr and Mrs Makaronis, were the victims of a breach of fiduciary duty committed by their solicitors. They wanted to purchase a chicken farm and retained the

18 (1955) 94 CLR 216; *Sourcebook* 5.4a, p 107.

19 Where property restored under the decree of rescission has been improved, the improver may be awarded an equitable allowance if the improvement increases the value of the property and was not made solely for the improver's personal enjoyment: *Brown v Smitt* (1924) 34 CLR 160, 165; *Jonval Builders Pty Ltd v Commissioner for Fair Trading* (2020) 104 NSWLR 1, [32] (Leeming JA).

20 [1939] 3 All ER 271, 288. In cases of fraud, a court of equity, acting in its concurrent jurisdiction, can award the plaintiff compensation for losses directly caused by the fraudulent misrepresentation: *Munchies Management Pty Ltd v Belperio* (1988) 58 FCR 274, 284–6.

21 (1997) 188 CLR 449; *Sourcebook* 5.4b, p 110.

defendant solicitors to negotiate a bank loan in order to buy the farm. The defendants lent the plaintiffs the purchase price, $250 000, at an interest rate of 24%. They then borrowed $250 000 from a bank at an interest rate of 22%. They therefore made a profit from the difference in interest rates. In so doing, they had placed themselves in a position of conflict between their self-interest and the duty they owed their clients. The plaintiffs lost money on their chicken farm venture and only made one loan repayment to the defendants.

The High Court held that the plaintiffs were entitled to rescind the contract of loan for breach of fiduciary duty. Rescission was made conditional on the plaintiffs repaying the $250 000 loan and interest initially at the bank interest rate of 22%, which was found to be the market interest rate for bridging finance loans at the time they obtained their loan. The aim of the order was to restore both parties to their pre-contractual position. However, failure to observe the repayment terms meant that the plaintiffs would continue to be bound by the original contract, including the provision stipulating a 24% interest rate.

The facts of *Maguire v Makaronis* were unusual, and the High Court's principal concern was to ensure that the defendant solicitors did not profit from their breach of fiduciary duty. The Court did not, in other respects, allow the plaintiffs to escape from the financial consequences of their imprudent decision to purchase the chicken farm. In later cases of contracts induced by fraudulent misrepresentation or by unconscionable conduct, the conditions imposed on the parties have been more favourable to a victim of exploitation. For example, in *Perpetual Trustees Victoria Ltd v Burns*,[22] the lender lent $266 849 on mortgage to a couple, each of whom was on a disability pension with no prospect of employment, as part of an $840 000 loan arrangement under a 'low doc[umentary]' mortgage scheme to enable the plaintiffs to invest in the stock market. The couple received no independent advice, and the loan contracts and mortgage over their home were rescinded on the ground that they had been procured by unconscientious conduct. It was a condition of rescission that the couple had to repay the $266 849 they had received, but the court held that only simple interest was payable on this amount and that the lenders were not entitled to security over the couple's home. The lenders, for their part, were ordered to repay the couple any interest in excess of simple interest they had received, as well as any charges the couple had paid the lenders under the rescinded loan agreement. [5.16]

The proprietary consequences of rescission

Prior to the election to rescind a voidable contract, the plaintiff has what is sometimes termed an 'equity', or 'mere equity', to have any property transferred under the contract returned to her. After she has elected to rescind, she has an equitable interest in the property.[23] Whereas an equitable interest entitles the holder to a vested proprietary interest, an 'equity' is a power, dependent on the exercise of equitable discretion, to obtain a proprietary interest in the subject-matter of the contract by electing to rescind the contract. The correct identification [5.17]

22 [2015] WASC 234.

23 *Latec Investments Ltd v Hotel Terrigal Pty Ltd (in liq)* (1965) 113 CLR 265; *Sourcebook* 8.3a, p 189.

of the plaintiff's interest as either an equitable interest or as an equity will be critical in the event of a priority dispute affecting the subject-matter of the contract.[24]

Bars to rescission and pecuniary restitution

[5.18] Like other equitable remedies, rescission in equity is discretionary and can be barred on grounds which include laches (delay), lack of 'clean hands', and the plaintiff's affirmation of the voidable contract.[25] Rescission will also be barred if the parties cannot be restored to their pre-contractual position. This will be rare because equity can usually order financial adjustments to be made where precise restoration is impossible. Rescission will be impossible if, for example, the subject-matter of the contract had been destroyed in an accidental fire.[26]

[5.19] An important bar to relief is 'third party rights' – that the legal or equitable title to the subject-matter of the voidable contract has been obtained by a good faith purchaser for value without notice of the plaintiff's ground of rescission. It would be unfair to leave the plaintiff without a remedy simply because the defendant has disposed of the property to the purchaser. In some cases where this has occurred, the defendant has been ordered to pay the plaintiff an amount based on the value of the property. The remedy has been described as pecuniary rescission.[27]

[5.20] *McKenzie v McDonald*[28] is an early example of pecuniary rescission. The plaintiff sold her farm at undervalue to the defendant, her estate agent, as part of an arrangement whereby she bought the agent's suburban shop and dwelling. In negotiating this contract, the defendant had acted in breach of fiduciary duty. The plaintiff was unable to recover the farm because the defendant had sold it to a good faith purchaser. Dixon AJ held that the defendant must pay the plaintiff the difference between the true value of the farm and the suburban shop and dwelling, or else take back the suburban shop and dwelling and repay the plaintiff the purchase price, together with a sum representing the true value of the farm.

[5.21] In *Hartigan v International Society for Krishna Consciousness Inc*,[29] pecuniary rescission was awarded where a gift had been made under undue influence. The plaintiff conveyed her farm to the defendant religious organisation while under undue influence. The organisation sold the farm to a good faith purchaser and used the proceeds of sale to pay off a bank loan. Bryson J held that the defendant was liable to pay the plaintiff a sum equal to the amount the defendant had received on sale of the farm.

24 See chapter 8.

25 Equitable bars to relief are discussed in chapter 6. The bars may apply even where ground for rescinding a contract is fraud: *Henjo Investments Pty Ltd v Collins Marrickville Pty Ltd* (1988) 39 FCR 546 (delay relevant to denying rescission for fraudulent non-disclosure).

26 See also *AH McDonald & Co Ltd v Wells* (1931) 45 CLR 506 (rescission impossible because contract included an option for one of the parties to obtain an interest in a patent from a third party, and by the time of the election to rescind the patent had expired).

27 P Birks, 'Unjust Factors and Wrongs: Pecuniary Rescission for Undue Influence' (1997) 5 *Restitution Law Review* 72.

28 [1927] VLR 134.

29 [2002] NSWSC 810.

Pecuniary rescission is a new development in the law of rescission and the principles have not yet been fully worked out.[30] One unresolved issue concerns the assessment of the monetary award. Should the plaintiff be entitled to the value of the property received by the defendant (in *Hartigan*, the value of the farm at the date of receipt), which is the usual method of valuing benefits in the law of unjust enrichment? Should she be entitled to an amount representing the actual sum received by the defendant on sale of the plaintiff's property – which is what Bryson J awarded in *Hartigan*? Or should the value of the farm be assessed at the date of election to rescind? Authority provides no clear answer to these questions. The court's overriding objective in ordering rescission is to place the parties substantially in the position they would have been if they had not entered into the voidable contract. How that objective can be best fulfilled in ordering pecuniary rescission will ultimately be a matter for the exercise of equitable discretion. [5.22]

Rectification

Equity can rectify a written instrument that does not reflect the true intentions of the parties who executed it. Their intentions are assessed as at the time of execution. The remedy of rectification corrects the instrument which can then be enforced according to its corrected terms. In *Bosaid v Andry*,[31] the parties intended 'No 75' Alma Road to be sold, but the written contract said 'No 15'. Sholl J ordered rectification of the contract and held that the defendant was liable to pay damages for breach of the rectified contract. [5.23]

Rectification must not be confused with rescission, although the principles applicable to rectification of a contract on the ground of unilateral mistake are based on *Taylor v Johnson*,[32] the leading decision on rescission for unilateral mistake. Rectification presupposes the existence of a valid contract whose terms are not accurately reflected by the written agreement, whereas rescission assumes that there was no valid agreement. Moreover, rescission, unlike rectification, can be ordered of an oral contract. [5.24]

The elements of rectification

Rectification will be ordered if the following criteria are satisfied: [5.25]

(a) There is a written instrument. Instruments are rectified, not contracts. The written instrument will often be a contract but it can be a conveyance of land, a lease, an insurance policy or any other document which affects legal rights.[33]

(b) A mistake has been made as to its content or effect. The mistake will usually be a *common* mistake relating to the content and terms of the contract, such as the mistake as to the house number in *Bosaid v Andry*. In *Commissioner of Stamp Duties (NSW) v Carlenka Pty Ltd*,[34] the New South Wales Court of Appeal held that

30 See [5.19]–[5.22].
31 [1963] VR 465.
32 (1983) 151 CLR 422.
33 Wills legislation in most States and Territories provides for the rectification of wills: see, eg, *Succession Act 2006* (NSW) s 27; *Wills Act 1997* (Vic) s 31.
34 (1995) 41 NSWLR 329 (CA).

a common mistake, not only as to the meaning of a term in a contract, but also as to its effect, can justify rectification. In that case, the parties intended to amend a trust deed so that a company would become an income beneficiary. Due to solicitor error, the amendment had the unintended effect of making the company a capital beneficiary as well as creating a liability to pay stamp duty. Rectification was ordered because there was a 'disconformity between the form or effect of the document executed and the intention of the parties … executing it'.[35] What must be proved in any case is a lack of correspondence between the parties' common intention and the words employed in the written instrument expressing that intention.[36]

A *unilateral* mistake will not usually entitle the mistaken party to rectification. But rectification will be ordered where the defendant has fraudulently or unconscientiously taken advantage of a mistake in the agreement. So where a purchaser of land deliberately takes advantage of the vendor's mistake in order to obtain a larger plot than the vendor intended to sell, the vendor will be entitled to rectification.[37] Rectification for unilateral mistake is based on *Taylor v Johnson*,[38] the leading High Court decision on rescission for unilateral mistake. The defendant must have actual knowledge of the plaintiff's mistake. In *Leibler v Air New Zealand Ltd*,[39] Kenny JA, in reviewing the criteria for rectification on the ground of unilateral mistake, left open the question whether 'something less' than actual knowledge might suffice.

(c) The instrument does not reflect the true intention of the parties (in the case of a common mistake) or of the mistaken party (in the case of a unilateral mistake). For this purpose, the subjective intentions of the contracting parties are relevant, in contrast to the objective approach of the courts in constraining the terms of the contract.[40] In applying a subjective test, however, a court will ascertain the parties' intentions from their objective words and actions.[41] In *Simic v New South Wales Land and Housing Corporation*,[42] the corporation required a building contractor to obtain a performance bond as security for demolition and construction work the contractor had agreed to undertake for the corporation. The contractor obtained a bond from a bank. The contract stated that the bond had been made in favour of the New South Wales Department of Housing. There was no such government department and the corporation was the intended beneficiary of the bond. The High Court held that the actual common intention of the representatives of both the

35 *Commissioner of Stamp Duties (NSW) v Carlenka Pty Ltd* (1995) 41 NSWLR 329 (CA), 336.
36 *Club Cape Schanck Resort Co Ltd v Cape Country Club Pty Ltd* [2001] 3 VR 526.
37 *Tutt v Doyle* (1997) 42 NSWLR 10.
38 (1983) 151 CLR 422.
39 (Victorian Court of Appeal, Winneke P, Phillips and Kenny JJA, 3 October 1997).
40 *Simic v New South Wales Land and Housing Corporation* (2016) 260 CLR 85, [19] (French CJ), [47]–[49] (Kiefel J). Cf the objective approach to ascertaining the parties' intentions proposed by Lord Hoffmann in *Chartbrook Ltd v Persimmon Homes Ltd* [2009] AC 1101, 1126 [59]–[60].
41 *Simic v New South Land and Housing Corporation* (2016) 260 CLR 85, [104] (Gageler, Nettle and Gordon JJ). Disagreement about the basis of rectification in subjective or objective intention may reflect misconceptions as to the meaning of 'subjective' and 'objective' in this context: R Stevens, 'What is an Agreement?' (2020) 136(4) *Law Quarterly Review* 599.
42 (2016) 260 CLR 85.

building contractor and thc bank was to provide security in performing the contract to the corporation and that the contract should be rectified to reflect that intention.

The time for assessing intention is the time when the instrument comes into force. In the case of rectification of a written contract, the parties need not have entered into an enforceable contract prior to executing the instrument. For example, a written contract can be rectified even if the prior agreement was unenforceable by reason of non-compliance with statutory writing requirements.[43]

(d) The court must be able to identify the precise variation which needs to be made to the wording of the instrument. Rectification will be refused if the correct words cannot be identified. In *Club Cape Schanck Resort Co Ltd v Cape Country Club Pty Ltd*,[44] an agreement referred disputes about sewage treatment charges to the Administrative Appeals Tribunal. The Tribunal did not, however, have jurisdiction to hear the dispute. The plaintiff applied to replace the reference to the Tribunal with a reference to an arbitrator. The Victorian Court of Appeal refused to rectify the instrument since the reference to the Administrative Appeals Tribunal exactly reflected the parties' erroneous wishes and there was no other word or words which would give effect to the parties' agreement.

Rectification and construction

Not all mistakes require rectification. Obvious typographical and grammatical errors can be corrected as a simple matter of interpretation of the contract. Courts regularly insert, delete, alter and interpret words so as to give documents a sensible meaning without recourse to rectification. So, for example, the word 'John' has been construed as 'Mary',[45] and the words 'The usual conditions of sale … shall so far as they are inconsistent herewith be deemed to be embodied herein' were read as if 'inconsistent' meant 'consistent'.[46] But courts will not lightly amend the wording of commercial contracts giving rise to undertakings which must be strictly performed by both parties to the contract. In *Simic v New South Wales Land and Housing Corporation*,[47] the High Court refused to construe references in a performance bond to the New South Wales Land and Housing Department to mean the New South Wales Land and Housing Corporation. As French CJ stated, '[s]uch a loose approach to construction would be inconsistent with the commercial purposes of the Undertakings as performance bonds'.[48] The contract was nevertheless rectified in order to reflect the parties' actual intentions. [5.26]

The construction of a document is distinct from rectification and an instrument will not be rectified if its true meaning can be determined by construing it. An important practical difference is that a court will take into account pre-contractual negotiations when deciding whether to rectify an instrument but cannot do so when construing a contract.[49] In [5.27]

43 *United States v Motor Trucks Ltd* [1924] AC 196; *Bosaid v Andry* [1963] VR 465.
44 [2001] 3 VR 526.
45 *Wilson v Wilson* (1854) 10 ER 811, 822.
46 *Fitzgerald v Masters* (1956) 95 CLR 420.
47 (2016) 260 CLR 85.
48 Ibid [11].
49 Ibid [20].

some cases, however, as in *Bosaid v Andry*, discussed above at [5.23], the court will order rectification of an instrument if there is an obvious error on the face of the instrument and the parties are litigating some other matter concerning the instrument.

Effect of rectification

[5.28] The effect of rectification is to relate the rectified document back to the time of its original execution; it is read as if it had originally been executed in its rectified form. Rectification will not be decreed if the contract has already been construed by the court in an unrectified form and money has been paid out pursuant to the construction.[50] It will also not be decreed where to do so would invalidate rights in the subject-matter of the contract obtained by a good faith purchaser.[51] Other equitable bars, such as delay or acquiescence, also apply to rectification.[52]

Declaration

[5.29] A declaration is a court order which finally declares the legal rights or obligations of the parties to the proceedings.[53] Because they must be final, declarations are not granted in interim or interlocutory proceedings.[54] Historically, declarations were an equitable remedy granted in conjunction with specific relief such as an injunction. Courts could not grant so-called 'naked' declarations that were not ancillary to a grant of specific relief. Statute now, however, empowers courts to grant 'stand alone' declarations. Typical of modern legislation is s 75 of the *Supreme Court Act 1970* (NSW) which provides:

> No proceedings shall be open to objection on the ground that a merely declaratory judgment or order is sought thereby and the Court may make binding declarations of right whether any consequential relief is or could be claimed or not.[55]

[5.30] The practical effect of the legislation is that declarations are the most comprehensively fused[56] of all equitable relief; it is irrelevant whether the right or obligation subject to the declaration is legal, equitable or statutory. A plaintiff need not have a legal or equitable right or cause of action in order to seek a declaration. There is apparently no limitation on the kinds of situations in which declarations can be made.[57] Declarations are perhaps most useful where the court can provide an answer to a single question in dispute between the

50 *Caird v Moss* (1886) 33 Ch D 22.

51 *Coolibah Pastoral Co v Commonwealth* (1967) 11 FLR 173.

52 *Simic v New South Wales Land and Housing Corporation* (2016) 260 CLR 85, [20] French CJ.

53 R French, 'Declarations: Homer Simpson's Remedy – Is There Anything They Cannot Do?' in K Dharmananda and A Papamatheos (eds), *Perspectives on Declaratory Relief* (Federation Press, 2009) 41.

54 *Re Elm* (2006) 69 NSWLR 145, 153.

55 Equivalent provisions are: *Federal Court of Australia Act 1976* (Cth) s 21; *Supreme Court Rules 1937* (ACT) ord 29 r 5; *Supreme Court Act 1979* (NT) s 18; *Supreme Court Act 1995* (Qld) s 128; *Supreme Court Act 1935* (SA) s 31; *Supreme Court Rules 2000* (Tas) r 103; *Supreme Court Act 1986* (Vic) s 36; *Supreme Court Act 1935* (WA) s 25(6).

56 For a discussion of the 'fusion' debate, see [1.19]–[1.20].

57 French (n 53) 28–9.

parties. Indeed, a declaration may be refused if it would fail to resolve the issues between the parties.[58] However, a declaration is not an enforceable order. If the defendant fails to respect the plaintiff's declared rights, other proceedings must be brought to protect them, such as an action for damages or an injunction. For these enforcement proceedings it will be necessary for the plaintiff to identify the correct jurisdictional basis of the right.

Criteria for the award of a declaration

There are three basic criteria for the award of a declaration: [5.31]

(a) *Jurisdiction*. A court will have jurisdiction to grant a declaration unless a statute has ousted the jurisdiction. Clear words are required to exclude the jurisdiction.[59] In the case of courts exercising federal jurisdiction, a declaration cannot be granted if it would amount to giving an advisory opinion because their jurisdiction is limited to the decision of 'matters' for the purpose of ch III of the *Constitution*.[60]

(b) *Standing*. Where the plaintiff alleges the existence of a private right the plaintiff must show that she is entitled to the right, such as the right of a beneficiary under a trust.[61] Outside of such cases, the applicant must have a 'real'[62] or 'special'[63] interest in the subject-matter of the dispute. For example, in *Onus v Alcoa of Australia Ltd*,[64] elders of an Aboriginal tribe were held to have standing to seek a declaration concerning the protection of cultural relics under the *Archaeological and Aboriginal Relics Prevention Act 1972* (Vic).

(c) *Discretion*. A declaration is a discretionary remedy. The view has often been expressed that '[i]t is neither possible nor desirable to fetter the broad discretion … by laying down rules as to the manner of its exercise'.[65] A discretionary factor particularly relevant to declarations is whether the court is being asked to decide a theoretical dispute, since courts will not grant declarations where the question raised is hypothetical and not part of a justiciable controversy.[66] In *CE Heath & General Insurance Ltd v Pyramid Building Society (in liq)*,[67] the Victorian Court of Appeal refused to grant a declaration that claims brought against the auditors of a failed building society, but not yet heard, were covered by insurance policies taken out by the auditors. Whether the claims were covered would depend on the

58 *Neeta (Epping) Pty Ltd v Phillips* (1974) 131 CLR 286, 307 (Barwick CJ and Jacobs J).

59 *Forster v Jododex Australia Pty Ltd* (1972) 127 CLR 421, 436 (Gibbs J).

60 *Re Judiciary Act 1903 and Navigation Act 1912* (1921) 29 CLR 257; *Momcilovic v The Queen* (2011) 245 CLR 1.

61 For standing in public law matters including criminal law, see MGL [19-45]–[19-50].

62 *Ainsworth v Criminal Justice Commission* (1992) 175 CLR 564, 581–2.

63 *Australian Conservation Foundation Inc v Commonwealth* (1980) 146 CLR 493.

64 (1981) 149 CLR 27.

65 *Forster v Jododex Australia Pty Ltd* (1972) 127 CLR 421, 437 (Gibbs J). An important function of the declaration is to vindicate a legal right where compensatory damages would be nominal: *Lewis v Australian Capital Territory* (2020) 381 ALR 375, [119] (Gordon J).

66 *Egan v Willis* (1998) 195 CLR 424; *Gladstone Ports Corporation Ltd v Murphy Operator Pty Ltd* (2020) 6 QR 497, [18]–[19]. Judicial advice to trustees is an exception to the principle that courts do not give advisory opinions: see [19.32]–[19.35].

67 [1997] 2 VR 256.

outcome of complex tort litigation in which the issues were still to be defined. No declaration could be granted while that litigation remained an 'uncertainly formulated dispute'.[68] Another reason to refuse to make a declaration is that the declaration sought will be useless, or have no real consequences for the parties to the dispute.[69] For example, there is no utility in a declaration concerning past acts, when current conditions make the history of the matter irrelevant.

Equitable bars to relief

[5.32] In general, the equitable bars to relief will not defeat an application for a declaration.[70] Because the modern source of the court's power to make a declaration is statutory, considerations such as unclean hands, delay and hardship are irrelevant to its award.[71] But where the plaintiff seeks a declaration that she is entitled to an equitable right, the court necessarily takes into account equitable principles. In *H Stanke & Sons Pty Ltd v O'Meara*,[72] the plaintiffs sought declarations of their equitable proprietary interests in land held by the defendants. The South Australian Full Court held that the defendants could plead the plaintiffs' lack of clean hands as a consideration in the exercise of discretion because, in seeking the declaration, the plaintiffs sought equity's assistance.

WHAT'S ONLINE?

Available at www.cambridge.org/highereducation/isbn/9781009232388/resources:

- Recommended further readings
- Discussion topics
- Practice problems

68 Ibid 272 (Ormiston JA).
69 *Gardner v Dairy Industry Authority of New South Wales* (1977) 52 ALJR 180.
70 *Mayfair Trading Co Pty Ltd v Dreyer* (1958) 101 CLR 428.
71 See chapter 6.
72 (2007) 98 SASR 450.

6

BARS TO RELIEF

Introduction

[6.1] One distinguishing feature of equitable remedies is their discretionary nature. Common law remedies accrue as of right once the plaintiff has made out her cause of action. However, equitable relief is not automatic. Equity acts to correct the defendant's conscience and sometimes this may not lead to full recovery, or indeed any recovery, for the plaintiff.[1] Because the court weighs factors from both the plaintiff's and defendant's perspectives 'that tend towards the justice or injustice of granting the remedy that is sought',[2] there is some unpredictability involved in equitable remedies.

[6.2] Nevertheless, it is a mistake to imagine that equitable remedies are entirely unpredictable. When the plaintiff is denied her remedy, or finds her remedy less than she hoped for, or given to her on terms, we are able to point to a set of well-identified grounds that will have informed the court's exercise of discretion. Because these grounds are used to reduce or deny the plaintiff's remedy, they are often referred to as 'equitable defences', but they are not defences in the common law sense. They are merely factors relevant to the exercise of remedial discretion. They include the doctrines of laches and acquiescence, unclean hands, and hardship to the defendant. These are by no means the only cases in which equity will deny a plaintiff a remedy. For example, a court exercising equitable jurisdiction will not make an order that is futile,[3] or impossible to supervise. Estoppel, discussed in chapter 7, can operate as a defence. Another highly relevant matter, which is discussed in this chapter, is the effect of the order on third parties.

Laches

[6.3] Laches is pleaded by defendants almost routinely, whenever a time gap can be identified between the alleged cause of action arising and commencement of suit. Broadly speaking, laches involves delay. Nowadays, limitations legislation prescribes time limits within which most claims must be brought.[4] But prior to statute, common law actions had no limitation periods, and equity's disdain of slothful plaintiffs distinguished it from the common law. Laches is only relevant to equitable causes of action.[5]

[6.4] 'Delay' may be the English word nearest in meaning to the term 'laches', but delay does not fully encompass the concept of laches in equity. On its own, it is unlikely to be sufficient to sustain a claim of laches. The classic statement of law comes from *Lindsay Petroleum Co v Hurd*.[6] In summary, the Court declared that, in some cases, it would be unjust to give a remedy because the plaintiff (a) has effectively waived her rights, or (b) by her conduct and neglect, has put the defendant in what would be a difficult position if the remedy were now to be granted. The two circumstances important in such cases are the length of the delay and the nature of the acts done during the interval which might

1 *Bridgewater v Leahy* (1998) 194 CLR 457, 494.
2 ICF Spry, *The Principles of Equitable Remedies* (Lawbook, 6th ed, 2001) 4.
3 N Witzleb, '"Equity Does Not Act in Vain": An Analysis of Futility Arguments in Claims for Injunctions' (2010) 32(3) *Sydney Law Review* 503.
4 See [6.10].
5 *Orr v Ford* (1989) 167 CLR 316, 340; *Sourcebook* 6.2c, p 124.
6 (1874) LR 5 PC 221, 239–40.

affect either party and cause injustice. The defendant bears the burden of proving both the delay and its effect.[7]

Elapsed time is not the only consideration here; equally important is the *effect* of the delay. It may have resulted in prejudice to the defendant – perhaps the defendant is now unable to gather witnesses or documents to help in its defence,[8] or has altered its position. Alternatively, granting the remedy may now prejudice third parties who have, in the intervening period, dealt with the defendant on the basis that there is no claim against it. The elapsed time may mean that it is now impossible to give equitable relief on terms that would be just to the defendant. A consequence of the focus on the effect of delay is that even relatively short periods can allow the defendant to claim laches. On the other hand, a long delay during which the relative positions of the plaintiff and defendant did not substantially change might prove to be irrelevant. [6.5]

The general principles are illustrated by *Baburin v Baburin (No 2)*.[9] A mother transferred shares in a family company to her sons. Nineteen years later, she sought to have the transaction set aside for unconscientious dealing.[10] During that time, one of the sons had died, documents had been lost or destroyed, and some of the shares had been transferred to third parties. Further, some of the shares' value was due to the sons' efforts over the years. Requiring return of the shares would be unjust to the defendants for all of those reasons. Rescission of the transaction was refused, despite unconscientious dealing being made out. In contrast, in *Orr v Ford*,[11] two men agreed that one would purchase land, and hold one half on trust for the other, the other contributing to the purchase price. The second man did nothing to assert his rights to the land for 20 years. The High Court majority held that the purchaser could not show laches, as during that period no crucial evidence had been lost and no prejudice to other parties had occurred. [6.6]

Where the defendant alleges that evidence has been lost through delay, the defendant must specify the evidence lost and show that it would have supported his case. In *Baburin*, one of the key witnesses might have been able to refresh his memory by reference to documents, but they had been lost in the interim. [6.7]

Delay is assessed from the time at which the plaintiff had knowledge of the facts that gave rise to her claim.[12] But laches is not limited to lack of urgency in commencing proceedings; it can also arise when the plaintiff is slow to prosecute a commenced action.[13] [6.8]

All cases in which laches is claimed are judged on their own circumstances. In addition to issues, such as length of any delay and the effect that delay had on the parties and others, relevant matters include the nature of the relief claimed, any property over which relief is claimed, and the identity of the parties. For example, delay is less understandable in cases where interlocutory injunctions are sought,[14] but where the claim involves reconstitution of [6.9]

7 *Voukidis v C & O Voukidis Pty Ltd (in liq)* [2018] VSC 267.
8 *Lowe v Pascoe (No 9)* [2021] NSWSC 163, [169]
9 [1991] 2 Qd R 240.
10 See chapter 7.
11 (1989) 167 CLR 316.
12 *Lindsay Petroleum Co v Hurd* (1874) LR 5 PC 221, 241; *Sourcebook* 6.2a, p 120.
13 *Lamshed v Lamshed* (1963) 109 CLR 440.
14 This is because they are frequently sought on an urgent basis. See [3.19].

a trust fund following misappropriation, the trustee has fewer reasons to resist the claim due to beneficiary delay. Finally, laches is a personal bar only and does not usually bind the plaintiff's successors in title.[15]

[6.10] The doctrine of laches must also be considered in conjunction with statute. Limitation statutes can, by their terms, either apply to equitable causes of action, or exclude application to equitable causes of action; this is an issue of statutory interpretation. But further, equity[16] acts by analogy to the law and may apply time limits in cases where a common law or statutory claim exists in addition to the equitable cause of action.

[6.11] Limitation of action by analogy is illustrated in *Gerace v Auzhair Supplies Pty Ltd (in liq)*.[17] Three directors of a company were accused of breaching fiduciary duty by transferring company assets improperly. This was also a breach of ss 181–3 of the *Corporations Act 2001* (Cth). The statute had a time limit of six years for the bringing of actions. The company commenced proceedings for the equitable breach after the six-year period had elapsed. Meagher JA said that in equitable proceedings, where there was a corresponding remedy at law arising from the same matter, equity will apply the statutory limitation bar, unless the defendant's reliance on the statutory bar would, in the circumstances, be unconscionable. His Honour denied that there was a broad equitable discretion whether or not to apply the bar, saying that the defendant's unconscionability in such a case would be identified according to the principles discussed by the High Court in cases such as *Australian Broadcasting Corporation v Lenah Game Meats Pty Ltd*[18] and *Australian Competition and Consumer Commission v CG Berbatis Holdings Pty Ltd*[19] An example of such unconscionability would be where the defendant's fraud denied the plaintiff the opportunity to sue within the time limit.

Meagher JA said that the doctrine of laches was directed to a different, broader question than that of refusal to apply limitation periods. He said that laches was concerned with whether 'as between the parties, it would be practically unjust to give relief which otherwise would be just'.[20] This was a different question to whether it would be unjust to allow the statutory bar to be applied.

Acquiescence

[6.12] Acquiescence 'is best understood as requiring calculated (that is, deliberate and informed) inaction by [the plaintiff] or standing by, which encouraged [the defendant] reasonably to believe that his omissions were accepted or not opposed by her'.[21] There is a clear overlap

15 *Nwakobi v Nzekwu* [1964] 1 WLR 1019, 1024.

16 Some limitations legislation specifically adopts the doctrine of analogy: see *Limitation Act 1969* (NSW) s 23; *Limitation of Actions Act 1974* (Qld) s 10(6)(b); *Limitation of Actions Act 1958* (Vic) s 5(8).

17 (2014) 87 NSWLR 435; *Sourcebook* note 5, p 126. See also *Port Ballidu Pty Ltd v Frews Lawyers* (2018) 1 Qd R 276.

18 (2001) 208 CLR 199, [45].

19 (2003) 214 CLR 51, [41]–[42].

20 (2014) 87 NSWLR 435, [73]. An application for special leave to appeal to the High Court was dismissed: *Auzhair Supplies Pty Ltd v Gerace* [2014] HCASL 231.

21 *Byrnes v Kendle* (2011) 243 CLR 253, [79].

between the doctrines of laches and acquiescence.[22] Conduct that amounts to laches in part because the plaintiff 'sits on her hands', failing to take steps to protect her rights, is conceptually very similar to acquiescence, where a plaintiff with knowledge of a breach acquiesces in it. One difference lies in acquiescence requiring the plaintiff to indicate some level of acceptance of the defendant's wrongful behaviour (either expressly or impliedly), while laches requires the delay to cause prejudice to the defendant or a third party. The doctrine of acquiescence does not depend on delay. Confusion arises, though, because one of the evidentiary indicators that a plaintiff *has* accepted the wrongful behaviour can be delay in commencing proceedings. Standing by without any positive acts or words can amount to acceptance. Equally, because acquiescence involves acceptance, it does not require positive prejudice to the defendant.[23]

Le Miere J explained the confusion surrounding the overlap between laches and acquiescence.[24] His Honour said there are three senses in which the word 'acquiescence' is used, namely: (a) refraining from interfering while a violation of your rights is in progress; (b) refraining from exercising your rights (of which you have full knowledge) over such a long period of time that it can be inferred you have abandoned them; and (c) where your delay causes prejudice to the defendant or a third party. His Honour indicated that while (a) and (b) are acquiescence, (c) is laches. An alternative explanation is that the delay involved in acquiescence and assent is simply one of the 'themes' of laches, the other being the delay involved in prejudicial change in circumstances.[25]

Gafford v Graham[26] provides an example of acquiescence. A landowner held a restrictive [6.13]
covenant over adjoining land. Its owner erected an indoor equestrian school on the adjoining land in breach of the covenant. The landowner stood by and took no steps to enforce his rights for three years after the structure was completed. He was denied an injunction that would have involved removal of the building.

A plaintiff cannot accept a wrong and acquiesce in it without full knowledge of her [6.14]
rights. However, it is not necessary that the defendant make the facts known to the plaintiff.[27] In *Nocton v Lord Ashburton*,[28] a client had two claims against a solicitor arising from the solicitor's involvement (and conflict of interest) in dealings with real estate. The client's first claim was unsuccessful. Viscount Haldane[29] and Lord Parmoor[30] held the client had acquiesced to the breach. The client knew of the solicitor's involvement and had been warned in writing by one of the solicitor's partners of the risks he was taking.

The onus of proving acquiescence falls on the defendant.[31] [6.15]

---

22 And other doctrines such as waiver, release and estoppel: see *Orr v Ford* (1989) 167 CLR 316, 339.

23 S Worthington, *Equity* (Oxford University Press, 2nd ed, 2006) 36.

24 *Middleton v King* [2004] WASC 103, [63]–[64]. Le Miere J adopted the analysis of MGL at [36-090].

25 *Streeter v Western Areas Exploration Pty Ltd (No 2)* (2011) 278 ALR 291, [635] (Murphy JA); *Gillespie v Gillespie* [2013] 2 Qd R 440, [80] (Margaret Wilson J).

26 [1998] TLR 272.

27 This may distinguish the doctrine from the defence of disclosure and fully informed consent in relation to breach of fiduciary duty.

28 [1914] AC 932. See also [4.10].

29 [1914] AC 932, 958.

30 Ibid 974.

31 *Permanent Trustee Co Ltd v Bernera Holdings Pty Ltd* (2004) 182 FLR 431.

Unclean hands

[6.16] Refusing a plaintiff the relief sought due to unclean hands tends to invoke images of Lady Macbeth. Unfortunately, the doctrine is far less colourful and much more restricted than the image suggests.[32] It does not address the unattractiveness of a plaintiff's *general* conduct, and is usually only concerned with the specific issues between the plaintiff and the defendant.[33]

[6.17] The equitable maxim that a person must come to equity with clean hands reflects other general equitable principles; namely, that he who seeks equity must do equity, and that equity will not assist a person to gain an advantage from their own wrong. These maxims[34] direct the focus to justice *between the parties*. There must be a direct connection between the 'unclean' conduct and the actual dispute between the parties. A lack of connection is the reason why most claims of unclean hands fail.

[6.18] For example, in *Black Uhlans Inc v New South Wales Crime Commission*,[35] a motorcycle club member convicted of drug trafficking was the registered proprietor of land on which the clubhouse had been built. His assets were forfeited to the Crown under confiscation of proceeds of crime legislation. However, other members of the club claimed a resulting trust over the land, alleging the club had supplied part of the purchase price. Campbell J held that a resulting trust was made out. The Crown argued that the relief should not be granted on the grounds of unclean hands. The 'uncleanliness' referred to was that the other members of the club were implicated in a false application by the convicted member to a bank for a loan in respect of the land. Campbell J held that the bar could only be established if it could be shown that there was 'an immediate and necessary relation to the equity sued for'. This was absent: the equity sued for was a resulting trust arising from payment of part of the purchase price. That had nothing to do with any fraud committed on the bank by the parties.

The fact that the club member who owned the land had been convicted of drug offences would, of course, be entirely irrelevant to the issue of clean hands. General immorality or dishonesty, even criminality, is insufficient to engage the doctrine.

[6.19] It is said that the second condition of unclean hands is that the plaintiff's 'unclean' conduct must constitute 'a depravity in a legal as well as a moral sense'.[36] It is far from clear what 'depravity' means. The formulation comes from a case that is now over 200 years old,[37] and, apart from indicating that moral depravity alone is not sufficient, it may not add much to the doctrine. Some sense of the sort of 'depravity' that will attract the doctrine is provided by *Hewson v Sydney Stock Exchange Ltd*.[38] The plaintiff, a stockbroker, sought an injunction against the receiver of his business to prevent the receiver sequestrating his assets. The receiver had previously given an undertaking to the stockbroker not to proceed against him, and the plaintiff sought to enforce this undertaking via a prohibitory injunction. However,

32 In *Kation Pty Ltd v Lamru Pty Ltd* (2009) 257 ALR 336, [148], Basten JA called 'unclean hands' a 'colourful but imprecise label'.

33 Further, 'unclean hands' is not a bar to a claim for statutory relief: *Lodge v National Union Investment Co Ltd* [1907] 1 Ch 300.

34 See chapter 1.

35 (2002) 12 BPR 22,421; *Sourcebook* 6.4a, p 129.

36 *Dering v Earl of Winchelsea* (1787) 1 Cox 318, 319–20; 29 ER 1184, 1185.

37 Ibid.

38 [1968] 2 NSWR 224.

the receiver claimed the plaintiff should be barred from the remedy on the basis of unclean hands. The receiver had only given the undertaking on the basis of false and misleading statements made to him by the plaintiff. The plaintiff was denied the injunction.

False and misleading statements are wrongs in the legal sense, so it is easy to justify the decision in *Hewson*. Actions such as misleading the court also satisfy the 'depravity' requirement.[39] However, there have also been cases where the plaintiff's breach of the contract between the plaintiff and defendant has barred the plaintiff from the equitable relief being sought. In *Harrigan v Brown*,[40] the plaintiff, a theatrical agent, sought an injunction to prevent her client breaching their contract. She was denied this relief because she had failed to perform her side of the contract properly, even though hers was not such a breach as would have allowed the client to rescind. In contrast, in *Geltch v MacDonald*,[41] it was held that a mere breach of a contract involving the issue of shares in contravention of a shareholders' agreement would not suffice to establish unclean hands. In this case, the breach did no injury to the defendant. As breaches of contract sometimes amount to 'depravity' and on other occasions do not, it is clear that what amounts to 'depravity' will be a question of degree in each case. [6.20]

Courts sometimes deny the application of unclean hands on the basis of proportionality. To put this colloquially, the plaintiff's hands might be slightly dirty, but not quite dirty enough to prevent a remedy being granted. Denying the plaintiff's remedy would be disproportionate to any wrong the plaintiff has previously inflicted on the defendant. For example, in *Duchess of Argyll v Duke of Argyll*,[42] the parties had been through a messy divorce. The Duke proposed to publish newspaper articles exposing details about the Duchess's sexual exploits. She sought an injunction to prevent publication of this confidential information, and the Duke claimed she should be denied her relief on the grounds of unclean hands. This was (a) because the Duchess had already breached confidence by publishing an article detailing the Duke's drug use, and (b) on the basis of the Duchess's infidelities.[43] The injunction was granted. The Duchess's general infidelities were irrelevant; and the exposé the Duke was planning would cause harm entirely disproportionate to the breach of confidence previously committed by the Duchess. [6.21]

The plaintiff's unclean conduct may not act as a permanent bar to relief. More images of Lady Macbeth are raised by the suggestion that sometimes the plaintiff is permitted to 'wash her hands' by taking steps to remove the uncleanliness, or by showing that the unclean conduct is unlikely to recur. This needs to be done prior to court proceedings,[44] and an offer to submit to such order as the court makes with respect to the conduct may not suffice.[45] [6.22]

Although the depravity complained of must usually be found in the dealings between the plaintiff and defendant, there are some cases in which the public interest is taken [6.23]

39 *Armstrong v Sheppard & Short Ltd* [1959] 2 QB 384, 397.
40 [1967] 1 NSWR 342.
41 [2007] NSWSC 1000.
42 [1967] Ch 302.
43 In the divorce proceedings, Lord Wheatley said that the Duchess's attitude to the sanctity of marriage was 'wholly immoral': see [1967] 1 Ch 302, 331.
44 *EDPI Pty Ltd v Rapdocs Pty Ltd* [2007] NSWSC 195.
45 *Kettles & Gas Appliances Ltd v Anthony Hordern & Sons Ltd* (1934) 35 SR (NSW) 108. But see *Plath v Plath* [2020] QCA 43, [69].

into account. In these cases, innocent members of the public might be affected by either the granting or refusing of the remedy. So, an order for delivery up and destruction of documents might be granted despite any unclean hands, or even illegality on the plaintiff's side, if others might be misled by the documents.[46] Conversely, in *Kettles & Gas Appliances Ltd v Anthony Hordern & Sons Ltd*,[47] a plaintiff was denied an injunction in respect of the tort of passing off because its grant would have assisted the plaintiff's attempts to mislead the public about the copyright and patent status of its product.

Hardship

[6.24] Apart from applications for interlocutory injunctions,[48] it is unusual to find modern examples of courts denying the plaintiff a remedy due to the hardship that will be caused to the defendant.[49] No doubt this is in part due to the many opportunities given to modern litigants to settle their disputes without a court hearing. Nevertheless, it has traditionally been the case that, if great hardship would result to the defendant due to the remedy granted, the court has a discretion to refuse the plaintiff's request. Generally, more than mere financial hardship to the defendant is required before relief will be denied.[50] Unpalatable commercial results are not hardship.[51] Further, when assessing claims of hardship, the court may not show much sympathy where the defendant is 'author of its own misfortune'.[52]

[6.25] If a court elects to exercise its discretion to deny the remedy sought, it is extremely rare that the plaintiff is denied a remedy altogether. In cases where hardship does bar the plaintiff's remedy, the plaintiff usually has some entitlement to damages. For example, an order for specific performance of a contract to purchase land might be denied, and yet the defendant may still be liable to pay damages for his breach.

[6.26] This is shown in *Patel v Ali*.[53] A couple contracted to sell a house they owned. For various reasons, completion was delayed for several years. During this time, the personal circumstances of one of the vendors changed dramatically. She gave birth to two more children and then lost a leg to cancer. As a result, she became dependant on family members and friends who lived close by, and would lose that support if required to vacate the premises. The purchasers had obtained an order for specific performance of the contract, but Goulding J held that, so long as damages for breach of contract were paid into Court, the order for specific performance would be discharged on the grounds of hardship.

46 *Money v Money (No 2)* [1966] 1 NSWR 348.

47 (1934) 35 SR (NSW) 108.

48 See [3.35]. Hardship to the party likely to be restrained or to third parties is specifically taken into account when interlocutory injunctions are sought.

49 Nevertheless, hardship due to the effect of COVID-19 was one of the factors taken into account in a case where specific performance of a contract was sought: *NTT Australia Digital Pty Ltd v Cover Genius Services Pty Ltd* (2020) 19 BPR 40,711, [187].

50 *Wong v Van Vlymen* [2016] NSWSC 161, [40]–[46].

51 *ANZ Executors and Trustees Ltd v Humes Ltd* [1990] VR 615; *Sourcebook* 6.5b, p 136.

52 *Linfield Developments Pty Ltd v Shuangxing Development Pty Ltd* [2016] NSWSC 68, [116].

53 [1984] 1 Ch 283.

Effect of order on third parties

The discretionary nature of equitable remedies is highlighted when we consider the manner in which equitable remedies can be moulded by reference to the effect the order may have on third parties. The common law only considers the parties to the dispute, and does not consider any effect orders for damages will have on persons 'upstream' or 'downstream' from the defendant. In equity, however, the effect of an order on a third party is a well-recognised reason to modify or deny the plaintiff's remedy. There are numerous cases where courts have refused to order specific performance of a contract where performance would entail a breach of trust or fiduciary duty by the party forced to perform it.[54] Equally, specific performance has been refused where that would require a breach of the defendant's contract with a third party.[55] Hardship that may be caused to third parties is also considered in appropriate injunction cases.[56] [6.27]

Giumelli v Giumelli[57] provides an example of third party interests being taken into consideration. Robert Giumelli was induced by his parents' promise to transfer part of their farm to him to stay working on the farm for a number of years for little or no wages. When it eventually became obvious they would not transfer the land to him, he claimed a proprietary interest in the land in estoppel. The Supreme Court of Western Australia found the parents were bound by their promise and ordered a constructive trust over a portion of the land. This order was altered on appeal to the High Court, in part because of the possible injustice that would result to another son, Stephen. Stephen had also worked on the farm and improved the property. Insisting the parents transfer the land to Robert might well adversely affect Stephen's interests. Robert had to be satisfied with an order for equitable compensation instead. The case also demonstrates that the Court can take the interests of third parties into account quite informally; Stephen was not made a party to the action and no evidence was led on his behalf. [6.28]

Following *Giumelli*, the High Court has stressed that, where it is proposed to order a constructive trust over land, the interests of third parties who may have acquired an interest in the land must be taken into account.[58] In such cases, constructive trusts should not be ordered if it is possible to order a lesser (monetary) remedy.[59] More remote interests can be taken into account too. In *Disctronics Ltd v Edmonds*,[60] Warren J refused to impose a constructive trust over land because she was concerned the order would unduly advantage the plaintiff over third party creditors of the defendant. [6.29]

The interests of third parties are not only taken into account in cases involving land. In *Victoria University of Technology v Wilson*,[61] two academics breached fiduciary duty by appropriating an opportunity to develop a software system that should have gone to [6.30]

54 *Kennedy v The Queen* (1864) 1 W W & a'B (E) 145, 156; *Wood v Richardson* (1840) 4 Beav 174, 176–7; 49 ER 305, 306.
55 *Manchester Ship Canal Co v Manchester Racecourse Co* [1901] 2 Ch 37.
56 *Miller v Jackson* [1977] QB 966; *Sourcebook* 3.3.3a, p 50.
57 (1999) 196 CLR 101; *Sourcebook* 6.6a, p 138.
58 *John Alexander's Clubs Pty Ltd v White City Tennis Club Ltd* (2010) 241 CLR 1, 45–6.
59 Ibid 45.
60 [2002] VSC 454, [213].
61 (2004) 60 IPR 392.

their employer, the university. A patent had been issued in respect of the system. Nettle J declined to order a constructive trust over the software system and the patent because of contributions of time and effort by a third party to development of the software, and the effect such an order would have on third party investors in the project. Constructive trusts were ordered, though, over shares in companies which held interests in the patent and which were controlled by the academics.

WHAT'S ONLINE?

Available at www.cambridge.org/highereducation/isbn/9781009232388/resources:

- Recommended further readings
- Discussion topics
- Practice problem

PART C

EQUITY, CONTRACT AND PROPERTY

7

EQUITY IN CONTRACT LAW

Introduction

Much equitable doctrine concerning contract law is now covered in contract law or property law subjects. Our coverage will therefore be brief. Equitable intervention into contract law takes one of four forms: [7.1]

(1) Equity enforces some promises which are unenforceable at common law. It may also modify or even prevent the enforcement of promises which would otherwise be enforceable at common law. These results are principally achieved by estoppel doctrines.

(2) Equity sets aside contracts[1] where the consent of a party to the contract has been impaired or vitiated by factors such as mistake, misrepresentation, undue influence or unconscionability.

(3) Equity intervenes in some cases where the contract is substantively unfair; for example where it contains a penalty clause or a clause authorising forfeiture of property.

(4) Equity provides remedies unavailable at common law (or, in the case of rescission, available on restrictive conditions) which:
   - enforce contracts (eg specific performance or injunctions);
   - set aside contracts where consent has been vitiated (rescission); or
   - correct contracts where they do not reflect the mutual intention of the parties (rectification).

The focus of this chapter will be on the first three examples of equitable intervention. Equitable remedies are discussed in Part B.

Estoppel and promise enforcement

Estoppels were originally developed as rules of evidence and some applications of estoppel (such as estoppel by deed, and judgment estoppel) remain evidential in character.[2] The equitable estoppels considered in this chapter have outgrown their evidential origins. In all cases, one party is prevented from enforcing a legal right, or from departing from an assumption relied upon by the other party, where it would be unconscionable to do so. [7.2]

This chapter focuses on two types of estoppel: common law estoppel and equitable or promissory estoppel. Proprietary estoppel is discussed in chapter 8.

Common law estoppel

This estoppel prevents a person who, by a representation of fact, has induced another to alter her position from denying the fact as represented. Common law estoppel is not a cause of action. It alters the basis on which other causes of action may be brought or defended.[3] It is confined to representations of existing fact, not to representations as to future intention. [7.3]

1 Gifts can also be set aside: *Louth v Diprose* (1992) 175 CLR 621.
2 DSK Ong, *Ong on Estoppel* (Federation Press, 2020).
3 *Commonwealth v Verwayen* (1990) 170 CLR 394, 439 (Deane J).

In *Jorden v Money*,[4] the plaintiff owed money to a solicitor. When the solicitor died, his sister, Mrs Jorden, who became entitled to payment of the debt, orally stated that she would not enforce it. A majority of the House of Lords held that Mrs Jorden could go back on her word and enforce the debt. This was because she had made a statement as to her future intention and not of existing fact.

Common law estoppel remains a rule of evidence. Some High Court judges have suggested that common law and equitable estoppel should be merged.[5] This is discussed at [7.12].

Equitable (or promissory) estoppel

[7.4] Equitable estoppel applies where the representation made, or assumption created, relates to a future state of affairs and not existing fact, and a party relies on the representation or assumption to her detriment.[6] The modern starting point for the development of the doctrine is the decision of Denning J in *Central London Property Trust Ltd v High Trees House Ltd* (the *High Trees* case)[7]. A landlord who had agreed to reduce the rent payable by the tenant on a block of flats for the duration of the war was held to be entitled to increase the rent at the end of the war. Denning J stated in obiter that during the war the landlord was estopped by his promise from claiming the full rent even though the tenant had provided no consideration for the variation. This version of equitable estoppel operates to modify or suspend the operation of legal rights: in other words (as was commonly said at the time), equitable estoppel operates as a shield and not as a sword.

[7.5] In Australia, the *High Trees* version of equitable estoppel was reviewed by the High Court in *Waltons Stores (Interstate) Ltd v Maher*.[8] Waltons negotiated with the Mahers to lease the Mahers' property, which Waltons intended to use as a supermarket. This required demolition of the building on the site and construction of new premises to Waltons' specifications. A draft contract was prepared and amendments negotiated between the parties. Waltons' solicitors indicated to the Mahers' solicitors that the amendments were probably acceptable but that client consent had not been obtained, concluding: 'We shall let you know tomorrow if any amendments are not agreed to.' Having heard nothing from Waltons' solicitors, the Mahers' solicitors forwarded an executed draft contract for exchange. The Mahers proceeded to demolish the existing buildings on the site. Meanwhile, Waltons had decided not to go ahead with the lease and instructed their solicitors to 'go slow' in the negotiations with the Mahers. When the supermarket was 40% complete, they informed the Mahers they would not lease the property.

4 (1854) 5HL Cas 185; 10 ER 868.

5 *Waltons Stores (Interstate) Ltd v Maher* (1988) 164 CLR 387, 448–9 (Deane J); *Sourcebook* 7.2.1a, p 143; *Commonwealth v Verwayen* (1990) 170 CLR 394, 410–11 (Mason CJ), 445 (Deane J).

6 Promissory estoppel arises where a party to a pre-existing relationship makes a representation that rights under that relationship will not be enforced: *Central London Property Trust Ltd v High Trees House Ltd* [1947] 1 KB 130. It has now been subsumed under the head of equitable estoppel expounded in *Waltons Stores (Interstate) Ltd v Maher* (1988) 164 CLR 387.

7 [1947] KB 130. See also *Combe v Combe* [1951] 2 KB 215. The earlier House of Lords decision of *Hughes v Metropolitan Railway Co* (1877) 2 App Cas 439 is arguably a decision on relief from forfeiture, not estoppel.

8 (1988) 164 CLR 387.

The High Court held that Waltons was estopped from denying either that an exchange of contracts had taken place (Deane and Gaudron JJ) or that an exchange of contracts would occur (Mason CJ, Wilson and Brennan JJ). Brennan J identified the criteria which, if met, will give rise to an estoppel:[9]

(a) *Assumption*. The plaintiff assumes that a particular legal relationship exists between the plaintiff and the defendant or that a particular relationship will exist between them. In either case, the plaintiff must reasonably assume that the defendant is not free to withdraw from the expected legal relationship.

(b) *Inducement*. The defendant has induced the plaintiff to adopt that assumption or expectation.[10]

(c) *Reliance*. The plaintiff acts or abstains from acting in reliance on the assumption or expectation.[11]

(d) *Knowledge*. The defendant knew or intended him to act on the assumption.

(e) *Detriment*. The plaintiff's action or inaction will occasion detriment if the assumption or expectation is not fulfilled.[12]

(f) *Failure to prevent detriment*. The defendant has failed to act to avoid that detriment whether by fulfilling the assumption or expectation or otherwise.

These criteria have been accepted and applied in later decisions with little modification.[13] [7.6]
The plaintiff's reliance on the assumption or expectation created must be reasonable.[14] Where the basis of the assumption is that a particular legal relationship exists between the parties, detriment may be avoided by the party who creates the assumption giving reasonable notice of an intended departure from the assumption.[15] The basis of equitable intervention is the defendant's unconscionable conduct,[16] but unconscionability by itself is not a substitute for Brennan J's criteria. If all the criteria are satisfied it will be unconscionable for the defendant to depart from the assumption or not to fulfil the expectation he has created.

9 Ibid 428–9.

10 The assumption is usually induced by a representation made by the defendant, but silence can also, as in *Waltons Stores*, constitute an inducement. A representation must be clear but need not attain the level expected of a valid commercial contract: *Crown Melbourne Ltd v Cosmopolitan Hotel (Vic) Pty Ltd* (2016) 260 CLR 1; *Wilson v Arwon Finance Pty Ltd* [2020] WASCA 137, [147]–[159].

11 *Sidhu v Van Dyke* (2014) 251 CLR 505. See [8.9].

12 In assessing detriment, account will be taken of benefits the plaintiff has received as a result of relying on the assumption induced by the defendant: *Q (a pseudonym) v E Co (a pseudonym)* (2020) 383 ALR 469, [154] (Meagher JA).

13 See *Silovi Pty Ltd v Barbaro* (1988) 13 NSWLR 466; *Milchas Investments Pty Ltd v Larkin* (1989) 96 CLR 464; *Giumelli v Giumelli* (1999) 196 CLR 101; *Sourcebook* 8.5a, p 198. See chapter 8 for the application of these criteria in proprietary estoppel. The criteria have, however, been described as 'subject to qualification and refinement' which may be necessary in order to give effect to the equitable principles on which they are based: *Wilson v Arwon Finance Pty Ltd* [2020] WASCA 137, [91] (Quinlan CJ and Vaughan J).

14 *Australian Securities Commission v Marlborough Gold Mines Ltd* (1993) 177 CLR 485. Cf *Wilson v Arwon Finance Pty Ltd* [2020] WASCA 137, [121] (Quinlan CJ and Vaughan J) (analysing 'reasonableness' as an aspect of the inquiry into whether permitting departure from an assumption would be unjust).

15 *Commonwealth v Verwayen* (1990) 170 CLR 394.

16 *Waltons Stores (Interstate) Ltd v Maher* (1988) 164 CLR 387, 453 (Deane J).

[7.7] Prior to *Waltons Stores*, it was thought that equitable estoppel could prevent or suspend the enforcement of legal rights but did not create enforceable legal rights. *Waltons Stores* established that equitable estoppel can create enforceable rights in circumstances in which no contractual or other common law claim can be brought. It is, however, unclear how far the *Waltons Stores* decision goes in recognising estoppel as a doctrine that creates rights. On one view, the decision is an application of the doctrine of proprietary estoppel (discussed in chapter 8).[17] On this view, only proprietary estoppel can create rights. Promissory estoppel operates only negatively to restrain the enforcement of existing legal or equitable rights. The alternative view is that *Waltons Stores* is authority for the proposition that promissory estoppel can create legal rights and that the decision was not argued and decided on the ground of proprietary estoppel.[18]

Commentators have expressed concern that the enforcement of promises by the application of estoppel doctrines will undermine the doctrine of consideration in contract law. The American judge, Oliver Wendell Holmes, expressed the view that '[i]t would cut up the doctrine of consideration by the roots if a promisee could make a gratuitous promise binding by subsequently relying on it'.[19] In *Waltons Stores*, Mason CJ and Wilson J emphasised that equitable estoppel was not a substitute for the doctrine of consideration which would render otherwise gratuitous promises enforceable.[20] A promise will only be enforceable through estoppel to the extent that enforcement prevents unconscionable conduct. The doctrine does not enable representations to be made good.

[7.8] Promises cannot be enforced in estoppel where enforcement would undermine the criteria for forming a valid contract. In *Austotel Pty Ltd v Franklins Selfserve Pty Ltd*,[21] a majority of the New South Wales Court of Appeal refused to recognise an estoppel on facts which were similar to those found in *Waltons Stores* except that the parties had not agreed some of the terms of the proposed lease. To enforce an estoppel in such a case would undermine the principle that a contract will not be valid if its essential terms are unclear or unsettled. Kirby P emphasised the importance of equity not filling in the gaps in commercial agreements which the parties have not agreed to fill in themselves. '[C]ourts should, in my view, be wary lest they distort the relationship of substantial, well advised corporations in commercial transactions by subjecting them to the overly tender consciences of judges.'[22]

[7.9] An important question in considering whether equitable estoppel undermines the doctrine of consideration is whether the relief granted enforces the plaintiff's reasonable expectations. The objective of a damages award in contract law is to place the plaintiff

17 *DHJPM Pty Ltd v Blackthorn Resources Ltd* (2011) 285 CLR 311; *Saleh v Romanous* (2010) 79 NSWLR 453; *Ashton v Pratt* (2015) 88 NSWLR 287; KR Handley, *Estoppel by Conduct and Election* (Sweet & Maxwell, London, 2006) [13.008].

18 *Walton Stores (Interstate) Ltd v Maher* (1988) 164 CLR 387, 404 (Mason CJ and Wilson J). Cf *Crown Melbourne Ltd v Cosmopolitan Hotel (Vic) Pty Ltd* (2016) 260 CLR 1, [134] (Keane J). A Robertson, 'Three Models of Promissory Estoppel' (2013) 7(3) *Journal of Equity* 226; M Bryan, 'Unifying Estoppel Doctrines: The Argument for Heresy' (2013) 7(3) *Journal of Equity* 209. Cf J Hudson, 'The True Purpose of Estoppel by Representation' 32(3) (2015) *Journal of Contract Law* 275.

19 *Commonwealth v Scituate Savings Bank*, 137 Mass 301, 302 (1884).

20 *Waltons Stores (Interstate) Ltd v Maher* (1988) 164 CLR 387, 400–5.

21 (1989) 16 NSWLR 582.

22 Ibid 586.

in the position in which she would have been if the contract had been performed,[23] an objective usually achieved by enforcing the plaintiff's reasonable expectation of benefit under the contract. In estoppel cases, the court's aim is to achieve practical justice between the parties. This may require the enforcement of expectations in some cases but giving effect to expectations is not automatic.

In *Commonwealth v Verwayen*,[24] the plaintiff sued the Commonwealth in negligence in respect of injuries sustained in a naval accident. The Commonwealth initially stated that it would not deny liability and would not rely on the statute of limitations as a defence. In 1986, the Commonwealth changed this policy, denying that it was liable to the plaintiff in negligence and relying on the statute of limitations to bar Verwayen's claim. A majority of those members of the High Court who considered the application of estoppel to the facts[25] held that any detriment Verwayen incurred as a result of the Commonwealth's change of policy could be met by requiring the Commonwealth to pay the plaintiff's legal costs incurred as a result of the change. The minority on this issue, Deane and Dawson JJ (in the majority as to outcome), held that the Commonwealth was estopped from changing its plea. The costs order proposed by the majority would have protected Verwayen's 'reliance interest' by compensating him for his wasted expenditure. The minority's order, on the other hand, enforced Verwayen's 'expectation interest' by placing him in the position he would have been in if the Commonwealth had not changed its policy. Despite the apparent preference for reliance relief, the Court's decision in practice enforced Verwayen's expectation interest. Other members of the Court disallowed the Commonwealth's change of heart on the basis of waiver. [7.10]

Verwayen was hardly clear authority, and subsequent cases have not consistently favoured an expectation-based or a reliance-based approach to the award of relief.[26] Instead, courts have preserved the flexibility of equitable relief by awarding the remedy that does the most complete justice to the parties on the facts of the case.[27] [7.11]

Should the distinction between common law and equitable estoppel be retained? In *Waltons Stores*, Deane J stated that '[t]here is no acceptable reason why the doctrine of promissory estoppel should be seen, in a fused system, as exclusively equitable or as raising some new or heightened conflict between law and equity'.[28] Similarly, Mason CJ argued for an 'overarching doctrine' which integrated common law and equitable estoppel.[29] These remarks were obiter, however, and other High Court judges firmly maintained the distinction between the two types of estoppel.[30] [7.12]

The case for amalgamating common law and equitable estoppel is strong. As Mason CJ and Wilson J pointed out, the distinction between a representation as to existing fact

23 *Robinson v Harman* (1848) 1 Ex 850, 855; 154 ER 363, 365.
24 (1990) 170 CLR 394.
25 Mason CJ, Brennan and McHugh JJ. Toohey and Gaudron JJ found for the plaintiff by applying the doctrine of waiver.
26 A Robertson, 'Satisfying the Minimum Equity: Equitable Estoppel Remedies after *Verwayen*' (1996) 20(3) *Melbourne University Law Review* 805.
27 *Giumelli v Giumelli* (1999) 196 CLR 101.
28 *Waltons Stores (Interstate) Ltd v Maher* (1988) 164 CLR 387, 451–2. See also *Foran v Wight* (1989) 168 CLR 385, 411–13.
29 *Commonwealth v Verwayen* (1990) 170 CLR 394, 410–11.
30 Ibid 422 (Brennan J), 499 (McHugh J).

and a representation as to future intention is often fine.[31] For example, in *Waltons Stores*, a majority of the High Court considered that Waltons had represented to the Mahers that a contract *would be* exchanged, providing the basis of an equitable estoppel.[32] On the other hand, Deane and Gaudron JJ were of the view that the representation was that the contract *had been* exchanged, thereby giving rise to a common law estoppel.[33] Both interpretations are plausible. The classification of estoppel should not depend on inferences drawn from what is sometimes ambiguous evidence. It is suggested that the correct analysis of estoppel is that the 'foundational principle on which equitable estoppel in all its forms is grounded is that equity will not permit an unjust or unconscionable departure by a party from an assumption or expectation of fact or law, present or future, which that party has caused another party to adopt for the purpose of their legal relations'.[34]

More recent decisions of the High Court, however, have shown no enthusiasm for merging common law and equitable estoppel.[35] One obstacle, apart from the High Court's suspicion of fusion,[36] is that the basis of a possible merger of the two types of estoppel has never been made clear. Deane J favoured merger on the basis of the common law version, based on estoppel not constituting a cause of action but enabling 'the assumed state of affairs' arising from the assumption or expectation created by the defendant to be enforceable in contract or other recognised cause of action.[37] Mason CJ, on the other hand, advocated a unified estoppel doctrine based on equitable estoppel, which would constitute an independent cause of action.[38] Regardless of merits, no fusion of common law and equitable estoppel is likely to occur until the precise juridical nature of the integrated doctrine is clarified.

Equity and voidable transactions

[7.13] Equity sets aside transactions where consent has been vitiated by unilateral mistake, misrepresentation, duress, undue influence and unconscionability. Contracts of guarantee voidable under the principle of *Yerkey v Jones*,[39] and contracts made in breach of fiduciary duty can also be set aside. Together, these grounds demonstrate equity's objective in promoting procedural fairness. Equity has no particular interest in ensuring that a contract is substantively fair but intervenes if the process of bargaining or making of a gift is not based on a genuine intention to transact.

Contracts voidable for breach of fiduciary duty are discussed in chapter 10. This section focuses on the doctrines of undue influence, unconscionable conduct, and the related rule in *Yerkey v Jones*.

31 *Waltons Stores (Interstate) Ltd v Maher* (1988) 164 CLR 387, 397.
32 Ibid 398 (Mason CJ and Wilson J), 432–3 (Brennan J).
33 Ibid 435 (Deane J), 463 (Gaudron J).
34 *Crown Melbourne Ltd v Cosmopolitan Hotel (Vic) Pty Ltd* (2016) 260 CLR 1, [217] (Nettle J).
35 *Giumelli v Giumelli* (1999) 196 CLR 101. *Crown Melbourne Ltd v Cosmopolitan Hotel (Vic) Pty Ltd* (2016) 260 CLR 1, [37] (French CJ, Kiefel and Bell JJ) where the issue was said to be 'as yet unresolved'. See also [139] (Keane J) and [217] (Nettle J).
36 For a discussion of 'fusion', see [1.19]–[1.20].
37 *Commonwealth v Verwayen* (1990) 170 CLR 394, 449.
38 Ibid 413.
39 (1939) 63 CLR 649.

Undue influence

Equity sets aside contracts and gifts procured by the exercise of undue influence.[40] The equitable doctrine of undue influence was developed in response to the limitations of common law duress, which was originally confined to threats of physical violence. Equity recognised that a person could be influenced by subtle pressures which lay outside the scope of duress. [7.14]

Although there is a close relationship between equitable intervention on the ground of undue influence and intervention on the ground of unconscionability, and the two grounds are often pleaded on the same facts, they are conceptually distinct. The distinction was explained by Deane J in *Commercial Bank of Australia Ltd v Amadio*: [7.15]

> Undue influence, [like] common law duress, looks to the quality of the consent or assent of the weaker party … Unconscionable dealing looks to the conduct of the stronger party in attempting to enforce, or retain the benefit of, a dealing with a person under special disability in circumstances where it is not consistent with equity or good conscience that he should do so.[41]

Nonetheless, the same circumstances can give rise to both a relationship of undue influence and to a position of special disadvantage which has been unconscionably exploited by the defendant.[42]

It is a mistake to assume that recent developments in the equitable and statutory grounds of relief for unconscionable conduct discussed at [7.29] have marginalised the law of undue influence. On the contrary, cases on the exploitation of the elderly have given greater prominence to the law of undue influence.[43]

Undue influence can arise in three ways. It can be: [7.16]

- actual undue influence exercised by one person over another;
- relationships which are presumed by equity to be relationships of undue influence; or
- relationships which are proven to be relationships of undue influence.

Actual undue influence

Actual undue influence is closely related to duress. It requires proof of four matters, discussed by Dixon J in *Johnson v Buttress*.[44] The defendant must have a capacity to influence the plaintiff; influence must have been exercised; the influence must have been undue; and it must result in the plaintiff's entry into the transaction. If any one of the elements is not made [7.17]

40 *Earl of Chesterfield v Janssen* (1751) 2 Ves Sen 125, 155–6; 28 ER 82, 100. This discussion only concerns contracts and gifts made inter vivos. Different principles apply to undue influence in the making of a will. The latter are discussed in estates and probate texts.

41 (1983) 151 CLR 447, 474; *Sourcebook* 7.3.3b, p 158.

42 *Thorne v Kennedy* (2017) 263 CLR 85; *Sourcebook* 7.3.3c, p 164.

43 F Burns, 'Undue Influence Inter Vivos and the Elderly in Australia' (2002) 26(3) *Melbourne University Law Review* 499.

44 (1936) 56 CLR 113, 134.

out, the claim fails. Since the boundaries between duress and undue influence are blurred, some dispositions of property which are voidable for actual undue influence will also be voidable for duress. Voidability on the ground of duress, however, requires proof that the party imposing pressure applied unlawful means, such as threatening to commit a tort or breach of contract.[45]

[7.18] In *Thorne v Kennedy*,[46] the plaintiff became engaged to the defendant, a 60-year-old property developer. She had no substantial assets and, had the relationship ended, would not have been entitled to secure migration status in Australia. The defendant made clear from the outset that his wealth would pass on his death to his children from a previous marriage. Less than a fortnight before the wedding, he arranged for the plaintiff to consult an independent solicitor to discuss his proposed prenuptial agreement. He told her that, unless she signed, the marriage would not go ahead. The plaintiff was advised by the solicitor that the agreement was 'entirely inappropriate', being the worst that the solicitor had seen.[47] The financial provision she would receive, in the event of their separation after three years without children, was described as 'piteously small'. In spite of this advice, the plaintiff, who wanted to have children and was under stress caused by the imminence of the wedding, signed the agreement.[48]

The couple separated, without children, after being married for less than four years. The agreement the plaintiff had signed entitled her to $50 000. Although provisions of the *Family Law Act 1975* (Cth) promote the enforcement of prenuptial contracts entered into with the benefit of legal advice, an agreement will be set aside under s 90K(1)(b) where the agreement is 'void, voidable or unenforceable'. The High Court upheld the primary judge's order invalidating the agreement. The primary judge found that the agreement had been vitiated by duress. The High Court rejected duress as the basis of intervention.[49] Instead, the Court set aside the agreement on the ground that it was unconscionable[50] and because it had been entered into as a result of undue influence, with Gordon J dissenting on the issue of undue influence.

[7.19] The High Court held that undue influence was established by the circumstances surrounding the plaintiff's signing of the prenuptial contract. The plurality judgment of Kiefel CJ, Bell, Gageler, Keane and Edelman JJ found that the plaintiff was not a free agent capable of protecting her interests in the negotiations with her future husband. It was not necessary for the plaintiff to be 'reduced entirely to an automaton, but judgmental capacity must be "markedly substandard" as a result of the influence exercised by the defendant'.[51] Among the factors contributing to the finding of undue influence were: the fact that the

45 *Thorne v Kennedy* (2017) 263 CLR 85, [29]–[30] (Kiefel CJ, Bell, Gageler, Keane and Edelman JJ). Nettle J at [70]–[73] doubted in obiter whether duress required proof of pressure exerted by unlawful means, suggesting that the preferable test was whether the pressure went beyond what was reasonably necessary to protect the defendant's legitimate interests.

46 (2017) 263 CLR 85. *Sourcebook* 7.3.3c, p 164.

47 *Thorne v Kennedy* (2017) 263 CLR 85, [12] (Kiefel CJ, Bell, Gageler, Keane and Edelman JJ).

48 Ibid [8].

49 Nettle J would have decided the case on the basis of duress but for the fact that the question whether duress required proof of a threat of unlawful conduct had not been explored in argument: see n 45.

50 See [7.32].

51 *Thorne v Kennedy* (2017) 263 CLR 85, [32].

agreement was offered to the plaintiff on the basis that it was not subject to negotiation; the emotional threat of not going ahead with the wedding unless the agreement was signed; the relative financial positions of the parties; and the absence of time to reflect on the independent legal advice.[52]

Gordon J, while agreeing that the agreement was unconscionable, rejected undue influence as the ground of rescission. In her opinion, the factors identified in the plurality judgment did not indicate a lack of will or of capacity to exercise independent judgment. The lack of practical options available to the plaintiff were relevant to a finding of unconscionability but not to relieving against undue influence.[53] Gordon J's judgment sets a higher threshold for invalidating contracts on the ground of undue influence: pressure which impairs but does not remove the plaintiff's decision-making capacity does not constitute undue influence.

Presumed undue influence

In some cases, equity *presumes* that a benefit conferred within a relationship is the result of the exercise of undue influence. There are two types of case. The first involves cases where the relationship between the donor and donee is such as to raise a presumption that the donee has exercised undue influence over the donor. The second type of case is where the court is satisfied that a relationship of undue influence has been proved on the facts. In both cases, the defendant must rebut the presumption that arises. [7.20]

Presumed relationships of influence

In the following relationships, equity rebuttably presumes that a benefit conferred by the weaker party (in italics) was procured by undue influence exercised by the stronger party (in bold): [7.21]

(a) *Child*, **parent**. The child need not be an infant. In *West v Public Trustee*,[54] a 41-year-old daughter, described as an 'experienced woman of the world, notwithstanding the seclusion of her home life', could rely on the presumption, which her mother could not rebut. The presumption also applies to the relationship of *guardianship* and **ward**. Gifts from parents to their children do not attract a presumption of undue influence although the parent, or her estate after her death, may be able to establish that the child actually exercised undue influence.[55]

(b) *Disciple*, **religious adviser**. Many of the classic authorities on undue influence have concerned gifts made to religious orders. In *Allcard v Skinner*, Lindley LJ stated that 'of all influences religious influence is the most dangerous and the most powerful, and to counteract it Courts of Equity have gone very far'.[56] In *McCulloch v Fern*,[57] the plaintiff and his wife gave money to a religious sect. Mrs Fern, the sect's

52 Ibid [60].
53 Ibid [106]–[107].
54 [1942] SASR 109.
55 *Spong v Spong* (1914) 18 CLR 544.
56 (1887) 36 Ch D 145, 183.
57 [2001] NSWSC 406. See also *Quek v Beggs* (1990) 5 BPR 11,761.

founder, who claimed to speak the word of God, or the 'Ascended Masters', exerted considerable influence over the plaintiff's wife. Palmer J held that a presumption of undue influence which arose had not been discharged.

(c) *Client*, **solicitor**. The presumption of undue influence is stronger and harder to rebut here than in other presumed relationships of influence.[58] The solicitor/client relationship is also recognised as fiduciary in nature,[59] and the solicitor is forbidden by the fiduciary rules from permitting conflicts or making unauthorised profits. The presumption of undue influence, however, will apply to *any* gift or transaction between the solicitor and client, even if it is outside the scope of the fiduciary relationship.

(d) *Patient*, **doctor**. The presumption has been applied to the relationship of patient and doctor, where the patient has provided benefits to the doctor not explicable as remuneration for the doctor's services.[60] It has also been applied to a **manager** of a mental institution.[61]

The relationship of husband and wife is not one of presumed influence, although it can be established on the facts that one spouse exercised undue influence over the other.[62] The husband and wife relationship is relevant, however, to the principle in *Yerkey v Jones*,[63] discussed further at [7.42].

In *Thorne v Kennedy*, the High Court rejected the plaintiff's submission, based on some previous authorities, that the relationship of fiancé and fiancée was a relationship of presumed influence.[64]

Proven relationships of influence

[7.22] If the parties are not in a relationship where undue influence is presumed, the plaintiff can nonetheless show that the other party to a transaction occupied a position of ascendancy and influence over her.

The leading authority here is *Johnson v Buttress*.[65] An elderly man, nicknamed 'Rocker', was of low intelligence and dependent on others. He was on close terms with the defendant, a distant relative. Near the end of his life, he transferred his home, being his only substantial asset, to her, receiving no independent advice. After Rocker's death, his son applied to have the transfer set aside on the ground of undue influence. The High Court held that the plaintiff had proved that the relationship between Rocker and the defendant was one of undue influence. The onus then shifted to the defendant to show that Rocker had been able to exercise independent judgement, free of any influence, in making the transfer. Since the defendant was unable to discharge this burden of proof, the transfer was rescinded.

58 *Haywood v Roadknight* [1927] VLR 512.

59 See [10.4].

60 *Dent v Bennett* (1839) 4 My & Cr 269; 41 ER 105.

61 *Re CMG* [1970] Ch 574.

62 *Thorne v Kennedy* (2017) 263 CLR 85. See [7.18]

63 (1939) 63 CLR 649.

64 *Thorne v Kennedy* (2017) 263 CLR 85, [36]. Dixon J in both *Johnson v Buttress* (1936) 56 CLR 113, 134 and *Yerkey v Jones* (1939) 63 CLR 649, 675 recognised the relationship as one of presumed undue influence.

65 (1936) 56 CLR 113.

There was no evidence that the defendant had exploited Rocker's incapacity and weakness. Rather, evidence showed that she had provided him with considerable support and that the transfer recognised the assistance she had provided. Relief against undue influence does not depend on proof of the actual victimisation of the weaker party by the stronger, although victimisation or exploitation is sometimes present. Instead, equitable intervention rests on the principle that it is against public policy to transact with persons who are incapable of protecting their own interests in the transaction, because their capacity for independent decision-making has been impaired.

It is not necessary for the vulnerable party in an undue influence case to suffer from some incapacity, such as illiteracy. It is possible for someone who makes informed and rational decisions in some matters to be subject to undue influence in other areas of her life. In *Union Fidelity Trustee Co of Australia v Gibson*,[66] Miss Dunn, 'a mature woman of education and business experience' loaned £15000 to the defendant, secured by a mortgage. Miss Dunn later forgave the debt and discharged the mortgage, allegedly in gratitude for the services the defendant had provided to her as her financial adviser. After her death, her executors successfully applied to have these transactions set aside on the ground of undue influence. It was irrelevant that Miss Dunn possessed business experience. In her own financial matters, she placed herself wholly under the control of the defendant, who could not rebut undue influence by showing, for example, that she had received independent legal advice. The fact that a substantial sum had been paid to someone who was not a close relative but a business adviser established that the relationship was, on the facts, one of undue influence. [7.23]

Although not decisive, the size of the payment or other gift made may be evidentially important in establishing whether it was made under undue influence. In *Quek v Beggs*,[67] Mrs Quek gave a relatively small sum of money to her pastor and his wife, as well as several very large gifts that in total constituted almost the whole of her estate, despite the fact she had two children who needed her support. It was held that the small gift was explained both by Mrs Quek's natural desire to support the defendants in their pastoral work and by the personal friendship which had grown between them. The larger gifts, however, were set aside as having been made under undue influence. [7.24]

Rebutting the presumption of undue influence

An undue influence claim will be defeated by proof that the donor was emancipated from undue influence at the time of the transaction. Independent advice remains the best proof. Proof that the donor received independent *legal* advice will defeat the undue influence claim, provided that the nature and effect of the transaction were so fully explained to the donor that the court is satisfied that she was acting independently. Purely formal consultation with a solicitor does not constitute independent legal advice for this purpose. In *Bester v Perpetual Trustee Co Ltd*,[68] the plaintiff had been left a considerable fortune under her father's will. When she was 21 years old, she was advised by the trustee company administering her father's estate, and by her uncles, that it would be in her best interests if [7.25]

66 [1971] VR 573.
67 (1990) 5 BPR 11,761.
68 [1970] 3 NSWR 30.

her fortune was settled on trust. The trust deed was read to her by a solicitor, who asked if she had any questions concerning the settlement but who otherwise gave her no advice. Street J held that the plaintiff had been subjected to undue influence and had not received independent advice. What the plaintiff needed, but did not receive, was 'advice upon the more general topic of whether a settlement should be entered into at all, and, if so, the general nature of the settlement'.[69]

Independent legal advice will not defeat an undue influence claim if the plaintiff had insufficient time to reflect on the advice, or if her circumstances prevented her from assessing it rationally.[70]

[7.26] Adequacy of consideration may also be relevant to rebuttal. A sale of property at full value is evidence that it was not made within a relationship of undue influence, but it is not decisive. In *Watkins v Coombes*,[71] Isaacs J stated that it would still be possible to show that the sale was made under undue influence. The decision to sell may have been the outcome of undue influence, regardless of the price paid for the property.

[7.27] While not strictly amounting to rebuttal, the equitable bars to relief apply to undue influence as they apply to other equitable claims. In *Allcard v Skinner*,[72] the plaintiff transferred her assets to a religious order on joining the order. After she left the order, she sought to recover her property. A majority of the Court of Appeal held that the claim failed because of her delay in bringing the action after she had left the order and had become emancipated from the undue influence.

Undue influence and third parties

[7.28] A third party who receives property transferred as a result of undue influence must return the property or its traceable proceeds unless the third party is a good faith purchaser for value without notice of the circumstances giving rise to the undue influence.[73] Where a spouse, de facto partner or elderly parent has been induced to guarantee repayment of a loan made by a bank to the other spouse, partner or child, a critical question will be whether the bank has notice of any undue influence practised by the borrower. In practical terms, the answer to the question will depend on whether the bank comes under a duty to adopt procedures aimed at identifying potential improper pressure imposed on the guarantor. Guarantees entered into by spouses, and perhaps by others in family relationships,[74] are liable to be set aside under the principle of *Yerkey v Jones*.[75] In other cases, there may be an issue as to whether the bank had notice of unconscionable conduct which induced the execution of the guarantee.[76]

69 Ibid 35.

70 *Thorne v Kennedy* (2017) 263 CLR 85, [60].

71 (1922) 30 CLR 180, 193.

72 (1887) 36 Ch D 145. Some of the plaintiff's shares had been sold by the religious order and were held to be irrecoverable even if the defence of laches had not applied. This may be an example of the restitutionary defence of change of position. See also *Cheese v Thomas* [1994] 1 WLR 129; J Edelman and E Bant, *Unjust Enrichment* (Hart Publishing, 2nd ed, 2016) 353.

73 *Bank of New South Wales v Rogers* (1941) 65 CLR 42; *Quek v Beggs* (1990) 5 BPR 11,761.

74 See [7.42].

75 (1939) 63 CLR 649; *Garcia v National Australia Bank Ltd* (1998) 194 CLR 395; *Sourcebook* 7.3.4a, p 166. See [7.42]–[7.48].

76 *Commercial Bank of Australia Ltd v Amadio* (1983) 151 CLR 447; *Sourcebook* 7.3.3b, p 158. See [7.31].

In *Royal Bank of Scotland v Etridge (No 2)*,[77] the House of Lords prescribed procedures which lenders must follow before accepting a family member's interest in property as security for a loan to another family member. The bank's knowledge that a solicitor is acting for the guarantor, and has advised about the nature and effect of the transaction, will generally entitle the bank to rely on the guarantor's agreement to put up the security for the loan even though it is later discovered that the guarantee was procured by undue influence or a misrepresentation. But if the bank is aware of any facts which increase the risk that the transaction may have been procured by undue influence or a misrepresentation, the bank must be satisfied that the guarantor has received legal advice from a solicitor who is independent of the borrower before it can rely on the guarantor's consent to the transaction. The *Etridge* procedures have not been considered by the High Court. In *Kranz v National Australia Bank Ltd*,[78] the Victorian Court of Appeal rejected the application of the *Etridge* procedures to security provided to a bank as a result of misrepresentations made by the brother-in-law of the security provider. Charles JA considered[79] that the burden rested on the party seeking to set aside the guarantee to prove that the bank was aware of circumstances which would justify setting aside the guarantee. Eames J stated[80] that there was merit in applying the *Etridge* guidelines, although they did not represent current law in Australia.

Unconscientious conduct

One of the major features of twentieth-century Australian equity was the re-invigoration of the doctrine of unconscionable, or unconscientious, conduct as a ground for setting aside transactions. Gageler J has explained that unconscionability [7.29]

> is an obscure English word which centuries of use by courts administering equity have transformed into a legal term of art. In Australia, the central concern of a court administering equity in identifying conduct as unconscionable has long been understood to be to relieve against a stronger party to a transaction exploiting some special disadvantage which has operated to impair the ability of a weaker party to form a judgment as to his or her interests.[81]

Equity will intervene to set aside transactions where the following conditions are met: [7.30]

(a) One party to the transaction is under a special disability when compared with the other party;

(b) The special disability is sufficiently obvious to the other party; and

(c) The other party takes unconscientious advantage of the first party's special disability in procuring the transaction.

77 [2002] 2 AC 773.

78 (2003) 8 VR 310. The High Court refused leave to appeal on the ground that the facts did not provide a suitable vehicle for examining whether the *Etridge* guidelines ought to apply in Australia: *Kranz v National Australia Bank Ltd* [2004] HCA Trans 211.

79 (2003) 8 VR 310, [31].

80 Ibid [89].

81 *Australian Securities and Investments Commission v Kobelt* (2019) 267 CLR 1, [81] ('*ASIC v Kobelt*').

Any kind of transaction can be attacked – examples have included gifts,[82] security transactions[83] and loans.[84]

[7.31] Much of the modern law comes from the landmark High Court decision of *Commercial Bank of Australia Ltd v Amadio*.[85] Mr and Mrs Amadio were an elderly couple with limited English language skills. Their son had a company that was in financial difficulty; it was being kept afloat through the assistance of its banker. The banker, concerned about the company's growing unsecured debt, indicated to the son that more security would be needed. The son convinced his parents to execute a personal guarantee and mortgage over their property to secure the company's bank overdraft. The Amadios believed the guarantee was limited as to both time and amount, but this was not the case. Execution of the documents was informal. The bank manager called on them at their home, and the documents were signed at the kitchen table. The son's company collapsed very shortly after, and the bank attempted to enforce the securities. The Amadios successfully resisted this claim.

In the High Court, a majority held that the Amadios had been in a position of special disability in their dealings with the bank. The nature of their special disability was their age and lack of English; their lack of knowledge and understanding of the contents of the documents they had signed; the circumstances in which the documents were signed; and their lack of assistance and advice when their conversation with the bank manager made it clear that they were in need of assistance. Their disability was obvious to the bank through its employee, the manager. Under those circumstances, it was unconscientious for the bank to take advantage of their position.

Special disability

[7.32] The kinds of disabilities that can place one party in a position of special disadvantage cannot be definitively listed. In *Blomley v Ryan*, Fullagar J said that relative disadvantage could arise from poverty or need, sickness, age, sex, infirmities, drunkenness, illiteracy, lack of education, or lack of assistance and explanation where those were needed.[86] Modern examples of disabilities have included 'the extraordinary vulnerability' of a highly infatuated man to manipulation by the object of his affection,[87] and addiction to gambling.[88] Frequently, more than one disabling factor will be present, as in the *Amadio* case. The circumstances amounting to a special disadvantage may also establish undue influence, although that will not necessarily be the case if the weaker party's capacity for exercising her judgment was not significantly impaired.[89] In *Thorne v Kennedy*, the undue influence exercised on the plaintiff, which left her powerless to negotiate a satisfactory prenuptial contract, also proved that she was specially disadvantaged in signing the contract.[90]

82 *Louth v Diprose* (1992) 175 CLR 621.
83 *Commercial Bank of Australia Ltd v Amadio* (1983) 151 CLR 447.
84 *Asia Pacific International Pty Ltd v Dalrymple* [2000] 2 Qd R 229.
85 (1983) 151 CLR 447. *Sourcebook* 7.3.3b, p 158.
86 (1956) 99 CLR 362, 405.
87 *Louth v Diprose* (1992) 175 CLR 621.
88 *Kakavas v Crown Melbourne Ltd* (2013) 250 CLR 392.
89 *Thorne v Kennedy* (2017) 263 CLR 85, [40] (Kiefel CJ, Bell, Gageler, Keane and Edelman JJ), [94] (Gordon J).
90 Ibid [64] (Kiefel CJ, Bell, Gageler, Keane and Edelman JJ). See [7.18].

A disadvantage is special if it amounts to more than inequality of bargaining power and seriously affects the ability of the weaker party to protect her own interests.[91] The factors that made up the Amadios' special disadvantage clearly deprived them of that ability.

Knowledge of the disability

The disability must be sufficiently obvious to the other contracting party. This means the defendant must have actual knowledge, or be in the position where he ought to have known of the disability. [7.33]

In *Amadio*, it was not entirely clear whether the bank, through its manager, had actual notice of all of the disabilities. Age and language difficulties may have been apparent. The manager knew of the son's position, and how important it was to him to re-finance. Mason J said it must have been obvious that the transaction was improvident, and it was inconceivable that the possibility did not occur to the manager that the Amadios were unable to judge what was in their best interests.[92] It was noted as being important that comments Mr Amadio made should have put the manager on notice.

In *Kakavas v Crown Melbourne Ltd*,[93] the plaintiff, a 'high roller' gambler, lost $20.5 million gambling at the defendant's casino. Although he was addicted to gambling, he appeared to casino employees to be someone capable of making decisions in his own interests, as far as gambling was concerned. The plaintiff was subject to an order made in New South Wales excluding him from casinos. One of the consequences of the order was that any winnings payable to him in Victoria were forfeited to the State. The plaintiff was unaware of the consequences of the order and the casino, which was aware of the order, did not appreciate its significance when paying him his winnings. One issue was whether, assuming that the plaintiff's addiction constituted a special disadvantage, the casino had sufficient knowledge of his condition. In finding that the knowledge requirement had not been satisfied, the High Court held that knowledge, for this purpose, did not include constructive notice. The Court stated that equitable intervention required proof of 'a predatory state of mind', and that 'heedlessness of, or indifference to, the best interests of the other party is not sufficient for this purpose'.[94] The requirement of a 'predatory state of mind' arguably imposes a more exacting knowledge requirement than the standard applied to the bank in *Amadio*. [7.34]

If the plaintiff cannot establish that the defendant had the required knowledge of his disability the plaintiff cannot succeed, no matter how vulnerable the plaintiff was to making a decision against his own interests. Without knowledge, the defendant cannot have exploited the plaintiff's situation. For example, in *Tessman v Costello*,[95] the plaintiff was elderly, in poor health, and suffered a reduced concentration span; however, no disability was obvious to the lender, and in fact no allegation was made that the lender had knowledge of the plaintiff's condition. The claim therefore failed. [7.35]

91 *Commercial Bank of Australia Ltd v Amadio* (1983) 151 CLR 447, 462 (Mason J).
92 Ibid 466–7.
93 (2013) 250 CLR 392.
94 Ibid [161].
95 [1987] 1 Qd R 283.

[7.36] An important question is whether a defendant who has deliberately avoided acquiring knowledge of a possible disadvantage will be held to have acted unconscionably. The answer to this question will be critical when a lender has no face-to-face dealing with a borrower, who has applied online for the loan, but leaves it to third parties to explain the legal and financial consequences of taking out the loan.[96]

In *Stubbings v Jams 2 Pty Ltd*,[97] a solicitor arranged for three clients to lend money to a company controlled by the defendant, who also guaranteed repayment of the loan. The purpose of the loan was to enable the defendant to buy a property as his home, although it was stated on the documentation to be a loan made for business purposes. The loan was secured by mortgages taken over two other properties owned by the defendant and occupied by other members of his family, as well as over the property the borrower was buying. At the time the loans were made, the defendant was unemployed and had no regular income. This was therefore an asset-lending arrangement, whereby a loan is made on the basis of the value of the assets securing the loan, without consideration of the borrower's ability to repay from his own income. The defendant took documents to appointments with a solicitor and an accountant which he signed in their presence. The documents acknowledged that he understood the effects of the mortgage arrangement and the financial risks he was incurring. Although the loan was sufficient to pay the first month's interest, the defendant was subsequently unable to make further repayments, and the lenders sought possession of his properties. The defendant argued that the mortgage was unconscionable because his lack of income made it inevitable that the loan would not be repaid.

The High Court upheld the trial judge's finding that the loan arrangement was unconscionable. The lenders had obtained knowledge of the borrower's special disadvantage through their agent's negotiations with the borrower, and the lenders could not avoid liability by reason of the fact that the agent had put in place a system designed explicitly to ensure that the lenders actually knew nothing of the borrower's financial circumstances. Moreover, the certificates obtained from the solicitor and accountant were simply 'window dressing' which did not address the reality of whether the borrower fully understood the risks he was assuming in entering into the asst lending agreements.

Exploitation of special disability

[7.37] Once the plaintiff establishes that a special disability was known to the defendant, an inference arises that the defendant has unconscientiously exploited that disability in transacting. It is then up to the defendant to show that no advantage was taken.[98] Exploitation does not necessarily entail positive action by the defendant; it is sufficient if the defendant merely accepts a benefit.[99] Unless the defendant can lead evidence that no unconscientious

96 Cf *Commonwealth Bank of Australia v Kojic* [2016] FCAFC 186, [153]: Edelman J suggesting in obiter that a corporation could not avoid liability by putting in place procedures intended to ensure that no particular individual could have the requisite knowledge.

97 (2022) 399 ALR 409. Cf *Elkofairi v Permanent Trustee Co Ltd* (2002) 11 BPR 20,841.

98 *Commercial Bank of Australia Ltd v Amadio* (1983) 151 CLR 447, 474 (Mason J); *Louth v Diprose* (1992) 175 CLR 621, 632.

99 *Bridgewater v Leahy* (1998) 194 CLR 457, 493.

advantage was taken, the transaction is likely to be set aside. Independent advice is the best method of showing that no unconscientious advantage was taken, as the assumption is that, in receiving advice, the plaintiff will have received any assistance necessary to negate the effect of the disability.[100]

Statutory unconscionability

Statute has made substantial inroads into the regulation of unconscionable contracts. The legislation is usually studied in contract and consumer law subjects. Chief among these is the *Australian Consumer Law*[101] (re-enacting the former *Trade Practices Act 1974* (Cth) pt IVA). Section 20 states that a person in trade or commerce must not engage in 'conduct that is unconscionable within the meaning of the unwritten law from time to time'. Section 21 applies to the provision of goods and services acquired for personal, domestic or household use, and prohibits conduct that is, in all the circumstances, unconscionable. Section 22 is similar, but applies to the provision of goods and services acquired for the purposes of trade and commerce. An application for equitable relief from unconscionability is often combined with a statutory claim. The latter entitles a successful plaintiff to a wider range of remedies, including damages awards.[102] [7.38]

Section 21 of the *Australian Consumer Law* enacts a broad prohibition on unconscionable conduct, in trade or commerce, in connection with the supply or acquisition of goods and services to a person (other than a listed public company). Section 21(4) states that the prohibition is not limited to unconscionable conduct under the unwritten (ie equitable) law, and s 22 enacts a number of matters to which the court may have regard, including the relative strengths of the bargaining positions of the supplier and customer. There have been a number of judicial attempts to describe conduct proscribed by s 21. In *ASIC v Kobelt*, Gageler J stated that the conduct must be 'so far outside societal norms of acceptable commercial behaviour as to warrant condemnation as conduct that is offensive to conscience'.[103] [7.39]

The jurisdictional scope of the *Australian Consumer Law* is both Federal and State.[104] In addition, equivalent provisions of the *Australian Securities and Investments Commission Act 2001* (Cth) deal with unconscionability in the provision of financial services.[105]

100 *Chen v Song* [2005] ANZ Conv R 130, [166]. But independent legal advice will not constitute a defence if circumstances prevent the plaintiff from giving proper consideration to the advice: *Thorne v Kennedy* (2017) 263 CLR 85.

101 *Competition and Consumer Act 2010* (Cth) sch 2. Unconscionable conduct in the provision of financial services is proscribed by ss 12CA(1) and 12CB of the *Australian Securities and Investments Commission Act 2001* (Cth). Credit contracts are separately covered by the *Consumer Credit Code* enacted by the *National Consumer Credit Protection Act 2009* (Cth) sch 1.

102 *Australian Consumer Law* (Cth) s 236.

103 (2019) 267 CLR 1, [92]. Cf Edelman J, dissenting, suggesting at [295] that s 21 sets a bar 'that is lower than that developed in equity' even if might not have been lowered to the standard of 'unreasonableness' or 'unfairness'.

104 *Fair Trading (Australian Consumer Law) Act 1992* (ACT) pt 2.2; *Fair Trading Act 1987* (NSW) pt 3; *Consumer Affairs and Fair Trading Act 1990* (NT) pt 4; *Fair Trading Act 1989* (Qld) pt 3; *Fair Trading Act 1987* (SA) pt 3; *Australian Consumer Law (Tasmania) Act 2010* (Tas) pt 2; *Australian Consumer Law and Fair Trading Act 2012* (Vic) pt 2.2; *Fair Trading Act 2010* (WA) pt 3.

105 *Australian Securities and Investments Commission Act 2001* (Cth) ss 12CB, 12CC.

[7.40] In *ASIC v Kobelt*,[106] a storekeeper who sold food, fuel and used cars to residents of remote Indigenous communities on credit used a 'book-up' system. Under that system, credit was advanced to purchasers if they supplied the storekeeper with their bank debit cards, together with PIN numbers so that he could access their accounts for payment. The funds would be taken for purchases made and on account of future purchases. There was no suggestion that the storekeeper took more money than he was owed. The customers had a basic understanding of the system although the storekeeper's record-keeping was obscure. Members of the community were characterised by poverty and low levels of literacy, including financial literacy. A majority of the High Court held that the 'book-up' system was not unconscionable under s 12CB of the *ASIC Act* which prohibits unconscionability in the provision of financial services.

All the High Court judges recognised that s 12CB took account of a broader range of considerations than were covered by the term 'special disadvantage' in equity. Gageler J, a majority judge, stated that the section is 'indicative of an intention that conduct of the requisite gravity need not be found only in a fact-pattern which fits within the equitable paradigm of a stronger party to a transaction exploiting some special disadvantage which operates to impair the ability of a weaker party to form a judgement as to his or her best interests'.[107] Similarly, Edelman J, dissenting, considered that 'statutory unconscionability permits consideration of, but no longer requires (i) special disadvantage, or (ii) any taking advantage of that special disadvantage'.[108]

Judicial disagreement centred on the application of the statutory unconscionability standard to the facts. For the majority, the book-up system had a long history in rural and remote Indigenous communities; it was used by members of those communities to acquire goods they would otherwise have been unable to acquire; and the defendant had not exploited customers in using the system. The dissenting judges emphasised the serious imbalance of bargaining power between the defendant and Indigenous customers; the absence of an alternative payment method available to the customers; and the obscure record-keeping which concealed from customers how the credit system operated. As Gageler J remarked, 'hard cases test and sometimes strain legal principle'.[109] The judgments in *ASIC v Kobelt* provide little precedential guidance on the application of s 12CB, and arguably illustrate the drawbacks of an unconscionability standard that is not based on the well understood equity authorities.

[7.41] New South Wales has legislation that deals with unjust contracts, the *Contracts Review Act 1980*. The Act applies to contracts which are 'unconscionable, harsh or oppressive', as determined by statutory criteria.[110] In contrast to s 20 of the *Australian Consumer Law*, which is directed at unconscionable conduct and is not limited to the formation or performance of contracts, relief under the *Contracts Review Act* is confined to contractual unconscionability. The unconscionability can relate to either the formation of a contract or its operation.[111]

106 (2019) 267 CLR 1. See also *Australian Competition and Consumer Commission v Quantum Housing Group Pty Ltd* (2021) 285 FCR 133, holding that the judgments in *ASIC v Kobelt* did not require proof of exploitation of disadvantage as a prerequisite to imposing liability under s 21.

107 *ASIC v Kobelt* (2019) 267 CLR 1, [89].

108 Ibid [295].

109 Ibid [95].

110 *Contracts Review Act 1980* (NSW) ss 4, 9.

111 *West v AGC (Advances) Ltd* (1986) 5 NSWLR 610, 620 (McHugh JA); *Kowalczuk v Accom Finance* (2008) 77 NSWLR 205; *Provident Capital Ltd v Papa* (2013) 84 NSWLR 231.

The rule in *Yerkey v Jones* and the *Garcia* case

The doctrines of undue influence and unconscientious conduct partially overlap in relation to one kind of transaction; namely, a surety given by one spouse to secure the borrowings of the other. The old rule in *Yerkey v Jones*,[112] which established special conditions for wives seeking to be relieved of surety obligations incurred to support their husbands' borrowings, was considered by the High Court in *Garcia v National Australia Bank Ltd*.[113] Although the spousal relationship is not one where undue influence is presumed, the doctrine recognises that there can be an 'invalidating tendency'[114] in transactions procured within that relationship. This doctrine is distinct from the *Amadio* doctrine, despite the fact that both address situations in which it will be unconscionable for a party to seek to enforce a contract. [7.42]

In *Garcia*, a physiotherapist executed several guarantees to secure the borrowings of her husband's company. Although she was a director of the company, she had no involvement in its activities and took no real benefit from its borrowings. She incorrectly believed the security to be for a limited amount. She signed the documents at the bank, but the documents were not explained to her, and she had no independent advice. The High Court held that the bank was prevented from enforcing the security. [7.43]

There are four preconditions to application of the *Yerkey* doctrine. It is unconscionable for a lender to attempt to rely on a security where: [7.44]

(a) The 'wife' is a 'volunteer';

(b) The 'wife' executes a security as a result of actual undue influence, or did not understand the effect of the security;

(c) The lender knows of the 'wife' and borrower's relationship, and is taken to understand that the borrower may not have accurately explained the transaction; and

(d) The lender has not taken 'sufficient steps' to explain the security to the 'wife', or does not reasonably believe they have been explained to her independently.

'Wife'

In *Garcia*, four judges thought it might be possible to extend the doctrine to long-term sexual relationships where the parties had not married.[115] Since then, other relationships such as parent and child have occasionally been given protection,[116] and there have been indications that more remote relationships might qualify.[117] [7.45]

112 (1939) 63 CLR 649.
113 (1998) 194 CLR 395.
114 *Yerkey v Jones* (1939) 63 CLR 649, 675.
115 (1998) 194 CLR 395, 404 (Gaudron, McHugh, Gummow and Hayne JJ).
116 Cf *State Bank of New South Wales v Layoun* (2001) NSW Conv R 55-984; *Permanent Mortgages Pty Ltd v Vandenbergh* [2010] WASC 10.
117 *Kranz v National Australia Bank Ltd* (2003) 8 VR 310, [24].

The greatest impediment to extension of the categories of relationship that might attract protection is that it is inherent in the doctrine that the guarantor is being protected from the risk that she may overly rely on the borrower due to the closeness of their marital relationship. If the lender knows of that relationship, it can be regarded as having notice that exploitation might occur. It is then the lender's responsibility to see sufficient steps are taken to ensure the guarantor's understanding. While more distant relationships can be exploited (as the doctrine of presumed undue influence shows), it is less likely that the lender would have reason to suspect exploitation. For example, if a patient guarantees a doctor's borrowings, the parties are likely to have different surnames, and reside at different addresses. There will be nothing to make the lender suspect the patient was at risk of exploitation.

'Volunteer'

[7.46] Under *Garcia*, the guarantor should be a volunteer, in that she takes no benefit from the transaction. 'Benefit' can be discussed on several levels. First, the wife may actually benefit from the contract underlying the surety. Where the borrowings are used to finance the family home, the wife is not a volunteer in the relevant sense.[118] Secondly, the wife may appear to benefit, in that she is a shareholder or director of the husband's company. If the company is really the alter ego of the husband, and the wife takes no personal benefit, she will still be a volunteer.[119] However, sometimes the husband's borrowings, or those of his company, deliver an indirect benefit to the wife, in the sense that her general standard of living is improved. Whether or not the wife is still a volunteer in the relevant sense is then a matter of degree.[120]

'Surety'

[7.47] The doctrine is presently limited to mortgages, charges and guarantees to support underlying borrowing.[121] Courts have not so far been prepared to extend the doctrine to transactions that are not security or guarantee arrangements and yet still operate to the husband's advantage.

'Sufficient steps'

[7.48] The lender will be able to enforce the surety where it has taken sufficient steps to ensure the wife understands the transaction. Sufficiency depends upon what caused the wife's entry into the transaction. If actual undue influence was asserted, the lender will not be able to enforce the security unless the wife received independent advice or is otherwise emancipated from the husband's ascendency. The lender is treated as affected by the husband's undue influence.

---

118 *Satchithananthan v National Australia Bank Ltd* [2009] NSWCA 268.

119 *Garcia v National Australia Bank Ltd* (1998) 194 CLR 395. Incidental benefits, which accrue to the family generally, will not constitute a benefit for this purpose: *Bank of Western Australia v Abdul* [2012] VSC 222, [59]–[61].

120 Cf *Radin v Commonwealth Bank of Australia* [1998] FCA 1361; *Agripay Pty Ltd v Byrne* [2011] 2 Qd R 501.

121 *Elkofairi v Permanent Trustee Co Ltd* (2002) 11 BPR 20,841; *Narain v Euroasia (Pacific) Pty Ltd* (2009) 26 VR 387.

However, where there has been no undue influence, but instead there is a failure in the wife's understanding of the transaction, the lender does not have to show independent advice was received. All that must be shown is that adequate steps were taken to inform the wife, and that the lender reasonably believed the wife had sufficient understanding. It may be sufficient for the lender to make the explanation itself,[122] or for it reasonably to believe the transaction has been fully explained to the wife by an independent person.

In practice, it is usual for lenders to insist on independent advice from a solicitor, who certifies that all necessary advice has been given and that the guarantor understands the transaction. This usually protects lenders from application of the *Amadio* and *Garcia* doctrines.

Equity and substantive fairness: penalties and relief from forfeiture

Provided that a contract or gift has not been vitiated by a procedural irregularity of a kind described above, equity generally is not concerned with whether a contract is substantively fair in its terms or operation. The aim of most equitable intervention is to achieve corrective, not distributive, justice. [7.49]

The equitable doctrine of penalties is an exception: equity sets aside penalty provisions in contracts because they are substantively unfair, not because there has necessarily been some deficiency in the bargaining process. This section also considers the principles governing equitable relief from forfeiture, where a party is prevented from exercising a contractual right to forfeit a property interest upon the other party's breach of contract. Relief from forfeiture raises questions of both procedural and substantive fairness. A theme common to both is the prevention of unconscientious enforcement of legal rights. Specifically, equity will prevent the unconscientious enforcement of a contractual remedy if enforcement would significantly exceed reasonable relief for the breach of contract the defendant has committed. [7.50]

The penalties doctrine

Commercial contracts often provide for the payment of an agreed amount of damages in the event of a breach or failure to comply with a condition in the contract. These are called 'liquidated damages'. If the payment constitutes a genuine attempt to pre-assess the loss incurred by the innocent party on breach the clause will be upheld. But if the clause is not a genuine pre-estimate of the loss suffered it will be unenforceable as a penalty.[123] Unenforceability does not mean that the innocent party will be denied a remedy for breach. Damages for the actual loss flowing from the breach will be recoverable.[124] [7.51]

It was at one time considered that the equitable principles for relief had become merged with, and superseded by, equivalent common law principles after the enactment of the

122 *Radin v Commonwealth Bank of Australia* [1998] FCA 1361.
123 N Tiverios, *Contractual Penalties in Australia and the United Kngdom* (Federation Press, 2019).
124 *AMEV-UDC Finance Ltd v Austin* (1986) 162 CLR 170.

judicature legislation in the nineteenth century. The decision of the High Court in *Andrews v Australia and New Zealand Banking Group Ltd*[125] confirmed, however, that equitable principles continue to be relevant to the exercise of the penalties jurisdiction.

[7.52] In determining whether a payment clause constitutes a penalty, two questions have to be answered. The first is whether the penalties doctrine applies to the clause in question. If the doctrine does apply, the second question is whether the clause is in fact a penalty. If the clause is found to be a penalty it will be unenforceable but the innocent party can recover damages for breach of any obligation to which it would have applied.

[7.53] It was long assumed that the penalties doctrine only applied where the sum specified in the contract was payable on breach of contract.[126]. In order to avoid thc application of the doctrine, many commercial and consumer contracts included provisions requiring a party to pay the other party upon the occurrence of a condition that did not constitute a breach of contract. In particular, contracts between banks and their customers required the customer to pay a charge in circumstances, such as a late payment or non-payment of credit card debt, which did not, according to the terms of the agreement, constitute a breach of contract. In *Andrews v Australia and New Zealand Banking Group Ltd*,[127] a class action was brought by some 38 000 customers who had incurred bank charges. The customers argued that the bank charges were penalties since the amounts payable by the customer were not referable to any loss suffered by the bank as a result of the acts or omissions which made the customer liable to pay the charge. A preliminary issue was whether bank charges attracted the application of the penalties doctrine since the customer's liability to pay did not depend on proof of a breach of contract. The High Court held that equitable relief was available even though no contractual obligation had been broken. The Court stated that the doctrine applies where, as a matter of substance, a contractual stipulation is secondary to another stipulation, and the secondary stipulation imposes, on failure of the primary stipulation, an additional detriment for failure to comply with that primary stipulation.[128] A bank charge for late payment of a credit card debt therefore comes within the scope of the penalties doctrine because the charge imposes an additional detriment (the charge) for failure to comply with the primary obligation to pay off credit card debt by the due date. On the other hand, the payment will not be a penalty if the payer receives an additional benefit in return for making the payment.[129]

The High Court decision in *Andrews* is controversial because many commercial contracts include clauses imposing obligations on a party to make payments to the other party upon the occurrence of a contingency. They include 'break clauses' whereby a party is entitled to

125 (2012) 247 CLR 205; *Sourcebook* 7.4.1a, p 172.

126 A penalty need not be monetary: see *Ringrow Pty Ltd v BP Australia Pty Ltd* (2005) 224 CLR 656 (provision requiring property to be transferred on breach); *Kay v Playup Australia Pty Ltd* (2020) 19 BPR 40,037 (the benefit of contractual warranties lost on breach).

127 (2012) 247 CLR 205. Claims were also brought under the unconscionability provisions of the *Australian Securities and Investments Commission Act 2001* (Cth), the 'fair terms' provisions of the *Fair Trading Act 1999* (Vic), and the 'unjust transactions' provisions of the *Consumer Credit (Victoria) Code* and the *National Credit Code*.

128 *Andrews v Australia and New Zealand Banking Group Ltd* (2012) 247 CLR 205, [10].

129 *Metro-Goldwyn-Mayer Pty Ltd v Greenham* [1966] 2 NSWR 717 (movie exhibitor to pay four times the ordinary rate of hire for unauthorised additional showing of the movie: held not to be a penalty since the unauthorised showing was an 'additional benefit').

terminate a contract prematurely in return for making a payment, additional establishment fees payable by a borrower exercising an option to take out a larger loan, and 'take or pay' clauses which require a customer to take goods from a supplier or to pay a prescribed amount if the goods are not taken. Many of these commercial payments will not be penalties because they confer an additional benefit on the payer. Nevertheless, the *Andrews* decision has created some uncertainty as to the limits of the penalties doctrine. It has been criticised for not taking into account the realities of commercial practice in structuring transactions.[130]

If the penalties doctrine applies to a payment provision, the court will next consider whether the provision is in fact a penalty. Until the recent High Court decision of *Paciocco v Australia and New Zealand Banking Group Ltd*,[131] Australian courts applied criteria laid down by Lord Dunedin in *Dunlop Pneumatic Tyre Co Ltd v New Garage & Motor Co Ltd*[132] to distinguish between a liquidated damages clause and a penalty. The essential question was whether the sum payable was extravagant and unconscionable in amount in comparison with the greatest loss that could conceivably be proved to have followed from the breach. A sum held to be extravagant and unconscionable was unenforceable as a penalty. The date of assessment for this purpose is the date of entry into the contract, and not the date of breach. [7.54]

In *Paciocco v Australia and New Zealand Banking Group Ltd*,[133] a majority of the High Court replaced Lord Dunedin's criteria with a broader test based on whether the payment provision protects a legitimate interest of the party seeking to rely on it. Following its decision in *Andrews*, the High Court in *Paciocco* had to determine whether the bank charges in fact amounted to penalties and were therefore unenforceable. Attention was focused on a late payment fee on a credit card account payable by a customer who did not pay the minimum monthly amount by a specified date.[134] The bank conceded that the amount of the late payment fee bore no relation to the costs incurred by a customer's late payment. However, the bank argued that it was entitled to take into account other costs in fixing the amount. These other costs were provisioning costs (being the provision made in the bank's accounts for the risk of customer default), regulatory capital costs (being the amount regulators required the bank to set aside as a buffer against unexpected losses) and operational costs (being part of the bank's costs in collecting debts it was owed). The primary judge held no account could be taken of these costs in determining whether the late payment fee was a penalty.

On appeal, the Full Federal Court disagreed and held that these costs were relevant to setting the amount of the fee.[135] That decision was upheld by the High Court, Nettle J

130 JW Carter et al, 'Contractual Penalties: Resurrecting the Equitable Jurisdiction' (2013) 30 *Journal of Contract Law* 99. Cf PS Davies and PG Turner, 'Relief Against Penalties Without a Breach of Contract' (2013) 72(1) *Cambridge Law Journal* 20. English law continues to apply the breach rule: *Cavendish Square Holding BV v Makdessi* [2016] AC 1172.

131 (2016) 258 CLR 525. *Sourcebook* 7.4.1b, p 174.

132 [1915] AC 79, 87–8.

133 (2016) 258 CLR 525. Statutory claims under the *Australian Securities and Investments Commission Act 2001* (Cth), the *Fair Trading Act 1999* (Vic) and the *National Credit Code* also failed.

134 The failure to pay the amounts by the due date constituted a breach of contract, so that the test laid down in *Andrews* for determining the applicability of the penalties doctrine (see [7.53]) was not engaged.

135 (2015) 236 FCR 199.

dissenting. The High Court reviewed *Dunlop v New Garage*, the majority holding that the appropriate test was whether the payment was out of all proportion to the payee's interest in enforcing the obligation to which the payment provision applied.[136] Nettle J dissented on the ground that the primary judge was entitled to conclude that the costs were irrelevant to determining whether the late payment fee was a penalty. He also held that Lord Dunedin's criteria were appropriate in cases, including *Paciocco*, where a straightforward comparison can be drawn between the sum specified in the payment clause and the amount of compensatory damages that the innocent party would be awarded on breach.[137] The 'legitimate interest' test should, in his view, be limited to more complex cases where compensatory damages could not easily be assessed.

[7.55] What constitutes a payee's legitimate interest, for the purpose of determining whether a payment provision is a penalty, is somewhat speculative and will have to be worked out on a case-by-case basis following the *Paciocco* decision. Likely candidates are a corporation's interest in the commercial reputation of its goods and services, and in maintaining customer good will.[138] In *Paciocco*, Keane J stated that a bank's interest in profitability was a legitimate interest.[139] But it cannot be the case that a contracting party has a legitimate interest in maximising profit to the exclusion of all other considerations. Such an 'interest' would render the penalties doctrine redundant.[140] Moreover, private law litigation is poorly suited to undertaking inquiries into the lines to be drawn between legitimate and illegitimate profit-making.

The practical effect of the High Court decision in *Paciocco* is that agreed payment provisions will be respected in most cases. The penalties doctrine is now limited to exceptional cases in which the sole purpose of the provision is to punish the party in breach of obligation and not to promote any legitimate interest of the innocent party.

[7.56] Finally, it should be noted that some common clauses which used to come within the penalties doctrine, such as resale price maintenance clauses, are now assessed under competition legislation and not in equity.[141]

Equitable relief against forfeiture

[7.57] Suppose a lease provides that if the tenant does not pay the rent by the due date the landlord is entitled to terminate the lease and repossess the property. The tenant pays the rent one day late and the landlord, relying on the forfeiture clause, purports to terminate the lease.

136 *Paciocco v Australia and New Zealand Banking Group Ltd* (2016) 258 CLR 525, [69] (Kiefel J), [271]–[279] (Keane J). Cf Gageler J at [166], who stated the test as being whether the provision had no other purpose other than to punish. The 'legitimate interest' test had been applied by Lord Atkinson in *Dunlop Pneumatic Tyre Co Ltd v New Garage & Motor Co Ltd* [1915] AC 79, 91–2. In *Cavendish Square Holding BV v Makdessi* [2015] UKSC 67, the UK Supreme Court adopted the test in preference to the criteria laid down by Lord Dunedin.

137 *Paciocco v Australia and New Zealand Banking Group Ltd* (2016) 258 CLR 525, [317]–[334] (Nettle J).

138 Cf the interests recognised on the sale of a business in *Cavendish Square Holding BV v Makdessi* [2016] AC 1172.

139 *Paciocco v Australia and New Zealand Banking Group Ltd* (2016) 258 CLR 525, [278] (Keane J).

140 See S Worthington, *Equity* (Oxford University Press, 2nd ed, 2006) 224–7 for the argument that the doctrine should be abolished.

141 *Competition and Consumer Act 2010* (Cth) pt VIII.

The tenant is entitled to apply for relief against forfeiture of the lease. The right to relief was originally equitable but, in the case of tenancies, is now governed by legislation.[142] The equitable right to relief remains important where an interest in property has been forfeited as a result of failure to perform a term in the contract.

Relief may be granted on equitable grounds where a contract provides for the forfeiture of a proprietary or possessory interest in property as a sanction for breach of contract, and the interest-holder has committed a breach. It is unclear whether relief can be granted where the contract provides that the contract-breaker will lose the benefit of conditions or warranties contained in the contract upon breach. On the one hand, the benefit of most contracts have some of the characteristics of property since they can be assigned or held on trust for third parties.[143] On the other hand, it is unclear why the principles of equitable relief from forfeiture ought to apply when a breach of contract causes the benefit of contractual provisions to be lost, given that the contract-breaker may anyway be protected by the doctrine of penalties in such a case.[144] Whether equity relieves against forfeiture of contractual rights ultimately depends on whether the forfeiture principles constitute a discrete equitable doctrine or, alternatively, can be considered as one application of a broader principle prohibiting the unconscientious enforcement of legal rights.[145] [7.58]

Until recently, it was unclear whether equity would relieve against a *substantively* unfair exercise of the right to termination; for example, where the basis for forfeiture is a comparatively trivial breach of contract. Alternatively, would relief only be granted where there is some *procedural* defect in the forfeiture process, such as a forfeiture procured by fraud or mistake? Recent authority favours the narrower, procedural analysis of equitable relief. [7.59]

Divisions of the High Court's judicial opinion on the scope of equitable relief were highlighted in *Stern v McArthur*.[146] The plaintiffs were vendors under a terms contract for the sale of land. The contract price was payable by a deposit and monthly instalments. In the event of the purchasers' default, the vendor was entitled to terminate the contract and sue for breach. The purchasers went into possession and built a house on the land. After about eight years, they defaulted in their repayments. They later offered to pay the outstanding arrears. The vendors rejected the offer and sought to terminate the contract. A majority of the High Court, Mason CJ and Brennan J dissenting, held that the purchasers were entitled to relief from forfeiture and to specific performance of the contract of sale. The judgments exhibited three distinct approaches to determining the availability of equitable relief: [7.60]

(1) Mason CJ and Brennan J would only have permitted relief if there had been some unconscionability, in the sense of shabby conduct, on the part of the vendors. Since there had been none, there were no grounds for equitable relief.

142 *Conveyancing Act 1919* (NSW) s 129; *Property Law Act 1958* (Vic) s 146.

143 See chapter 9.

144 See [7.54] and *Kay v Playup Australia Pty Ltd* (2020) 19 BPR 40,03, Brereton JA at [82]–[93] on the application of the penalties doctrine to accrued contractual obligations.

145 Cf *Mineralogy Pty Ltd v Sino Iron Pty Ltd (No 6)* (2015) 329 ALR 1, Edelman J obiter at [980]–[991]; *Kay v Playup Pty Ltd* (2020) 19 BPR 40,037, Brereton JA obiter at [103]–[122], Macfarlan JA and Simpson AJA not expressing an opinion. See also *Manchester Ship Canal Co Ltd v Vauxhall Motors Ltd* [2020] AC 1161, [49]–[51] (Lord Briggs), [77]–[88] (Lady Arden). F Di Lizia, 'The Requirement of Property or Possessory Rights for Relief against Forfeiture' (2021) 95(8) *Australian Law Journal* 641.

146 (1988) 165 CLR 489.

(2) Deane and Dawson JJ held that the forfeiture provision was intended as security for payment of the purchase price under the instalment purchase contract. It was therefore analogous to a mortgage of land. The purchasers were in the position of mortgagors entitled to equitable relief from foreclosure of the mortgage provided that they paid the mortgagee the outstanding mortgage arrears, interest and costs. Since the purchasers were prepared to pay these amounts to the vendors, they were entitled to relief from forfeiture.[147]

(3) Gaudron J held that the vendors had acted unconscionably and that the purchasers were therefore entitled to equitable relief. The vendors had chosen to forfeit the purchasers' interest in the property even though they could have pursued the alternative remedy of suing for specific performance to recover the outstanding purchase moneys. Forfeiture was unconscionable because the purchasers had built a house on the property and the property had considerably appreciated in value. These matters went to the substantive fairness of the instalment purchase contract and the vendors' exercise of rights under the contract. On this approach, deciding which party ought to enjoy the benefit of the increase in the value of the land is a critical consideration.

[7.61] The division of opinion in *Stern v McArthur* left open the question whether equitable relief was based on procedural unconscionability, as Mason CJ and Brennan held, or on substantive unconscionability, adopting the approach of Gaudron J. The later decision of the High Court, *Tanwar Enterprises Ltd v Cauchi*,[148] construed unconscionability in a narrow, procedural sense. The purchaser bought land under a contract which stipulated 4pm on 25 June 2001 as settlement time. Time was stated to be of the essence of the contract. The purchaser failed to complete the purchase by the stipulated time because Singaporean authorities delayed an international money transfer. The funds were released and paid over to the purchaser a day later, but the vendor refused to accept the tender of the purchase price and terminated the contract of sale.

The High Court held that the purchaser was not entitled to relief from forfeiture of the contract. The vendors had not acted unconscientiously in exercising their right to termination. The majority judgment[149] stated that, generally speaking,[150] relief from forfeiture will only be granted in cases of 'fraud, accident, mistake or surprise'.[151] In this context, 'accident' means unforeseen circumstances. 'Surprise' means that the party terminating the contract takes advantage of the other party's ignorance of a relevant fact. On the facts, there was no accident since the history of the negotiations between the parties and the final contract showed that the purchaser took the risk of delay in accessing funds sourced overseas.

147 The mortgage analogy in cases of instalment purchase contracts was also recognised, although on the facts not applied, in the later High Court decision of *Tanwar Enterprises Pty Ltd v Cauchi* (2003) 217 CLR 315; *Sourcebook* 7.4.2a, p 182.

148 (2003) 217 CLR 315; *Sourcebook* 7.4.2a, p 182.

149 Kirby J delivered a separate judgment identifying a broader basis for the principles of equitable relief. Callinan J also delivered a separate judgment dismissing the appeal.

150 The grounds were said not to be exhaustive: (2003) 217 CLR 315, 373.

151 Citing *Shiloh Spinners Ltd v Harding* [1973] 2 AC 691, 723 (Lord Wilberforce).

The application of the principles of equitable relief to contracts for the sale of land is arguably unnecessarily complex. The principles apply because, upon signing the contract, the vendor holds the land on constructive trust for the purchaser.[152] The purchaser seeks relief from the forfeiture of the equitable interest arising under the constructive trust. However, the existence of the constructive trust, where the purchase price has not been paid, was doubted in *Tanwar*.[153] The critical question ought not to be whether the purchaser's interest under the constructive trust should be forfeited. Rather, it ought to be whether the purchaser is entitled to specific performance of the vendor's obligation to convey the land, even though the vendor purported to terminate the contract on account of the purchaser's failure to pay the purchase price by the contractual deadline, time being of the essence of the contract. [7.62]

WHAT'S ONLINE?

Available at www.cambridge.org/highereducation/isbn/9781009232388/resources:

- Recommended further readings
- Discussion topics
- Practice problems

152 *Lysaght v Edwards* (1876) 2 Ch D 499, 506 (Jessel MR).
153 (2003) 217 CLR 315, 370–1.

8

EQUITABLE PROPRIETARY INTERESTS

Introduction

We saw in Part B that equity developed an armory of personal remedies, such as specific performance and injunctions, directed at the person of the defendant. Their principal function is to enforce *personal* rights, such as performance of a contract. However, over time, equity proved willing to award personal relief almost routinely – not only against owners of property but also against third parties who had received the property.[1] This regular award of equitable personal relief was eventually perceived as having created a proprietary interest in favour of the party entitled to the relief. For example, if A signs a contract to purchase land from B, but B refuses to complete the contract, equity will grant the remedy of specific performance against B, and B will have to transfer the land to A. This happened so routinely that eventually A was treated in equity as if she held a property interest in the land once the contract was signed. Similarly, the regular awards of personal relief against trustees in breach of trust eventually gave rise to a proprietary interest in the beneficiary. All equitable property rights are sourced in a personal obligation enforced in equity. [8.1]

The availability of an equitable remedy does not necessarily mean that the interest protected by the remedy constitutes property; for example, equity grants injunctions and other relief to prevent the unauthorised use of confidential information.[2] But confidential information is not recognised as a species of equitable property. Information is only protected against misuse by parties who act in breach of an equitable obligation of confidence. A person who has confidential information has only a personal right to protection in equity. Equitable property, like common law property, must be of a kind that is recognised as property in law.[3] [8.2]

Equity recognises and enforces interests in property which are not recognised or enforced at common law. Interests include: [8.3]

(a) a beneficiary's interest under a fixed trust;[4]

(b) a partner's interest in the partnership;[5]

(c) proprietary interests that are counterparts to common law interests, such as the equitable fee simple and the equitable lease. (These differ from equivalent common law interests in their method of creation and the extent of their enforceability);

(d) equitable security interests, such as the equitable charge. An equitable charge is created more informally than the common law mortgage. It also entitles the chargee to more limited relief in the event of the chargor's default; and

(e) equitable rights over land such as the equitable easement or restrictive covenant over land which, unlike common law interests over land, do not have to be created by deed.

1 FW Maitland, *Lectures on Equity*, rev J Brunyate (Cambridge University Press, rev ed, 1929) 29–30.

2 See chapter 12.

3 There is some circularity involved in defining what constitutes property entitled to equitable protection. See Kevin Gray, 'Property in Thin Air' (1991) 50(2) *Cambridge Law Journal* 252, analysing property in terms of excludable resources.

4 See [13.6] for the distinction between fixed and discretionary trusts.

5 While a partner has an equitable interest in partnership property, it is distinct from the type of interest held by a beneficiary under a fixed interest trust. In *Commissioner for State Revenue v Rojoda Pty Ltd* (2020) 268 CLR 281, 302, a majority of the High Court stated 'a partner's equitable interest is not accurately expressed as a "beneficial interest", at least in the sense of being a right to any proportion of, or for the personal use of, or for the benefit from, any particular asset'.

[8.4] Equitable interests in property can be created in one of three ways:

(1) By agreement; for example, an equitable mortgage is created by an agreement between a lender and a borrower;

(2) By express trust;[6] or

(3) By court order or operation of law. A constructive trust, for example, derives its efficacy from a court order and not from a settlor's expression of intention to create a trust.[7] Another equitable interest created by operation of law is the equitable lien. It is a court-ordered security interest imposed over the defendant's property.[8] If the defendant fails to perform an obligation owed by the plaintiff, the property will be sold off and the plaintiff's debt discharged out of the proceeds. One example is the trustee's lien over trust property to secure repayment of sums expended by the trustee for the trust.[9] The doctrine of proprietary estoppel is another example of equity's flexible approach to the creation of proprietary interests. A plaintiff who is successful in an action for proprietary estoppel may obtain a proprietary interest by way of constructive trust or lien, or the court may award a monetary remedy.

[8.5] Equitable interests over property and their enforcement will only be discussed briefly here.[10] They share the following features:

(a) Equitable interests in property are created more informally than the equivalent legal interests. Interests in land usually have to be created by registration (for land under the Torrens system) or by deed at common law.[11] In equity, a deed is not required; the equitable interest will be enforceable if there is a specifically enforceable contract to create the interest.[12] Equity assists those who pay valuable consideration for property. Even where valuable consideration has not been paid, some transfers of property may be enforceable in equity. A transfer will be effective in equity where the transferor has done all that it is necessary for her to do to complete the transfer.[13] Alternatively, equity looks to the intent and not the form of a legal transaction.[14] These principles are discussed further in chapter 9. The doctrine of proprietary estoppel allows for the creation of proprietary interests in certain circumstances where a party has relied on an assumption or expectation

6 See chapter 13.

7 See chapter 23.

8 *Hewett v Court* (1983) 149 CLR 639, 663 (Deane J). Liens can also arise by agreement between the parties.

9 See chapter 19 and *Boensch v Pascoe* (2019) 268 CLR 593.

10 More detail can be found in specialist property law texts, such as BJ Edgeworth et al (eds), *Sackville & Neave: Australian Property Law* (LexisNexis Butterworths, 10th ed, 2016).

11 There are exceptions to the requirement of a deed. See, eg, *Property Law Act 1958* (Vic) s 54(2). Implied periodic tenancies are also not created by deed but by the regularity of payment by the occupier to the landowner.

12 *Walsh v Lonsdale* (1882) 21 Ch D 9; *Sourcebook* 8.3b, p 195; *Chan v Cresdon Pty Ltd* (1989) 168 CLR 242. The lease must be in writing (but see n 11) or be enforceable by virtue of the equitable doctrine of part performance: *McBride v Sandland* (1918) 25 CLR 69.

13 *Corin v Patton* (1990) 169 CLR 540; *Sourcebook* 1.4a, p 13.

14 *Norman v Federal Commissioner of Taxation* (1963) 109 CLR 9, 30 (equitable assignment of equitable property); *Sourcebook* 9.3a, p 212. See chapter 9.

that an interest will be granted to them. The creation of proprietary interests under the principles of proprietary estoppel is discussed below.

(b) Equity acts on the conscience of the holder of the legal title to property. This means that an equitable interest can be enforced against the person who created the interest or who, by his conduct, is bound by the interest, as well as against any volunteer who takes from that person; but it will not be enforceable against a good faith purchaser for value of the legal estate or interest in the property who does not have notice of the equitable interest. For example, a purchaser of property from a landlord who does not have notice of an equitable lease will not be bound by the lease. In contrast, legal interests in property 'bind the world'. They are binding on any recipient of that property, even one who is unaware of the interest. Where the property interest consists of land or a security interest over personal property, legislation has largely displaced the application of the doctrine of notice. This development is discussed below.

Proprietary estoppel

Proprietary estoppel is a sub-set of equitable estoppel, discussed more generally in chapter 7. [8.6]
Equity has long exercised a jurisdiction to prevent a holder of an interest in property from insisting upon his legal rights to property where he has encouraged another to act to her detriment on the faith of her belief that she had, or would be granted, some rights over the property in question. In *Dillwyn v Llewelyn*,[15] a father allowed his son to possess some of his land and conveyed the land to him under a conveyance which proved to be defective. The son occupied the land and built a house on it with the father's knowledge and approval. On the father's death, the son obtained a declaration that he was the equitable owner of the land and Lord Westbury directed that the land be conveyed to him. Equity also recognises proprietary estoppel by acquiescence, where no promise is made, but the owner of the property stands by and allows another to make improvements on the relevant property. Estoppel by encouragement occurs more often than estoppel by acquiescence.

To establish proprietary estoppel, it must be demonstrated that: [8.7]

(a) an assumption was created that the plaintiff would be entitled to an interest in land;[16]

(b) the defendant encouraged that assumption by a making a promise or by their acquiescence;[17]

(c) the plaintiff reasonably relied on the assumption to their detriment;

(d) the defendant knew of the plaintiff's reliance.

15 (1862) 4 De GF & J 517; 45 ER 1285.

16 Including a promise to leave property by will: *Delaforce v Simpson-Cook* (2010) 78 NSWLR 483; *Thorner v Major* [2009] 1 WLR 776.

17 The High Court in *Sidhu v Van Dyke* (2014) 251 CLR 505 used the language of promises and representations interchangeably but some writers see promises and representations as distinct: see B McFarlane, *The Law of Proprietary Estoppel* (Oxford University Press, 2nd ed, 2020) and K Handley 'Estoppel' (2006) 20(2) *Commercial Law Quarterly* 29. The distinction between representations and promises was rejected by White J in *Construction Technologies Australia Pty Ltd v Doueihi* (2014) 17 BPR 33,457.

If the plaintiff is relying on the defendant's acquiescence as the relevant encouragement, classic formulations also require that the plaintiff has a mistaken belief as to her current rights in the property.[18] In *Q (a pseudonym) v E Co (a pseudonym)*,[19] the classic formulation was discussed with apparent approval.

[8.8] While the elements of equitable estoppel as stated by Brennan J in *Waltons Stores* are still a 'useful check', care must be taken to apply those elements to the type of estoppel in question. The first element as formulated by Brennan J is that 'the plaintiff assumed that a particular legal relationship then existed between the plaintiff and the defendant or expected that a particular legal relationship would exist between them and, in the latter case, that the defendant would not be free to withdraw from the expected legal relationship'.[20] The New South Wales Court of Appeal has since clarified that this element was formulated in the context of promissory estoppel and will not be applied to proprietary estoppel in a mechanical fashion. In proprietary estoppel, the correct question is whether the plaintiff assumed that an interest in property would be granted. It is not necessary to demonstrate that the plaintiff intended to enter into a legal relationship with the defendant.[21]

[8.9] Although the High Court in *Waltons Stores* said that promissory estoppel and proprietary estoppel doctrines were merged into a single doctrine of equitable estoppel,[22] it can no longer be said that this is the case.[23] The *Waltons* version of equitable estoppel had, at its heart, that a successful plaintiff receive the minimum necessary relief, or the 'minimum equity'.[24] The lack of endorsement of the 'minimum equity' approach in the later High Court case of *Giumelli v Giumelli*[25] was interpreted by writers[26] and subsequent courts to be a rejection of it. Decisions in appellate State courts stated that proprietary estoppel has a different rationale, and consequently, a different remedial operation than promissory estoppel.[27] The High Court of Australia has now endorsed this view.

In *Sidhu v Van Dyke*, the appellant and respondent had previously been in an extra-marital relationship. The respondent lived in a cottage on property owned by the appellant and his wife. During the relationship, the appellant told the respondent, on numerous occasions, that the cottage would be hers. After the relationship broke down, the appellant

18 *Ramsden v Dyson* (1866) LR 1 HL 12. This requirement is criticised by White J in *Construction Technologies Australia Pty Ltd v Doueihi* (2014) 17 BPR 33,457 and *Priestley v Priestley* [2016] NSWSC 1096.

19 (2020) 383 ALR 469, 476 (Meagher JA, Leeming and Payne JJA agreeing).

20 *Waltons Stores (Interstate) Ltd v Maher* (1988) 164 CLR 387, 428; *Sourcebook* 7.2.1a, p 143.

21 *Doueihi v Construction Technologies Australia Pty Ltd* (2016) 92 NSWLR 247. See also *Currie v Currie (No 2)* [2019] WASCA 2.

22 *Waltons Stores (Interstate) Ltd v Maher* (1988) 164 CLR 387; *Sourcebook* 7.2.1a, p 143. See also *Silovi Pty Ltd v Barbaro* (1988) 13 NSWLR 466.

23 See chapter 7 at [7.4] for more detailed discussion of developments post-*Waltons*.

24 (1988) 164 CLR 387. The term 'minimum equity' is drawn from the statement of Scarman LJ in *Crabb v Arun District Council* [1976] Ch 179, 198 that the Court must determine 'the minimum equity to do justice to the plaintiff'.

25 (1999) 196 CLR 101; *Sourcebook* 8.5a, p 198.

26 The authors of *On Equity* take the view that *Giumelli* rejected the minimum equity approach: PW Young, C Croft and M Smith, *On Equity* (Lawbook, 2009) 957.

27 See *Donis v Donis* (2007) 19 VR 577, 594; *Harrison v Harrison* [2013] VSCA 170, [159] (Garde AJA, Harper and Tate JJA agreeing); *Delaforce v Simpson-Cook* (2010) 78 NSWLR 483; *Walsh v Walsh* [2012] NSWCA 57.

refused to transfer the property to the respondent. In relation to the rationale for proprietary estoppel by encouragement, the plurality stated: 'This category of equitable estoppel serves to vindicate the expectations of the representee against a party who seeks unconscionably to resile from an expectation he or she has created'[28] and 'the relief which is necessary … is usually that which reflects the value of the promise.'[29] The Court held that it was reasonable for the respondent to rely on the statements, even though the appellant's ability to carry them out was conditional on the approval of third parties.[30]

An example of 'expectation based' relief is provided by *Arfaras v Vosnakis*.[31] In this case, the parties were a man (the respondent) and his mother-in-law (appellant). The respondent's wife (appellant's daughter) died. The appellant told the respondent that he could bury his wife in the burial plot to which she held rights. The burial licence permitted two people to be buried in the plot. The appellant also promised that she would transfer the burial licence to her son-in-law so that he could be buried next to his wife when he died. Mr Vosnakis accepted the offers and his wife was buried in the plot. His mother-in-law later resiled from the promise to transfer the burial licence to him. The New South Wales Court of Appeal confirmed the trial judge's decision that proprietary estoppel had been established and that the appropriate remedy was an order to transfer the burial licence. His reliance was irreversible. [8.10]

Although it is now clear that the purpose of proprietary estoppel is to vindicate the expectation, this does not necessarily mean that the plaintiff will obtain a proprietary interest in the promised property. The Court may exercise its remedial discretion to decide that a personal remedy of equitable compensation is preferable in the circumstances of the case. Consistent with the rationale of equitable estoppel, the starting point for determining the amount of monetary relief will be the value of the promised interest. [8.11]

In *Sidhu v Van Dyke*,[32] the plaintiff obtained a money remedy, because the trial judge held that to award her the expected interest would affect the interests of a third party (the respondent's wife) who was a co-owner of the land. The respondent made no claim on appeal for a proprietary remedy.

A similar concern that the remedy not affect third parties was evident in the earlier High Court case of *Giumelli v Giumelli*.[33] In that case, parents encouraged the plaintiff, one of their sons, to work for their business without pay by promising him that he would be given a part of a block of land they had acquired, and that he could build a house on the land. The plaintiff did considerable work on the land. The parents refused to transfer a share of the land to him after he married a woman of whom they disapproved. The High Court held that the requirements of proprietary estoppel had been established. The plaintiff had relied

28 *Sidhu v Van Dyke* (2014) 251 CLR 505, [77] (French CJ, Kiefel, Bell and Keane JJ); *Sourcebook* 8.5b, p 201. Gageler J gave a separate judgment which agreed with the joint reasons.

29 (2014) 251 CLR 505, [85].

30 Ibid. Council approval was required to subdivide the land and the appellant had to obtain his wife's consent to the transfer as she was a joint owner of the land. On the facts, the respondent's reliance was reasonable. The plurality stated [86]: 'His assurances to the respondent were expressed categorically so as to leave no room for doubt that he would ensure that the subdivision would proceed and that the consent of the appellant's wife would be forthcoming.'

31 (2016) 18 BPR 35,819.

32 (2014) 251 CLR 505.

33 (1999) 196 CLR 101.

to his detriment on the expectation created by his parents that he would be awarded a share in the property. He was not, however, awarded a proprietary interest in the land. Instead, the parents were ordered to pay him a sum representing the present value of the promised plot of land – the sum being charged on the whole block of land in order to secure its payment. Relevant factors included the fact that a partnership action was still pending between the parties in which the proprietary rights of all the parties would be clarified and the fact that other members of the family had worked on the land. An award of a proprietary interest to the plaintiff, by way of constructive trust, would defeat any interest those family members had in the land.[34]

[8.12] While the starting point for assessing compensation will be the value of the promised property, the court will not grant relief in the expectation measure if that is inappropriate on the facts. In *Sidhu*, the plurality stated: 'The requirements of good conscience may mean that in some cases the value of the promise may not be the just measure of relief.'[35] The plurality cited Deane J's statement in *Commonwealth v Verwayen* that expectation relief will not be granted if such relief is disproportionate to the plaintiff's expenditure on the property.[36]

Other reasons may require reduction or adjustment of the award. Where, for example, an interest was promised to the plaintiff promisee on the death of the promisor, but the award entitles the plaintiff to an immediate property interest, the court award accelerates the promisee's receipt of the interest. In such a case, the award may be reduced[37] or conditions may be imposed on the award to reflect the fact that the promisee has received the benefit of the promise early.[38] In *Q (a pseudonym) v E Co (a pseudonym)*, the New South Wales Court of Appeal imposed conditions when granting accelerated relief. Meagher JA stated:

> to impose conditions on relief in this case is to do no more than shape relief according to the requirements of conscience, in circumstances where it is accepted that the making good of the encouraged expectation should be brought forward. In substance there is no distinction between qualifying relief by imposing a condition on the party relying on the estoppel and qualifying relief by giving effect only in part to the underlying expectation.[39]

His Honour explained that, in framing the appropriate condition on relief, it was necessary to consider what the position of the parties would have been if the promise had not been accelerated.[40]

An award may also be reduced because the promisee has already received benefits as a consequence of her reliance.[41]

---

34 See also [6.27].

35 *Sidhu v Van Dyke* (2014) 251 CLR 505, [83].

36 (1990) 170 CLR 394, 441.

37 *Quinn v Bryant* [2012] NSWCA 377; *Gillett v Holt* [2001] Ch 210.

38 See, eg, *Currie v Currie (No 2)* [2017] WASC 312, upheld on appeal: [2019] WASCA 2; *Q (a pseudonym) v E Co (a pseudonym)* (2020) 383 ALR 469.

39 *Q (a pseudonym) v E Co (a pseudonym)* (2020) 383 ALR 469, 510 (Meagher JA; Leeming and Payne JJA agreeing).

40 Ibid.

41 *Milling v Hardie* [2014] NSWCA 163.

The nature of equitable ownership

An absolute owner of property does not hold two estates, one legal and the other equitable. She holds only the legal interest in the property. In *DKLR Holding Co (No 2) Pty Ltd v Commissioner of Stamp Duties (NSW)*, Aickin J stated: [8.13]

> If one person has both the legal estate and the entire beneficial interest in the land he holds an entire and unqualified legal interest and not two separate interests, one legal and the other equitable ... It is a fundamental principle of both the common law and of equity that the holder of an estate in fee simple cannot be a trustee of that fee simple for himself for what he holds is a single estate, being the largest estate in land known to the law.[42]

It follows that an owner of property cannot reserve equitable title in the property to herself while transferring legal title to another. If S, a settlor, transfers property to T, to be held on trust for S, S does not keep her equitable title while transferring the legal title in the property to T. Instead, S transfers the full beneficial ownership in the trust property to T who is then subjected to the obligations of a trustee administering the trust for S. As Brennan J stated in the same case, '[a]n equitable interest is not carved out of a legal estate but impressed upon it'.[43]

The scope of an equitable interest is commensurate with the relief equity will grant to enforce it, whether by specific performance, injunction or other remedy. In some cases, equitable protection takes the form of conferring a property interest on the party entitled to enforce the equitable obligation. A property interest is conferred, for example, on the beneficiary of a fixed trust. But in other cases, the party enforcing the equitable obligation has no proprietary interest in the subject-matter of the obligation. So a beneficiary of a discretionary trust is entitled to enforce the trust against both the trustees and third parties who have obtained title to the property but has no proprietary interest in any specific trust asset.[44] As Viscount Radcliffe put it, '[e]quity ... calls into existence and protects equitable rights and interests in property only where their recognition has been found to be required in order to give effect to its doctrines'.[45] [8.14]

Priority disputes and the doctrine of notice

When the legal system recognises a duality of property ownership (legal and equitable) it is inevitable that disputes as to entitlement will arise. The enforceability of equitable [8.15]

42 (1982) 149 CLR 431, 463. See also *Commissioner of Stamp Duties (Qld) v Livingston* [1965] AC 694, 712 (Viscount Radcliffe); *Westdeutsche Landesbank Girozentrale v Islington London Borough Council* [1996] AC 669, 706 (Lord Browne-Wilkinson).

43 *DKLR Holding Co (No 2) Pty Ltd v Commissioner of Stamp Duties (NSW)* (1982) 149 CLR 431, 473; *Sourcebook* 8.2a, p 187. Brennan J's formulation was quoted with approval in *Boensch v Pascoe* (2019) 268 CLR 593, [4] (Kiefel CJ, Gageler and Keane JJ).

44 See [13.9].

45 *Commissioner of Stamp Duties (Qld) v Livingston* [1965] AC 694, 712.

interests in property under general law depends on the application of the doctrine of notice. Equitable interests in or over property are binding on later legal title-holders except a good faith purchaser for value of the legal estate in the property without notice of the equitable interest.[46] The interest therefore binds a donee of the property or a squatter on land.[47] If valuable consideration[48] is given it is irrelevant that the consideration was inadequate. The purchaser bears the onus of showing that she is not affected by an adverse equitable interest.[49] The 'good faith purchase' defence destroys the equitable interest involved. It cannot be revived even against a subsequent purchaser who has notice of the equitable interest.[50] Notice can be actual, constructive or imputed.[51]

[8.16] In significant areas of property law, the enforceability of equitable property interests is determined by registration and not the doctrine of notice. Under the Torrens system of title by registration, a purchaser of land obtains indefeasible title to the land subject to entries on the register unless one of the so-called 'exceptions' to indefeasibility applies. A beneficiary under an express trust of land, for example, will be unable to enforce the trust against a later registered proprietor of the land unless that proprietor was party to fraud committed by the trustee or where the trust is protected by entry on the register. Trusts of land are commonly protected by the entry of a caveat on the certificate of title.[52]

[8.17] The *Personal Property Securities Act 2009* (Cth) creates a statutory system for enforcing security interests in personal property. The legislation establishes a register of security interests and, where an interest is required to be registered in order to be enforceable against third parties, priority is in general determined by the date of registration of the interest and not by the doctrine of notice.

Equities and equitable interests

[8.18] If property has been transferred under a contract or as a gift[53] which is voidable in equity, the party entitled to set aside the transaction has an 'equity', sometimes described as a 'mere' or 'personal' equity, to have the transaction rescinded and the property returned to her. The grounds of rescission are discussed in chapter 5. The plaintiff must elect to have the transaction rescinded. If she fails to make an election within a reasonable time after transferring the property, she will be held to have affirmed the disposition. Once the election to rescind has been made, the defendant holds property received under the transaction, or its traceable proceeds, on constructive trust for the plaintiff, subject to the application of the

46 Disputes can also occur between two parties who each hold an equitable interest in property: see the discussion in [8.19] below.

47 *Re Nisbet & Potts' Contract* [1906] 1 Ch 386.

48 Consideration includes money, money's worth, marriage consideration and the satisfaction of an existing debt: *Thorndike v Hunt* (1859) 3 De GF & J 563, 569; 44 ER 1386, 1388. Consideration must have been paid by the time of the receipt of the legal estate: *Story v Windsor* (1743) 2 Atk 630, 631; 26 ER 776.

49 *Barclays Bank plc v Boulter* [1999] 4 All ER 1002, 1008.

50 *Wilkes v Spooner* [1911] 2 KB 473.

51 See the online resources.

52 BJ Edgeworth et al (eds), *Sackville & Neave: Australian Property Law* (LexisNexis Butterworths, 10th ed, 2016) [5.168].

53 *Allcard v Skinner* (1887) 36 Ch D 145.

equitable bars to relief.[54] Before election, the plaintiff has an equity to have the property transferred under the voidable transaction returned to her. After election, she holds an equitable interest in the property under the constructive trust. Priority disputes can arise in respect of these rights.

Suppose the plaintiff conveys property to the defendant under a contract voidable for the defendant's fraudulent misrepresentation. The defendant sells the property to a third party before the plaintiff discovers the fraud. The third party will be entitled to the property if she can show that she is a good faith purchaser without notice of the fraud.[55] Alternatively, suppose the defendant grants an equitable mortgage over the property before the plaintiff rescinds the contract for fraud. This was essentially the situation which occurred in *Latec Investments Ltd v Hotel Terrigal Pty Ltd (in liq)*.[56] A mortgagor of a hotel applied to have the sale of the hotel by the mortgagee set aside on the ground that the power of sale had been exercised fraudulently. Before the mortgagor elected to rescind, however, the purchaser of the hotel from the mortgagee created an equitable charge over it in favour of a financier. The question for the High Court was whether the mortgagor's equity to rescind for fraud prevailed over the later equitable charge. It was unanimously held that the equitable charge prevailed over the earlier equity, although each judge reached this result by a different route. [8.19]

Kitto J held that the later equitable interest in the hotel prevailed over the earlier equity to rescind: a good faith purchaser for value of an *equitable* interest in property without notice of the equity has priority over the equity.[57] Taylor J held that the plaintiff had an equitable interest in the hotel, not a mere equity.[58] Although the usual rule applied in a priority dispute is that the first equitable interest prevails unless there is good reason for preferring the second interest, Taylor J held that the plaintiff needed the assistance of the Court in order to enforce his interest and that the assistance would not be provided against a good faith purchaser. Menzies J attempted to reconcile the two approaches by holding that whether the right to rescind constitutes an equity or an equitable interest depends on the purpose for which the inquiry is made. For the purpose of determining a priority dispute, a right to rescind is classified as an equity.

There is less than meets the eye to these diverse analyses of the plaintiff's right to rescind. Even if Taylor J was correct to characterise the plaintiff's interest as an equitable interest, it is obviously an interest whose properties differ from the equitable interest of, say, a beneficiary under a fixed trust who does not ordinarily require any assistance from equity in order

54 *Daly v Sydney Stock Exchange Ltd* (1986) 160 CLR 371; *Sourcebook* 5.3a, p 102.

55 Alternatively, she may have indefeasible title under one of the statutory title regimes discussed in [8.16]–[8.17]. See, eg, *Super Jacobs Pty Ltd v Faalogo* [2019] VSC 778 where the former registered proprietors of property had granted a general power of attorney to their mortgage broker. They alleged that their mortgage broker fraudulently used the power of attorney to sell the property to the plaintiff, who was the new registered proprietor. The purchaser had indefeasible title unless an exception applied.

56 (1965) 113 CLR 265. Even though *Latec* holds that the equity-holder cannot recover the property, she may be entitled to an award of equitable compensation, assessed as the value of the property, against the party responsible for vitiating the contract or gift: *Hartigan v International Society for Krishna Consciousness Inc* [2002] NSWSC 810. See [5.21].

57 Applying *Phillips v Phillips* (1861) 4 De GF & J 208; 45 ER 1164.

58 Applying *Stump v Gaby* (1852) 2 De GM & G 623; 42 ER 1015.

to assert priority against a subsequent equitable holder.[59] A distinction between equitable interests which require the assistance of the court and others which need no such assistance presupposes that the former category is weaker than the latter. It is therefore convenient to give them different labels to reflect that difference, such as 'equity' and 'equitable interest'.[60] Likewise, while it is true, as Menzies J noted, that a right to rescind a contract for fraud can be characterised as a chose in action[61] (a full property interest) which can be devised by will, as can other assignable legal and equitable rights to recover property in legal proceedings, the critical question is the extent to which the interest can be enforced against other claimants of the property. Since the enforceability of the right to rescind is more limited than the enforceability of a beneficiary's interest under an express trust, a different label, such as an 'equity', is needed to express that difference.

The judgment of Kitto J provides the most convincing analysis in *Latec*, since it clearly recognises that the right to rescind in equity is different in character from established equitable interests such as interests under fixed trusts, and therefore must not be confused with such interests. The difference justifies the application of a different priority rule from that applicable to competing disputes between equitable interests. The judgment has been identified in later cases as providing the ratio of the decision.[62]

WHAT'S ONLINE?

Available at www.cambridge.org/highereducation/isbn/9781009232388/resources:

- Recommended further readings
- Discussion topics
- Practice problem

59 The earlier equitable interest may lose priority to a later interest based on an assessment of the merits of the claimants: *Rice v Rice* (1853) 2 Drew 73, 78; 61 ER 646, 648 (Kindersley V-C), but deferral is not based on the inherent nature of the plaintiff's interest.

60 The labels are confusing since the word 'equity' is used to describe several concepts. Some recent analysis has described the 'equity' as a 'power'; that is, a power to have a contract or gift set aside. But the word 'power' is also ambiguous. See Birke Häcker, 'Proprietary Restitution after Impaired Consent Transfers: A Generalised Power Model' (2009) 68(2) *Cambridge Law Journal* 324.

61 See [9.4].

62 *Double Bay Newspapers Pty Ltd v AW Holdings Pty Ltd* (1996) 42 NSWLR 409.

9

EQUITABLE ASSIGNMENTS

Introduction

[9.1] In chapter 8 we saw that equity recognises as property certain assets not recognised at common law, such as the beneficiary's interest in a trust. We also saw that property interests can be created more informally in equity than at law. One aspect of this is equity's attitude to assignments of property.

Assignments are transfers of property either for consideration or as gifts. The question whether property has been effectively assigned is of considerable commercial significance.[1] It is not always an easy question to answer. The law of assignments stands at the intersection of common law, equity and statute. The common law developed basic rules for the transfer of property. Equity acts as a 'gloss'[2] and recognises assignments in various cases where the common law would not. Many assignments are also effected by statute. So when we consider whether an assignment has been effective, we need to be able to apply law from all three sources.

[9.2] A transfer or assignment of property is a transfer of wealth, whether it is in exchange for value or by gift. Common law assumes that people do not part with their wealth lightly or accidently. It treats assignments of property formally, in the sense that it does not recognise that a transfer has occurred unless and until all formal requirements have been met.

[9.3] There are several differences in equity's approach to property assignments. First, equity may regard a transfer of property as complete in equity even though the law would regard the transfer as incomplete. Secondly, equity may regard a transfer as effective even though the property is not transmissible at common law. Finally, equity adopts a wider definition of property for the purpose of recognising and enforcing the transfer of property. The guiding principle behind these different approaches to assignment is that equity steps in when the assignor's conscience *ought* to be bound by the assignment.[3]

Equity's approach to assignment should not, however, be seen as so informal as to be discretionary. Principles governing when equity will (or will not) recognise an assignment have been developed and consistently applied. Equity's relative lack of formality has played an important role in economic development. Equity has been able to respond more quickly to new forms of property and wealth, and recognise assignments of such property, where the common law lagged behind. But there are costs associated with this system. First, lack of formality can also equate to a lack of certainty. Secondly, the interaction of multiple sets of rules (common law, equity and statute) may be criticised for excessive complexity.

1 For example, the use of assignments of property interests as securitisation for major borrowings. See P Rajapakse, R Copp and J Gardner, 'Assessment of Insolvency Issues for the Mortgage Originator and Trustee-insurer in Securitisation Programs' (2008) 34(2) *Monash University Law Review* 370. In Australia, the *Personal Property Securities Act 2009* (Cth) ('PPSA') deals with security interests in personal property. An 'interest in personal property' provided by an assignment is caught as a 'security interest' under the PPSA 'if the transaction, in substance, secures payment or performance of an obligation': s 12(2)(j).

2 See [1.15].

3 See [8.5].

Property terminology

The assignment rules focus on the traditional classifications of property. There are several ways of categorising property interests. [9.4]

The earliest distinction drawn by the common law was between land (real property) and chattels or goods (personal property). As commerce became more complex, other distinctions appeared, such as the distinction between tangible and intangible property, or choses in possession and choses in action. Tangible property is property that has a physical presence, such as a car. Intangible property lacks a physical presence, although it often has value and represents an asset to its owner. Company shares are an example. '*Chose*' is a French word meaning 'thing'. A chose in possession is a thing which can be physically held (ie is tangible). The terminology 'chose in action' indicates that the asset cannot be possessed (ie is intangible). It can only be enforced by legal action. An example is a contractual debt, a right which must be enforced in court if the debtor fails to pay.

Another distinction is between legal and equitable property. Legal property is all forms of property that the common law recognises, including land, interests in and over land such as tenancies, chattels, and legal choses in action such as debts and company shares. Equitable property is a right recognised in a court exercising equitable jurisdiction prior to the judicature reforms, and was unknown to the common law. Examples include the beneficiary's interest in a trust and the partner's interest in a partnership. All equitable rights are intangible. All forms of equitable property are therefore equitable choses in action[4] as rights can only be enforced by action.

Property rights can obviously fall into more than one of the categories mentioned above.

Assignment of legal property

Over time, the common law developed methods of transfer for different kinds of legal property; these methods were common sense responses to the type of property in question, and the relative importance of that property. For example: [9.5]

- Ownership of bank notes generally passes with possession.[5]
- Title to chattels (in the absence of statutory input[6]) passes either by deed, or by delivery with the intention to confer ownership.[7]
- Company shares sold off-market require a transfer form signed by the transferee and transferor to be registered in the company books.[8]
- Legal choses in action could not originally be assigned at law. This can now be done by statutory methods, which are described at [9.30].

4 *Commissioner of Stamp Duties (Qld) v Livingston* [1965] AC 694.
5 *Ilich v The Queen* (1987) 162 CLR 110.
6 Statutory input is extensive. For example, the transfer of motor cars, boats and certain livestock is regulated by statute.
7 *Thomas v The Times Book Co Ltd* [1966] 1 WLR 911.
8 *Corporations Act 2001* (Cth) pt 7.11.

- Transfer of title to land has always required strict compliance with formalities, reflecting the historical importance of land. Transfer methods depend on the relevant land-holding system.
  (a) The transfer of general law land originally relied on a strict system of proof of chain of title. This was succeeded by a deed registration system, under which land is transferred by deed under seal in most Australian States.[9]
  (b) Most land in Australia is held in a second land-holding method, the Torrens registration system. This requires that the details of a sale of land be registered.[10] Only registration completes a legal transfer of title.[11]

[9.6] Assignment methods are now frequently specified by statute. Some transfer methods require numerous steps for completion of the transfer, as in the case of Torrens system land. This system requires an instrument of transfer in the proper form, signed by both the transferee and transferor. Stamp duty must be paid on this instrument, and then the instrument must be lodged for registration, together with the title deed. Nowadays, this process can be completed by electronic lodgement. Once lodged, a governmental registry registers the transfer. Title passes to the transferee on registration, and failure at any step along the way invalidates the transfer at law.

The same formal approach to assignments is evident whenever legal title to any kind of legal property is being considered; unless every required step is completed, the law will not regard the transfer as effective.

Equity and legally ineffective assignments

[9.7] Even though an assignment of legal property is legally ineffective, equity may regard the transfer as complete and make orders giving effect to it. This depends on whether equity regards the assignor's conscience as bound by the transaction. There are two situations to consider: first, where the assignee has given consideration; and secondly, where the transaction is a gift.

The relevance of consideration

[9.8] A critical issue in equity's attitude to the purported assignment is whether consideration for it has been given by the assignee. Common law regards the receipt of consideration as a valid reason for assigning property. Nevertheless, unless all relevant steps to complete the transfer at law are taken, the common law would not regard the transfer as complete. Equity assists an assignee who has given consideration in such cases. Assuming that the asset can be assigned (discussed below), consideration is equity's cue to attempt to

---

9 *Conveyancing Act 1919* (NSW) s 23B; *Law of Property Act 1936* (SA) s 28; *Conveyancing and Law of Property Act 1884* (Tas) s 60; *Property Law Act 1958* (Vic) s 52; *Property Law Act 1969* (WA) s 33. In Queensland and the Northern Territory, land can be conveyed by deed or mere writing: *Property Law Act 1974* (Qld) s 10; *Law of Property Act 2000* (NT) s 9.

10 *Transfer of Land Act 1958* (Vic) ss 40–44N. See also *Land Titles Act 1925* (ACT); *Real Property Act 1900* (NSW); *Land Title Act 2000* (NT); *Land Title Act 1994* (Qld); *Real Property Act 1886* (SA); *Land Titles Act 1980* (Tas); *Transfer of Land Act 1893* (WA).

11 *Breskvar v Wall* (1971) 126 CLR 376, 385–6 (Barwick CJ).

do whatever may be required to enforce the transaction, so long as the contract can be specifically performed.[12] Equity regards the assignor's conscience as 'bound' by the receipt of consideration and the assignor holds the property on trust for the assignee until the transfer is complete. This is the converse of the maxim 'equity will not assist a volunteer'.

Receipt of consideration also attracts equity's intervention where the property assigned is 'future property'. This is discussed below. Again, equity regards the assignor's conscience as bound by the consideration. Once the future property comes into the hands of the assignor, equity will deem done that which ought to be done and will insist the assignor complete the transfer, so long as the contract can be specifically performed.

Gifts

In the absence of consideration, equity regards the donor's conscience as bound when the donor has done all that she alone must do to make the assignment effective. This is the rule in *Milroy v Lord*,[13] as refined for Australian purposes by statute and the High Court decision in *Corin v Patton*.[14] [9.9]

In *Milroy v Lord*, an uncle attempted to assign shares to a trustee to hold on behalf of his niece. He executed a deed assigning the shares to the intended trustee and gave the intended trustee the share certificates. However, this was not the method required to legally assign shares. At law, the shares were not transferred until the assignment was recorded in the company books, following receipt of a transfer executed by both the assignee and assignor. Failure to comply with the relevant procedure was not discovered until after the uncle's death. The uncle had clearly intended his niece get the benefit of the shares, but had the uncle done enough so that, in equity, his conscience (and therefore his estate) would be regarded as bound by the gift?

It was held that he had not done enough. The test was said to be whether the assignor had done 'everything which, according to the nature of the property comprised in the settlement, was necessary to be done in order to transfer the property and render the settlement binding on him'.[15] The uncle had taken no steps to sign the relevant transfer, and he had not armed his agent with sufficient authority to sign it without further reference to him.

The phrase 'everything which … was necessary to be done in order to transfer the property and render the settlement binding on him' begs a question. By whom must these steps be taken? Has the assignor done all that is necessary when he has taken all the steps that he *alone* must take to transfer the property, even if that leaves some outstanding step which the assignee or some third party will have to perform, or does the term mean 'all that can possibly be done to transfer the property'?

The difference can be illustrated by reference to *Re Rose*.[16] Here, a husband assigned shares to his wife. He executed all the necessary forms and forwarded them to the company. The transfer was eventually registered. The husband died soon afterwards, and the question arose as to which of the husband or wife had been entitled to the shares on a certain date

12 See chapter 3.
13 (1862) 4 De GF & J 264; 45 ER 1185; *Sourcebook* 9.2a, p 207.
14 (1990) 169 CLR 540; *Sourcebook* 9.2b, p 208.
15 *Milroy v Lord* (1862) 4 De G F & J 264, 274–5; 45 ER 1185, 1189.
16 [1952] Ch 449.

some months prior to his death. (Taxation on the shares would have been payable by the husband's estate if he had been entitled to them.) On the relevant date, the transfer forms had been forwarded to the company, but registration had not yet occurred. If the test from *Milroy v Lord* meant 'all that had to be done by the assignor alone', then the husband had done all that he had to do (as the remaining steps were to be taken by the company secretary), and the wife would be the owner of the shares in equity.[17] But if the test meant 'all that can possibly be done to transfer the property', the wife would not be the owner in equity until the company secretary registered the transfer.

[9.10] In all Australian States bar Queensland (where legislation adopted the first interpretation[18]), this question was resolved in *Corin v Patton*.[19] A dying woman attempted to assign her interest in land, held as joint tenant with her husband, to her brother on trust. She was to be the beneficiary of the trust, and she would then leave her beneficial interest to her children in her will. The aim was to ensure that her husband would not be entitled to the whole of the land as surviving joint tenant. She executed all the necessary transfer documents. However, the land was mortgaged, and the woman died without making arrangements for the production of the title deed by the mortgagee[20] to allow registration of the transfer to occur.

The High Court held by majority that she had not done all that she alone had to do to allow the assignment to be recognised in equity. Three members of the court considered the meaning of the test in *Milroy v Lord*. In a joint judgment, Mason CJ and McHugh J held that equity regarded the assignment as complete when the donor had taken all the steps that she *alone* had to take to ensure the effectiveness of the transaction. As long as the donee could complete any remaining steps without the assistance of the court, equity would regard the transfer as binding.[21] This would have required the woman to have executed all necessary transfer forms *and* arranged for the production of the title for registration, or at least armed her brother with authority to request production of the title deed from the mortgagee. Her brother would then have been able to take any other steps necessary for registration himself.

Deane J adopted a more complex explanation of the meaning of the rule in *Milroy v Lord*. His Honour held that, in addition to showing that the donor has taken all steps that she alone must take to ensure the assignment, she also had to put the gift 'beyond the recall or intervention of the donor'.[22] Mrs Patton had not put the transaction beyond her recall as she had not arranged for production of the title document.[23] When the donor has done all that she alone must do to enable the donee to perfect the assignment, usually the gift will coincidentally be beyond the donor's recall. But, on the facts of this case, it could be argued that another objection to the assignment structure employed was that, even if the assignment had been successful, Mrs Patton would *not* have put the property beyond recall. If the assignment to the trustee was effective, Mrs Patton would have become the

17 The husband would hold the shares on trust for the wife until registration was complete.

18 *Property Law Act 1974* (Qld) s 200.

19 (1990) 169 CLR 540.

20 In some jurisdictions, the assignee can insist the mortgagee produce the title for registration of subsequent dealings: see, eg, *Transfer of Land Act 1958* (Vic) s 86.

21 *Corin v Patton* (1990) 169 CLR 540, 559. Their Honours endorsed the view of Griffith CJ in the earlier decision of *Anning v Anning* (1907) 4 CLR 1049.

22 *Corin v Patton* (1990) 169 CLR 540, 582.

23 Ibid 583.

only person beneficially entitled to the trust property. She could then have called for the property to be transferred to her under the rule in *Saunders v Vautier*.[24] As she could so simply reclaim the land, then according to Deane J, she would not have put the gift of the land 'beyond her recall'.[25]

Since *Corin v Patton*, broad support for the position that equity will recognise an assignment of legal property as binding on the assignor when the assignor has taken all steps that she alone can take has emerged. This has the advantage of certainty. It is usually possible to consider the assignment of all types of legal property and identify the point at which the assignor will have met those requirements. [9.11]

However, sometimes there can be factual doubts concerning whether the donee *has yet* been placed in a position where he can complete the gift to him without assistance. This kind of problem can arise where there is doubt about the extent of the authority given to a donor's agent to complete a transaction.[26] In *Marchesi v Apostolou*,[27] one solicitor acted for both the transferor and the transferee in an attempted gift of land to a trustee. Transfer documents were executed but no other steps were taken. Never having been registered, the transfer was incomplete at law. It was later argued that the transfer was nevertheless complete at equity. It was argued that the transfer was complete in equity once the solicitor held the executed documents on behalf of the transferee; thereafter, the transferee could have completed the assignment itself. Jessup J held that, where a solicitor acted for both parties in the transaction, the solicitor would not hold the transfer documents on behalf of the transferee until he had the transferor's authority to treat them as the property of the transferee. On the facts, the solicitor did not have such authority; the transferor had intended to pay stamp duty on the transaction himself and it could not be inferred that the transfer documents were the property of the transferee until stamping had occurred. The solicitor had always held the transfer documents as the transferor's agent only.[28]

A gift was also held to be incomplete in *Isin v Ozen*.[29] Sons had attempted to transfer property to their mother as a gift. The transfer documents were signed by the sons and returned to the solicitors who signed on behalf of the mother. However, the transfer could not complete as the mortgage over the property had not been discharged, and the mortgagee had not been instructed to release the certificate of title. When the mortgage was later discharged, the solicitors obtained the certificate of title. The sons by then had formed an intention to give their mother a life interest instead and signed a transfer in registrable form. The issue was whether the mother held only a life interest or whether the gift of the fee simple was complete in equity. The Court of Appeal held that the transfer was not complete when the mortgage was discharged and the certificate returned, as the solicitors needed further instructions from the sons to register the transfer.[30] [9.12]

---

24 (1841) 4 Beav 115; 49 ER 282. See [13.3].

25 *Corin v Patton* (1990) 169 CLR 540, 583.

26 This was a problem in *Milroy v Lord* itself. It was held the uncle's attorney did not have sufficient authorisation to allow him to complete the transaction without further reference to the uncle.

27 [2007] FCA 986.

28 For the impact of electronic conveyancing on gifts of land, see: S Barkehall Thomas, 'Electronic conveyancing and incomplete gifts of Torrens Land' (2018) 27(1) *Australian Property Law Journal* 87.

29 (2017) 19 BPR 38,123.

30 Ibid 38,134 [48]–[51] (White JA, Macfarlan and Leming JJA agreeing). See also *Stone v Registrar of Titles* [2012] WASC 21.

[9.13] In summary, the law in Australia is clear. Equity regards the transfer as complete where the transferor has done all she alone must do to perfect the assignment. The transferee must be in a position to complete any outstanding steps for legal assignment without the assistance of the transferor or the court. This requires delivery of any necessary document to the transferee in that capacity.

Non-assignable rights

[9.14] Some assets or rights cannot be assigned at law or equity. If the transaction in question is an attempted assignment of one of these kinds of rights, the assignment will fail.

[9.15] Equity generally takes a robust view and allows the assignment of rights that are unassignable at common law.[31] There are, however, some limitations. The benefit of contracts of personal service cannot be assigned because the identity of the person for whom the service is to be performed may matter to the person who has to perform it. Further, most assignments of bare rights of action have historically been regarded as void on the basis of public policy unless the assignee has a genuine commercial interest in the litigation.[32] The reason for the policy is said to be 'procedural sin: the law disapproves of it because it thinks it is a misuse of the legal process when people muscle in on lawsuits that are none of their business'.[33] The Queensland Court of Appeal in *Gladstone Ports Corporation Ltd v Murphy Operator Pty Ltd*[34] recently questioned the policy basis for the disapproval. The Court noted that '[T]he instinctive aversion of judges to any encouragement of a trade in certain causes of action is justified'.[35] The Court then acknowledged that the law permits the assignment of some forms of choses in action such as shares and debts, and stated:

> The law concerning the assignability of choses in action has developed upon the basis of changing foundations and, in the course of changing apperceptions accompanying changing social conditions, this has resulted in a degree of doctrinal incoherence ...[36]

The Court added:

> The development of litigation in Australia has not yet reached the stage at which there is a general trade in tort claims, for example, by offering for sale claims for damages for personal injuries or for defamation on an open market underwritten by the judiciary's preparedness to vindicate claims in the hands of plaintiffs whose only interest in the wrongdoing lies in the recoupment of an investment. Such a development would

31 Part choses in action, such as part of a debt, are unassignable at common law.

32 *Trendtex Trading Corporation v Credit Suisse* [1982] AC 679, considered in *Equuscorp Pty Ltd v Haxton* (2012) 246 CLR 498; *Sourcebook* 9.5b, p 222. The meaning of 'genuine commercial interest' is not settled in Australia. See the discussion in *Bakewell v Anchorage Capital Master Offshore Ltd* (2019) 372 ALR 349.

33 Andrew Tettenborn, 'Assignment of Rights to Compensation' [2007] *Lloyd's Maritime and Commercial Law Quarterly* 392, 403.

34 (2020) 384 ALR 725.

35 Ibid 746, [78] (Sofronoff P, Morrison JA and Davis J).

36 Ibid 747, [79]. See also *Bakewell v Anchorage Capital Master Offshore Ltd* (2019) 372 ALR 349, 361 where Bell P (Macfarlan and White JJA agreeing) in the New South Wales Court of Appeal said: 'The proper extent of the prohibition on the assignment of bare causes of action cannot, in my opinion, be regarded as settled beyond argument. Indeed, the public policy case for the continued existence of the prohibition at all may be open to argument and critical appraisal.'

> depend upon whether it would affect public confidence in the integrity of the courts if they were to cease to be [the] place in which an injured party's rights were vindicated and were to become, instead, a clearing house for a general speculation in claims.[37]

Contracts can also stipulate that contractual rights cannot be assigned.[38]

Non-assignability often arises by statute. Statutes may expressly or impliedly make an asset unassignable. In *Re Bruynius*,[39] legislation expressly forbade assignment of superannuation pensions.[40] In contrast, the statute in *Tasmanian Seafoods Pty Ltd v MacQueen*[41] impliedly restricted assignments of abalone diving licences. It provided that licences were for personal diving and had to be surrendered when the diver ceased to be a commercial diver, thus indicating the licences were unassignable. [9.16]

Nevertheless, equity does not completely quarantine non-assignable benefits. A holder of a contractual right can, by self-declaration, hold that right on trust for another. So, for example, the benefit of a contract of personal service can be held by the contracting party on trust for a beneficiary.[42] In this way, equity recognises a limited form of interest in the beneficiary even though neither the common law nor equity would allow the contractual right to be assigned directly to the beneficiary. [9.17]

Some rights cannot be assigned or form the subject-matter of a trust by self-declaration[43] because they are in no sense property. Instead, they are mere expectancies. Although the would-be assignor may one day receive property, there is no assignable right. For example, an object of a discretionary trust or power of appointment only has a mere expectancy. This expectancy is not a property interest capable of assignment.[44] [9.18]

Future property

Future property cannot be assigned at common law because the assignor has no title to assign.[45] Future property cannot be effectively assigned without consideration in equity. Thus, the absence of consideration renders an assignment of future property entirely ineffectual. [9.19]

Property can be 'future' in two senses. The property may presently exist, but not yet be owned by the would-be assignor; for example, shares owned by A, that B is expecting A to transfer to B on B's next birthday. The shares are 'future' to B; although they exist, B does not own them. Or property may not yet be in existence. An example of property not [9.20]

---

37 (2020) 384 ALR 725, 747.

38 *Linden Gardens Trust Ltd v Lenesta Sludge Disposals Ltd* [1994] 1 AC 85, 108.

39 [1995] 1 Qd R 492.

40 See also *Carmody v Superannuation Complaints Tribunal* [2020] FCA 291. The superannuation benefit in this case was also non-assignable. The trustee deducted child support from the member's invalidity payments in compliance with a garnishee order from the Child Support Agency. The question was whether this had effected an impermissible assignment of his benefit. It had not. For discussion of the difference between an assignment and a garnishee order, see [121].

41 (2005) 15 Tas R 1.

42 *Don King Productions Inc v Warren* [2000] Ch 291; *St Vincent de Paul Society Qld v Ozcare Ltd* (2009) 1 Qd R 457.

43 See chapter 13.

44 *Kennon v Spry* (2008) 238 CLR 366, 417 (Heydon J in dissent).

45 Note that under the PPSA '[a] security agreement may provide for security interests in after-acquired property': s 18(2).

yet in existence is afforded by a broodmare in foal. The unborn foal is property that is not yet in existence. A recent case example is provided by *Exotic Retirement Living v Construct By Design Commercial*.[46] The plaintiff and defendant were involved in the construction of residential apartments. The defendant had entered into a contract with a third party for the manufacture of a car stacker for the apartments. The contract between the plaintiff and defendant was brought to an end, and the defendant assigned its 'rights, title and interest … (if any)'[47] in the car stacker to the plaintiff. The plaintiff sought an order that it was entitled to possession and an order for delivery up of the stacker. This was refused. At the date of the assignment, the defendant had no title to the stacker which 'was presumably in the course of construction somewhere outside this country'.[48]

[9.21] It can be difficult to determine whether property presently exists or is 'future'. Most problems arise over what can generally be called 'income cases'. Here it is crucial to determine whether the assignor is attempting to assign the income not yet earned only, which is future property, or the underlying property that gives rise to the income, which is presently existing property.

[9.22] Many forms of property produce income. For example, X owns a mare in foal and attempts to assign the unborn foal to Y. The unborn foal cannot be assigned for value or by gift at common law. If X has received consideration, equity will recognise the assignment of the unborn foal; when it is born, X will have to transfer it to Y because X's conscience is bound in equity.[49] Equity will not enforce an attempted gift of the unborn foal because there is no consideration that binds X's conscience. Equity will not assist a volunteer here. But X can voluntarily assign by gift the broodmare to Y. That assignment will have the effect of carrying with it the foal; when the foal is born it will belong to Y. The foal is 'income' or, more correctly, natural increase, and the broodmare is the underlying pre-existing property that gives rise to the 'income' of the foal when it is born.

[9.23] The leading cases in the area concern more complicated facts than those given above. In *Norman v Federal Commissioner of Taxation*,[50] a taxpayer tried to assign income. The deed of assignment voluntarily assigned dividends to be earned on shares. The High Court held unanimously that the yet-to-be declared dividends were future property and could not be assigned without consideration.[51] They were 'future' in that the dividend did not yet exist and indeed might never be declared by the company. Another clause of the deed of assignment attempted voluntarily to assign the right to interest to be earned on a loan. The loan had some unusual features. Interest only became payable on an annual basis, but the borrower could repay the loan at will. This meant that if the borrower chose to repay the loan in a particular year, no interest would become payable in the following year. It could not be said at the time of the assignment that the interest would ever be payable. A majority of the High Court held that this was therefore an assignment of future property and, as it was not for consideration, it was ineffective.[52]

46 [2018] NSWSC 860.
47 See clause 2.2 set out at [13].
48 [19]. The assignment was for value but not all the consideration had been paid. See [9.25].
49 See [9.8].
50 (1963) 109 CLR 9; *Sourcebook* 9.3a, p 212.
51 (1963) 109 CLR 9, 16 (Dixon CJ), 18 (McTiernan J), 23 (Menzies J), 40 (Windeyer J), 41 (Owen J).
52 Ibid 16 (Dixon CJ), 21 (Menzies J), 41 (Owen J).

Norman can be contrasted with *Shepherd v Federal Commissioner of Taxation*.[53] The inventor of a furniture castor granted a licence to produce the castors to a manufacturer who was to pay him royalties based on the number produced. He attempted to assign voluntarily a percentage of royalties. The Commissioner argued that this was an assignment of future property. As the manufacturer was not obliged to produce any castors at all, it could not be said with certainty that any royalties would be earned under the agreement. However, the High Court held by majority[54] that the transaction here was an assignment of part of the *contractual right* to receive royalties, rather than an assignment of the yet unearned royalties themselves. The metaphor used to explain this was that this was an assignment of part of the 'tree' (or asset) that produced the 'fruit' (or income). The 'tree' was presently existing property.[55] *Shepherd* and *Norman* are difficult to reconcile and ultimately turn on the wording of the assignments. However, *Shepherd* appears good authority for the proposition that assignments of assets that may produce income in the future can be made voluntarily. [9.24]

Should a person who has a mere expectancy or an interest that is 'future property' attempt to assign it to another for valuable consideration, equity treats the transaction as a contract to assign. If and when the assignor receives the property, equity deems done that which ought to have been done and regards the property as owned beneficially by the assignee.[56] This is because the assignee has given consideration, and the assignor's conscience is bound.[57] [9.25]

Assignment of equitable property

Property that is only recognised in equity can only be assigned in equity. Equitable proprietary interests grew out of the willingness of courts of equity to grant relief against those who bound their conscience by agreeing to perform obligations in respect of property.[58] For example, at common law the trustee is the legal owner of land but is subject to an obligation to hold it for the benefit of another. As the beneficiary's interest in land can only be enforced in equity, it can also only be assigned in equity. [9.26]

Unlike the common law rules on transfer of property, equity does not differentiate between varieties of equitable property. There is only one method of equitable assignment, regardless of whether the equitable property is, for example, a beneficial interest in a trust, a [9.27]

53 (1965) 113 CLR 385; *Sourcebook* 9.3b, p 216.

54 (1965) 113 CLR 385, 393 (Barwick CJ), 397 (Kitto J).

55 The two decisions, taken together, have attracted criticism: see MGL [6-235]. The decisions seem to turn on a deeply theoretical dissection of the words used in the deeds of assignment rather than on the effect of the transactions.

56 *Holroyd v Marshall* (1862) 10 HL Cas 191; 11 ER 999; *Sourcebook* 9.3c, p 218. The property must be sufficiently described so that when it comes into existence, it can be identified as property to which the contract applies: *Tailby v Official Receiver* (1888) 13 App Cas 523, 543 (Lord Macnaghten). Equally, an agreement to assign a chose in action for valuable consideration is enforceable in equity without compliance with the statutory requirements: *Jaeger v Bendigo and Adelaide Bank Ltd* [2018] NSWCA 116, [41] per Leeming JA (Payne JA and Sackville AJA agreeing).

57 In *Exotic Retirement Living v Construct by Design Commercial* [2018] NSWSC 860, discussed at [9.20], the assignment was expressed to be for valuable consideration. It was argued that the document could be valid as an agreement to assign future property for consideration. Consideration included the requirement for the plaintiff to make outstanding payments to the supplier of the stacker. The payments had not been made and McDougall J refused to enforce the assignment.

58 See [8.5].

partnership share or another equitable chose in action. The equitable method of assignment was discussed by Windeyer J in *Norman's case*:

> If the interest to be assigned is a creature of equity, such as the beneficial interest of a cestui que trust, then, apart from any statutory provisions, an assignment of it can, of course, only be effected in equity; for the common law does not know it. Any present assignment of such an interest, that is to say of a chose in equity, is therefore necessarily an equitable assignment. Such an assignment can be by way of gift; and, except that writing is required by s 9 of the Statute of Frauds, no formality is necessary beyond a clear expression of an intention to make an immediate disposition.
>
> ...
>
> It seems to me that, in principle ... the delivery of a deed couched in terms of present gift manifests, in the best possible way, the intention of the assignor to make an immediate and irrevocable transfer.[59]

[9.28] Thus, a *gift* of equitable property is complete in equity when the assignor has manifested an immediate, irrevocable intention to assign that property. At that point equity regards the assignor's conscience as bound by the gift. Despite equity's acceptance that beneficial title has passed, the transaction is still subject to statutory requirements concerning the need for writing, as Windeyer J noted in the passage quoted above. Without the necessary writing the assignment may be rendered invalid or at least unenforceable. These provisions come from the old Statute of Frauds and are discussed below at [9.36].

[9.29] As all equitable property can be described as equitable choses in action,[60] an issue is whether statutory transfer methods for choses in action apply to them. Statutory assignment, and its application to equitable choses in action, is discussed in the following section.

Statutory assignment

[9.30] One of the Judicature Act reforms was to provide a statutory method of assignment of debts and other choses (or things) in action that had previously been unassignable at common law.[61] Many kinds of legal choses in action such as bills of exchange and insurance policies have specific statutory methods of transfer, but additionally the legislature had provided a 'default' mechanism for other legal choses. The first part of the current New South Wales provision, contained in s 12 of the *Conveyancing Act 1919* is used as an example:

> **Assignments of debts and choses in action**
>
> Any absolute assignment by writing under the hand of the assignor (not purporting to be by way of charge only) of any debt or other legal chose in action, of which express notice in writing has been given to the debtor, trustee, or other person from whom the assignor would have been entitled to receive or claim such debt or chose in action, shall be, and be deemed to have been effectual in law (subject to all equities which would have been entitled to priority over the right of the assignee if this Act had not passed) to pass and

59 *Norman v Federal Commissioner of Taxation* (1963) 109 CLR 9, 31–2.

60 *Commissioner of Stamp Duties (Qld) v Livingston* [1965] AC 694.

61 See [1.18], n 25.

> transfer the legal right to such debt or chose in action from the date of such notice, and all legal and other remedies for the same, and the power to give a good discharge for the same without the concurrence of the assignor …[62]

A practical example of use of the section is the assignment of a debt. D has a personal loan for $5000 from XYZ Bank. XYZ Bank decides to sell its entire personal loan portfolio to ABC Bank. This can be formally accomplished by use of the statutory assignment legislation. Express written notice of the assignment must be given to D. The provision only applies to 'absolute' assignments.[63] An assignment will not be absolute if only part of the chose in action is being assigned; for example, a letter from XYZ Bank assigning to ABC Bank $2500 of the $5000 owed by D would not be caught by the provision because it is not an absolute assignment.[64] Similarly, if XYZ Bank only intended D's debt to be used as security for a debt XYZ Bank owed to ABC Bank, the section would not be enlivened.[65] [9.31]

While there is no particular form of assignment dictated by the legislation, the instrument must be in writing and signed by the assignor.[66] It has been held that an absolute assignment governed by the legislation would usually be expressed in the form of 'the assignor "hereby assigns"' and a document expressed as 'the assignors "will assign"' has been held to not effect an absolute assignment.[67]

The assignment of the chose takes effect when 'express notice in writing' has been given to the person who is liable to pay the assignor. There are, however, no statutory time limitations on the giving of notice.[68] It has been said that *receipt* of notice is not technically required; under evidence legislation, a presumption will arise that notice was received a certain time after posting unless evidence is presented that this was not so.[69] Notice to the debtor can be given by either the assignee or the assignor.[70] Therefore, a statutory assignment of an entire legal chose in action is complete at law when either (a) the assignor has given notice to the debtor of the assignment, or (b) the assignor has armed the assignee with the ability to give notice, and the assignee has duly given notice.[71] [9.32]

---

62 Equivalent provisions are: *Civil Law (Property) Act 2006* (ACT) s 205; *Law of Property Act 2000* (NT) s 182; *Property Law Act 1974* (Qld) s 199; *Law of Property Act 1936* (SA) s 15; *Conveyancing and Law of Property Act 1884* (Tas) s 86; *Property Law Act 1958* (Vic) s 134; *Property Law Act 1969* (WA) s 20.

63 In Western Australia, partial assignments are also covered by the legislation: see *Property Law Act 1969* (WA) s 20(3).

64 See, eg, the observation of Gleeson JA in *Segal v Sharma* [2020] NSWCA 192, [7] that 'the weight of authority favours the view that an assignment of part of a debt is necessarily an equitable assignment because the statutory method of assignment is not available.' Partial assignments are discussed below at [9.35].

65 See now *Personal Property Securities Act 2009* (Cth).

66 The statute does not allow an agent to sign; however, it has been held that the signature of the liquidator of the assignor suffices: *Carob Industries Pty Ltd (in liq) v Simto Pty Ltd* (2000) 23 WAR 515.

67 *Hazard Systems Pty Ltd v Car-Tech Services Pty Ltd (in liq)* [2013] NSWCA 314, [19] (Basten JA).

68 Ibid [21].

69 *Leveraged Equities Ltd v Goodridge* (2011) 191 FCR 71; *Szepesvary v Weston* (2018) 363 ALR 379.

70 *Anning v Anning* (1907) 4 CLR 1049, 1059.

71 If the assignment is not complete at law, for example, because notice has not been given, the assignment may be complete in equity if there is compliance with the rules for incomplete gifts, discussed at [9.9] onwards or if consideration has been paid. In *Szepesvary v Weston* (2018) 363 ALR 379, 385, the Full Federal Court (Perry, Moshinsky and Lee JJ) noted 'the giving of notice to a debtor is not, of course, essential to the validity of an assignment of a debt in equity'. The Court discussed at 389 how an equitable assignee can recover the debt.

[9.33] It is unclear whether the statutory method of assignment was intended to apply to equitable choses in action in addition to legal choses in action. At first glance, this suggestion seems unlikely. The legislation in most Australian jurisdictions states that the section applies to debt (which is a legal chose in action) 'or other thing in action', and discusses when an assignment will be deemed to have been effectual in law. As equitable choses in action are only recognised in equity, there would never have been an occasion on which an assignment of an equitable chose *could* have been regarded as effective in law. On the other hand, the terminology under the provisions in place in the ACT is more general, referring only to a 'thing in action' and arguably includes both legal and equitable choses in action. Where the legislature could have specified 'legal things in action', the broader term 'thing in action' was employed.[72]

[9.34] The better view is that the legislatures did not intend the statutory method to be the *only* transfer mechanism for equitable choses in action. There are High Court dicta that equitable choses *may* be assigned by the statutory method but it would appear the statutory method is not a compulsory formality.[73] Instead, the section provides an optional method for the assignment of equitable choses in action, in addition to the method described above,[74] which, if followed, will be regarded as effective. Compliance with the statutory assignment method, including giving notice to the person required to discharge the obligation, would be a very clear manifestation of an immediate intention to assign. Nevertheless, an equitable chose in action can still be assigned by the assignor manifesting an intention to immediately assign the chose by some other method.

Legal property that can only be assigned in equity

[9.35] Because the statutory assignment method described above only applies to *absolute* assignment of legal choses in action, the law still does not allow the *partial* assignment of a legal chose in action.[75] Debts cannot be assigned in parts at common law,[76] and partial assignment is excluded by the statutory assignment mechanism. Nevertheless, equity may be able to recognise a partial assignment. A part legal chose in action is treated in the same manner as equitable property for assignment purposes.[77] So it will be sufficient if there is a clear expression of an intention to make an immediate disposition of the part chose.

Statutory formalities

[9.36] Despite all that has been said above, an assignment might still be void or unenforceable if it fails to comply with any relevant statutory formalities. For over 300 years, assignments of some interests in property have been subject to statutory writing requirements. The *Statute of Frauds* was originally enacted in 1677 to guard against 'the great danger of parol

72 The provisions in New South Wales, Queensland, South Australia, Tasmania, Victoria and Western Australia (see n 62) use the adjective 'legal'.

73 *Federal Commissioner of Taxation v Everett* (1980) 143 CLR 440, 447; *Sourcebook* 9.6.1a, p 225.

74 See [9.27].

75 In Western Australia, partial assignments are also covered by the legislation: see *Property Law Act 1969* (WA) s 20(3).

76 A partial legal chose in action is the only kind of legal property that cannot be assigned at law.

77 *Norman v Federal Commissioner of Taxation* (1963) 109 CLR 9, 33.

declarations'[78] in a time when the laws of evidence were still unsettled. All Australian States have current versions of what was originally the *Statute of Frauds*.[79] In Victoria, for example, this is contained in s 53 of the *Property Law Act 1958*, which is reproduced below.

> **Instruments required to be in writing**
>
> **(1)** Subject to the provisions hereinafter contained with respect to the creation of interest in land by parol–
>
> **(a)** no interest in land can be created or disposed of except by writing signed by the person creating or conveying the same or by his agent thereunto lawfully authorised in writing or by will or by operation of law;
>
> **(b)** a declaration of trust respecting any land or interest therein must be manifested and proved by some writing signed by some person who is able to declare such trust or by his will;
>
> **(c)** a disposition of an equitable interest or trust subsisting at the time of disposition must be in writing signed by the person disposing of the same, or by his agent thereunto lawfully authorised in writing, or by will.
>
> **(2)** This section shall not affect the creation or operation of resulting, implied or constructive trusts.

These provisions will only be discussed briefly here.[80]

Many assignments are caught by this legislation. An assignment of an asset to another is one method of 'disposition'.[81] It would seem that the general words 'interest in land' in subsection (a) include both legal and equitable interests in land.[82] Unless it is reduced to writing at time of disposition, the assignment of an equitable or legal interest in land is void. [9.37]

There are several exceptions to this. Dispositions of land by will, or by resulting, implied or constructive trusts are excluded explicitly.[83] The sections have no effect on the law relating to part performance of contracts.[84] [9.38]

78 *Forster v Hale* (1798) 3 Ves Jun 696, 707 (Lord Alvanley).

79 *Civil Law (Property) Act 2006* (ACT) s 201; *Conveyancing Act 1919* (NSW) s 23C; *Law of Property Act 1936* (SA) s 29; *Conveyancing and Law of Property Act 1884* (Tas) s 60(2); *Property Law Act 1969* (WA) s 34. Note that under the *Civil Law (Property) Act 2006* (ACT) s 201, declarations of trust over land must be in writing. Note also that in Queensland and the Northern Territory, dispositions of subsisting equitable interests need only be manifested and proved in writing: *Property Law Act 1974* (Qld) s 11(1)(c); *Law of Property Act 2000* (NT) s 10(1)(c).

80 See also [15.5].

81 However, care must be taken to ensure the transaction in question is a final disposition, and not just a mandate given to a person to apply the property which is liable to revocation: *Comptroller of Stamps (Vic) v Howard-Smith* (1936) 54 CLR 614; *Sourcebook* 9.7b, p 229.

82 *Adamson v Hayes* (1973) 130 CLR 276.

83 See *Property Law Act 1958* (Vic) ss 53(1)(a), 55; see also *Civil Law (Property) Act 2006* (ACT) ss 201(4), 203; *Conveyancing Act 1919* (NSW) s 23C(2); *Law of Property Act 2000* (NT) s 10(2); *Property Law Act 1974* (Qld) s 11(2); *Law of Property Act 1936* (SA) ss 29(2), 31; *Conveyancing and Law of Property Act 1884* (Tas) s 60(2), (5); *Property Law Act 1969* (WA) ss 34(2), 36.

84 This is explicitly stated in *Property Law Act 1958* (Vic) s 55; see also *Civil Law (Property) Act 2006* (ACT) s 203; *Conveyancing Act 1919* (NSW) s 23E; *Law of Property Act 1936* (SA) s 31; *Conveyancing and Law of Property Act 1884* (Tas) s 60(5); *Property Law Act 1969* (WA) s 36.

[9.39] In contrast to the provisions of subsection (a), subsection (b) only requires that the transaction be manifested and proved in writing.[85] This means that a trust of an interest in land can be created orally, and later reduced to writing. Until it is manifested and proved in writing, the trust is valid but unenforceable. There is no particular form of writing required, but the writing must set out the terms of the trust.[86]

[9.40] As subsection (a) applies to the *creation* of interests in land as well as the *disposition* of such interests, it would appear there is a potential overlap in operation between subsections (a) and (b). Declarations of trust *create* new equitable interests in land. As subsections (a) and (b) impose different formal requirements, this overlap had the potential of making subsection (b) otiose. The problem has been solved in recent years by treating subsection (b) as an exception to subsection (a).[87] Although all dispositions of interests in land and creations of other interests in land must be done in writing, interests in land created by declaration of trust need only be manifested and proved by some writing.

[9.41] Subsection (c) applies to dispositions of subsisting equitable interests in either land or personalty.[88] It requires that the disposition be made in writing.[89] What is important is that the equitable interest exists *prior* to the disposition. The subsection is not concerned with the creation of new equitable interests. As all existing equitable property can be assigned by the manifestation of an immediate intention to assign,[90] subsection (c) invalidates purely oral manifestations of an intention to assign.[91] One effect of the subsection is that, although assignments of personal property do not need to be made in writing, assignments of equitable interests in personal property do require writing.

[9.42] Issues arise concerning the effect of subsection (c) on declarations of trust. For example, a person who holds an equitable interest as beneficiary under a trust might declare a sub-trust over it. Is such a transaction required to be done in writing? The question turns on whether a declaration of sub-trust amounts to a 'disposition' of a subsisting equitable interest. In *Howard-Smith*,[92] Dixon J listed declarations of sub-trust as one of the methods of disposing of an equitable interest. *Grey v Inland Revenue Commissioners* treats a declaration of trust as a 'disposition' of a subsisting equitable interest.[93] However, another view is to the effect that a settlor who declares a trust over a subsisting equitable interest may or may not be 'disposing' of all her title and interest, depending on the facts of the case. Where the settlor intends to retain duties as a trustee, it is hard to argue that a complete disposition has occurred.[94] If this is so, then the declaration of trust should not be treated as a disposition of a subsisting equitable interest, and would not need to be done in writing.

85 Except in the ACT: see n 79.

86 *Re McGowan & Valentini Trusts* (2021) 63 VR 449.

87 *Secretary, Department of Social Security v James* (1990) 20 ALD 5; *Sourcebook* 15.2b, p 390; *Hagan v Waterhouse* (1991) 34 NSWLR 308.

88 *Grey v Inland Revenue Commissioners* [1960] AC 1; *Sourcebook* 9.7c, p 230.

89 In Queensland and the Northern Territory, the disposition only need be manifested and proved by some writing: *Property Law Act 1974* (Qld) s 11(1)(c); *Law of Property Act 2000* (NT) s 10(1)(c).

90 See [9.27].

91 *Shepherd v Federal Commissioner of Taxation* (1965) 113 CLR 385.

92 *Comptroller of Stamps (Vic) v Howard-Smith* (1936) 54 CLR 614, 621–2.

93 [1960] AC 1. The case involved a subsisting equitable interest in personalty, rather than land.

94 MGL [7-205].

Summary

The following is a summary of the principles discussed in this chapter: [9.43]

(1) The asset or right in question may not be assignable either in equity or at common law. If that is the case, neither law nor equity can recognise an attempted assignment.

(2) Assuming the asset can be assigned, the question whether the assignee has given valuable consideration is crucial. If consideration has been given, equity will usually deem done that which ought to have been done, and recognise beneficial title in the assignee.

(3) If no consideration has been given, it is necessary to determine whether the property being assigned is legal or equitable property before we can determine whether the property has been assigned, either at law or equity.

We will first consider the attempted gifts of equitable property. Equitable property is only recognised in equity and can only be assigned in equity. Equitable property is assigned when the assignor demonstrates or manifests an immediate intention to dispose of the property. According to Windeyer J in *Norman's case*, this is best demonstrated by deed, although a deed is not essential.[95] Writing of some form, however, is essential because of the statutory formality requirements which apply to the disposition of subsisting equitable interests.[96] [9.44]

Figure 9.1 Gift of equitable property

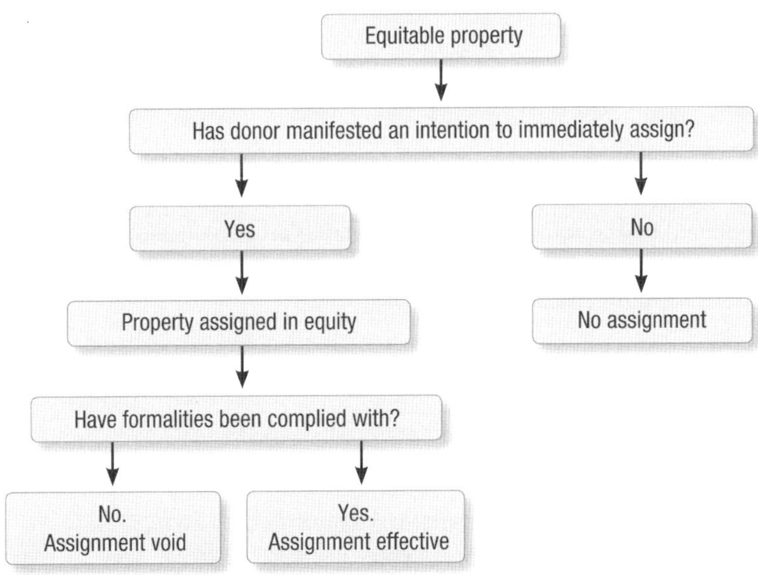

95 *Norman v Federal Commissioner of Taxation* (1963) 109 CLR 9, 32.

96 In Queensland and the Northern Territory, the disposition only need be manifested and proved by some writing: *Property Law Act 1974* (Qld) s 11(1)(c); *Law of Property Act 2000* (NT) s 10(1)(c).

[9.45] Legal property is assigned according to the transfer rules applicable to that kind of property. A gift of legal property is complete at law when all the steps required for completion of the assignment have occurred. When only some of those steps have occurred, equity may still regard the transaction as complete if the assignor has done all the necessary things that can *only* be done by her. Any outstanding steps must be able to be performed without her assistance. The assignor must have put the gift beyond recall. Statutory formalities apply to some assignments of legal property too, as s 53(1)(a) applies to dispositions of interests in land. However, assignments of personal property are not affected.

Figure 9.2 Gift of legal property

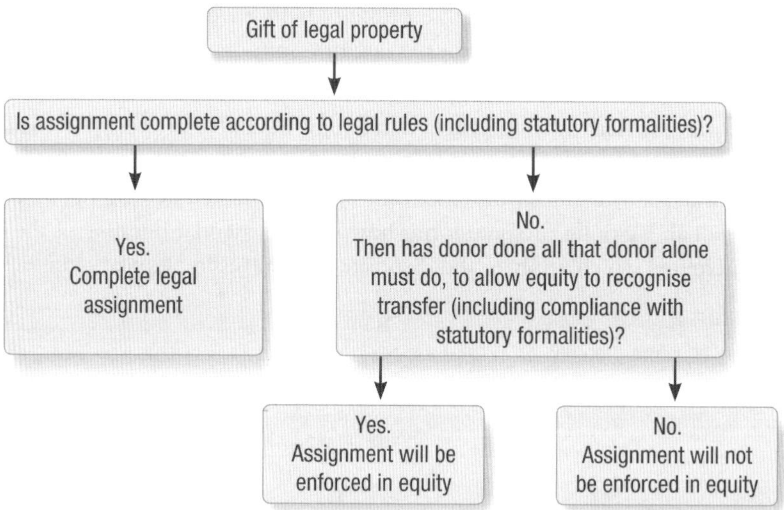

[9.46] One form of legal property, partial legal choses in action, cannot be assigned at law. These are assigned by the same method as equitable property. Statutory formalities do not impact on assignments of partial legal choses; they are not dispositions of land and are not dispositions of subsisting equitable interests.

Figure 9.3 Partial legal chose in action: unassignable at law

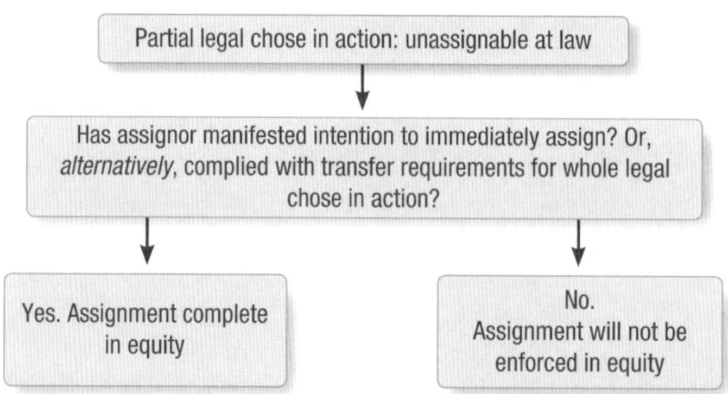

WHAT'S ONLINE?

Available at www.cambridge.org/highereducation/isbn/9781009232388/resources:

- Recommended further readings
- Further commentary
- Discussion topics
- Practice problem

PART D

EQUITABLE OBLIGATIONS

10

FIDUCIARY RELATIONSHIPS AND OBLIGATIONS

Introduction

Equity closely scrutinises relationships in which one party places trust and confidence in another. There are many examples of trust in human interaction, but equity cannot grant relief against every breach of trust and confidence, any more than contract law can enforce all promises. Only some trusting relationships[1] and some obligations of confidence[2] are protected. The relationships which equity protects are known as fiduciary relationships. [10.1]

A relationship of trust and confidence will be recognised as fiduciary where it arises from F (fiduciary) undertaking to act in the interests of B (beneficiary) in a matter which confers a discretion on F, and in respect of which the exercise of discretion affects B's economic interests. B may hand over property to F, such as an investor handing over money to an investment adviser. A settlor may hand property to F to hold on trust for B. Alternatively, B may entrust F with the task of negotiating a contract on behalf of B so that F is B's agent. Or F may be entrusted with the task of obtaining information on behalf of B which will enable B to exploit a commercial opportunity. This is also an example of agency. [10.2]

In all these cases, the relationship between F and B constitutes a fiduciary relationship. F will owe fiduciary obligations to B. If, in the second example, F negotiates to take the benefit of a contract for himself, and not for B, he has committed a breach of fiduciary obligation. Fiduciary relationships do not – or do not simply – require the fiduciary, F in these examples, to act reasonably, as may be the case in tort or contract. The essence of a fiduciary relationship is that the fiduciary must act *exclusively* in the interests of the beneficiary in matters coming within the scope of the relationship. [10.3]

The central concern of fiduciary law is the division between the management and enjoyment of property, which is broadly defined for this purpose to include such matters as information and the opportunity to obtain the benefit of a contract. (These latter are sometimes called 'soft property'.) Fiduciary obligations regulate managers' behaviour where their activities cannot be properly supervised by those on whose behalf they act, whom we will refer to as 'the beneficiaries'. This is achieved by imposing on them obligations which limit their pursuit of self-interest. The core obligations, discussed at [10.31], are the duty not to make a profit out of the relationship, and the duty not to place themselves in a position of conflict between self-interest and the duty owed to the beneficiary, or in a position where they owe conflicting duties to several beneficiaries.

Fiduciary relationships

Recognised fiduciary relationships

Like most legal concepts, the concept of the fiduciary does not lend itself to a dictionary definition.[3] It is more easily described than defined. Some legal relationships have long been [10.4]

1 Limited protection is given in respect of relationships affected by undue influence. See [7.18].
2 See chapter 12.
3 For discussions of the fiduciary concept, see PD Finn, *Fiduciary Obligations* (Law Book Co, 1977); PD Finn, 'The Fiduciary Principle' in TG Youdan (ed), *Equity, Fiduciaries and Trusts* (Carswell, 1989) 1; M Conaglen, *Fiduciary Loyalty* (Hart Publishing, 2010); J Edelman, 'When Do Fiduciary Duties Arise?' (2010) 126(2) *Law Quarterly Review* 302.

recognised as fiduciary. These relationships have been described as the 'first circle' of fiduciary relationships.[4] In each, the first party owes fiduciary obligations to the second. They are:

- Trustee–Beneficiary
- Solicitor–Client
- Director–Company
- Employee–Employer
- Agent–Principal
- Partner–Co-partner
- Executor–Beneficiaries of deceased's estate

[10.5] The list of established (or presumed) fiduciary relationships is not closed and other relationships can be added. A prime candidate is the relationship of investment adviser and client.[5] Moreover, there is no uniformity in the list of core fiduciary relationships across the common law world. The Canadian Supreme Court has held that the relationship between parent and child is 'intuitively fiduciary',[6] but no Australian court has held that parents are recognised fiduciaries. Even so, there may well be circumstances in which a parent managing a child's money will be subject to fiduciary obligations.

[10.6] The trust is regarded as the paradigm fiduciary relationship, although it has some special features not shared with the other fiduciary relationships.[7] The history of the law of fiduciary relationships has to a considerable extent involved the extension of trustees' obligations to other relationships perceived by courts to be 'trust-like'. What the relationships have in common is that the fiduciary is expected to act exclusively in the interests of another on matters covered by the relationship and is not permitted to pursue self-interest.[8]

[10.7] In most legal relationships self-interest is expected, and even considered desirable in a capitalist society; there is no expectation that one party will act in the other's interests. A relationship which could be argued to be diametrically opposed to a fiduciary relationship is that of vendor and purchaser. Although legislation and the general law impose basic requirements on contracting parties to avoid misleading and unconscionable conduct,[9] a sales contract is the classic legal relationship in which the pursuit of self-interest is legitimate and socially approved. The more closely a legal relationship approximates to that of vendor and purchaser, the less likely it is to be fiduciary.

4 See Finn, 'The Fiduciary Principle' (n 3) 33.

5 It is probable that the relationship is already established as fiduciary, but the development has been obscured by contractual exclusions of fiduciary obligations in contracts entered into with clients. See *Australian Securities and Investments Commission v Citigroup Global Markets Australia Pty Ltd (No 4)* (2007) 160 FCR 35; *Sourcebook* 10.6a, p 284. S Degeling and J Hudson, 'Credit Advisers, Consumer Credit, and Equitable Fiduciary Obligations' (2019) 47(1) *Federal Law Review* 64; S Degeling and J Hudson, 'Financial Robots as Instruments of Fiduciary Loyalty' (2018) 40(1) *Sydney Law Review* 63.

6 *M(K) v M(H)* 96 DLR (4th) 289, 323 (La Forest J); L Smith, 'Parenthood is a Fiduciary Relationship' (2020) 70(4) *University of Toronto Law Journal* 395.

7 In particular, trustees may come under a duty to act for unborn (and therefore unidentified) beneficiaries. *Breen v Williams* (1996) 186 CLR 71, 137 (Gummow J).

8 See Finn, 'The Fiduciary Principle' (n 3). The remedies for breach of fiduciary obligation were developed from those traditionally available against a trustee who committed a breach of obligation: *Ancient Order of Foresters in Victoria Friendly Society Ltd v Lifeplan Australia Friendly Society Ltd* (2018) 265 CLR 1, [74] (Gageler J).

9 *Competition and Consumer Act 2010* (Cth) sch 2.

Outside the recognised relationships

'Vertical' relationships

Other relationships outside of those recognised as fiduciary relationships will be held to be fiduciary, either whole or in part, where there is a reasonable expectation that one party should subordinate self-interest in a particular matter to the interests of another. [10.8]

Most commercial relationships do not attract fiduciary obligations; contracts in these cases enable parties to cooperate for the pursuit of individual self-interest. But some contracts give rise to an expectation that one party will act exclusively in the interests of the other. In *News Ltd v Australian Rugby League Ltd*,[10] Gummow J identified criteria which assist in establishing whether a commercial relationship gives rise to fiduciary obligations. A distinction was drawn between 'vertical' fiduciary relationships where one party has greater access to resources, skill or information than the other, and 'horizontal' fiduciary relationships where resources, skill and information are shared for the purpose of achieving a common goal. Trust and agency relationships typify vertical fiduciary relationships, whereas a professional or business partnership is an example of a horizontal fiduciary relationship. [10.9]

The High Court decision *Hospital Products Ltd v United States Surgical Corporation*[11] is the leading authority on the application of fiduciary obligations to vertical business relationships. USSC manufactured surgical stapling products. The first defendant, Blackman, realised that USSC's products were not patented in Australia and offered to become its distributor. He obtained exclusive distribution rights in Australia under an oral contract. Blackman established his own company, Hospital Products, which competed with USSC by repackaging USSC's products and selling them as its own, and by reverse engineering USSC's products to enable competing products to be developed. This was so successful that Hospital Products began competing with USSC in the USA as well as Australia. USSC terminated its contract with Blackman and sued him and Hospital Products for breach of contract and breach of fiduciary obligation. [10.10]

The High Court unanimously held that Blackman's conduct in developing a business which competed with USSC's was a breach of contract. However, the majority held that Blackman did not owe fiduciary obligations to USSC, and that therefore no constructive trust could be imposed over Hospital Products' assets. Mason J dissented on the ground that the defendants were under a limited fiduciary obligation to protect USSC's Australian product goodwill. The test of a fiduciary relationship proposed by Mason J in *Hospital Products* was accepted by the majority judges even though they disagreed on the application of the test to the facts. It has also been applied in many subsequent cases. The essential features of fiduciary relationships were explained as follows:

> The critical feature of these relationships is that the fiduciary undertakes or agrees to act for or on behalf of or in the interests of another person in the exercise of a power or discretion which will affect the interests of that person in a legal or practical sense.[12]

10 (1996) 64 FCR 410.
11 (1984) 156 CLR 41; *Sourcebook* 10.2a, p 235.
12 *Hospital Products Ltd v United States Surgical Corporation* (1984) 156 CLR 41, 96–7.

[10.11] This summary of the elements of a fiduciary relationship is often termed the 'undertaking test'. It would, however, be a serious oversimplification to assume that a fiduciary relationship exists whenever one person undertakes to act for another in some matter. Suppose A undertakes to buy theatre tickets for B with his own money. A is not acting in a fiduciary capacity. The position will be different if B entrusts A with her money so that A can buy theatre tickets. In that case, A has temporary control (or power) over B's money and any misapplication of the money will constitute a breach of fiduciary obligation. A's expenditure of B's money will affect B in both a legal and a practical sense. All elements of Mason J's test have to be applied to a relationship to determine whether it is fiduciary; it is not enough to conclude that A is a fiduciary just because A has undertaken to act for B.

In *Hospital Products*, the majority held that Blackman and Hospital Products had not undertaken to act in USSC's interests so as to justify the imposition of fiduciary obligations. The latitude Blackman enjoyed under the distributorship agreement with USSC was inconsistent with the existence of a fiduciary relationship. Blackman was not obliged to sell any specific quantity of USSC's products, could determine the sale price of the products, and was permitted to make a profit on his own account.[13] Moreover, the contract was terminable by either party at will. These factors all indicated that the defendants were free to promote their own interests and had not exclusively agreed to act in the interests of USSC. If USSC had wanted more effective protection for its product goodwill in Australia it should, in the view of the majority, have negotiated a detailed confidentiality agreement.[14] Although it is sometimes argued that the function of fiduciary law is to insert hypothetical 'implied terms' into contracts, to which the parties would have agreed if they had been a matter for negotiation,[15] *Hospital Products* demonstrates that courts will not, by the application of fiduciary principles, make agreements for parties which they have not made for themselves.

[10.12] Situations to which the undertaking test has been applied include professional advisory relationships.[16] Relationships such as banker–customer and accountant–client are primarily governed by contract law, supplemented by legislation. Incompetent performance in these relationships attracts liability for breach of contract or in negligence.[17] For example, the relationship between bank and customer is contractual, being the relationship of debtor and creditor (the customer being the creditor if her account is in credit). It is not ordinarily a fiduciary relationship and the taking of deposits from customers does not attract fiduciary obligations.[18] But a bank advising a customer on the investment of the customer's money may owe fiduciary obligations to the customer if it has undertaken to provide wholly disinterested advice and to act exclusively in the customer's interests.

[10.13] In *Commonwealth Bank of Australia v Smith*,[19] the plaintiffs – longstanding customers of a branch of the bank who often relied on its advice in their business dealings – sought the

13 Ibid 72–3 (Gibbs CJ).

14 Ibid 72.

15 FH Easterbrook and DR Fischel, 'Contract and Fiduciary Duty' (1993) 36(1/2) *Journal of Law & Economics* 425; A Duggan, 'Contracts, Fiduciaries and the Primacy of the Deal' in E Bant and M Harding (eds), *Exploring Private Law* (Cambridge University Press, 2010) 275.

16 *Daly v Sydney Stock Exchange Ltd* (1986) 160 CLR 371; *Sourcebook* 10.2b, p 236; *Hodgkinson v Simms* [1994] 3 SCR 377.

17 *Henderson v Merrett Syndicates* [1995] 2 AC 145.

18 *Foley v Hill* (1848) 2 HLC 28; 9 ER 1002.

19 (1991) 42 FCR 390; *Sourcebook* 10.5.2c, p 273.

bank's advice in buying the lease of a hotel from another of the bank's customers. The bank was also interested in arranging the sale of the hotel so that loans it had made to the vendor would be repaid. The branch manager told the plaintiffs that the purchase was a 'good buy', even though the bank's mortgage valuation showed that the hotel was worth less than the price the plaintiffs had agreed to pay. He also represented that the lease of the hotel would be renewed, despite having no grounds for making the representation. The plaintiffs bought the hotel and lost considerable money operating it. Moreover, the landlord refused to renew the lease. The Full Federal Court held that the bank had so completely identified its interests with those of the plaintiffs that it owed the plaintiffs fiduciary obligations – it had undertaken to act exclusively in their interests in advising them on the purchase of the hotel. It had acted in breach of fiduciary obligation when it placed itself in a position of conflict between the advisory duties it owed the plaintiffs and its interest in ensuring the sale of the lease. The bank had made no profit from the conflict of interest. Nevertheless, it was ordered to pay equitable compensation to the plaintiffs for their financial losses incurred in running the hotel.

'Horizontal' relationships

We have seen that some fiduciary relationships can be described as vertical because *one* party possesses more skill or resources, or superior access to information, than the other party. Other commercial relationships are structured as horizontal in that *both* parties bring resources, skill and information to the pursuit of a common goal. [10.14]

The paradigm of a horizontal commercial relationship which also imposes fiduciary obligations is a business or professional partnership. A partner does not undertake to act exclusively in the interests of the co-partners in matters within the scope of the partnership unless the partnership agreement makes provision for a partner to act as an agent for the others in some matter. Rather, all the partners undertake to act in the interests of the partnership. The *Hospital Products* test is therefore not apt to determine whether a partnership imposes fiduciary obligations. Other horizontal commercial relationships will create fiduciary obligations if they are analogous to a partnership. In determining whether they are fiduciary, the test is not whether one party has undertaken to act in the interests of another party (or other parties). The question will be whether the parties have placed a high degree of mutual trust and confidence in each other in the pursuit of their common goal. The precise degree of trust and confidence required to justify the imposition of fiduciary obligations is a matter for judicial assessment and cannot be quantified. In general terms, the degree of trust that one partner expects of another will also be expected in any horizontal commercial relationship alleged to be fiduciary.

The leading authority on the fiduciary status of horizontal fiduciary relationships is *United Dominions Corporation Ltd v Brian Pty Ltd*.[20] Brian, operating through his company, invested money under an agreement, described as a joint venture agreement, with UDC and SPL to construct a shopping centre near Brisbane. SPL owned the land on which the shopping centre was constructed. Although the shopping centre was successfully developed, Brian was neither repaid its financial contribution nor paid a share of the profits. Unknown to Brian, UDC had taken a mortgage over SPC's land and claimed payment of the profits under [10.15]

20 (1985) 157 CLR 1; *Sourcebook* 10.3.4a, p 248. See also *Farah Constructions Pty Ltd v Say-Dee Pty Ltd* (2007) 230 CLR 89, [101]–[105]; *Sourcebook* 11.2.2a, p 292.

a collateralisation clause in the mortgage. The High Court held that the collateralisation clause was unenforceable against Brian to the extent that it deprived it of its share of the profits. Mason, Brennan and Deane JJ held that the joint venture agreement was in substance a partnership even though it was not labelled a partnership in the documentation. Moreover, it was irrelevant that the co-venturers had embarked on partnership or joint venture activities before formally executing the agreement. The relationship between the parties at that stage was fiduciary since the willingness of the parties to proceed with the project prior to executing the agreement demonstrated a high degree of mutual trust and confidence. The parties owed each other fiduciary obligations at the time the mortgage was executed so that UDC could not obtain for itself a collateral advantage without the knowledge and consent of the other parties.

Concurrent contractual and fiduciary relationships

[10.16] Many fiduciary relationships are created by contract. Alternatively, they may evolve from a relationship which was initially a contract permitting the pursuit of self-interest but which over time became a relationship of trust and confidence.[21] Contract and fiduciary obligations often co-exist. The solicitor–client relationship, for example, is established by a contract under which the client retains the services of the solicitor.

Three aspects of the relationship between contract law and the law of fiduciary obligations deserve emphasis:

(1) Fiduciary obligations can be modified or even excluded by the terms of a contract. A dictum of Mason J in *Hospital Products Ltd v United States Surgical Corporation*[22] emphasises the role of contract law in determining the content of fiduciary obligations:

> The fiduciary relationship, if it is to exist at all, must accommodate itself to the terms of the contract so that it is consistent with, and conforms to, them. The fiduciary relationship cannot be superimposed upon the contract in such a way as to alter the operation which the contract was intended to have according to its true construction.

A commercial contract may exclude or limit liability for breach of fiduciary obligation. This will be achieved by (a) an acknowledgement that the contract does not impose fiduciary obligations, or (b) limiting the areas to which fiduciary duties apply, or (c) excluding the application of remedies for breach of fiduciary obligation. In *Australian Securities and Investments Commission v Citigroup Global Markets Australia Pty Ltd (No 4)*,[23] an investment bank agreed to advise a company on its proposed takeover bid for another company. The day before the takeover bid was announced, a bank employee purchased shares in the target company on behalf of the bank. The employee did not have insider information about the takeover,

21 The principal theme of Conaglen (n 3) is that fiduciary obligations protect and reinforce the performance of non-fiduciary legal, equitable or statutory duties.

22 (1984) 156 CLR 41, 97.

23 (2007) 160 FCR 35; *Sourcebook* 10.6a, p 284; J Getzler, '*ASIC v Citigroup*: Contractual Exclusion of Fiduciary Duties' (2007) 2(1) *Journal of Equity* 62.

and the bank had procedures in place to restrict the flow of commercially sensitive information. The statutory regulator, ASIC, argued that the bank acted in a fiduciary capacity in advising on the takeover bid, and that it had committed a breach of fiduciary obligation by permitting the shares to be bought. The claim failed because the letter of engagement under which the bank agreed to act expressly excluded the existence of fiduciary obligations and allowed the bank to trade on its own account. A claim that someone is acting in the interests of another rings hollow if the contract between the parties excludes the existence of fiduciary obligations.

If a contract does not exclude the application of fiduciary obligations, a later attempt by one party to exclude their application will fail unless the other party agrees to their modification, in accordance with recognised principles of contract modification.

(2) Not every breach of duty committed by a fiduciary amounts to a breach of fiduciary obligation. The breach may constitute a breach of contract or a tort without necessarily involving any fiduciary failure. Only if it constitutes a breach of the fiduciary prohibitions of unauthorised conflicts of interest and unauthorised profit-making (discussed below) will a breach of fiduciary duty have been committed. [10.17]

An example of a breach of contract which also constituted a breach of fiduciary obligation occurred in *Farrington v Rowe McBride & Partners*.[24] Solicitors acted for the plaintiff in a personal injury claim. The plaintiff recovered damages and sought the firm's advice on the investment of the damages. The firm had a major corporate client which was in financial difficulties, and the solicitor advising the plaintiff had a financial interest in the corporation. The solicitor persuaded the plaintiff to invest his money with the corporation. Two years later the corporation went into liquidation. The New Zealand Court of Appeal held that the solicitors had placed themselves in a position of conflict between the duty owed to the plaintiff and the duty owed to its corporate client, and had therefore committed a breach of fiduciary obligation. The firm was ordered to compensate the plaintiff for his lost investment. The case shows how a conflict may arise between a fiduciary's duty to two different principals – the plaintiff and the corporation – as well as the conflict between the fiduciary's own interest and that of the principal.

Farrington v Rowe McBride & Partners is distinguishable from the High Court decision in *Hill v Van Erp*.[25] A solicitor negligently failed to ensure that a will complied with statutory formalities, with the result that the plaintiff failed to receive a legacy she expected. The High Court held that the solicitor had acted in breach of a duty of care she owed the plaintiff and was liable in tort. The solicitor was also in breach of the contractual duty of care and skill she owed to her client's estate, although damages for this breach would have been nominal since the estate suffered no loss. The solicitor was not, however, liable for breach of fiduciary obligation since she owed no duty to the plaintiff to protect her interests, and there was no element of conflict of interest or unauthorised profit-making in her negligent conduct.

24 [1985] 1 NZLR 83.
25 (1997) 188 CLR 159.

[10.18] (3) Following from (2) above, fiduciary obligations differ in character from obligations, including obligations of good faith and fair dealing, created by or implied into contracts. Equity does not recognise a fiduciary obligation to perform the duties which the parties must already perform by the terms of the contract.[26] In *Streetscape Projects (Australia) Pty Ltd v City of Sydney*,[27] the City council licensed to Streetscape the right to exploit intellectual property and know-how relating to multi-purpose poles, known as 'smartpoles'. The City later alleged that Streetscape had exploited the rights beyond the limits set by the licence agreement by supplying 'smartpoles' to the United Arab Emirates and elsewhere in the Middle East, and by not returning items at the termination of the licence agreement. The unauthorised acts of exploitation constituted breaches of contract. The New South Wales Court of Appeal held that they did not also constitute breaches of fiduciary obligation. The allegation of a breach of fiduciary obligation added nothing to the finding of a breach of contract. Barrett JA stated:

> The case ... was one of breach of a detailed commercial contract. The circumstances in which the contract had been made and in which performance was required did not indicate in any way that remedies for breach of contract would not be adequate for the vindication of the rights and the protection of the interests involved. There was simply no need for equity to provide supplementation in the form of fiduciary obligation.[28]

The remedies for breach of fiduciary obligation are different from, and more extensive than, the remedies for breach of contract. But they cannot be invoked simply because contractual remedies are perceived to be inadequate; they will be awarded for breaches of the specific obligations described later in this chapter.

[10.19] Fiduciary obligations can survive the termination of the contract that brought them into existence. As we will see, the survival of such obligations is a hotly contested question when a solicitor acts for one party in litigation, having previously acted under a contract of retainer for the other party[29] But it is well established that fiduciary duties can survive the termination of the relationship that brought the duties into being, such as the dissolution of a partnership or joint venture[30] or the resignation of a company director,[31] where the fiduciary later exploits an opportunity to obtain a benefit which should have been secured for the partnership, joint venture or company in question.

A fiduciary who terminates her contract with the beneficiary for the sole purpose of obtaining a personal benefit which she was under a duty to obtain for the other beneficiary will be accountable for breach of fiduciary duty even though the contract is at an end. An injunction will be granted to prevent her from deriving any benefit or advantage from her

26 *Re Goldcorp Exchange Ltd* [1995] 1 AC 74, 98 (PC).

27 (2013) 295 ALR 760. P Finn, 'Fiduciary Reflections' (2014) 88(2) *Australian Law Journal* 127, 135–6.

28 (2013) 295 CLR 760, [128].

29 *Spincode Pty Ltd v Look Software Pty Ltd* (2001) 4 VR 501; *Kallinicos v Hunt* (2005) 64 NSWLR 561; *Técnicas Reunidas SA v Andrew* [2018] NSWCA 192.

30 *Chan v Zacharia* (1984) 154 CLR 178; *Edmonds v Donovan* (2005) 12 VR 513.

31 *Schmidt v AHRKalimpa Pty Ltd* [2020] VSCA 193.

resignation.[32] If she has obtained such a benefit, she will be accountable to the other party for the value of the benefit and may be ordered to hold property traceable to her breach of duty on constructive trust for the other party.[33] A fiduciary is not permitted to 'shake off the character of a fiduciary'[34] by resigning her office in order to obtain a personal advantage. Indeed, proof that she resigned for this reason indicates that she was not acting exclusively in the interests of the beneficiary prior to her resignation.

More difficult are cases in which termination occurs before the opportunity to act against the interests of the beneficiary arises. A solicitor who acts in litigation against a former client will not usually have terminated the contract of retainer with the former client solely in order to obtain a more lucrative retainer from the new client. The solicitor may, nevertheless, have obtained information in the course of acting for the former client which can be exploited advantageously for the benefit of the new client, and correspondingly to the detriment of the former client. Does the solicitor's agreement to act against the former client constitute a breach of fiduciary duty? [10.20]

In *Prince Jefri Bolkiah v KPMG*,[35] Lord Millett held that the solicitor in such a case does not owe fiduciary obligations to the former client. Any protection to which the former client was entitled rests either on the contractual and equitable principles governing the disclosure of confidential information[36] or on the court's inherent jurisdiction to regulate solicitors as officers of the court. Where breach of confidence is the basis of the claim, a plaintiff seeking to restrain a solicitor from acting must show (a) that the solicitor is in possession of the former client's confidential information and (b) that the information is or may be relevant to the new matter, in which the interests of the solicitor's new client may be adverse to those of the former client. [10.21]

Lord Millett's analysis has had a mixed reception in Australia. Most State and Territory jurisdictions have adopted the analysis. In these jurisdictions, while solicitors owe a fiduciary duty of loyalty to existing clients, any duty owed to former clients rests on either breach of confidence law or on the inherent jurisdiction of the court to regulate its officers.[37] The analysis has also been adopted by the Federal Court.[38] But in *Spincode Pty Ltd v Look Software Pty Ltd*,[39] the Victorian Court of Appeal declined to follow *Prince Jefri*, holding that solicitors can owe fiduciary obligations to their former clients. Brooking JA drew attention to authorities recognising that solicitors may, in certain circumstances, owe fiduciary obligations [10.22]

32 'Benefit' for this purpose is broader than the legal definition of property: *Ancient Order of Foresters in Victoria Friendly Society Ltd v Lifeplan Australia Friendly Society Ltd* (2018) 265 CLR 1, [75] (Gageler J). See [10.3].

33 See chapter 21.

34 *Ex parte James* (1803) 32 ER 337, 348 (Lord Eldon). See also *Gould v O'Carroll* (1964) NSWR 803, 805 (Jacobs J).

35 [1998] UKHL 52; [1999] 2 AC 222, 234–5.

36 See chapter 12.

37 *Beach Petroleum NL v Abbott Tout Russell Kennedy* (1999) 48 NSWLR 1, [205]; *Técnicas Reunidas SA v Andrew* [2018] NSWCA 192; *PDP Group Pty Ltd v Bennett & Philp* [2013] QSC 231; *Lyons v Legalese Pty Ltd* (2016) 126 SASR 232; *A v Law Society of Tasmania* [2001] 10 Tas R 152; *Ismail-Zai v Western Australia* (2007) 34 WAR 379, [23] (Steytler P); *Birkett Investments Pty Ltd v Streatfield Investments Pty Ltd* [2016] ACTSC 323.

38 *Dealer Support Services Pty Ltd v Motor Trades Association Ltd* (2014) 228 FCR 252.

39 (2001) 4 VR 501. See also *Schmidt v AHRKalimpa Pty Ltd* [2020] VSCA 193.

to their former clients that had not been considered by the House of Lords in *Prince Jefri*. But he also asserted that 'the equitable obligation of "loyalty" is not observed by a solicitor who acts against a former client in the same matter'.[40] In his opinion, the former client may be disadvantaged not only by the potential misuse of confidential information but also by the exploitation by the solicitor of personal but non-confidential knowledge of the client obtained during the currency of the retainer.[41]

Lord Millett's reasoning in *Prince Jefri,* and the analysis of that reasoning in Australian decisions, have not yet been considered by the High Court. An appropriate vehicle for considering these issues would be a case in which an application was made to disqualify a solicitor from acting in litigation against a former client where no confidential information had previously been communicated to the solicitor but where it was alleged that the former client would nonetheless incur detriment if the solicitor was allowed to act.

Abuse of the fiduciary concept

[10.23] The fiduciary concept sometimes risks becoming distorted in cases where the plaintiff is considered to deserve an award of a remedy for breach of fiduciary obligation, such as an account of profits or a constructive trust, but where the requirements for a fiduciary relationship have not been met. In these cases, courts may impermissibly 'read equity backwards'[42] by artificially finding the existence of a fiduciary relationship as the key that unlocks the door to the preferred remedy.

[10.24] An example of a distortion of the fiduciary obligation is *Chase Manhattan Bank NA v Israel-British Bank (London) Ltd.*[43] An employee of the plaintiff bank mistakenly made a double payment of $2 million to the defendant bank. A mistaken payment can be recovered by the payer in a claim for money had and received.[44] This is a personal claim, however, which means that if the payee is insolvent the payer will be an unsecured creditor in the payee's insolvency. The defendant bank in this case was in liquidation. The payer successfully argued that the payee owed a fiduciary duty to repay the mistaken payment and therefore held the payment on constructive trust for the payer. The practical effect of the imposition of the constructive trust was that the plaintiff became the equitable owner of the payment and was entitled to keep the money in priority to the defendant's unsecured creditors.

There was no pre-existing fiduciary relationship on the facts of the *Chase Manhattan* case except in the artificial sense that payment created a relationship between the parties. Neither the 'undertaking' nor the 'mutual trust and confidence' tests, described above, were satisfied. A fiduciary duty to return the payment was recognised because the Court considered that the defendant's insolvency should not prevent the plaintiff from recovering its money.

---

40 (2001) 4 VR 501, [53].

41 The discussion of *Prince Jefri* in *Spincode* was obiter since the Court of Appeal upheld the decision of the primary judge who granted an injunction on the basis of the potential misuse of confidential information: *Spincode* at [24]. But later Victorian authority has confirmed the application of fiduciary principles to prevent solicitors acting against their former clients: *Schmidt v AHRKalimpa Pty Ltd* [2020] VSCA 193, [142].

42 *Lac Minerals Ltd v International Corona Resources Ltd* [1989] 2 SCR 574, 651 (La Forest J).

43 [1981] Ch 105.

44 *David Securities Pty Ltd v Commonwealth Bank of Australia* (1992) 175 CLR 353.

Scope of the fiduciary relationship

It is important to distinguish between aspects of the parties' relationship which are fiduciary and those which are not. This is done by reference to the 'scope' of the relationship. Suppose A is the trustee of a family trust, of which B is a beneficiary. The trust property is company shares. Coincidentally, A owns a house which he leases to B. The fact that A owes fiduciary obligations to B in respect of the trust will not constitute him a fiduciary towards B in respect of the lease. A is perfectly entitled to act in his own self-interest in negotiating the terms of the lease. [10.25]

The decision of the High Court in *Howard v Commissioner of Taxation (Cth)*[45] is a more complex illustration of fixing the scope of a fiduciary relationship. Howard had been involved in a joint venture to buy and later resell a golf course. He was a director of a company, Disctronics, which was intended to be the investment vehicle for the acquisition of the golf course. The joint venture failed when the golf course was sold to other co-venturers who had acted in breach of the fiduciary duties they owed to Howard. In subsequent litigation, Howard was awarded a substantial sum of equitable compensation for the breach. He did not include the compensation in his tax return, arguing that, as a director of Disctronics, he held the compensation on trust for Disctronics. [10.26]

The High Court held that Howard was assessable to tax on the compensation because he had received it on his own account, and not in his capacity as a director owing a fiduciary duty to account for the compensation to Disctronics. If Disctronics had purchased the golf course, Howard would have had to account for any benefits he received from the joint venture, in his capacity as director, to the company. But Disctronics had not acquired the property, and the scope of the fiduciary obligations Howard owed to the company did not extend to compensation he had been awarded in a personal capacity. In the words of French CJ and Keane J, Howard had 'attempted to stretch the fiduciary mantle attaching to his position as director to his membership of the joint venture … His purpose had nothing to do with the vindication or protection of Disctronics' interests'.[46]

Courts determine the scope of the fiduciary relationship by reference to the fiduciary's undertaking and do not impose obligations beyond that undertaking. However, equity is not limited to any written record of the parties' agreement, if there is one. The conduct of the parties can be considered in full. In *Birtchnell v Equity Trustees Executors and Agency Co Ltd*,[47] the deceased had entered into a real estate partnership with others. A partnership client introduced a land development opportunity to him which he took up personally, not informing his co-partners of it. After his death, the other partners alleged that, in exploiting the opportunity, he had committed a breach of fiduciary duty. The High Court closely examined the written agreement between the partners; from that, it appeared that the partners were entitled to pursue such opportunities personally. However, when the course of conduct of the partners over the years was considered, it appeared that the partners had in fact regarded themselves as bound to offer such opportunities to the partnership. The opportunity was therefore held to be within the scope of the partnership. [10.27]

45 (2014) 253 CLR 83; *Sourcebook* 10.4b, p 261.
46 *Howard v Commissioner of Taxation (Cth)* (2014) 253 CLR 83, [35].
47 (1929) 42 CLR 384.

[10.28] Questions of scope usually only arise in cases involving recognised categories of fiduciary relationships. If a relationship is alleged to be fiduciary outside of those relationships, the nature and extent of the fiduciary's undertaking will determine its scope.

Fiduciary obligations

[10.29] A fiduciary is expected to act in in the interests of the other party, or parties, to the fiduciary relationship, to the exclusion of her own interests. It is sometimes asserted that the fiduciary must act in the best interests of the other party, but this formulation should not be understood as imposing an abstract duty to ensure that the beneficiary's interests are promoted. What constitutes 'best interests' in a given case depends on the nature of the relationship, the terms of any legally dispositive document governing the relationship and, in some cases, upon the course of dealings between the parties. Fiduciary obligations are not applied in the abstract; they promote objectives which a settlor or drafter of a contract will have set out in a trust instrument or contract, or which may be implied from the dealings between the parties.[48] Moreover, Australian equity does not recognise all duties imposed on the fiduciary as being specifically fiduciary in character but only those duties discussed in the following paragraphs.

[10.30] It is often said that a fiduciary owes a duty of loyalty to the beneficiary. At a high level of generality, this is correct. But the duty of loyalty is not a specific fiduciary obligation. It is a policy which expresses the aim of other, more detailed, obligations. The duty of loyalty is a positive obligation, but the High Court has consistently emphasised the proposition that the core specific fiduciary obligations are proscriptive, or negative, in character.[49]

[10.31] The core fiduciary obligations are:

(1) The fiduciary's obligation not to permit a conflict, or a potential conflict, between the duty owed to the beneficiary and personal interest. The duty reflects the basic principle that the fiduciary must subordinate personal interest to the interests of the beneficiary in matters coming within the scope of the fiduciary relationship. Equity will intervene to prevent a potential conflict arising even though the fiduciary may have obtained no profit or other advantage.[50]

(2) The duty also applies to the situation in which the fiduciary has a conflict between the interests of two beneficiaries – a 'duty–duty' dispute, as opposed to

48 See Conaglen (n 3); M Conaglen, 'The Nature and Function of Fiduciary Loyalty' (2005) 121(3) *Law Quarterly Review* 452. Cf L Smith, 'Fiduciary Relationships: Ensuring the Loyal Exercise of Judgment on Behalf of Another' (2014) 130(4) *Law Quarterly Review* 608.

49 *Breen v Williams* (1996) 186 CLR 71; *Sourcebook* 10.3.2a, p 244 and 10.5.2d, p 276; *Pilmer v Duke Group Ltd (in liq)* (2001) 207 CLR 165; *Ancient Order of Foresters in Victoria Friendly Society Ltd v Lifeplan Australia Friendly Society Ltd* (2018) 265 CLR 1, [74] (Gageler J). Whether fiduciary obligations are, or should be, confined to negative obligations is a controversial question. See the dissenting judgment of Kirby J in *Pilmer v Duke*, [128]: '[O]missions quite frequently shade into commissions'. The Australian model of proscriptive fiduciary obligations contrasts with some Canadian Supreme Court decisions which have recognised an affirmative duty of loyalty. See, eg, *McInerney v MacDonald* [1992] 2 SCR 138, disapproved in *Breen v Williams*.

50 *Breen v Williams* (1996) 186 CLR 71; *Sourcebook* 10.5.2d, p 276; *Agricultural Land Management Ltd v Jackson (No 2)* (2014) 48 WAR1, [268] (Edelman J).

an 'interest–duty' dispute, although many conflicts between the interests of two beneficiaries, when examined closely, also involve an element of fiduciary self-interest. An example of a conflict between the interests of two beneficiaries is that of a solicitor who is placed in a position of conflict between the interests of two clients.[51] The aim of the prohibition of unauthorised conflicts of interest in both cases is to ensure that the fiduciary's exercise of discretion on behalf of the beneficiary is wholly disinterested.

(3) The fiduciary's obligation not to make a profit at the expense of the beneficiary. Like the 'no conflict' rule, the 'no profit' rule has several applications. For example, a trustee must not appropriate trust property for his personal benefit. In addition, he must not exploit for his personal benefit a business opportunity which should have been offered to the beneficiary.[52] The aim of the prohibition on unauthorised profit-making is to prevent a fiduciary from exploiting his position for personal gain.

It is not always easy to distinguish between the 'no conflict' and the 'no profit' principle. [10.32]
A breach of one obligation will often constitute a breach of the other. But a fiduciary can place himself in a position of conflict without necessarily profiting from the conflict. For example, an injunction will be granted to prevent a solicitor acting for one client against another client even if there is no proof that the solicitor has benefited from representing conflicting interests.

The 'no conflict' and 'no profit' principles are proscriptive, and not prescriptive. In other [10.33]
words, they impose negative obligations on fiduciaries, preventing them from engaging in prohibited conduct; they do not impose positive obligations requiring fiduciaries actively to promote the beneficiaries' best interests. Since the High Court decision in *Breen v Williams*,[53] the proposition that Australian law recognises proscriptive, but not prescriptive, fiduciary obligations has become judicial orthodoxy.

The plaintiff in *Breen v Williams* had a bilateral breast augmentation in which silicone [10.34]
breast implants were inserted. Complications developed and the plaintiff consulted the defendant, a plastic surgeon, who performed surgery but did not remove the implants. The plaintiff suffered further complications. She wanted to participate in a United States class action against the manufacturers of the implants. It was a condition of participating in the action that the plaintiff submit copies of her medical records to the American court. The defendant offered to allow her access to the records on condition that she released him from any claim that might arise in relation to the procedures he had performed, but he denied that the plaintiff had any right to access her medical records. The plaintiff sought a declaration that she had contractual and proprietary rights to her medical records. Alternatively, she claimed that the defendant owed her a fiduciary obligation to disclose the records to her. The High Court refused to grant the declaration. In rejecting the fiduciary claim, the High Court held that, while there might be circumstances in which a doctor would owe fiduciary obligations to a patient, equity did not recognise the existence of an affirmative fiduciary obligation on the part of the doctor to act in the best interests of the patient. Gaudron and

51 See [10.19].
52 *Cook v Deeks* [1916] AC 554.
53 (1996) 186 CLR 71.

McHugh JJ made reference to the proscriptive obligations discussed above, and continued that 'the law of this country does not otherwise impose positive legal duties on the fiduciary to act in the interests of the person to whom the duty is owed'.[54] Dawson and Toohey JJ stated that there was 'a tendency, not found in this country, but to be seen in the United States and to a lesser extent in Canada, to view a fiduciary relationship as imposing obligations which go beyond the exaction of loyalty'.[55]

[10.35] A possible narrow reading of *Breen v Williams* is that the High Court rejected the plaintiff's attempt to establish the existence of a freestanding obligation resting on fiduciaries, including doctors, to disclose material facts relating to the protection of the beneficiary's interests, particularly where there were alternative legal processes, such as invoking the Court's discovery procedures, which would have enabled the plaintiff to obtain disclosure of her medical records. It is usual, however, to interpret *Breen v Williams* as authority for the wider proposition that Australian law recognises proscriptive, but not prescriptive, fiduciary obligations. The difficulty with accepting the wider proposition is that equity recognises and regulates obligations in addition to the 'no conflict' and 'no profit' prohibitions, which require the fiduciary to take affirmative steps to ensure the loyal performance of his obligations. These other obligations, and the enforcement of them in equity, are discussed in the following paragraphs.

[10.36] An essential characteristic of fiduciary relationships is that the fiduciary exercises powers and discretions which will affect the interests of the beneficiary. The exercise is subject to review in equity. The basis of intervention was explained by the Full Federal Court in *Grimaldi v Chameleon Mining NL (No 2)*:

> Its essential concern is with judicial review of the exercise of powers, duties and discretions given to a fiduciary to be exercised in the interests of another ('the beneficiary') where the beneficiary does not have the right to dictate or to veto how the power, discretion etc is exercised by the fiduciary. Here the law channels and directs how 'fiduciary discretions' are exercised.[56]

For example, a discretion will be conferred on the trustees of a discretionary trust to select some members of a class of beneficiaries to receive a distribution of trust income. Any payment to a beneficiary which fails to take into account relevant considerations, including a law which affects the tax treatment of the payment, or which takes into account irrelevant considerations in making the selection, is liable to be set aside.[57] Similarly, company directors are subject to duties to act in good faith and for the proper purposes for which their powers were conferred.[58] Decisions taken in breach of these duties are liable to be set aside in equity and attract additional sanctions under the *Corporations Act 2001* (Cth).

54 Ibid 113.
55 Ibid 95.
56 (2012) 200 FCR 296, [174].
57 *Futter v Futter* [2013] 2 AC 108. English decisions describe this judicial review function as applying the rule in *Re Hastings-Bass (deceased)* [1975] Ch 25.
58 R Langford, *Directors' Duties: Principles and Application* (Federation Press, 2014) 16–31.

In *Westpac Banking Corporation v Bell Group Ltd (in liq) (No 3)*,[59] the Western Australian Court of Appeal considered the fiduciary status of company directors' obligations in complex litigation arising out of the collapse of the Bell Group of companies. Shortly before the collapse, the directors transferred securities from the companies to banks which had lent money to the companies. The effect of the transfers was to convert the banks from unsecured creditors to partially secured creditors. The position of the banks vis-à-vis other creditors was thereby improved. Non-bank creditors were excluded from access to the securities when the companies were wound up. The liquidators of the companies in the Bell Group instituted proceedings seeking to recover the money raised by the banks when they sold their securities after the companies had been placed in liquidation. One of the key issues raised by the litigation was whether the directors had committed breaches of their fiduciary duties in transferring the securities to the banks. It was alleged that the directors, in making the transfers, had not acted in good faith or for the proper purposes of the companies concerned. [10.37]

Different views were expressed in the Court of Appeal on whether these obligations were fiduciary in character. Lee AJA[60] and Drummond AJA[61] were prepared to recognise that these obligations were fiduciary, and that the 'no conflict' and 'no profit' prohibitions were not the only fiduciary obligations. In the opinion of Drummond AJA: [10.38]

> [U]ntil the High Court declares the law to be otherwise, long established authority requires the duties of company directors to act bona fide in the interests of the company and to exercise their powers for proper purposes to be accepted to be fiduciary ones even though they may require the directors to take positive action.[62]

Lee AJA and Drummond AJA considered that *Breen v Williams* was authority for the narrow proposition that Australian law does not recognise the American and Canadian model of fiduciary obligations which requires the fiduciary to act in the best interests of the beneficiary. Carr AJA also thought that *Breen v Williams* was not the last word on the reach and content of fiduciary duties but considered that the directors had not acted in breach of these duties.[63] The subsequent appeal to the High Court was settled, so the views expressed in the *Bell Group* decision on whether Australian law recognises prescriptive fiduciary obligations are, for the time being, binding on other intermediate appellate courts, unless held to be clearly wrong (eg because a court considers that *Breen v Williams* was misinterpreted in *Bell Group*).

59 (2012) 44 WAR 1. Special leave to appeal to the High Court was given but the case was settled before the appeal could be heard: [2013] HCATrans 49; R Langford, 'Solving the Fiduciary Puzzle – The Bona Fide and Proper Purposes Duties of Company Law' (2013) 41(3) *Australian Business Law Review* 127; L Firios, 'Precluding Prescriptive Duties in Fiduciary Relationships: The Problems with the Proscriptive Delimitation' (2012) 40(3) *Australian Business Law Review* 166.

60 (2012) 44 WAR 1, [897].

61 Ibid [1962]–[1969].

62 Ibid [1978].

63 Ibid [2720], taking the view that *Breen v Williams* was not concerned with, and was therefore irrelevant to, a consideration of a director's fiduciary duties.

[10.39] In addition to the core fiduciary obligations, fiduciaries are subject to a number of other *equitable* obligations.[64] They include the duty to act in good faith (which may in fact be a core fiduciary obligation if the reasoning in *Westpac Banking Corporation v Bell Group Ltd (in liq) (No 3)* is accepted[65]), the equitable duty of care (or business prudence, in the case of trustees) and the equitable duty of confidence. They differ from the fiduciary duties previously discussed in this chapter in that the justification for their imposition is not the need to ensure the fiduciary's loyal performance of his duties. The imposition of other duties will depend on the fiduciary relationship in question. For example, trustees are subject to a number of specific obligations, such as the duty to comply with the terms of the trust instrument and the duty to invest trust moneys.[66] These obligations are inapplicable to some other fiduciary relationships which can be of limited duration and do not necessarily require the fiduciary to invest beneficiary money. These duties are considered in detail in chapters 17 and 18.

Authorisation and ratification

[10.40] Almost all fiduciary and equitable obligations can be excluded by the terms of the trust instrument, contract or other document defining the obligations of the fiduciary.[67] A principal can also ratify what would otherwise constitute a breach of fiduciary obligation. An exception is the fiduciary's obligation of good faith, since good faith is central to the fiduciary notion of subordinating personal interest to the interest of the beneficiary.[68] Further, the beneficiary can authorise or consent to what would otherwise constitute a breach of obligation. In *Queensland Mines Ltd v Hudson*,[69] the plaintiff company was initially interested in developing iron ore mining operations in Tasmania. Hudson, who was managing director of QML, succeeded in obtaining the necessary licences to develop the mines. QML, however, was in financial difficulties and unable to proceed with the project. Hudson resigned his position as managing director and, with the full knowledge of the directors of QML, successfully developed the mines. Eleven years later, QML sought to hold Hudson accountable for the profits he had made on the ground that he had exploited his fiduciary position as managing director to make the profits. The Privy Council held that

64 Whether obligations listed in this paragraph are fiduciary or, alternatively, equitable (but not fiduciary) is a disputed question: *Permanent Building Society (in liq) v Wheeler* (1994) 11 WAR 187; *Bristol & West Building Society v Mothew* [1998] Ch 1. But see *Youyang Pty Ltd v Minter Ellison Morris Fletcher* (2003) 212 CLR 484, [38]–[40]; *Sourcebook* 4.3.3b, p 78, suggesting that the trustee's duty of care is fiduciary. See also JD Heydon, 'Are the Duties of Company Directors to Exercise Care and Skill Fiduciary?' in S Degeling and J Edelman (eds), *Equity in Commercial Law* (LawBook, 2005) 185. No practical consequences, in terms of the availability of equitable relief, turn on the resolution of the dispute, although the *Wheeler/Mothew* distinction clarifies the aims of specifically fiduciary obligations. See Conaglen, 'The Nature and Function of Fiduciary Loyalty' (n 48) 478–9.

65 (2012) 44 WAR 1. See also *Armitage v Nurse* [1998] Ch 241, 253–4 (Millett LJ), holding that the duty of good faith was a core 'non-excludable' obligation; DJ Hayton, 'The Irreducible Core Content of Trusteeship' in AJ Oakley (ed), *Trends in Contemporary Trust Law* (Oxford University Press, 1996) 47, 57–8.

66 See chapters 18 and 19.

67 See [10.16].

68 *Armitage v Nurse* [1998] Ch 241, 253–4 (Millett LJ).

69 (1978) 52 ALJR 399.

Hudson was not liable to account: first, because QML's rejection of the opportunity to develop the mines took the venture outside his fiduciary obligations; and, secondly, because Hudson had acted with full knowledge of the directors of the company who must be taken to have consented to his activities.

The reasoning is open to criticism. By holding that the decision of the directors not to proceed took the project outside the scope of the defendant's fiduciary obligations, the Privy Council effectively permitted the board of directors to define the scope of a director's fiduciary obligations. The defendant's activities should have been authorised by shareholder approval. In *Queensland Mines*, however, there was a substantial identity between directors and shareholders. Moreover, the merits of the case were on Hudson's side. Queensland Mines had waited 11 years, until the profitability of the mine had been secured, before issuing a writ. Hudson had taken the commercial risks, but the company was seeking to reap the profit. Even if the defence of implied consent had not prevailed it is likely that the defence of laches would have succeeded.[70] [10.41]

How strict are fiduciary obligations?

The primary goal of enforcing fiduciary obligations is deterrence (sometimes referred to as prophylaxis).[71] Deterrence comprises both *general deterrence*, where fiduciaries generally, or a particular class of fiduciaries such as trustees or company directors, are deterred from misappropriating trust property or neglecting their responsibilities; and *individual deterrence*, in that relief is designed to deter a particular fiduciary from committing a breach of duty (assuming that the fiduciary is permitted to continue acting in a position of trust). Equity judgments abound with dicta emphasising the stringency of fiduciary obligations. For example, in *Meinhard v Salmon*, Cardozo CJ described the fiduciary's duty of loyalty as a: [10.42]

> tradition that ... is unbending and inveterate. Uncompromising rigidity has been the attitude of courts of equity when petitioned to undermine the rule of undivided loyalty by the 'disintegrating erosion' of particular exceptions ... Only thus has the level of conduct for fiduciaries been kept at a level higher than that trodden by the crowd.[72]

The stringency of fiduciary obligations has also been emphasised in Australian decisions. The strictness is justified not only because the harm suffered by the beneficiary from a breach of fiduciary obligation can be substantial, but also because it is in the nature of fiduciary relationships that beneficiaries cannot easily monitor fiduciary activity. Wrongdoing is notoriously hard to discover until the damage has been done. For these reasons, equity presumes that any benefit or gain made by a fiduciary was made from his fiduciary position.[73] But although fiduciary standards are enforced stringently, they are also applied sensitively; otherwise socially and economically desirable behaviour will be discouraged by an overly [10.43]

70 See [6.3].

71 L Smith, 'Deterrence, Prophylaxis and Punishment in Fiduciary Obligations' (2013) 7(2) *Journal of Equity* 87. The reversal of unjust enrichment may in some cases be a relevant consideration: see G Jones, 'Unjust Enrichment and the Fiduciary Duty of Loyalty' (1968) 84(4) *Law Quarterly Review* 472; but the High Court rejected the unjust enrichment approach as an exclusive justification: *Warman International Ltd v Dwyer* (1995) 182 CLR 544, 557; *Sourcebook* 4.2a, p 64.

72 249 NY 456, 464 (1928).

73 *Chan v Zacharia* (1984) 154 CLR 178, 201–2 (Deane J).

deterrent approach to fiduciary obligations. If a fiduciary is held accountable for exploiting a profit-making opportunity for personal gain *and* to the advantage of the beneficiaries, skilful entrepreneurs will be discouraged from taking on fiduciary responsibilities, to the ultimate detriment of the beneficiaries. In reading the authorities on fiduciary obligations, the student should consider whether the court has applied the deterrent rationale appropriately in enforcing the obligations.

The following decisions illustrate the stringency of fiduciary obligations.

KEECH V SANDFORD[74]

[10.44] *Keech v Sandford* contains the classic, albeit concise, justification for the strict 'no conflict' and 'no profit' fiduciary principles. The defendant held the lease of the profits of a market on trust for an infant beneficiary. The landlord did not want to renew the lease to the infant and the defendant took the renewal of the lease in his own name. Chancellor King ruled that a trustee who renewed a lease, being trust property, in his own name rather than as trustee held the lease on constructive trust for the beneficiary. The basis of the fiduciary principles in general deterrence is well brought out by the Chancellor's short judgment:

> I very well see, if a trustee, on the refusal to renew, might have a lease to himself, few trust-estates would be renewed to *cestui que* use; ... This may seem hard, that the trustee is the only person of all mankind who might not have the lease: but it is very proper that rule should be strictly pursued and not in the least relaxed; for it is very obvious what would be the consequences of letting trustees have the lease, on refusal to renew to *cestui que* use.[75]

It was irrelevant that the trustee had acted in good faith in taking the renewal of the lease, and that the landlord encouraged him to take the renewal. Moreover, the Court did not inquire into whether the defendant had made a profit from taking the renewal; it was sufficient that he obtained the opportunity to make a profit from his position as trustee. A striking feature of the decision is that, although the landlord did not want to renew the lease in favour of the infant beneficiary because of the difficulties of enforcing covenants in leases against infant tenants, the practical effect was to restore the infant as equitable tenant of the property under the constructive trust.

BOARDMAN V PHIPPS[76]

[10.45] The decision of the House of Lords in *Boardman v Phipps* is one of the most controversial in the law of fiduciary obligations. Its critics argue that the majority decision applied the 'no conflict' and 'no profit' rules too harshly; a fiduciary whose skill and effort secured considerable benefits to the beneficiaries was nonetheless held accountable for breach of fiduciary obligation.

A trust held a minority holding of shares in a poorly managed textile company. Boardman, the solicitor to the trustees, together with one of the beneficiaries, Tom Phipps, developed a

---

74 (1726) Sel Cas T King 61; 25 ER 223. See J Getzler, 'Rumford Market and the Genesis of Fiduciary Obligations' in A Burrows and A Rodger (eds), *Mapping the Law* (Oxford University Press, 2006) 577.

75 (1726) Sel Cas T King 61, 62; 25 ER 223, [62].

76 [1967] 2 AC 46; *Sourcebook* 10.5.2a, p 268. See Jones (n 71).

plan for gaining control of the company. Boardman and Phipps attended company meetings, purporting to represent the trust although they had not been given formal authority to do so. At the meetings, they obtained a great deal of information about the company. The trust was unable to purchase more shares in the company; it had no money to do so, and even if it had it would have been imprudent for the trustees to make the purchase. Boardman and Phipps used the information about the company to make an offer, which was accepted, to buy the shares of the directors of the company with their own money. The purchase meant that, between them, the trust, Boardman and Phipps had a majority shareholding in the company. They used their control to sell off loss-making assets and reorganise the company, ultimately making it profitable. The shareholders, including Boardman, Phipps and the beneficiaries of the trust, made considerable profits on their shares. Boardman and Phipps did not obtain the trustees' consent to their course of action. Two of the trustees were aware of their plans but one trustee, the testator's widow, was senile and not legally competent to consent.

A beneficiary, John Phipps, sued Boardman and Tom Phipps for breach of fiduciary duty, even though he had benefited from the reorganisation of the company. The House of Lords held by majority that the defendants had acted in breach of fiduciary duty although they also directed that Boardman be 'liberally remunerated' for the work he had done. The principal points to emerge from the decision are as follows:

(1) Boardman and Tom Phipps had, in the view of the majority, acted in breach of the 'no profit' and 'no conflict' rules. Both profited from their position as 'self-appointed agents' of the trust, obtaining information about the company, which enabled them to negotiate to purchase the directors' shares and to reorganise the company, and ultimately make a profit. In addition, Boardman was in a position of conflict between his duty as solicitor to advise the trustees on the purchase of additional shares and his interest in buying shares in his own name.[77] The minority judges considered that the defendants were not acting as agents but in their own right in obtaining information about the company and negotiating for the purchase of shares. They had therefore not acted in a fiduciary capacity in buying the shares.

(2) According to the majority, a fiduciary acts in breach of obligation if there is the slightest possibility of conflict between self-interest and the duty owed to the beneficiaries. Lord Upjohn, however, in dissent, held that the 'no conflict' rule applied only if there was 'a real sensible possibility of conflict'.[78] In his view, the conflict of interest identified by the majority was hypothetical in the absence of any proof that Boardman had been asked to advise the trustees about the trust purchasing additional shares. The requirement that there must be 'a real sensible possibility of conflict' is now recognised as an accurate statement of the 'no conflict' principle.[79]

77 See Finn, *Fiduciary Obligations* (n 3) 244–6, where the author points out that Boardman was under no duty to advise the trustees on this matter, and, if consulted, could have refused to act.

78 [1967] 2 AC 46, 124.

79 *Queensland Mines Ltd v Hudson* (1978) 52 ALJR 399, 401; *Beach Petroleum NL v Abbott Tout Russell Kennedy* (1999) 48 NSWLR 1, [425]; *Bell Group Ltd (in liq) v Westpac Banking Corporation (No 9)* (2008) 39 WAR 1, [4506]–[4507].

(3) The majority held that the defendants had not obtained the fully informed consent of the beneficiaries before purchasing the shares in their own name. In particular, they had not obtained the consent of the testator's widow or applied to the court to have her consent dispensed with on account of her senility.[80]

(4) The defendants were ordered to hold their shares on constructive trust for the beneficiaries of the trust and to account for the profits they had made. In calculating profit, a deduction was made for the price the defendants had paid for the shares. Although the imposition of a constructive trust for breach of fiduciary obligation is common and was awarded in *Keech v Sandford*,[81] the remedy in *Boardman* was controversial since it entitled the plaintiff to shares and dividends which he could not have obtained for himself. Another controversial feature of the remedy is that, in the event of the fiduciary's bankruptcy, the beneficiary is entitled to property held on constructive trust to the exclusion of the fiduciary's creditors.[82] There was, however, no question in *Boardman v Phipps* of either defendant being insolvent. An advantage of the constructive trust is that it is a convenient remedy. It enables specific property to be transferred to the plaintiff without the court having to engage in complex questions of computing the balance of receipts over expenditure, which would otherwise be necessary if an account of profits were to be ordered.[83]

(5) The House of Lords unanimously agreed that Boardman should be awarded 'liberal remuneration' for his considerable skill and effort in securing the purchase of the shares and reorganising the company. Equity has an inherent jurisdiction to award an allowance or remuneration to a fiduciary. The argument for remunerating Boardman was strong; his efforts on behalf of the Phipps trust went far beyond his retainer as solicitor to the trustees, and he had committed an honest breach of trust. In later cases, even dishonest fiduciaries have been awarded allowances provided that they can demonstrate that their special skill, effort and resources were responsible for making the profit.[84]

Critics of *Boardman v Phipps* argue that the decision over-deters fiduciaries. By insisting all gains be stripped from the fiduciaries, the majority of the House of Lords removed incentives for entrepreneurs to undertake fiduciary roles.[85] On the other hand, supporters argue that Boardman and Phipps should have been more active in consulting the trustees

80 The widow died before the shares were purchased but she had not previously been asked to approve the plan which culminated in the purchase of the shares. Wilberforce J at first instance preferred to rely on the fact that the plaintiff had not been consulted on the plan to buy the shares: [1964] 1 WLR 993, 1012–17.

81 See [10.44].

82 A Hicks, 'The Remedial Principle of Keech v Sandford Reconsidered' (2010) 69(2) *Cambridge Law Journal* 287.

83 See [4.2].

84 See, eg, *Warman International Ltd v Dwyer* (1995) 182 CLR 544. For a criticism of the causative basis for awarding allowances, see Matthew Harding, 'Justifying Fiduciary Allowances' in A Robertson and Tang Hang Wu (eds), *The Goals of Private Law* (Hart Publishing, 2009) 341.

85 Boardman never again advised a trust but instead became a Member of Parliament within a year of the House of Lords decision, and was later a government minister and chairman of a bank. See MW Bryan 'Boardman v Phipps' in C and P Mitchell (eds), *Landmark Cases in Equity* (Hart Publishing, 2012) 581.

and beneficiaries for whom they purported to act. In holding the fiduciaries accountable but ordering they be liberally remunerated, the majority judges may have achieved a reasonable compromise between the deterrent rationale of the law of fiduciary obligations and promoting socially valuable fiduciary behaviour.

CHAN V ZACHARIA[86]

The High Court decision in *Chan v Zacharia* applied *Keech v Sandford* to a professional partnership. The plaintiff and defendant were doctors who worked as partners. They rented premises as joint tenants under a three-year lease with an option to renew for a further two-year term. At the end of the three-year term, the doctors agreed to dissolve their partnership. The defendant, Dr Chan, was invited to join with the plaintiff in exercising the option to renew the lease but declined to do so. Shortly afterwards, Chan obtained a new lease of the premises, in his name only, in return for paying the landlord a premium of $10 000. A majority of the High Court, Murphy J dissenting, held that in obtaining the new lease the defendant had exploited his fiduciary position as co-partner of the plaintiff. He was ordered to hold the lease on constructive trust for both parties. [10.46]

A feature of *Chan v Zacharia* was the importance that Deane J, for the majority, attached to presumptions. Where a trustee obtains renewal of a lease to himself, the lease being trust property, it is irrebuttably presumed (ie it is a rule of law) that the trustee has obtained the renewal by use of his position as trustee. Where other fiduciaries, including partners, obtain renewal of a lease for themselves, the lease being the subject-matter of the fiduciary relationship, it is rebuttably presumed that the renewal was obtained by use of the fiduciary position.[87] The purpose of the presumptions is to overcome difficulties experienced by beneficiaries in showing that the gain made by the fiduciary was caused by the breach of obligation. In the case of fiduciaries other than trustees, the onus rests on the fiduciary to show that he did not obtain renewal of the lease by exploiting his fiduciary position. Dr Chan was both a co-trustee with the plaintiff of the doctors' legal rights under the lease, and a co-partner of the medical practice. In the capacity of co-partner, he was unable to rebut the presumption that he had obtained the new lease by reason of his fiduciary position.

Deane J also examined the role of deterrence in enforcing fiduciary obligations. In an important passage, he indicated his support for the reasoning of the minority judges in *Boardman v Phipps*,[88] essentially restating Lord Upjohn's test in *Boardman v Phipps* that there must be a 'real sensible' possibility of conflict of interest and not a remote possibility of conflict which is unlikely to harm the beneficiary.

86 (1984) 154 CLR 178; *Sourcebook* 10.5.4a, p 279.

87 (1984) 154 CLR 178, 201–2 (Deane J). A fiduciary who has obtained a benefit can avoid having to account for the benefit by showing either that it was obtained outside the scope of the fiduciary relationship, or if obtained within the scope of the relationship, that it was not caused by the breach. A 'but for' test will be sufficient to establish causation even if other causes contributed to obtaining the benefit. A dishonest fiduciary will be accountable for a benefit if the dishonest conduct contributed materially to obtaining the benefit, even if the 'but for' test is not satisfied: *Ancient Order of Foresters in Victoria Friendly Society Ltd v Lifeplan Australia Friendly Society Ltd* (2018) 265 CLR 1, [9]–[16] (Kiefel CJ, Keane and Edelman JJ), [84]–[89] (Gageler J).

88 *Chan v Zacharia* (1984) 154 CLR 178, 204–5.

Informed consent as a defence to an action for breach of fiduciary obligation

[10.47] Claims of breach of fiduciary obligation can be defeated on a number of grounds. These include:

(a) The equitable bars to relief, such as laches, unclean hands and hardship, which apply to all equitable claims.[89]

(b) Statutory defences to breaches of trust available to trustees under trustee legislation or to company directors under the *Corporations Act 2001* (Cth).[90]

(c) The beneficiary's informed consent. A fiduciary who obtains the beneficiary's consent to placing himself in a position of conflict between his interest and the duty he owes the beneficiary, or to making a profit from his fiduciary position, will not be liable for breach of fiduciary duty. Consent may be given prior to the transaction (authorisation) or subsequently (ratification).[91] It is convenient to refer to informed consent as a defence, but the correct analysis is that the beneficiary's informed consent prevents any liability for breach of fiduciary obligation from arising.

[10.48] In *Boardman v Phipps*,[92] the defendant Boardman argued that the trustees and beneficiaries of the Phipps trust, on whose behalf he was acting in buying shares and reorganising a company, had consented to his purchase of shares in the company. The majority of the House of Lords held that Boardman had not adequately explained the reasons for the purchase to the beneficiaries. Moreover, he had not consulted one of the trustees – the testator's widow, who was senile and who would not have understood Boardman's plan. It may seem harsh to hold a fiduciary accountable for failing to obtain the consent of a trustee who was legally incapable of consenting. But Boardman should have taken steps to remove the widow from the trusteeship prior to embarking on his scheme to reorganise the company.

[10.49] In order to obtain the beneficiary's consent, the fiduciary must have made full disclosure of all the facts to the beneficiary. The extent of the disclosure required will depend on 'the sophistication and intelligence of the persons to whom disclosure must be made'.[93] In *Farah Constructions Pty Ltd v Say-Dee Pty Ltd*,[94] the plaintiff and defendant entered into a fiduciary joint venture agreement to redevelop a property. The defendant was informed by the council that only a plan to redevelop the property in amalgamation with adjoining properties would be approved. The defendant also received information that some adjoining properties were available for purchase. The defendant disclosed the information to the plaintiff at different times and in different ways; for example, by mailing the council's notice of refusal of initial planning permission to the plaintiff. It was held that, since the plaintiff had considerable business experience, the disclosure had been sufficient.[95]

89 See chapter 6.
90 See chapter 20 for the trustee legislation.
91 See [10.41].
92 [1967] 2 AC 46; *Sourcebook* 10.5.2a, p 268.
93 *Farah Constructions Pty Ltd v Say-Dee Pty Ltd* (2007) 230 CLR 89, 139.
94 Ibid.
95 Ibid 139–40.

Remedies for breach of fiduciary obligation

The extensive relief available for breach of fiduciary obligation is one of the distinctive features of this head of equitable liability. The remedies available for breach are more numerous than the remedies available for, say, breach of contract or tort. Moreover, where a breach of obligation also amounts to a breach of contract or tort, equitable compensation for breach of the equitable obligation is not subject to the limitations that apply for damages, such as remoteness rules.[96] [10.50]

The remedies for breach of fiduciary obligation are distinguishable in terms of the objectives that their award achieves. They may be summarised as follows: [10.51]

- Compensation for loss: equitable compensation (a personal remedy) (chapter 4);
- Disgorgement of gain: account of profits (a personal remedy) (chapter 4); constructive trust (a proprietary remedy) (chapter 23); and
- Restitution of property obtained by the fiduciary in breach of obligation: rescission of gift or contract between the fiduciary and the beneficiary, together with constructive (or resulting) trust over property transferred or its traceable proceeds (a proprietary remedy) (chapters 5, 22 and 23).[97]

The list of remedies above is not comprehensive because the full range of equitable relief is, in principle, available to relieve against the consequences of a fiduciary duty. The beneficiary may, for example, also be awarded an injunction to prevent future breaches of fiduciary obligation. A common case is where an injunction is awarded to restrain a solicitor from acting against a former client in litigation where the solicitor's involvement would create a real and sensible possibility of conflict of interest.[98]

WHAT'S ONLINE?

Available at www.cambridge.org/highereducation/isbn/9781009232388/resources:

- Recommended further readings
- Further commentary
- Discussion topics
- Practice problems
- FAQs

96 See [4.12].
97 See chapter 2 for the distinction between personal and proprietary remedies.
98 See [10.19].

11

PARTICIPANTS IN A BREACH OF FIDUCIARY OBLIGATION

Introduction

The fiduciary may not be the only person who is accountable for a breach of fiduciary obligation. Other parties may also be liable. Suppose a solicitor misappropriates client money and then pays it into his wife's bank account. The solicitor might also have been helped to commit the breach by an accountant who gave the solicitor access to the client account. Will these third parties – the wife and accountant – be liable in equity for their participation in the fiduciary's breach? If the solicitor is solvent, the answer to this question may not matter much. The solicitor will be ordered to restore the money to the fund, together with compound interest to compensate for the loss of investment opportunity caused by the misappropriation.[1] But if the solicitor is insolvent the client will look to other participants in the fraud with 'deep pockets' to recover her funds.[2] [11.1]

Potential liability for participating in a breach of fiduciary obligation is illustrated by the following example: [11.2]

Solicitor S withdraws $10 000 of client C's money from the client account in breach of duty. He is assisted by A, the firm's accountant. S gives $10 000 to X, who spends $2000 on a family holiday, and pays the remaining $8000 to Y. Y uses $4000 to buy a valuable painting and gives the balance of $4000 to Z, who pays it into his bank account. S is insolvent. Leaving aside the worthless claim against S, C has potential claims against A, X, Y and Z. C may be able to recover against them, either because equity regards them as wrongdoers too (which is discussed in this chapter), or because equity will allow C to trace and claim property from them (discussed in chapter 21).

These claims are both *personal* and *proprietary*. C can claim a constructive trust over Y's painting as representing part of the stolen money.[3] This is a *proprietary* claim. C can also claim the $4000 paid into Z's bank account. This involves a tracing (or identification) exercise to identify the money in Z's account. C can then elect to take the money from the account.[4] On the other hand, C's claims against A and X will be *personal*. A never received C's money and X no longer has the money he received from S.

All the third parties in this example can be held liable *as constructive trustees*. They are not express trustees because they have not been appointed to hold the money they have received as trustees. Nevertheless, they are accountable in equity *as if* they were express trustees; this is the simple idea that the term 'constructive trust' is intended to express.[5] The duties which a constructive trustee must perform have never been authoritatively laid down[6] but, at a [11.3]

1 *Re Dawson (deceased)* [1966] 2 NSWR 211.

2 Some of the limitations imposed by the High Court in *Farah Constructions Pty Ltd v Say-Dee Pty Ltd* (2007) 230 CLR 89, on liability for knowing assistance, may be based on disapproval of pushing the 'deep pocket' analogy too far: see especially [184]. See also [11.17].

3 If the painting is worth less than $4000, C can claim equitable compensation of $4000 secured by an equitable lien over the painting. See chapter 22 and *Foskett v McKeown* [2001] 1 AC 102, 130 (Lord Millett).

4 *Stephens Travel Service International Pty Ltd v Qantas Airways Ltd* (1988) 13 NSWLR 331, 347 (Hope JA).

5 See chapter 23.

6 See Charles Mitchell and Stephen Watterson, 'Remedies for Knowing Receipt' in Charles Mitchell (ed), *Constructive and Resulting Trusts* (Hart, 2010) ch 4 for a discussion of the duties imposed in knowing receipt cases. Cf William Swadling, 'The Fiction of the Constructive Trust' (2011) 64(1) *Current Legal Problems* 399.

Figure 11.1 Client account

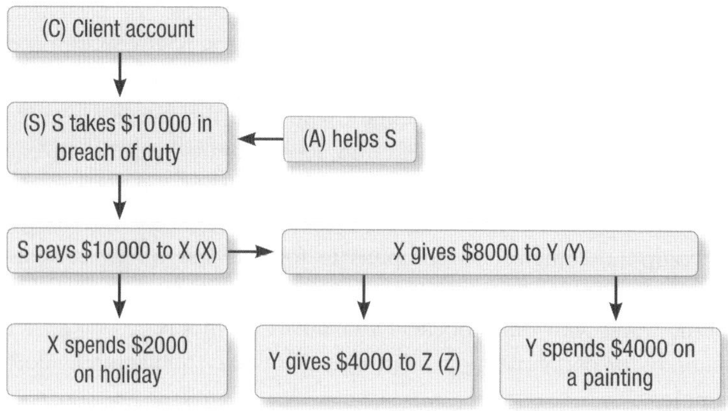

minimum, they include restoring the property received in breach of fiduciary obligation, and compensating the trust or principal for loss caused by the breach.[7] The duty to compensate the trust or principal should be particularly noted. We usually think of a constructive trustee as someone who is ordered by a court to hold property on trust for the plaintiff, but this need not be the case.[8] A defendant can be accountable as constructive trustee, and therefore liable to pay for loss caused by a breach of fiduciary duty even though he never received property from the fiduciary and so has nothing to return. In the example, A can be held accountable as constructive trustee for having helped S commit the breach even though he received none of the proceeds of the breach. A will be required to pay equitable compensation to C or to account for any gains made.

C cannot recover more than the amount S misappropriated, including compound interest to reflect the loss of its investment value. If C obtains full recovery from A, questions will arise as to whether A can obtain a contribution from X, Y and Z.[9]

Third party liability: the rule in *Barnes v Addy*

[11.4] The foundation case on third party liability for participating in a breach of fiduciary obligation is *Barnes v Addy*.[10] Addy, the trustee of a family trust, appointed Barnes sole trustee of half the trust fund. Barnes misapplied trust money and became bankrupt. Addy's solicitor, Duffield, had advised Addy not to appoint Barnes trustee, since placing trust money under the control of a sole trustee created a serious risk of misappropriation. Another solicitor, Preston, was

7 See chapter 23 for further discussion.
8 See chapter 23.
9 Alison Gurr, 'Accessory Liability and Contribution, Release and Apportionment' (2010) 34(2) *Melbourne University Law Review* 481.
10 (1874) LR 9 Ch App 244.

employed to execute the documents appointing Barnes sole trustee. After the trust money had been lost, the beneficiaries attempted to hold Duffield and Preston accountable for the loss. It was not a deserving claim and the Court of Appeal in Chancery rejected it in short order. Lord Selborne LC laid down the principles applicable to third party liability:

> [S]trangers are not to be made constructive trustees merely because they act as the agents of trustees in transactions within their legal powers, transactions, perhaps of which a Court of Equity may disapprove, unless those agents receive and become chargeable with some part of the trust property, or unless they assist with knowledge in a dishonest and fraudulent design on the part of the trustees.[11]

This dictum distinguishes between two types of third party liability:

(a) liability for *knowingly receiving* property in breach of trust or other fiduciary obligation (sometimes referred to as liability under the 'first limb' of *Barnes v Addy*); and

(b) liability for *knowingly assisting* a fiduciary to commit a breach of obligation (sometimes referred to as liability under the 'second limb' of *Barnes v Addy*).

Liability for knowing receipt and knowing assistance does not cover the entire field of third party liability. The final section of this chapter briefly considers other instances. Moreover, the liability of recipients must be read in conjunction with the tracing rules, leading to the recovery of specific property, discussed in chapter 21. [11.5]

Knowing receipt

A recipient of property transferred in breach of fiduciary obligation, or of the proceeds of such property, is liable to account as constructive trustee to the party to whom the fiduciary obligation is owed when the following criteria are satisfied: [11.6]

A breach of fiduciary obligation

This need not be a breach of trust but can consist of a breach of some other fiduciary obligation, such as the misappropriation of company property by a director or of client money by a solicitor.[12] The breach need not be dishonest.[13]

Receipt of property by the defendant

The property must have been received either directly from the fiduciary (as X did from S in the example above at [11.2]) or from someone who has directly or indirectly received the property from the fiduciary (as in the case of Y and Z in the example). The property may be the original property or the traceable proceeds of that property; for example, the painting purchased with client money in the example.

11 Ibid 251–2. See also *Fyler v Fyler* (1841) 3 Beav 550; 49 ER 221.

12 The point was left open by the High Court in *Farah Constructions Pty Ltd v Say-Dee Pty Ltd* (2007) 230 CLR 89, 144, but there is abundant authority applying recipient liability to breaches of obligation committed by company directors and other fiduciaries. See *Kalls Enterprises Pty Ltd (in liq) v Baloglow* [2007] 63 ACSR 557, [152]–[159] (Giles JA). See also *Grimaldi v Chameleon Mining NL (No 2)* (2012) 200 FCR 296 and *Hasler v Singtel Optus Pty Ltd* (2014) 87 NSWLR 609, [57] ('*Hasler*').

13 Cf liability for 'knowing assistance' discussed at [11.17].

The defendant must have *beneficially* received the property in question. This means that he must have received the property as principal, and not as agent for another party. An agent who deals with the property within the scope of the agency relationship will not be liable for 'knowing receipt'. Liability in such a case will be imposed on the principal, assuming that the other criteria for its imposition have been met. The practical importance of the requirement that receipt of property must be beneficial is that when the proceeds of fiduciary wrongdoing have been paid into a bank account, the bank will not be accountable in equity for having received the money provided that it applies the money in accordance with its customer's instructions. So, if F, a fiduciary, pays the proceeds of a fiduciary breach into his account at X bank, and later withdraws and spends the money, X bank will not have *received* the money for the purposes of third party liability. However, X bank will be accountable as constructive trustee if it applies the money for its own purposes; for example, by using the money to reduce F's overdraft with the bank, assuming that it is also aware of the breach of duty.

[11.7] In *Stephens Travel Service International Pty Ltd v Qantas Airways Ltd*,[14] Stephens, a travel agency, was required by the terms of its contract with Qantas to hold the proceeds of sale of Qantas tickets on trust for the airline. However, the proceeds were paid into Stephens' general trading account which was overdrawn. After a large payment had been made into the account from Qantas tickets sales, the bank closed the account and used the proceeds to reduce Stephens' overdraft. The New South Wales Court of Appeal held that the bank had knowingly received the money held on trust for Qantas which Stephens had, in breach of trust, paid into its general trading account. The bank's application of the money to reduce the overdraft constituted 'beneficial receipt' for the purpose of holding the bank accountable as constructive trustee. The bank had applied the money not as its customer's agent, but in its own right.

Knowledge of the breach of fiduciary duty

Two questions have to be answered under this heading.

(1) What did the recipient know of the breach of fiduciary duty? This is a question of fact. Answering it may be difficult, particularly if the recipient is a corporation and knowledge of the relevant facts is dispersed among different directors or employees.

(2) What type of knowledge must be proved in order to hold the recipient accountable as constructive trustee? This is a question of law. Numerous judgments and a voluminous academic literature have attempted to answer this question. In Australia, the answer is now clear as a result of the decision of the High Court in *Farah Constructions Pty Ltd v Say-Dee Pty Ltd*.[15] A brief sketch of the background to the decision remains necessary, however, in order to understand the Court's conclusion.

14 (1988) 13 NSWLR 331. See also *Quince v Varga* [2009] 1 Qd R 359, [50] where the issue is framed as whether the recipient had control over how property was used, rather than beneficial ownership. In this case, a trustee was liable for knowing receipt on the basis of his ability to control the disbursement of funds.

15 (2007) 230 CLR 89; Robert Chambers, 'Knowing Receipt: Frozen in Australia' (2007) 2(1) *Journal of Equity* 40; Joachim Dietrich and Pauline Ridge, 'Receipt of What? Questions Concerning Third Party Recipient Liability in Equity and Unjust Enrichment' (2007) 31(1) *Melbourne University Law Review* 47; Pauline Ridge and Joachim Dietrich, 'Equitable Third Party Liability' (2008) 124(1) *Law Quarterly Review* 26.

What type of knowledge?

Most decisions on knowing receipt have rejected the application of the doctrine of notice[16] to recipients of the proceeds of a breach of fiduciary duty. Under the doctrine, the recipient would be liable if he had actual, constructive or imputed notice of the breach of fiduciary duty.[17] There would be few objections to making a recipient liable if he had actual knowledge, or if his agent's knowledge was imputed to him, but courts have generally refused to apply the doctrine of constructive notice to commercial transactions. That doctrine imposes a duty on transferees of property to make reasonable inquiries into the existence of potential adverse equitable interests. Courts have acknowledged that it is unrealistic to expect recipients of money to investigate the possibility that the money represents the proceeds of a breach of fiduciary duty. In *Port of Brisbane Corporation v ANZ Securities Ltd*, McPherson JA made this point in connection with the receipt of money by a stockbroker: [11.8]

> A stockbroker who refused to receive or to deal with money from his client without first checking the client's title to it would soon find himself out of business. He is, after all, conducting a stockbroking business and not a detective agency. The same is true of a host of other activities, including the practice of accountants, solicitors and estate agents, in which funds are constantly being received from clients on trust to be applied for particular purposes. In many instances, the exigencies of the contemplated transaction would not permit a thorough, or indeed any, investigation as to the original source of the funds or their true ownership at the time of their receipt.[18]

In place of the doctrine of notice, courts have formulated a 'knowledge-based' test of liability which takes into account the context in which money or other property was received and the actual knowledge possessed by the recipient either at the time of receipt or subsequently. In *Baden, Delvaux and Lecuit v Société Générale*,[19] Peter Gibson J set out a scale of knowledge relevant to determining liability for 'knowing receipt' and 'knowing assistance' (the *Baden* scale). There are five points on the scale: [11.9]

(1) actual knowledge;

(2) wilfully shutting one's eyes to the obvious;

(3) wilfully and recklessly failing to make such inquiries as an honest and reasonable person would make;

(4) knowledge of circumstances which would indicate the facts to an honest and reasonable person; and

(5) knowledge of circumstances which would put an honest and reasonable person on inquiry.[20]

16 See [8.5].

17 *Consul Development Pty Ltd v DPC Estates Pty Ltd* (1975) 132 CLR 373 (a decision on 'knowing assistance', but the objections to notice-based liability extend to 'knowing receipt' claims).

18 [2003] 2 Qd R 661, [17].

19 [1992] 4 All ER 161 (a 'knowing assistance' case).

20 Ibid 235.

The advantage of the scale is that it confines liability to cases where the recipient was genuinely at fault in failing to uncover the breach of fiduciary duty. Its principal drawback is that it is not always easy to distinguish between the points on the scale. The lines drawn between the second, third and fourth points on the scale, in particular, are so fine as to be illusory in some cases.

[11.10] Reacting against the complex and contradictory authorities on knowledge-based liability, unjust enrichment writers have argued that recipients should be strictly liable to return property, or to pay the value of property if they no longer have it, to the principal to whom the fiduciary duty is owed. Liability here resembles the tort of conversion for the unauthorised taking of goods which is strict and does not depend on proof that the taker was at fault. Likewise, liability in an action for money had and received (or unjust enrichment) is also strict: a recipient of a mistaken payment is strictly liable to make restitution of the value of the payment unless a recognised restitutionary defence such as change of position applies.[21] It has been argued that equitable liability for 'knowing receipt' should also be strict, by analogy to liability in conversion and unjust enrichment.[22] Strict liability is not the same as absolute liability. Defences are available to the recipient in a strict liability claim, including change of position, which defeats a claim in unjust enrichment when the recipient has in good faith changed his position to his detriment.[23]

[11.11] In *Say-Dee Pty Ltd v Farah Constructions Pty Ltd*,[24] the New South Wales Court of Appeal held that the recipient was strictly liable to return property received in breach of fiduciary obligation. The plaintiff and defendant had entered into a joint venture agreement to develop a property. Elias, who controlled Farah Constructions, applied for council planning permission. The council refused permission as the site was too narrow for the proposed development, but Elias was informed that approval might be given if adjoining houses were purchased and incorporated into the development. Elias purchased the two adjoining properties and completed the development. Title to units in the adjoining properties was taken in the name of Elias's wife and their daughters.

On appeal, in *Farah Constructions Pty Ltd v Say-Dee Pty Ltd*,[25] the High Court rejected the application of unjust enrichment theory to determine recipient liability. The analysis was said by the High Court to be 'unhistorical' and inconsistent with the system of equitable titles to property recognised in Australia.[26] The High Court held that Elias was under a fiduciary duty to disclose to Say-Dee the council's opinion that planning approval would be given if the property were to be developed in amalgamation with adjoining properties, and that adjoining properties were for sale. Elias had made full disclosure of these matters to Say-Dee, so no breach of fiduciary duty had been committed. Even assuming, however, that Elias

21 An action for money had and received can sometimes coincide with an equitable 'knowing receipt' claim: *Spangaro v Corporate Investment Australia Funds Management Ltd* (2003) 47 ACSR 285.

22 P Birks, 'Misdirected Funds: Restitution from the Recipient' (1989) *Lloyd's Maritime & Commercial Law Quarterly* 296; Lord Nicholls, 'Knowing Receipt: The Need for a New Landmark' in W Cornish et al (eds), *Restitution Past, Present and Future* (Hart, 1998) 231.

23 *David Securities Pty Ltd v Commonwealth Bank of Australia* (1992) 175 CLR 353, 385; Elise Bant, *The Change of Position Defence* (Hart, 2009); Hon Justice WMC Gummow, '*Moses v Macferlan*: 250 Years On' (2010) 84(11) *Australian Law Journal* 756, 762–3.

24 [2005] NSWCA 309.

25 (2007) 230 CLR 89.

26 Ibid 256–8.

had failed to make full disclosure, his wife and daughters were not liable for having received property in breach of fiduciary obligation.

The High Court gave two reasons why the wife and daughters were not liable for knowing receipt. First, they had not received property. They had received information enabling them to purchase units in the adjoining properties and to benefit from their redevelopment. But information is not, in law, property,[27] and only recipients of property are liable under the first limb of *Barnes v Addy*.[28] Secondly, the wife and daughters had no knowledge of the (assumed) breach of fiduciary obligation.[29] Applying dicta in the earlier High Court decision of *Consul Development Pty Ltd v DPC Estates Pty Ltd*,[30] the High Court held that a recipient is only liable if he has knowledge on any of the first four points of the *Baden* scale. A recipient will therefore be liable if he has knowledge of circumstances which would indicate a breach of fiduciary duty to an honest and reasonable person. Elias's wife and daughters had no such knowledge of Elias's assumed breach of fiduciary obligation.

The recipient's knowledge must be of the breach of fiduciary obligation. He will not be liable if he was aware that he had received property from a fiduciary but was unaware of the breach.[31] Liability is imposed from the time he becomes aware of the breach. So a recipient of money from a fiduciary who spends some of the money prior to becoming aware of the fiduciary's breach will not be accountable for the amount spent.[32] [11.12]

Although *Farah* rejected strict liability for the equitable receipt claim, subsequent case law has held that recipients of property can be held liable for money had and received at common law.[33]

Remedies for knowing receipt

The choice of remedy for knowing receipt will depend on whether the recipient is still holding the property taken in breach of fiduciary duty. If the recipient no longer holds the property, the principal will be limited to the personal remedies of equitable compensation or account of profits. [11.13]

If the recipient still holds the property, the position is more complicated and, in part, depends on the property involved.[34] In some cases, the principal will not have to rely on the rule in *Barnes v Addy*. She will be entitled to trace the property to the recipient and claim it.[35] This is also easier for the principal to establish. If the principal claims property traced, the onus of proof will rest on the recipient to defeat the claim by showing he is a good faith purchaser for value without notice of the trust. Conversely, if the principal [11.14]

27 See [8.2].

28 (2007) 230 CLR 89, 145–6. Even assuming that information was property, Elias had not transferred it to his wife and daughters: 144.

29 Ibid 145.

30 (1975) 132 CLR 373, 396 (Gibbs J); 409–10 (Stephen J).

31 *Spangaro v Corporate Investment Australia Funds Management Ltd* (2003) 47 ACSR 285, [55].

32 *Re Blundell* (1888) 40 Ch D 370.

33 See *Fistar v Riverwood Legion and Community Club Ltd* (2016) 91 NSWLR 732; *Sourcebook* 11.2.5a, p 300; *Great Investments Ltd v Warner* (2016) 243 FCR 516.

34 The nature of the breach of duty is also relevant. If the breach is one of fiduciary duty, other than a breach of trust, proprietary relief is not available unless the transaction is rescinded: *Grimaldi v Chameleon Mining NL (No 2)* (2012) 200 FCR 296, [277].

35 See chapter 21.

wishes to establish that the recipient is liable for knowing receipt, she will bear the burden of establishing the recipient had sufficient knowledge. In *Farah Constructions Pty Ltd*,[36] the High Court assumed that proprietary remedies were available for knowing receipt, and that relief was not purely personal. It is unclear where the burden of proof is placed when a principal tries to recover specific property from a third party recipient.

[11.15] Where the misappropriated property is registered land, the recipient will be entitled to the benefit of indefeasible title and will not have to return it unless one of the so-called exceptions to indefeasibility can be established.[37] Two exceptions are relevant here:

(1) The recipient was party to the trustee's fraud,[38] in which case the land must be returned; and

(2) The 'in personam' principle.[39] A registered proprietor is bound by interests he has created which affect his title, such as an express trust over the land. The proprietor is also bound where his conduct entitles another to enforce an interest against him.[40] In *Farah Constructions Pty Ltd*, the High Court held that the principle only applied where the constructive trustee was the 'primary wrongdoer'.[41] The recipient will usually be the secondary wrongdoer.

[11.16] It is not clear whether a defendant who has knowingly received land in breach of fiduciary duty, and who has obtained indefeasible title, must instead pay equitable compensation to the principal.[42] It has been argued that enforcing a personal claim against the recipient would undermine the principle of indefeasibility which is the cornerstone of the Torrens land registration system.[43]

Liability for knowing assistance

[11.17] One who knowingly assists the commission of a breach of fiduciary duty is liable to compensate for loss or account for gains caused by the breach if the following criteria are met:

(a) *A dishonest and fraudulent breach of trust.* In *Barnes v Addy*, Lord Selborne stated that strangers are accountable if they 'assist with knowledge in a dishonest and fraudulent design on the part of the trustees'.[44] Whether the breach of trust, or of other fiduciary obligation, must be dishonest and fraudulent has been a controversial question. In *Royal Brunei Airlines Sdn Bhd v Tan*,[45] the Privy Council held that an

36 *Farah Constructions Pty Ltd v Say-Dee Pty Ltd* (2007) 230 CLR 89.

37 BJ Edgeworth et al (eds), *Sackville & Neave: Australian Property Law* (LexisNexis Butterworths, 10th ed, 2016) 470–504. Note that it will be relevant in some States whether the recipient was a volunteer: *King v Smail* [1958] VR 273; *Bogdanovic v Koteff* (1988) 12 NSWLR 472; *Conlan v Registrar of Titles* (2001) 24 WAR 299; *Land Title Act 1994* (Qld) s 180. See also [21.28].

38 *Assets Co Ltd v Mere Roihi* [1905] AC 176, 210 (Lord Lindley).

39 Edgeworth et al (n 37) 496–508.

40 See *Baumgartner v Baumgartner* (1987) 164 CLR 137. See also chapter 23.

41 (2007) 230 CLR 89, [195] quoting Pullin J in *LHK Nominees Pty Ltd v Kenworthy* (2002) 26 WAR 517, 571.

42 *Super 1000 Pty Ltd v Pacific General Securities Pty Ltd* (2008) 221 FCR 427, [235].

43 But see recent case law on the interaction between tracing, indefeasibility and personal restitutionary claims, discussed at chapter 23.

44 (1874) LR 9 Ch App 244, 251–2.

45 [1995] 2 AC 378.

assister will be liable even if the breach is honest. In the opinion of Lord Nicholls, it would make no sense if 'a dishonest third party is liable if the trustee is dishonest, but if the trustee did not act dishonestly that of itself would excuse a dishonest third party from liability'.[46]

However, in *Farah Constructions Pty Ltd*, the High Court insisted on strict fidelity to Lord Selborne's dictum: the breach of duty must be dishonest and fraudulent.[47] It was pointed out that breaches of trust and fiduciary obligation vary widely in their seriousness, and that it would be unduly onerous to impose equitable liability on professional advisers where the breach of duty was entirely innocent. Otherwise, if a trustee negligently breached trust on the (incorrect) advice of a solicitor, the solicitor could be liable as a knowing assistant. The meaning of 'dishonest and fraudulent' for the purposes of this limb has been the subject of some judicial disagreement post-*Farah Constructions Pty Ltd*. In *Westpac Banking Corporation v Bell Group Ltd (in liq) (No 3)*,[48] the Western Australian Court of Appeal held that a breach would be 'dishonest and fraudulent' if (a) it is 'characterised as dishonest or fraudulent according to equitable principles', and (b) it 'is more than a trivial breach and is also too serious to be excusable because the fiduciary has acted honestly, reasonably and ought fairly to be excused'.[49]

The New South Wales Court of Appeal in the later decision of *Hasler v Singtel Optus Pty Ltd*[50] refused to follow *Bell* on this point, on the basis that it was 'plainly wrong'.[51] In *Hasler*, Leeming JA held that the 'dishonest and fraudulent' component requires dishonesty on the part of the fiduciary. His Honour stated:

> Dishonesty amounts to a transgression of ordinary standards of honest behaviour … it is not necessary to demonstrate that the person thought about what those standards were.[52]

Gageler J endorsed the *Hasler* test in *Ancient Order of Foresters in Victoria Friendly Society Ltd v Lifeplan Australia Friendly Society Ltd*.[53] The *Hasler* formulation has also been approved by the Full Federal Court.[54]

While the High Court in *Farah Constructions Pty Ltd* insisted on retaining the traditional formulation of liability, the Court did not directly answer Lord Nicholls' objection to permitting a third party to escape liability when he had dishonestly assisted an honest fiduciary to commit a breach of obligation. It may be that the third

46 Ibid 385.

47 (2007) 230 CLR 89, 159, 163.

48 (2012) 44 WAR 1.

49 Ibid [2112] (Drummond AJA).

50 (2014) 87 NSWLR 609.

51 Ibid [102] (Leeming JA), Gleeson JA agreed at [10]. The decision was followed in *Cornerstone Property & Development Pty Ltd v Suellen Properties Pty Ltd* [2015] 1 Qd R 75.

52 (2014) 87 NSWLR 609, [124], paraphrasing Lord Hoffman in *Barlow Clowes International Ltd (in liq) v Eurotrust International Ltd* [2006] 1 WLR 1476, [16].

53 (2018) 265 CLR 1, [11.22]. Citing *Hasler*, His Honour stated: 'The requisite element of dishonesty and fraud on the part of the fiduciary is met where the conduct which constitutes the breach transgresses ordinary standards of honest behaviour': [71].

54 *Zibara v Ultra Management (Sports) Pty Ltd* (2021) 283 FCR 18, [106].

party could be held liable in this case for a distinct equitable wrong of knowingly inducing a breach of fiduciary obligation.[55]

(b) *Assistance in the breach*. There is little authority on the meaning of assistance. It is suggested that the third party will be liable as an assister where either the breach would not have occurred without the assistance or where the breach was committed earlier than would have been the case because of the assistance received. In *Harstedt Pty Ltd v Tomanek*,[56] the Victorian Court of Appeal identified two principles regarding assistance:

> First, there will be assistance where, but for the action or inaction of the third party, the breach of fiduciary duty would not have occurred … Secondly, there may also be assistance where the third party has facilitated a breach of fiduciary duty that would have occurred in any event.[57]

The Court did not address whether an omission or acquiescence could amount to assistance.[58]

(c) *Knowledge of the breach of fiduciary duty*. The meaning of knowledge for the purpose of imposing liability for knowing assistance has proved to be as difficult to determine as it has been in the law of *knowing* receipt. Here also, the High Court decision in *Farah Constructions Pty Ltd* has removed some of the uncertainty.

What type of knowledge?

[11.18] The earlier High Court decision of *Consul Development Pty Ltd v DPC Estates Pty Ltd*[59] established that equitable liability for assistance would only be imposed upon proof of knowledge. A solicitor controlled a property company whose manager identified and recommended properties to the solicitor that were suitable for purchase and redevelopment. The solicitor also employed an articled clerk in his law practice, who controlled his own property company. The manager of the solicitor's property company informed the articled clerk about properties which were suitable for redevelopment, saying that the solicitor's company was unable to buy them. Having confirmed from other sources that the solicitor's company could not afford to buy them, the articled clerk's company purchased the properties and redeveloped them profitably. The High Court, McTiernan J dissenting, held that the articled clerk was not liable for having knowingly assisted the manager to commit a breach of fiduciary obligation by giving the opportunity to buy the properties to the clerk, and not to the solicitor.

55 *Farah Constructions Pty Ltd v Say-Dee Pty Ltd* (2007) 230 CLR 89, 159. See [11.24].
56 (2018) 55 VR 158.
57 Ibid [117]–[118] citations omitted. In *Re-Engine Pty Ltd (in liq) v Fergusson* (2007) 209 FLR 1, Dodds-Streeton J at [120] held that the assistance should 'forward or advance the primary breach or misconduct in some way. Mere passive acquiescence in the breach would not, in the ordinary case, suffice to establish liability on the ground of assistance'. The English authorities on the meaning of 'assistance' are collected in Charles Mitchell, 'Assistance' in Peter Birks and Arianna Pretto (eds), *Breach of Trust* (Hart, 2002) 171–82.
58 *Harstedt Pty Ltd v Tomanek* (2018) 55 VR 158, [119].
59 (1975) 132 CLR 373.

The majority rejected application of the doctrine of notice as the test of whether an assister knew of the breach of fiduciary obligation. Knowledge rather than notice was required. But the majority judges formulated the knowledge test in different terms. Gibbs J stated that '[i]t would not be just that a person who had full knowledge of all the facts could escape liability because his own moral obtuseness prevented him from recognizing an impropriety that would have been apparent to an ordinary man'.[60] Stephen J, with whom Barwick CJ agreed, defined the knowledge requirement in these terms: 'If a defendant knows of facts which themselves would, to a reasonable man, tell of fraud or breach of trust the case may well be different [i.e., the defendant will be liable], as it clearly will be if the defendant has consciously refrained from enquiry for fear lest he learn of fraud. But to go further is, I think, to disregard equity's concern for the state of conscience of the defendant.'[61]

Consul Development was decided before the *Baden* scale of knowledge was formulated,[62] and it was unclear how the dicta of Gibbs and Stephen JJ could be converted to points on the scale. Moreover, the exercise of drawing fine distinctions between degrees of knowledge has been criticised by judges for being overelaborate. In *Royal Brunei Airlines Sdn Bhd v Tan*,[63] the Privy Council discarded the knowledge test, replacing it with a test of dishonesty, so that the equitable wrong consists of dishonestly assisting a fiduciary to commit a breach of duty. Lord Nicholls described dishonesty as an objective standard: 'The individual is expected to attain the standard which would be observed by an honest person placed in those circumstances.'[64] His aim in replacing 'knowledge' with 'dishonesty' was to treat the mental requirement as a question of fact, and not as a question of law dependent on the precise judicial meaning ascribed to knowledge. Following the *Tan* decision, some Australian courts applied the dishonesty test on the basis that it was not inconsistent with the tests laid down in *Consul Development*.[65] [11.19]

In *Farah Constructions Pty Ltd*,[66] the High Court rejected, at least for the time being, the dishonesty test laid down in *Royal Brunei Airlines Sdn Bhd v Tan*, and reaffirmed the knowledge test applied in the *Consul Development* case. The judgments in *Consul* were restated in terms of the *Baden* scale of knowledge. An assister will be accountable as constructive trustee for having knowingly assisted the commission of a breach of fiduciary obligation if he has knowledge of the breach of duty on any of the first four points of the *Baden* scale, the fourth point being that the assister knows of circumstances which would put an honest and reasonable person on inquiry as to the existence of a breach of fiduciary obligation. The High Court did not completely rule out acceptance of the dishonesty test, but only a later High Court decision can introduce the test into Australian law.[67] [11.20]

60 Ibid 398.
61 Ibid 412.
62 See [11.9].
63 [1995] 2 AC 378.
64 Ibid 399.
65 The dishonesty test has in turn arguably become overelaborate: *Twinsectra Ltd v Yardley* [2002] 2 AC 164; *Barlow Clowes International Ltd (in liq) v Eurotrust International Ltd* [2006] 1 WLR 1476.
66 (2007) 230 CLR 89.
67 Ibid. The Victorian Court of Appeal in *Harstedt Pty Ltd v Tomanek* (2018) 55 VR 158 rejected dishonesty on the part of the assister as the applicable test at [84].

Remedies for knowing assistance

[11.21] Only personal relief can be awarded in a claim for knowing assistance. Although the assister is described as a constructive trustee, the term 'constructive trust' does not imply that he holds identified property on trust. It is a shorthand expression for stating that he is personally liable to account as if he were an express trustee.

[11.22] The usual remedy awarded is equitable compensation. The objective of the remedy is to compensate the beneficiary for loss caused by the breach of duty. The assister is liable to compensate for all the loss caused by the breach, although he can obtain a contribution from the fiduciary and other assisters.[68]

Exceptionally, an assister will be liable to account for profits made by the breach of obligation.[69] For the purpose of imposing liability for knowing assistance, the profits must have been made by the assister, not by the fiduciary.[70] If the assistance has caused both a loss to the beneficiary and a gain to the assister, the beneficiary must elect between compensation and an account of profits.[71]

The High Court decision of *Ancient Order of Foresters in Victoria Friendly Society Ltd v Lifeplan Australia Friendly Society Ltd*[72] is an example of an account of profits being awarded against a knowing assister in a breach of fiduciary duty. In this case, two fiduciaries employed by Lifeplan Australia Friendly Society Limited (Lifeplan) worked with the competitor of their employer (Foresters) to set up a competing business, while they were still employed. The business model for the competitor's business was based directly on Lifeplan's business plan and on the acquisition of the business connections of Lifeplan. The new business was highly successful, to the detriment of Lifeplan's business.

At trial, the judge awarded no account of profits against Foresters on the basis that the breaches might have allowed the competing business to be established earlier than would otherwise have been the case, but 'did not lead to the profits earned'.[73] On appeal to the Full Court, it was held that Foresters should account for over $6 million in profits, being the value of contracts written in a prescribed period. In the High Court, a majority of the Court ordered Foresters to account for over $14 million, being the total capital value of the new business.[74]

In a joint judgment, Kiefel CJ, Keane and Edelman JJ stated: 'where causation is sufficiently established the onus is upon the errant fiduciary or participant to show that he or she should not account for the full value of the advantage'.[75] Foresters could not identify any factor that explained the success of its new business aside from the strategy implemented by Foresters and the fiduciaries.

---

68 Gurr (n 9) 481.

69 See also *Warman International Ltd v Dwyer* (1995) 182 CLR 544, where an account of profits was awarded against companies controlled by the fiduciary, as well as against the fiduciary. An account of profits was recognised as a potential remedy in *Farah Constructions Pty Ltd v Say-Dee Pty Ltd* (2007) 230 CLR 89, 172. See also Steven B Elliott and Charles Mitchell, 'Remedies for Dishonest Assistance' (2004) 67(1) *Modern Law Review* 16.

70 *Chameleon Mining NL v Murchison Metals Ltd* [2010] FCA 1129, reversed in part in *Grimaldi v Chameleon Mining NL (No 2)* (2012) 200 FCR 296.

71 *Chameleon Mining NL v Murchison Metals Ltd* [2010] FCA 1129.

72 (2018) 265 CLR 1. See also chapter 4.

73 *Lifeplan Australia Friendly Society Ltd v Woff* (2016) 259 IR 384, [444].

74 Per the joint judgment Kiefel CJ, Keane and Edelman JJ, and Gageler J; Nettle J dissented.

75 (2018) 265 CLR 1, [13] (Kiefel CJ, Keane and Edelman JJ).

Other forms of participatory liability

Claims based on tracing

Tracing is the process of identifying the claimant's property in the hands of the defendant. It is discussed in detail in chapter 21. Tracing claims can be combined with claims under both limbs of *Barnes v Addy*. In the example given at the beginning of this chapter, C may be able to trace her money into the painting Y has bought and into Z's bank account. [11.23]

A defence to a tracing claim in equity is that the claimant's property has been acquired by a good faith purchaser for value without notice of the claimant's interest in the property. If a knowing receipt claim also entitles a successful claimant to recover the property, it is uncertain whether a knowledge test or the doctrine of notice will be applied to determine whether a purchaser is entitled to retain this property. This question is discussed at [11.14] above.

Inducing a breach of trust

Before *Barnes v Addy* established the modern dichotomy of knowing receipt and knowing assistance, other forms of participatory liability were recognised in equity. For example, liability was imposed in some cases for knowingly inducing or procuring a breach of trust where the trustee had not acted with an improper motive.[76] In *Farah Constructions Pty Ltd*,[77] the High Court noted the existence of liability for knowing inducement. Although the High Court did not clearly state that the action is recognised in Australia, later decisions have proceeded on the basis that the cause of action exists in modern Australian equity. In *Grimaldi v Chameleon Mining NL (No 2)*, the Federal Court regarded the action of knowing inducement as an available cause of action[78] and the Victorian Court of Appeal has upheld the imposition of liability under this cause of action.[79] [11.24]

In *Pittmore v Chan*, Leeming JA outlined two elements for this action: 'The first is the intentional conduct which causes, and is intended to cause, the breach of trust or fiduciary duty. The second is that the third party knew that he or she was bringing about a breach of trust or fiduciary duty.'[80]

There is no difference between inducing and procuring a breach of duty.[81] An important feature of this basis of liability is that it is not necessary to show that the fiduciary's breach was dishonest and fraudulent.[82] It appears that level (4) knowledge on the *Baden* scale is also sufficient for liability under this head.[83]

---

76 *Fyler v Fyler* (1841) 3 Beav 550, 561–2, 567–8; 49 ER 221, 223–4; *Eaves v Hickson* (1861) 30 Beav 136; 54 ER 840. See C Harpum, 'The Stranger as Constructive Trustee' (1986) 102(1) *Law Quarterly Review* 114, 141–4.

77 (2007) 230 CLR 89, 159.

78 *Grimaldi v Chameleon Mining NL (No 2)* (2012) 200 FCR 296, [245]. See also *Hasler v Singtel Optus Pty Ltd* (2014) 87 NSWLR 609, [77], [106].

79 *Marriner v Australian Super Developments Pty Ltd* [2016] VSCA 141. See also the extensive discussion by Sloss J at first instance: *Australian Super Developments Pty Ltd v Marriner* [2014] VSC 464, [284]–[310].

80 *Pittmore Pty Ltd v Chan* (2020) 104 NSWLR 62, [186] ('*Pittmore*'). The action failed on the facts.

81 Ibid [161] (Leeming JA, Bell P and Brereton JA agreeing).

82 Ibid. See also *Chickabo Pty Ltd & Ors v Zphere Pty Ltd* (2019) 57 VR 406.

83 *Pittmore* [192].

If these cases are correct and the knowing inducement action exists, it fills a gap in knowing assistance liability created by *Farah Constructions* where an innocent trustee is persuaded by a dishonest third party to commit a breach of trust. After *Farah Constructions*, the third party will not be liable for knowing assistance because the trustee's breach is not dishonest and fraudulent, but he might nonetheless be liable for knowing inducement. Remedies for inducement are personal only.

Trusteeship de son tort

[11.25] Someone who acts in the capacity of trustee without being properly appointed, and administers the trust, will be personally liable to compensate for any loss caused by the administration as if he had been properly appointed a trustee. Such a person is known as a 'trustee de son tort', meaning a 'trustee by his own wrong'. The defendant will not be held liable as a trustee de son tort unless he has sufficient control over the trust property to enable him to dispose of it.[84]

Equity recognises the concept of 'executor de son tort', where a third party assumes the role of an executor of an estate,[85] and 'agency de son tort',[86] where the role of agent is assumed without proper appointment. By acting without authority, such persons find themselves subject to the fiduciary obligations for which they would have been accountable if they had been properly appointed.

WHAT'S ONLINE?

Available at www.cambridge.org/highereducation/isbn/9781009232388/resources:

- Recommended further readings
- Further commentary
- Discussion topics
- Practice problem

84 *Re Barney* [1892] 2 Ch 265. See also *Nolan v Nolan* [2004] VSCA 109.

85 *Nolan v Nolan* [2004] VSCA 109; *Re Estate of Daisy May Phillips (deceased)* [2009] SASC 200.

86 *Lyell v Kennedy* (1889) 14 App Cas 437. The defendants in *Boardman v Phipps* were agents de son tort insofar as they acted as agents of the Phipps trust without authority: *Phipps v Boardman* [1965] 1 Ch 992, 1017–18 (Lord Denning MR).

12

BREACH OF CONFIDENCE

Introduction

[12.1] The equitable obligation of confidence is used to protect information from unauthorised misuse or exploitation by others. The action now has two significant aspects: it is traditionally used to protect commercially valuable information such as trade secrets, and it is increasingly used to protect personally private information. Whether the same considerations apply to these two aspects of the action is an open question. Though the obligation of confidence is one of the oldest in equitable jurisdiction,[1] it has only recently been called upon to protect interests previously thought to be ineffectively protected.

[12.2] The long hiatus between the action's origins and its current development is partly due to the unusual position confidentiality has occupied. Whereas many equitable responsibilities, such as trust or fiduciary obligations, have no direct common law counterparts, confidentiality can be regulated by regimes other than equity.[2] Up until the mid-twentieth century, most cases concerning the equitable obligation of confidence also involved a breach of an obligation of confidence not sourced in equity.[3] For this reason, the courts were not particularly rigorous in their discussions of the doctrine.[4] In older cases, it can be hard to discern whether courts are referring to an equitable obligation, a contractual obligation, or perhaps both. This is particularly noticeable in respect of remedies.

The equitable obligation of confidence

[12.3] A comprehensive statement of the law of confidential information for Australian purposes was given in *Smith Kline & French Laboratories (Australia) Ltd v Secretary, Department of Community Services*.[5] Gummow J identified the four elements of the obligation that must be demonstrated by the plaintiff:

(1) The information said to be confidential must be identified with *specificity* and not merely in global terms;

(2) The information has the *necessary quality of confidentiality* (and is not, for example, common or public knowledge);

(3) The information was received by the defendant in *such circumstances as to import an obligation of confidence*; and

(4) That there is actual or threatened *misuse of that information*, without the consent of the plaintiff.[6]

1 See *Coco v AN Clark (Engineers) Ltd* [1969] RPC 41, 46; *Sourcebook* 12.2a, p 318.

2 Such as contract or statute; see, eg, *Health Records and Information Privacy Act 2002* (NSW); *Privacy and Personal Information Protection Act 1998* (NSW); *Privacy Act 1988* (Cth).

3 The first superior court decision to rely exclusively on an equitable obligation of confidence was *Saltman Engineering Co Ltd v Campbell Engineering Co Ltd* (1948) 65 RPC 203: see MGL [42-060].

4 See, eg, *Duke of Queensberry v Shebbeare* (1758) 2 Eden 329; 28 ER 924. The case was decided in Chancery, but there is no discussion of the nature of the jurisdiction. The decision appears to conform to a modern understanding of the action of breach of confidence.

5 (1990) 22 FCR 73.

6 Ibid 87 (emphasis added).

Unless the defendant can establish some valid defence, equity will restrain the unauthorised misuse. If the misuse has already occurred, a wide range of remedies, including an account of profits and equitable compensation, is available.

It is possible for the equitable obligation of confidence to overlap with other equitable obligations. For example, if a senior employee takes confidential information from his employer and uses it for his own profit, he will be in breach of confidence and in breach of the fiduciary profits rule.[7] Fiduciary obligations are discussed in chapter 10.

Specificity

The plaintiff must be able to precisely specify the information she claims is protected because the court has to assess whether that information is, in fact, confidential or whether any confidentiality it once had has been destroyed by publication. A second reason for specificity relates to remedy. If called upon to restrain a misuse by injunction, the court must determine the scope of the injunction, otherwise it will be impossible to enforce. It is relatively unusual for plaintiffs to be unable to specify what information is claimed to be confidential.[8] [12.4]

Quality of confidentiality

To be protected, information must have the necessary quality of confidentiality. Sometimes confidentiality is implicit in the information itself. Hence, medical records are taken to be confidential.[9] Alternatively, the nature of the relationship between the parties implies the necessary quality of confidence. This was so where a man threatened to expose marital secrets concerning his ex-wife.[10] Sometimes the manner and detail in which the information is recorded can give it a quality of confidentiality.[11] Information contained in documents for which legal professional privilege is claimed will often, but not always, be confidential in nature.[12] Whether or not privilege attaches to a communication is not the same question as whether the information in the communication has the necessary quality of confidence.[13] [12.5]

The term 'quality of confidentiality' should not imply that the information must be secret, as the concepts of secrecy and confidentiality do not completely overlap. Complete secrecy is not necessary: information may be known in its entirety by some and still be

7 Remedial consequences can attach to the choice of cause of action; in Australia, constructive trusts are available in cases of breach of fiduciary duty, but not for breach of confidence.

8 *O'Brien v Komesaroff* (1982) 150 CLR 310; *Sourcebook* 12.2.1a, p 321; *Borgese v Cater & Blumer Pty Ltd (No 3)* [2017] NSWSC 92; *Bluescope Steel Ltd v Kelly* (2007) 72 IPR 289. If complete specification of the information in pleadings would have the effect of destroying the quality of confidence in the information, plaintiffs may be allowed some lack of specificity.

9 *W v Egdell* [1990] 1 All ER 835; *Australian Football League v The Age Co Ltd* (2006) 15 VR 419; *Sourcebook* 12.2.1.1a, p 323. The same is true of company board papers: *NRMA Ltd v Geeson* (2001) 40 ACSR 1.

10 *Duchess of Argyll v Duke of Argyll* [1967] Ch 302.

11 In *Giller v Procopets* [2004] VSC 113; (2008) 24 VR 1 sex videos of a couple were held to be confidential, even though it was well known that the couple had a sexual relationship.

12 *Lord Ashburton v Pape* [1913] 2 Ch 469.

13 *Cowell v British American Tobacco Australian Services Ltd* [2007] VSCA 301, [32]–[34].

confidential.[14] The real concern is with accessibility of the information.[15] Information that was originally confidential loses protection when it enters the public domain because it is readily accessible.[16] However, so long as information retains its confidential nature, there is no restriction on the type of information that can be protected or the form that information can take. For example, plans,[17] photographs,[18] drawings,[19] customer lists,[20] concepts for television shows,[21] fruit-tree cuttings,[22] sex videos,[23] and recipes for drinks[24] have all been held to be or contain confidential information.

[12.6] While information retains its confidential nature, the obligation not to misuse it continues. This means that, in some cases, the obligation can continue indefinitely.[25]

[12.7] Whether information has entered the public domain is a question of fact and is invariably one of degree. In *Australian Football League v The Age Co Ltd*,[26] a newspaper wanted to publish names of footballers who had recorded multiple positive drug tests. This information was prima facie confidential to the AFL and the footballers. The names had been broadcast on cable television (to a small audience); they were also known to AFL officials. Additionally, there had been extensive internet speculation concerning the footballers' identities, some of which correctly identified them. The newspaper argued that publication had destroyed the information's confidentiality. Kellam J held that it had not; the limited actual publication that had occurred did not amount to public knowledge. A distinction was drawn between gossip and innuendo on the one hand, and public knowledge on the other, internet speculation falling into the former category.[27]

[12.8] Alternatively, information may be known in part and still be confidential. Compilations of well-known information may be confidential if sufficient effort has gone into the compilation. For example, land sizes and sale prices are matters of public record, and building plans can be inspected by the public. There will be little or no confidentiality attaching to those individual pieces of information. However, a valuation report compiled for the owner of the land will have the requisite quality of confidence due to the effort that has gone into its preparation.

[12.9] Originality per se is not protected by equity;[28] the equitable obligation of confidence does not seek to quarantine knowledge permanently or to encourage the plaintiff to suppress it. Information recreated by independent effort or reverse engineering[29] does not have the

---

14 *Australian Football League v The Age Co Ltd* (2006) 15 VR 419.
15 John Glover, *Equity, Restitution and Fraud* (LexisNexis Butterworths, 2004) 329.
16 *Jane Doe v Fairfax Media Publications Pty Ltd* [2018] NSWSC 1996.
17 *Saltman Engineering Co Ltd v Campbell Engineering Co Ltd* (1948) 65 RPC 203.
18 *Douglas v Hello! Ltd (No 3)* [2003] 3 All ER 996.
19 *Saltman Engineering Co Ltd v Campbell Engineering Co Ltd* (1948) 65 RPC 203.
20 *Ithaca Ice Works Pty Ltd v Queensland Ice Supplies Pty Ltd* [2002] QSC 222.
21 *Talbot v General Television Corporation Pty Ltd* [1980] VR 224.
22 *Franklin v Giddins* [1978] Qd R 72.
23 *Giller v Procopets* [2004] VSC 113; (2008) 24 VR 1.
24 *Cadbury Schweppes Inc v FBI Foods Ltd* (1999) 167 DLR (4th) 577.
25 *Faccenda Chicken Ltd v Fowler* [1984] Ch 589; *Prince Jefri Bolkiah v KPMG* [1999] 2 AC 222.
26 (2006) 15 VR 19.
27 Information alleged to be 'a farrago of lies' is not confidential in nature: *Duthie v Nixon* (2015) 47 VR 355, [28] (Beach JA). When a plaintiff wants protection against *untrue* information being circulated against her, the appropriate cause of action may be defamation, rather than breach of confidence.
28 Originality is protected by intellectual property regimes such as copyright and patent.
29 Reverse engineering occurs when a confidant or perhaps a third party 'picks the product apart' to discover its components or the process of its production.

necessary quality of confidence to enable it to be protected by the doctrine. The obligation of confidence guards against unauthorised misuse of confidential information. Information that has been independently recreated is not confidential and has not been misused.

Circumstances importing an obligation of confidence

The action for breach of confidence originally assumed that the information would be imparted within a confidential relationship.[30] As many early cases of breach of confidence also involved contract law (where information was confided during a contractual relationship or negotiations)[31] or relationships that were naturally confidential (such as a solicitor–client relationship),[32] this was easily made out. However, when the focus moved to cases where there was no concurrent obligation of confidence sourced outside of equity, the requirement that the information be imparted in a confidential relationship was relaxed, to the point where it is now no longer necessary at all. The obligation to observe confidentiality arises in circumstances where the recipient of the information knows or ought to know that the information cannot be used without the authority of the confider. The test is whether a reasonable person in the position of the confidant would have realised the information was confidential.[33] [12.10]

This objective standard allows the obligation of confidence to be imposed on persons who receive information outside of a confidential relationship. Thus attempts to use information obtained by surreptitious or unlawful means constitutes a breach of confidence.[34] In commercial cases, relevant indicators of confidentiality include express claims of confidentiality, evidence as to the extent the information is known in the industry, measures taken to guard the secrecy, the value of the information to its creator and its competitors, and the amount of effort and capital invested in acquiring the information.[35] The standard also allows an obligation of confidence to be imposed on third parties who innocently receive information from the original confidant. In *Wheatley v Bell*,[36] third parties paid for information concerning a confidential business idea from the person in whom the information had been confided. The third parties did not realise that the information was confidential to the plaintiff. There was obviously no relationship of confidence between the third parties and the plaintiff. Nevertheless, a duty of confidence was imposed upon the third parties from the time they became aware of the plaintiff's claim of confidentiality. Accidental recipients may also be caught by the objective standard. This was originally not the case,[37] but was recognised by Lord Goff as including: [12.11]

30 See N Witzleb, 'Money Remedies for Breach of Confidence in Privacy Cases' (2007) 27 *Legal Studies* 430, 432.

31 *Talbot v General Television Corporation Pty Ltd* [1980] VR 224.

32 *Lord Ashburton v Pape* [1913] 2 Ch 469. See also *Breen v Williams* (1996) 186 CLR 71 (doctor–patient); *Duchess of Argyll v Duke of Argyll* [1967] Ch 302 (marriage); *Hartigan Nominees Pty Ltd v Rydge* (1992) 29 NSWLR 405 (trust); *NRMA Ltd v Geeson* (2001) 40 ACSR 1 (director–company board).

33 *Coco v AN Clark (Engineers) Ltd* [1969] RPC 41, 48.

34 *Franklin v Giddins* [1978] Qd R 72, where a rival farmer stole cuttings of a competitor's nectarine tree.

35 *A-G (UK) v Heinemann Publishers Australia Pty Ltd* (1987) 10 NSWLR 86, 189–90 (McHugh JA).

36 [1982] 2 NSWLR 544.

37 *Malone v Commissioner of Police* [1979] Ch 344, 376 (Megarry V-C).

> ... situations beloved of law teachers – where an obviously confidential document is wafted by an electric fan out of a window into a crowded street, or where an obvious confidential document, such as a private diary, is dropped in a public place, and is then picked up by a passer-by.[38]

[12.12] As the obligation of confidence can arise in the absence of any pre-existing relationship between the parties, equitable liability now resembles tort: the obligation is owed in similar circumstances to the duty of care. However, the tort analogy should not be over-emphasised. The equitable obligation of confidence is more than a responsibility to be careful when using another's information; it is an obligation not to make unauthorised use of the information. In one respect, the extent of the similarity between breach of confidence and tort is unsettled. There is very little authority concerning whether employers can be vicariously liable for breaches of confidence by their employees. In *Coulthard v South Australia*,[39] it was assumed that employers could be held liable. As many reported cases involve employers sued in respect of the actions of their employees, this is likely to be correct.

Misuse of confidential information

[12.13] The obligation of confidence protects information from unauthorised misuse; that is, use against the wishes of the party to whom the information is confidential. Protection is also given where misuse is still only threatened.[40] There is no element of mens rea required of the defendant. Liability can attach if the misuse was accidental or unintentional.[41] In the *Prince Jefri Bolkiah* case, Lord Millett explained that the duty was 'unqualified',[42] not to be satisfied by taking reasonable steps.

Further, the term 'misuse' encompasses more than just unauthorised disclosure or publication. The confidant is stopped from using information imparted to her for her own purposes unless that use is authorised by the confider. In *Cadbury Schweppes v FBI Foods*,[43] a drink producer manufactured a drink under licence from the recipe owners. After the licence was terminated, the producer continued to use the recipe to produce a competing product and was held liable for breach of confidence. In *British American Tobacco Australia Ltd v Gordon*,[44] it was said that an intellectual use of confidential information to guide a decision on a course of action was just as much an unauthorised use as publication or dissemination.

[12.14] The confidant is sometimes permitted to use the information for some purposes but not others. Where the confider has directly confided information to the confidant, the court's focus is on whether the confider can be said to have placed any relevant restrictions on the confidant's use of the information. If the confider has imparted the information without

38 *A-G v Guardian Newspapers Ltd (No 2)* [1990] 1 AC 109, 281.

39 (1995) 63 SASR 531, 535 (King CJ). But see *Lifeplan Australian Friendly Society Ltd v Woff* (2016) 259 IR 384, [362]–[372].

40 If the plaintiff does not plead an actual or threatened misuse of confidential information, breach of confidence will not be made out: *Moran v Atrum Coal NL (No 5)* [2016] WASC 23, [11].

41 *Talbot v General Television Corporation Pty Ltd* [1980] VR 224.

42 *Prince Jefri Bolkiah v KPMG* [1999] 2 AC 222, 235.

43 *Cadbury Schweppes Inc v FBI Foods Ltd* (1999) 167 DLR (4th) 577.

44 [2007] NSWSC 230, [28].

placing any restrictions on its use, the confidant is free to use it at will.[45] Where the plaintiff has not directly confided information to the defendant (as where the defendant accidently or surreptitiously comes by the information, or obtains it through a third party), it is more likely that a blanket prohibition on use will be assumed,[46] as the plaintiff never considered passing the information to the defendant at all.

Restrictions can be explicit or implicit. Some information is obviously of such a nature that no use can be made of it against the confider's wishes.[47] Alternatively, the restrictions placed on the use of certain information may not mean that its use for any purpose whatsoever is prohibited. The confider's intention is not conclusive. Instead, the question is whether the confidant should have known that use for *all* purposes was restricted. In *Smith Kline & French Laboratories (Australia) Ltd v Secretary, Department of Community Services*,[48] Gummow J said:

> [T]he circumstances that the person who imparted the information in question intended to do so for a limited purpose, will not necessarily of itself be sufficient to bind the conscience of the party to whom the information was imparted. ... [W]here the defendant neither knew nor ought to have known of the alleged limited purpose of the disclosure, it is difficult to see on what footing equity should bind his conscience.[49]

On the other hand, in some instances, statutes permit or even mandate use of what would otherwise be confidential information. If this is so, an action for breach of confidence cannot succeed.[50] Alternatively, any obligation of confidence owed can be limited for reasons of public policy. *AB v CD & EF*[51] provides an example. A barrister acting for accused criminals was, without their knowledge, acting as a registered police informer. Her activities may have denied those accused a fair trial. The Victorian Court of Appeal said that the trial judge was correct to say that any obligation of confidence owed by the police to the informer was qualified by the public interest in ensuring fair trials. This would mean that the obligation of confidence could not prevent the information concerning her role being available to those accused.[52] [12.15]

Does the plaintiff need to show a detriment will be suffered?

In *Coco v AN Clark (Engineers) Ltd*,[53] Megarry J left open the question whether the plaintiff must have suffered detriment as a result of the breach of confidence. Subsequent English courts have rejected the suggestion that detriment must be positively demonstrated.[54] Australian courts do not require detriment as a precondition to relief,[55] except perhaps in [12.16]

45 *Fractionated Cane Technology Ltd v Ruiz-Avila* [1988] 1 Qd R 51.
46 *Franklin v Giddins* [1978] Qd R 72.
47 See, eg, solicitor–client letters: *Lord Ashburton v Pape* [1913] 2 Ch 469.
48 (1990) 22 FCR 73, 112.
49 Ibid 114.
50 *Commissioner of Taxation v Donoghue* (2015) 237 FCR 316.
51 [2017] VSCA 338.
52 Ibid [220].
53 [1969] RPC 41, 47.
54 *A-G v Observer Ltd* [1990] 1 AC 109, 256 (Lord Keith), 282 (Lord Goff).
55 *NRMA Ltd v Geeson* (2001) 40 ACSR 1.

the case of governmental information. Gummow J explained why this was so in the *Smith Kline* case. Equity, his Honour said, 'intervenes to uphold an obligation and not necessarily to prevent or recover loss … The obligation of conscience is to respect the confidence, not merely to refrain from causing detriment to the plaintiff'.[56]

However, a government which tries to protect its secrets via the equitable obligation of confidence must show that there will be some detriment to the public interest if information is released. This difference between private confidences and public information recognises the need to preserve a level of transparency in governmental dealings in a democratic system. Mason J said in *Commonwealth v John Fairfax & Sons Ltd*:

> It is unacceptable in our democratic society that there should be a restraint on the publication of information relating to government when the only vice of that information is that it enables the public to discuss, review and criticize government action.
>
> Accordingly, the court will determine the government's claim to confidentiality by reference to the public interest. Unless the disclosure is likely to injure the public interest, it will not be protected.[57]

His Honour commented that disclosure in non-prejudicial circumstances is in the public interest as it promotes public awareness and discussion. Disclosure will be restrained where it is contrary to public interest due to prejudice to national security, foreign relations or the ordinary business of government. These conflicting public interests may be finely balanced.[58]

Defences to breach of confidence

[12.17] There are few effective defences to a claim of confidentiality. The defendant's best chance lies in showing that the information is not, in fact, confidential, or that the use was not unauthorised. Nevertheless, defences relating to public interest and change of position may be available.

Public interest

[12.18] A defence of disclosure in the public interest is accepted in England.[59] Australian reaction to this defence has been more restrained, and its availability 'remains uncertain'.[60] Courts have tended to regard public interest as going to the question of the quality of confidence in the information. Gummow J commented in *Corrs Pavey Whiting & Byrne v Collector of Customs (Vic)*, 'information as to crimes, wrongs and misdeeds … lacks "the necessary quality of confidence"'.[61] This negates the need for a defence.

56 *Smith Kline & French Laboratories (Australia) Ltd v Secretary, Department of Community Services* (1990) 22 FCR 73, 112.

57 (1980) 147 CLR 39, 52.

58 Ibid.

59 *Norwich Pharmacal Co v Commissioners of Customs and Excise* [1972] RPC 743.

60 M Handler, 'Reconsidering the Need for Defences to Permit Disclosures of Confidential Copyright Material on Public Interest Grounds' (2018) 12(2) *Journal of Equity* 195, 197.

61 (1987) 13 ALD 254, 274.

'Crimes, wrongs and misdeeds' are collectively referred to as 'iniquity'. Whether 'iniquity' is regarded as a defence, or a bar to the information having the quality of confidence, the concept is strictly applied. In *Australian Football League v The Age Co Ltd*,[62] the defendant newspaper argued that information concerning footballers' drug use could be published as it exposed an iniquity. Kellam J held that in order to rely on the iniquity rule the defendant had to establish that: (a) the proposed disclosure would disclose an iniquity that was a crime, civil wrong or serious misdeed of public importance; (b) the iniquity had a character of public importance in the sense that it affected the community as a whole or public welfare; and (c) the proposed disclosure was to be made to a person with a real and direct interest in redressing the alleged crime, wrong or misdeed.[63] The newspaper failed to satisfy the court on all three grounds. However, in *AB v CD & EF*,[64] the Victorian Court of Appeal stated that the subject matter of the confidence qualified as an iniquity. There, a barrister representing those charged with criminal offences was a registered police informer passing on information about those she represented to the police. This was, of course, a gross abuse of professional standards.

It is unclear whether the notion of 'public interest' is a broader concept than that of disclosure of iniquity. Are disclosures of matters impacting on public health and welfare also disclosures in the public interest, despite not revealing any crime, wrong or misdeed? Common sense suggests that, as a matter of public policy, some defence should be available if there is a real risk to the public in suppression of the information. But this remains an unsettled part of the law of breach of confidence.[65] [12.19]

In *Australian Broadcasting Corporation v Lenah Game Meats Pty Ltd*, Gleeson CJ indicated that a defence of public interest existed;[66] later, the High Court appeared to endorse a 'public interest' defence wider in scope than disclosure of an iniquity.[67]

Change of position

It is sometimes suggested that a defence of change of position should be available.[68] The defence is discussed in *David Securities Pty Ltd v Commonwealth Bank of Australia*[69] in relation to the mistaken receipt of money. When a person mistakenly receives funds, and acts to his detriment in reliance on that receipt in good faith, he has 'changed his position' and should not have to return the funds he has spent. In the context of breach of confidence, the defence could be made available to innocent third party recipients of information. Australian decisions on the availability of the defence are inconclusive. In *Wheatley v Bell*,[70] (discussed at [12.11]), innocent purchasers of confidential information were restrained from [12.20]

62 (2006) 15 VR 419.
63 Ibid [69]–[71].
64 [2017] VSCA 338
65 M Handler, 'Reconsidering the Need for Defences to Permit Disclosures of Confidential Copyright Material on Public Interest Grounds' (2018) 12(2) *Journal of Equity* 195, 197.
66 (2001) 208 CLR 199, 224.
67 *Minister for Immigration and Citizenship v Kumar* (2009) 238 CLR 448, 457.
68 Gareth Jones, 'Restitution of Benefits Obtained in Breach of Confidence' (1970) 86(4) *Law Quarterly Review* 463.
69 (1992) 175 CLR 353.
70 [1982] 2 NSWLR 544.

using it, and were not allowed to set up a bona fide purchaser claim to defeat the plaintiff.[71] In *Retractable Technologies Inc v Occupational and Medical Innovations Ltd*,[72] Greenwood J held that the defendant's changes in position could be taken into account by the court in determining appropriate relief. This approach does not destroy the plaintiff's right to protect confidentiality in its information so long as the information has not lost its quality of confidence. Moulding an appropriate remedy to the situation at hand is consistent with equity's overall discretionary approach to remedies.[73]

Protection of private information

[12.21] The equitable obligation of confidence has always been able to protect private information, in addition to trade and commercial secrets, where the requirements of the action have been met. In *Giller v Procopets*,[74] where the defendant attempted to distribute sex videos of himself and the plaintiff, the plaintiff succeeded in a claim of breach of confidence. The information had been created inside a relationship of confidence; it had the necessary quality of confidence about it; and the man's attempt to distribute the information was an unauthorised use of that information. This was a relatively straightforward example of a breach of confidence.

[12.22] More complicated examples of breaches of confidence have arisen outside of accepted relationships of confidence. For example, in England the action for breach of confidence has been used to protect celebrities against an intrusion into their wedding by a paparazzo.[75] It is far harder to fit this kind of case into a traditional understanding of the law of confidentiality. The relevance of these decisions to Australian law is discussed below.

English developments

[12.23] The use of the doctrine of breach of confidence where information has been surreptitiously, accidentally or innocently obtained has been noted above. This has allowed the doctrine to be used to protect what would otherwise be regarded as private information as confidential information even if it was not imparted in a relationship of confidence. English and Australian law has typically denied the existence of a tort of invasion of privacy,[76] but use of the doctrine of breach of confidence this way has allowed some measure of protection of privacy.

[12.24] In England, this expansion was referable to the 'horizontal effect'[77] of adoption of the *European Convention on Human Rights* ('*ECHR*'). Article 8(1) of the *ECHR* states:

71 This was because the defence of bona fide purchase for value was used to settle priority disputes with respect to property rights, and was not appropriate to the obligation of confidence.

72 (2007) 72 IPR 58.

73 See chapter 2.

74 (2008) 24 VR 1. See also *Wilson v Ferguson* [2015] WASC 15. A defendant who posted explicit photographs of the plaintiff on a social media site was ordered to pay equitable compensation for the plaintiff's distress caused by breach of confidence.

75 *Douglas v Hello! Ltd (No 3)* [2003] 3 ALL ER 996.

76 *Victoria Park Racing and Recreation Grounds Co Ltd v Taylor* (1937) 58 CLR 479. But see *Australian Broadcasting Corporation v Lenah Game Meats Pty Ltd* (2001) 208 CLR 199.

77 J Morgan, 'Privacy, Confidence and Horizontal Effect: "Hello" Trouble' (2003) 62 *Cambridge Law Journal* 444. The term 'horizontal' refers to the outward-spreading effect of a requirement that domestic law be interpreted in light of the Convention.

> Everyone has the right to respect for his private and family life, his home and his correspondence.

Under the *Human Rights Act 1998* (UK), which annexes and applies the *ECHR*, English courts are required to interpret existing law in a manner consistent with the human rights established in the *ECHR*. In the absence of a tort of invasion of privacy, courts have interpreted the action for breach of confidence in a manner which provides some protection for privacy of individuals in line with art 8.

This is demonstrated by *Douglas v Hello! Ltd*.[78] Michael Douglas and Catherine Zeta-Jones married in New York in 2000, having sold *OK! Magazine* exclusive rights to publish wedding photographs. The couple went to considerable lengths to ensure (unsuccessfully) that unauthorised photographs were not taken. A rival magazine, *Hello!*, obtained unauthorised photographs from a paparazzo and intended to publish them in its next issue. [12.25]

After failing to obtain an injunction, the plaintiffs ultimately recovered damages for the distress caused to them by the publication of the unauthorised photographs. There was no confidential relationship between them and the paparazzo. Nevertheless, the action for breach of confidence, interpreted in the light of the *ECHR*, allowed the Court to protect the couple's privacy.[79]

Some commentators believe that the action for breach of confidence in England has developed into two actions. McCamus says that the traditional action 'remains standing and presumably will continue to apply to the kinds of cases to which it has traditionally applied'.[80] However: [12.26]

> [t]he new doctrine of breach of confidence, freed from any requirement to establish that information has been confided in circumstances importing an obligation of confidence, appears to be designed to apply in circumstances where the publication of sensitive personal information threatens to undermine the moral authority of the individual in question or is highly offensive to the moral sensibilities of a reasonable person in a similar situation.[81]

This split is particularly noticeable when defences are considered. Article 10 of the *ECHR* also protects the right to freedom of expression. It requires English courts to balance the plaintiff's right to privacy against any rights the defendant has to freedom of expression. A general position has been reached where use of information is regarded as being in breach of confidence when it 'threatens to undermine the moral autonomy of the individual in question or is highly offensive to the moral sensibilities of a reasonable person'.[82] These kinds of considerations do not come into account when the information involved is of the 'trade secret' variety.

The recent exit of the United Kingdom from the European Union is not expected to cause changes to the law relating to confidentiality.

78 *Douglas v Hello! Ltd (No 3)* [2003] 3 All ER 996.

79 *OK! Magazine* also succeeded in its action for breach of confidence: see *OBG Ltd v Allen* [2005] QB 762; *Douglas v Hello! Ltd (No 3)* [2003] 3 All ER 996; *Mainstream Properties v Young* [2008] 1 AC 1.

80 JD McCamus, 'Celebrity Newsgathering and Privacy: The Transformation of Breach of Confidence in English Law' (2006) 39(4) *Akron Law Review* 1191, 1214.

81 Ibid.

82 Ibid.

Australian developments

[12.27] There are frequent calls in Australia for effective privacy protection, and High Court comments seem broadly supportive of development of a tort of invasion of privacy.[83] Several Law Reform Commissions have recommended a statutory right to privacy.[84] Some lower court decisions have claimed to recognise a tort of invasion of privacy,[85] although its existence has been denied in higher courts.[86] Limited protection has also been provided in Australia via the action for breach of confidence.

[12.28] *Giller v Procopets*[87] is a landmark decision in that it goes much further than previous decisions to offer redress to a plaintiff (whose privacy has been invaded) by use of the equitable obligation of confidence. One of the difficulties of using the traditional action for breach of confidence to protect privacy is remedying the breach. Before private confidential information has been misused, an injunction is an appropriate and usually sufficient remedy; it stops disclosure and protects the plaintiff against any harm such as humiliation and distress. But once information is disclosed, an injunction cannot undo the damage done. Previously, unless the disclosure of the information also caused economic loss to the plaintiff, equity had no useful compensatory remedy against humiliation and distress. The Victorian Court of Appeal held in *Giller* that the plaintiff was entitled to compensation for distress, including aggravated damages, both as equitable compensation and as damages under the local equivalent of *Lord Cairns' Act*.[88] This was despite the absence of any economic loss.[89]

[12.29] *Giller* only offers limited protection of privacy, however. The equitable action of breach of confidence offers no protection if the information was not obtained in circumstances where the defendant ought reasonably to have known that the information was confidential. So, for example, there is nothing, apart from good taste, preventing a photographer taking and publishing shots of a distressed parent leaving the trial of their child's murderer. The photograph has been taken in a public place, so the defendant cannot reasonably be expected to know the information contained in the photo is confidential.[90] Moreover, if information can be reconstructed or discovered independently it will not be confidential,

83 *Australian Broadcasting Corporation v Lenah Game Meats Pty Ltd* (2001) 208 CLR 199, 225–6, 230–1 (Gleeson CJ), 254–5 (Gummow and Hayne JJ).

84 Australian Law Reform Commission, *For Your Information: Australian Privacy Law and Practice* (Report No 108, 2008), vol 3, ch 74; Law Reform Commission New South Wales, *Invasion of Privacy* (Report No 120, 2009); Victorian Law Reform Commission, *Surveillance in Public Places* (Final Report No 18, 2010); Australian Law Reform Commission, *Serious Invasions of Privacy in the Digital Era: Final Report* (Report No 123, 2014).

85 *Grosse v Purvis* (2003) Aust Torts Reports 81–706; *Jane Doe v Australian Broadcasting Corporation* [2007] VCC 281.

86 *Kalba v Commonwealth* [2004] FCA 763; *Giller v Procopets* (2008) 24 VR 1.

87 (2008) 24 VR 1.

88 See [3.41].

89 See also *Wilson v Ferguson* [2015] WASC 15. A defendant who posted explicit photographs of the plaintiff on a social media site was ordered to pay equitable compensation for the plaintiff's distress caused by breach of confidence. The plaintiff made no claim for *Lord Cairns' Act* damages.

90 This is the Australian position. In England, author JK Rowling successfully sued when photographs of her son taken in a public place were sold to the media: *Murray v Big Pictures* [2008] EWHC Civ 446. At first instance, it was held that the photographs were not private, having been taken in a public place. The Court of Appeal held that the child had a reasonable expectation of privacy.

even though it may be intensely private. In the New Zealand decision of *P v D*, a journalist was able to establish through independent research that a public figure had spent time in a psychiatric institution. The plaintiff could not prevent its publication on the grounds of breach of confidence.[91]

Australian law reform commissions have recommended that a statutory action of invasion of privacy be established.[92] A statutory right to privacy can offer better protection than can be obtained in equity as it can catch factual situations left unprotected by the obligation of confidence. Further, greater doctrinal coherence is achieved; it would remove doubts about whether breach of confidence has become two distinct causes of action, one protecting economic interests and one protecting privacy, each potentially subject to different rules and remedies. A third advantage is that a wider range of defences,[93] and perhaps remedies,[94] could be accommodated by a statutory action. To date, these recommendations have not been adopted. All Australian jurisdictions except Tasmania, however, have legislated to make the kind of publication that occurred in *Giller* a criminal offence.[95] [12.30]

Remedies for breach of confidence

The most common remedy employed in breach of confidence cases is the injunction. Where an injunction is inappropriate, other remedies can be claimed. These include an account of profits and compensation for loss. Controversially, the Supreme Court of Canada has awarded a constructive trust.[96] English and Australian courts have to date resisted the temptation to award proprietary relief for breaches of confidence. [12.31]

Injunctions

Injunctions are granted if a breach is threatened, or where the breach has already occurred and is likely to be repeated. There are no essential differences in this respect between commercial and personal information. The plaintiff will have a strong claim to injunctive relief where an order preventing the defendant's misuse of information will protect the plaintiff from all subsequent harm. Once information has been misused, an injunction will not be awarded unless the plaintiff can show the likelihood of repetition.[97] The criteria for its award are discussed in chapter 3. [12.32]

In the case of an injunction sought for breach of the equitable obligation of confidence, the court is not required to consider whether damages will be an adequate remedy, as common law damages will not be available in any event.

91 [2000] 2 NZLR 591.

92 Law Reform Commission New South Wales, *Invasion of Privacy* (Report No 120, 2009); Australian Law Reform Commission, *Serious Invasions of Privacy in the Digital Age: Final Report* (Report 123, 2014).

93 Such as freedom of expression or fair reporting.

94 Such as an order that the defendant apologise to the plaintiff.

95 *Criminal Code Act 1995* (Cth) s 474.17; *Crimes Act 1900* (ACT) s 72C; *Crimes Act 1900* (NSW) ss 91P, 91Q, 91R; *Criminal Code 1983* (NT) div 7A; *Criminal Code 1899* (Qld) s 223; *Summary Offences Act 1953* (SA) ss 26B, 26C; *Summary Offences Act 1966* (Vic) ss 40–41DB; *Criminal Code 1913* (WA) Ch XXVA;.

96 *Lac Minerals Ltd v International Corona Resources Ltd* [1989] 2 SCR 574.

97 *A-G (UK) v Heinemann Publishers Australia Pty Ltd* (1987) 8 NSWLR 341.

Account of profits

[12.33] Misuse of commercially valuable information may attract the award of a monetary remedy. Whether the plaintiff seeks an account of profits or compensation will depend on how successfully the defendant has used the information. An account of profits will be particularly appropriate where the defendant has used the plaintiff's information to obtain a 'head start'[98] in getting its product to the market.

[12.34] An account of profits is said to be an unpopular remedy for breach of confidence, as the remedy is 'extraordinarily difficult and expensive to administer'.[99] Nevertheless, it is not an uncommon remedy in such cases. In *Bluescope Steel Ltd v Kelly*,[100] for example, an injunction to prevent further disclosure of the confidential information and an account of profits was ordered, despite the fact that calculation of quantum was 'not without difficulties'.[101] Emmett J said that the Court was required to make an approximation of profit,[102] having made allowances for expenses, and also for the skill and expertise of the defendants.

In 'head start' or 'springboard' cases, it is common to limit the account of profits to the period in which the defendant was able to use the plaintiff's information as a stepping stone, without going to the trouble of producing the information itself.

Compensatory remedies

[12.35] Sometimes the defendant's misuse of the information causes loss to the plaintiff rather than a profit for the defendant. Equitable compensation for breach of confidence, sourced in equity's inherent jurisdiction, is in principle available in these cases. Nevertheless, it has been held in several Victorian cases that there is a jurisdiction to award compensation as damages under *Lord Cairns' Act*, in lieu of or in addition to the award of an injunction.

[12.36] The principle behind the awarding of equitable compensation is restoration of the value of the plaintiff's right that has been lost.[103] Compensation is usually assessed at time of trial, with the benefit of hindsight.[104] Common law considerations such as contributory negligence,[105] punitive damages,[106] and mitigation[107] are not used to adjust quantum.[108]

The court must try to assess how much compensation it takes to restore the plaintiff to her former position. For example, in *Talbot v General Television Corporation Pty Ltd*,[109] the plaintiff's idea for a television series was misused; he lost the opportunity to profit

98 See, eg, *Cadbury Schweppes Inc v FBI Foods Ltd* (1999) 167 DLR (4th) 577.

99 J Glover, *Commercial Equity: Fiduciary Relationships* (Butterworths, 1995) 338, citing S Ricketson, *Law of Intellectual Property* (Lawbook, 1984) 841–2.

100 (2007) 72 IPR 289.

101 Ibid [160].

102 Ibid [161].

103 *Nocton v Lord Ashburton* [1914] AC 932. See [4.10].

104 *Canson Enterprises Ltd v Boughton & Co* (1991) 85 DLR (4th) 129, 162–3.

105 *Pilmer v Duke Group Ltd (in liq)* (2001) 207 CLR 165.

106 *Giller v Procopets* (2008) 24 VR 1.

107 See [4.27].

108 However, the Victorian Court of Appeal ordered a component of aggravated damages in *Giller v Procopets* (2008) 24 VR 1.

109 [1980] VR 224.

from his concept. Compensation was ordered to reflect the possible profit the plaintiff might have made, reduced by such contingencies as might have prevented the profit being realised.

With commercially valuable information, compensation is naturally concerned with economic loss. But the same is not necessarily true of private confidential information. The harm that results from disclosure of this sort of information is often embarrassment and humiliation rather than an identifiable financial loss. Until very recently, equity has had no way of addressing this kind of damage. *Giller v Procopets*[110] may have changed the landscape here. The Victorian Court of Appeal held that compensation for distress is available for breach of the equitable obligation of confidence, both pursuant to equity's inherent jurisdiction and under the local equivalent of *Lord Cairns' Act*.[111] [12.37]

Miscellaneous orders

In some cases of breach of confidence, the plaintiff risks further damage unless the information in question is removed from the defendant's possession or otherwise destroyed. Orders for delivery up and destruction achieve this aim. In *Franklin v Giddins*,[112] an orchardist surreptitiously removed cuttings of a rival orchardist's new nectarine variety and grafted them onto his own trees. The confidential information was, in effect, the DNA of the new variety. An order was made for the delivery up and destruction of the grafted trees. A modern variation of this order is one directing the defendant to delete electronic copies of confidential information as well as destroying hard copies.[113] [12.38]

WHAT'S ONLINE?

Available at www.cambridge.org/highereducation/isbn/9781009232388/resources:

- Recommended further readings
- Discussion topics
- Practice problem

110 (2008) 24 VR 1.

111 An application for special leave to appeal was refused: *Procopets v Giller* [2009] HCASL 187. *Giller* was followed in *Wilson v Ferguson* [2015] WASC 15, with respect to recovery in equity's exclusive jurisdiction.

112 [1978] Qd R 72.

113 *Smartways Logistics Holdings Pty Ltd v O'Sullivan* [2020] NSWSC 189.

PART E

EXPRESS TRUSTS

13

THE CONCEPT OF THE EXPRESS TRUST

Introduction

Express trusts are a form of wealth management. Ownership and management of the property is split from the enjoyment of the property. In its simplest terms, the trustee manages the property but not for his own benefit. Express trusts emerged from medieval 'uses' of land and have been recognised and enforced in common law systems for over 700 years.[1] They are no longer limited to land; any form of property can be held on trust. [13.1]

Today, the express trust is used for a wide variety of purposes, both private and commercial, where it is necessary or desirable to split management from benefit.

These include:

- Managing family wealth under a family trust;
- Managing property for those unable to do so themselves, such as children or those under disabilities;
- Group investment trusts, such as unit trusts;
- Trading trusts;
- Trusts set up under wills;
- Superannuation trusts, which operate for the benefit of large numbers of members; and
- Trusts used as security for borrowings.

Almost all Australians over the age of 18 will have some involvement in a superannuation trust. Many kinds of trusts are now largely regulated by statute,[2] but all are based on the equitable principles for supervising the administration of trusts. Except where otherwise stated, we will use the simplest form of express trust as an example – that set up under a will for the benefit of the testator's relatives.

Definition

The express trust has never been authoritatively defined. Indeed, the very lack of definition has been partly responsible for its evolution as a flexible and effective method for managing wealth. The principal features of a trust can nevertheless be described in general terms. Ford and Lee describe it as: [13.2]

> an obligation enforceable in equity which rests on a person (the trustee) as owner of some specific property (the trust property) to deal with that property for the benefit of a certain person (the beneficiary) or persons, or for the advancement of certain purposes.[3]

1 Prior to the *Statute of Uses 1535* (Imp), and for several centuries afterwards, trusts were known as 'uses'. The term 'trust' was originally a synonym for 'use' but later came to mean a use not executed by the *Statute of Uses*. See JH Baker, *An Introduction to English Legal History* (Oxford University Press, 4th ed, 2002) 290–2.

2 For example, superannuation trusts are regulated by the *Superannuation Industry (Supervision) Act 1993* (Cth).

3 F & L [1.010].

The important elements in this definition are:

(a) A trust imposes an *obligation* or duty on a title-holder of property to apply the property for the purposes specified by the creator of the trust. This contrasts with the concept of a power which confers a *discretion* on the person on whom the power is conferred to apply property for purposes specified by the creator of the power.

(b) A trust is *enforceable in equity*, which simply means it is enforced by courts which have power to apply equity as administered by the Court of Chancery prior to the *Judicature Acts* reforms.[4]

(c) The *trustee* holds legal or equitable title to the trust property.[5] Functionally, the trustee is the manager of the trust property. The trust document, equity, and statute confer obligations on the trustee, such as the duty to invest trust money, as well as powers (or discretions) which he can exercise if he considers it in the interest of the trust to do so, such as the power to sell trust property.

(d) There must be *trust property* (often referred to as the 'subject-matter'). The trustee will usually hold legal or equitable title to the property, but a possessory title, such as a title held by a thief or an adverse possessor of land, can also be the subject-matter of a trust.[6]

(e) The trustee is not simply the owner of property; he *deals with the property* and manages it. Management duties are not uniform; they vary according to the nature of the trust in question. For example, the trustee of a superannuation trust comes under extensive statutory and equitable obligations; whereas the trustee of a bare trust is a nominee trustee, with no active duties to perform, who must act at the direction of the beneficiaries.

(f) The trustee manages the trust property *for the benefit of another person* – the beneficiary. The beneficiary holds equitable title to the trust property. Trusts can be created for unborn beneficiaries as well as for the living. In functional terms, the beneficiaries enjoy the property the trustee manages. The beneficiaries are sometimes termed the 'objects' of the trust.

(g) Not all trusts are established for the benefit of human beneficiaries. Some are created *for the advancement of purposes*. The most common category of trusts for purposes is the charitable trust,[7] but it is also possible to create, within judicially prescribed limitations, some trusts for non-charitable purposes such as trusts to maintain a testator's pet or gravestone.[8]

---

4 See [1.3], [1.18].

5 The title will be equitable when A holds property on trust for B, and B declares a trust of the equitable interest for C. The trust B has declared is termed a sub-trust.

6 Cf the constructive trust of stolen money discussed in chapter 23: *Black v S Freedman & Co* (1910) 12 CLR 105; *Sourcebook* 23.6a, p 624; S Barkehall Thomas, 'Thieves as Trustees: The Enduring Legacy of *Black v S Freedman & Co Ltd*' (2009) 3(1) *Journal of Equity* 1; R Chambers, 'Trust and Theft' in E Bant and M Harding (eds), *Exploring Private Law* (Cambridge University Press, 2010) 223, 228–30.

7 See chapter 16.

8 See [16.44].

Some essential characteristics of the express trust

The wealth-management purposes for which express trusts are created are remarkably varied. Trusts can be set up to provide for infants, to run businesses, or provide superannuation. As we will see shortly, different structures and terms can be utilised to achieve these results. Nevertheless, some basic propositions apply to all express trusts. They include the following: [13.3]

(1) A trust is distinguishable from a gift to beneficiaries. Once a gift has been made, all legal rights affecting the subject-matter of the gift vest in the donee. Beneficiaries of a trust are not entitled, as is the donee of a gift, to the full ownership of the trust property, although a beneficiary of a fixed trust has equitable ownership of her share of the trust property. The subject-matter of the trust vests in the trustee until the time it is transferred to the beneficiary or otherwise disposed of on termination of the trust. In the meantime, the property will be applied to the beneficiaries' benefit.[9]

(2) A trust has no legal personality. The trustee is the person who holds the property on behalf of the trust, and the trust activities are conducted through him. Actions in contract and tort can be brought by or against the trustee but not by or against the trust. Because the trustee is likely to incur liabilities while acting as trustee and managing the property for the beneficiaries, the trustee may have recourse to the trust fund to pay 'properly incurred' liabilities.[10]

(3) A trustee owes fiduciary obligations to the beneficiaries of the trust. A trustee is a classic fiduciary; to a considerable extent, the law of fiduciary obligations has been developed by analogy from the core trustee–beneficiary relationship. But in some respects, a trustee is not a typical fiduciary. For example, whereas other fiduciaries owe their obligations to an identified principal, a trustee may owe fiduciary obligations to unascertained beneficiaries, such as unborn children. Such beneficiaries will not have reposed any trust and confidence in the beneficiary. It will be the settlor, not the beneficiaries, who will have entrusted the trustee with the management of the trust property.[11] Nevertheless, the trustee will be subject to the 'no conflict' and 'no profit' prohibitions which apply to all fiduciaries. In addition, trustees will be subject to equitable and statutory duties, the latter mainly prescribed by State and Territory trustee legislation, which do not apply to other fiduciaries.

(4) The conception of the trust as a legal device for separating the management of property from its enjoyment is qualified in an important respect. The rule in *Saunders v Vautier*[12] provides that, where all the beneficiaries are of full age and capacity, they may terminate the trust by requiring the trustees to transfer the assets to them or at their direction. The importance of the rule is that it overrides any terms contained in the trust instrument. So if a settlor settles property on trust for A, B and C, the beneficiaries, if adult, can agree to terminate the trust and divide the

9 A trust is not, like a cake, divisible into two pieces, the legal and equitable. When a trust is created, the trustee obtains full ownership, but equitable obligations are imposed on the trustee, enforceable for the benefit of the beneficiary. See [13.12].

10 See chapter 19.

11 *Breen v Williams* (1996) 186 CLR 71, [69] (Gummow J); *Sourcebook* 10.3.2a, p 244.

12 (1841) 4 Beav 115; 49 ER 282. See chapter 24.

trust property between themselves.[13] It is irrelevant that the trustees are opposed to the termination or that it is not authorised by the trust instrument.

The parties to a trust

[13.4] There are three parties to an express trust:

(1) The *settlor* who creates the trust. If a trust is created by will, the settlor will also be testator of the will. Once the settlor has created the trust, he typically has no rights in respect of the trust property. He 'drops out of the picture'. It is possible for the settlor to retain some influence over the management of a trust after it has been created; for example, by expressly reserving a power in the trust instrument to vary or revoke the trust. It is in practice rare for settlors to reserve powers of revocation in a trust instrument. Section 102 of the *Income Tax Assessment Act 1936* (Cth) imposes potentially adverse tax consequences on settlors who create such a power. Another method for the settlor to retain control is for the settlor to be named as the 'appointor'.[14]

Many trusts are created after an initial settlor settles a nominal sum, say $2, on trust, substantial amounts being added to the trust fund by another provider at a later date. The later provider is not, at least for the purpose of tax law, a settlor.[15] But when deciding whether an arrangement constituted in form as a trust is in reality a sham or illusory, a court can ignore a nominal settlor and instead determine whether the provider of substantial funds to the trustee in fact exercises practical control of the funds so as, in reality, to remain their owner.[16] This is an example of the law looking at the substance of a transaction and not its form.

(2) The *trustee* who holds title to the trust property and who must perform the trust obligations. A trustee may be an individual or a corporation. A trustee does not have to consent to his appointment but if he does not want to act as trustee he must disclaim the trusteeship.[17]

In New South Wales, the Australian Capital Territory, Queensland, Victoria and Western Australia there are statutory provisions limiting the number of trustees of a trust to four in prescribed circumstances.[18] There is some art to choosing the number of trustees. It is inadvisable to create a trust with fewer than two individuals as trustee. Placing the administration of the trust in the hands of one person increases the possibility of fraud, and the administration can be seriously impaired by the death of the sole trustee. However, the appointment of numerous

13 *Sir Moses Montefiore Jewish Home v Howell & Co (No 7) Pty Ltd* [1984] 2 NSWLR 406.
14 See [13.19].
15 *Truesdale v Federal Commissioner of Taxation* (1970) 120 CLR 353.
16 *Webb v Webb* [2020] UKPC 22, [88].
17 *Mallot v Wilson* [1903] 2 Ch 494.
18 *Trustee Act 1925* (ACT) s 6(5)(b); *Trustee Act 1925* (NSW) s 6(5)(b); *Trusts Act 1973* (Qld) s 11; *Trustee Act 1958* (Vic) s 40; *Trustees Act 1962* (WA) s 7(2)(a). The provisions only deal with the appointment of substitute trustees. The Victorian provision is limited to trusts of land. In Queensland, the Attorney-General may authorise the appointment of additional trustees above the number to which they are normally restricted by statute: *Trusts Act Amendment Act 1981* (Qld) s 8(b).

trustees can obstruct trust administration since trustees of express trusts (except charitable trusts) must act unanimously and not by majority decision.

It is possible for a trust to subsist without a trustee at all, relying on the maxim that 'no trust shall fail for want of a trustee'. In such a case, the court will supervise the administration of the trust until trustees are appointed.

In the ACT and New South Wales, trustee legislation provides that a person under the age of 18 may not be a trustee.[19] In other jurisdictions, a minor is not disqualified from being appointed a trustee but the lack of capacity to exercise the discretions conferred on a trustee will provide grounds for his removal, as will the inability of the minor to enter into contracts which bind the trust. Similar considerations apply to the appointment of a person of unsound mind as a trustee. There is no rule that a bankrupt may not be a trustee although bankruptcy provides grounds for the trustee's removal.[20]

(3) The *beneficiary* who benefits from the administration of the trust. A beneficiary can be an individual or a corporation. A trust can also benefit charitable objects or, exceptionally, non-charitable objects.[21] There are no limits on the number of beneficiaries of a trust, although if the beneficiaries of a discretionary trust are too numerous or too widely dispersed, the trust may be held void for being administratively unworkable.[22] The fact that a beneficiary is a minor or is under some other legal incapacity is not a disqualification from being a beneficiary. On the contrary, the need to protect persons lacking legal capacity is an important reason for creating a trust. We have already noted that unborn children can be beneficiaries.

The roles of settlor, trustee and beneficiary can be combined. A settlor becomes a trustee by declaring herself trustee of her own property for another. These are sometimes known as 'self-declared trusts'.[23] A settlor can also be a beneficiary of a trust, although combining these roles may attract adverse tax consequences. A trustee can also be a beneficiary; however, a trust cannot be created where a person is intended to be the sole trustee and beneficiary, and a trust will terminate when one person becomes sole trustee and beneficiary.[24] [13.5]

Different types of trust

All express trusts conform to one of two basic structures: [13.6]

(a) *Fixed trust*. Under a fixed trust, the share of the trust property which each beneficiary is to receive is determined by the trust instrument. For example, a direction to trustees 'to pay the income to A for life, and then to divide the capital equally

19 *Conveyancing Act 1919* (NSW) s 10(1)(b); *Minors (Property and Contracts) Act 1970* (NSW) s 10(1); *Conveyancing Act 1919* (ACT) s 151A.

20 *Miller v Cameron* (1936) 54 CLR 572; *Sourcebook* 20.5a, p 515; *Weir v Matthews* [2001] NSWSC 824.

21 See chapter 16.

22 See [14.47].

23 See chapter 15.

24 *DKLR Holding Co (No 2) Pty Ltd v Commissioner of Stamp Duties (NSW)* (1982) 149 CLR 431, 463–4; *Sourcebook* 8.2a, p 187.

between B, C and D on A's death' creates a fixed trust because the trust instrument, and not the trustees, determines the existence and share of each beneficiary's interest under the trust.

(b) *Discretionary trust.* Under a discretionary trust, the share, if any, which each beneficiary is to receive is determined by the trustees and not by the trust instrument. Although the trustees have a *discretion* as to which beneficiary, among the class of beneficiaries, is to receive income or capital under the trust, they are under a *duty* to distribute the trust money. The duty to distribute will not necessarily be immediate. The trustees will usually be given a power under the trust instrument to accumulate trust income – in other words, to add the income to capital. They must distribute the capital and income in accordance with the terms of the trust instrument by the date (usually referred to as the termination or vesting date) specified in the instrument. The trust must not be of indefinite duration. The rule against perpetuities prescribes the maximum duration of a trust.[25] An example of a discretionary trust is a direction 'to pay the income and capital to whichever of E, F and G the trustees shall select'. Members of the class of potential beneficiaries of a discretionary trust are often referred to as 'objects' of the class.

[13.7] The terminology of discretionary trusts is one of the most confusing aspects of the law of express trusts. Although the term 'discretionary trust' is commonly used, it is not a legal term of art.[26] The discretionary trust is more accurately known as a 'trust power'. There is a 'trust', because the trustee is obliged to distribute property by the termination date of the trust, but it is coupled with a 'power' to choose which beneficiaries will receive the distribution. A discretionary trust is sometimes described as an 'exhaustive trust', a term which draws attention to the fact that the trustees are under a duty to exhaust, or distribute, the trust property.[27]

[13.8] Charitable trusts may be fixed or discretionary. It is possible, for example, for money to be settled on trust 'for the Suburbia Animal Protection Society' (a fixed trust) or on trust 'for such animal protection societies as my trustees shall select' (a discretionary trust).

[13.9] From the beneficiary's point of view, there are great differences between a fixed trust and a discretionary trust. The beneficiary will have a proprietary interest in property where a fixed trust has been created. The interest may be vested or contingent. The beneficiary's interest might also be of limited duration, such as a life estate. Where a discretionary trust has been created, no member of the class of eligible beneficiaries has a proprietary interest in the trust property or any part of it. Because of this, the term 'beneficiary' is usually confined to persons to benefit under a fixed trust, or who have received a share from a discretionary trust. While all persons who can benefit from a trust can be accurately termed 'objects', not all 'objects' are 'beneficiaries'. They are 'potential' or 'eligible' beneficiaries only.

25 See [15.34].

26 *Chief Commissioner of Stamp Duties (NSW) v Buckle* (1998) 192 CLR 226, 234; *Sourcebook* 19.2a, p 476.

27 See J Hudson, 'Mere and Discretionary Objects in Australia' in Y Liew and M Harding eds, *Asia-Pacific Trust Law and Practice* (Hart Publishing, 2021) 19.

All beneficiaries of fixed trusts and objects of discretionary trusts have the right to due administration of the trust. They can compel the trustee to perform the trust and to compensate the trust for losses caused by a breach. A beneficiary of a fixed trust can insist that the trustee perform his duties and distribute property to the beneficiary in accordance with the terms of the trust. But an object of a discretionary trust can only insist the trustee perform his duties; she cannot insist the trustee exercise his discretion in *her* favour. [13.10]

Beneficiaries and objects can also have a non-performing trustee removed and a new trustee appointed.[28] In certain circumstances, the beneficiaries can recover trust property or its traceable proceeds from third parties who have received the property or proceeds from a trustee who has committed a breach of trust,[29] and can sue third parties who have helped the trustee to commit the breach.[30] [13.11]

If a beneficiary has a proprietary interest in trust property, the interest is not 'carved out' of the trustee's legal interest, in the sense that the trustee and beneficiary have separate legal and equitable interests in the property. Rather, the trust property is impressed with obligations which the beneficiary is entitled to enforce against the trustee.[31] They are personal obligations attached to the trust property and, depending on the nature of the trust and its terms, can include the right to claim the trust property from the trustee or from a third party who has received the property in breach of trust without being a good faith purchaser for value without notice. To say that a beneficiary has an equitable proprietary interest in trust property is a convenient shorthand expression, but it is more exact to say that the proprietary interest is the consequence of the beneficiary's entitlement to enforce personal rights attaching to the trust property against the trustee. [13.12]

Trusts and powers

We have noted that there is a distinction between a fixed trust – where the beneficiaries and their shares are known at the outset – and a discretionary trust – where the trustee has a discretion to select the beneficiaries, although he is under an obligation to distribute the property. The latter is called a 'trust power' because there is a trust obligation coupled with discretion. [13.13]

A 'trust power' is distinguishable from a 'bare power' which also confers a discretion on the trustees. Two types of power are relevant in the trusts context. The first are powers of appointment, empowering the trustee or other person to appoint property among a class of potential beneficiaries. The second are administrative, or managerial, powers conferred on trustees to facilitate the administration of the trust property. Administrative powers include the trustee's power to invest trust funds, discussed in chapter 18. The focus of this chapter is on powers of appointment. [13.14]

A bare power of appointment gives a discretion to appoint trust property among the specified class of beneficiaries but places no obligation on the trustee to exercise this discretion. These are sometimes called 'non-exhaustive' trusts, as the trustee is not under an obligation to distribute the property.[32] Frequently, these powers specify who will receive the [13.15]

28 See chapter 19.
29 See chapter 21.
30 See chapter 11.
31 *DKLR Holding Co (No 2) Pty Ltd v Commissioner of Stamp Duties (NSW)* (1982) 149 CLR 431, 474.
32 Y Grbich, 'Baden: Awakening the Conceptually Moribund Trust' (1974) 37(6) *Modern Law Review* 643.

property if the trustee does not exercise the discretion. The nominated beneficiary's right to the property is known as a 'gift over', being a shorthand expression for 'gift over in default of the trustee's exercise of discretion'. It can be difficult to tell whether a particular clause creates a trust power or a bare power of appointment, as the cases on certainty of objects demonstrate.[33] However, the presence of a 'gift over' clause is determinative of a bare power. If the settlor has made arrangements for what is to happen to the property if the trustee does not exercise its discretion, the trustee is not obliged to exercise it. An example of a bare power of appointment is as follows: 'I leave my house to my trustees to appoint the same to whichever of A, B and C they select; and in default of appointment, to C'. In this example, C is entitled to the gift over if the trustees do not select among the class of beneficiaries.

[13.16] Trust instruments creating a trust may include both trust obligations and powers of appointment. For example, superannuation trusts established for retired employees of a company will usually confer a power on the trustees to pay income to former employees who leave their employment before retirement age because they are totally and permanently incapacitated.[34]

[13.17] A person, such as the settlor of a trust, who confers a power of appointment on another person, such as a trustee, is known as the 'donor' of the power. The person given the power is the 'donee' of the power. The persons who can potentially benefit from the donee's exercise of discretion are known as the 'objects' of the power.

[13.18] It is possible for a settlor to confer a power on a person who is not the trustee. For example, a testator's will might appoint a professional trustee company as the trustee, but confer power to appoint property to the testator's children on the testator's brother, who can be expected to know the children personally. Powers conferred on non-fiduciaries attract no legal sanctions if the donee of the power fails to exercise the power, as powers do not need to be exercised. However, a trustee who is the donee of a fiduciary power must consider the exercise of her discretion. If she fails to do so, or applies the property for purposes not within the scope of the power, she will not have performed her obligations and any exercise of discretion will be set aside.[35]

[13.19] It is quite common for discretionary trust deeds to confer a power of appointment onto a specified person, known as the 'appointor'. The appointor may be given power to replace the trustee and to add or remove people from the class of eligible beneficiaries. This is a device to allow the settlor to retain a measure of continued power over the assets held on trust.

Types of powers of appointment

[13.20] There are three basic types of power of appointment, determined by the class of objects to whom property can be appointed:

(a) A *general power of appointment* entitles the donee to appoint property to *anyone*, including the donee herself; for example, a gift 'to X for life, remainder to whomsoever X shall appoint' is a general power. It can be suggested that the donee of a general power is for all practical purposes the owner of property subject

33 See chapter 14.

34 Cf *Finch v Telstra Super Pty Ltd* (2010) 242 CLR 254 where the invalidity benefit was construed as a fixed entitlement. *Sourcebook* 17.3.10.1b, p 450.

35 See chapter 17.

to the power. This will certainly be true if the donee appoints the property to herself. But the courts have nonetheless insisted that there is a distinction between owning property and having a power to own property.[36] Moreover, if the power is exercisable only by will, it will still be a general power of appointment even though the donee would then be unable to appoint to herself during her lifetime.

(b) A *special power of appointment* entitles the donee to make an appointment among a class of objects selected by the settlor; for example, a power conferred on X to appoint trust income among the settlor's children is a special power of appointment. The power will be special even though the donee is herself a member of the specified class.[37] A special power is usually defined by inclusion but may be defined by both inclusion and exclusion; for example, a power to appoint trust income 'among the settlor's children, but not to X' will still be a special power.

(c) A *hybrid, or intermediate, power of appointment* entitles the donee to appoint to anyone *except* a specified class of persons;[38] for example, a power conferred on X to appoint to anyone except the settlor and the settlor's spouse will be a hybrid power of appointment. Tax considerations usually explain the identity of the class of persons who are excluded from benefiting from the exercise of the power. A settlor of trust property who is entitled to benefit from the exercise of a general power of appointment might be deemed, for tax purposes, to be the beneficial owner of the trust property.[39]

The student must be able to distinguish the different types of power. The principles governing certainty of objects for special powers of appointment differ in some respects from the principles governing general and hybrid powers.[40]

Trusts and related concepts

It is not always easy to distinguish a trust from other legal or equitable concepts which perform similar functions. Nevertheless, a lawyer may have to choose between the trust and some other legal structure as devices for holding and managing wealth. The following is a brief summary of the differences between the trust and core related legal concepts. [13.21]

Trust and agency[41]

The role of trustees and agents is to act not in their own interests but for the benefit of others. Both owe fiduciary obligations in performing their respective roles. An agent who comes under a duty to hold property for a principal may be held to be a trustee of that property, so that he must keep the property separate from his own.[42] [13.22]

36 *Kennon v Spry* (2008) 238 CLR 366, [176] (Heydon J). See also *Fonu v Merrill Lynch Bank & Trustee Co (Cayman) Ltd* [2011] UKPC 17.
37 *Re Penrose* [1933] Ch 793.
38 *Re Park* [1932] 1 Ch 580; *Re Byron's Settlement* [1891] 3 Ch 474.
39 *Income Tax Assessment Act 1936* (Cth) s 102.
40 See chapter 14.
41 P Watts and FMB Reynolds (eds), *Bowstead and Reynolds on Agency* (Sweet & Maxwell, 15th ed, 2010).
42 *Cohen v Cohen* (1929) 42 CLR 91; *Sourcebook* 13.4.1a, p 350.

[13.23] Differences between trust and agency include the following:

(1) Whereas title to property under a trust must be vested in a trustee, an agency relationship can be created without vesting any property in the agent. For example, where an agent is appointed to negotiate a contract on behalf of the principal, no transfer of property from principal to agent is involved.

(2) A trustee who makes a contract in the administration of the trust contracts as principal, whereas an agent who makes a contract within the scope of his authority creates a contract between his principal and the party with whom he is dealing.[43] The agent himself is not a party to the contract.

(3) At common law, the relationship of principal and agent terminates on the death of either. If a trustee dies, however, the trust is not terminated. Instead, a new trustee is appointed.

Trust and equitable charge

[13.24] An equitable charge arises where A gives B the right to have property belonging to A made available to secure a payment or other benefit to B.[44] For example, A may leave Blackacre in his will to his wife but charge Blackacre with payment of $10 000 to B.

[13.25] Both the trust and the charge create equitable interests, in the beneficiary and the chargee respectively. In both cases, the equitable interest will be lost if the underlying property is sold to a good faith purchaser for value without notice of the interest. In this eventuality, however, personal remedies will still be available to the beneficiary and chargee. Both will also be entitled to the consideration paid by the purchaser to the trustee and chargor.

[13.26] The fundamental difference between a trust and a charge is that the trust entitles the beneficiary to equitable ownership of the trust property, or of a share of the property, whereas the charge confers only a security interest on the chargee, who can only claim the amount secured by the charge from a sale of the charged property. The remedies for failure to discharge the obligation secured by the charge are therefore more limited than those available to a beneficiary. A chargee can never claim the property subject to the charge by a foreclosure order. The normal judicial remedy is sale of the charged property, although a receiver can be appointed to manage the property. Charges over personal property require registration pursuant to statute.[45]

[13.27] The distinction between a charge and a trust is obscured by drafters of commercial lending agreements who purport to give the lender the status of a beneficiary rather than the more limited rights of a chargee. Whether a secured loan creates a trust or a charge is a matter of substance, not form, although the parties' objectively ascertained intention will be respected if they genuinely intend to create a trust.[46] The distinction is less significant under the *Personal Property Securities Act 2009* (Cth), since both are registrable under the Act if created as security interests.

43 *Vacuum Oil Co Pty Ltd v Wiltshire* (1945) 72 CLR 319.
44 See E Sykes and S Walker, *The Law of Securities* (Law Book Co, 5th ed, 1993) 187.
45 See *Personal Property Securities Act 2009* (Cth).
46 *Associated Alloys Pty Ltd v ACN 001 452 106 Pty Ltd (in liq)* (2000) 202 CLR 588; *Sourcebook* 13.4.2a, p 351.

Trust and condition

Property may be given upon condition that the recipient pays a third party a sum of money or performs some other obligation in favour of the third party. It will be a question of construction whether the arrangement creates a trust for the third party, a charge in favour of the third party, or whether a gift has been made subject to a condition precedent in favour of the third party which must be performed if the gift is to be effective. [13.28]

Courts are reluctant to construe a disposition as a gift subject to a condition precedent. This is because if the recipient fails to perform the condition, not only will the recipient not receive the gift but the third party will obtain no benefit. The party for whose benefit the condition precedent was made has no equitable interest in the property, unlike a beneficiary under a trust, and has no security interest, in contrast to a chargee. There have nevertheless been cases where gifts have failed because of the intended donee's failure to comply with a condition precedent to the making of the gift. In *Re Gardiner*,[47] a will provided that the testator 'give devise and bequeath all my estate both real and personal unto my son Ivor ... subject to my said son paying the sum of $1000 within two years of my death to my son Albert'. It was held that when he failed to make the payment within the two years, Ivor forfeited his interest and the estate vested in the testator's next of kin.[48] [13.29]

In *Re Gardiner*, the gift was held to be subject to a condition precedent. In other cases, the condition may be construed as a condition subsequent, relating to the use of the property after the gift has been received. If the donee fails to observe the condition, the gift will fail and once again the intended beneficiary of the condition will lose her expected benefit. An alternative to total invalidity where a condition subsequent has not been performed is to place the donee under a personal obligation to compensate the beneficiary of the condition for any loss caused by non-performance. Whether this is possible depends on the construction of the instrument conferring the conditional gift. In *Gill v Gill*,[49] a farm with homestead was devised to a son on terms 'that he keep the homestead as a home and provide board and residence for his sisters' if they were unmarried. Harvey J held that any failure to observe the condition might give rise to a personal obligation to compensate his sister who was not provided for in accordance with the condition. The term did not create a trust, so the sister had no proprietary interest in the property, but a breach of condition could give rise to an award of equitable compensation. An equitable condition was also held to arise in *Cobcroft v Bruce*[50] from the words 'I give to my wife ... my shares in public companies, to deal with as she in her absolute discretion sees fit, but otherwise on condition that she ultimately gives those shares, or the remainder thereof, to my nephews'. The words 'deal with' were interpreted as only conferring on the wife the right to deal with the shares during her lifetime. [13.30]

Trust and contract

Contracts are capable of creating 'trust-like arrangements'. For example, a contract may provide that A is to pay $1000 to B for the benefit of C. There is no public policy objection [13.31]

47 [1971] 2 NSWLR 494.

48 As Ivor received property on the settlor's intestacy, he was not completely deprived of benefit.

49 (1921) 21 SR (NSW) 400.

50 (2013) 9 ASTLR 39; *Sourcebook* 14.2c, p 372.

to contracts for the benefit of third parties, but in most cases they will be unenforceable by the third party (C) under the doctrine of privity of contract. Furthermore, the promisee (B) cannot recover more than nominal damages for breach because she has suffered no loss.[51] In spite of being the intended beneficiary of A's performance, C has no beneficial interest in any payment made to B and cannot invoke the remedies available to the beneficiary of a trust.

[13.32] The position changes if A and B intend B to hold the benefit of A's contractual performance on trust for C. B's right to sue for breach of contract is then a chose in action which B holds on trust for C.[52] As beneficiary of the trust, C will be entitled to sue for A's non-performance of his promise to pay B. If B, as trustee of the benefit of the promise, fails to sue A for breach of contract, C will join him as co-defendant for having committed a breach of trust. The important question in this case will be whether A and B intended to create a trust for C's benefit.[53] If the contract expressly or by implication manifests an intention to create a trust, C will enjoy the rights of a beneficiary.

Trust and debt

[13.33] Suppose that A pays $100 to B, with whom A has had no previous dealings. This simple transaction is susceptible to at least five analyses:[54]

(1) A gift to B if A intends B to become beneficial owner of the $100.

(2) A bailment of the $100 if A intends B to retain possession of the notes and coins for a specified period.

(3) A loan of the $100 if the intention of the parties is that B should be free to use the money as B's own, but that B is to repay an equivalent amount to A either on demand or at some prescribed time.

(4) A transfer to B of $100 on trust for persons or for recognised charitable or non-charitable purposes.

(5) B will hold the $100 on resulting trust for A where there is no evidence that A intended any of the other four outcomes to apply.[55]

[13.34] In this section, we are concerned with the difference between (3) above (a loan) and (4) above (a trust). Where a loan has been made, the borrower becomes the absolute owner of the money lent, subject to a contractual obligation to repay the loan or to perform some other obligation specified in the loan agreement. The borrower is free to spend the money

51 *Trident General Insurance Co Ltd v McNiece Brothers Pty Ltd* (1988) 165 CLR 107; *Sourcebook* 13.4.3a, p 353. Inadequacy of damages may provide grounds for awarding C specific performance of A's promise: *Coulls v Bagot's Executor & Trustee Co Ltd* (1967) 119 CLR 460; *Beswick v Beswick* [1968] AC 58.

52 *Fletcher v Fletcher* (1844) 4 Hare 67; 67 ER 564; *Trident General Insurance Co Ltd v McNiece Brothers Pty Ltd* (1988) 165 CLR 107.

53 See chapter 14.

54 *Dewar v Dewar* [1975] 2 All ER 728.

55 See chapter 22. Where the amount of money is small, as in this example, the presumption will be one of gift: *Joaquin v Hall* [1976] VR 788. The presumption of resulting trust will be stronger where the property consists of shares: *Vandervell v Inland Revenue Commissioners* [1967] 2 AC 291.

as he pleases even if the parties assume that the loan will be applied for a specific purpose. In the event of the debtor's bankruptcy, the lender is an unsecured creditor, entitled only to share rateably with the debtor's other creditors such of the debtor's assets as are available for distribution among the unsecured creditors.

When a trust has been constituted of a sum of money, the trustee holds only the legal title to the money – the equitable title being held by the beneficiary of the trust. The trustee is not free to spend the money as he wishes but must keep it separate from his own money and apply it only for the purposes of the trust. In the event of the trustee's bankruptcy or insolvency, the money will not be divisible among the trustee's creditors but will continue to be held on trust for the beneficiary.[56] **[13.35]**

The simple distinction between debt and trust informs a great deal of the legal structuring of commercial activity. The relationship between bank and customer, for example, is a contractual relationship of debtor and creditor; money deposited at the bank is not trust money unless it is expressly deposited on the terms of an express trust. If the customer's account is in credit, the customer is the creditor and the bank is the debtor.[57] **[13.36]**

In recent years, some loan contracts have been drafted in such a way that the agreement creates an enforceable trust as well as a contract. The trusts created by these agreements are known as '*Quistclose* trusts' after the leading case of *Barclays Bank Ltd v Quistclose Investments Ltd*.[58] Under a *Quistclose* trust, money is lent on terms that it is only to be applied for a purpose specified by the lender and should be segregated from the borrower's own funds. An express or implied term of a *Quistclose* arrangement is that if the money is not applied for the specified purpose, it will be held on trust for, and returned to, the lender. If the money is applied for the agreed purpose, the lender only has a contractual claim to repayment from the borrower. But if the money is not applied for the purpose, or is misapplied by the borrower, the lender can invoke the remedies available to a beneficiary of a trust to recover it from the borrower or from a third party recipient. *Quistclose* trusts are discussed in chapters 14 and 22. **[13.37]**

WHAT'S ONLINE?

Available at www.cambridge.org/highereducation/isbn/9781009232388/resources:

- Recommended further readings
- Further commentary
- Discussion topics
- Practice problem
- FAQs

56 *Bankruptcy Act 1966* (Cth) s 116; *Corporations Act 2001* (Cth) s 553E.

57 *Foley v Hill* (1848) 2 HLC 28; 9 ER 1002. A bank may, however, come under fiduciary obligations in giving investment advice to a customer: *Commonwealth Bank of Australia v Smith* (1991) 42 FCR 390; *Sourcebook* 10.5.2c, p 273. See [10.13].

58 [1970] AC 567; *Sourcebook* 13.3.1a, p 346.

14

CERTAINTY REQUIREMENTS IN THE LAW OF TRUSTS

Introduction

All dispositions that are intended to transfer property, such as contracts, gifts, trusts and wills, must be clearly defined if they are to be legally effective. In the event of a dispute, a court may have to ascertain whether the property owner intended to dispose of her property and, if so, on what terms. In some cases, the court may have to determine the identity, or identities, of the recipients of the property, or the quantum of property transferred. A recipient of property will need to know if the transfer constitutes a gift, a loan or a trust. [14.1]

All trusts, whether or not they also have to satisfy writing requirements,[1] must be sufficiently certain in order to be enforceable. The certainty requirements for trusts are more demanding than for contracts because trusts can affect the rights of parties who did not agree to, or participate in, its creation. These parties may include the beneficiaries and third parties who do business with the trustee. [14.2]

An express trust must be certain in three distinct respects, sometimes called the 'three certainties'.[2] They are: [14.3]

(a) Certainty of intention. The settlor must have intended to create a trust of her property, as opposed to making a gift of it or lending it to another.

(b) Certainty of subject-matter. The subject-matter of the trust must be specified with reasonable certainty.

(c) Certainty of objects. The beneficiaries of the trust must be sufficiently identifiable.

Charitable trusts[3] are not required to satisfy the requirement of certainty of objects. Resulting and constructive trusts,[4] which are judicially imposed rather than created by a settlor, will not satisfy the requirement of certainty of intention, although the other two certainty requirements are still applicable to them.

The certainty requirements build upon each other in the sense that failure to satisfy one of the certainties may cast doubt on whether one of the other requirements has been met. For example, if the subject-matter of a trust is uncertain, it may well also be the case that the settlor did not truly intend to make the recipient of her property a trustee.[5] [14.4]

Certainty of intention to create a trust

The settlor must have intended to create a trust of her property, as opposed to making a gift or a loan. The settlor need not have used the word 'trust'. If a trust is the most appropriate legal mechanism for giving effect to the settlor's wishes, an inference will be drawn that the settlor intended to create a trust. [14.5]

In *Re Armstrong*,[6] shortly before his death, a father deposited £1500 for each of his two sons on a two-year term deposit at the bank, the title of the accounts being 'George [14.6]

1 See chapter 15.
2 *Knight v Knight* (1840) 3 Beav 148, 173 (Lord Langdale MR).
3 Discussed in chapter 16.
4 See chapters 22 and 23.
5 *Mussoorie Bank v Raynor* (1882) 7 App Cas 321, 331.
6 [1960] VR 202.

Armstrong in re William Armstrong' and 'George Armstrong in re Bernard Armstrong'. When he died, before the deposit term expired, Herring CJ held that the father had intended to create a trust. A trust had been created even though the word 'trust' did not appear in the title of the accounts. The father did not intend to make an immediate gift of the money in the accounts to his sons because he intended to collect the interest on the accounts. A trust, conferring a life interest in the money on the father and remainder interests on the sons, was the most appropriate method of giving effect to the father's wishes with respect to the money.

[14.7] A similar result was reached in *Paul v Constance*.[7] Constance, who was separated but not divorced from his wife, lived with the plaintiff, Mrs Paul. He received damages for a workplace accident and paid the money into an account in his name. At various times, Constance said to the plaintiff and others about the money: 'This is as much yours as mine'. Small amounts were paid into and withdrawn from the account which was not actively used. Constance died without making a will. At law, his widow was entitled to all the money in the account. The Court of Appeal held that Constance's intention was to create a trust of the money in the account, for himself and the plaintiff as beneficiaries. Constance had never used the word 'trust' in his conversations with the plaintiff but this was irrelevant, bearing in mind 'the unsophisticated character of the deceased and his relationship with the plaintiff during the last few years of his life'.[8] Although it might have been thought that Constance had tried to make a gift of half the money in the account, the Court held that a trust was the most appropriate machinery for giving effect to his intention.[9]

Objective or subjective intention?

[14.8] The intention to create a trust is determined by reference to the settlor's objective intention: would a reasonable person consider that in all the circumstances the settlor intended to create a trust? Although earlier High Court authority suggested that the test of intention to create a trust was subjective,[10] the High Court decision of *Byrnes v Kendle*[11] has confirmed that the settlor's intention must be determined objectively.

[14.9] In *Byrnes v Kendle*, the parties were a married couple who purchased a house in the defendant's name because he was able to obtain a loan at favourable rates. The plaintiff paid for some of the renovations to the house. The defendant signed a deed of acknowledgement which stated that he held an undivided half-interest in the property as tenant in common on trust for the plaintiff. Each acknowledged that, upon the death of one of them, the survivor was entitled to the use of the property for life. After the couple separated, the defendant permitted his son from his previous marriage to occupy the house without paying the agreed rent.

The defendant in *Byrnes v Kendle* argued that he had never intended to create a trust for the plaintiff's benefit, notwithstanding the wording of the acknowledgement. In rejecting the argument, the High Court held that he had manifested an objective intention to create a trust

7 [1977] 1 WLR 527.

8 Ibid 532.

9 There was no gift because Constance had not paid any of the money to the plaintiff. A valid trust cannot be construed out of an invalid gift: *Richards v Delbridge* (1874) LR 18 Eq 11.

10 *Commissioner of Stamp Duties (Qld) v Jolliffe* (1920) 28 CLR 178.

11 (2011) 243 CLR 253; *Sourcebook* 14.2a, p 367.

and that his mental reservations were irrelevant in construing the document the parties had signed. As Gummow and Hayne JJ observed, the question which must be answered is 'What is the meaning of what the parties have said?', not 'What did the parties mean to say?'[12] The objective construction of the document was that the defendant had declared a trust of an undivided half share in the property for the plaintiff.

The settlor in *Byrnes v Kendle* had used explicit words to create the trust. However, in some cases, ambiguous words are used, as occurred in *Paul v Constance*. In these cases, the court must consider the words and actions of the settlor to assess whether she has manifested a sufficient objective intention to create a trust. [14.10]

The only circumstances in which a settlor's subjective intention is relevant is where it is alleged that the trust is a sham, or voidable for mistake, misrepresentation, duress, undue influence or unconscionability, or where rectification of the trust instrument is sought on the ground that it does not represent the parties' actual intentions.[13] In *Markopoulos v Marco*,[14] the plaintiff sought summary judgment and a declaration that funds invested with the defendant were held on trust as well as an account. The defendant argued that there was only a debtor-creditor relationship. Tottle J held that there was intention to create a trust as each investment was evidenced with a 'Declaration of Trust'. The defendant argued that he subjectively had misunderstood the term 'trust' and the matter should not be determined summarily. The issue of his subjective intention was held to be a non-triable issue, and irrelevant.[15] [14.11]

Sham trusts

A trust may be created for the purpose of avoiding potential claims of creditors, the Tax Office, or Centrelink. Upon execution of the trust deed, the settlor may insist that he no longer beneficially owns the property so that it is not available for distribution to his creditors and does not form part of his taxable assets. If such trusts are 'shams', subjective intention is relevant. This means that the circumstances surrounding the execution of the trust instrument can be examined. A court can also take into account evidence that the settlor, subsequent to the execution of the trust instrument, treated the trust property as though he was still the absolute owner. [14.12]

A trust is a sham where the settlor deals with property otherwise than in accordance with the terms of the trust he has created, with the intention of deceiving third parties as to the settlor's real interest in the property.[16] A sham has been defined as [14.13]

> acts done or documents executed by the parties to the "sham" which are intended by them to give to third parties or to the court the appearance of creating between the parties legal rights and obligations different from the actual legal rights and obligations (if any) which the parties intend to create.[17]

12 (2011) 243 CLR 253, [53].
13 See [5.23].
14 [2020] WASC 79.
15 Ibid [48].
16 Matthew Conaglen, 'Sham Trusts' (2008) 67(1) *Cambridge Law Journal* 176.
17 *Snook v London & West Riding Investments Ltd* [1967] 2 QB 786, 802 (Diplock LJ). See also *Equuscorp Pty Ltd v Glengallan Investments Pty Ltd* (2004) 218 CLR 471.

Sham trusts intended to deceive creditors are liable to be set aside; for example, under State and Territory legislation providing that 'every alienation of property with intent to defraud creditors shall be voidable at the instance of any person thereby prejudiced'.[18]

[14.14] In *Midland Bank plc v Wyatt*,[19] Mr and Mrs Wyatt executed a formal declaration of trust over their family home in favour of their children. Soon after, Mr Wyatt put the family home up as security for a bank loan to support his business. He did not tell the bank about the trust deed. The business failed, and when the bank sought to enforce its security, the trust was held to be a sham. Wyatt had not intended to act on the trust deed, executing it only in case it was later needed to defeat creditors. The Wyatts had no real intention to benefit their children.

[14.15] This can be contrasted with *Lewis v Condon*[20] where a trust was created for an improper motive, but was intended to have legal effect. The trust was not a sham. Ms Lewis wished to hide her beneficial ownership of property to deceive the Family Court and her ex-husband. Despite her improper intent, the New South Wales Court of Appeal held that she did intend for the trust to take effect. An intention to deceive third parties existed, but that intent could only be carried out if the trust operated according to its terms.

What intention has to be proved?

[14.16] An intention to create a trust is an intention to impose on a property owner[21] an obligation to apply the property for the benefit of identified beneficiaries or for recognised charitable purposes. The essence of a trust is that an owner of property is *obliged* to apply the property for another.[22] As we have seen, it is unnecessary for the word 'trust' to be employed. But there must be evidence that the owner was under an obligation with respect to the property, and therefore not entitled to deal with it as absolute owner. So, in *Re Armstrong*,[23] the Court was satisfied that the father did not intend to be absolute owner of the term deposits which he had bought, and held them as trustee. This imposed an obligation on his executor to have them applied for the benefit of his sons after his death. And in *Paul v Constance*,[24] Constance had imposed an obligation on himself to apply half the money in the bank account for the benefit of the plaintiff.

[14.17] An *obligation* to apply property for another must be contrasted with a *discretion* to apply the property for another, which is insufficient to create a trust. The distinction between trusts and powers was discussed in chapter 13. For example, 'I give $10 000 to A to be used by A for B's maintenance and education' creates an obligation on A to use the fund for B – a trust.

18 *Conveyancing Act 1919* (NSW) s 37A. Anti-avoidance provisions in the *Corporations Act 2001* (Cth) and the *Family Law Act 1975* (Cth) may also be relevant. See the online resources.

19 [1995] 1 Fam Law R 697.

20 (2013) 85 NSWLR 99.

21 Title can be legal or equitable. The title-holder may be the settlor, in the case of a settlor who declares herself trustee of her own property, or a person or persons to whom the settlor has transferred the property. See chapter 15.

22 The fact that a trustee must apply the property for another does not prevent the trustee from also being one of the beneficiaries. See [13.5].

23 [1960] VR 202.

24 [1977] 1 WLR 527.

But, 'I give $10 000 to C. She may use it for D's education or anything else she likes' creates a discretion that C can exercise or not, as she sees fit. This does not create a trust for D.[25]

Precatory trusts

In the nineteenth century, a husband would sometimes leave his property to his wife upon his death, his will indicating how he wanted the property to be applied. For example, he might leave money to his wife 'hoping', or 'in full confidence', that she would use the money to maintain and educate their children. Such words were known as precatory words (words of prayer). For a time, courts construed such provisions as imposing trust obligations on the wife even though words such as 'hoping' are not obligatory.[26] Trusts at that time were economic devices for spreading investment income among the family as a whole, and equity judges construed wills so as to promote this objective.[27] By the end of the nineteenth century, however, strict rules of construction had been adopted and the wife would not be held to be a trustee unless the will clearly imposed an obligation on her to apply property received for the benefit of the children. In *Re Williams*,[28] a testator left his residuary estate in his will to his wife 'in fullest confidence' that she would leave insurance moneys to their daughter, Lucy. A majority of the Court of Appeal held that the words 'in fullest confidence' did not create a trust for Lucy and that the wife was entitled to keep the insurance moneys for herself. [14.18]

Intention to create an immediate trust

A settlor must intend to create a trust which takes effect immediately. In the case of a trust created by deed or will, it must take effect from the date when the document creating the trust takes legal effect. A trust can take effect immediately even though the beneficiaries' enjoyment of property under the trust is deferred; for example, where a settlor settles property on trust for himself for life, with remainder to his children after his death. But equity will not enforce a trust stated to take effect in the future because it might be cancelled, and alternative dispositions of the property made, after it has been declared. In *Harpur v Levy*,[29] a deed of trust executed in August 1997 was expressed to come into effect on the 'commencement day' of 1 October 1997. A majority of the Victorian Court of Appeal held that no trust had been created because the settlor had not expressed a clear intention to create an immediately operative trust. [14.19]

A contract to create a trust in the future will, if valuable consideration has been provided, be enforceable. It will be specifically enforceable by the intended trustee unless a bar to specific performance, such as lack of clean hands or delay, applies.[30] [14.20]

25 For some of the rules of construction applied in determining whether a disposition of property constitutes a trust, see [13.15].

26 *Thorp v Owen* (1843) 2 Hare 607; 67 ER 250.

27 RJ Morris, *Men, Women and Property in England 1780–1870* (Cambridge University Press, 2005) 372–3.

28 [1897] 2 Ch 12; *Sourcebook* 14.2b, p 370. For a modern (inter vivos) application of the principles, see *Chang v Tjiong* [2009] NSWSC 122.

29 (2007) 16 VR 587; *Sourcebook* 14.2d, p 374.

30 The contract may also be enforceable by the beneficiary if a nominal damages award in favour of the intended trustee would be inadequate, applying the principles of *Coulls v Bagot's Executor & Trustee Co Ltd* (1967) 119 CLR 460; *Beswick v Beswick* [1968] AC 58.

Contract and trust: questions of certainty of intention

[14.21] Historically, there was little overlap between trusts and contracts. Trusts law developed within a context of family trusts: typically, the beneficiaries of the trust were volunteers, meaning that they had not provided consideration for their beneficial interests. Nowadays, many trusts are created as part of a commercial arrangement. The arrangement may provide that the trustee pays the settlor for the trust property or that the beneficiaries purchase their interests under the trust. Examples of such trusts, which combine trust, contract and statutory regulation, are superannuation and managed investment trusts.[31]

[14.22] Whether a contract creates a trust is determined objectively, conformably with the principles applied in contract and trust law. In *Shortall v White*,[32] the plaintiff agreed to pay the defendant $20 000 in return for the defendant's agreement to hold 222 000 shares in a public company for her. The defendant argued that he never intended to create a trust for the plaintiff. The New South Wales Court of Appeal held that the circumstances surrounding the transaction showed that the defendant objectively intended to create a trust.

[14.23] A trust enables the doctrine of privity of contract to be avoided in cases where A contracts with B, and B promises to hold the benefit of the contract on trust for C. C can enforce the contract against A by joining B as co-plaintiff, or as co-defendant if B refuses to join C in suing A. B must have intended to create the trust for the benefit of C, but, in ascertaining B's intention, a court will examine the contract between A and B in its commercial context.[33] An intention to create a trust will be established if the contract expressly or by necessary implication provides that B is to hold the benefit of the contract on trust for C.[34]

[14.24] In *Korda v Australian Executor Trustees (SA) Ltd*,[35] members of the High Court reinforced the proposition that, in the absence of express words of trust, intention to create a trust must be able to be imputed from the contract, the parties' oral dealings, and the surrounding commercial circumstances.[36]

The co-existence of contract and trust: the *Quistclose* trust

[14.25] An important, if controversial, example of an express trust created by contract is the '*Quistclose*' trust, named after the leading case of *Barclays Bank Ltd v Quistclose Investments Ltd*.[37] *Quistclose* trusts usually arise out of contracts of loan (although other contexts are possible).[38] Under an ordinary contract of loan where A lends money to B, B will obtain full beneficial title to the money and can apply it for any purpose he wishes, even if the contract envisages that it will be applied for a specific purpose. For example, if A lends B $20 000 to assist B in buying a car, B will, in the absence of special terms in the contract, obtain full

31 See [13.1].

32 [2007] NSWCA 372, [30].

33 *Trident General Insurance Co Ltd v McNiece Brothers Pty Ltd* (1988) 165 CLR 107, 121 (Mason CJ and Wilson J), 147 (Deane J); *Sourcebook* 13.4.3a, p 353.

34 (1988) 165 CLR 107, 147 (Deane J). See [13.31].

35 (2015) 255 CLR 62.

36 Ibid [11] (French CJ), [109] (Gageler J).

37 [1970] AC 567; *Sourcebook* 13.3.1a p 346, 22.1 p 553 and 22.5 p 577. The academic writing on the *Quistclose* trust is extensive. See, especially, the essays in William Swadling (ed), *The Quistclose Trust: Critical Essays* (Hart Publishing, 2004).

38 *Re Kayford Ltd* [1975] 1 All ER 604; *Djmal v Cemal* [2015] NSWSC 1125.

beneficial title to the money and can use it as he wishes, so long as he repays the loan by the due date. A misapplication of the loan may entitle the lender to damages for breach of contract if she can prove that she has suffered loss, but it has no proprietary consequences. But if money is lent under a contract which establishes a *Quistclose* trust, the borrower does not become the beneficial owner of the money. Instead, he receives it as trustee to apply it solely for the purpose specified by the lender. From the lender's perspective, the advantage of a *Quistclose* trust is that, in the event of the borrower's bankruptcy, the borrower's creditors will not be entitled to any part of the loan.

The ingredients of the *Quistclose* trust are illustrated by the *Quistclose* case. Rolls Razor Ltd, which was in financial difficulties, had declared a dividend payable to its shareholders. Quistclose, a finance company, agreed to lend Rolls Razor £209 000 for the sole purpose of paying the dividend. Quistclose paid the money into a special account opened by Rolls Razor at Barclays Bank. The Bank was Rolls Razor's principal creditor. Before the dividend could be paid, Rolls Razor went into voluntary liquidation. The Bank claimed the right to set off the money in the special account against Rolls Razor's overdraft. It would be entitled to exercise this right of set-off unless the money was trust money and the Bank had notice of the trust. [14.26]

The House of Lords held:

(1) The money lent was held on trust, first, to pay the dividend to the shareholders and, secondly, in the event that the dividend could not be paid, to repay Quistclose; and

(2) The bank had notice of the terms of the trust and was therefore not entitled to exercise its right of set-off.

The loan was made on condition 'that it is used to pay the forthcoming dividend due on July 24 next'.[39] The contract therefore did not specify that Rolls Razor, the borrower, was to receive the loan in the capacity of trustee. The words nevertheless showed that Rolls Razor was not to obtain beneficial title to the loan: it had to use the money to pay the dividend or, if the dividend could not be paid, return it to Quistclose. Moreover, since Rolls Razor had not received the money beneficially, the Bank, which was aware of the terms of the loan, was not entitled to apply the money to reduce Rolls Razor's overdraft.

Lord Wilberforce saw no inconsistency in holding that a contract was also enforceable as a trust.[40] The trust enabled the dividend to be paid; it also ensured that the borrower's creditors could not claim the money since the borrower had received it as trustee and not as beneficial owner. If the dividend had been paid, however, the lender could only rely on his contractual right to repayment from the borrower. Once the dividend had been paid the trust came to an end.

The *Quistclose* trust has been recognised in other cases where money has been lent on terms that the borrower is not to become beneficial owner. In *Twinsectra Ltd v Yardley*,[41] a solicitor received money from a lender under a contract which provided that 'the loan moneys will be utilised solely for the acquisition of property on behalf of our client [the borrower] and for no other purpose'. The House of Lords held that the solicitor had received [14.27]

39 *Barclays Bank Ltd v Quistclose Investments Ltd* [1970] AC 567, 569; *Sourcebook* 13.3.1a, p 346 and 22.5a, p 577.

40 *Barclays Bank Ltd v Quistclose Investments Ltd* [1970] AC 567, 581.

41 [2002] 2 AC 164; *Sourcebook* 22.5b, p 578.

the money as trustee and not as beneficial owner. Lord Millett stated that: '[t]he question in every case is whether the parties intended the money to be at the free disposal of the recipient'.[42] This is answered by reference to the terms of the loan agreement, objectively construed. In both *Quistclose* and *Twinsectra*, the loan was paid into a separate bank account opened by the borrower. An arrangement whereby a loan is paid into a separate account, and not mixed with the borrower's own funds, provides strong but not conclusive evidence that the loan is not intended to be at the free disposal of the borrower.

[14.28] The *Quistclose* trust has not been considered in detail in any High Court decision.[43]

In *Re Australian Elizabethan Theatre Trust*,[44] the Theatre Trust accepted donations for a number of arts organisations. Donors gave their money unconditionally to the Theatre Trust but could indicate their preference as to which arts organisation they wished to benefit. The Theatre Trust was not bound to give effect to the preference. The donations were deposited by the Theatre Trust in its general operating account at its bank, and not in a special account. When the Theatre Trust went into liquidation, Gummow J held that the donations did not create an express trust for the preferred arts organisations because there was no certainty of intention to create a trust. The Theatre Trust was not obliged to give effect to the donor's preference.

Gummow J noted that *Quistclose* lending arrangements can be rationalised in terms of a number of equitable structures. He saw Lord Wilberforce's characterisation in the *Quistclose* case as 'indicative of an express trust with two limbs rather than an express trust in favour of the shareholders'.[45] Later English decisions, in contrast, have analysed the *Quistclose* trust as a resulting trust: the borrower holds the money on resulting trust for the lender, subject to any directions the lender gives him on applying the loan.[46] A majority of the New South Wales Court of Appeal in *Salvo v New Tel Ltd* preferred the express trust explanation.[47] Whether *Quistclose* trusts are express or resulting in character may depend on the precise terms on which the money has been lent. Arguably, an express trust analysis can only be applied where money has been lent solely for the purpose of an identified third party beneficiary. Such an express trust must satisfy the certainty rules for the creation of express trusts, including the rules for certainty of objects, discussed below. Where these rules are not satisfied – for example, where money is lent to the borrower solely to enable the borrower to buy equipment for his business – a resulting trust analysis may be more convincing, since the absence of identified beneficiaries will preclude the recognition of an express trust. However, the authors of *Jacobs* argue that an express trust is still possible in this situation[48]

42 *Twinsectra Ltd v Yardley* [2002] 2 AC 164, 185. In *Bellis v Challinor* [2015] EWCA Civ 59, the Court applied the resulting trust analysis from *Twinsectra* but held that only the transferor's intention was relevant.

43 In *Legal Services Board v Gillespie-Jones* (2013) 249 CLR 493, the High Court rejected a *Quistclose* trust on the facts and the various judgments contain no substantive discussion of its nature. Bell, Gageler and Keane JJ noted at [112] that *Quistclose* trust 'terminology is not helpful if taken to suggest the possibility apart from statute of a non-express trust for non-charitable purposes'.

44 (1991) 30 FCR 491; *Sourcebook* 13.4.4a, p 355.

45 *Re Elizabethan Theatre Trust* (1991) 30 FCR 491, 691.

46 *Twinsectra Ltd v Yardley* [2002] 2 AC 164, 192–3 (Lord Millett); *Sourcebook* 22.5b, p 578. See chapter 22 for a discussion of the analysis of the *Quistclose* trust as a resulting trust.

47 [2005] NSWCA 281.

48 JD Heydon and MJ Leeming, *Jacobs' Law of Trusts in Australia* (LexisNexis, 7th ed, 2006) [216] discussed in *Westgem Investments Pty Ltd (recs and mgrs apptd) (admin apptd) v Saracen Project Management Pty Ltd (No 2)* (2012) 8 ASTLR 578, [50]. The argument is maintained in the 8th edition (LexisNexis, 8th ed, 2016) [2-16].

and there appears to be little interest in the courts in resolving the issue. What is clear, however, is that on either analysis the contract of loan will only be construed as creating a trust if the intention of the parties, as objectively manifested by their agreement, was not to confer on the borrower full beneficial title to the money lent.

Because a *Quistclose* trust arises from contractual relationships, the question of intention is considered by looking at the intention of both parties to the contract. This can be contrasted to the usual method of determining intention, where only the intention of the settlor is relevant.

Certainty of subject-matter

The subject-matter of a trust must be certain if the trust is to be enforceable. The requirement of certainty of subject-matter conflates several distinct issues. [14.29]

(a) The subject-matter of a trust (trust property) must constitute legally recognised property. It can be real or personal tangible property, such as land or a painting, or intangible property, such as a patent or the right to enforce a debt (which is a chose in action). It can be legal or equitable property. The settlor must also have present property rights. An expectancy, such as the expectation of receiving property under a will, does not constitute property and therefore cannot be held on trust.[49] Similarly, the expectation of receiving property as a beneficiary under a discretionary trust cannot be held on trust.[50] An expectation of receiving property can be frustrated, for example, by the testator changing his will or the trustees of the discretionary trust failing to exercise their discretion in favour of a particular beneficiary. Because an expectation of receiving property is uncertain, it does not constitute property capable of being held on trust.

(b) The quantum, or amount, of property to be held on trust must be clearly defined. In *Palmer v Simmonds*,[51] the testator left 'the bulk of my estate' to be held on trust. The trust failed because the word 'bulk' did not clearly indicate how much of the testator's property was to be held on trust.

This does not mean that the subject-matter of a trust will be uncertain just because it cannot be precisely quantified. Take a typical testamentary family trust under which the testator settles property on trust for his widow for life, with remainder to their children after her death. During the widow's lifetime, the children's interest cannot be precisely valued. Variables affecting valuation include the longevity of the widow, the distribution of trust income to her, and the success of the trustees' investment policy. Nevertheless, the children have a vested interest in reversion which will take effect in possession on the widow's death. The reversionary interest is sufficiently certain to constitute the subject-matter of the trust.[52] [14.30]

49 *Norman v Federal Commissioner of Taxation* (1963) 109 CLR 9, 24 (Windeyer J); *Sourcebook* 9.3a, p 212.

50 *Kennon v Spry* (2008) 238 CLR 366, [160]–[162] (Heydon J).

51 (1854) 2 Drew 221; 61 ER 704.

52 The same is true of the interest of a beneficiary of a residuary estate.

[14.31] The subject-matter of a trust can be certain even if the quantum of property the beneficiary is to receive will be determined by the trustee, provided that the criteria applied by the trustee can be objectively assessed. In *Re Golay's Will Trusts*,[53] a gift directing the testator's executors to allow a beneficiary to 'enjoy one of my flats during her lifetime and to receive a reasonable income from my other properties' was upheld. The term 'reasonable income' was held to be certain since it was to be interpreted objectively. A difficulty with the decision is that the standard for assessing 'reasonable income' was not laid down. Was it to be determined by reference to the beneficiary's needs or to a proportion of the trust income?

[14.32] Where a trust is created of a proportion of goods which form part of a bulk the subject-matter of the trust will not be certain until the goods which are to be held on trust have been segregated from the bulk. In *Re Goldcorp Exchange Ltd*,[54] a company sold unascertained gold bullion to customers for future delivery. Each customer received a certificate verifying his ownership. The customers were told that the company would maintain a sufficient stock of bullion to satisfy all orders but it failed to do so. The company experienced financial difficulties and a floating charge held by a bank over all the company's assets crystallised. This meant that the bank could claim all the unallocated bullion held by the company unless title had passed to the customers under the contracts for sale or a trust had been declared for them. The Privy Council held that no title to the bullion had passed to the customers and no valid trust had been created. Until the bullion had been segregated from the bulk and appropriated to each customer's contract, title remained with the company. Lord Mustill recognised that it would be possible to create a trust of the bulk of the bullion or of a specified percentage of the bulk;[55] but the contracts of sale of the bullion did not specify a particular percentage of the stock which would be held on trust. The bullion would have to be segregated from the bulk and appropriated to the trust if the subject-matter of the trust was to be certain.

[14.33] In *Hunter v Moss*,[56] the English Court of Appeal held that a trust is sufficiently certain if the trust property consists of a percentage or fraction of fungible property (ie property which is identical to, and interchangeable with, property of the same description, such as coins of the same value or shares of the same class). The defendant owned 950 shares in a company which had an issued share capital of 1000 shares. He orally declared himself trustee of 5% of the share capital (ie 50 shares) for the plaintiff. The Court of Appeal held that the trust was valid. Provided that the shares were of the same class and in the same company there was no need to segregate them before declaring the trust.

[14.34] In *White v Shortall*,[57] Campbell J reached the conclusion that a declaration of trust over 222 000 shares from a holding of 1.5 million was valid; however, he did not follow the reasoning in *Hunter*, as he was not satisfied by the analogies drawn with transactions involving other forms of property. In *Ellison v Sandini Pty Ltd*,[58] the Full Federal Court

53 [1965] 1 WLR 969.

54 [1995] 1 AC 74. See also *Re London Wine Co* [1986] PCC 121.

55 *Re Goldcorp Exchange Ltd* [1995] 1 AC 74.

56 [1994] 1 WLR 452; *Sourcebook* 14.3a, p 376; Sarah Worthington, 'Sorting Out Ownership Interests in a Bulk: Gifts, Sales and Trusts' [1999] *Journal of Business Law* 1; Roy Goode, 'Are Intangible Assets Fungible?' [2003] *Lloyds Maritime & Commercial Law Quarterly* 379.

57 *White v Shortall* (2006) 68 NSWLR 650; *Sourcebook* 14.3b, p 377.

58 (2018) 263 FCR 460.

approved *White*.[59] Jagot J (Siopis J agreeing) discussed the reasoning in *White*, as well as later English and New Zealand case law on the issue. Her Honour noted that in *White*, Campbell J held that the trust operated over the declarant's entire shareholding, in certain proportions for himself and for his former partner. Jagot J stated:

> In terms of principle, the weight of authority is that there can be a valid trust over a fungible pool of assets provided the assets and relevant proportions for the different beneficiaries are identified with sufficient certainty. The better view is that for the requirement of certainty to be satisfied the trust must be over all of the fungible assets in the pool, the beneficial co-ownership proportions reflecting the respective interests of the beneficiaries.[60]

Her Honour also noted a 'conceptual difficulty'[61] which did not arise on the facts of the case. If the shares were not all acquired at the same time, they may be subject to different capital gains tax liability. This may mean that the shares are not interchangeable for the purposes of the certainty of subject matter analysis.

Certainty of objects

The third respect in which a trust must be certain is that of certainty of objects: the beneficiaries of a trust must be identifiable.[62] This 'certainty' has given rise to more difficulty than the other two in recent years, mainly due to the expanding use of discretionary trusts. [14.35]

In applying the rules governing certainty of objects, it is important to distinguish between bare powers of appointment and trust powers, discussed in chapter 13. It will be recalled that, whereas a trust imposes an *obligation* to apply the trust property in accordance with the settlor's directions, a power is a *discretion* exercisable with respect to property to which the person exercising the power (the appointor or donee of the power) is not solely entitled. [14.36]

As explained in chapter 13, the power of appointment may be *general*, empowering the trustees to appoint trust money to anyone, including themselves. It may be *special*, empowering the trustees to appoint to members of a class specified by the settlor, such as the settlor's relatives and dependants. Such persons are known as the objects of the power. Finally, a power may be *hybrid*, entitling the trustees to appoint to anyone except members of a specified class, as where trustees have a discretion to appoint to anyone except the settlor and the settlor's spouse. [14.37]

Another important distinction in this context is between fixed trusts and trust powers (or discretionary trusts).[63] A fixed trust is one in which the share or interest of each beneficiary [14.38]

---

59 The case dealt with capital gains tax consequences of Family Court orders that the trustee of a trust transfer 2 115 000 shares in a particular company to Mrs Ellison. The trustee held more than 2 115 000 shares in the company. The shares were all of the same class, and uncertificated. Logan J (in the minority) also approved *White* generally.

60 (2018) 263 FCR 460, [148].

61 Ibid [149]. The impact of capital gains tax on the analysis discussed above was also noted by Campbell J in *White v Shortall* (2006) 68 NSWLR 650, [259]. The issue did not arise on the facts.

62 P Creighton, 'Certainty of Objects of Trusts and Powers: The Impact of *McPhail v Doulton* in Australia' (2000) 22(1) *Sydney Law Review* 93.

63 See [13.6].

is specified in the trust instrument. A trust power is a trust in which the share of the trust property, if any, which each potential beneficiary is to receive is determined by the trustees. So if S settles $500 000 on T to be divided equally between S's children, a fixed trust has been created. But if S settles $500 000 on trust to be divided among such of S's children as T considers deserving, S has established a discretionary trust.

[14.39] Many trust instruments contain both trust obligations and powers. For example, a testatrix might settle her property on discretionary trust for her children and also confer a power on her trustees to pay income to such of her nephews and nieces as may be in need. It is essential to consider the validity of the trust obligations and powers separately. This is not only because the tests for determining certainty of objects for a trust and a power may be different, but also because courts must be satisfied that trusts are workable if the trustees are obliged to administer them.

Powers and certainty

[14.40] A special power of appointment will be valid if the trustees can say with certainty that any given individual is or is not a member of the class of objects of the power. This is known as the 'criterion certainty' test. The test was laid down by the House of Lords in *Re Gulbenkian's Settlement Trusts*.[64] A trust was constituted with power to appoint property for 'any person or persons in whose house or apartments or in whose company or under whose care or control or by or with whom the said Nubar Sarkis Gulbenkian may from time to time be employed or residing'.[65] The House of Lords held that the power was valid. It was possible to say of any individual that he was or was not a person with whom Nubar Gulbenkian was residing, or that he had or had not employed Nubar Gulbenkian.

[14.41] A hybrid power of appointment will be valid if the members of the excluded class of beneficiaries satisfy the criterion certainty test. So a clause empowering the trustees to distribute to anyone in the world except the settlor, her spouse, and the trustees is valid.[66]

Conceptual and evidential uncertainty

[14.42] Conceptual certainty relates to whether the words used to define a class have objective meaning.[67] Criteria such as 'residence' used in a trust instrument are imprecise. Whether A resides with B, as opposed to staying with B temporarily, depends on establishing as a question of fact how long A occupied B's home, and then determining whether it amounts to 'residence' within the terms of the trust instrument. Lord Upjohn in *Re Gulbenkian's Settlement Trusts* distinguished between conceptual and evidential uncertainty. He gave as an example of conceptual uncertainty a trust for 'my old friends'.[68] A power which is conceptually uncertain is invalid, since insufficient information has been given to allow the

64 [1970] AC 508; *Sourcebook* 14.4a, p 380. The decision has been applied in Australia: *Gerhardy v South Australian Auxiliary to the British & Foreign Bible Society* (1982) 30 SASR 12. See also Creighton (n 62) 102.

65 As the House of Lords noted, the clause was ungrammatical: [1970] AC 508, 517.

66 *Re Manisty's Settlement* [1974] Ch 17; *Re Hay's Settlement Trusts* [1982] 1 WLR 202.

67 Conceptual uncertainty is sometimes referred to in the cases as linguistic or semantic uncertainty.

68 [1970] AC 508, 524. In *Re Barlow's Will Trusts* [1979] 1 WLR 278, a gift to friends was upheld, but in the context of a gift subject to a condition precedent where a less strict test applies.

trustee or the court to exercise the power. In other cases, there may be evidential difficulties identifying the objects of a power. This is evidential uncertainty. Concepts employed in the power considered in *Re Gulbenkian's Settlement Trusts*, such as 'residence', 'employed' and 'care and control' may have been evidentially uncertain but they were held not to be conceptually uncertain.[69] Evidential uncertainty will not cause a power to fail. Application can be made to the court, if necessary, to resolve any ambiguity.[70]

One method of overcoming conceptual uncertainty is for the trust instrument to provide that the opinion of a third party is to resolve the ambiguity. The third party can be the trustees, although it will not be assumed that the trustees have the power to resolve conceptual ambiguity solely from the fact that the settlor has conferred on them discretion to administer the power. In *Re Tuck's Settlement Trusts*,[71] a will which required the beneficiary to be of the Jewish faith and married to an 'approved wife', with any disputes being resolved by a chief rabbi, was upheld. However, a settlor or testator cannot oust the jurisdiction of the Court by giving the trustees or any other third party conclusive power to construe the terms of the trust.[72] [14.43]

Fixed trusts

If trust property is to be divided among a class of beneficiaries in shares determined by the settlor in the trust instrument, the trust is only valid if the identity of all the beneficiaries is known. This is known as 'list certainty': at the time of distribution the trustees must be able to draw up a list of all the beneficiaries entitled to a share of the trust property.[73] If the existence or whereabouts of a beneficiary is unknown, her share can be paid into court until the uncertainty is resolved. [14.44]

Trust power (discretionary trust)

The criterion certainty test determines whether the objects of a trust power are certain. The trust power is valid if the trustees can say with certainty that a given individual is or is not a member of the class. The leading case on certainty of objects for trust powers is the House of Lords decision in *McPhail v Doulton*.[74] The settlor executed a trust instrument 'for the benefit of any of the officers and employees or ex-officers or ex-employees of Matthew Hall [14.45]

69 For a recent example, see *Wright v Stevens* [2018] NSWSC 548 where the discretionary class was: 'Such persons, Trustees of Trusts (but excluding any Trusts which would result in a breach of the rule against perpetuities or the rule against accumulations) companies or charities, residing in or otherwise carrying on business in Dorrigo in New South Wales or surrounding area as defined by post code 2453.' Hallen J said that the objects were certain even though a list of all objects may not have been able to be made: [196].

70 *Re Gulbenkian's Settlement Trusts* [1970] AC 508, 523.

71 [1978] Ch 49. The condition was held to be certain without any need to make any reference to a chief rabbi.

72 *Re Wynn* [1952] Ch 271.

73 *Inland Revenue Commissioners v Broadway Cottages Trust* [1955] Ch 20; *Kinsela v Caldwell* (1975) 132 CLR 458; Creighton (n 62) 95–9. Cf application of the criterion certainty test to a fixed trust in *West v Weston* (1998) 44 NSWLR 657, criticised by Creighton (n 62) 97–8.

74 [1971] AC 424; *Sourcebook* 14.4b, p 382; JW Harris, 'Trust, Power and Duty' (1971) 87(1) *Law Quarterly Review* 31.

and Company or to any relatives or dependants of any such persons in such amounts at such times and on such conditions (if any) as they think fit'.[75] After the settlor's death, the validity of the will was challenged by his next of kin.

The House of Lords held:

(a) (unanimously) that the instrument created a trust power, and not a bare power;

(b) (by a majority) that the test of certainty of objects for trust powers was the criterion certainty test;

(c) (unanimously) that the trust should be remitted to the Chancery Division to determine whether it satisfied the criterion certainty test.

The trust power would have failed if list certainty was required since it was impossible to draw up a complete list of all the employees, former employees and (more crucially) their relatives and dependants. Large employment welfare trusts, of the kind created in *McPhail v Doulton*, are only likely to be upheld if criterion certainty rather than list certainty is required.

When the case was remitted it was held by the Court of Appeal in *Re Baden's Deed Trusts (No 2)*[76] that the trust satisfied the criterion certainty test. The word 'dependants' in the trust deed simply referred to anyone who was dependent on an employee or former employee of the company. The word 'relatives' in the deed was more problematic because it is impossible to prove that someone is *not* a relative of another person for the purpose of applying the criterion certainty test. Sachs and Megaw LJJ overcame the difficulty by holding that the term referred to persons descended from a common ancestor,[77] while Stamp LJ construed it more narrowly to mean 'next of kin' or 'closest relatives'.[78] In practice, any dispute as to whether a claimant is a relative of a person identified in a trust instrument could now be solved by DNA testing.

Status of the criterion certainty test in Australia

[14.46] The High Court has not considered *McPhail v Doulton*[79] but State courts have applied its reasoning. In *Horan v James*,[80] the New South Wales Court of Appeal expressly applied *McPhail v Doulton* to a clause construed as a trust power. *Re Blyth*[81] is a controversial application of the criterion certainty principle. The testator established a trust to be distributed in his 'uncontrolled discretion … among such Organizations as in the Public Trustee's opinion are working for the elimination of war and … such Organizations as in the Public Trustee's opinion are formed for the purpose of raising the standard of life throughout the world'.[82] Thomas J upheld the first disposition as it was possible to show whether or not an organisation was working for the elimination of war even though it was impossible to draw up a list of all such organisations. On the other hand, the second disposition failed because the criteria for inclusion in the class were too uncertain; 'raising the standard of life' is an ambiguous concept.

75 [1971] AC 424, 428.
76 [1973] Ch 9.
77 Ibid 22.
78 Ibid 29.
79 [1971] AC 424.
80 [1982] 2 NSWLR 376. Even though it satisfied the certainty of objects test the gift failed as an improper delegation of testamentary power.
81 [1997] 2 Qd R 567. See also *McCracken v A-G (Vic)* [1995] 1 VR 67.
82 [1997] 2 Qd R 567, 569–70.

Validity of a trust power when the settlor has selected two classes of beneficiaries, one class being certain and the other uncertain, was also considered in *Re Blyth*. Where a settlor has created two distinct trusts, the failure of one trust for lack of certainty of objects will not cause the failure of the other. So if S leaves $1000 to be held on discretionary trust for persons satisfying condition A, and $1000 to be held on discretionary trust for persons satisfying condition B, the criterion certainty test will be applied independently to each trust. If condition A is uncertain, the trust including that condition will fail, but the trust containing condition B will not fail unless it independently fails the test. [14.47]

Where, however, a trust power is created, the trustee having discretion to select among two groups of beneficiaries, and one group is uncertain, the whole trust fails. Where the class of beneficiaries of a trust power consists of several sub-classes all the sub-classes must satisfy the criterion certainty test if the trust is to be valid.[83] It would defeat the intention of the settlor to enforce a trust power for some, but not all, of the class of beneficiaries she had specified. In *Re Blyth*, however, Thomas J severed the valid part of the trust power, relating to organisations working for the elimination of war, from the invalid part, relating to organisations formed for the purpose of raising the standard of life throughout the world. The trust power was enforceable for the former purpose but not the latter. The decision on this point is inconsistent with previous authority holding that an invalid subclass of beneficiaries under a private trust cannot be severed from the valid part.

Administrative unworkability

Even if a trust power satisfies the criterion certainty test, it will be void if it is administratively unworkable. The requirement of administrative unworkability was laid down by Lord Wilberforce in *McPhail v Doulton*. He identified cases where 'the definition of beneficiaries is so hopelessly wide as not to form "anything like a class" so that the trust is administratively unworkable', suggesting 'all the residents of Greater London' as an example.[84] He went on to hold that the trust power in *McPhail v Doulton* was not void for administrative unworkability. [14.48]

Courts have not found it easy to interpret the administrative unworkability test.[85] Lord Wilberforce's objection was to beneficiaries not constituting a coherent class, whereas in some later cases trusts have been held to be administratively unworkable on the ground that the beneficiaries were too numerous to have their claims properly considered. In *R v District Auditor; Ex parte West Yorkshire Metropolitan County Council*,[86] a council resolved to set up a trust 'for the benefit of any or all or some of the inhabitants of the County of West Yorkshire'. There were 2.5 million potential beneficiaries of the trust. The trust was held to be void for administrative unworkability as the class of beneficiaries was too large to be enforceable. [14.49]

A bare power will not be void for administrative unworkability.[87] This is because trustees of a bare power have a discretion to exercise the power but are not required to exercise [14.50]

83 *Tatham v Huxtable* (1950) 81 CLR 639. There is an exception for charitable trusts which meet statutory criteria for severance. See [16.35].

84 [1971] AC 424, 457.

85 Creighton (n 62) 107–10.

86 (1986) 26 RVR 24.

87 *Re Manisty's Settlement* [1974] Ch 17, disapproving *Blausten v Inland Revenue Commissioners* [1972] Ch 256. See also *Re Hay's Settlement Trusts* [1982] 1 WLR 202.

it by making a distribution of trust money. Their duty is only to consider the exercise of their discretion.

[14.51] It is unclear whether Australian law applies an administrative workability test.[88] The trust in *Horan v James*[89] was for all the world except specific named persons. This was held to satisfy the criterion certainty test without any consideration of administrative unworkability. On the other hand, in *McCracken v Attorney-General (Vic)*,[90] it was held that a trust for 'such Christian organisations and societies as my trustees shall select' did not satisfy the criterion certainty test and was therefore void. JD Phillips J held that, even if the trust had satisfied the test for certainty of objects, it would have been void for administrative unworkability.

[14.52] It is suggested that administrative unworkability should be confined to invalidating attempts to create hybrid trusts, such as a trust to appoint to anyone except X. Trustees of such trusts cannot sensibly exercise their discretion. But, such cases apart, trusts which satisfy the test of certainty of objects should not be invalidated on the ground of unworkability, assuming that the trustees consider that they can administer them.

Capricious trusts and powers

[14.53] An unsettled question is whether a trust or power will be void if the class of beneficiaries has been selected capriciously by the settlor.[91]

Generally speaking, there is nothing to prevent a property owner from making a capricious disposition of her property.[92] A trustee may, however, be unable to exercise her fiduciary duties properly if the terms of a trust or fiduciary power are arbitrary or capricious. A trustee is under a duty to consider exercising her discretion in good faith and upon a proper consideration of all relevant factors. The duty may be hard to fulfil if the beneficiaries have been selected capriciously; for example, where the beneficiaries have no connection with the settlor, and selection among a class of beneficiaries will be random. Such cases are, however, rare. There are many cases in which the selection of the class of beneficiaries appears to be random but which on close inquiry turns out to be entirely rational. We have seen that in *R v District Auditor; Ex parte West Yorkshire Metropolitan County Council*[93] a trust established by a local council 'for the benefit of any or all or some of the inhabitants of the County of West Yorkshire' was held void for administrative unworkability.[94] It was, however, held not to be a capricious trust because the local authority, as settlor, had every reason for wanting to benefit the inhabitants in the ways specified.

[14.54] In *Re Manisty's Settlement*,[95] Templeman J, in upholding a hybrid power, stated that a power of selection among the 'residents of Greater London' would be void as being capricious, not because the class of potential beneficiaries was numerous, but because the terms of the power negatived any sensible intention on the settlor's part and any

88 Creighton (n 62) 110.
89 [1982] 2 NSWLR 376.
90 [1995] 1 VR 67.
91 On capriciousness as a separate ground of invalidity, see Creighton (n 62) 106.
92 Testators' maintenance legislation – for example, pt IV of the *Administration and Probate Act 1958* (Vic) – limits capricious testamentary dispositions where the testator had a responsibility to make provision for the applicant.
93 (1986) 26 RVR 24.
94 See [14.48] above.
95 [1974] Ch 17.

sensible selection by the trustees. But it is hard to see why a special power should fail for capriciousness when the much broader hybrid power in that case was held not to be capricious. It is suggested that capriciousness should not be recognised as an independent ground for invalidating trusts or powers. Assuming that they satisfy the test of certainty of objects, and, in the case of trusts, they are administratively workable, they should not be invalidated on a ground which necessarily involves second-guessing, and interfering with, a settlor's intentions.

Certainty of objects and trustees' duties

The purpose of rules for certainty of objects is to enable trustees to identify the beneficiaries correctly, so that trust property is only distributed to those entitled under the trust instrument. Since the 'list certainty' principle does not apply to trust powers, the trustees of many trust powers containing broadly defined classes of beneficiaries will be unable to identify all potential recipients of trust money. In *McPhail v Doulton*, Lord Wilberforce emphasised that trustees are under a duty to survey the class of beneficiaries and inquire into the needs and qualifications of any beneficiary to whom an appointment of trust money was being considered.[96] Trustees must adopt a strategy for selecting beneficiaries; for example, by dividing them into categories of beneficiary and selecting individual beneficiaries in each class. [14.55]

Trustees exercising a special or hybrid power also come under a duty to survey the range of objects of the power. In these cases, the duty is less extensive than for a trust power. This is because a trustee who has to distribute the whole of a fund's income must necessarily make more systematic inquiries than a trustee who only has a discretion to apply trust money. [14.56]

Executing a trust power

It is not only trustees who must be able to identify the beneficiaries of a trust. A court may have to distribute trust property if the trustees fail to do so. The court's aim in distributing the property is to give effect to the settlor's intentions; uncertainty as to the identity of the beneficiaries may result in the frustration of the settlor's wishes. [14.57]

Prior to *McPhail v Doulton*, it was assumed that if the trustees failed to exercise their discretion under a trust power, the court had to divide the trust property equally among all the beneficiaries, applying the maxim 'equality is equity'.[97] It would be impossible to divide the property equally unless the court could identify every beneficiary. The justification for applying the 'list certainty' rule of certainty of objects to trust powers was that it enabled the court to identify every beneficiary sharing in the equal distribution. [14.58]

In *McPhail v Doulton*,[98] Lord Wilberforce rejected the principle of equal division of trust property in the event of default by the trustees. A settlor's intention in creating a trust power is not to benefit the beneficiaries equally; the whole point of conferring a discretion on the trustees is to authorise unequal treatment of the beneficiaries, whether on the basis of need, qualifications, or some other criterion specified by the settlor. If the trustees fail [14.59]

96 [1971] AC 424, 449.
97 *Inland Revenue Commissioners v Broadway Cottages Trust* [1955] Ch 20.
98 [1971] AC 424.

to exercise their discretion a court may give effect to the settlor's intentions in one of the following three ways:

(1) by appointing new trustees;[99]

(2) by authorising a representative class of beneficiaries to prepare a scheme of distribution; or

(3) if the settlor's basis for distribution is clear, by distributing the trust property itself.[100]

The same orders can be made if trustees fail to consider the exercise of a power.[101] But a court will not intervene if the trustees, having properly considered the exercise of their discretion, decide not to appoint trust property to an object of the power. In that eventuality, the party entitled in default of the exercise of discretion will be entitled to the property.[102]

WHAT'S ONLINE?

Available at www.cambridge.org/highereducation/isbn/9781009232388/resources:

- Recommended further readings
- Further commentary
- Discussion topics
- Practice problem

99 Some subsequent Australian decisions have indicated this is the extent of the court's power: see *Knudsen v Kara Kar Holdings Pty Ltd* [2000] NSWSC 715, [62]; *Hay v Total Risk Management Pty Ltd* [2004] NSWSC 94, [60].

100 [1971] AC 424, 457. The distribution must be in favour of those who were objects at the time the discretion should have been exercised: *Re Locker's Settlement* [1977] 1 WLR 1323.

101 *Mettoy Pension Trustees Ltd v Evans* [1990] 1 WLR 1587.

102 See [13.15].

15

CREATING AN EXPRESS TRUST

Introduction

[15.1] In chapter 14, we saw that enforceability of an express trust depends on proof of certainty in three matters: intention to create a trust, subject-matter, and objects. In addition to satisfying the certainty requirements and not infringing public policy prohibitions on creating trusts,[1] an express trust must have been validly created (or constituted); that is, the trust must be properly declared, and title to the trust property must be properly vested in the trustee.

Additionally, some trusts must comply with statutory formalities. Unless they meet these requirements, they will be unenforceable or void, depending on the statutory provision in question.

Methods of creating a trust

[15.2] Testamentary trusts are created by will, and only come into effect on the death of the testator. Inter vivos trusts are trusts that come into effect during the settlor's life. Inter vivos trusts can be created by a declaration of trust of the settlor's own property, or by transfer of property to a trustee.

Self-declaration of trust

[15.3] A settlor can declare herself trustee of her own property. The settlor already holds title to the property, and all that she has to do is to make a valid declaration of trust. A declaration of trust is simply a way of saying that the requirement of certainty of intention to create a trust has been satisfied.[2] The authorities on certainty of intention are therefore also authorities on declaration of trust.[3] In trusts created by declaration, the settlor must intend to impose trustee obligations upon herself.

[15.4] A court will not, however, construe a declaration of trust out of an invalid gift. In *Richards v Delbridge*,[4] a grandfather who was the lessee of business premises wanted to benefit his grandson. He wrote on the back of the deed of lease: 'This deed and all thereto belonging I give to [my grandson] from this time forth, with all the stock-in-trade'. The lease was delivered to the grandson's mother. The grandfather died, making no mention of the property in his will.

The writing did not constitute a valid gift of the lease to the grandson. A gift would have required execution of a separate deed under seal. Jessel MR held that the words were also inappropriate for the declaration of trust: '[F]or a man to make himself a trustee there must be an expression of intention to become a trustee, whereas words of present gift shew an intention to give over property to another, and not retain it in the donor's own hands for any purpose, fiduciary or otherwise'.[5]

1 See [15.26]–[15.39].

2 See [14.5].

3 See especially *Re Armstrong* [1960] VR 202, discussed at [14.6]; *Paul v Constance* [1977] 1 WLR 527, discussed at [14.7].

4 (1874) LR 18 Eq 11.

5 Ibid 15.

Formalities for inter vivos trusts by declaration

The formalities relevant to express trusts created by declaration depend upon the nature of the trust property. Only some inter vivos trusts must comply with formalities. None are required to create a trust of *personal property* where the trust is intended to take effect during the settlor's lifetime. In the case of a trust of land, however, the evidence required to prove the existence of the trust must be distinguished from the evidence which will enable the beneficiaries to enforce it. The *existence* of the trust can be proved by oral evidence. But the trust cannot be *enforced* by the beneficiaries unless the statutory requirements based on the *Statute of Frauds 1677* (Eng) have been met.[6] In most Australian jurisdictions, this requires the declaration of trust to be manifested and proved by writing signed by the person able to declare the trust.[7] [15.5]

The writing is required as evidence of declaration; the declaration need not itself be in writing. So, trusts over land can be created orally and later reduced to writing. Failure to comply with the writing requirement renders the trust unenforceable, not void.[8] If an oral trust over land is later reduced to writing it can then be enforced and is treated as taking effect at the date of the declaration, not the date of the writing.[9] Under the terms of the legislation, constructive, implied and resulting trusts are not required to satisfy writing requirements. [15.6]

There is no particular form of writing required, and it can be contained in more than one document.[10] The legislation requires that the writing be signed by the person able to declare the trust. In most cases, that will mean the settlor, but not her agent. Writing signed by a trustee who is also the settlor is sufficient to enforce the trust against the trustee.[11] [15.7]

It is unclear what formalities apply to declarations of trust over subsisting equitable interests. Suppose S wishes to declare a trust over her interest as a beneficiary of a trust. If, by doing so, S is *disposing* of a pre-existing equitable interest, this declaration might be required to be made in writing. This is discussed at [9.42]. [15.8]

Trust created by transfer

Alternatively, a settlor can create an express trust by transferring property to a trustee to hold on trust. Where a trust is created by transfer of property to an intended trustee, two requirements must be satisfied: [15.9]

(1) *A declaration of trust*. The declaration must establish that the recipient of the property was intended to take the property in the capacity of trustee and not beneficially. The words used by the settlor in transferring the property will be

6 *Re McGowan & Valentini Trusts* (2021) 63 VR 449, [68]–[69].

7 See *Civil Law (Property) Act 2006* (ACT) s 201(2); *Conveyancing Act 1919* (NSW) s 23C(1)(b); *Law of Property Act 2000* (NT) s 10(1)(b); *Property Law Act 1974* (Qld) s 11(1)(b); *Law of Property Act 1936* (SA) s 29(1)(b); *Conveyancing and Law of Property Act 1884* (Tas) s 60(2)(b); *Property Law Act 1958* (Vic) s 53(1)(b); *Property Law Act 1969* (WA) s 34(1)(b). The ACT provision requires declarations of trust of land to be 'in writing', and not 'manifested and proved by writing', as in other jurisdictions., but it has been held, by reason of the provision's basis in the *Statute of Frauds*, that a declaration will be valid if it is manifested and proved by writing: *Hurst–Meyers v Public Trustee and Guardian for the ACT* [2018] ACTSC 61, [24]–[32]; *Sourcebook* 15.2a, p 388.

8 *Gardner v Rowe* (1828) 5 Russ 258; 38 ER 1024.

9 *Secretary, Department of Social Security v James* (1990) 20 ALD 5; *Sourcebook* 15.2b, p 390.

10 *Secretary, Department of Social Security v James* (1990) 20 ALD 5; *Sourcebook* 15.2b, p 390.

11 *Hagan v Waterhouse* (1991) 34 NSWLR 308.

construed in the context of the transfer itself. In *T Choithram International SA v Pagarini*,[12] the settlor executed a trust deed establishing a charitable foundation. He then made statements which appeared to indicate an intention to make outright gifts of property to the intended trustees. The Privy Council held that in the context of the creation of a charitable foundation, the words used should be taken to establish an intention to transfer property on the terms of the charitable foundation the settlor had set up, and not to make absolute gifts. He had therefore validly declared a trust.

(2) *A valid transfer of the intended trust property to the intended trustee.* The transfer will be valid if it complies with the common law or statutory formalities required to transfer legal or statutory title. These are discussed in chapter 9.

[15.10] A transfer may be invalid at law but valid in equity applying the principle of *Corin v Patton*,[13] discussed at [9.10]. Applying the principle to express trusts, a transfer of property by a settlor to the intended trustee will be valid in equity if the settlor has done all those things, prescribed by statute or by common law for the transfer of the legal or statutory title, that have to be done by the settlor and cannot be done by anyone else. So, if S transfers 1000 shares to T to be held on trust for B but dies before the transfer is registered, the transfer will be valid in equity. S's estate will hold the shares on constructive trust for T[14] until all the legal requirements for transfer of the legal title have been satisfied and the transfer is complete at law. T will, in turn, hold the equitable interest under the constructive trust on the terms of the express trust for B. Any dividends paid to S's estate before the transfer of shares has been registered will also be payable to T and held on trust for B.

Formalities for inter vivos trusts by transfer

[15.11] Trusts of land created by transfer must be evidenced in writing, as required by provisions derived from the *Statute of Frauds*, discussed at [15.5]. They are unenforceable if they are not evidenced in writing. However, suppose A conveys Blackacre to B on the faith of B's oral promise that B will hold Blackacre on trust for A. After the conveyance, B claims to be full beneficial owner of the land and that the trust is unenforceable because it is not evidenced in writing. It would be unfair for B to rely on the absence of writing to deny that he is bound by his promise. Equity will enforce the trust, applying the maxim that equity will not allow a statute to be used as an instrument of fraud.

[15.12] In *Last v Rosenfeld*,[15] the plaintiffs and defendants owned a house as joint tenants. The plaintiffs transferred their share to the defendants at cost price as part of an oral agreement that, if the defendants did not personally occupy the house within 12 months, they would re-transfer the plaintiffs' former share of the property to the plaintiffs at the same price. The defendants neither occupied the house nor re-transferred the plaintiffs' share. Instead, they

12 [2001] 1 WLR 1 (PC); *Sourcebook* 15.3a, p 392. It was also held that a trust of the property had been created even though title had been vested in only one of the trustees of the foundation. See also *Bowack v Saxton* [2020] EWHC 1049 (Ch), [43]–[46].

13 (1990) 169 CLR 540; *Sourcebook* 9.2b, p 208. See [9.10].

14 *Re Rose* [1952] Ch 499. See [9.9].

15 [1972] 2 NSWLR 923; *Sourcebook* 15.4a, p 394.

sold the house to a third party with a mortgage back to the defendants. Even though the oral agreement between the plaintiffs and the defendants was unenforceable under the *Statute of Frauds*, Hope J applied the maxim that equity will not allow a statute to be used as an instrument of fraud. He ordered the defendants to pay the plaintiffs half of the proceeds of sale, and awarded the plaintiffs a half interest in the mortgage, subject to the plaintiffs repaying the defendants the price they had received on sale of their half interest in the property.

The 'cloak for fraud' doctrine operates within carefully defined limits. An oral trust over land will only be enforceable by an application of the doctrine if the plaintiff has relied to her detriment on the trust's assumed enforceability; for example, by transferring land to the defendant who has declared himself trustee. It will not apply where an owner of land orally declares himself trustee of the land for another and the intended beneficiary has not acted to her detriment. In *Wratten v Hunter*,[16] a father transferred land to one of his sons shortly before the father died. On the day of the funeral, the son said to his sisters and brothers: 'I promise to live in the house and care for the home and the property for us all'.[17] Needham J held that the oral declaration of trust was not enforceable. It did not attract the application of the 'cloak for fraud' principle because the other siblings could not show that they had acted to their detriment in reliance on their brother's promise. [15.13]

The 'cloak for fraud' doctrine overlaps with the law of constructive trusts,[18] particularly the common intention constructive trust, and with estoppel.[19] Developments in these other areas of equity have meant that the doctrine is nowadays invoked only rarely. But it will be relevant where the facts of a case cannot be accommodated within one of the recognised categories of constructive trust, or where the requirements for a valid estoppel have not been established. [15.14]

Testamentary trusts

Special rules apply to a trust which is intended to take effect on the death of the creator of the trust.[20] Such trusts are known as 'testamentary trusts'. The will creating the trust must comply with the formalities for creating a will specified in State and Territory legislation[21] rather than the *Statute of Frauds* formalities. The testator must have legal capacity to make a will, must have an unimpaired intention to execute a will (eg, not being under the undue influence of another), and must comply with the formalities for execution. In general terms, the formalities require: [15.15]

(a) the will to be in writing;

(b) signature of the will by the testator or by some person in the testator's presence and by the testator's direction;

16 [1978] 2 NSWLR 367.

17 This statement also failed to manifest an intention to create a trust.

18 See *Halloran v Minister Administering National Parks and Wildlife Act 1974* (2006) 229 CLR 545, [69]–[82].

19 See chapters 7 and 23.

20 The rules do not apply to a trust which takes effect during the settlor's lifetime but where there is a transfer of equitable interest upon the settlor's death; for example, where property is settled on trust for the settlor during her life and on trust for another after the settlor's death: *Russell v Scott* (1936) 55 CLR 440, 454 (Dixon and Evatt JJ).

21 See RF Croucher and P Vines, *Succession: Families, Property & Death* (LexisNexis Butterworths, 5th ed, 2018) ch 7 for the statutory requirements for a valid will, and exceptions to the requirements.

(c) location of the signature in a special position on the material bearing the writing;

(d) making of the signature in the presence of two or more witnesses;

(e) the presence of the witnesses together at the same time when the signature is made; and

(f) signature by the witnesses.

[15.16] All States and Territories have amended their wills legislation to permit a court to admit to probate a document which the court is satisfied was intended by its maker to constitute a will, notwithstanding that it has not been executed in complete conformity with the statutory requirements.

The doctrine of incorporation by reference

[15.17] A will may refer to another document so as to incorporate that document into the will. A document can be validly incorporated into a will if:

(a) the document to be incorporated is in existence at the time of execution of the will; and

(b) the will refers to the document as an existing document.[22]

[15.18] A testator who has previously created a trust may later make a will disposing of part or all of his estate to the trustees of the trust to be held on its terms. Provided that the will refers to the trust instrument as an existing document, the trust will be incorporated into the will. It may also be possible for the terms of a will to be construed as including a direction to the testator's personal representatives to create trusts of property disposed of by the will. In *Abbs v Abbs*,[23] the testator made gifts by will to several trusts which were not in existence when he died. He should have made a gift to his personal representatives with a direction that they set up a fund to be held on the terms of the particular trusts. As the testator's intentions were clear and the identity of the beneficiaries was not in dispute, the Court construed the will as giving the testator's personal representatives directions to establish the trusts. The Court treated the way in which the will was expressed as providing defective machinery to give effect to the testator's intention.

Secret trusts

[15.19] If X induces a testator to make a will leaving property to X on the faith of X's promise to hold the property on trust for Y, X will not be permitted to take the property under the will beneficially but must hold it on trust for Y. The trust is termed a 'secret trust' because the existence of the trust is not disclosed by the terms of the will. A secret trust differs from the doctrine of incorporation of reference in that the latter is a method of incorporating a non-testamentary document into the provisions of a valid will, including a will creating a trust, whereas a secret trust imposes trust obligations on a legatee which are not expressed in the

22 *In bonis Smart* [1902] P 238.

23 [2003] NSWSC 1202.

will.[24] Under a fully secret trust the legatee must accept the obligation prior to the testator's death. Acceptance can occur either before or after the execution of the will.

In *Voges v Monaghan*,[25] the testator, who had carried on a successful business as a chemist in Hamilton, Victoria, left his entire estate to the defendant who had helped in managing the business. The testator left nothing to the first plaintiff, who had worked in the testator's household as a domestic servant for 35 years for low pay although the testator had informed her that she would be looked after when he died. The testator also left nothing to the second plaintiff, a niece of the testator's wife, whom the testator had assisted financially for many years. The testator had also promised that provision would be made for her after his death. The evidence showed that the defendant had promised the testator to provide for both plaintiffs from the estate. For four years after the testator's death the defendant made regular payments to the plaintiffs, accompanied by letters stating that the payments had been made in accordance with the testator's wishes. The payments ceased after a claim for unpaid tax had been made on the testator's estate, the defendant stating that they had been made on a discretionary basis. The High Court held that the defendant's promise had created a secret trust for both plaintiffs. Although the testator had left his estate absolutely to the defendant, the latter had accepted the obligations imposed by the testator to provide for both plaintiffs. Equity would prevent fraud by ordering the defendant to resume making the payments to the plaintiffs. [15.20]

A half-secret trust arises where the will discloses that the legatee takes property as trustee but does not set out the terms of the trust. The legatee will be ordered to hold the property on the terms he had previously agreed to with the testator. For example, if a testator leaves property to X 'on the terms communicated by me' or 'for the purposes indicated by me', and there is evidence to show that X promised the testator to hold the property for the benefit of Y, X will take the property as trustee for Y.[26] English authority holds that the terms of a half-secret trust must have been communicated to, and accepted by, the legatee prior to the execution of the will.[27] However, in *Ledgerwood v Perpetual Trustee Co Ltd*,[28] Young J held that, in conformity with the rule applicable to fully secret trusts, the obligation will be enforceable if accepted by the legatee at any time before the testator's death. [15.21]

The justification for enforcing secret trusts is said to be the prevention of fraud. A high standard of proof is required to prove fraud, and some authorities require proof of a secret trust to a more exacting standard than on the balance of probabilities.[29] If the evidence establishes the existence of the secret trust but not the identity of the beneficiaries, the legatee will hold the property received on resulting trust for the testator's estate.[30] Neither [15.22]

24 Secret trust obligations can also be imposed on a recipient of property under an intestacy where the intestate was induced not to make a will by a promise made by the next-of-kin to hold property received on intestacy on trust terms: *McCormick v Grogan* (1869) LR 4 HL 82, 88.

25 (1954) 94 CLR 231; *Sourcebook* 15.5a, p 396.

26 Cf *Re Estate of Badger (deceased)* [2021] SASC 25 ('as [the executor] shall know to be in accordance with my wishes').

27 *Blackwell v Blackwell* [1929] AC 318; *Re Bateman's Will Trusts* [1970] 1 WLR 1463.

28 (1997) 41 NSWLR 532.

29 *McCormick v Grogan* (1869) LR 4 HL 82, 87 (Lord Westbury). Cf *Re Snowden* [1979] Ch 528, 537, where the ordinary civil burden of proof was applied. These authorities must, in applicable jurisdictions, be construed within the context of the provisions of the uniform *Evidence Act* dealing with the civil burden of proof: *Edwards v Crawford* [2020] TASSC 20.

30 *Re Boyes* (1884) 26 Ch D 531. See chapter 22.

secret nor half-secret trusts are testamentary trusts, in the sense of being trusts created by the testator's will. They are said to arise outside the will. So, in jurisdictions in which a witness of the signing of a will is not allowed to take a legacy under the will, it has been held that a witness can be a beneficiary of a half-secret trust imposed on a legatee.[31]

Incompletely constituted trusts

[15.23] A valid trust is not created if the steps necessary to create it have not been followed. But the consequences of non-compliance will depend on the nature of the intended trust in question and the precise steps which have not been taken. An obstacle that the beneficiary of an incomplete trust wanting to enforce it must overcome is the principle expressed in the maxim that equity will not assist a volunteer. The principle does not apply to a fully constituted trust, but it will defeat most attempts by the beneficiary to enforce an incomplete trust if the beneficiary has not provided consideration.

[15.24] These are the general principles applicable to incomplete trusts:

- If an attempt to create a trust *by declaration* fails for lack of certainty of subject, object or intention, or failure to comply with a statutory formality, the would-be settlor simply continues to hold the property on her own behalf. If the settlor is dead, the property returns to her estate under a resulting trust (discussed in chapter 22).
- If an attempt to create a trust *by transfer* fails for lack of certainty of subject, object or intention, or failure to comply with a statutory formality, but the property has been successfully transferred to the would-be trustee, the trustee will hold the property on resulting trust for the settlor, and must re-transfer it to the settlor.[32]
- If an attempt to create a testamentary trust fails the property will revert to the testator's estate, to be disposed of according to his will, or on a partial intestacy.

Non-simultaneous declaration and vesting

[15.25] Where property is transferred with the intention that the transferee holds the property on trust, the declaration of trust should be made at the same time as the transfer. A declaration of trust made *subsequent* to the transfer will be ineffective; the transferee will already have obtained full beneficial title to the property and the declaration will be ineffective to create a trust. But if a declaration of trust is made *before* the transfer of property to the intended trustee, the subsequent transfer will be sufficient to complete the previously incomplete trust. In *Re Bowden*,[33] a settlor promised to settle property she might receive upon the death of her father on trust for the religious order she was about to join. The promise was not enforceable by the trustees or the religious order who were volunteers. Nevertheless, upon

31 *Re Young* [1951] Ch 344. A witness is not disqualified from taking a benefit under a will in Victoria (*Wills Act 1997* (Vic) s 11) and may take a benefit in some circumstances in New South Wales (*Succession Act 2006* (NSW) s 10).

32 In the case of lack of certainty of intention to create a trust, the property will only be held on resulting trust for the settlor if the court is satisfied that the settlor did not intend to make a gift.

33 [1936] Ch 71. See also *Re Adlard* [1954] Ch 29; *Re Ralli's Will Trusts* [1964] Ch 288 (extending the principle to the case of a trustee of an incomplete trust who receives property in the capacity of trustee of another trust).

her father's death the settlor transferred money she had received under his will. Many years later, the settlor sought to recover the money from the trustees. It was held that it could not be recovered once it had been paid to the trustees and applied for the purposes of the trust. While equity will not assist a volunteer to enforce an incomplete trust the assistance of equity is no longer required once the property had been received by the trustees and impressed with the terms of the trust.

Trusts and public policy

A properly constituted trust may fail because it offends against: [15.26]

(a) the public policy recognised by the general law; or

(b) a statutory provision.

Grounds of public policy which invalidate contracts will also invalidate trusts. The following are examples of public policy which has been held to invalidate a trust: [15.27]

(a) Trusts prejudicial to the administration of justice. A trust to commit a legal wrong is void for illegality. For example, in *Thrupp v Collett*,[34] it was held that a trust to pay the fines of convicted poachers was void for public policy reasons.

(b) Trusts prejudicial to the status of marriage. At common law any contract or trust created for the purpose of prejudicing marriage was void as being contrary to public policy. For example, a trust including a general condition prohibiting marriage by the beneficiary will be invalid, although a condition prohibiting marriage to a particular person is permissible.[35] Trusts to promote divorce are also contrary to public policy.[36] A trust created as part of a divorce settlement, or upon termination of a de facto relationship, will, however, be enforceable provided that it meets the requirements of the *Family Law Act 1975* (Cth).[37]

(c) Restrictions on alienation. A *condition* prohibiting alienation of an interest in property will be void. It is irrelevant for this purpose whether the alienation is voluntary or whether it arises by operation of law, such as on the beneficiary's bankruptcy. For example, a provision in a trust that the beneficiary shall be entitled to the trust income on the condition that he does not go bankrupt will be void.[38] But a provision that an interest shall be *determinable* upon the occurrence of an event which will have the effect of alienating her interest will be valid.[39] So a provision in a trust settling property on a beneficiary until he shall become bankrupt will be valid. The distinction between conditional and determinable interests has been criticised on

34 (1858) 26 Beav 125; 53 ER 844.

35 *Lloyd v Lloyd* (1852) 2 Sim (NS) 255; 61 ER 338. Cf *Jenner v Turner* (1880) 16 Ch D 188.

36 *Church Property Trustees, Diocese of Newcastle v Ebbeck* (1960) 104 CLR 394. Cf *Ramsay v Trustee Executors & Agency Ltd* (1948) 77 CLR 321, where a direction by the testator that his son be absolutely entitled to the corpus of the trust estate when no longer married to his present wife was held not to be contrary to public policy.

37 Trusts established with the aim of defeating an actual or anticipated court order on divorce, or having that effect, may be set aside: *Family Law Act 1975* (Cth) s 106B.

38 *Hall v Busst* (1960) 104 CLR 206.

39 *Brandon v Robinson* (1811) 18 Ves 429; 34 ER 379.

the ground that it is purely terminological. But it is recognised in Australian law.[40] A trust determinable on the bankruptcy of the beneficiary supplies the conceptual foundation of the protective trust which enables trust income to be applied, in spite of the bankruptcy, to provide for the beneficiary's spouse, children or remoter issue.[41]

[15.28] A trust may also be expressly or impliedly prohibited by statute. In *Sykes v Stratton*,[42] foreign exchange regulations made under the *Banking Act 1959* (Cth) prohibited entry into a contract or arrangement which had the effect of evading the operation of the regulations. The defendant, a solicitor, received money as a trustee for the plaintiff in connection with a transaction which contravened the regulations. Helsham J held that the receipt directly contravened the regulations. Alternatively, the trust was void because it was created with the aim of defeating the scheme of statutory regulation.

Trusts and bankruptcy

[15.29] A trust established for the sole purpose of avoiding payment of the settlor's creditors is likely to be set aside as a sham.[43] But even if the trust is not a sham, State and Commonwealth legislation provides that dispositions of property, including property transferred to trustees, made with intent to defraud the settlor's creditors are voidable. Section 37A(1) of the *Conveyancing Act 1919* (NSW) provides that:

> every alienation of property ... with intent to defraud creditors, shall be voidable at the instance of any person thereby prejudiced.

Section 37A(3) provides that the section does not extend to any estate or interest in property alienated to a purchaser in good faith not having, at the time of the alienation, notice of the intent to defraud creditors.[44]

In *Marcolongo v Chen*,[45] the High Court held that s 37A 'should receive a liberal construction in effecting [the] purpose of suppressing fraud'.[46] In order to achieve this objective, the word 'defraud' was held to include delaying or hindering payment to creditors, as well as preventing creditors from being paid. A settlor's 'intent to defraud' creditors need not be expressly shown; it can be inferred from the fact that defrauding the settlor's creditors is a necessary consequence of creating the trust. The High Court upheld the decision of the trial judge who had found that a transfer of land owned by a corporation had been made with intent to defraud the corporation's creditors even though there was no direct proof

40 *Caboche v Ramsay* (1993) 119 ALR 215, 226.
41 See [15.31].
42 [1972] 1 NSWLR 145.
43 See [14.11] and *Millar v Federal Commissioner of Taxation* (2016) 243 FCR 302.
44 See also *Civil Law (Property) Act 2006* (ACT) s 239; *Law of Property Act 2000* (NT) s 208; *Property Law Act 1974* (Qld) s 228; *Law of Property Act 1936* (SA) s 86; *Conveyancing and Law of Property Act 1884* (Tas) s 40; *Property Law Act 1958* (Vic) s 172; *Property Law Act 1969* (WA) s 89. The burden of proof rests on the party relying on *Conveyancing Act 1919* (NSW) s 37A(3) to establish the defence of good faith purchase: *Super Vision Resources Ltd v AC Holdings Co Pty Ltd* [2020] NSWCA 319.
45 (2011) 242 CLR 546.
46 Ibid [20].

that the director who had arranged the transfer intended to prevent the creditors from being paid. The necessary intention was inferred from the circumstances surrounding the transfer, including the fact that the land was the only substantial asset available to meet a large damages claim brought against the corporation.

In addition to the State and Territory anti-creditor avoidance provisions, s 121(1) of the *Bankruptcy Act 1966* (Cth) provides that a transfer of property by a person who later becomes a bankrupt is void against the trustee in the transferor's bankruptcy if: [15.30]

(a) the property would probably have become part of the transferor's estate or would probably have been available to creditors if the property had not been transferred; and

(b) the transferor's main purpose in making the transfer was:

  (i) to prevent the transferred property from becoming divisible among the transferor's creditors; or

  (ii) to hinder or delay the process of making property available for division among the transferor's creditors.[47]

Section 121 is similar, but not identical, to the State and Territory provisions. The principal difference is that a transfer caught by s 121 is void whereas a transfer attracting the operation of the State and Territory legislation is voidable. The State and Territory legislation will normally be invoked where the assets of the settlor, if the property settled on trust can be recovered, will exceed his liabilities. But where the settlor's liabilities will exceed his assets even after the trust property has been recovered, the settlor will usually be made bankrupt, and recovery of the assets will be a function of the trustee in bankruptcy under the *Bankruptcy Act 1966* (Cth).

Paragraphs [15.29]–[15.30] set out the principles applicable to the statutory avoidance of a trust where the settlor has attempted to create a trust in order to defeat the claims of his creditors. Suppose that it is not the settlor, but the trustee or a beneficiary who is bankrupt? In the case of a bankrupt trustee, the trust assets are not divisible among the trustee's creditors because they are not beneficially owned by the trustee.[48] The interest of a beneficiary under a fixed trust can, however, be claimed by the beneficiary's trustee in bankruptcy. Moreover, any capital advanced or income paid to the beneficiary, whether under a fixed or discretionary trust, is property divisible among the beneficiary's creditors. But it is possible for a settlor to establish a protective trust (see [15.27]) whereby property is held on trust for a beneficiary (the principal beneficiary) determinable on that beneficiary's bankruptcy. In that event the trust income becomes payable to the principal beneficiary's spouse, children and remoter issue. Trustee legislation, except in South Australia, the Australian Capital Territory and the Northern Territory, makes provision for protective trusts even though these trusts are expressly designed to divert trust property away from the beneficiary's creditors.[49] [15.31]

47 Other relevant provisions of the *Bankruptcy Act 1966* (Cth) include s 120 (undervalued transactions) and s 122 (avoidance of preferences). Part 5.7B of the *Corporations Act 2001* (Cth) enacts an equivalent provision for transfers made by corporations.

48 *Bankruptcy Act 1966* (Cth) s 116(2).

49 *Trustee Act 1925* (NSW) s 45 (the definition of spouse includes a de facto partner); *Trusts Act 1973* (Qld) s 64; *Trustee Act 1898* (Tas) s 30; *Trustee Act 1958* (Vic) s 39; *Trustees Act 1962* (WA) s 61.

Trusts and discrimination

[15.32] An express trust can define the class of beneficiaries in terms of gender, religion, sexual orientation or in some other way.[50] Such trusts will be upheld on the ground that the law favours freedom of disposition. As Lord Wilberforce stated in *Blathwayt v Baron Cawley*, 'neither by express provision nor by implication has private selection yet become a matter of public policy'.[51]

A recent example of equity's preference for freedom of disposition is *Hickin v Carroll (No 2)*[52]. The testator left a portion of his residuary estate to four of his children who were Jehovah's Witnesses. The testator, who disapproved of their adherence to that faith, made the gifts conditional on the children attending his funeral and becoming Roman Catholics within three months of his death. It was held that the gift was not void as being contrary to public policy.

[15.33] Modern equal opportunity and anti-discrimination legislation does not apply to private trusts. It also expressly provides that the legislation does not affect provisions which confer charitable benefits, or acts done in order to give effect to such provisions.[53] In the case of trusts for charitable purposes, however, there may be an issue as to whether a discriminatory trust satisfies the public benefit requirement. Moreover, the existence of a discriminatory condition in a trust may afford grounds for exercising the court's cy-près jurisdiction to remove the condition.[54]

Trusts and perpetuity

[15.34] Two rules, which together are known as 'the rule against perpetuities', limit a settlor's or testator's power to regulate the disposition of property for a period of time that the law considers excessive. They are the rule against remoteness of vesting and the rule against indestructible trusts (sometimes termed 'the rule against perpetual duration').

[15.35] The common law rule against remoteness of vesting provided that no interest in property was valid unless it could vest, if at all, no later than 21 years after the death of some 'life

50 M Harding, 'Some Arguments Against Discriminatory Gifts and Trusts' (2011) 31(2) *Oxford Journal of Legal Studies* 303.

51 [1976] AC 397, 425–6 (HL) (the case concerned a testamentary disposition that discriminated against Roman Catholics). See also *Kay v South Eastern Sydney Area Health Service* [2003] NSWSC 292 (a testamentary gift for the treatment of 'white babies'), Young CJ in Eq at [18]: 'generally speaking testators can be as capricious as they like.' In jurisdictions such as Victoria, which have enacted variation of trusts legislation (*Trustee Act 1958* (Vic) s 63A), a discriminatory provision can provide grounds for varying the trust: *Re Remnant's Settlement Trusts* [1970] Ch 560.

52 [2014] NSWSC 1059.

53 *Anti-Discrimination Act 1977* (NSW) s 55; *Equal Opportunity Act 2010* (Vic) ss 51, 80. Cf *Wilkinson v Crawford* [2021] ZACC 8 (Constitutional Court of South Africa), a majority holding that a provision in a trust discriminating against adopted children contravened the right to equal treatment under s 9 of the *Constitution*. Mhlantla J stated at [73] that '[the] private and public divide in trust law does not mean that a court is permitted to countenance any kind of unfair discrimination in a trust simply because it is considered private. That being said, … the private nature of the trust must be given due consideration.'

54 See chapter 16; *Re Lysaght* [1966] 1 Ch 191 (successful cy-près application where bequest to found medical studentships excluded persons of Jewish or Roman Catholic faiths); M Harding, 'Charitable Trusts and Discrimination: Two Themes' (2016) 2(1) *Canadian Journal of Comparative & Contemporary Law* 227.

in being' (in other words, someone whose life is relevant to the vesting of the interest in property) who was alive when the instrument creating the interest took effect.[55] The rule applied to all dispositions of property, and not just to interests created under trusts. The vice at which the rule was directed was not the excessive duration of property interests (there is no objection, eg, to creating a lease for 999 years), but at the creation of interests taking effect at a date much later than the instrument creating the interest. The common law rule has been reformed or abolished by modern perpetuities legislation in all States and Territories. Where it survives, it represents a compromise between a settlor's interest in freedom of disposition and the interest of future generations in not having the destination of family wealth controlled by the wishes of a long-deceased settlor.

An example of the application of the common law rule against perpetuities is a gift made by will of property to trustees to be held on trust for X for life, and then for such of X's children as marry. Assuming that X survives the testator, the gift to X will be valid, but the gift to his children will be void at common law. This is because X may have children after the will takes effect, who could marry more than 21 years after the death of X and of any of X's children who were alive when the will took effect. It will be obvious from this example that the common law was concerned with the possibility, however remote, of a contingency occurring outside the perpetuity period; it was not concerned with whether a contingency was likely to occur. It would be irrelevant, for example, if X was instead a 90-year-old woman, since the realities of human gestation were ignored by the common law. On the other hand, the gift would have been valid at common law if X had predeceased the testator, since all X's children constituted lives in being for the purpose of applying the 'life and 21 years' rule.[56]

In New South Wales and the ACT, the common law 'life and 21 years' period has been **[15.36]** replaced by a statutory period of 80 years running from the date when the disposition takes effect.[57] In Queensland, Tasmania, Victoria, Western Australia and the Northern Territory, legislation gives settlors the option to choose either the common law period or a fixed period up to 80 years as the applicable perpetuity period.[58] All the legislation has enacted a 'wait and see' rule, whereby a gift is treated as valid until it becomes established that it must vest outside the perpetuity period. Most well-advised settlors avoid the complexity of the common law rule by specifying the statutory 80-year period. South Australia has followed some American states and Canadian provinces in abolishing the perpetuity rule entirely.[59]

As a result of the legislation considered in this paragraph, the gift considered in [15.35] of property on trust for X for life, and then to such of X's children as marry, will now be valid in South Australia. In New South Wales and the ACT, the gift to X will be valid, as will the gift over to such of X's children as marry within the statutory 80-year perpetuity period. In

55 *Cadell v Palmer* (1833) 1 Cl & F 372; 6 ER 956.

56 The common law allowed a period of gestation to be added, where necessary, to allow for the possibility that X might have a child born after his death.

57 *Perpetuities Act 1984* (NSW) s 7(1); *Perpetuities and Accumulations Act 1985* (ACT) s 8(1).

58 *Property Law Act 1974* (Qld) s 209; *Perpetuities and Accumulations Act 1992* (Tas) s 6(1); *Perpetuities and Accumulations Act 1968* (Vic) s 5; *Property Law Act 1969* (WA) s 101; *Law of Property Act 2000* (NT) s 187.

59 *Law of Property Act 1936* (SA) s 61. Section 62 confers a power on the court to vary the terms of a disposition so as to vest an interest that has not vested after 80 or more years. See LW Waggoner, 'US Perpetual Trusts' (2011) 127(3) *Law Quarterly Review* 423 for analysis of the USA experience of abolishing the rule against remoteness of vesting.

the remaining States and the Northern Territory, if the testator does not specify the 80-year perpetuity period, the gift to X will be valid but it will be necessary to 'wait and see' how many of X's children marry within 21 years of X's death and the death of any of X's children who were alive when the will took effect.[60]

[15.37] The rule against indestructible trusts (or rule against perpetual duration) applies to non-charitable purpose trusts.[61] The 'life and 21 years' rule was inapt for trusts lacking human beneficiaries, so the straightforward common law rule is that such a trust cannot endure more than 21 years. An example of its application is *Pedulla v Nasti*,[62] where the testator, who in his will had stated his intention not to provide for his widow or children, left his residuary estate to be applied towards the erection and maintenance of a vault or chapel in which his ashes were to be housed. One of the reasons why the trust was held to be invalid was that maintenance of the vault or chapel might be required after the perpetuity period had expired.[63]

[15.38] Some perpetuity legislation reforming the rule against remoteness of vesting has also modified the rule against indestructible trusts. Section 16(2) of the *Perpetuities Act 1984* (NSW) provides that where, by a settlement, there is a disposition for a purpose, the perpetuity period applicable to the disposition shall be 80 years from the date when the settlement takes effect. In Queensland, Tasmania, Victoria and the Northern Territory, a testator may specify the statutory 80-year perpetuity period; otherwise, the common law 21-year period of maximum duration continues to apply.[64] The common law 21-year period is still applicable in Western Australia and South Australia, with no 80-year alternative, even though the rule against remoteness of vesting has been abolished in the latter State.

[15.39] A trust for charitable purposes is subject to the rule against the remoteness of vesting and must vest within the perpetuity period.[65] However, the trust is not subject to the rule against indestructible trusts and can endure for as long as there is trust property that can be applied for the specified charitable objects.[66]

WHAT'S ONLINE?

Available at www.cambridge.org/highereducation/isbn/9781009232388/resources:

- Recommended further readings
- Further commentary
- Discussion topics
- Practice problem

60 The legislation also enacts 'class closing' rules to limit the gift to those members of a class of beneficiaries who have satisfied the condition specified by the settlor: *Perpetuities Act 1984* (NSW) s 9(4); *Perpetuities and Accumulations Act 1968* (Vic) s 9(4).

61 See [16.44]–[16.48].

62 (1990) 20 NSWLR 720.

63 The same provision applies in the ACT: see *Perpetuities and Accumulations Act 1985* (ACT) s 17(2).

64 *Property Law Act 1974* (Qld) ss 209(1), 210, 221; *Perpetuities and Accumulations Act 1992* (Tas) ss 6, 18; *Perpetuities and Accumulations Act 1968* (Vic) ss 5, 18; *Law of Property Act 2000* (NT) s 198 (enacting a presumption in favour of the 80-year period).

65 *Re Lord Stratheden and Campbell* [1894] 3 Ch 265.

66 See chapter 16.

16

TRUSTS FOR CHARITABLE AND NON-CHARITABLE PURPOSES

Introduction

[16.1] Students tend to approach the law of charitable trusts with a sense of relief. After the fairly dry and technical case law of private trusts, the eccentricities of numerous testamentary trusts created for charitable purposes provide some colour.

For example, when Beryl Campbell died, she wanted her house to be used in perpetuity, apparently for the purpose of keeping the garden for the benefit of native birds. Two kind, thoughtful, Protestant, garden-loving, non-drinking non-smokers who did not take drugs or gamble were to be installed as caretakers. They were not to have cats or dogs and were not to paint polished furniture.[1] This attempted trust failed, however. A valid charitable trust must be for a charitable purpose, and for the benefit of the public. This was neither, as the principles discussed in this chapter make clear.

Despite the colour provided by facts in cases such as that above, the law with respect to charitable trusts deserves deeper consideration. The charities and not-for-profit sector is now a major component of the Australian economy. Philanthropy and the effective control of charitable organisations raise important policy considerations.

Regulation of charitable trusts is a problematic area, in part due to the Australian federal system. Potential charitable trusts are validated (or invalidated) according to the general law as administered by State courts and local statute. Additionally, the Commonwealth regulates many financial aspects of the charities and not-for-profit sector.[2] The focus of this chapter will be upon the establishment of trusts for valid charitable purposes rather than their later regulation.

A valid trust for a purpose

[16.2] Charitable trusts differ from other express trusts in several important features. First, they are trusts for a *purpose* rather than for the benefit of identified or identifiable individuals. Trusts for purposes are usually invalid, as there is no person with standing to enforce them.[3] The exception is trusts that are for valid charitable purposes, and for the benefit of the public. This has an important impact on tests for certainty. As there is no identifiable person who benefits from the trust, the usual tests for beneficiary identification (list certainty and criterion certainty) are irrelevant. What is important is that the settlor intended to create a trust recognised at law as being *for a valid charitable purpose*. As there is no person who has sufficient standing to see the trust performed, *locus standi* is given to the Attorney-General. The question of intention to create a trust is approached in a technical manner. Although the settlor or testator may well have been attempting to support some philanthropic aim, the question asked is, 'Do the words used indicate that the gift is to be used for a valid charitable purpose?'[4] However, in all other respects, the usual rules relating to the establishment of trusts discussed in chapter 15 apply.

1 *Campbell v Sherwill* [1999] VSC 508.
2 For a discussion of regulation of charities generally, students are advised to consult a specialist text.
3 *Morice v Bishop of Durham* (1804) 9 Ves 399; 32 ER 656.
4 This is nevertheless consistent with the approach to private express trusts. The question is not what the settlor meant to say, it is the meaning of the words used.

Unlike private express trusts, charitable trusts can run indefinitely. Once the trust fund has been applied for a charitable purpose, it can only ever be available for a charitable purpose and cannot be returned to the settlor, unless that is expressly provided for in the trust instrument.[5] This remains so even if the original charitable purpose has ceased or is no longer needed. In such cases, the court applies the doctrine of cy-près and directs a charitable usage that is as near as possible to the original charitable purpose.[6] [16.3]

Practically, the most significant difference between private trusts and charitable trusts concerns their treatment under taxation legislation. State and Federal legislation grants exemptions from levies such as income tax and local government rates to charities. Federal legislation also allows tax deductibility in respect of donations made to charitable institutions. For Commonwealth purposes, the definition of 'charitable purposes' is wider than at common law.[7] Criticisms of charity law frequently involve objections concerning the tax benefits acquired through charitable status. These benefits have long been controversial, as they result in money that would have gone to government coffers being redirected to the charity in question. If charitable status is too easily achieved, concerns can arise that it is being used illegitimately.[8] [16.4]

Historical development of the charitable trust

As Australian charity law is derived from English law, our discussion starts with English history. Alms-giving was positively encouraged by the medieval Christian church, and this gave rise to what became the jurisprudence of charitable trusts. By Tudor times, 'uses' (trusts) for charitable or beneficent purposes were well established. [16.5]

However, administrative abuses were commonplace and the *Statute of Charitable Uses 1601* was enacted to combat these. The Act was not intended to define 'charitable purposes' but its Preamble contained a list of purposes regarded as charitable. Although long since repealed, the 'Statute of Elizabeth' (as it is called) remains important. The statement in its Preamble of valid charitable purposes forms the basis of our law of charities.

The Preamble referred directly to trusts for the relief of the aged, the impotent and poor people; the maintenance of sick and maimed soldiers and mariners; the maintenance of schools of learning, free schools and scholars in universities; the repair of bridges, ports, havens, causeways, churches, sea-banks and highways; the education and preferment of orphans; the relief, stock and maintenance of houses of correction; the marriage of poor maids; the support, aid and help of young tradesmen, handicraftsmen, and persons decayed; the relief or redemption of prisoners or captives; the aid or ease of any poor inhabitants concerning payment of fifteens, setting out of soldiers or other taxes. [16.6]

This was not intended to be a complete list, and within a short period the Act was being applied to unlisted purposes. It is therefore said that purposes are regarded as charitable when by analogy they are within the spirit and intendment of the Preamble.

5 *Re Sir Colin and Lady MacKenzie Trust* [2019] VSC 834.
6 The doctrine of cy-près discussed further at [16.39]–[16.43].
7 *Charities Act 2013* (Cth) s 12(1).
8 See, eg, 'Push for inquiry into Scientology's tax-free riches', *The Age*, 7 April 2021, p 10.

[16.7] At the end of the nineteenth century, the list was refined into four subdivisions by Lord Macnaghten in *Pemsel's Case*[9] as:

(a) trusts for the relief of poverty;

(b) trusts for the advancement of education;

(c) trusts for the advancement of religion; and

(d) trusts for other purposes beneficial to the community not falling under any of the preceding heads.

Valid charitable purposes are those that can be classified into one or more of the above subdivisions. These are commonly referred to as the four 'heads' of charity.

[16.8] While the Preamble is not referred to today with respect to charitable purposes under the first three heads, it is still relevant when considering whether a purpose can be regarded as charitable under the fourth head. Purposes that can be regarded as analogous to those listed in the Preamble will usually be valid as being for purposes beneficial to the community. The High Court has said that courts should interpret the Preamble liberally according to community standards; this allowed a free local car park to be regarded as within the spirit and intendment of the Preamble, and therefore charitable.[10]

More recently, the Commonwealth has enacted the *Charities Act 2013* (Cth). Section 12(1) defines charitable purposes for the purposes of Commonwealth legislation. This definition includes topics such as health, education, social or public welfare, culture, human rights, animal welfare and environmental matters. It has been suggested that this wider definition may eventually have a flow-on effect to decisions concerning what is a charitable purpose at general law.[11]

Where possible, courts tend to interpret doubtful clauses so as to ensure their validity as charitable trusts. However, a trust for a valid charitable purpose will not be enforced as a charitable trust unless the trust is for the benefit of the public. We will briefly discuss the 'heads' of charity before turning to the question of public benefit.

Trusts for the aged, impotent and poor

Poverty

[16.9] The relief of poverty was one of the matters directly mentioned in the Preamble, and is probably the aim most people consider charitable. The original grouping was 'aged, impotent and poor', but it is clear that each of these words has independent operation.[12] Ford and Lee say that this charitable head is wide enough to include the advancement of social and community welfare such as support of the disadvantaged, disabled or aged, and refugees and prisoners, among many others.[13]

9 *Commissioners for Special Purposes of Income Tax v Pemsel* [1891] AC 531, 583.
10 *Bathurst City Council v PWC Properties Pty Ltd* (1998) 195 CLR 566.
11 Matthew Harding, 'Equity and Statute in Charity Law' (2015) 9(2) *Journal of Equity* 167.
12 *Le Cras v Perpetual Trustee Co Ltd* [1969] 1 AC 514.
13 F & L [19.1010].

The terms 'poverty' and 'destitution' are not synonymous.[14] Trusts for the relief of poverty are not limited to supplying necessities such as food and housing. Any kind of want or inequality can possibly qualify as poverty. In *Trustees of the Indigenous Barristers' Trust v Commissioner of Taxation*,[15] a trust's purposes were 'the relief of poverty, suffering, helplessness, misfortune or other disability of indigenous persons and in particular the relief of any such disabilities which may constitute an impediment to their pursuit of a career at the New South Wales bar'. The fund was to be used for education, living expenses, books, apparel and chamber leases, among other things. It was argued that this was not a trust to relieve poverty, for practising as a barrister was hardly a 'necessity'. Gyles J held the trust was charitable, noting that 'the mere fact that the person has shown academic ability and some perseverance above the norm ... does not mean that the person does not need help'.[16] [16.10]

In short, trusts for the relief of poverty attempt to provide those who are in need *relative to the rest of the community* with some means of support they might otherwise not receive. Poverty is not judged by world-wide conditions (otherwise little poverty relief would be called for in developed countries).

The term 'relief of poverty' does not have to be used in order to demonstrate an intention to relieve poverty. However, the words used must indicate some relief of want. In *Downing v Commissioner of Taxation (Cth)*,[17] a clause stated that funds were to be used 'for the amelioration of the condition of the dependents of servicemen or ex-servicemen'. The High Court held this description was sufficient to indicate the relief of poverty. Words such as 'low income' and 'households in need' also imply relief from poverty.[18] [16.11]

Charities for the relief of poverty are presumed to be for the public benefit. [16.12]

Age and impotence

The term 'impotence' implies some sort of lack of strength, whether through ill-health, disability, mental impairment, injury or otherwise. Agedness will always be a relative concept; case law suggests, however, that trusts aimed at potential beneficiaries who exceed retirement age are likely to be valid as trusts for the support of the aged.[19] [16.13]

Although the Preamble listing 'aged, impotent and poor' is read disjunctively, there is doubt about whether trusts for the support of the aged must also relieve poverty. Case law is divided as to whether age without poverty can be a charitable purpose.[20] The same does not appear to be true of relief of the impotent. Disabilities such as blindness[21] are worthy of assistance per se. Thus, trusts for hospitals and treatment of the sick are charitable [16.14]

14 *Re Gillespie* [1965] VR 402, 406.

15 (2002) 127 FCR 63, [2].

16 Ibid [43].

17 (1971) 125 CLR 185.

18 *Community Housing Ltd v Clarence Valley Council* (2015) 90 NSWLR 292, [51]–[52] (Leeming JA).

19 *Re Robinson* [1951] Ch 198.

20 In *City of Hawthorn v Victorian Welfare Association* [1970] VR 205, a trust for accommodation of aged Christian Scientists was charitable despite the fact not all were poor. The terms 'aged' and 'poor' were read disjunctively. However, in *Church of England Property Trust v Imlay Shire Council* [1971] 2 NSWLR 216, a retirement village for the housing of the aged without means testing was held not to be a charitable purpose.

21 *Re Inman (deceased)* [1965] VR 238.

even though the wealthy may use their services. In *Le Cras v Perpetual Trustee Co*,[22] it was held that a trust for a private hospital was charitable. It was not problematic that the hospital made a profit so long as the profits were directed to the charitable purpose. Lord Wilberforce noted that there was an indirect public benefit in treating trusts for private hospitals as charitable, as treatment of patients in private hospitals freed up bedspace in the public hospital system. In any event, trusts for most hospitals would now satisfy the fourth head of charitable purposes.

Trusts for the advancement of education

[16.15] Education is a very broad concept. The purpose must advance learning and the dissemination of knowledge. This includes the provision of scholarships, prizes, educational facilities and equipment, the support of research and the encouragement of all manner of formal and informal education, training and instruction whether academic, vocational, social or cultural. For example, in *Re Shaw's Will Trust*,[23] a trust for 'the teaching, promotion and encouragement in Ireland of self control, elocution, oratory, deportment, the arts of personal contact, of social intercourse and the other arts of public, private, professional and business life' was held to be a valid educational trust.

[16.16] While the public benefit of educational purposes is usually assumed, the court must decide whether the purpose in question has any educational value if the validity of the purpose is questioned. Judgment is made on the basis of the evidence before the court.[24] In *Re Pinion*,[25] a testator left his artist studio and its contents to the National Trust to be kept as a museum. Expert evidence was given to the effect that the contents were of negligible artistic merit. This was not a valid educational purpose. Russell LJ said[26] that no member of the public would ever extract one iota of education from the disposition.[27] In contrast, when a well-known artist left his home to be retained and used as a place where people could be educated concerning his works and other artistic works, a valid charitable trust for education was created. Stevenson J said that the 'merit of the opportunity to preserve the work in situ of a major Australian artist is obvious'.[28]

Trusts for the advancement of religion

[16.17] The only reference in the Preamble of a religious nature was a single mention of churches in a phrase concerning repair of public buildings and utilities. Nevertheless, there was a long tradition in England of support of religious houses before the dissolution of religious institutions by Henry VIII, and charitable trusts for religion were enforced prior to 1601.

22 *Le Cras v Perpetual Trustee Co Ltd* [1969] 1 AC 514.
23 [1952] 1 All ER 49, 52.
24 *Re Hummeltenberg* [1923] 1Ch 237, 242.
25 [1965] Ch 85.
26 Ibid 111.
27 See also *Johansons v ANZ Executors & Trustee Co Ltd* [1999] VSC 219.
28 *Sharp v A-G (NSW)* [2015] NSWSC 1580, [35]. This was despite the testator's wish that the public also be educated about 'the as yet unrecognized significance of Luna Park and the work of Tiny Tim'.

A primary question is whether the purpose concerns 'religion'. Australian law differs from English law in defining religion. In the High Court decision *Church of the New Faith v Commissioner for Pay-Roll Tax (Vic)*,[29] the Church of Scientology sought an exemption from pay-roll tax, claiming it was a religion. Scientology comes from the writings of L Ron Hubbard, a twentieth-century science-fiction writer. The High Court held that Scientology was a religion for the purposes of the tax exemption. However, the members of the Court defined 'religion' differently. Mason ACJ and Brennan J's test is most widely accepted. Their Honours thought that a religion must satisfy two criteria: [16.18]

(1) Belief in a supernatural Being, Thing or Principle; and

(2) Acceptance of canons of conduct to give effect to that belief (though any canons of conduct which offended the ordinary law would be outside any immunity or privileges afforded on the grounds of religion).

Wilson and Deane JJ applied a more exacting list of criteria, and thought that there were five identifiable indicia of a religion. Murphy J took a more robust approach, and denied the state's jurisdiction to judge the truth or falsity of a religion. His definition of religion was very wide indeed. He commented that 'any body which claims to be religious, and offers a way to find meaning and purpose in life, is religious' unless it was shown to be a hoax, pointing out that 'if each purported religion has to show that its doctrines were true, then all might fail'.[30]

Charitable religious trusts are required to advance religion. 'Advancement' is given a wide meaning. Payment of clergy's salaries, church-building, support of missionary work and support of pilgrimages have all been included. Nevertheless, the religion must be advanced by the purported trust. In *Roman Catholic Archbishop of Melbourne v Lawlor*,[31] a testator wished to establish a trust to found a daily Catholic newspaper. Dixon J said that a daily newspaper was a secular activity, and not for the advancement of religion. It was not sufficient that the secular activity arise out of, or be connected with, a religion. The purpose had to be directly and immediately religious, involving the spreading or strengthening of spiritual teaching. By definition, a daily newspaper would have to report general news. [16.19]

Trusts for other purposes beneficial to the community

Trusts for other purposes beneficial to the community are judged according to the spirit and intendment of the Preamble, as interpreted in contemporary conditions. Purposes regarded as beneficial to the community will therefore change over time. Trusts for hospitals, ecological conservation, libraries, museums, parks, animal welfare and disaster relief have all been included under this head. It must be positively established that the purpose will be beneficial to the community. [16.20]

29 (1983) 154 CLR 120.

30 Ibid 150. In *Watkins v Commissioner for Corporate Affairs* [2021] SACAT 10, The Church of the Flying Spaghetti Monster Australia was refused incorporation under the *Associations Incorporation Act 1985* (SA) on the grounds that it was a parody of a religion, rather than a religion.

31 (1934) 51 CLR 1.

[16.21] The kind of benefit that is expected under this head is that of improving conditions prevailing in a settled community. So, not-for-profit law reporting was held to be a charitable purpose in *Incorporated Council of Law Reporting (Qld) v Commissioner of Taxation (Cth)*.[32] Barwick CJ and McTiernan J held that law reporting was important to the administration of justice and therefore a valid purpose under the fourth head. Similar reasoning is demonstrated in *Aid/Watch Inc v Commissioner of Taxation (Cth)*.[33] A High Court majority held that encouragement of debate about political and legislative issues was essential to a vibrant democracy and therefore was in the public interest, at least where the debate concerned charity.

[16.22] A criticisim of 'fourth head' charitable trusts is that the standard required for public benefit is too easily satisfied. Indeed, it is easier to find examples of purposes recognised under the fourth head than to find cases where the purpose is not regarded as beneficial to the community. However, in *Re Marks*,[34] a testator's attempt to create a facility for displaying her painting, books and other collectibles, such as her sewing machine, was not of any benefit to the public.[35]

Political purposes

[16.23] In England, trusts that promote the aims of political parties, promote amendment of the law, or agitate for change in government policy are invalid on the basis that political purposes are not valid charitable purposes. This is no longer the law in Australia.

Trusts that agitated for legislative change were previously not regarded as valid charitable purposes because they were thought not to be for public benefit.[36] Dixon J gave one explanation in *Royal North Shore Hospital of Sydney v Attorney-General (NSW)*.[37] His Honour said that the requisite public benefit could not be established in trusts which called for changes in the law as it was impossible for a coherent system of law to admit that the law required changing. The alternative explanation is that courts have no means of determining whether the suggested change will be of benefit to the public.[38] This reasoning was thought to be particularly compelling when the purpose is to procure changes in the law in other countries.[39]

[16.24] Difficulties occurred where an organisation had charitable aims but also had political aims. This was solved by allowing the trust to stand where the political aim could be said to be merely ancillary to the charitable purpose. For example, in *Victorian Women Lawyers' Association Inc v Federal Commissioner of Taxation*,[40] the primary aim of the association was to assist women to enter, and advance in, the legal profession. There was a secondary aim of achieving law reform. The Association was entitled to charitable status. Charitable funds could be directed to the charitable purpose but not to the political purpose.

32 (1971) 125 CLR 659.
33 (2010) 241 CLR 539.
34 [2017] VSC 665.
35 See also *Re Boning* (1997) 2 Qd R 12; *Campbell v Sherwill* [1999] VSC 508.
36 *Bowman v Secular Society Ltd* [1917] AC 406, 442 (Lord Parker).
37 (1938) 60 CLR 396, 426.
38 *Bowman v Secular Society Ltd* [1917] AC 406, 442 (Lord Parker).
39 *McGovern v A-G* [1981] 3 All ER 493.
40 (2008) 170 FCR 318.

The question whether agitation for legislative change is in the public interest was settled by the High Court in *Aid/Watch Inc v Commissioner of Taxation (Cth)*.[41] Aid/Watch's activities were described as seeking to influence government policy as to the nature, extent and means of delivery of overseas aid. The Full Court of the Federal Court[42] had noted that courts are not in a position to consider all the policies relevant to the distribution of foreign aid, and expressed the opinion that courts were not entitled to enter into such debates.[43] The High Court felt quite differently on the matter. The majority[44] noted that Australia's system of law is founded on the *Constitution*. As the electoral system allows for the amendment of the *Constitution* itself, public debate on statutory amendment is 'an indispensable incident'[45] of the constitutional system. The legal system therefore calls for debate and agitation concerning legislative change. As for the argument that the court would have no means of judging whether a proposed change would be of benefit or not, the majority commented that a court does not have to consider whether or not public benefit follows from a proposed change; the operation of the constitutional processes contributes to the public welfare. [16.25]

The majority interpreted Aid/Watch's activities as generating debate about the efficiency of foreign aid for the relief of poverty, and held that this was a purpose beneficial to the community under the fourth head of charity.[46] Their Honours added that it was 'unnecessary for this appeal to determine whether the fourth head encompasses the encouragement of public debate respecting activities of government which lie beyond the first three heads (or the balance of the fourth head) identified in *Pemsel*,[47] and, if so, the range of those activities'.[48]

Kiefel J agreed with the majority that there should be no blanket disqualification for political purposes[49] otherwise in the public benefit, but commented that 'reaching a conclusion of public benefit may be difficult where the activities of an organisation largely involve the assertion of its views'.[50] Her Honour accepted that public discussion and debate about the law was of value, but held it was necessary that benefits of this kind would flow from the pursuit of change before charitable status was achieved.[51] She thought that Aid/Watch's activities failed that test. The organisation was merely asserting its views and not generating public debate: 'Its pursuit of a freedom to communicate its views does not qualify as being for the public benefit'.[52]

The implication of the majority decision is that any purpose that can be said to encourage debate concerning whether the law should change is automatically in the

41 *Aid/Watch Inc v Commissioner of Taxation (Cth)* (2010) 241 CLR 539.
42 *Federal Commissioner of Taxation v Aid/Watch Inc* (2009) 178 FCR 423.
43 Ibid 431–2.
44 French CJ, Gummow, Hayne, Crennan and Bell JJ.
45 *Aid/Watch Inc v Commissioner of Taxation (Cth)* (2010) 241 CLR 539, [44] (citing *Lange v Australian Broadcasting Corporation* (1997) 189 CLR 520, 559–60).
46 (2010) 241 CLR 539, 557.
47 *Commissioners for Special Purposes of Income Tax v Pemsel* [1891] AC 531.
48 (2010) 241 CLR 539, 557 [48].
49 Ibid 565.
50 Ibid.
51 Ibid 564–6.
52 Ibid 568–9.

public interest, and therefore charitable, at least where the object can be linked to the relief of poverty, the advancement of religion or education, and possibly other matters covered by the fourth head.[53]

The decision leaves open the question whether the 'political purposes' exception retains any real force. One possible limitation on the reach of the decision is to be found in the judgments of Heydon and Kiefel JJ. Both were of the view that Aid/Watch's activities were not encouraging or fostering public debate but merely seeking to impose its views on the government; on this factual issue, their Honours disagreed with the majority. A distinction can perhaps be drawn between attempts to encourage debate on one hand, and lobbying on the other. On other facts, a claim to charitable status by a lobbyist might be rejected. Another possible limitation is to be found in the majority judgment. Their Honours admitted the possibility that some purposes that appeared to be charitable might not contribute to the public welfare 'by reason of the particular ends and means involved'.[54] Thus, a purpose that encouraged debate about laws concerning a recognised charitable head (say, the relief of poverty) might nevertheless fail the public benefit test because highly objectionable ends or means were suggested. The court will consider any public detriment that might flow from the proposed purpose.[55]

Sporting and recreational purposes

[16.26] Sport and recreation have not been traditionally regarded as charitable purposes, not being referable to the spirit and intendment of the Preamble. In *Said v Barrington*,[56] a testator's will provided that the residue of his estate could be 'used for sailing trophies in youngsters sailing, possibly sabots and that type of boat'. The testator was possibly unaware that the residue would have provided over $300 000 worth of trophies. It was held that this would have been a trust for the encouragement of sport per se, and therefore was not charitable.

[16.27] However, it is possible to link the sporting or recreational activity with a purpose recognised under the accepted heads of charity in order to validate the trust. So, in *Kearins v Kearins*,[57] a trust to support a rugby union club at Sydney University was valid as a trust for the advancement of education; participation in sporting clubs at university was regarded as enhancing the experience of a tertiary education. Similarly, a trust that in part provided tennis courts at a provincial Presbyterian church was validated as advancing part of the work of the church.[58] However, in more modern cases, such as *Re Irving*,[59] on similar facts, tennis courts associated with local churches were not held to advance religion in the necessary sense.[60]

[16.28] Public sporting grounds or community facilities are sometimes charitable on the basis that they represent an enhancement of community welfare and are therefore for a purpose

53 An example might be relief following natural disasters.

54 (2010) 241 CLR 539, 557. For an example of reasoning of this kind, see *Re Greenpeace of New Zealand Inc* [2013] 1 NZLR 339, [73].

55 *National Anti-Vivisection Society v Inland Revenue Commissioners* [1948] AC 31.

56 [2001] NSWSC 576.

57 (1956) 57 SR (NSW) 286.

58 *Re James Stewart's Will Trusts* [1962] QWN 24.

59 [2019] VSC 594.

60 *A-G (NSW) v Cahill* [1969] 1 NSWLR 85, 93.

beneficial to the public.[61] Some States have also legislated to allow charitable status to trusts for the provision of sporting and recreational facilities, as long as there is sufficient public benefit.[62] Tasmania goes further, presuming gifts for sporting and recreational activities to be charitable.[63]

The 'public benefit'

In addition to the requirement that the purpose of the trust must be a valid charitable purpose, the trust must also be for the public benefit in order to qualify as a charitable trust. Public benefit is a twofold test. The charitable purpose must *benefit* the public, and it must be of benefit to the *public*, or at least a section of the public. Both aspects of the test must be satisfied. [16.29]

Benefit

Benefit to the public is positively presumed in the case of trusts for the relief of poverty. Society benefits when the poverty of its members is alleviated. Benefit is assumed in cases of trusts for the advancement of education and religion,[64] but it can be negatived.[65] This occurred in the case of *Re Pinion*[66] mentioned above. The 'benefit' of religious charities is generally assumed to be that the spiritual advancement of adherents improves society as a whole, through the adherents' interactions with society. A small number of trusts for the advancement of religion have failed on the basis that the purpose will only be of benefit to the persons carrying out the purpose, and not to the public. In *Gilmour v Coats*,[67] an attempted trust for the purpose of prayers being said in a Carmelite convent (where the nuns had no contact whatsoever with the outside world) was said to be of no benefit to the public. Lord Simonds commented that the public benefit of intercessory prayers could not be proved. This reasoning was doubted by Gobbo J in *Crowther v Brophy*[68] who saw some public benefit derived from the comfort believers took from the knowledge intercessory prayers were being said for themselves or others. [16.30]

For Commonwealth purposes, 'benefit' is determined in accordance with the *Charities Act 2013* (Cth). Section 6 identifies benefit by consideration of possible benefit to be achieved and potential detriment. Section 7 provides that certain purposes are presumed to be of benefit to the public, unless contrary evidence is shown. These purposes include the relief of poverty, distress or disadvantage, advancement of education, advancement of religion, care of the aged and disabled, and preventing or relieving sickness or disease.

Trusts that are justified under the fourth head must be shown to be of benefit to the public.[69] [16.31]

61 *Monds v Stackhouse* (1948) 77 CLR 232.
62 *Trusts Act 1973* (Qld) s 103; *Trustee Act 1936* (SA) s 69C; *Variation of Trusts Act 1994* (Tas) s 4(1); *Charitable Trusts Acts 1962* (WA) s 5.
63 *Variation of Trusts Act 1994* (Tas) s 4(1).
64 'Benefit' is no longer assumed in the United Kingdom and must be positively established: *Charities Act 2006* (UK).
65 *Re Watson (deceased)* [1973] 3 All ER 678, 688; *Public Trustee v A-G (NSW)* (1977) 42 NSWLR 600, 604.
66 [1965] Ch 85.
67 [1949] AC 426.
68 [1992] 2 VR 97, 100.
69 *Re Blyth* [1997] 2 Qd R 567, 58.

Public, or a section of the public

[16.32] Trusts for charitable purposes are not intended to be for the benefit of specific individuals or to be enforceable by specific individuals. They will therefore be invalid unless they benefit the public as a whole, or a significant section of the public. Determining what constitutes a section of the public is not always an easy task. The guiding principles were most clearly stated by Lowe J in *Re Income Tax Acts (No 1)*.[70] His Honour said that large groups defined by a common calling, faith or geographical location would constitute a section of the public. Groups which imposed a bar to membership such as clubs, literary societies and trade unions would not constitute a section of the public despite their large numbers. Likewise, religions must be open to all, in order to constitute a section of the public.

The relevant 'section of the public' is not limited to the Australian public. Trusts for charitable purposes overseas can be valid. Validity is assessed according to Australian law, and the Attorney-General's role as protector of charitable trust extends to trusts that are to take effect outside of the jurisdiction.[71]

[16.33] What is generally required is that the potential objects of benefit cannot be linked to one (or perhaps a few) identifiable persons or bodies. If a trust can only benefit the direct descendants of certain families, it will not benefit a significant section of the public. In the *Compton* case,[72] a trust was set up to educate the Montague, Powell and Compton children. Lord Greene MR said that where all the potential beneficiaries were defined by reference to a relationship to a named individual, family or association, the public benefit requirement was not satisfied. This was so whether the relationship was near or distant or extended across generations. A similar outcome was reached in *Oppenheim v Tobacco Securities Trust Co Ltd*.[73] Even though the pool of potential beneficiaries were the children of over 110 000 employees and former employees, the limitation to the single tie (in this case, British American Tobacco Co Ltd) prevented the group being regarded as a section of the public.[74]

[16.34] An exception relates to trusts for the relief of poverty. From early times, trusts for the relief of poor relatives of the testator or settlor were held to be valid. This was extended to a trust for poor employees of a company in *Dingle v Turner*.[75] The reasoning appears to be that the relief of poverty, however it occurs, is of benefit to the public generally. It relieves the public purse and pressure on other organisations relieving poverty. Nevertheless, a trust directed to poor relatives will be invalid if the class of potential beneficiaries is so small that the gift is really for the persons themselves, rather than for the purpose of relieving their poverty. This is a matter of construction. The court must decide whether '(a) the gift is for the

70 [1930] VLR 211, 222–3. See also *Thompson v Federal Commissioner of Taxation* (1959) 102 CLR 315, 321–4 (Dixon CJ).

71 *Lever v A-G (NSW)* [2018] NSWSC 838.

72 *Re Compton* [1945] Ch 123.

73 [1951] AC 297.

74 But see *Groote Eyelandt Aboriginal Trust Inc v Deloitte Touche Tomahatsu (No 2)* (2017) 169 NTR 1, where Hiley J dismissed an argument that a trust for the benefit of Aboriginal people of ten named traditional clans resident on Groote Eylandt and Bickerton Island and their successor generations was not for a section of the public. Hiley J drew a distinction at [220] between descent from ascertainable persons known at a particular time, and descent under complicated traditional law and custom, which included being based on mythical ancestry.

75 [1972] AC 601.

relief of poverty amongst poor people of the particular description, or (b) a gift to particular poor persons, the relief of poverty being the motive of the gift'.[76]

Trusts for multiple purposes

A purported trust may have been set up for both charitable and non-charitable purposes. This situation is governed by 'severing' legislation in most Australian jurisdictions.[77] This legislation allows the non-charitable aspect of the trust to be severed from the charitable aspect. The legislation can be used in three situations. These are: [16.35]

(a) a trust for both charitable and non-charitable purposes;
(b) a trust expressed so broadly that it is potentially for charitable and non-charitable purposes; and
(c) gifts on trust for organisations that have both charitable and non-charitable purposes.

In the first situation, the legislation allows the court to simply 'pencil out' the non-charitable purpose. The trust is then construed as if the non-charitable purpose was not there. For example, a trust might be set up to alleviate poverty in Woolloongabba and to provide for the education of the employees of the Gabba Cricket Ground. The first part of the clause is a valid charitable trust for the relief of poverty. The second part of the clause is an invalid trust as it is not for the benefit of a section of the public. The second part would be pencilled out, leaving the trust for the relief of poverty in Woolloongabba. [16.36]

In the second situation, a broadly expressed purpose could cover both charitable and non-charitable purposes. This occurred in *Chichester Diocesan Fund v Simpson*.[78] The trust was expressed to be for 'such charitable institutions or other benevolent objects' as the executors selected. The House of Lords disallowed the trust on the basis that the funds might be directed to 'benevolent' purposes, and 'benevolent' purposes are not necessarily purposes that are charitable at law. Under English law, severance was not possible. In Australia, the severing provision would be used to pencil out the 'benevolent' purposes, leaving only the charitable purposes. [16.37]

Thirdly, statutory severance applies to gifts on trust to organisations that have both charitable and non-charitable aims. This occurred in *Victorian Women Lawyers' Association*.[79] The severing legislation here allows for the gift to be used for the charitable purposes of the organisation, but not for the non-charitable purposes. [16.38]

Administrative and cy-près schemes

Despite best intentions, the efforts of settlors and testators who try to establish charitable trusts or make charitable gifts are frequently met with failure. In some cases, their plans are [16.39]

76 *Re Segelman (deceased)* [1996] Ch 171, 188 (Chadwick J).
77 *Charitable Trusts Act 1993* (NSW) s 23; *Trusts Act 1973* (Qld) s 104; *Trustee Act 1936* (SA) s 69A; *Variation of Trusts Act 1994* (Tas) ss 4(2), (3); *Charities Act 1978* (Vic) s 7M; *Trustees Act 1962* (WA) s 102.
78 [1944] AC 341.
79 (2008) 170 FCR 318. See [16.24].

impossible to achieve at the outset. Initial failure can occur because the proposed project is illegal, has already been accomplished, or is no longer necessary. In *Re Slatter's Will Trust*,[80] a testator left her estate on trust to a tuberculosis hospital. By the time she died, however, the hospital had closed, as tuberculosis had been largely eradicated. In other cases, although a valid charitable trust is established, it may over time become impossible, difficult or unnecessary to carry out. In *University of New South Wales v Attorney General of New South Wales*,[81] a trust was established to construct and operate student accommodation at the university in 1962. Over time, health, safety and financial issues meant that there could no longer be a suitable and effective use of the trust property. This is an example of subsequent failure of the charitable purpose.

[16.40] If the charitable purpose fails, the doctrine of cy-près allows the funds to be applied to a purpose 'close by' that originally specified by the creator of the trust. In some States, trustees are under a statutory duty to seek a cy-près scheme once failure occurs,[82] and, in any event, will be in breach of trust if they do not apply the funds they hold for the specified charitable purpose.

[16.41] The doctrine of cy-près operates differently depending upon whether the charitable purpose has failed at the outset or subsequently. In cases of initial failure, the court must determine whether or not the settlor had a general charitable intention. A cy-près scheme will be ordered if a charitable intention can be discerned. Courts favour an interpretation that discerns a general charitable intent.[83] The settlor will often have demonstrated a general charitable intention, but if the purpose behind the gift or the trust is highly specific the court may not be able to discern a general charitable intention. The property in such a case will be returned to the settlor. In *Re Marks*,[84] a woman left money partially for the construction of rental units, expressing preference that the units be rented to indigenous returned servicemen. The project was not financially viable. The woman's will and other communications specifically linked the project to use of a particular piece of land. The Court was unable to discern a general charitable intention, and the property passed to her next of kin.

[16.42] In cases of subsequent failure, a cy-près scheme must be ordered. As the trust fund has been applied in the past for a valid charitable purpose, it must always be applied for a charitable purpose. The trust fund is not returned to the settlor or testator's estate. Once validly applied to charity, the fund will always be applied to charity unless express provision is made by the terms of the trust for a non-charitable application.[85]

[16.43] Cy-près schemes covering initial or subsequent failure of the charitable purpose are only one example of the kind of administrative schemes that may be necessary for the administration of a trust. As Hamilton J stated in *Hunter Region SLSA Helicopter Rescue Service Ltd v Attorney-General (NSW)*,[86] administrative schemes may also be needed where

80 [1964] Ch 512.
81 [2019] NSWSC 178.
82 See, eg, *Charities Act 1978* (Vic) s 2(4); *Trusts Act 1973* (Qld) s 105; *Charitable Trusts Act 1993* (NSW) s 11.
83 *Re Daniels* [1970] VR 72.
84 [2017] VSC 665.
85 *A-G (NSW) v Perpetual Trustee Co* (1940) 63 CLR 209, 223–4 (Dixon and Evatt JJ).
86 [2000] NSWSC 456, [3].

there is lack of clarity as to the particular objects, where there are no trustees, where there is no machinery for management and control of the trust property, or for its distribution and application.

Trusts for non-charitable purposes

Students are often told that charitable trusts are the only exception to the principle that a trust must have identifiable human beneficiaries. The proposition is an exaggeration. It is possible to impose responsibilities on persons to carry out purposes that are not recognised as charitable purposes. These responsibilities are not, strictly speaking, trusts. The best-known instances of such purpose trusts are trusts in favour of animals, trusts for graves and other monuments, and trusts for unincorporated associations. It is useful to consider first why these purpose trusts do not satisfy the requirements for express private trusts. [16.44]

Problems with purpose trusts

There are three basic conceptual objections to enforcing a trust for non-charitable purposes. They are: (a) lack of an identifiable beneficiary; (b) the absence of anyone, whether a beneficiary or an official such as the Attorney-General, to enforce the trust; and (c) possible infringement of the rule against perpetuities. The first two issues, lack of an identifiable beneficiary and difficulties of enforcement, are two sides of one coin. [16.45]

Let us consider the trust for an animal. Many of us love our family pets so much we want to provide for them after we are gone; and indeed, in some jurisdictions, this is valid.[87] But in the Anglo-Australian legal system, an animal (even a beloved pet) is a chattel and not a legal 'person'. The beneficiary principle[88] requires that a trust be for an identifiable person, not least because there must be someone who can enforce the trust. [16.46]

The charitable trust provides an exception to the beneficiary principle. The Attorney-General is given standing to enforce a charitable purpose trust, and the problem of lack of a person to enforce the trust is avoided. But the Attorney-General has no interest in matters that do not concern the public benefit, and cannot enforce a private trust for an animal. The court will not be in a position to step in to see that the trustee performs the trust.

Nevertheless, there are some cases where trusts for animals have been recognised and the beneficiary principle not applied. Most cases are English and of some age.[89] In *Re Astor's Settlement*,[90] Roxburgh J called these cases 'anomalous and exceptional',[91] and this description has largely stuck. The older decisions are now generally regarded as not [16.47]

---

87 Most jurisdictions in the United States now allow trusts for named animals to be established. See, eg, Georgia Code 2010 53–12–28 *Trusts for Animals*. These provisions commonly exclude such trusts from the rule against perpetuities and give certain persons power to enforce the trusts. Most such provisions also contain 'reasonable amount' terms, whereby the amount left on trust for the animal can be reduced by court order where it is in excess of what is required for the animal's care. Under the statutory schemes, money left over after the death of the named animal is distributed according to a statutory formula and is frequently settled on a charitable purpose.

88 *Morice v Bishop of Durham* (1804) 9 Ves 399; 32 ER 656.

89 See, eg, *Pettingall v Pettingall* (1842) 11 LJ Ch 176; *Re Dean* (1889) 41 Ch D 552.

90 [1952] Ch 534.

91 Ibid 547.

conforming to the law concerning the beneficiary principle. Roxburgh J's explanation of the older cases was that, in each, there was a taker in default who had a sufficient interest to see whether or not the trust had been performed. However, courts more commonly treat non-charitable purpose trusts as invalid whether or not there is a taker in default of non-performance.[92]

[16.48] Similar issues arise in the case of trusts for the purpose of grave maintenance and monument erection. There is no one who has sufficient interest in the performance of the obligation who can enforce it.[93] It can also be difficult to find public benefit in a gift to maintain certain graves, as opposed to the upkeep of a cemetery as a whole.[94] Most decisions concerning graves and monuments, however, are concerned with the rule against perpetuities.[95] Private express trusts are not intended to have an indefinite operation. The exception, again, is trusts for a charitable purpose which can operate indefinitely. Trusts expressed to be for purposes such as graves and monuments that may operate forever have been disallowed in both England and Australia,[96] although again, there are anomalous decisions.[97] Trusts for non-charitable purposes which would have offended the rule against perpetuities have sometimes been interpreted as valid trusts for a period of 21 years.[98] Perpetuities rules are now largely covered by statute, discussed at [15.38].

The *Quistclose* trust

[16.49] The *Quistclose* trust[99] is a 'mechanism by which one person may allow use of his money by another for a stated purpose without losing his right to the money more than necessary to achieve the purpose'.[100] Most analyses treat the *Quistclose* trust as either express trust or resulting. Nevertheless, Ford and Lee[101] point out that the explanation of the *Quistclose* trust in *Twinsectra Ltd v Yardley*[102] is that the agreement permitted the trustee to apply money loaned for a non-charitable purpose, being the purchase of land. But even though a *Quistclose* trust can be created to carry out a non-charitable purpose, it is not a purpose trust in the strict sense since the beneficiary is an identifiable person; namely, the lender of the money to the trustee. As Bell, Gageler and Keane JJ commented in *Legal Services Board v*

92 *Re Shaw (deceased)* [1957] 1 WLR 729; see also L McKay, 'Trusts for Purposes: Another View' (1973) 37 *Conveyancer and Property Lawyer* 420, 433.

93 In *Public Trustee v Nolan* (1943) 43 SR (NSW) 169, a trust to erect a set of bells near Sydney Harbour failed on the ground that there was no person who could enforce it.

94 *Phillips v McCabe* [2016] SASC 27, [29] (Gray J).

95 See, eg, *Phillips v McCabe* [2016] SASC 27. The relevant perpetuity period for an animal will be 21 years. See [16.46]. Trusts for most animals will not exceed this period except in the case of a long-living species such as a cockatoo. Legislation in the United States frequently specifies that the rule against perpetuities does not apply to trusts for animals, to make provision for these long-living species.

96 *Re Endacott* [1960] Ch 232; *Muir v Archdall* (1918) 19 SR (NSW) 10.

97 *Re Lambell* (1870) 9 SCR (NSW) Eq 94.

98 *Re Hooper* [1932] 1 Ch 38.

99 See [14.25].

100 Lord Millett, 'Foreword' in W Swadling (ed), *The Quistclose Trust: Critical Essays* (Hart Publishing, 2004).

101 F & L [1.3930, 1.3950].

102 [2002] 2 AC 164.

Gillespie-Jones,[103] '(t)he terminology of a "*Quistclose* trust" is helpful as a reminder that legal and equitable remedies may co-exist. The terminology is not helpful if taken to suggest the possibility apart from statute of a non-express trust for non-charitable purposes'. *Quistclose* trusts are discussed in chapter 14.

Gifts to unincorporated associations

There are many unincorporated associations in Australia, such as school parents' associations, sporting clubs, cultural groups, or interest groups such as birdwatchers. Many of these will not attract charitable status. What is to be done when a testator or a living settlor wishes to give property to such an association? As it is unincorporated the association is not a legal person; being unable to hold property, it is in theory unable to receive gifts. [16.50]

There have been occasional cases where such gifts were treated as valid trusts, but these are exceptional.[104] The most important Australian decision on point is *Bacon v Pianta*.[105] A testator left the residue of his estate 'to the Communist Party of Australia for its sole use and benefit'. One way of interpreting such a provision is to presume that the gift is to the members of the association; indeed, this is the prima facie presumption made. If that interpretation is possible, the gift is valid, and the property passes to each and every individual member at the time of the bequest. The gift cannot be interpreted as a trust for the benefit of current and *future* members, as that would offend the rule against perpetuities.[106] [16.51]

However, it can be hard to interpret such provisions as gifts to each and every member, especially where the membership is large, or where the wording of the provision suggests otherwise. Thus, the presumption is easily rebutted. For example, in *Leahy v Attorney-General (NSW)*,[107] two of the factors that led the Court to hold that the presumption was rebutted were the subject-matter of the gift itself, a large grazing property, and the potential recipients of the gift, an order of nuns. It was unlikely the testator had intended to split a grazing property among a large group of people.

In *Bacon v Pianta*,[108] the High Court held that the testator had not made a gift to the individual members but had attempted to create a trust for the purposes of the Communist Party. The High Court held that the gift for a purpose failed, as the purpose was not a charitable purpose.

Most Australian jurisdictions have legislated to allow unincorporated associations to benefit from gifts on trust. These provisions are to the effect that gifts on trust to the current and future members of an association, or on trust for the aims and purposes of the association, are treated as a gift in augmentation of the general funds of the association.[109] [16.52]

103 (2013) 249 CLR 493, [112].

104 See, eg, *Re Drummond* [1914] 2 Ch 90.

105 (1966) 114 CLR 364.

106 The term 'future' might also make the class uncertain: *McPhail v Doulton* [1971] AC 424. However, note *Alston v Cormack Foundation Pty Ltd* (2018) 358 ALR 236 where Beach J held that such a gift could be in favour of the members from time to time. This would not breach the rule against perpetuities as it would be possible to identify the members at any relevant point in time.

107 (1959) 101 CLR 611.

108 (1966) 114 CLR 364.

109 *Succession Act 2006* (NSW) s 43; *Wills Act 2000* (NT) s 42; *Succession Act 1981* (Qld) ss 33Q(1), (2); *Wills Act 2008* (Tas) s 57; *Wills Act 1997* (Vic) s 47.

WHAT'S ONLINE?

Available at www.cambridge.org/highereducation/isbn/9781009232388/resources:

- Recommended further readings
- Discussion topics
- Practice problem

PART F

PERFORMING THE TRUST

17

TRUSTEES' DUTIES AND POWERS

Introduction

A trustee owns the trust property and can exercise an owner's legal rights to manage and dispose of the property.[1] But the exercise of these rights is not absolute. It is subject to the beneficiary's equitable rights to compel the proper performance of the trust and, in accordance with principles described in chapter 24, to bring the trust to an end and become owner of the property. Legal ownership present opportunities for the trustee to betray and exploit the trust for personal gain. It also exposes the beneficiary to the risk that the trustee may neglect the trust property. Equity therefore imposes strict obligations on the trustee to ensure that the trust is carried out strictly according to its terms. Even when a trustee holds property on a bare trust for a single, adult beneficiary, so that an adult beneficiary can claim the trust property under the rule in *Saunders v Vautier*,[2] the trustee will have active duties to perform, including a duty of care with respect to the property.[3] The duties are enforceable by the remedies discussed in chapter 20. A breach of duty can also result in the imposition of a constructive trust, described in chapter 23. The remedies are designed to provide complete relief for the trust, as well as to deter future wrongdoing. [17.1]

A significant number of positive duties are imposed on a trustee. Failure to perform these duties constitutes a breach of trust. Additionally, the trustee is subject to the fiduciary obligations explained in chapter 10. Instead of requiring positive action from a trustee, these require the trustee to refrain from making an illicit profit from the trust, or from exercising discretions which may be vitiated by a real and sensible possibility of conflict of interest. Fiduciary obligations apply equally to trustees and other fiduciaries and will not be discussed further in this chapter except where they are relevant to the discussion of the duties which are specific to trustees. [17.2]

In addition, both equity and trustee legislation confer powers on the trustee to enable the trustee to carry out the trust according to its terms. Some powers are dispositive, meaning that they confer a discretion on the trustee to distribute some or all of the trust property. Other powers are administrative, meaning that they are concerned with the management of the trust property. Typical powers of the latter kind are the power to insure trust property; to appoint agents, such as lawyers, accountants and investment advisers; to maintain infant beneficiaries; and to advance capital to a beneficiary entitled to a share of the capital. The powers may be extended or limited by the express terms of the trust instrument. [17.3]

It is not uncommon for a duty to be coupled with a power. For example, a trust to sell land and invest the proceeds will usually include a power entitling the trustees to postpone sale until market conditions are advantageous. Moreover, the exercise of a power is subject to the application of trusteeship duties. For example, a trustee's power to distribute trust income to beneficiaries is subject to the trustee's duty to consider its exercise. Similarly, the administrative powers available to the trustee in managing the trust property are subject to the application of the trustee's duty of care. In summary, a trustee must have regard to the duties of a trustee in exercising a power, save to the extent that the duty has been validly limited or excluded by the terms of the trust instrument. Failure to comply with the duty constitutes a breach of trust.

1 A trustee will usually own the legal or registered interest in property, but a trustee holding as a sub-trustee (see chapter 13, [13.2], n 5]) holds the equitable interest in the trust property.

2 (1841) 4 Beav 115; 49 ER 282. See chapter 24.

3 *Byrnes v Kendle* (2011) 243 CLR 253, [21] (French CJ).

[17.4] The first part of this chapter explains the obligations imposed on a trustee. This is followed by an examination of a trustee's discretionary powers. In both cases, the focus will be on express trusts, both private and charitable. Resulting and constructive trustees are also subject to duties. These trusts do not, however, impose extensive obligations on the trustee. The principal obligation is to transfer property to the beneficiary entitled under the resulting or constructive trust.[4]

Sources of the trustee's duties and powers

[17.5] The trustee's powers and duties are sourced in the trust instrument (if one exists), in statute and in equity. Most modern trusts have trust instruments. In those cases where there is a valid trust without a trust instrument; for example, where an oral trust has been created, the obligations will be deduced from evidence of the intention of the settlor, as well as being imposed by equity and statute.[5]

[17.6] All Australian jurisdictions have legislation regulating trustees' duties and powers.[6] The legislation codifies many equitable principles[7] and modifies others.[8] In general terms, the duties imposed and powers conferred by the legislation are intended to supplement the provisions of the trust instrument, but their application can be modified or excluded by the terms of that instrument. There is no uniformity, however, as to which duties and powers can be altered by the trust instrument, and students are advised to peruse their local legislation carefully.[9]

Duties on assumption of trusteeship

Duty to adhere to the terms of the trust

[17.7] The primary duty of trustees is to adhere strictly to the terms of the trust. These terms reflect the settlor's wishes. Where the trust has been created by contract, as in the case of a superannuation trust where beneficiaries have contractual (as well as equitable) entitlements against trustees, the terms of the trust will be reinforced by the terms of the contract.

This duty continues for the entire duration of the trust but has particular resonance when a trustee assumes office. The trustee must obtain complete information about the terms of

4 See chapters 22 and 23.

5 See chapter 15.

6 *Trustee Act 1925* (ACT); *Trustee Act 1925* (NSW); *Trustee Act 1980* (NT); *Trusts Act 1973* (Qld); *Trustee Act 1936* (SA); *Trustee Act 1898* (Tas); *Trustee Act 1958* (Vic); *Trustees Act 1962* (WA).

7 For example, the equitable duty to act impartially towards beneficiaries and between different classes of beneficiaries when investing is reproduced in the legislation in each jurisdiction: ACT s 14B; NSW s 14B; NT s 7; Qld s 23; SA s 8; Tas s 9; Vic s 7; WA s 19.

8 For example, the standard of care expected when investing has been altered: this is discussed in chapter 18.

9 Tas s 64; Vic s 2(3); WA s 5. Qld s 4(2) gives primacy to the statutory powers by enacting that any powers conferred by the trust instrument are additional to the powers conferred by the Act. Section 4(4) provides, however, that the statutory powers (though not the duties imposed by the Act) apply only insofar as a contrary intention is not expressed in the trust instrument. Cf Vic s 2(3) which permits duties, as well as powers, imposed on trustees by the Act to be modified or excluded by the terms of the trust instrument unless the statute provides otherwise.

the trust, the trust property, and the identity of the beneficiaries, assuming that they can be identified.[10]

If any question arises about the construction of the provisions of the trust, the trustee should approach the court for determination of the question.[11] The trustee risks being in breach of trust if he does not seek the court's advice on the matter. This occurred in *Re Diplock*.[12] Trustees believed a provision of the trust gave them power to distribute trust assets to various charities. After they had distributed a large amount, the testator's next of kin challenged the validity of the distributions. It was held that the trustees' interpretation of the provision was incorrect. The provision was invalid, and therefore the next of kin were entitled to receive the assets. Having distributed to the wrong objects, the trustees were personally liable for breach of trust. [17.8]

Nevertheless, the obligation to adhere to the terms of the trust is not absolute. Departures from the strict terms of a trust instrument are sometimes allowed or even required. Trustee legislation, other statutory law, or public policy may mandate some other course of action.[13] It may not be possible to perform the trust exactly according to the terms of the instrument.[14] Alternatively, the trustee can act contrary to the trust's terms at the request of all *sui juris*[15] beneficiaries. Additionally, in cases of failure to comply with the terms of the trust, the court has power to excuse what would otherwise be a breach of trust. This is discussed in chapter 20. [17.9]

Duty to get in the trust assets

Incoming trustees are under a duty to ensure that trust assets are under their control. This may require the trustee to take steps to perfect its title; for example, by completing formal registration of its interest. Title documents must also remain within the trustee's control.[16] Failure to take control of assets may expose the trustee to liability to reconstitute the trust property if it is lost.[17] [17.10]

10 The identity of the entire class of the beneficiaries of a trust power may not be ascertainable: see [14.44]. The burden of proving whether an individual is a beneficiary rests on that individual: *Jordan v Goldspring* [2021] NSWSC 7.

11 ACT s 63; NSW s 63; Qld s 96; SA s 91; *Supreme Court (General Civil Procedure) Rules 2015* (Vic) ord 54; WA s 92. There are no equivalent provisions in Tasmania or the Northern Territory, but these courts have an inherent power to give advice and directions. The court can give advice on any matter concerning the trust. The advice is binding on all parties. For a full discussion of the court's jurisdiction, see *Macedonian Orthodox Community Church St Petka Inc v His Eminence Petar the Diocesan Bishop of the Macedonian Orthodox Diocese of Australia and New Zealand* (2008) 237 CLR 66; *Sourcebook* 19.5a, p 492.

12 [1948] 1 Ch 465; *Sourcebook* 21.6a, p 538. The House of Lords interpreted the will in the earlier decision of *Chichester Diocesan Fund v Simpson* [1944] AC 341.

13 For example, in *Orr v Ford* (1989) 167 CLR 316, the *Land Act 1962* (Qld) prevented the holder of land declaring a trust over it. Equity's 'salvage' jurisdiction to authorise the trustees to take steps, not otherwise permitted by the trust instrument, to protect the interests of the beneficiaries can sometimes be invoked, but the scope of this jurisdiction is limited: see [24.13].

14 In the case of charitable trusts, the cy-près doctrine may apply in this situation: see [16.40]. Variation of trusts legislation may be relevant in some jurisdictions: [24.20]–[24.31].

15 *Sui juris* beneficiaries are those of full age and full capacity.

16 *Field v Field* [1894] 1 Ch 425; *Sourcebook* 17.3.2a, p 428.

17 *Caffrey v Darby* (1801) 6 Ves 488; 31 ER 1159.

There will be no difficulties where the trust has been created by self-declaration, as the trustee will already control the asset. Where a trust has been created by transfer of property, some steps may remain to be taken to perfect the trustee's title to the property. Where the trustee is replacing a former trustee or is appointed as an additional trustee, this duty extends to checking whether the original trustee has breached the trust. If so, the new trustee is required to pursue the former trustee or any third party involved in the breach for compensation.[18]

A trustee must also enforce payment of debts owing to the trust. The duty is not, however, absolute. It will be reasonable, for example, for the trustee not to pursue the debtor if the cost of collection is likely to exceed to amount owing to the trust. Likewise, a trustee may legitimately decide not to litigate against a third party who has caused loss to the trust if the practical possibility of obtaining compensation is highly speculative.[19]

Ongoing management duties

Investment of trust funds

[17.11] Possibly the most important ongoing duties relate to investment of the trust funds. This is now largely regulated by important statutory provisions, and is discussed in the next chapter.

Duty to keep assets separate

[17.12] Trust assets must be kept strictly separate from the trustee's own assets. Where the trustee is trustee of multiple trusts, each trust's assets must be maintained separately unless the terms of the trust instruments permit mixing. This duty has been described as 'a hallmark duty of a trustee'.[20] The global financial crisis exposed cases of investors' money not being segregated in accordance with either the terms of the investment trust deed or investor protection legislation. In these cases, complex inquiries are needed to identify an investor's beneficial interest.[21] If asset mixing does occur, the tracing rules are enlivened.[22] These may not, however, entitle the beneficiaries to full recovery, depending on the circumstances of the case.

Keeping and rendering accounts

[17.13] The trustee of a trust is information-rich and the beneficiary information-poor. One of the methods employed to limit the risk of mismanagement is the trustee's duty to keep and render accurate accounts. This is a core duty that cannot be excluded by a contrary term in the trust instrument.[23]

18 *Young v Murphy* [1996] 1 VR 279; *Sourcebook* 20.2a, p 501.

19 *Australian Prudential Regulation Authority v Kelaher* (2019) 138 ACSR 459, [154] (Jagot J).

20 *Associated Alloys Pty Ltd v ACN 001 452 106 Pty Ltd (in liq)* (2000) 202 CLR 588, [34] (Gaudron, McHugh, Gummow and Hayne JJ) adopting the terminology of McPherson ACJ in *Puma Australia Pty Ltd v Sportsman's Australia Ltd (No 2)* [1994] 2 Qd R 159, 162.

21 *Re Lehman Brothers International (Europe) (No 2)* [2012] 1 BCLC 487; *Sourcebook* 17.3.4a, p 429.

22 See chapter 21.

23 F & L [929]. Cf ss 49–55 of the New Zealand *Trusts Act 2019*, which enacts a statutory presumption that a beneficiary is entitled to be given requested trust information but also recognises circumstances in which the presumption is inapplicable.

The trustee is expected to keep proper accounts and be in a position to render them to the beneficiaries when asked.[24] If the trustee is unable to render the account, a beneficiary can apply for an order that they be prepared; the trustee is then liable for the costs of the application. Failure to keep accounts may also be a ground for removal of the trustee.[25] The beneficiary's status is irrelevant; even those who are discretionary objects, or have only a contingent or limited interest, may complain.[26] [17.14]

Accounts must include all relevant information concerning the property and financial affairs of the trust, such as information about assets, investments, appointments made by the trustee, income and expenditure, capital and income allocation and taxation. Documents proving those figures, such as receipts, bills and tax returns, also form part of the trust accounts. [17.15]

The trustee's duty to keep accounts and the beneficiary's interest in inspecting trust documents can overlap.[27] One reason for denying beneficiaries access to trust documents is that disclosure might tend to reveal the trustee's confidential decision-making processes. But that reason will not excuse the trustee from disclosing the financial accounts to the beneficiaries. As the Privy Council remarked in *Schmidt v Rosewood Trust Ltd*, beneficiaries have a strong claim to see trust accounts so that they can assess the propriety of the trustee's conduct.[28] [17.16]

Legislation in some States amplifies the trustee's duty to keep and render accounts.[29] The most comprehensive scheme is that in operation in South Australia.

Duty to give information to beneficiaries

Information concerning entitlements

Whether trustees are under a duty to inform beneficiaries about their entitlements under the trust depends on whether the trust is fixed or discretionary, and, if it is discretionary, on the social or commercial purpose of the trust. In *Hawkesley v May*,[30] trustees were in breach when they failed to inform a beneficiary of his entitlement when he became an adult. The position of discretionary objects in this regard is less certain.[31] Where the class is small, it can be argued that all potential objects should be informed so that the trustee's performance can be monitored. On the other hand, in some cases it would be pointless to inform potential objects of a possible interest. For example, objects of a family trust might include the settlor's [17.17]

24 *Kemp v Burn* (1863) 4 Giff 348; 66 ER 740; *Sourcebook* 17.3.5a, p 431; *Re Craig* (1952) 52 SR (NSW) 265, 267.

25 *Hackett v Hackett* [1922] NZLR 24.

26 *Chan v Valmorbida Custodians Pty Ltd* [2020] VSC 590, but noting at [124]–[128] that the proximity of the beneficiary to the trust, and the likelihood of the beneficiary receiving benefits under the trust, are relevant considerations when a beneficiary applies for disclosure of trust information. See also *Erceg v Erceg* (2017) 1 NZLR 320, [56].

27 Trust accounts are usually regarded as trust documents: *Global Custodians v Mesh* [2002] NSWSC 47, [80].

28 [2003] 2 AC 709, 735.

29 ACT s 102; NSW s 102; NT s 8; SA ss 84A–84F; Tas s 28.

30 [1956] 1 QB 304. Remarkably, the trustees had received legal advice that they were not obliged to inform the beneficiary.

31 *Spellson v George* (1987) 11 NSWLR 300; *Sourcebook* 17.3.6a, p 432; *Hartigan Nominees Pty Ltd v Rydge* (1992) 29 NSWLR 405, 432 (Kirby J).

parents, children, and nieces and nephews. The settlor's primary intention might be to benefit her children. There may not be much sense in informing nieces and nephews of their status when it is unlikely that a distribution in their favour would ever be made.[32] However, if the policy of ensuring performance of a trust is paramount, there may nonetheless be reason to impose such a duty. If a class was so wide as to make it impractical for a trustee to inform all discretionary objects, a court could excuse[33] any complaint about failure to inform a particular person, so long as the most relevant potential objects had been informed.

[17.18] In *Segelov v Ernst & Young Services Pty Ltd*,[34] the New South Wales Court of Appeal held that the trustee of a discretionary trust, established as part of a remuneration package for partners of an accountancy practice, was not under a duty to disclose to the plaintiff that she had been nominated as an object of the trust by her husband shortly before he became a partner. The trustee made payments from the trust into two bank accounts opened by the husband in their joint names. The plaintiff was unaware that she had been appointed an object of the trust and derived no benefit from the payments. She later separated from her husband. In the opinion of Gleeson JA, the proposition that a trustee was under a duty to inform an object of her entitlements under the trust did not have 'regard to the nature and terms of the relevant trust and the social or business environment in which it operates'.[35] In this case, the trust was a service trust operated as part of a remuneration package provided by the accountancy firm to its partners. Its primary purposes were to provide benefits for partners and tax advantages for the partnership, and not to make continuing provision for the objects. Moreover, the trustee was not in possession of the contact details of individual objects. These practical considerations meant that the plaintiff was not entitled to be informed of her status as an object of the trust.

Other information concerning the trust

[17.19] It is doubtful whether a trustee is under a *duty* to give beneficiaries other information concerning the trust. Until fairly recently, it was thought that beneficiaries had a right to inspect trust documents on the basis that they were, in a sense, owners in equity of the trust documents.[36] This justification is now not generally accepted.[37] Whatever the status of the beneficiaries' right to inspect trust documents it is not proprietary. It is only a personal right and cannot be separately assigned.[38]

[17.20] Recent cases have suggested that allowing beneficiaries to inspect trust documents is an application of the court's inherent jurisdiction to supervise trusts. In *Schmidt v Rosewood*

32 *Chan v Valmorbida Custodians Pty Ltd* [2020] VSC 590, [124]–[128], holding that the proximity of the beneficiary to the trust is relevant to the level of disclosure required.

33 See [20.20].

34 (2015) 89 NSWLR 431.

35 Ibid [130]. An exemption clause in the trust instrument would have protected the trustee from liability in the event of non-disclosure being held to constitute a breach of trust.

36 See *O'Rourke v Darbishire* [1920] AC 581, 626 (Lord Wrenbury).

37 *Hartigan Nominees Pty Ltd v Rydge* (1992) 29 NSWLR 405, 417–22 (Kirby J); F & L [9290]; TH Tey, 'Letters of Wishes' (2009) 21(1) *Singapore Academy of Law Journal* 193; JC Campbell, 'Access by Trust Beneficiaries to Trustees' Documents Information and Reasons' (2009) 3(2) *Journal of Equity* 97. The proprietary explanation is still accepted in Victoria: *Deutsch v Trumble* (2016) 52 VR 108; *Chan v Valmorbida Custodians Pty Ltd* [2020] VSC 590.

38 *Global Custodians v Mesh* [2002] NSWSC 47, [84].

Trust Ltd,[39] a father had established discretionary trusts under which his son was one of the beneficiaries. After the father's death, the son, suspecting that misappropriations had occurred, applied for disclosure of documents relating to the administration of the trust. The trustees rejected his application on the ground that he did not have a vested interest in the trust property. The Privy Council, allowing the son's application, rejected the argument that a beneficiary had to show a proprietary interest in the trust in order to seek disclosure of documents. The right to seek disclosure of trust documents was held to be one aspect of the Court's inherent jurisdiction to supervise the administration of trusts. The right to seek the Court's assistance does not depend on the beneficiary having a vested interest in the trust.[40] On the other hand, the Court's power to order inspection was discretionary, and it would not be in every case that a beneficiary would be given access to documents. Decisions are based on balancing the beneficiary's interest in disclosure against the trustee's interest in preserving confidentiality.

It is still uncertain whether *Schmidt* will be followed in Australia. In *Avanes v Marshall*[41] and *McDonald v Ellis*,[42] the New South Wales Supreme Court reached contrary conclusions on the question. In *Murray v Schreuder*,[43] Newnes J refused to apply *Schmidt* to a case involving a beneficiary with a vested interest. In an appeal from that decision, Buss JA (with McLure JA agreeing), in the Western Australian Court of Appeal, declined to express an opinion on whether the *Schmidt* approach represents the law in Australia. In Victoria *Schmidt* was not applied in *Deutsch v Trumble*.[44]

Leaving aside *Schmidt*'s status in Australia, any right the beneficiaries have to inspect trust documents is not an unqualified right to see *all* documents.[45] Although the right probably extends to essential trust documents, such as the trust deed, trust accounts and records of distributions made under the trust, the right does not extend to documents in possession of trustees created for their own purposes. These can include correspondence between co-trustees, and between trustees and beneficiaries, and agendas and minutes of trustee meetings.[46]

Further, where an inspection of trust documents would tend to reveal the trustee's reasons for reaching a decision, the trustee is not obliged to allow inspection. Trustees are generally not obliged to provide reasons for the exercise of their discretions,[47] and the beneficiary's right to inspection gives way to the trustee's right to confidentiality of reasons

---

39 [2003] 2 AC 709; *Sourcebook* 17.3.6c, p 434.

40 [2003] 2 AC 709, 729.

41 (2007) 68 NSWLR 595; *Sourcebook* 17.3.6d, p 435. See also *Silkman v Shakespeare Haney* (2011) 8 ASTLR 117, [27].

42 (2007) 72 NSWLR 605; *Sourcebook* 17.3.6e, p 437.

43 (2009) 1 ASTLR 340.

44 (2016) 52 VR 108. See also *Chan v Valmorbida Custodians Pty Ltd* [2020] VSC 590 (but applying a discretionary approach on the facts). *Schmidt* is good law in New Zealand: *Erceg v Erceg* (2017) 1 NZLR 320.

45 The right to see trust documents is a continuing right to allow the beneficiaries to inspect accounts and records from time to time: *Hancock v Rinehart* (2015) 106 ACSR 207, [365].

46 *Hartigan Nominees Pty Ltd v Rydge* (1992) 29 NSWLR 405, 432–3 (Mahoney JA).

47 The trust instrument may require that reasons be given. This is more common in superannuation trusts than private family trusts. Additionally, some statutes require that reasons be given; see, eg, *Trustee Companies Act 1988* (SA) s 15B(1).

in cases of clash.[48] The reasoning behind this principle was explained by Salmon LJ in *Re Londonderry's Settlement*, where he said: 'It might indeed well be difficult to persuade any persons to act as trustees were a duty to disclose reasons, with all the embarrassment, arguments and quarrels that might ensue, added to their present not inconsiderable burdens.'[49] This argument does not justify all cases of non-disclosure of reasons, given the rise of public trusts such as superannuation trusts and of professional trustees. Moreover, trustees are not entirely insulated from exposure of their thought processes to the court; trustees sued for breach of trust might be required to disclose the relevant documents showing their reasons in pre-trial discovery.[50]

[17.21] Trustees may also wish to avoid disclosing documents if the disclosure will reveal confidential information. Protection of confidentiality has been described as 'one of the most important limitations on the right to disclosure of trust documents'.[51] Recent case law on disclosure of information has frequently concerned 'memoranda or letters of wishes'.[52] These are documents provided by the settlor at the time of creation of the trust. Although the trust instrument may define the class of objects widely, the letter of wishes commonly 'narrows down' the class to a group the settlor primarily intends to benefit, giving 'guidance'[53] to the trustee by stating the settlor's preferences. In *Hartigan Nominees Pty Ltd v Rydge*,[54] two members of the New South Wales Court of Appeal held that the beneficiaries were not entitled to inspect the memorandum. Kirby P, dissenting, also regarded confidentiality as of some importance; however, he would have required an express request from the settlor that the letter remain confidential, and there was none on the facts.[55]

In *Breakspear v Ackland*,[56] an English decision post-*Schmidt*, Briggs J held that a letter of wishes delivered separately to the trust instrument is inherently confidential in nature. This confidentiality indicates that beneficiaries are not entitled to inspect the document, subject to the Court's overriding discretion to oversee administration of trusts.[57] Briggs J nevertheless ordered disclosure of the letter of wishes, largely due to the futility of doing otherwise, as the letter of wishes would necessarily be disclosed at a later point in litigation.

48 *Tierney v King* [1983] 2 Qd R 580; *Re Londonderry's Settlement* [1965] Ch 918; *Sourcebook* 17.3.6b, p 432; *Mandie v Memart Nominees Pty Ltd* [2014] VSCA 181, [21] (beneficiaries not entitled to interrogate a trustee's reasoning processes).

49 [1965] Ch 918, 937.

50 It is unclear whether discovery in a hostile action would require access to documents. In *Hartigan Nominees Pty Ltd v Rydge* (1992) 29 NSWLR 405, 437, Mahoney JA said that the principle of trustee non-disclosure of reasons should not be circumvented by an order for discovery. In *Breakspear v Ackland* [2009] Ch 32, the fact that the document in question would eventually be disclosed in litigation was regarded as relevant to granting access to it at an earlier stage. But the beneficiary's equitable right to disclosure of trust documents is distinct from discovery and need not be exercised in support of litigation: *Chan v Valmorbida Custodians Pty Ltd* [2020] VSC 590, [138]–[139]; *Kayler-Thomson v Colonial First State Investments Ltd (No 2)* (2021) 153 ASCR 663, [11]–[12]. In some Australian jurisdictions, this issue is covered by legislation requiring trustees to give reasons if required by court order: Qld s 8; WA s 94.

51 *Schmidt v Rosewood Trust Ltd* [2003] 2 AC 709, 728 (Lord Walker).

52 The difference between a memorandum and a letter is that the memorandum may not be signed.

53 If the terms of the letter are binding on the trustee, the letter forms part of the trust instrument.

54 (1992) 29 NSWLR 405.

55 Ibid 420.

56 [2009] Ch 32.

57 See Tey Tsun Hang, 'Letters of Wishes' (2009) 21(1) *Singapore Academy of Law Journal* 193, 209–12.

Finally, the trustee might need to restrict access to trust documents where disclosure is contrary to the interests of the trust. In *Rouse v IOOF Australia Trustees Ltd*,[58] a beneficiary was involved in a legal dispute with trustees. It sought access to the trustees' brief to legal counsel and correspondence between the trustees and other beneficiaries. The Court held that a trustee could, in limited circumstances, decline to give information to beneficiaries 'where the trustee has reasonable grounds for considering that to do so will not be in the interests of the beneficiaries as a whole, and will be prejudicial to the ability of the trustee to discharge its obligations under the trust'.[59] [17.22]

Duties of performance

Duty of care

It is often forgotten that equity developed a trustee's duty of care long before the common law was bothered by a snail in a ginger beer bottle.[60] While tortious and equitable duties of care are largely co-extensive, there are some differences in the application of the standard of care. The standard applicable to trustees recognises their role and position. The tort of negligence generally imposes the level of care expected of a reasonable person. Equity requires the trustee to carry out duties according to the standards of an ordinary prudent businessperson, regardless of the personal attributes of the trustee. This will be discussed further below. [17.23]

Remedial outcomes between tort and equity differ too. As in tort, there must be a loss to the trust estate before the trustee is liable to pay compensation. In tort, negligence that causes no loss is not actionable. But if a trustee fails to exercise sufficient care, the beneficiary may still be able to complain of a breach of trust in spite of suffering no financial loss. Trustee negligence can be grounds for seeking the trustee's removal and replacement, although this remedy is at the discretion of the court.[61]

The trustee's standard of care

The standard of the ordinary prudent businessperson was laid down in *Speight v Gaunt*.[62] A trustee employed a stockbroker to invest trust money. The stockbroker stole the trust funds given to him to pay for the purchases. The beneficiaries later sued the trustee. Jessel MR held the trustee not liable for breach of trust. He said that a trustee 'ought to conduct the business of the trust in the same manner that an ordinary prudent man of business would conduct his own, and beyond that there is no liability or obligation on the trustee'.[63] As it was in the ordinary course of business to employ a stockbroker to carry out brokerage, the trustee had acted with sufficient care. [17.24]

The 'ordinary prudent business person' standard applies to the day-to-day management of the trust. The standard of care to be exercised by trustees when *investing* is now defined by trustee legislation, discussed in chapter 18. The legislation applies a differential standard [17.25]

58 (1999) 73 SASR 484, 501. See also *Avanes v Marshall* (2007) 68 NSWLR 595.

59 *Rouse v IOOF Australia Trustees Ltd* (1999) 73 SASR 484, 501. See also *Marigold Pty Ltd v Belswan (Mandurah) Pty Ltd* [2001] WASC 209.

60 *Donoghue v Stevenson* [1932] AC 562.

61 See [20.43].

62 (1883) 22 Ch D 727; *Sourcebook* 17.3.7a, p 440.

63 (1883) 22 Ch D 727, 739.

of care, a higher standard being imposed on professional trustees than on other trustees. It is arguable that professional trustees are judged as professionals in relation to all their duties.[64]

Duty to act impartially

[17.26] There are two aspects to this duty. First, the trustee must act impartially between individual beneficiaries. Secondly, the trustee must act impartially between different classes of beneficiaries.

Favouring one beneficiary over another was the problem in *Tanti v Carlson*.[65] After the Second World War, the government regulated land-sale prices. A trust decided to sell land and to divide the proceeds among the beneficiaries. One of the beneficiaries was the wife of a trustee. She was allowed to purchase the property from the trust at the regulated price, far below its true market value. Other beneficiaries had also offered to purchase the property at that price. Allowing one beneficiary to purchase at the greatly reduced rate gave her an advantage at the expense of the other beneficiaries. The correct course of action the trustees should have taken was to apply to the court for directions.[66]

Allegations of lack of impartiality concerning different classes of beneficiaries often involve disputes between income and capital beneficiaries. Income beneficiaries are interested in the income produced by the trust estate; capital beneficiaries are concerned to see the corpus grow. The two classes may disagree on investment strategies. It may not be possible for a trustee to act in a way that benefits all *individual* beneficiaries, but this is not the duty imposed. The trustee is required to act in the interests of all beneficiaries as a whole. It is sometimes said that what is required is that the trustee exhibits 'fairness' between beneficiaries when exercising its discretions.[67] In some cases, the relevant considerations will be finely balanced, and a decision either way, for example, whether or not to pay income to a beneficiary, will be fair.[68]

The duty to act impartially further requires that the trustee fairly apportion capital and income coming into the trust, and any expenses and losses made by the trust, between capital and income beneficiaries.[69]

Duty to act personally

[17.27] Trustees must act personally and cannot delegate their decision-making powers. Where there are multiple trustees, they must also act unanimously; therefore, trustees cannot

64 *Bartlett v Barclays Bank Trust Co Ltd* [1980] Ch 515 (failure to supervise management of a company in which the trust had a majority shareholding); *Sourcebook* 17.3.7b, p 441. *Australian Securities Commission v AS Nominees Ltd* (1995) 62 FCR 504, 517 (Finn J); *Sourcebook* 17.3.7, note 4, p 443.

65 [1948] VLR 401; *Sourcebook* 17.3.8a, p 444.

66 The court might have ordered that the sale be delayed until post-war restrictions were lifted, as this would likely have been in the best financial interests of the beneficiaries as a whole.

67 *Re Mulligan (deceased)* [1998] 1 NZLR 481, 501; *Nestle v National Westminster Bank plc* [1993] 1 WLR 1260, 1279; *Sourcebook* 17.3.8b, p 445.

68 *Nestle v National Westminster Bank plc* [1993] 1 WLR 1260, 1270; *Australian Prudential Regulation Authority v Kelaher* (2019) 138 ACSR 459, [65].

69 *Nestle v National Westminster Bank plc* [1993] 1 WLR 1260. The trustees may seek judicial approval to create a sinking fund to maintain property for the capital beneficiaries: *Davidson v Cameron* (2016) 2 Qd R 340.

delegate their decision-making to one of their number. This is discussed below. The duty to act personally has several overlapping aspects to it:

- non-delegation;
- not acting under dictation;
- not fettering discretion;
- acting unanimously; and
- appointing agents.

Although trustees are under a duty *not to delegate* their decision-making powers, this duty is subject to exceptions. Trustee legislation in all Australian jurisdictions gives trustees some power to appoint delegates to act in their place. The legislation is far from uniform. In some States, the legislation is designed to cover short-term absences from the jurisdiction;[70] in others, permanent absence is catered for.[71] The most limited delegation power is contained in the Tasmanian statute.[72] [17.28]

In addition to statutory powers to delegate, the trust instrument itself might allow delegation.[73]

Trustees must *not act under dictation* of others. This duty extends to attempts by beneficiaries to dictate action to trustees. In *Re Brockbank*,[74] one of the two trustees of the Brockbank trust wished to retire. The beneficiaries wanted a professional trustee appointed to replace him. The continuing trustee disagreed, believing the professional trustee's fees would be too high. The beneficiaries sought an order directing the continuing trustee's consent to the appointment, but the Court held that the beneficiaries could not dictate the exercise of the trustee's discretionary powers. The beneficiaries either had to 'put up' with the trustee's exercise of power or wind up the trust. [17.29]

It is possible for a trust instrument to allow for dictation. It is common for commercial trusts to allow the beneficiaries, or perhaps a third party such as a lender, to dictate a course of action to the trustee.[75]

Trustees are under a duty *not to fetter their discretion* by binding themselves to a make a decision at some time in the future or make it in a predetermined fashion. In *Re Vestey's Settlement*,[76] trustees of a discretionary trust decided that they would make distributions of trust money to objects in predetermined proportions. It was held that a decision taken *now* to distribute in a given way *until further notice* is void as it is an attempt to bind the trustees at the time the discretion should be exercised. Evershed MR commented that this could not be an effective exercise of a discretion for the future.[77] The rule against fettering discretion also applies to a trustee's contractual agreement to act in a certain way in the future.[78] [17.30]

---

70 ACT s 64; NSW s 64; SA ss 17, 17A.

71 Qld s 56; Vic s 30; WA s 54.

72 Tas s 25AA.

73 *Doyle v Blake* (1804) 2 Sch & Lef 231. The Queensland legislation follows a different model to other jurisdictions. The statutory power to delegate applies 'whether or not a contrary intention is expressed in the instrument': s 31(1).

74 [1948] Ch 206.

75 *Citibank NA v MBIA Assurance SA* [2007] 1 All ER (Comm) 475; *Hancock v Rinehart* (2015) 106 ACSR 207, [162]–[167].

76 [1950] 2 All ER 891.

77 Ibid 895.

78 *Moore v Clench* (1875) 1 Ch D 447.

[17.31] Where there are multiple trustees, they *must act unanimously*.[79] The trustees must take their decisions jointly. If the trustees defer to one trustee who makes all the decisions, they may be liable for breach of trust for having failed to properly consider the exercise of their discretions.[80]

In *Sky v Body*, Street J described the principle in the following terms:

> Inherent in this basic system of trusts is the principle that trustees must act unanimously. They do not hold several offices – they hold a single, joint, inseparable office. If conflicting business considerations lead to such a divergence that the trustees are not able to act unanimously, then the simple position is that they cannot act.[81]

One result of the unanimity rule is that trustees are jointly (as well as severally) liable for trust decisions. Where one of the trustees commits a breach of trust, the rest will also be personally liable unless otherwise excused by the court,[82] or able to invoke the 'wilful default' provision, discussed in chapter 20.

There are other dangers too for the trustee who acts without the unanimous agreement of co-trustees. A joint trustee cannot carry out any act or incur any liability on behalf of the trust in the absence of unanimous agreement from all of the trustees. The trustee will not be entitled to claim indemnification unless the trust benefitted from the expense, and will incur the liability personally.[83]

A dysfunctional group of trustees which is unable to agree should seek the court's advice as to what steps to take in order to avoid committing a breach of trust.[84] Trustee disagreement occurred in *Cowan v Scargill*.[85] Half the trustees of a miners' pension trust were appointed by the miners' union and the other half by employers. The trustees were unable to unanimously agree on adoption of a proposed investment plan. In an application for directions, it was ordered that the plan be adopted.

[17.32] Trustees are permitted to *appoint agents* to implement the decisions the trustees have made.[86] If trustees appoint agents, their duty of prudence requires they take sufficient care in the agents' appointment and supervision. Trustees must appoint an appropriate agent, suitably qualified to perform the task in question,[87] and must properly supervise that performance.[88]

Equitable principles on appointment of agents are now supplemented by statute. There is significant variation between Australian jurisdictions.[89] Generally, however, legislation in

79 *Re Mayo* [1943] Ch 302. In the case of a charitable trust, decisions may be made by majority vote. It is also possible for a trust instrument to allow majority decision-making: *Dawson v Dawson* [1945] VLR 113.

80 See [17.34].

81 (1970) 92 WN (NSW) 934, 935.

82 See [20.12].

83 *Beath v Kousal* [2010] VSC 24.

84 See [17.8] and comment above in n 11.

85 [1985] Ch 270; *Sourcebook* 18.5a, p 467. See [18.21].

86 *Speight v Gaunt* (1883) 22 Ch D 727; *Sourcebook* 17.3.9a, p 447.

87 The agent must be employed to act within what is the agent's usual line of business. If the agent is appointed to perform an act outside of its ordinary business, the trustee may be liable for any loss that ensues: *Fry v Tapson* (1884) 28 Ch 268, 279.

88 *Graham v Gibson* (1882) 8 VLR (Eq) 43.

89 ACT s 53; NSW s 53; NT s 17; Qld s 54; SA s 24; Tas s 20; Vic s 28; WA s 53.

Victoria, Queensland and Western Australia allows the greatest latitude to trustees in their appointment of agents. New South Wales takes the middle ground, and narrow powers are given by the statutes in South Australia, Tasmania and the Northern Territory. The legislation in the last three States effectively limits trustees to employing solicitors and bankers to receive trust moneys.

All jurisdictions have a statutory limit on a trustee liability where an agent has been appointed.[90] These provisions are discussed in chapter 20.

Duty to consider exercise of powers

The principal distinction between the concepts of a trustee's duty and a trustee's power is that a duty *must* be performed; as its performance is mandated by the terms of the trust, performance can be demanded by any object and will be enforced by the court. A power, however, entails a discretion to act or not, as the trustee sees fit. An object cannot demand that a trustee exercise a discretionary power, and a court will not insist on it. The limit of the court's power is to ensure that the power, if exercised, is exercised properly.[91] [17.33]

A trust instrument may give the trustee power to distribute capital and income to one or more of a class of objects. The trustee's fiduciary status means that the trustee cannot merely ignore the power given. As Megarry V-C observed in *Re Hay's Settlement Trusts*,[92] a trustee is required to consider periodically whether or not to exercise the power, to consider the range of objects of the power, and to consider the appropriateness of individual appointments. In *Turner v Turner*,[93] a settlor established a trust and installed various relatives as trustees, none of whom understood the duties imposed on them by the trust. They effectively 'rubber-stamped' all of the decisions the settlor took concerning the running of the trust. The trustees signed documents making appointments under their power of appointment. Mervyn Davies J held that the appointments had been invalidly made as the trustees had not considered the exercise of their power before making them. Indeed, the trustees did not even appreciate that they had a discretion upon which to act. [17.34]

The consequences of a court's decision to set aside a trustee's exercise of discretion are discussed at [17.62]–[17.65].

Particular aspects of the trustee's fiduciary obligations

Fiduciary obligations are discussed in chapter 10. The fiduciary principles have some specific applications in the trust field. They arise so commonly that they are generally referred to as if they are separate duties, and it is convenient to discuss them that way. However, it should be borne in mind that their underpinnings are the loyalty required of a fiduciary. [17.35]

We will be discussing the most important of these, namely:

- the duty to act gratuitously;
- the self-dealing rule; and
- the fair dealing rule.

90 ACT s 53(3); NSW s 53(3); NT s 26; Qld s 54(2); SA s 24(2); Tas s 20(1); Vic s 28(2); WA s 53(2).
91 See [13.10].
92 [1982] 1 WLR 202.
93 [1984] Ch 100.

Duty to act gratuitously

[17.36] The 'no-profit' rule forbids unauthorised profit-making by fiduciaries.[94] Unless the trustee's profit has been authorised, the trustee must perform its duties free of charge, no matter how arduous or time-consuming they are. As a fiduciary, the trustee must act solely in the interests of the beneficiary, and not in its own interests. A trustee is not, however, required to underwrite a trust and can always obtain recompense for outlays incurred in the running of the trust. The trustee's right to reimbursement is discussed in chapter 19 at [19.17].

There are exceptions to the requirement that trustees must act gratuitously. This duty can be altered by an express term in the trust instrument, and most trust instruments are drafted so as to allow a trustee to charge for services rendered, especially if the trust involved is commercial. If a charging clause has not been inserted at time of drafting, it is possible for the trustee and *sui juris* beneficiaries to agree on remuneration for the trustee.

Additionally, courts can award trustees fair compensation for carrying out their duties even if there is no such allowance in the trust instrument.[95] The award can be made both in the court's inherent jurisdiction and pursuant to statute. Statutory provisions may explicitly allow the award of remuneration;[96] however, courts have also relied on their general statutory power to make orders where it is expedient in the administration of the trust.[97]

The advantage of applying for remuneration under statutory provisions rather than the inherent jurisdiction is that awards may perhaps be made more readily and calculated more generously. Awards under the inherent power are usually only made in special cases. In *Re Moore*,[98] a trustee gave all his time to running the business of the trust, which included running a profitable department store chain that employed over 700 people. The Court granted him remuneration, but it was at a modest level, given the work involved.

By contrast, explicit statutory provisions usually give the court great discretion as to the award of compensation to trustees, although there is often a percentage-based cut-off point above which awards cannot be made. For example, the *Trustee Act 1958* (Vic) s 77 provides that a court can order commission or percentage not exceeding 5% for the trustee's pains and trouble as is just and reasonable. Courts take into account a range of concerns when deciding whether to award recompense, such as the time and effort the trustee has put into performing the trust and the difficulties faced, as well as the size of the fund and its capacity to pay.[99] However, a breach of trust may influence the court to deny or limit trustee compensation.[100]

The self-dealing rule

[17.37] The trustee is uniquely placed to appreciate the true value of trust assets. The risk of the trustee using that information for personal advantage is so great that he is forbidden from

94 See [10.31].

95 *Re Queensland Coal & Oil Shale Mining Industry (Superannuation) Ltd* [1999] 2 Qd R 524, 526.

96 NT s 78; Qld s 101; *Administration and Probate Act 1919* (SA) s 70(1); Tas s 58; Vic s 77; WA s 98. *Zevering v Callaghan* [2012] 1 Qd R 194, [49], Peter Lyons J emphasising that payment to a trustee under the statutory provision does not require proof of exceptional circumstances.

97 ACT s 81; NSW s 81; NT s 50A; Qld s 94; SA s 59B; Tas ss 47, 55; Vic s 63; WA s 89.

98 [1956] VLR 132.

99 *Re Kerr* (1904) 24 NZLR 1.

100 *Will of Greer* (1911) 11 SR (NSW) 21.

purchasing trust assets from the trust. This is called the 'self-dealing rule', because the trustee as legal owner of the trust asset would be selling the asset to himself.[101]

It is irrelevant whether or not the trustee has paid full market value for the asset, or the sale was otherwise fair in all respects. A sale in breach of the rule can be rescinded[102] at the suit of a beneficiary. In *Calvo v Sweeney*,[103] it was held that rescission will not be refused merely because the court believes the transaction to be fair.

There are some exceptions to the self-dealing rule. Self-dealing may be expressly permitted by the trust instrument. Moreover, the court can give permission for the dealing. There is both an inherent power and, in some jurisdictions, a statutory power to allow such transactions.[104] The court's permission is usually granted in cases where the sale will be of obvious benefit to the beneficiaries. In *Patros v Patros*,[105] a husband who was the sole registered owner of the family home died. His widow (and trustee of his estate) was allowed to purchase the family home from the trust in order to provide accommodation for the couple's children.

If the voidable sale cannot be set aside because the trustee has on-sold the property to a bona fide purchaser for value without notice, the trustee must account to the beneficiary for profits or compensate the beneficiary for any loss.[106]

Fair dealing rule

The self-dealing rule does not apply where a trustee purchases a beneficiary's interest in the trust. Instead, equity applies the 'fair dealing rule'. Under this rule, a sale by a beneficiary to a trustee of a beneficial interest in a trust is not forbidden except in limited circumstances.[107] Equity recognises the beneficiary's right to trade in the asset which belongs in equity to her (the beneficial interest). For example, a farm might be left on trust to three siblings in equal shares, with one of the siblings also a trustee. The beneficiaries who are not also trustees may have no interest in carrying on farming, whereas the trustee may wish to retain the asset. The trustee cannot purchase two-thirds of the farm from the trust, but he can purchase his siblings' beneficial interests. [17.38]

There is still a risk that the trustee could misuse his superior knowledge. Equity guards against that risk by overseeing the transaction at the suit of the beneficiary. The transaction is not automatically set aside (as is the case with breaches of the self-dealing rule) but will be set aside unless the trustee can satisfy the court that the transaction was proper. In particular, the onus is on the trustee to show that:

- he has not taken advantage of his position as trustee;
- he has made full disclosure to the beneficiary; and
- the transaction is fair, honest and at arm's length.[108]

101 The self-dealing rule also applies to fiduciaries who deal with property that is the subject-matter of fiduciary obligations.
102 See [5.1].
103 [2009] NSWSC 719.
104 NT s 7; SA s 49. Other States also use the expediency provision: see n 97.
105 (2007) 16 VR 182. See also *Tagliaferri v Tagliaferri* [2013] WASC 321.
106 *McKenzie v McDonald* [1927] VLR 134; *Sourcebook* 2.2b, p 19.
107 *Haywood v Roadknight* [1927] VLR 512.
108 Ibid 521. The purchase of a beneficial interest by a party associated with the fiduciary, such as the fiduciary's spouse, is also covered by the fair dealing principle: *Real Estate and Business Agents Supervisory Board v Landa* [2009] WASCA 191.

Duties on the winding up of a trust

[17.39] Express private trusts continue for a finite time.[109] The trust property must vest in those who are entitled to it at the termination (or vesting) date. However, it is also possible for a trust to be terminated earlier by the exercise of a right of revocation of the trust contained in the trust instrument, a court-ordered termination, or termination by the beneficiaries under the rule in *Saunders v Vautier*.[110]

In order to terminate the trust, the trustee must ensure that all outstanding claims against the trustee relating to the trust are satisfied. The trustee must make enquiries to ascertain these claims. The enquiries are usually made by published notice. Statute permits the trustee to rely on the responses received. For example, the *Trustee Act 1936* (SA) s 29(1) provides that a trustee who has given notice requiring interested persons to submit their claims can, at the expiration of the time mentioned in the notice, distribute the fund. Further, the trustee is not liable to any person of whose claim he had no notice before distribution of property is made.[111]

The trustee is entitled to have the trust accounts examined by the beneficiaries, so that a formal discharge can be obtained from them.

Once the outstanding claims are settled, distribution of the trust assets can take place. Any amount owed to the trustee pursuant to a right of indemnity has priority over the interests of the beneficiaries,[112] and the trustee will reimburse himself first. The remaining property is then distributed to the correct beneficiaries.

If a potential beneficiary cannot be found, trustees can apply to the court for an order permitting them to distribute the trust fund as if the beneficiary were dead,[113] but without prejudice to the beneficiary's rights should they return or be found to have acquired a vested interest in the trust. Alternatively, the trustee can take out a 'missing beneficiary' insurance policy. In *Re Evans*,[114] a beneficiary had been missing for about 30 years and was presumed dead. His sister, the trustee, wanted to wind up the trust, and took out an insurance policy to pay him his share of the trust should he return, which he did. She was allowed to claim the insurance premium as a valid trust expense.

Trustees' powers

[17.40] A power, for the purpose of the law of trusts, is simply an authority or discretion conferred on a trustee to deal with property held on the terms of the trust. Powers can be distinguished in a number of ways. Some powers are dispositive, meaning that they authorise the distribution of trust income or capital to the beneficiaries. An example of a dispositive power is a power of appointment. The validity of a power of appointment will depend on the application of the principles governing certainty of objects (see [14.39]). Other powers are administrative, in the sense that they authorise the trustee to enter into transactions for the benefit of the trust, such as powers to sell, lease or insure trust property.

---

109 See [15.34].
110 (1841) 4 Beav 115; 49 ER 282. See [13.3] and chapter 24.
111 See also ACT s 60; NSW s 60; NT s 22; Qld s 67; Tas s 25A; Vic s 33; WA s 63.
112 See chapter 19.
113 These are called 'Benjamin orders': *Re Benjamin* [1902] 1 Ch 723. In Western Australia, the court's power is statutory: WA s 66.
114 [1999] 2 All ER 777.

There are three sources of trustees' powers: the trust instrument (if any), statute and court order (if any). It is common for the trust instrument to confer a wide variety of administrative powers, depending on the particular features of the trust in question. For example, a trust to carry on a business and a trust to maintain infant beneficiaries will require different powers. Modern trust instruments usually contain a very extensive list of powers (possibly more than a trustee could ever imagine using). [17.41]

Trustee legislation in all Australian jurisdictions also confers administrative powers on trustees. In the event that the trustee requires a power not already conferred by statute or the trust instrument for the better management or administration of the trust, the trustee can apply to the court for further powers.[115] [17.42]

The exercise of a power is distinguishable from the trustee's duty to identify and evaluate factual matters. In *Finch v Telstra Super Pty Ltd*,[116] under the terms of a superannuation trust, a member was entitled to a benefit for total and permanent invalidity if 'in the opinion of the Trustee … the Member has ceased to be an Employee and is unlikely ever to engage in any gainful Work for which the Member is for the time being reasonably qualified by education, training or experience'.[117] The High Court held that forming an opinion under this provision 'was not a matter of discretionary power to think one thing or the other; it was an ingredient in the performance of a trust duty'.[118] The Trustee was held not to have complied with the duty of inquiry required by the provision. The principles governing judicial review of a trustee's exercise of discretion, discussed below, did not apply to the breach of duty. [17.43]

Exercise of power and review

Use of the word 'power' indicates that the trustee has discretions to exercise in decision-making. These are contrasted with obligations that are placed upon a trustee. The discretions given to trustees are many and various. The exercise of trustees' discretions may be crucial to the proper administration of the trust, such as identifying which beneficiary should be paid trust money under a discretionary trust.[119] They also include such matters as choosing an agent or selecting an investment. [17.44]

Courts have traditionally intervened in the exercise of a discretion on narrow grounds. First, if the trustee has been given a *discretion* as opposed to being under an *obligation*, the court will not insist that the trustee exercise it. The decision to exercise, or not to exercise, a discretion is solely a matter for the trustee. However, if a trustee exercises a power the court will insist that it is not exercised improperly. In *Tempest v Lord Camoys*, Jessel MR said: 'It is settled law that when a testator has given a pure discretion to trustees as to the exercise of a power, the court does not enforce the exercise of the power against the wishes of the [17.45]

115 ACT s 81; NSW s 81; Qld s 95; SA s 59B; Tas s 47; Vic s 63; WA s 89.
116 (2010) 242 CLR 254; *Sourcebook* 17.3.10.1b, p 450.
117 *Finch v Telstra Super Pty Ltd* (2010) 242 CLR 254, [7].
118 Ibid [30].
119 The High Court has disapproved of the term 'discretionary trust' on the basis that it lacks precision: *Chief Commissioner of Stamp Duties (NSW) v Buckle* (1998) 192 CLR 226; *Sourcebook* 19.2a, p 476. But see *Commissioner of Taxation (Cth) v Bamford* (2010) 240 CLR 481, [6] for an example of the usage.

trustee, but it does prevent them from exercising it improperly. The Court says that the power, if exercised at all, is to be properly exercised.'[120]

[17.46] Proper exercise involves exercise which is:

(a) in good faith;

(b) upon a real and genuine consideration of the discretion given;

(c) for the purpose for which the powers were given; and

(d) not for an ulterior purpose.[121]

[17.47] A discretion will not be exercised upon a real and genuine consideration if the trustee (whether innocently or not) considered the wrong question, did not really apply his mind to the question at all or perversely shut his eyes to the true facts.[122] Dishonesty and lack of good faith also indicate that no real decision has been made.[123] In *Klug v Klug*,[124] a daughter benefited from a trust set up under her father's will. Her mother was one of the two trustees. The second trustee wished to exercise a power of advancement to the daughter. Her mother refused to agree on the basis that the daughter had married a Frenchman without her consent. It was held that there had been no exercise of discretion; the Court itself proceeded to exercise the discretion in the daughter's favour.

[17.48] In *Re Hay's Settlement Trusts*,[125] trustees attempted to exercise a power for a purpose other than that for which it had been given. Trustees had a power to appoint property. If the power was not exercised within 21 years, the settlor's nieces and nephews were to receive the property. After 11 years, the trustees purported to appoint the property to themselves as trustees of a new trust, effectively extending the original term of the power to 32 years. Megarry V-C held this was an improper exercise of discretion. The power had been conferred to allow the trustees to appoint the property to persons or purposes. Instead, what they had done was set up a new mechanism for appointment at some later time. That was not the purpose for which the power had been given.

[17.49] The trustee cannot exercise its discretion for an ulterior motive. In *Re Pauling's Settlement Trusts*,[126] a wealthy woman married a penniless navy officer. To stop him frittering away her fortune, her money was settled on trust. The beneficiaries were the woman for life, and then her children. The trustee had power to advance part of the children's expected shares to them during their mother's lifetime. That power could only be exercised for the benefit of the children. Money was regularly advanced by the trustee (at the husband's request), ostensibly to the children. These advances went 'straight into the banking account of the mother' and were used for family living expenses. These were breaches of trust.

[17.50] What is important here is the trustee's *motive*. The trustee's decision may have the *outcome* of indirectly benefiting those who are not beneficiaries. This is not objectionable. If the sums advanced in *Re Pauling's Settlement Trusts* had been used by the children to

120 (1882) 21 Ch D 571, 578.
121 *Karger v Paul* [1984] VR 161; *Sourcebook* 17.3.10.1a, p 449.
122 *Dundee General Hospitals Board of Management v Walker* [1952] 1 All ER 896, 905.
123 Ibid.
124 [1918] 2 Ch 67.
125 [1982] 1 WLR 202.
126 [1961] 3 All ER 713.

benefit the parents indirectly, this would have been acceptable. But the trustee knew that the funds were being used by the parents and were not primarily benefiting the children.

Courts have had in general very limited powers to review the trustee's exercise of a discretion. Except in States where there is a statutory right of review of trustees' decisions,[127] this is still the case with private or family trusts. Scope for court review is not quite so limited in superannuation trusts. [17.51]

In a traditional trust, courts have little scope to review a trustee's discretionary decision-making, and even less to overrule it. As McGarvie J said, 'the Court examines whether the discretion was exercised but does not examine how it was exercised'.[128] If the trustee's discretion has been exercised 'in good faith, upon real and genuine consideration and in accordance with the purposes for which the discretion was conferred',[129] courts will not examine or review the decision. These three 'essential components' indicate that the trustee has exercised the discretion. [17.52]

The court will not examine the exercise further unless the trustee has chosen to give reasons for her decision. Review when reasons are given is discussed further below. Absent reasons, the court only checks to see what enquiries the trustee might have made or what information the trustee might have been acting on for the purposes of establishing that the three essential components are present, not 'for the independent purpose of impugning the exercise of the discretion on the grounds that their inquiries, information or reasons or the manner of exercise of that discretion, fell short of what was appropriate and sufficient'.[130]

This is illustrated by *Karger v Paul*.[131] A testamentary trust appointed the testatrix's husband and solicitor trustees of a trust. The husband was the life tenant, with capital to go to the testatrix's niece. The trustees had, however, an 'absolute and unfettered' discretion to transfer the capital to the husband upon his request. He requested that it be transferred to him. The trustees obtained no independent information about the niece's financial position, relying on the husband's knowledge. It was inferred in court that the request might not have been made to benefit the husband but instead to benefit his girlfriend. The niece challenged the trustees' decision to transfer capital as not being honest, in good faith, or for the purposes for which the power was given.

McGarvie J considered the position of the two trustees separately. There was insufficient evidence that the husband's exercise of discretion was intended to benefit his friend. He had not acted dishonestly or in bad faith by exercising the discretion in his own favour; the testatrix had clearly intended that he *could* exercise in his own favour. Further, it was not shown that he had not given a real and genuine consideration to the exercise of his discretion. The solicitor had exercised the discretion on the basis of inaccurate and incomplete information about the niece's situation. These 'gaps and errors' were not so extensive that he had not been able to give a real and genuine consideration to the exercise of the discretion. He had not acted negligently, and even gross negligence did not show a lack of good faith.

127 Qld s 8(1); WA s 94. See [17.61].
128 *Karger v Paul* [1984] VR 161, 164.
129 Ibid 163.
130 Ibid 164.
131 Ibid.

This decision illustrates the leeway that courts give trustees in reviewing the exercise of discretion.

[17.53] The discretion given in *Karger v Paul* was 'absolute and unfettered'. It is common, however, for discretions to be given to a trustee in such a way as to indicate points of reference for their exercise – in other words to be 'fettered'. If the trustee does not refer to such points, there will not have been a real and genuine consideration, and any purported exercise may not be in accordance with the purpose for which the power was given. The trustee has to consider those matters which *must* be taken into account according to the nature of the discretion.

[17.54] In *Sinclair v Moss*,[132] a testator's will established a discretionary trust. Income, and if necessary, capital, was to be paid to the testator's widow in 'such generous and appropriate sums as may in the opinion of my trustees be necessary or desirable after taking into account the income of which she is in receipt from any other source to support my wife … in the same style of life as that to which she was accustomed immediately prior to my death'. The widow and two others were trustees. After the widow's death, one of the other trustees alleged that the trustees had continually failed to take into account the widow's other income and failed to turn their minds to the level of support the widow needed to keep her in the intended style. This was established in respect of several years' distributions. The trustees had not given 'genuine consideration to the matter entrusted to their discretion'; the exercise of discretion had therefore miscarried.[133]

[17.55] A distinction can be drawn between matters the trustee *must* take into account and matters the trustee *might have* taken into account. The trustee is not under an obligation to consider every possible matter so long as all necessary matters are considered. As Hayne J said in *Esso Australia Ltd v Australian Petroleum Agents' and Distributors' Association*:

> The bare fact that there was material that was not placed before the trustee and which the trustee *might* have taken into account is not to say that the trustee should have considered it. Thus proof that there was material not considered by the trustee and which was material that the trustee might have taken into account does not show that the decision is ill founded.[134]

[17.56] It is not particularly difficult to establish that trustees took a matter into consideration when exercising discretion. It is not necessary that the trustee take any formal step to gather information to allow it to exercise its discretion. Courts approach the question by assuming the trustee's discretion has been exercised correctly; anyone wishing to complain bears the burden of proof that the situation is otherwise.[135]

[17.57] If the trustee chooses to give reasons for exercising its discretion, the court is entitled to review those reasons. This does not, however, give the court the power to reopen the exercise of the discretion. Instead, the reasons are examined so that the court can see that the discretion was exercised properly (ie, in good faith, without ulterior purpose, and for the purpose for which the discretion was given) and to satisfy itself that the reasons are

132 [2006] VSC 130.

133 Ibid [78].

134 [1999] 3 VR 642, 652.

135 *Sinclair v Moss* [2006] VSC 130, [36]; *Wendt v Orr* [2004] WASC 28, [50].

relevant to the discretion being exercised and reasonably support the conclusion reached by the trustee.[136]

The law referred to above was developed in the context of family or testamentary trusts. The bulk of funds now held in trusts in this country are in superannuation trusts. These differ in some fundamental respects from the family-style trust. The beneficiaries of these funds are not 'volunteers' in the way that beneficiaries of family trusts usually are. Employers make contributions on behalf of employee-beneficiaries in amounts proportionately linked to the employees' salaries. The employee-beneficiaries themselves may have made direct contributions to the fund, 'topping up' their 'accounts' as a method of saving for retirement. [17.58]

In a real sense, employee-beneficiaries have an entitlement to their beneficial interest. Further, although the trustees usually have discretions to exercise concerning early payments to beneficiaries (on injury or disablement), the trustees will not have unfettered discretion to refuse to pay a beneficiary their 'entitlement' absolutely. [17.59]

In *Finch v Telstra Super Pty Ltd*,[137] the High Court discussed whether the *Karger v Paul* test for reviewing the exercise of discretion applies to superannuation trusts, or whether a more intensive level of judicial scrutiny is required. The Court acknowledged the essential differences between a superannuation trust and a traditional family trust.[138] 'Superannuation', they said, 'is not a matter of mere bounty, or potential enjoyment of another's benefaction'.[139] The importance of superannuation and its differences from a traditional trust indicated that 'the decisions of superannuation trustees are not likely to be largely immunised from judicial control without clear contrary language in the relevant trust documents'.[140]

The High Court declined, however, the opportunity to determine exactly how the *Karger v Paul* test should be qualified, save in one respect. Their Honours commented that the trustee's responsibility to make enquiries for information, evidence and advice to enable it to form opinions concerning the entitlement of the applicant is more intense in the case of superannuation trusts than for family trusts. The trustee's decision can be reviewed by the court for want of properly informed consideration because, if the consideration is not properly informed, it is not genuine. Failure to seek relevant information that would allow the trustee to resolve conflicting evidence as to the condition of the applicant is a breach of trust.[141] [17.60]

The superannuation context also presents a partial exception to the principle that trustees are not required to give reasons for the exercise of their discretions. Courts take into account the trustee's failure to give reasons as some evidence of improper exercise.[142]

Two Australian States give a statutory right of review to beneficiaries.[143] Any person who has a vested or contingent interest in the trust property can apply to the court to review any [17.61]

136 *Meat Industry Superannuation Fund Pty Ltd v Petrucelli* (Supreme Court of Victoria, Nathan J, 28 February 1992) 48.

137 (2010) 242 CLR 254; *Sourcebook* 17.3.10.1b, p 450.

138 *Finch v Telstra Super Pty Ltd* (2010) 242 CLR 254, 272.

139 Ibid.

140 Ibid.

141 Ibid 280–1. For an example of the application of *Karger v Paul* to a self-managed superannuation trust, see *Wareham v Marsella* [2020) 61 VR 2662.

142 *Maciejewski v Telstra Super Pty Ltd* (1998) 44 NSWLR 601, 604; *Knudsen v Kara Kar Holdings Pty Ltd* [2000] NSWSC 715, [61]; *Hay v Total Risk Management Pty Ltd* [2004] NSWSC 94, [33].

143 Qld s 8(1); WA s 94.

act, omission or decision of the trustee. The formulations of the rights to review, however, differ. The Western Australian review process is limited to review of exercise of powers conferred by the Act.[144] It has been held that where a power is conferred by both the Act and the trust instrument, the statutory right of review can be invoked.[145] It would seem that exercise of powers conferred solely by the trust instrument fall to be reviewed (if at all) under the general law.[146] The Queensland provision, in contrast, applies to powers conferred either by the Act or by the trust instrument.[147]

It appears that the court's attitude when reviewing the trustees' decisions under the statutory power is much the same as at general law, and courts are reluctant to intervene.[148] However, as both provisions allow the court to require the trustee to substantiate its grounds for decision-making, the statutory power to review enables the court to insist that the trustee provide reasons.

Effect of improper exercise of discretion

[17.62] We have seen that a decision taken by a trustee who has not independently considered her exercise of discretion – for example, because she was acting on the instructions of a third party – will be void.[149] This is an obvious case of a trustee failing to understand her obligations. In other cases, the trustee recognises that she has discretions to exercise but takes into account irrelevant considerations or ignores relevant considerations. In these cases, the matter will generally be remitted by the court to the trustee for a new determination to be made, with directions as to the considerations which ought, or ought not, to be taken into account. In exceptional cases, the court may lack confidence in the trustee's competence or impartiality to exercise the discretion properly. This is likely to result in the removal of the trustee from office and replacement by a competent trustee who can be relied upon to exercise the discretion appropriately.[150] In *Finch v Telstra Super Pty Ltd*,[151] where the trustee had misapplied the criteria for an award of a benefit for total and permanent invalidity under a superannuation scheme, the decision was remitted to the trustee for a redetermination in accordance with the principles laid down by the High Court. The trustee had not acted in bad faith and was competent to apply the correct criteria for determining invalidity benefit, as identified by the High Court.[152]

[17.63] In *McPhail v Doulton*, Lord Wilberforce suggested that in an appropriate case the court could make the decision itself, if necessary by ordering the trustees to distribute to those entitled to a distribution, provided that the basis of distribution clearly appeared in the trust instrument.[153] This dictum was applied in *Meat Industry Superannuation Fund Pty Ltd*

144 *Wendt v Orr* [2004] WASC 28, reversed on other grounds [2005] WASCA 199.
145 *Wendt v Orr* [2004] WASC 28, [26].
146 *Pope v DPR Nominees Pty Ltd* (1999) 74 SASR 78, [57]; *Tonkin v Western Mining Corporation Ltd* (1998) 10 ANZ Ins Cas 61-397; *Wendt v Orr* [2004] WASC 28, [30].
147 *Re Faulkner* [1999] Qd R 49, 53.
148 *Wendt v Orr* [2004] WASC 28, [56].
149 *Turner v Turner* [1984] Ch 100. See [17.34].
150 See [20.43].
151 (2010) 242 CLR 254.
152 Ibid [68].
153 [1971] AC 424, 452, 457.

v Petrucelli.[154] In older cases, such as *Klug v Klug*,[155] the Court was prepared to exercise the trustee's discretion. But in *Finch v Telstra Super Pty Ltd*, the High Court declined an invitation to make its own determination, suggesting that this step should only be taken where there was only one possible conclusion to be reached.[156] A determination in favour of the applicant for benefit in that case was not the inevitable result of the trustee's exercise of discretion.

In a number of English cases, trustees have impugned their own exercises of discretion where they have ignored or misunderstood tax liabilities arising from the decisions they have taken. The trustees have invited the court to invalidate the exercise of discretion so that they can make a new determination which has regard to relevant fiscal consequences. The decisions have invoked the so-called 'rule in *Re Hastings-Bass*'[157] which governs the circumstances in which a trustee will be permitted to challenge their own exercise of discretion when made under a misapprehension. In *Pitt v Holt; Futter v Futter*,[158] the United Kingdom Supreme Court considered two cases of this type. In *Futter v Futter*, the trustees, acting on the advice of solicitors, had distributed all the capital of the trust in the exercise of a power of appointment. The trustees believed that the beneficiaries would not incur a tax liability as a result of the distribution. A considerable liability to capital gains tax was in fact incurred because a relevant statutory provision had been overlooked. In *Pitt v Holt*, a victim of a road accident received a substantial damages award. The damages were settled on trust. In structuring the trust, the victim's wife, who was acting as receiver for the victim and therefore in a fiduciary capacity, took no account of the trust's tax liability. A significant liability to inheritance tax was incurred. [17.64]

The Supreme Court refused to set aside either exercise of discretion. Lord Walker, giving the judgment of the Court, stated that tax considerations were relevant to the exercise of a trustee's discretion, and that a decision that ignored these considerations would be voidable if it amounted to a breach of fiduciary duty. But although the trustees (in *Futter*) and the wife (in *Pitt v Holt*) had made incorrect decisions, they had not, in relying on apparently competent advice, acted in breach of fiduciary duty.[159]

Australian equity has not recognised the rule in *Re Hastings-Bass*, and Australian trusts are not taxed on the same basis as trusts under English law.[160] Possible tax consequences are obviously relevant to a trustee's exercise of discretion, but permitting trustees to rely on their own breach of duty in order to avoid adverse fiscal consequences is unattractive.[161] Moreover, there is no good reason for allowing a trustee's decision to be set aside if it turns out to have tax disadvantages when a gift cannot be set aside for this reason.[162] It is [17.65]

154 (Supreme Court of Victoria, Nathan J, 28 February 1992) 48.

155 [1918] 2 Ch 67.

156 (2010) 242 CLR 254, [68].

157 [1975] Ch 25. The principle was in fact developed in *Mettoy Pension Trustees Ltd v Evans* [1990] 1 WLR 1587.

158 [2013] 2 AC 108.

159 In *Pitt v Holt*, the trust was set aside on the ground of mistake entitling the plaintiff to equitable relief.

160 J Campbell, 'Should the 'rule in Hastings-Bass' be followed in Australia? Trustees' duties to enquire and trustees' mistakes' (2011) 34(3) *Australian Bar Review* 259.

161 *Futter v Revenue and Customs* [2010] EWHC 449, [2].

162 *Futter v Revenue and Customs* [2013] UKSC 26, [8] (Lord Walker).

suggested that the grounds for reviewing a trustee's exercise of discretion should be limited to those set out in *Karger v Paul*.[163]

WHAT'S ONLINE?

Available at www.cambridge.org/highereducation/isbn/9781009232388/resources:

- Recommended further readings
- Discussion topics
- Practice problem

163 [1984] VR 161. See [17.52].

18

INVESTMENT OF TRUST FUNDS

Introduction

[18.1] As we saw in chapter 13, express trusts are created to manage assets. Asset management means *active* asset management. Thus, the trustee is under a duty to invest trust funds rather than to simply hold them safe.[1] Resulting or constructive trustees[2] are usually not under a duty to invest funds as their responsibility is to transfer the property to the person entitled to it. However, they can come under a duty to invest if the period of time for which the asset is held allows investment.[3] It has been held that a trust fund should be invested within six months, although there are occasions when funds should be invested more promptly.[4] Failure to actively manage the trust is a breach of trust and can result in personal liability for the trustee.[5] If a trustee under a resulting or constructive trust invests the funds, the trustee is under the same investment duties as a trustee of an express trust.[6]

Sources of trustees' investment powers

[18.2] Trustees' investment powers derive from the trust instrument, statute or court order. Early trusteeship legislation gave trustees limited investment powers. Unless the trust instrument contained extended investment powers, the trustee could only invest in securities authorised by statute or obtain an order of the court allowing another form of investment. By the middle of the twentieth century, this scheme exhibited a number of disadvantages. One major flaw concerned the statutory list of authorised investments in which a trustee was permitted to invest. This required investment in highly conservative assets, such as government bonds. Most Australian jurisdictions did not even permit investment in land. Further, the prudence of each independent investment was considered separately. This was called 'line by line' analysis. As no individual investment could be at all speculative, the conservative nature of authorised list investments was magnified.

[18.3] Investment in authorised securities worked well enough when inflation was low and returns on permitted investments were stable and aligned to the inflation rate. However, as the nature of capital markets changed and inflation became 'a persistent phenomenon',[7] investment in authorised investments no longer protected beneficiaries. They found that the capital value of their trust funds was eroded over time. Ford and Lee note that part of the difficulty arose from 'list investments' being unsuited to the range of modern trust structures. They were not sufficiently flexible to meet the needs of large superannuation trusts, for example.[8]

1 *Adamson v Reid* (1880) 6 LLR (E) 164. The terms of the trust can limit the trustee's duties to merely holding the property safe, as is the case in a 'bare' trust.
2 See chapters 22 and 23.
3 *Adamson v Reid* (1880) 6 LLR (E) 164; *Fan v Tang* (2010) 3 ASTLR 580.
4 *Cann v Cann* (1884) 51 LT 770; *Adamson v Reid* (1880) 6 LLR (E) 164.
5 Failure to invest trust funds usually exposes the trustee to liability for interest that could have been expected to be earned on the fund if properly invested: *Hutchings v Snowden* (1897) 23 VLR 118. If the fund is lost, the trustee is liable to reinstate it: *Caffrey v Darby* (1801) 6 Ves 488; 31 ER 1159.
6 *Fan v Tang* (2010) 3 ASTLR 580. The trustee of funds held on resulting trust was liable for failing to invest prudently.
7 *Nestle v National Westminster Bank plc* [1993] 1 WLR 1260, 1276 (Staughton LJ).
8 F & L [10.030].

During the twentieth century, economic research gave rise to two important theories: efficient market hypothesis, and modern portfolio theory. Modern portfolio theory has been called 'a mathematical interpretation of the old adage "don't put all your eggs in one basket"'.[9] The theory encourages maximisation of returns through the minimisation of risk. Returns and risks can be calculated so that 'optimisation' is achieved. The theory aims to eliminate as far as possible industry risk[10] and specific firm risk,[11] leaving the investor open only to market risk.[12] This is achieved by investment in a diversified portfolio of investments. Over the last few decades portfolio theory has become an accepted theory of investment, given its statistical success. [18.4]

Efficient market hypothesis posits that an efficient market is characterised by skilled buyers and sellers who have all publicly available information concerning an asset. These parties can rapidly establish a market price. As all buyers and sellers have similar information, none are disadvantaged.[13] Assuming that those who trade in an efficient share market are rational decision-makers, then 'no investor with published information can outperform the market by picking undervalued securities'.[14] This hypothesis is controversial but has some empirical basis.[15] Efficient market hypothesis suggests that the most efficient form of investment is in index-linked funds (funds that completely reflect the listed share market). This also achieves complete diversification under modern portfolio theory, as it only exposes investors to market risk. As it is possible to invest relatively small amounts in index-linked funds, even small investors can achieve near-complete portfolio theory diversification. Alternatively, significant diversification can be achieved without index-linking. Some empirical research has shown that 87% diversification can be achieved with as few as ten well-selected securities.[16] [18.5]

The best returns for trustees may be achieved by a diversified portfolio (and possibly investment in index-linked funds) insofar as that is appropriate to the trust.[17] This is a far cry from investment in a small range of conservative, authorised investments, each of them independently prudent.

Trustee legislation adopted in every Australian State, based on New Zealand statute and influenced by the theories discussed above, has replaced the earlier investment model. [18.6]

9 Ian Shipway, 'Modern Portfolio Theory' (2009) 15(2) *Trusts & Trustees* 66, 67.

10 Industry risk is the risk to which a given industry is susceptible. For example, severe prolonged drought resulting in water-use bans will impact negatively on the pool construction and maintenance industry.

11 Specific firm risk is the risk that impacts on a single firm or company, such as the unexpected death of a key manager.

12 Market risk is the risk that is common to all securities in the market; for example, a global financial crisis.

13 Achieving market efficiency is one of the policy drivers of measures such as insider trading prohibition and continuous disclosure requirements.

14 F Philip Manns Jr, 'New Zealand Trustee Investing: Reflecting on Modern Portfolio Theory and the Ancient Distinction of Principal and Income' (1998) 28(4) *Victoria University of Wellington Law Review* 29.

15 Ibid 34.

16 RA Brealey, *An Introduction to Risk and Return from Common Stocks* (MIT Press, 2nd ed, 1983) 112, cited in WA Lee, 'Trustee Investing: Homes and Hedges' (2001) 1(1) *Queensland University of Technology Law and Justice Journal* 3, 10.

17 High diversification may not be appropriate to all trusts. Trustees must first consider the degree of diversification required in their particular circumstances. This is discussed below at [18.27].

The legislation now allows trustees to invest in any form of investment, unless prohibited by the terms of the trust instrument.[18] Some other statutes give trustees power to invest in specified investments,[19] but given the width of the general investment power now in place they are probably unnecessary.

[18.7] It is not clear to what extent the legislation adopts modern portfolio theory, as its terms send mixed signals. Butler, writing shortly after the introduction of the ground-breaking New Zealand legislation,[20] concluded that its terms encouraged, and possibly even mandated, modern portfolio theory, especially in the case of large funds.[21]

The statutory model

[18.8] Although there are some differences between trustee investment legislation in Australian States, the legislation is sufficiently similar for it to be discussed generally.

The provisions applicable in New South Wales will be used as examples; significant discrepancies between States will be noted.

[18.9] The provisions of the Act apply unless there is a contrary term in the trust instrument.[22] The general format of the legislation is to give trustees a wide discretion as to investment selection, restricted by certain limitations on its exercise. Many of these limitations merely reproduce the standards applied in equity, though others have no equitable equivalent. The legislation first sets out a wide *power to invest*. This is followed by certain positive duties with respect to investment. These include a duty to *invest carefully*, and a duty to *review trust investments*. Additionally, equitable rules and principles are preserved insofar as they are not inconsistent with the legislation. Four equitable duties are specifically included:

(a) to exercise the powers of the trustee in the best interests of beneficiaries;

(b) to invest in investments that are not speculative;

(c) to act impartially towards beneficiaries; and

(d) to take advice.

The trustee is also directed to a list of *matters to which the trustee must have regard when investing*. Later, the statutes provide *exculpatory provisions* in the case of breach of the investment provisions. We will now discuss these matters in more detail.

18 ACT ss 14, 14C(3); NSW ss 14, 14C(3); NT s 5; Qld s 21; SA s 6; Tas s 6; Vic s 5; WA s 17. A trust instrument can either direct a trustee to invest in a particular investment, or deny the trustee the right to invest in a given investment. In either case, the direction is a term of the trust. However, in some cases the express alteration may need to post-date the new provisions of the trustee legislation. In *AXA Trustees Ltd v A-G (Vic)* [2000] VSC 530, it was held that a provision in a will that specifically denied trustees the ability to invest in certain investments was of no effect in light of the statutory amendments as it formed part of a clause extending the trustees' power to invest (to beyond list-investments). As the statutory amendments allow investment in 'any form of investment', the entire clause extending the investment powers (to investments A, B and C, but not D) was otiose.

19 See, eg, *Treasury Bills Act 1914* (Cth) s 11.

20 New Zealand has since abandoned the legislation upon which Australian statutes were based, and has adopted a simplified approach to trustee investments: see *Trusts Act 2019* (NZ) s 30.

21 Andrew Butler, 'Modern Portfolio Theory and Investment Powers of Trustees: The New Zealand Experience' (1995) 7(1) *Bond Law Review* 119, 147–50.

22 See, eg, *Australian Securities and Investments Commission v Drake (No 2)* (2016) 340 ALR 75.

The power to invest

Trustee Act 1925 (NSW) [18.10]

14 Powers of investment

A trustee may, unless expressly forbidden by the instrument (if any) creating the trust:

(a) invest trust funds in any form of investment, and

(b) at any time vary any investment.[23]

The term 'investment' is not defined in the legislation.[24] Originally, the term meant the acquisition of income-producing assets,[25] and later, assets that produce income and/or capital gain.[26] Most writers believe the term 'investment' must be construed more widely under the current statutory provisions, given the extensive changes from the previous investment model.[27] Nevertheless, it should not be regarded as entirely unrestricted. Although a trustee can 'invest ... in any form of investment' the width of trustees' discretion is limited by statutory requirements such as the duties of review, of prudence, of acting in the best interests of the beneficiaries, and of not speculating.[28] An investment that does not comply with these duties may not be 'an investment' at all. To date, there is little case law concerning the meaning of the term 'investment' in the current statutory scheme.[29] Trustees' liability has instead focused on other duties imposed by the new legislation. It would therefore appear that the term 'investment' does not limit the kind of return the trustee can seek; any restrictions on the trustee's choice of investment emerge from the context of the trustee's duties.

Investing prudently

Prior to the enactment of the current statutory scheme, equity developed a two-level duty of prudence to be imposed on trustees. In day-to-day management of the trust, the standard of care required was that of the 'ordinary prudent man of business'.[30] When investing, a higher standard of care was expected, namely that of 'a reasonably prudent business man investing for those for whom he felt morally obliged to provide'.[31] A man of business might take more risks with his own funds than with the funds of those for whom he felt a moral obligation. This indicated that a degree of caution and conservatism was called for when investing. [18.11]

23 See also ACT s 14; NT s 5; Qld s 21; SA s 6; Tas s 6; Vic s 5; WA s 17.

24 In the case of the English *Trustee Act 2000*, this was deliberate. The Law Commission commented, 'The notion of what constitutes an investment is an evolving concept, to be interpreted by the Courts'. The Law Commission, *Trustees' Powers and Duties* (Report No 260, 1999) [2.28] n 61.

25 *Re Somerset* [1894] 1 Ch 231, 247.

26 *Harris v Church Commissioners for England* [1992] 1 WLR 1241, 1246 (Nicholls V-C).

27 F & L [10.1000]; Jacobs [1807].

28 See, eg, *Antill v Mostyn* [2010] NSWSC 587, [17].

29 In *Byrnes v Kendle* (2011) 243 CLR 253, [120], Heydon and Crennan JJ commented that 'letting of land is an "investment" within the meaning of s 6(a)' of the South Australian legislation. Their Honours had previously noted (at [119]) that the trustee was under a duty to obtain income from property that can produce it. It is assumed their Honours meant that the land itself represented the 'investment'. French CJ thought the power to lease a house came from the general law: [11]. For competing dicta as to the meaning of the term compare *Perpetual Trustee Co Ltd v Cheyne* (2011) 42 WAR 209, [26]; *Public Trustee of Queensland v Tracey* [2013] QSC 183, [3].

30 *Speight v Gaunt* (1883) 22 Ch D 727, 739. See [17.24].

31 *Bartlett v Barclays Bank Trust Co Ltd* [1980] Ch 515, 531. *Sourcebook* 18.4b question, p 466.

[18.12] Towards the end of the twentieth century, some authorities suggested that this was not always the appropriate model against which prudence in investing should be tested. Trustees were once individuals connected with the beneficiaries or settlor; now they are more commonly professional trustees, to whom a more rigorous standard of care might appropriately be applied.[32] The legislation adopted this suggestion, enacting a bifurcated standard of prudence in investment, depending on the professional attributes of the trustee in question. More is expected of a professional trustee than an unpaid family trustee. The standard of care imposed on a trustee can be altered by express terms in the trust instrument.[33]

> ***Trustee Act 1925*** **(NSW)**
>
> **14A Duties of trustee in respect of power of investment**
>
> **(1)** This section has effect subject to the instrument (if any) creating the trust.
>
> **(2)** A trustee must, in exercising a power of investment:
>
> **(a)** if the trustee's profession, business or employment is or includes acting as a trustee or investing money on behalf of other persons, exercise the care, diligence and skill that a prudent person engaged in that profession, business or employment would exercise in managing the affairs of other persons, or
>
> **(b)** if the trustee is not engaged in such a profession, business or employment, exercise the care, diligence and skill that a prudent person would exercise in managing the affairs of other persons.[34]
>
> ...

[18.13] The standard of prudence imposed on non-professional trustees appears lower than was the case at common law. Amateur trustees are no longer expected to behave as 'business persons' when investing. Arguably, the prudence standards for professional trustees may also be lower than common law expectations, as the reference to 'moral obligation' has not been retained. Professionals are, however, judged as professionals, which will be informed by industry standards.

[18.14] The bifurcated prudence standards expected of professional and non-professional trustees may be difficult to reconcile with the trustees' duty to act unanimously where there is more than one trustee.[35] It is not uncommon for a professional trustee company and a non-professional trustee, who is known to the settlor or testator, to be appointed.[36] Trustees are required to reach decisions unanimously, and yet a professional and a non-professional trustee are apparently subject to different standards of care with respect to investment decisions. Where professional and non-professional trustees have been appointed, it is suggested that their investment decisions must be judged according to the professional standard. Allowing a professional trustee to be judged by a lower standard simply because another trustee is an amateur contradicts the obvious intention of the legislature to impose a higher standard of care on the professional. Further, it might have the unintended effect

32 See, eg, *Bartlett v Barclays Bank Trust Co Ltd* [1980] Ch 5, 534; *Australian Securities Commission v AS Nominees Ltd* (1995) 62 FCR 504, 517–18.

33 *Australian Securities and Investments Commission v Drake (No 2)* (2016) 340 ALR 75.

34 See also ACT s 14A; NT s 6; Qld s 21; SA s 7; Tas s 7; Vic s 6; WA s 18.

35 See [17.31].

36 *Re Mulligan (deceased)* [1998] 1 NZLR 481.

of encouraging professional trustees to insist on the appointment of a non-professional co-trustee in order to avoid the application of the higher standard of prudence.

Personal liability will not necessarily attach to the amateur trustee in this situation. A court can excuse an amateur trustee from personal liability under the general statutory defence available where that trustee has been honest, reasonable and ought fairly to be excused the breach of trust.[37] Where the amateur trustee had been both honest and reasonable, a court might excuse a breach that could not be excused in a professional. The application of this defence is, however, discretionary, and an amateur trustee will not necessarily be excused in cases where the professional co-trustee is held liable.

The question as to whether the trustee has acted prudently will, at least in part, be determined by an assessment of whether the trustee has met other criteria laid down by the legislation. For example, consideration of the statutory list of matters to be taken into account[38] is relevant to the question whether a trustee has acted prudently. In *HBL v Trust Co Ltd*,[39] the trustee's failure to address one of the listed matters (diversification) was indicative of the trustee's failure to achieve the relevant standard of prudence, given the size of the trust fund.[40] Similarly, in *Re CCR*,[41] lack of diversification and risks involved with the proposed investments were regarded as indicative of lack of prudence. [18.15]

Review of investments

Regardless of whether the trustee is a professional or an amateur, the careful trustee is required to regularly review trust investments unless that duty is otherwise altered by the trust instrument. [18.16]

> ***Trustee Act 1925* (NSW)**
> **14A Duties of trustee in respect of power of investment**
>
> ...
>
> **(4)** A trustee must, at least once in each year, review the performance (individually and as a whole) of trust investments.[42]

The legislation requires review 'at least' annually; whether that is sufficient to discharge the duty of prudence will depend upon the facts of the case. In *HBL v Trust Co Ltd*,[43] a single investment of nearly $4 million was held for a period of approximately 12 months at low interest. The trustee (a professional) gave evidence that investments were reviewed every six months unless circumstances changed dramatically. The Tribunal indicated that this review was insufficient, given the size of the investment and the poor return.[44] [18.17]

Review of the investments requires a review of the performance of trust investments individually and as a whole. This is generally interpreted as an indication that 'line by line' [18.18]

37 See [20.20]–[20.22].
38 See [18.27].
39 [2010] QCAT 40.
40 A failure to diversify is not of itself actionable: *Gregson v HAE Trustees* [2008] All ER 105.
41 [2006] QGAAT 45.
42 See also ACT s 14A(4); NT s 6(3); Qld s 22(3); SA s 7(3); Tas s 7(3); Vic s 6(3); WA s 18(3).
43 [2010] QCAT 40.
44 Ibid [36]. The case was brought under the *Guardian and Administration Act 2000* (Qld). This Act applies trustee legislation investment standards with respect to investment on behalf of those under a guardianship order.

analysis has been replaced by modern portfolio theory, given that the performance of the portfolio as a whole must be considered.[45]

[18.19] In all States, except New South Wales,[46] trustees must review investments each time a new investment is made, in addition to conducting the minimum annual review. A review of existing investments is one of the matters that need to be taken into account by trustees when investing.[47] In these jurisdictions, the section refers to 'the results of a review of existing trust investments', whereas the New South Wales provision makes it apparent that the trustee should consider the annual review. The matters that need to be taken into account by a trustee when investing are of importance when the court is considering relieving the trustee from liability.[48] In order to avoid liability for breach of trust, a prudent trustee should review existing trust investments each time an investment is made, rather than relying on the annual review.

Applying other duties of law and equity to investing

[18.20] Certain equitable duties imposed on trustees when investing are preserved by the legislation unless inconsistent with the statutory provisions or negated by express words in the trust instrument.

> ***Trustee Act 1925* (NSW)**
>
> **14B Law and equity preserved**
>
> **(1)** Any rules and principles of law and equity that impose a duty on a trustee exercising a power of investment continue to apply except to the extent that they are inconsistent with this or any other Act or the instrument (if any) creating the trust.
>
> **(2)** Without limiting the generality of subsection (1), a duty imposed by any rules and principles of law or equity includes the following:
>
> **(a)** a duty to exercise the powers of a trustee in the best interests of all present and future beneficiaries of the trust,
>
> **(b)** a duty to invest trust funds in investments that are not speculative or hazardous,
>
> **(c)** a duty to act impartially towards beneficiaries and between different classes of beneficiaries,
>
> **(d)** a duty to take advice.[49]
>
> ...
>
> **(4)** If a trustee is under a duty to take advice, the reasonable costs of obtaining the advice are payable out of trust funds.

These duties will be considered separately.

45 J Debeljak, 'Trustees' Power of Investment: The Impact of the *Trustees and Trustee Companies (Amendment) Act 1995* (Vic)' (1997) 5 *Current Commercial Law* 99.

46 See [18.27].

47 Ibid.

48 Ibid.

49 See also ACT s 14B; NT s 7; Qld s 23; SA s 8; Tas s 9; Vic s 7; WA s 19.

Duty to act in best interests of beneficiaries

At least in the case of the trustee's duty to invest[50] (and probably more generally), the duty to act in the best interests of the beneficiaries is taken as meaning in their best *financial* interests. This is illustrated by two English cases, *Cowan v Scargill*[51] and *Harries v Church Commissioners for England*.[52] In *Cowan v Scargill*, a coalminers' pension fund was managed by industry-appointed trustees and union-appointed trustees. The investment subcommittee proposed an annual investment plan. One of the reasons the union-appointed trustees objected to the plan was that some of the proposed investments were in industries in competition with coalmining. Megarry V-C held that their objections were unreasonable. The paramount duty of trustees of a trust to provide pension benefits to members was to maximise those financial benefits. The union-appointed trustees were not entitled to object to the plan on grounds of personal or political preference. [18.21]

As private express trusts exist to provide financial benefits, trustees must act in the best financial interests of the beneficiaries unless that obligation is modified by the trust instrument. Even though charitable trusts promote charitable purposes and may not be directly concerned with providing financial benefits, the position with respect to financial interests is much the same. In *Harries*, a large trust fund was used to support the clergy of the Anglican Church. The applicant sought a declaration that the investment policy of the trustees was too focused on financial considerations and not sufficiently focused on Christian moral concerns. The Court held in favour of the trustees. Nicholls V-C said that prima facie the purposes of the charitable trust would be best served by the trustees seeking to obtain maximum returns on their investments. In rare cases, such as where the objects of the charity conflicted with a certain kind of investment, the trustees should not make the investment, even if it resulted in financial detriment to the trust. The examples given were temperance charities investing in alcohol production and cancer charities investing in tobacco. [18.22]

However, the worldwide movement towards 'ethical' investment appears to be growing, perhaps as part of an increasing interest in environmental, social and governance issues.[53] It can be argued that financial concerns may not be the only matter that a trustee can take into account when considering what is in the best interests of the beneficiaries.[54] In any event, it is possible for the trust instrument itself to allow investment in 'ethical' investments, even if that is to the financial detriment of the trust. This explains the numerous 'ethical' investment unit trusts being marketed in Australia. Further, beneficiaries are able to consent to a trustees' investment policy, if they are all in agreement. [18.23]

50 The duty appears in the part of the Act concerning trustee investment.

51 [1985] Ch 270. *Sourcebook* 18.5a, p 467.

52 [1993] 2 All ER 300. *Sourcebook* 18.5b, p 469.

53 UN Global Compact, *Conference Report, Investing for Long-Term Value: Integrating environmental, social and governance value drivers in asset management and financial research* (Conference Report, 25 August 2005); *Sourcebook* 18.5, p 467.

54 See, eg, P Ali and M Gold, 'Investing for Good: The Cost of Ethical Investment' (2002) 10(5) *Companies & Securities Law Journal* 307; R Thornton, 'Ethical Investments: A Case of Disjointed Thinking' (2008) 67(2) *Cambridge Law Journal* 396. See chapter 24 – matters other than financial concerns can be taken into account when variation of a trust is being considered.

Duty to invest in non-speculative investments

[18.24] The previous statutory model ensured safe, conservative investments. Speculation was anathema to 'line by line' analysis as each investment had to independently satisfy the prudence requirement. Whether any degree of speculation is currently permitted is an open question. Despite what appears to be a clear indication that speculative or hazardous investments will not be tolerated, it can be argued that some degree of speculation could be allowed under the new statutory model.

This argument is underpinned by reference to modern portfolio theory discussed above. A trustee might put together an investment portfolio that has a variety of investments, from the ultra-safe through to the inherently risky. Risky investments can achieve the greatest returns[55] (when they achieve a return at all), whereas safe investments are expected to have lower returns. A portfolio that contains a range of both safe and risky investments might arguably be balanced and diversified. The portfolio *when judged as a whole* might then be prudent, according to modern portfolio theory, and on this basis some degree of speculation might be allowed. It is obviously easier to justify a more hazardous investment where it is, contextually, a small piece of a large fund.[56]

But what is meant by the term 'speculation'? The term is not defined in the Act, and there are no reported cases under the current regime which have considered its meaning. What little case law there is arose under the earlier scheme.[57] It is relevant that the current statutory regime was drafted by those with a full knowledge of efficient market hypothesis and modern portfolio theory. It is also significant that modern portfolio theory has been industry practice in the investment sphere for a considerable time. Despite the fact that legislators apparently approved[58] of the application of portfolio theory to trust investments, a duty not to invest in speculative or hazardous investments made its way into the Act. This suggests that there will be some investments that are simply too speculative or hazardous to have a place in a trust portfolio even though the portfolio is otherwise diversified. Such cases will probably be highly fact dependent.[59] Perhaps there are some 'investments' that are so inherently hazardous they cannot be called investments at all.[60]

On the other hand, it is arguable that the duty not to speculate merely reflects modern portfolio theory in any event. Modern portfolio theory advocates the elimination of specific risks, leaving the portfolio exposed to market risk alone;[61] thus, portfolio theory

55 Computer technology was originally considered risky. Ronald Wayne sold his 10% stake in the Apple computer corporation two weeks after its establishment in April 1976 for $US1500 because he feared the risks associated with the investment. In 2016, 10% of Apple was worth approximately US$60 billion: David Lee, 'Apple at 40: The forgotten founder who gave it all away' *BBC* (online, 1 April 2016) www.bbc.com/news/technology-35940300.

56 *Trustees of the British Museum v A-G* [1984] 1 All ER 337, 343 (Megarry V-C).

57 See, eg, *Re Buckland* (Supreme Court of Victoria, Nathan J, 13 July 1993); *Sourcebook* 18.4a, p 461.

58 Butler (n 21) 147–50.

59 For example, in *Bartlett v Barclays Bank Trust Co Ltd* [1980] Ch 515, it was held that investment in a land development scheme was speculative where there was no certainty that the necessary council approval could be obtained.

60 Such as racehorses, lottery tickets and cryptocurrency.

61 Manns Jr (n 14) 33.

too would reject some investments as being too risky. Arguably, on that basis, a trustee who properly follows modern portfolio theory is not speculating.[62]

Duty to act impartially between beneficiaries

The general duty to act impartially between beneficiaries was discussed in chapter 17. Its relevance in the context of investment relates to trusts with different classes of beneficiaries. Where a trust has capital and income beneficiaries, choice of one kind of investment may benefit one class at the expense of the other. This is what occurred in *Re Mulligan (deceased)*.[63] A testamentary trust had a life tenant (the testator's widow) and capital beneficiaries. The widow, who was also a co-trustee along with a professional trustee, insisted on income-producing investments, rather than investments attracting capital appreciation. The real value of the capital dropped considerably. The New Zealand High Court held that the trustees had breached the duty to act impartially between different classes of beneficiaries when investing. They had completely failed to consider the capital beneficiaries at all. The rule is that trustees must act in the interests of the beneficiaries as a whole, not preferring one class of beneficiaries over another in selecting investments.[64] [18.25]

It has been argued that there is inherent tension between the duty to act impartially when investing and the adoption of modern portfolio theory.[65] This is because portfolio theory is neutral concerning whether a return on an investment is regarded as a capital or income return;[66] the theory is only concerned with total return. However, as the legislation specifically requires trustees to act impartially between different classes of beneficiaries when investing, it must be assumed that trustees are not free to adopt portfolio theory completely. This appears to be the case even though 'it ensures that trusts will earn lower returns'.[67] This interpretation is strengthened by inclusion of the statutory list of matters trustees may consider when investing (discussed at [18.27]). Trustees are specifically directed to consider the need to maintain the real value of capital or income of the trust, and the risks of capital or income losses or depreciation.

The problem of balancing capital and income has been the subject of a Law Commission Report in England. The Commission recommended that trustees of private trusts be permitted to invest on a 'total return basis', rather than have to apportion between capital and income beneficiaries.[68]

62 In other jurisdictions, it has been held that trustees who follow modern portfolio theory are acting properly: see *Dominica Social Security Board v Nature Island Investment Co Ltd* [2008] UKPC 19, [30]; *Jones v AMP Perpetual Trustee Co New Zealand Ltd* [1994] 1 NZLR 690.

63 [1998] 1 NZLR 481.

64 Ibid 501; *Wendt v Orr* [2004] WASC 28, [103]–[104].

65 Manns Jr (n 14).

66 While there are established understandings of the concepts of 'capital' and 'income' receipts the trust instrument itself can specify whether a receipt is to be regarded as capital or income: see *Commissioner of Taxation (Cth) v Bamford* (2010) 240 CLR 481.

67 Manns Jr (n 14) 37.

68 The Law Commission, *Capital and Income in Trusts: Classification and Apportionment* (Report No 315, 2009) [1.22].

Duty to take advice

[18.26] Is a trustee under a *positive* duty to take advice, or is this duty better expressed as a duty to obtain advice if it is needed? The legislation itself seems to imply that the trustee is under a positive duty; however, other provisions in the same part of the legislation are inconsistent with this interpretation. Section 14B(4)[69] and its equivalents state that if a trustee is under a duty to take advice the costs of the advice are recoverable. Further, s 14B(2) allows, but does not mandate, a trustee to take advice with respect to investment. It therefore seems that not all trustees will be under a duty to take investment advice. This might possibly depend on the nature of the trust. For example, a unit trust set up to run a shopping centre may have only that purpose, with no scope for other investment. In such a case, it would be an unreasonable expense to insist on independent advice being taken.

The better view is probably that a trustee is under a duty to take advice if advice is necessary in the circumstances of the case. For example, in *Re CCR*,[70] a tribunal applying the investment provisions of the Queensland *Trusts Act 1973* regarded the applicant as under a positive duty to take advice. The applicant had no relevant financial or investment expertise, and in the view of the Tribunal needed independent advice in order to act prudently.

Since the extent to which trustees followed independent advice is one of the matters a court can take into account when assessing liability for breach of trust, trustees will be well advised to take advice unless satisfied it is unnecessary in their particular circumstances.

Matters to be considered by the trustee when investing

[18.27] The statutory model sets out a list of matters to be considered by the trustee when investing. States differ as to whether consideration of these matters can be excluded by the trust instrument. New South Wales and the ACT require express negation in the trust instrument. In Victoria, it seems the list cannot be excluded.[71]

> ***Trustee Act 1925* (NSW)**
>
> **14C Matters to which trustee is to have regard when exercising power of investment**
>
> **(1)** Without limiting the matters that a trustee may take into account when exercising a power of investment, a trustee must, so far as they are appropriate to the circumstances of the trust, if any, have regard to the following matters:
>
> **(a)** the purposes of the trust and the needs and circumstances of the beneficiaries,
>
> **(b)** the desirability of diversifying trust investments,
>
> **(c)** the nature of, and risk associated with, existing trust investments and other trust property,
>
> **(d)** the need to maintain the real value of the capital or income of the trust,
>
> **(e)** the risk of capital or income loss or depreciation,

69 See also ACT s 14B(4); NT s 7(4); Qld s 23(4); SA s 8(4); Tas s 9(4); Vic s 7(4); WA s 19(4).

70 [2006] QGAAT 45.

71 In contrast to other sections in this part, the *Trustee Act 1958* (Vic) s 8 does not include the words 'subject to the instrument creating the trust'.

> (f) the potential for capital appreciation,
>
> (g) the likely income return and the timing of income return,
>
> (h) the length of the term of the proposed investment,
>
> (i) the probable duration of the trust,
>
> (j) the liquidity and marketability of the proposed investment during, and on the determination of, the term of the proposed investment,
>
> (k) the aggregate value of the trust estate,
>
> (l) the effect of the proposed investment in relation to the tax liability of the trust,
>
> (m) the likelihood of inflation affecting the value of the proposed investment or other trust property,
>
> (n) the costs (including commissions, fees, charges and duties payable) of making the proposed investment,
>
> (o) the results of a review of existing trust investments in accordance with s 14A(4).[72]
>
> ...

The list is not intended to be exhaustive; nor is reference to every stated consideration mandatory. Only those considerations appropriate to the circumstances of the trust need be taken into account. Some listed matters may be appropriate for all trusts. It is, for example, doubtful that the purposes of the trusts and circumstances and needs of the beneficiaries could ever be safely ignored by a trustee when investing. The effect of the inclusion of this consideration is the subject of some academic disagreement. The authors of *Jacobs* take the view that this imposes a de facto duty to consult the beneficiaries concerning their needs and circumstances on trustees.[73] The authors of *Ford & Lee* are not entirely convinced. While commenting that it is appropriate and sensible to consult beneficiaries, they deny trustees are under any duty to do so.[74]

Some of the matters trustees should take into account when investing have been mentioned above. The desirability of diversifying trust investment is the legislative provision that most clearly adopts modern portfolio theory. One of the hallmarks of that theory is that diversified portfolios best reduce risk while simultaneously reducing costs. It would appear from the few decided cases in the area that diversification is taken seriously.[75] This is not surprising. As Tony Lee has commented, 'except where the purposes of the trust or the needs of the beneficiaries justify the maintenance of an under-diversified portfolio, failure to diversify is a first sign of mismanagement'.[76]

Diversification is not, however, always necessary or even desirable. For example, in a farming trust where the only asset is the farm there can be no real question of diversification. Very small trust funds may find it difficult to achieve diversification although empirical evidence suggests that diversification is achieved by index funds, some of which do not

72 See also ACT s 14C; NT s 8; Qld s 24; SA s 9; Tas s 8; Vic s 8; WA s 20.

73 Jacobs [1816].

74 F & L [10.2540].

75 *Re CCR* [2006] QGAAT 45; *HBL v Trust Co Ltd* [2010] QCAT 40. In both cases, lack of diversification was considered imprudent.

76 Lee (n 16) 13.

require large funds to be invested.[77] There is some recognition of this possibility in New South Wales, where the regulations suggest appropriate investments for small funds.[78]

As indications are that courts will regard failure to consider the listed matters as evidence of imprudence,[79] trustees are well advised to consider each matter on the list, if only for the purpose of avoiding liability for breach of trust.

Exculpatory provisions

[18.28] In addition to the general exculpatory powers that allow courts to excuse a breach of trust,[80] the statutory scheme allows courts to take specific matters into account when considering trustee liability for breaches concerning the trustees' powers of investment.

> ***Trustee Act 1925* (NSW)**
>
> **90 Court may take into account investment strategy in action for breach of trust**
>
> In proceedings against a trustee for breach of trust in respect of a duty under Division 2 of Part 2 relating to the trustee's power of investment, the Court may, when considering the question of the trustee's liability, take into account the following:
>
> **(a)** the nature and purpose of the trust,
>
> **(b)** whether the trustee had regard to the matters set out in section 14C so far as is appropriate to the circumstances of the trust,
>
> **(c)** whether the trust investments have been made pursuant to an investment strategy formulated in accordance with the duty of a trustee under Division 2 of Part 2,
>
> **(d)** the extent the trustee acted on the independent and impartial advice of a person competent (or apparently competent) to give the advice.[81]

This provision is generally regarded as endorsing or encouraging trustee adoption of modern portfolio theory in that it refers back to the statutory list of considerations for investing, such as diversification.

[18.29] Subsection (c) deserves separate comment. It allows courts to consider whether the impugned investment was made 'pursuant to an investment strategy formulated in accordance with the duty of the trustee under this Part'. This is the only reference to an investment strategy in the legislation, so it is difficult to read the provision as imposing a positive duty to formulate an investment strategy.[82] The absence of a positive obligation is perhaps understandable given that the trustee legislation is universal in application to all trusts. It would be unnecessarily onerous to require trustees to formulate an investment strategy where no new investments were to be made. It is more likely that the provision encourages formulation of an investment strategy where that is appropriate to the trust.

77 Manns Jr (n 14) 34.
78 *Trustee Regulation 2020* (NSW) reg 4.
79 See [18.26].
80 See [20.20]–[20.25].
81 See also ACT s 89; NT s 10E; Qld s 30B; SA s 113C; Tas s 12D; Vic s 12C; WA s 26B.
82 Superannuation legislation, however, positively requires formulation of an investment strategy. See also Debeljak (n 45) 113. The author argues that the Victorian legislation (which is not materially different) imposes a duty on trustees to formulate and follow an investment strategy.

The exculpatory provision probably offers some real protection to trustees. If the trustee considers all relevant matters specified in the legislation, formulates a sensible investment strategy and follows it, and has at least considered whether or not to obtain independent advice, it would be hard to show the trustee had acted imprudently. To date there have been no cases where the section has been successfully relied upon by a trustee, but this may well be because compliance with those factors may make a trustee 'suit-proof'. On the other hand, it is possible to find examples of tribunals considering failure to achieve acceptable standards in respect of subsections (c) and (d) as indicative of imprudence. This reinforces the point that all trustees should be advised to formulate an investment strategy. [18.30]

Additionally, courts are permitted by statute to set off investment losses against investment gains. [18.31]

***Trustee Act 1925* (NSW)**

90A Power of Court to set off gains and losses arising from investment

(1) The Court may, when considering an action for breach of trust arising out of or in respect of an investment by a trustee where a loss has been, or is expected to be, sustained by the trust, set off all or part of the loss resulting from that investment against all or part of the gain resulting from any other investment whether in breach of trust or not.[83]

...

This goes further than the limited provision for set-off permitted before the investment provisions were enacted. When business prudence was assessed on a 'line by line' basis, set-off seems to have only occurred within each 'line'. Traditionally, this meant the same transaction, but was later extended to the same class of investment. For example, in *Bartlett v Barclays Bank Trust Co Ltd*,[84] the trustee was allowed to set off losses against gains made in a property development scheme, although more than one transaction was involved. Under s 90A, one investment can be set off against any other investment. This 'setting-off' provision also indicates that modern portfolio theory is tacitly supported by the trustee legislation.[85] However, as the section only applies to losses made *in breach of trust*, the position is unclear. A loss made by a trustee while applying modern portfolio theory prudently would probably not be in breach of trust.

The relative absence of reported case law concerning trustee investment may be a sign that the legislative provisions are working effectively. If beneficiaries are not complaining about imprudent investments, perhaps trustees who are complying with their statutory duties are investing both prudently and as well as anyone can. This is probably more clearly the case with professional trustees. Industry practice applies portfolio theory, and professional trustees will run risks in ignoring its most obvious element – diversification. Amateur trustees may not understand the ins and outs of investment theory but will be expected to take advice if they lack expertise. On the other hand, the proliferation of exculpatory clauses in professionally drawn trust instruments, which excuse the trustee from liability to compensate the trust in certain circumstances[86] may be the real reason why few cases appear in the reports. [18.32]

83 See also ACT s 89A; NT s 10F; Qld s 30C; SA s13D; Tas s 12F; Vic s 12D; WA s 26C.
84 [1980] Ch 515.
85 Butler (n 21) 144.
86 See chapter 17.

WHAT'S ONLINE?

Available at www.cambridge.org/highereducation/isbn/9781009232388/resources:

- Recommended further readings
- An 'investment strategy'
- Discussion topics
- Practice problem

19

TRUSTEES' RIGHTS AND LIABILITIES

Introduction

[19.1] Both equity and trustee legislation confer rights on trustees which enable them to perform their obligations effectively and protect them from some of the more onerous aspects of the responsibilities of trusteeship. Only selected rights are covered in this chapter, the most important of which is the trustee's right of indemnity.

[19.2] The trustee's most significant liability is for breach of trust;[1] however, the trustee is also liable at law to incur the expenses of the trust. This liability gives rise to the trustee's right[2] of indemnity. The trustee's exposure to liability must therefore be understood before his or her rights can be considered.

Trustee's liabilities

[19.3] A trust is not a legal entity.[3] This can be contrasted with the position of a corporation, for example. At law the trustee is the legal owner (or holder) of the trust property. The trustee is therefore legally liable for all expenses incurred in respect of that property, whether those expenses arise in contract, tort[4] or otherwise.[5]

[19.4] Intentionally incurred expenses usually arise in contract; for example, contracts for legal services. It is sometimes possible for a trustee to limit or avoid personal liability under the contract. The trustee and other contracting party can agree that the other party will be limited to the trust assets for debt recovery, with the trustee not exposed to personal liability for breach. Very clear language is required. It is not sufficient for the contract to state that the trustee signs 'as trustee'. That term is descriptive only and does not indicate the parties' intention to restrict the trustee's personal exposure.[6] An example of words indicating that the trustee is not exposing itself to personal liability is a signature 'as trustee and not otherwise'.[7]

Trustee's right of indemnity

[19.5] Expenses the trustee incurs in managing the trust property are in equity incurred on behalf of the beneficiaries. The beneficiaries must do equity in return for the expenditure incurred by the trustee; the trustee must be reimbursed, if necessary by the beneficiaries themselves.[8] At general law,[9] and under statute,[10] the trustee is entitled to reimburse himself for expenses

1 See chapter 20.
2 Suggestions are sometimes made that the trustee's 'right' is better described as a 'power'. See HAJ Ford, 'Trading Trusts and Creditors' Rights' (1981) 13(1) *Melbourne University Law Review* 1, 4–5, 14, 17 and discussion in *Carter Holt Harvey Woodproducts Australia Pty Ltd v Commonwealth* (2019) 268 CLR 524 ('*Carter Holt Harvey*'), [30] (Kiefel CJ, Keane and Edelman JJ), [80]–[84] (Bell, Gageler and Nettle JJ). We will use the term in more general use: 'right'.
3 See [13.3].
4 *Re Raybould* [1900] 1 Ch 199.
5 Income tax, stamp duty, land tax and rates are all examples of statutory expenses.
6 *Helvetic Investment Corporation Pty Ltd v Knight* (1984) 9 ACLR 773.
7 *Re Robinson's Settlement* [1912] 1 Ch 717.
8 The situations in which a beneficiary must personally reimburse the trustee are discussed at [19.18].
9 *Worrall v Harford* (1802) 8 Ves Jun 4, 8; 32 ER 250, 252.
10 ACT s 59(4); NSW s 59(4); NT s 26; Qld s 72; SA s 35(2); Tas s 27(2); Vic s 36(2); WA s 71.

already discharged out of trust property, and is also entitled to discharge the expense directly out of trust property. This is the trustee's right of indemnity,[11] and is of immense practical importance. Expenses that attract indemnification include all the properly incurred costs of running the trust, such as rates, taxes, agent's fees and out-of-pocket costs. This includes legal expenses incurred on behalf of the trust,[12] and can extend to a trustee's legal fees incurred in defending an allegation of breach of trust.[13]

'Expenses' can be far-reaching. In *Re Raybould*,[14] trustees running a colliery had to compensate a neighbour when works at the colliery affected the neighbour's building. The damages for negligence and costs ordered against the trustees were held to be the subject of a right of indemnity. There was nothing untoward in the trustee running the trust business, and the trust had to indemnify the trustee out of the trust estate.[15] [19.6]

In addition to the trustee's right of indemnity out of trust assets, the trustee may be entitled to be indemnified by the beneficiaries personally. This is discussed below at [19.18]. [19.7]

The status of the trustee's right of indemnity

The trustee is the legal owner of the trust property. However, the trustee may obtain a proprietary interest in the trust property if it is entitled to a right of indemnity.[16] The right of indemnity is not itself property, but gives rise to an interest in the trust property enforced by way of lien or charge. The trustee's interest is given priority to the trust property over all other claimants, including the beneficiary. The trustee's lien does not operate as an encumbrance[17] on the beneficiary's equitable title to the trust property; instead, the beneficiary's title can only be assessed once the indemnity is discharged. In *Chief Commissioner of Stamp Duties (NSW) v Buckle*,[18] the High Court stated that the trustee cannot be compelled to surrender the trust property to the beneficiary until the right of indemnity is satisfied. This right survives the trustee's removal from office.[19] A court may authorise the sale of trust assets held by the trustee in order to satisfy a right of indemnity.[20] [19.8]

Upon a trustee's insolvency, property held on trust by the trustee vests in the bankrupt's trustee in bankruptcy (or liquidator).[21] This is because the trustee's right of indemnity gives [19.9]

11 This is frequently referred to as the 'right to reimbursement and exoneration'. A trustee is reimbursed when it has already discharged the debt out of personal funds; when the debt is not yet discharged, the trustee is entitled to apply the trust property to repay the debt in exoneration: see *Chief Commissioner of Stamp Duties (NSW) v Buckle* (1998) 192 CLR 226 ('*Buckle*'); *Sourcebook* 19.2a, p 476.

12 *Re Beddoe* [1893] 1 Ch 547.

13 *Macedonian Orthodox Community Church St Petka Inc v His Eminence Petar the Diocesan Bishop of the Macedonian Orthodox Diocese of Australia and New Zealand* (2008) 237 CLR 66; *Sourcebook* 19.5a, p 492.

14 [1900] 1 Ch 199; *Sourcebook* 19.3a, p 478.

15 The judgment creditor was subrogated to the trustee's right to recover indemnification from the trust assets.

16 Whether or not the trustee is entitled to indemnification is discussed at [19.11]–[19.14].

17 An example of an encumbrance on title is a mortgage.

18 (1998) 192 CLR 226. See also *Carter Holt Harvey* [29].

19 *Belar Pty Ltd (in liq) v Mahaffey* [2000] 1 Qd R 477.

20 *Buckle* 247 [50]: *Carter Holt Harvey* [32], [83].

21 *Carter Holt Harvey* [94]; *Boensch v Pascoe* (2019) 268 CLR 593. Complications arise when the trust property is registered land, as vesting is then subject to statutory rules: [5] (Kiefel CJ, Gageler and Keane JJ), [94] (Bell, Nettle, Gordon and Edelman JJ).

rise to a proprietary interest in *all* of the trust property. However, the trust property is held subject to the equities it was subject to in the original trustee's hands.[22] Insofar as the trust property exceeds the trustee's interest in it referable to the trustee's right of indemnity, it will not be available for distribution among the trustee's creditors. So, for example, if a trust fund of $100 vests in the trustee in bankruptcy, but the bankrupt trustee's interest is only valued at $20, the trustee in bankruptcy will hold the remaining $80 for the beneficiaries. The exception here is where the bankrupt trustee had no beneficial interest in the trust property;[23] in such cases, it is not necessary for the trust property to vest in the trustee in bankruptcy, as the bankrupt trustee will have no claim over the trust property.

[19.10] The trustee's priority in the trust estate has interesting consequences. While the trustee's right of indemnity remains unsatisfied, it is not possible to attribute ownership of an asset held by the trust to a beneficiary for taxation purposes, as it is not possible to conclusively establish the extent of the trust property.[24] Further, the trustee's undischarged indemnity can operate as a bar to the beneficiaries winding up the trust pursuant to the rule in *Saunders v Vautier*.[25] The trustee's right of indemnity also impacts on the rights of third parties. This is discussed below at [19.17].

Calculating the value of the trustee's right of indemnity

[19.11] The limitation placed on the trustee's right to be indemnified is that the expense has to be an expense properly incurred in the administration of the trust. Courts start on the assumption that the expense had been properly incurred, and it is for the claimant to show otherwise.

Some expenses are not properly incurred. In *Beath v Kousal*,[26] two joint trustees could not agree on the appointment of a solicitor to represent the trust in litigation. One of the trustees appointed a solicitor without the other's agreement. As trustees must act unanimously,[27] she was in breach of trust in making a unilateral appointment and had to bear the costs incurred personally.

[19.12] There is considerable doubt as to what must be shown to disqualify an expense, and the law in Australian jurisdictions varies here. Traditionally, indemnity arises in respect of expenses that are not improperly incurred. In *Re Beddoe*,[28] Lindley LJ said:

> a trustee is entitled as of right to a full indemnity out of his trust estate against all his costs, charges, and expenses properly incurred; such an indemnity is the price paid by cestui que trust for the gratuitous and onerous services of trustees; and in all cases of doubt, costs incurred by a trustee ought to be borne by the trust estate and not by him personally. The words 'properly incurred' in the ordinary form of order are equivalent to not improperly incurred.[29]

22 *Carter Holt Harvey* [94]; *Boensch v Pascoe* (2019) 268 CLR 593.
23 *Boensch v Pascoe* (2019) 268 CLR 593.
24 See *Chief Commissioner of Stamp Duties (NSW) v Buckle* (1998) 192 CLR 226.
25 (1841) 49 ER 282. See [13.3].
26 [2010] VSC 24.
27 See [17.31].
28 [1893] 1 Ch 547.
29 Ibid 558.

In the same case, Bowen LJ indicated that costs that had been 'unreasonably incurred'[30] would not be the subject of indemnification and that the question was not simply solved by reference to bona fides. This has been interpreted as meaning that properly incurred expenses are those that are honestly *and reasonably* incurred; expenses incurred negligently are not properly incurred. This test has been adopted in a number of jurisdictions,[31] and is supported by some writers,[32] but has not met with favour in all courts.

In *Gatsios Holdings Pty Ltd v Nick Kritharas Holdings Pty Ltd (in liq)*,[33] the New South Wales Court of Appeal considered whether damages payable for trustee's breaches of trade practices legislation could be indemnified as 'properly incurred expenses'. The Court held unanimously that the trustee should be indemnified. Meagher JA indicated that it was not necessary to show that the expense in question was both 'reasonable' and 'proper'. In his view, the only limitation on the expense was that the trustee's activity should not have been fraudulent.[34]

The Victorian Court of Appeal unanimously rejected the 'reasonable' test in *Nolan v Collie*,[35] though for reasons different from the New South Wales Court of Appeal. Ormiston JA said the question of whether the expense was proper or improper had to be considered in the circumstances of the duty or power the trustee was seeking to perform in incurring the expense. He drew a distinction between trustees' duties that require strict compliance (such as the duty to keep and render accounts, the fiduciary obligations, the investment power and the duty to adhere to the terms of the trust) and more day-to-day functions of trust management that call for a reasonable standard of care. If the trustee's duty requires strict compliance, and this has not been achieved, the inevitable conclusion is that any expenses incurred in (failure of) performance of the duty are necessarily improperly incurred. But the same is not necessarily true of a more commonplace performance. Here, lack of care does not necessarily determine the question whether the trustee should be indemnified. An expense incurred technically in breach of trust (for being below the required standard of care) can still be the subject of indemnification.

This idea requires illustration. The duty to adhere to the terms of the trust is strict. If a trust instrument requires Blackacre to be transferred to A, but instead, the trustee transfers it to B, the trustee will be in breach of trust. Any expense incurred in that breach (such as solicitor's fees for the transfer and registration) will not be properly incurred and cannot be indemnified. Alternatively, the trustee may be in breach of trust for lack of care. Suppose trust property includes antique furniture worth $5000. The trustee might consider whether to insure the furniture. If annual insurance premiums are $2500, a reasonably prudent trustee might decide *not* to insure the furniture as the value of the trust fund will diminish too quickly when compared to the asset being protected. The decision to insure might therefore be in

30 Ibid 562.

31 *Kirwan v Cresvale Far East Ltd (in liq)* (2002) 44 ACSR 21, [259]; *National Trustees Executors and Agency Co of Australasia Ltd v Barnes* (1941) 64 CLR 268.

32 F & L [14.3030]. But see M Scott Donald, 'The "proper" approach to a trustee's right to indemnity out of trust assets' (2014) 8(3) *Journal of Equity* 283.

33 (2002) ATPR 41-864; *Sourcebook* 19.3b, p 479.

34 (2002) ATPR 41-864, [47].

35 (2003) 7 VR 287; *Sourcebook* 19.3c, p 482. An application for special leave to appeal to the High Court was refused: [2004] HCATrans 22.

breach of trust due to imprudence. However, Ormiston JA's analysis suggests that the trustee will not automatically be denied indemnity for the premium payments. Reasonableness is not a part of the test as to whether the expense is proper, but it can impact upon quantum.[36] In this case, perhaps *part* of the premiums could be the subject of indemnification.[37]

[19.13] The trustee's right of indemnity for properly incurred expenses may be subject to reduction if there is an outstanding breach of trust. Suppose a trustee has properly incurred expenses of $2000. However, in breach of trust the trustee has misapplied $1000. Should the trustee have a lien over $2000 of trust assets (albeit with personal liability to repay $1000 to the trust) or should the lien be reduced to $1000? In *RWG Management Ltd v Commissioner for Corporate Affairs*,[38] Brooking J indicated that the trustee's right of indemnity was liable to reduction where the trustee had caused a loss to the trust in breach of trust. The court strikes a balance between what the trustee owed the trust, and what the trust owed the trustee, 'netting-off reciprocal monetary obligations'.[39] The Court would not demand that the trustee reinstate the trust fund before claiming indemnification, reducing the indemnity accordingly.

[19.14] To the extent that third parties can claim to be subrogated to the trustee's right of indemnity, the amount available to them is necessarily reduced by an unremedied breach of trust.[40]

Can the trustee's right to indemnity out of trust assets be excluded by the trust instrument?

[19.15] Australian courts have not reached consensus on this point. In Queensland, New South Wales and South Australia, the view is taken that the right of indemnification out of trust assets cannot be excluded, as the right is an intrinsic element of the trustee's office. Queensland's position is statutory.[41] In *JA Pty Ltd v Jonco Holdings Pty Ltd*,[42] Santow J stated that the right of indemnity arose as a necessary incident to the office of trustee, was integral to the institution of the trust, and was for the benefit of the trust and its creditors, whether or not the creditors were aware that they were dealing with a trust.[43] In a South Australian decision, it was said that exclusion of a right to indemnity was contrary to public policy.[44] In *Buckle,* the High Court referred to the 'rights conferred upon the trustee as a necessary incident of the office

36 (2003) 7 VR 287, 308.

37 In 2015, the Victorian Court of Appeal commented that a trustee would not be indemnified where a liability was incurred in breach of the trustee's obligation to perform the trust with reasonable diligence and care. However, the standard of care expected was that 'which might reasonably be expected of a trustee objectively but not over-zealously enforced': *Wales v Wales* (2015) 16 ASTLR 236, [41]–[42].

38 [1985] VR 385.

39 *Re Kaupthing Singer & Friedlander Ltd [No 2]* [2012] 1 AC 804, 813 [8]; *Carter Holt Harvey* [31].

40 This position is not without its critics. See HAJ Ford, 'Trading Trusts and Creditors' Rights' (1981) 13(1) *Melbourne University Law Review* 1.

41 Qld s 65. See also *Kemtron Industries Pty Ltd v Commissioner of Stamp Duties (Qld)* [1984] 1 Qd R 576; *Jessup v Queensland Housing Commission* [2002] 2 Qd R 270, 275 [14].

42 (2000) 33 ACSR 691; see also *Agusta Pty Ltd v Provident Capital Ltd* (2012) 16 BPR 30,397.

43 Ibid 713.

44 *Moyes v J & L Developments Pty Ltd (No 2)* (2007) LSJS 61, [40].

of trustee'.[45] More recently, Bell, Gageler and Nettle JJ commented in *Carter Holt Harvey* that the trustee's lien over trust assets in support of a right of indemnity 'arises endogenously as an incident of the office of trustee in respect of trust assets'.[46] In both instances, the comments were obiter.

This does not, however, appear to be the position in all Australian jurisdictions. In Victoria, s 2(3) of the *Trustee Act 1958* allows statutory provisions to be overridden by an express term in the trust instrument. In *RWG Management Ltd v Commissioner for Corporate Affairs*,[47] Brooking J held that, as a matter of statutory interpretation, the statutory right to indemnification could be altered or excluded by appropriate provision in the trust instrument. His Honour considered the arguments raised in other Australian jurisdictions but took a different approach. He reasoned that if the trustee's personal rights for indemnification against a beneficiary could be excluded by the trustee's agreement,[48] it was difficult to see why the right to indemnification out of trust assets should be treated differently. His Honour commented: 'If a trustee is willing to accept office where the trust instrument ousts his indemnity, I do not see why he should not be free to do so'.[49] In Western Australia, it has been held that the trustee's right of indemnity can be excluded by the trust instrument, or released by the trustee, unless the purpose of the exclusion or release is to fraudulently defeat trust creditors.[50]

The position in Victoria and Western Australia[51] may not be ideal for trust creditors. It will often be impractical to expect trade creditors to insist on inspection of the trust instrument, especially if they have no notice of the trust.[52] Nevertheless, as the following section shows, there appears to be relatively widespread acceptance that, absent statutory prohibition, exclusion clauses are effective in trusts law.

Liability of directors of trustee companies

Many trustees are corporations, particularly in the case of unit trusts and trading trusts. [19.16]
Instruments setting up these trusts may contain provisions excluding indemnification from trust assets. The insolvency of the corporation raises the real prospect that unsecured creditors will not recover debts incurred by the corporation acting as trustee even though the trust may have assets to cover the debts.[53]

Federal legislation to overcome this problem makes directors of corporate trustees liable for debts in certain cases where the right of indemnity is excluded or lost. Section 197 of the *Corporations Act 2001* (Cth) holds a director of a corporation acting as a trustee liable to

45 *Buckle* [50].
46 *Carter Holt Harvey* [83].
47 [1985] VR 385.
48 See [19.21].
49 [1985] VR 385, 395.
50 *Franknelly Nominees Pty Ltd v Abrugiato* (2013) 10 ASTLR 558, [235].
51 It is likely that this is also the position in Tasmania: see *Trustee Act 1898* (Tas) s 64.
52 An exclusion of the right to indemnity may not be enforceable against trust creditors: see Ford (n 40) 14, 17–18.
53 This presents fewer difficulties where the trustee is an individual because, even if the trust instrument contained a clause restricting recovery from trust assets, the trustee would remain personally liable for the debt.

discharge the debts of the corporation if the corporation has not and cannot discharge the liability, and the corporation is not entitled to indemnification out of trust assets for reasons including breach of trust and the inclusion of an exclusion clause in the trust instrument.

The section accepts the validity of such exclusion clauses (contrary to the views discussed at [19.15] above), but instead attacks the directors who have overseen the incurring of the trust's debt. Subsection (b) suggests that the view that the trustee's right of indemnity can be set off against the trustee's liability for breach of trust is correct[54] in that it anticipates that the right of indemnity might only be lost in part.

Section 197 does not apply, however, merely because the corporate trustee lacks the funds to discharge its debts. Personal liability only attaches to the directors where the directors' right of indemnity is compromised by breach of trust, actions outside the scope of its powers, or the presence of a clause excluding the right of indemnity. The protection offered by s 197 may therefore be of little comfort to trust creditors. If the corporate trustee has a full right of indemnity, but the trust assets are insufficient to discharge the indemnity, its directors will not incur personal liability for the debts.

Third parties and the trustee's right of indemnity

[19.17] Parties who have advanced credit to a trust by contracting with a trustee are entitled to be subrogated to the trustee's right of recoupment out of the trust assets. (This means that they effectively 'stand in the trustee's shoes' and can access the property represented by the trustee's right of indemnity.) Creditors are limited to the assets secured by the lien in respect of the properly incurred expenses, as discussed in [19.8]. Matters become complicated, however, where the *trustee* is insolvent.

Upon insolvency, and after secured creditors have satisfied their securities, the trustee's remaining assets will be available for distribution among his unsecured creditors. Because the trustee's interest in the trust assets raised by the right of indemnity is proprietary, that interest passes to the trustee in bankruptcy on insolvency.[55] The trust assets that are needed to discharge the indemnity may therefore be available for distribution among the trustee's own personal creditors.

Nevertheless, the question whether the property received via the trustee's right of indemnity can be used to pay the trustee's general creditors (no matter how those debts arose) or whether it should only be used to discharge debts incurred by the trustee on behalf of the trust has been much debated. In *Re Byrne Australia Pty Ltd*,[56] Needham J held that the proceeds of a right of indemnity could only be used to discharge trust debts and were not available for distribution among general creditors. In contrast, in *Re Enhill Pty Ltd*,[57] the Full Court of the Supreme Court of Victoria held that the trustee's liquidator could be paid its fees out of the proceeds of a right of indemnity. It was said that the trustee's lien is a personal asset of the trustee and available for distribution among all creditors.[58]

54 See [19.12].
55 *Octavo Investments Pty Ltd v Knight* (1979) 144 CLR 454.
56 [1981] 1 NSWLR 394.
57 [1983] 1 VR 561.
58 See also *Nolan v Collie* (2003) 7 VR 287, 313 where *Re Enhill* was distinguished at 313.

The liquidator was also allowed to recover costs in *Re Suco Gold Pty Ltd*;[59] however, the reasoning used by the Court appears to support the *Re Byrne* position that the proceeds of a right of indemnity can only be used to discharge trust debts. Further, the Court was critical of the *Re Enhill* reasoning.[60] In *Re Suco Gold Pty Ltd*, a corporate trustee of two unit trusts was insolvent. Its only assets were its rights to be indemnified for trust expenses. If the rights of indemnity could only be used to discharge existing trust debts, the company's winding-up could not proceed, as there would be no funds for the liquidator's fees. The Full Court in South Australia drew a distinction between cases where the trustee was seeking reimbursement for expenses already paid and cases where the debts had not been discharged. If the debt had been discharged, and the trustee sought reimbursement, then the proceeds of that reimbursement could be distributed among the trustee's general creditors. But if the trust debt had not been discharged, moneys coming into the liquidator's hands on behalf of the trust could only be used to discharge trust debts. King CJ classified the liquidator's expenses as trust expenses. His Honour noted that the trust could not be performed unless the liquidation proceeded; therefore, it was 'reasonable to regard the expenses mentioned above as debts of the company incurred in discharging the duties imposed by the trust and as covered by the trustee's right of indemnity'.[61]

The matter has now been settled in the High Court in *Carter Holt Harvey,* where the *Suco Gold* reasoning was preferred. In *Carter Holt Harvey,* a company called Amerind Pty Ltd went into liquidation. Its sole business was as a trustee of a trading trust. Apart from a nominal paid-up capital, it had no assets of its own. All of its creditors were trust creditors. A dispute arose about distribution of the remaining surplus, and in particular, whether s 433 of the *Corporations Act 2001* (Cth) applied so as to determine that distribution. It was not necessary for the Court to decide whether *Suco Gold* was to be preferred to *Re Enhill.* Nevertheless, the Court was unanimous in its obiter support of the *Suco Gold* approach[62]. If the trustee has discharged a trust liability out of its own pocket and is seeking reimbursement from trust assets, the interest in the trust assets raised by the right of indemnity is the trustee's own asset and available for general distribution. But if the trust debts have not been discharged by the trustee, and the trustee is seeking exoneration out of trust assets, the trust assets can only be used to discharge trust creditors. The trustee personally has no right to that money and the trustee's creditors cannot be in a better position than the trustee itself was.

Indemnification by the beneficiaries

Since the trustee assumes personal risk for the benefit of the beneficiaries of the trust, the beneficiaries may be liable to indemnify the trustee personally where the indemnity cannot be satisfied out of trust assets. This liability can arise in a number of ways. First, there is a rule that where a trustee is acting as trustee at the request of one or more beneficiary, those beneficiaries are liable to indemnify the trustee for losses made performing [19.18]

59 (1983) 33 SASR 99.
60 Ibid 105.
61 Ibid 110.
62 *Carter Holt Harvey* [42]–[44] (Kiefel CJ, Keane and Edleman JJ), [94]–[96] (Bell, Gageler and Nettle JJ), [153]–[154] (Gordon J).

the trust.[63] Secondly, there is statutory protection for a trustee who commits a breach of trust at the instigation or with the consent of a beneficiary. Here, the court may make an order impounding the beneficiary's interest in the trust estate (or part thereof) in order to indemnify the trustee.[64] More generally, in most Australian jurisdictions,[65] beneficiaries are liable to indemnify the trustee on the basis that justice requires that beneficiaries who have the benefit of the trust should bear its burdens.[66]

[19.19] In *Hardoon v Belilios*,[67] the plaintiff held partly-paid shares in a bank on behalf of the defendant. When the bank went into liquidation, the plaintiff was liable to pay the subscription price on the shares in full. He sought indemnification from the defendant. The Privy Council held that the trustee's right of indemnity included an *in personam* right against the beneficiary in addition to the *in rem* right against the trust assets.

[19.20] The *Hardoon* principle was extended to multiple *sui juris* beneficiaries in *JW Broomhead (Vic) Pty Ltd (in liq) v JW Broomhead Pty Ltd*.[68] The trustee of a unit trust incurred debts of around $70 000, and was otherwise insolvent. Units in the unit trust were held in differing proportions. Three companies held 42%, 10% and 24% units respectively. The company holding 24% was itself in liquidation. The remaining 24% unit was held by a husband and wife jointly. The wife had no knowledge of the trust and disclaimed her interest. The husband claimed that he held the units as trustee for a sub-trust, the beneficiaries of which were infants. The question arose whether the individual beneficiaries were liable to reimburse the trustee, and if so, the proportions in which they were liable.

McGarvie J held that the beneficiaries were only liable to indemnify the trustee to the extent that they benefited from the trust, and were not required to make up the shortfall caused by one beneficiary's insolvency. Under the circumstances where the wife had disclaimed the trust, the husband should only be liable to indemnify the trustee for the liability attaching to one half of their joint interest, as he had never expected being entitled to the interest in full. However, holding his interest on sub-trust for infant beneficiaries did not exempt him from liability. Although, on the basis of the rule in *Hardoon*, a trustee cannot recover from infant beneficiaries (discussed below), the trustee here was entitled to ignore any sub-trust an adult beneficiary may have declared. In effect, the trustee is entitled to 'rule a line' across the chain of beneficial entitlement. The trustee can recover from the beneficiaries (assuming they are *sui juris*) and can leave it to those beneficiaries to recover from their sub-beneficiaries if there is a sub-trust.

In *Broomhead*, all beneficiaries of the primary trust had the same interest (albeit in different proportions) and were together absolutely entitled to the trust estate. The decision in *Hardoon* indicates that in other cases there will be limitations on the principle of allowing the trustee to recover against beneficiaries. Lord Lindley said that where there were trusts for life tenants or infants, or where the trust itself limited the right of indemnity, the beneficiaries would not be required to indemnify the trustee personally.[69]

63 *Matthews v Ruggles-Brise* [1911] 1 Ch 194.
64 ACT s 86; NSW s 86; NT s 50; Qld s 77; SA s 57; Tas s 53; Vic s 68; WA s 76.
65 See discussion below at [19.23]
66 *Hardoon v Belilios* [1901] AC 118; *Sourcebook* 19.4a, p 486.
67 [1901] AC 118.
68 [1985] VR 891; *Sourcebook* 19.4b, p 487.
69 *Hardoon v Belilios* [1901] AC 118, 127.

Strictly speaking, Lindley LJ's comment only indicates that a life tenant would not be liable to indemnify a trustee personally, and says nothing about the position of the capital beneficiaries. It would seem strange that the presence of life tenants could completely destroy a trustee's right to seek indemnity from all the beneficiaries when the trust property was insufficient. As the law is otherwise able to apportion expenses between capital and income beneficiaries, it is unclear why a similar process could not be employed to allocate responsibility for trustee indemnification to both income and capital beneficiaries. If capital beneficiaries *never* receive a benefit, however, because the trust becomes insolvent during the life tenancy, it is hard to argue that they should carry responsibility for the burden.

It is also unclear why the presence of infant beneficiaries necessarily destroys the trustee's rights against adult beneficiaries of the trust. Infant beneficiaries are protected from the liability to indemnify in that they cannot be held in equity to have accepted the benefit of the trust while under the age of majority. Assuming the trust was insolvent prior to the infant turning 18 years of age, the infant could simply disclaim the trust on majority and thus avoid liability. Where all beneficiaries are infants, all can obviously disclaim. But there is little justification for protecting adult beneficiaries where a trust has both infant and adult beneficiaries. If the adult beneficiaries have received a benefit, the *Hardoon* principle should extend to them on the basis that they should also bear the burden.

Where a trustee agrees to act as trustee under an instrument that limits its rights of recovery to trust assets, he cannot be heard to complain when trust property is insufficient to discharge the indemnity. The issue becomes more complicated, however, when the trustee is insolvent. Creditors who deal with the trustee on trust business may not know of the limitation in the instrument. Although it was accepted in *Hardoon* and subsequent cases[70] that such limitations are possible, it has sometimes been argued that they should be invalid. In *McLean v Burns Philp Trustee Co Pty Ltd*,[71] it was held that limitation clauses are valid although equity will not allow such clauses to be used as a vehicle for fraud. [19.21]

The rule in *Hardoon v Belilios* only applies to beneficiaries who have a vested interest in the trust. It does not apply to objects of a discretionary trust. As they cannot insist the trustee distribute in their favour, they cannot be expected to bear the burdens of the trust. Nor does the rule apply to the shareholders of a corporate beneficiary[72]. [19.22]

However, the rule in *Hardoon v Belilios* no longer applies in New South Wales. Section 100A of the *Trustee Act 1925* (NSW),[73] which came into effect in November 2019, abolished it, albeit with some minor exceptions. The change is apparently referrable to a view that the rule is 'an obstacle to the use of trusts in commerce'.[74] Section 100A(2) states that a beneficiary is not liable to indemnify a trustee unless the beneficiary has agreed in writing to be liable; however, under subsection (3) the trustee can still recover from the beneficiary an amount the beneficiary is liable to pay for a right, interest, or entitlement to profits, income or trust returns in relation to an investment trust.[75] [19.23]

70 *RWG Management Ltd v Commissioner for Corporate Affairs* [1985] VR 385, 395.
71 (1985) 2 NSWLR 623, 640–1.
72 *Chief Commissioner of State Revenue v CCM Holdings Trust Pty Ltd* [2014] NSWCA 42, [74]–[76].
73 See *Sourcebook* 19.4c, p 491.
74 J Campbell, 'The New s 100A *Trustee Act 1925* (NSW): When a Beneficiary is Personally Liable to Indemnify a Trustee' (2020) 14(2) *Journal of Equity* 103, 106.
75 For a discussion of when a beneficiary may or will still be liable to the trustee see Campbell (n 74).

Creditor's rights to be subrogated to the trustee's personal indemnification by beneficiaries

[19.24] Although creditors can be subrogated to a trustee's right of indemnity out of trust assets it is not clear whether they can be subrogated to the trustee's personal rights against beneficiaries. The decisions on this point are contradictory. In *Marginson v Ian Potter & Co*,[76] it was assumed that creditors could be subrogated to the trustee's personal right against beneficiaries. In *Ron Kingham Real Estate Pty Ltd v Edgar*,[77] McPherson JA in the Queensland Court of Appeal thought that creditors could subrogate to the rights against beneficiaries without first seeking to recover trust assets. However, in another decision of the same court,[78] the *Ron Kingham* case was distinguished on its facts. It was said that a creditor had to exhaust its claim against the trustee (ie in respect of the lien over trust assets) before proceeding against beneficiaries. Moreover, it was suggested that the creditor's rights were limited to the trustee's proprietary right over trust assets.[79] This later decision has been the subject of some criticism.[80]

Trustee's right to impound beneficiary's interest

[19.25] Where a beneficiary has participated in a breach of trust by instigating it or requesting it, the court has statutory power to impound all or part of the beneficiary's interest in the trust in order to indemnify the trustee.[81]

[19.26] The statutory power is thought to be wider than the power that existed at general law.[82] Nevertheless, the protection given to trustees here is relatively limited. In *Re Somerset*,[83] two life tenants requested that the trustees alter trust investments. Some negligence occurred in the reinvestment, causing loss to the trust. Later, one life tenant and the capital beneficiaries sued for breach of trust. The Court of Appeal held that the section had no application where the trustee's act was not in itself a breach of trust but became one because of the trustee's negligence. The life tenants had here asked the trustees to act within their powers and they were entitled to expect that the trustees would act with the appropriate level of care. Therefore, the trustee could not impound the life tenant's interest.

Trustee's right of contribution from co-trustees

[19.27] Multiple trustees are jointly and severally liable for breach of trust. Frequently, only one of several trustees will discharge a liability for breach of trust. The general rule is that the

76 (1976) 136 CLR 161.
77 [1999] 2 Qd R 439.
78 *Belar Pty Ltd (in liq) v Mahaffey* [2000] 1 Qd R 477.
79 Ibid 488.
80 G Dal Pont, *Equity and Trusts in Australia* (Lawbook Co, 5th ed, 2011) 681, n 144.
81 ACT s 86(1); NSW s 86(1); NT s 50; Qld s 77; SA s 57; Tas s 53; Vic s 68; WA s 76.
82 *Bolton v Curre* [1895] 1 Ch 544, 549.
83 [1894] 1 Ch 231.

trustee who discharges the debt can seek contribution and recoupment from the other trustees of their appropriate share.

A trustee can sometimes call for full indemnification from his co-trustees, rather than simple contribution. In *Goodwin v Duggan*,[84] two trustees were liable for a breach of trust. One had misused trust funds for his own benefit, but the other was liable for having improperly delegated her duties to him. While both trustees were liable to the beneficiary for the breach of trust, the honest (but passive) trustee was entitled to be indemnified fully by the trustee who had benefited from the breach. Further, one trustee might be required to indemnify fellow trustees in full where the fellow trustees were entitled to, and did, rely upon the first trustee's advice which proved to be negligent.[85] Solicitor-trustees are usually required to indemnify co-trustees, but the principle is not limited to solicitors.[86] **[19.28]**

Finally, there is an overlap between the law relating to a trustee's right to impound a beneficiary's interest, and the trustee's right to contribution in the situation where one of the trustees in breach of trust is also a beneficiary and acquiesced in the breach. The loss for breach of trust is here discharged first out of the interest of the trustee/beneficiary. That person cannot seek contribution from co-trustees until the loss exceeds the beneficiary's interest. In *Chillingworth v Chambers*,[87] a joint trustee was also one of the beneficiaries. The trustees lost trust money through unauthorised investments. Although the trustees were held to be jointly and severally liable for the breach, the loss was paid out of the trustee/beneficiary's share of the estate. The trustee/beneficiary was not entitled to contribution from his co-trustee. The usual principle of contribution did not apply because the trustee/beneficiary (in his role as beneficiary) had been a party to the breach of trust and was liable to indemnify the trustee out of his share of the trust. **[19.29]**

Trustee's right to recover overpayment from a beneficiary

Should a beneficiary be overpaid,[88] the trustee can withhold payments from that beneficiary's share of the trust fund, if any.[89] If that beneficiary's share of the trust fund has been exhausted, however, the trustee will need to recover the overpayment directly from the beneficiary. Equity was generally unsympathetic to trustees in that position,[90] especially if repayment would cause hardship to the beneficiary. **[19.30]**

The modern position is that the beneficiary is liable to a common law action of money had and received for money paid by mistake, subject only to a defence of change of position.[91] The trustee can also trace funds into the hands of the beneficiary, as the beneficiary is a **[19.31]**

84 (1996) 41 NSWLR 158.
85 *Re Linsley* [1904] 2 Ch 785.
86 *Bahin v Hughes* (1886) 31 Ch D 390, 395–7.
87 [1895] 1 Ch 685.
88 For example, a life tenant could be paid more income than that to which they were entitled.
89 This extends to income later received into the trust fund: *Burns v Leda Holdings Pty Ltd* [1988] 1 Qd R 214, 227.
90 See *Merriman v Perpetual Trustee Co Ltd* (1895) 17 LR (NSW) Eq 325.
91 *Wendt v Orr* [2004] WASC 28.

volunteer, and may be able to recover the funds, depending on the use the beneficiary has made of them.[92] The right to trace is lost by dissipation of the trust property,[93] and in that eventuality the trustee may have to resort to the common law action.

Trustee's right to seek directions from the court

[19.32] One of the most valuable rights possessed by a trustee is the right to approach the court for advice and direction. The trustee who seeks the court's advice is in a highly protected position. The advice given by the court is decisive, and binding on all parties. So long as the trustee follows the advice (and made full disclosure of all relevant facts to the court when seeking advice), the trustee will not liable for breach of trust. In most States, approaching the court for advice is regulated by statute,[94] though the terminology differs between jurisdictions. Tasmania lacks legislation on the point, but it is possible its court exercises an inherent or implied jurisdiction to give advice.[95]

[19.33] In the *Macedonian Church case*, the High Court said that the right to seek advice must be read in conjunction with the statutory power to relieve a trustee wholly or in part for a breach of trust.[96] This indicated that it was desirable that trustees who were unsure what to do should seek the court's advice first, rather than seek relief from personal liability later.[97] Advice can be sought as to construction of the terms of the trust, the management and administration of the trust, and as to whether or not to commence or defend litigation. The court will not necessarily give the advice sought; the decision to withhold advice will depend on the circumstances of the case.

[19.34] The advice the court gives is private advice to the trustee, designed to give personal protection to the trustee. Nevertheless, the advice binds all parties. It is not necessary to give notice of the application for advice to any person unless the advice concerns the identity or rights of the beneficiaries, or unless the court requires notice to be given. A person who claims to be prejudiced as a beneficiary by any distribution of the trustee pursuant to the court's advice can apply to the court for any appropriate order.

[19.35] Seeking the court's advice delivers another advantage to the trustee. If the trustee follows the court's advice, the trustee will not have committed a breach of trust, and expenses incurred in steps taken to follow that advice will be properly incurred expenses for the purposes of the trustee's right of indemnity. This includes the costs of defending an action for breach of trust against the trustee. A trustee who fails to seek the court's advice concerning litigation may not be able to claim costs incurred as properly incurred expenses.[98] In the *Macedonian*

92 See chapter 21.

93 *Re Diplock* [1948] Ch 465.

94 *Trustee Act 1925* (ACT) s 63; *Trustee Act 1925* (NSW) s 63; *Supreme Court Rules* (NT) ord 54.02; *Trusts Act 1973* (Qld) s 96; *Trustee Act 1936* (SA) s 91; *Supreme Court (General Civil Procedure) Rules 2005* (Vic) ord 54.02(2); *Trustees Act 1962* (WA) s 92.

95 *Macedonian Orthodox Community Church St Petka Inc v His Eminence Petar the Diocesan Bishop of the Macedonian Orthodox Diocese of Australia and New Zealand* (2008) 237 CLR 66 ('*Macedonian Church case*'); *Sourcebook* 19.5a, p 492.

96 This legislation is common to all Australian jurisdictions: see ACT s 85; NSW s 85; NT s 49A; Qld s 76; SA s 56; Tas s 50; Vic s 67; WA s 75. See [20.20].

97 *Macedonian Church case* (2008) 237 CLR 66, 93.

98 Failure of a trustee to seek advice does not necessarily preclude it from being indemnified for its legal costs as a properly incurred expense: *Grizonic v Suttor* [2011] NSWSC 471.

Church case, the majority of the High Court said that 'a trustee who is sued should take no step in defence of the suit without first obtaining judicial advice about whether it is proper to defend the proceedings.'[99] Well-advised trustees now commonly seek the court's advice as to whether or not to defend an action for breach of trust, or to commence proceedings on behalf of the trust, in order to preserve the trustee's right of indemnity for its legal costs.[100]

WHAT'S ONLINE?

Available at www.cambridge.org/highereducation/isbn/9781009232388/resources:

- Recommended further readings
- Discussion topics
- Practice problem

99 *Macedonian Church case* (2008) 237 CLR 66, 94. See also S Kiefel, 'Judicial Advice to Trustees: Its Origins, Purposes and Nature' (2019) 42(3) *Melbourne University Law Review* 993.

100 See, eg, *Re Bideena* (2016) 334 ALR 146; *Bianca Rinehart trading as trustee of the Hope Margaret Hancock Trust* [2017] NSWSC 282.

PART G

BREACH OF TRUST

20

BREACH OF TRUST: DEFENCES AND REMEDIES

Introduction

Put simply, a breach of trust occurs whenever the trustee fails to perform one of the duties or obligations discussed in earlier chapters. This chapter is not, therefore, principally concerned with *how* a breach of trust occurs. Instead, the focus is on the *consequences* of a breach of trust. [20.1]

There are many different duties that can be breached by a trustee; the consequences that attend a breach will depend on the nature of the breach.

A breach of trust does not automatically mean that the trustee must compensate the trust, in the sense that breach of a common law obligation exposes the defendant to liability for damages. First, the breach may be of a minor or merely technical nature or may not call for relief in monetary terms. Secondly, no matter how poorly the trustee has performed his obligations, if he has not been dishonest, he may be protected by a valid exculpation given by the trust instrument. Further opportunities for relief are given by explicit statutory provisions and by the general law. Finally, it must always be borne in mind that equity's remedies are discretionary.[1] Courts try to give effect to the terms of the trust and will utilise the appropriate remedy to achieve that aim. Exculpatory provisions, defences and remedies for breach of trust are discussed below. [20.2]

Exculpation and defences

There are three sources of trustees' defences. Nowadays, the most important of these is the trust instrument itself. Professionally drawn trust instruments invariably contain provisions excusing breaches of trust or limiting liability in the case of loss. Statutory provisions also provide some protection to trustees. Finally, as the law of trusts is a branch of equity, general equitable defences such as laches and acquiescence apply. [20.3]

Exculpation in the trust instrument

Most, but not all, liability for breach of trust can be excluded by specific provision in the trust instrument. The trustee bears the burden of establishing that the loss in question is covered by any exemption clause.[2] Such clauses are always interpreted strictly, according to the natural meaning of the words used, and any ambiguities are resolved against the interests of the party seeking to rely on the clause. In *Wight v Olswang*,[3] professional trustees decided to sell a parcel of shares held by the trust in stages. This strategy made a lower return to the trust than if the shares had all been sold at the outset. When the beneficiaries sought compensation for breach of trust, the trustees attempted to rely on exemption clauses contained in the trust instrument. The instrument was ambiguous as to whether paid trustees (as these were) could claim the benefit of the clauses. It was held that, while exemption clauses should be fairly construed according to the natural meaning of their words, the Court should not construe the clause broadly. On the construction of the clauses in this case, the trustees were not protected. [20.4]

1 See chapter 2.
2 *Reader v Fried* [2001] VSC 495.
3 [1999] EWCA Civ 1309.

[20.5] Exemption clauses in trust instruments are controversial. It is frequently argued that such clauses are over-generous to trustees and prejudicial to the interests of beneficiaries. This concern is magnified where professional trustees who are paid for their services attempt to rely on such clauses. These arguments were considered in *Armitage v Nurse*.[4] A beneficiary sued in relation to breaches causing loss to the trust fund. Clause 15 of the trust instrument exempted the trustees from liability for any loss or damage to the income or capital of the fund unless such loss or damage was caused by *their own actual fraud*.

The Court of Appeal held that allowing a trust instrument to exclude or restrict a trustee's liability for breach of trust was not contrary to public policy. A trustee's liability for negligence could therefore be excluded. It would, however, offend public policy to allow an exemption clause to exclude liability for actual fraud or dishonesty.

The words 'actual fraud' used in *Armitage* were contrasted to 'equitable fraud'. Actual fraud involves some form of conscious wrongdoing by the trustee in the sense of knowing his actions are contrary to the beneficiary's interests or being recklessly indifferent to those interests. The exemption clause in this case still excluded liability for 'equitable fraud', such as an innocent breach of fiduciary obligation.[5]

The beneficiary argued that this interpretation would mean that the trustee's responsibilities would fall below 'the irreducible core of obligations owed by trustees to beneficiaries', and thus not conform to the concept of a 'trust'. Millett LJ agreed that there was an 'irreducible core' of obligations that a beneficiary must be able to enforce, without which there would be no trust. But he did not accept that these core obligations included 'duties of skill and care, prudence and diligence'. He said that 'the duty of the trustees to perform the trust honestly and in good faith for the benefit of the beneficiaries is the minimum necessary to give substance to the trusts'. As none of the allegations against the trustee involved actual fraud, he was entitled to rely on the clause for protection.

[20.6] What obligations constitute the 'irreducible core' of a trust is uncertain. In addition to the duty to perform the trust honestly and in good faith (if that is an independent obligation, as opposed to being a standard which all trustees must observe in performing all their obligations), the duty to adhere to the terms of the trust is recognised as a core obligation.[6] On the other hand, it has been held that a trustee's duty to provide information to an object of a discretionary trust is not 'core' for the purpose of determining the scope of an exculpation clause.[7]

4 [1998] Ch 241; *Sourcebook* 20.3.1a, p 504. See also *Ausralian Securities and Investments Commission v Drake (No 2)* (2016) 340 ALR 75, [281]–[285] (Edelman J), confirming the application of *Armitage v Nurse* to assumed obligations but declining to consider whether it applied to fiduciary duties and duties only to engage in authorised transactions. *Armitage v Nurse* also applies to a statutory duty of care unless the statute prohibits exclusion: *Australian Securities and Investments Commission v Drake (No 2)* (2016) 340 ALR 75, [260] (Edelman J).

5 The use of the term 'actual fraud' was important, as the clause thereby extended protection to losses caused by mere constructive or equitable fraud. See also *Green v Wilden Pty Ltd* (2009) 38 WAR 429, [162]: a breach of an equitable obligation was not necessarily an act of 'personal conscious fraudulent bad faith' where the exculpation clause did not cover such an act.

6 *Crossman v Sheahan* (2016) 115 ACSR 130, [308] (Ward JA). See chapter 17.

7 *Segelov v Ernst & Young Services Pty Ltd* (2015) 89 NSWLR 431. The Court of Appeal also held that the trustee was under no obligation to inform a beneficiary of a discretionary trust of her entitlement. See also *Citibank NA v MBIA Assurance SA* [2007] 1 All ER (Comm) 475 (contractual fettering of trustee's exercise of discretionary powers); A Trukhtanov, 'The Irreducible Core of Trust Obligations' (2007) 123(3) *Law Quarterly Review* 342.

Although the protection given by an exemption clause such as the *Armitage* clause is extensive, it is not absolute. First, loss-causing breaches that are dishonest or committed in bad faith will attract liability. Millett LJ indicated that a trustee acts dishonestly if he acts in a way he does not honestly believe is in the beneficiary's interests or acts with the intention of benefiting himself or others who are not objects of the trust.[8] [20.7]

Secondly, and this may depend upon the wording of the clause, protection is limited to excluding liability for loss or damage. If the breach complained of does not result in loss or damage, the exemption clause is not engaged. Millett LJ gave the example of a claim for rescission of a contract of sale of trust property to the trustee in breach of the self-dealing rule.[9] A beneficiary is entitled to rescission in such a case without having to show that a loss has been caused; a trustee would not be able to rely on an exemption clause to preserve the contract. [20.8]

For the same reason, a clause excluding liability for loss will not excuse the trustee from liability to account for the management of a trust; for example, where the trustee has been ordered to make restitution of money misappropriated from the trust.[10] In such a case, no loss has to be proved beyond the fact that the trustee made an unauthorised payment from the trust. Likewise, a clause in *Armitage* terms would not excuse a breach of the profits rule, as the beneficiary's complaint is that the trustee has made an unauthorised profit, not that the trustee has caused a loss to the trust fund. [20.9]

Finally, a trustee who deliberately prefers his own interests to the duty owed to the trust would be dishonest in the sense employed by Millett LJ in *Armitage*. In the Victorian decision of *Reader v Fried*,[11] it was held that trustees who had preferred their own interests had not established that they had acted honestly and were therefore not entitled to rely on an exemption clause. The burden of proof rested on the trustees to show that they had not acted dishonestly in preferring their own interests. [20.10]

Millett LJ in *Armitage* construed dishonesty narrowly. Even deliberate breaches of trust were not dishonest if the breach was committed in good faith and in the honest belief the step was in the best interests of the beneficiaries. Indolence, imprudence, lack of diligence, negligence and wilfulness did not of themselves amount to dishonesty.[12] However, in the later decision of *Walker v Stones*,[13] the Court of Appeal appeared to retreat slightly from the *Armitage* view. The beneficiaries under a trust set up by their father complained that professional trustees (solicitors) had invested, in breach of trust, with the primary intention of benefiting their father who was not an object of the trust. An exemption clause excluded liability for anything other than 'wilful fraud or dishonesty' of the trustee. The Court of Appeal held that it was dishonest for a trustee/solicitor deliberately to commit a breach of trust which no reasonable trustee/solicitor could have thought to be in the interests of the beneficiaries. This decision applies an objective test of dishonesty.[14] [20.11]

8 [1998] Ch 241, 251.

9 Ibid 712.

10 *Crossman v Sheahan* (2016) 115 ACSR 130, [313] (Ward JA). See chapter 4.

11 [2001] VSC 495. Cf *Lehtimäki v Cooper* [2020] UKSC 33, [83] (Lady Arden): '[T]here must be some fiduciary duty which the court can enforce but it need not extend to the full range of fiduciary duties which a fiduciary might owe.'

12 [1998] Ch 241, 251.

13 [2001] 2 WLR 623.

14 Cf the definition of dishonesty applied in *Royal Brunei Airlines Sdn Bhd v Tan* [1995] 2 AC 378 for the purpose of imposing liability for dishonestly assisting a breach of fiduciary duty. See [11.17].

[20.12] The clause in *Armitage* was an express exemption clause. Sometimes, exemption from liability is implied from the terms of the trust. In *Wilkins v Hogg*,[15] individual trustees were given an express power to receive trust property. When one trustee absconded with the trust property, it was held that the remaining two were not liable for breach of trust. Because the trust instrument explicitly allowed one trustee to receive property, it impliedly exempted from liability the trustees who had not received the property.

[20.13] A matter for concern is the protection that exemption clauses give trustees from liability for negligence,[16] particularly where a trust is managed by a professional trustee. It can be argued that exemption clauses remove the incentives for trustees to act in the best interests of the beneficiaries. Millett LJ identified these concerns in *Armitage*, but expressed the view that any step to reduce the efficacy of exemption clauses should be taken by Parliament, not the courts.[17] Since the *Armitage* decision, several law reform agencies have recommended reform of the law concerning exemption clauses.[18] In Australia, however, except in cases of dishonesty, the efficacy of an exemption clause depends on its construction.

[20.14] Finally, it may in some contexts be important to distinguish between a provision that has the effect that there is no breach of trust (eg, a clause entitling the trustees to act in the interests of parties other than the beneficiaries in particular circumstances) and a clause which excuses a trustee from liability for a breach of trust. The cases discussed in this section have concerned the latter type of clause. The distinction will be relevant to a claim brought against a third party for knowingly receiving property in breach of trust or for knowingly assisting a breach of trust.[19] In the absence of a breach of trust, the third party will not be accountable for 'knowing receipt' or 'knowing assistance'. But the third party will be liable if a breach of trust has been committed even though the trustee is exonerated by the terms of an exemption clause from having to compensate for the breach.[20]

Statutory exculpation

[20.15] There are numerous ways in which trustee legislation across Australia modifies, or removes, liability for breach of trust. In some situations, a trustee is only responsible for its personal default and not for the defaults of others. In relation to investment, statute provides some specific limitations on liability.[21] In addition to these specific exemptions, courts have a general discretionary power to relieve against liability for breach of trust.

15 (1861) 31 LJ Ch 41; 3 Giff 116; 66 ER 346.
16 The concern was expressed by the dissenting judges in *Spread Trustee Company Ltd v Hutcheson* [2011] UKPC 13.
17 [1998] Ch 241, 256.
18 See British Columbia Law Institute, *Exculpation Clauses in Trust Instruments* (Report No 17, March 2002); New Zealand Law Commission, *Some Problems in the Law of Trusts* (Report No 79, April 2002); Law Commission (UK), *Trustee Exemption Clauses* (Report No 301, June 2000).
19 See chapter 11.
20 *Crossman v Sheahan* (2016) 115 ACSR 130, [332] (Ward JA).
21 See [18.28].

Wilful default

Legislation in all Australian jurisdictions provides that a trustee who employs an agent is, generally speaking, not liable for the agent's default, and is only liable for his own wilful default. For example, s 70 of the *Trustees Act 1962* (WA) provides: [20.16]

> **Trustees liable for own defaults etc. only**
> A trustee shall be chargeable only for money and securities actually received by him, notwithstanding his signing any receipt for the sake of conformity; and shall be answerable and accountable only for his own acts, receipts, neglect or defaults, and not for those of any other trustee, nor those of any bank, broker or other person with whom any trust money or securities may be deposited, nor for the insufficiency or deficiency of any securities, nor for any other loss, unless the insufficiency, deficiency or loss occurs through his own wilful default.[22]

The 'wilful default' provisions also protect a trustee from liability for the actions of a co-trustee. The trustee is not protected, however, if the co-trustee's breach is causally linked to the trustee's own breach. For example, if a trustee improperly delegates authority to a co-trustee, she will not be protected from liability for the co-trustee's misdeeds.[23] [20.17]

The meaning of the term 'wilful default' is not entirely clear. It is not certain whether it was intended to exempt negligent trustees. The better view is that 'wilful default' includes negligence, and that, therefore, a trustee who is careless in appointing or supervising an agent will not obtain the protection of the section. In *Dalrymple v Melville*,[24] the defendant trustee allowed a co-trustee control of the trust property. The co-trustee misappropriated trust funds and the defendant trustee was sued for breach of trust. Long Innes J found that the defendant trustee understood what was required of an ordinary prudent man; his failure to act in accordance with the standard amounted to wilful default. On this construction, the word 'wilful' adds nothing to the section. [20.18]

Legislation enacted in Queensland and South Australia has simplified the issue. The relevant section in Queensland requires 'default' rather than 'wilful default'.[25] The South Australian legislation imposes a higher standard than other jurisdictions, imposing liability on the trustee for losses that could be reasonably expected to be foreseen.[26]

Other statutory provisions protect trustees in specific situations, such as where they advertise correctly for missing claimants before they distribute the trust estate.[27] [20.19]

The general statutory defence

Courts have statutory power to relieve trustees from liability where the trustee has been honest, reasonable and ought fairly to be excused the breach of trust, and for failure to [20.20]

22 ACT s 59(2); NSW s 59(2); NT s 26; Qld s 71; SA s 35(1); Tas s 27(1); Vic s 36(1); WA s 70.
23 *Dalrymple v Melville* (1932) 32 SR (NSW) 596; *Sourcebook* 20.3.2d, p 510.
24 (1932) 32 SR (NSW) 596. Cf *Re Vickery* [1931] 1 Ch 572 (construing 'wilful default' to mean a conscious or reckless breach of duty); *Segelov v Ernst & Young Services Pty Ltd* (2015) 89 NSWLR 431, [150]; *Re Bogdanov (No 2)* [2019] VSC 836, [69] (where the issue was said to be whether an executor was 'recklessly careless'). See also G Jones, 'Delegation by Trustees: A Reappraisal' (1959) 22(4) *Modern Law Review* 381.
25 Qld s 71.
26 SA s 35(1A).
27 See, eg, NSW s 61A; Qld s 75; SA s 31; Vic s 34; WA s 74.

obtain the court's directions prior to the breach. The court can excuse the trustee either wholly or in part for such a breach. Courts originally had no power to excuse breaches of trust unless one of the equitable bars such as laches or acquiescence could be made out.[28] This led to harsh results. No matter how diligent, honest and hard-working a trustee had been, a breach of trust resulting in a loss meant that the trustee was obliged to make the loss good personally. The general statutory defence was enacted to remove the injustice by conferring judicial discretion to excuse trustees in certain circumstances. All Australian jurisdictions have a version of the excuse provision.[29]

[20.21] Section 67 of the *Trustee Act 1958* (Vic) provides:

> **Power to relieve trustee from personal liability**
> If it appears to the Court that a trustee, whether appointed by the Court or otherwise, is or may be personally liable for any breach of trust, whether the transaction alleged to be a breach of trust occurred before or after the commencement of this Act, but has acted honestly and reasonably, and ought fairly to be excused for the breach of trust and for omitting to obtain the directions of the Court in the matter in which he committed such breach, then the Court may relieve him either wholly or partly from personal liability for the same.

[20.22] The provision sets a high threshold for excusing trustees from liability. The onus is on the trustee seeking relief to show that she has acted honestly and reasonably.[30] Honesty on its own is insufficient; the trustee's actions must be both honest *and* reasonable. This is demonstrated in *Dalrymple v Melville*,[31] discussed at [20.18]. A trustee was not excused for breach of trust when his co-trustee absconded with the trust assets. Although he had acted honestly, his action of leaving his co-trustee in control of trust property was risky, and he had appreciated the risk. He could not be said to have acted reasonably. Courts commonly refuse to excuse trustee behaviour that has been negligent on the basis it cannot have been reasonable.[32] A trustee who is in breach of the fiduciary profits rule will usually not have acted honestly and cannot claim relief.[33] In *Reader v Fried*,[34] a conflict of duty and interest was held to disqualify a trustee from relief.

[20.23] Even if a trustee can establish that the actions in question were both honest and reasonable, excuse is not automatic. The provision also requires that the trustee ought fairly to be excused. Circumstances may suggest that a trustee should not be excused because it would be unfair to blameless beneficiaries. The court is less likely to excuse professional trustees who are in breach of trust.[35] Conversely, where the trustees have been honest,

28 See chapter 6.

29 ACT s 85; NSW s 85; NT s 49A; Qld s 76; SA s 56; Tas s 50; WA s 75.

30 *Re Stuart* [1897] 2 Ch 583.

31 (1932) 32 SR (NSW) 596.

32 *Bartlett v Barclays Bank Trust Co Ltd* [1980] Ch 515; *Sourcebook* 17.3.7b, p 441; *Pateman v Heyen* (1993) 33 NSWLR 188; *Re Mulligan (deceased)* [1998] 1 NZLR 481.

33 *Boardman v Phipps* [1967] 2 AC 46. See [10.42]. No application for statutory relief could have been made in *Boardman* because the defendants were not trustees. The provision does not apply to other fiduciaries.

34 [2001] VSC 495.

35 *National Trustees of Australasia Ltd v General Finance Co of Australasia Ltd* [1905] AC 375; *Sourcebook* 20.3.2b, p 508; *Bartlett v Barclays Bank Trust Co Ltd* [1980] Ch 515.

sensible if not reasonable, and have caused no real damage to an identifiable beneficiary, the court may excuse the breach. In *Re Umpherstone (deceased)*,[36] a will established two charitable trusts for the award of scholarships. In breach of trust, the trustees mixed the funds of the two trusts and failed to make any appointments in about 40 years. The trustees were unsure what to do – there was no question of dishonesty; the mixing of the funds was sensible although wrong; there was no loss to the corpus of the fund; and no one had been disadvantaged by the failure to make appointments, except perhaps those unidentifiable persons who might otherwise have received a distribution from the charities. Under these circumstances, excuse was appropriate.

It is unclear whether trustees who have acted in accordance with poor legal advice ought fairly to be excused. Cases on this issue turn on their own facts. In *Marsden v Regan*,[37] a trustee administering a small estate took legal advice on the discharge of debts due to the estate. Loss was caused to the estate by the release of some debts. The Court held that the trustee ought fairly to be excused the breach, having taken and relied upon legal advice. In *Re Evans*,[38] however, the trustee was not completely excused for having relied on legal advice. The trustee and her long-lost brother were residuary beneficiaries of an estate. The trustee wished to wind up the estate and, not having heard from her brother for over 30 years, thought it possible he was dead. Acting on legal advice, she took out missing beneficiary insurance to cover the possibility of his return after the estate had been paid out. The brother did return and was paid by the insurer, but the trustee had failed to arrange insurance to cover interest payable on her brother's share. She was excused the breach of trust in respect of having paid out his share and allowed the cost of the insurance policy as a trust expense but was not forgiven the breach in respect of the interest due on the capital despite the fact she had acted on legal advice. [20.24]

The provision also allows the court to excuse the trustee's failure to obtain the directions of the court in the matter in which he committed such breach. This is a reminder to the trustee that the best protection against liability comes from approaching the court for directions in cases of doubt. The trustee's ability to obtain directions is discussed at [17.8].[39] Nevertheless, if the trustee fails to seek the court's directions first, the court is not precluded from excusing the subsequent breach merely on that ground. It is usually the case that a court asked for directions would probably have given permission for the trustee to act as the trustee did. If the trustee would have been given advance approval, he is likely to be given retrospective exculpation for the breach.[40] [20.25]

36 (1990) 53 SASR 293. The trustee may be relieved from having to compensate the trust for some, but not all, the consequences of a breach: *Re Sir Colin and Lady MacKenzie Trust (No 2)* [2020] VSC 335.

37 [1954] 1 WLR 423. A trustee's failure to consult a solicitor may well be unreasonable, even if honest: *Partridge v Equity Trustees, Executors & Agency Co Ltd* (1947) 75 CLR 149. See also [20.16]–[20.18] for the relevance of the 'wilful default' provision in trustee legislation to this situation.

38 [1999] 2 All ER 777.

39 For a full discussion of the jurisdiction to give advice, see *Macedonian Orthodox Community Church St Petka Inc v His Eminence Petar the Diocesan Bishop of the Macedonian Orthodox Diocese of Australia and New Zealand* (2008) 237 CLR 66; *Sourcebook* 19.5a, p 492; S Kiefel, 'Judicial Advice to Trustees: Its Origins, Purposes and Nature' (2019) 42(3) *Melbourne University Law Review* 993.

40 *Kerferd v Perpetual Executors and Trustees Association of Australasia Ltd* (1893) 19 VLR 700, 706 (Holroyd J).

Equitable defences

[20.26] All discretionary considerations that influence the granting of an equitable remedy apply to remedies for breaches of trust. These were discussed in chapter 6. In this section, we discuss the defence of consent and the associated topics of acquiescence and release, as some issues are particular to the trust. The general position is that a trustee will not be liable when the beneficiary[41] consents to the breach of trust, acquiesces in the breach, or later releases the trustee from its obligations. The onus of proof lies on the trustee to establish such a defence.

Consent

[20.27] A beneficiary can validly consent to a breach of trust where a trustee has made full disclosure of the circumstances of the breach and of the legal consequences of committing it. The leading Australian decision is *Spellson v George*.[42] A beneficiary found himself in a difficult position with his overbearing and wealthy father-in-law. The son-in-law was an object of a family trust. The assets of that trust were transferred to a second family trust in breach of trust. It was claimed that the son-in-law had consented to the breach. His father-in-law had sent him a memo outlining the proposed scheme of rearrangement, and he had later been given a copy of an accountant's advice. However, he was not given notice of the trustee's meetings at which the rearrangement was to take place and was unsure whether the scheme would even proceed.

Young AJA in the New South Wales Court of Appeal held that the beneficiary's disentitling conduct could occur prior to the breach, simultaneously with it or after the breach. It was not, however, sufficient to show that the beneficiary had knowledge of a pending breach and did not protest about it. A clearer act of concurrence in the breach would be required. Handley JA stated that the defence of consent would fail unless the beneficiary had prior knowledge of all material facts constituting the breach of trust.[43]

In *Spellson*, two members of the Court (Hope AJA and Handley JA agreeing) indicated that consent was a discretionary defence. Even if consent was established, the Court was still under a duty to consider whether it was fair and equitable to allow the beneficiary to sue the trustee.[44] This observation was referred to without criticism by French CJ in *Byrnes v Kendle*.[45] In that case, it was held that unwillingness to insist that the trustee recover lost sums was not consent to the trustee's inaction.[46]

Acquiescence and release

[20.28] Acquiescence has been discussed generally in chapter 6. To establish acquiescence, it is necessary to show that the beneficiary had full knowledge of the breach of trust, and that,

41 Only beneficiaries who are *sui juris* are in a position to consent, acquiesce or give a release to a trustee.
42 (1992) 26 NSWLR 666; *Sourcebook* 20.4a, p 512.
43 (1992) 26 NSWLR 666, 670.
44 Ibid 676.
45 (2011) 243 CLR 253, [25]; *Sourcebook* 14.2a, p 367.
46 (2011) 243 CLR 253, [26].

by her actions or inactions, must be taken to have accepted the breach. Inaction involves what is referred to in the cases as 'standing by'. The defence has overtones of equity's traditional concern with conscience. For example, in *Re Kerr*,[47] the trustees of a trust over a sheep farming property successfully applied for an ex parte order giving them remuneration for their efforts. From 1899 to 1904, the trustees included the amount of remuneration in the trust accounts provided to the beneficiaries. Five years after the original order, the beneficiaries successfully had it set aside; the trustees were being overpaid as they were really only overseeing the work done by the farm manager, and the order should never have been made ex parte. However, it was held that the trustees were not liable to repay the beneficiaries the amounts they had received. The beneficiaries had full notice of the amounts received and had not raised any objection for nearly five years.

Release following a breach of trust is, in one sense, more formal than acquiescence. [20.29] Lord Westbury said that it required the trustee to show that the beneficiary 'deliberately and advisedly, with full knowledge of all the circumstances, and of his own rights and claims against the trustee ... freely and without pressure or undue influence of any description'[48] released the trustee from the trust obligation. A written release is not required. It can be given orally or even by conduct.[49] When the alleged release is by conduct, there is little to distinguish it from acquiescence in a breach. Release will obviously be easier to establish if it is provided in writing.

Remedies in the context of breach of trust

When equity relieves against breaches of trust, any remedy granted, or order made is [20.30] intended to achieve due administration of the trust. Equity can, in this respect, be contrasted with the common law. Taking the tort of trespass as an example, we see that a successful plaintiff is entitled to damages as of right. The quantum may be small if damage is slight, but the entitlement cannot be ignored. Breaches of trust can range from the trivial to the catastrophic. The court's remedial selection (and not merely quantum) will reflect the nature and severity of the breach and will be aimed at having the trust performed as its creator intended, so far as that is possible. Equity's range of remedies is not limited to compensation for loss. But equally, there is no right to a remedy, as there is at common law.

It is common to distinguish between breaches of trust that require remedies of a [20.31] monetary nature and breaches that can be remedied by other orders. Some non-monetary orders are relatively straightforward. The court often makes the orders necessary to make the trust effective. For example, the court might order a trustee in a position of conflict of interest to be removed and replaced with a neutral trustee.[50] Other breaches of trust may result in proprietary orders, which attach to specific property. These proprietary remedies are discussed in chapters 2 (equitable remedies) and 23 (constructive trusts).

47 (1904) 24 NZLR 1.
48 *Farrant v Blanchford* (1863) 1 De G J & S 107; 46 ER 42, 46–7.
49 Jacobs [2236].
50 *Monty Financial Services Ltd v Delmo* [1996] 1 VR 65; *Porteous v Rinehart* (1998) 19 WAR 495.

[20.32] Other considerations are relevant when we turn to monetary orders for breach of trust. First, it must be determined whether the beneficiary's complaint is that the trustee made an unauthorised profit or that the trustee's actions have caused loss to the trust fund. If the complaint concerns a loss, it may be necessary to examine the breach further. Was the trustee's act prohibited by the terms of the trust? Or did the trustee perform its duties negligently? Was the breach a breach of the fiduciary 'no profit' and 'no conflict' rules? These matters impact on the trustee's personal liability.

Monetary remedies for breach of trust

Unauthorised profits

[20.33] Trustees are fiduciaries[51] and cannot make an unauthorised profit from their position. If such a profit is made, it will be stripped totally from the trustee, subject only to such allowances as the court sees fit. Profit-stripping can be achieved via an account of profits or by an order for a constructive trust where the trustee's profit has been to acquire property. These matters are discussed in chapters 4 (monetary remedies) and 23 (constructive trusts).

Prohibited breaches

[20.34] As we saw in chapter 17, there are some duties the trustee *must* perform in order to execute the trust. One of the trustee's most important duties is to account to the beneficiaries for the trust property. If the trustee cannot account to the beneficiaries because the trust fund has been misapplied, the trustee is strictly liable to restore the trust fund in full. Since the duty of the trustee is to reinstate the trust fund completely, 'common law rules of damage and remoteness are out of place'.[52] Causation is established by reference to the simple 'but for' test. What would have been the value of the trust fund 'but for' the trustee's breach? The trustee must then reconstitute that value.

[20.35] Reinstatement of the trust fund will usually be made by way of payment of the monetary equivalent of the missing asset. This is referred to in equity as 'equitable compensation', rather than 'damages'. However, use of that term poses some difficulties. Its usage is now so wide in equity that it can refer to any monetary order made, whether in response to breach of confidence, undue influence, breach of fiduciary duty or breach of trust.[53] Further, it is used in cases of reinstatement of the trust fund, as in *Re Dawson (deceased)*[54] and *Youyang*,[55] as well as in cases where the trust fund has not been misapplied but instead has been managed negligently.[56]

51 See chapter 10.

52 P Millett, 'Equity's Place in the Law of Commerce' (1998) 114(2) *Law Quarterly Review* 214, 226. See chapter 4.

53 See [4.8].

54 [1966] 2 NSWR 211.

55 *Youyang Pty Ltd v Minter Ellison Morris Fletcher* (2003) 212 CLR 484; *Sourcebook* 4.3.3b, p 78. See chapter 4.

56 See *Re Mulligan (deceased)* [1998] 1 NZLR 481.

It is increasingly recognised that greater precision is called for when describing equity's monetary award.[57] Elliott and Edelman suggest that it might be necessary to use terms that distinguish between cases where the trust fund must be reinstated in money due to misapplication of the trust funds, sometimes referred to as 'substitutive compensation', and other cases where the trustee's negligent performance of its duties has caused some loss to the fund, known as 'reparative compensation'.[58]

Considerations of these matters can be traced back to an influential extra-judicial article written by Lord Millett[59] which re-examined the traditional right of the beneficiary to call for an account of the state of the trust fund. The accounts produced could be reviewed, and the beneficiary could accept, falsify or surcharge the account. Acceptance indicates the beneficiary's satisfaction with the trustee's performance. Accounts are 'falsified' when the beneficiary identifies a misappropriation or misapplication. The disbursement made by the trustee is then disallowed, and the trustee must reinstate the trust fund in full. The term 'surcharge' refers to the situation where the trustee is said to have mismanaged the trust fund, and not received all that a prudent trustee would have. This kind of negligence in performance is discussed below. The article demonstrates that equity's response to a breach of trust depends on the nature of the breach. Reinstatement may only be appropriate where misapplication has occurred. [20.36]

The distinction between substitutive compensation and reparative compensation was rejected by the United Kingdom Supreme Court in *AIB Group (UK) plc v Mark Redler & Co Solicitors*.[60] The plaintiff bank agreed to lend £3.3 million to borrowers, taking security over the borrowers' home. The money was transferred to the defendant firm of solicitors to hold as trustee until paid out to the borrowers, which was only to occur after the defendant had taken a first charge over the borrowers' home. Another bank held a charge over the home, so it was necessary for the loan secured by that bank's charge to be paid off before the plaintiff's intended first charge could be taken over the property. Due to the defendant's negligence only part of the earlier loan was paid off, so that the earlier charge retained its priority over the property for £309 000. The plaintiff therefore never obtained the first charge it had instructed the defendant to obtain. The borrowers failed to repay the loan, and the plaintiff received £876 697 from the proceeds of sale of the home. The plaintiff sued the defendant for breach of trust in releasing the loan to the borrowers without taking the first charge. The plaintiff claimed substitutive compensation, being the amount wrongly paid out by the solicitors to the borrowers (£3.3 million) minus the amount the plaintiff had received on sale of the borrowers' home (£867 697). The United Kingdom Supreme Court, [20.37]

57 See J Edelman and S Elliott, 'Money Remedies Against Trustees' (2004) 18(3) *Trust Law International* 116.

58 Ibid 116. *Agricultural Land Management Ltd v Jackson (No 2)* (2014) 48 WAR 1, [334]–[349] (Edelman J); *Sourcebook* 4.3.2a, p 73; *Crossman v Sheahan* (2016) 115 ACSR 130, [313] (Ward JA). See chapter 4.

59 Millett (n 52). See also Lord Millett's judgment in *Libertarian Investments v Hall* (2013) 16 HKCFAR 681; *Sourcebook* 4.3.1a, p 71. A similar argument was made slightly earlier by P Birks, 'Equity in the Modern Law: An Exercise in Taxonomy' (1996) 26(1) *University of Western Australia Law Review* 1, 44–8. See *Youyang Pty Ltd v Minter Ellison Morris Fletcher* (2003) 212 CLR 484, 502; *Sourcebook* 4.3.3b, p 78.

60 [2015] AC 1503.

however, awarded the plaintiff reparative compensation, being the amount of £309 000 that should have been paid in order to discharge the earlier charge but which had in fact been paid to the borrowers. The Court applied the 'but for' test of causation in reaching this conclusion: the plaintiff would only have lost £309 000 but for the solicitors' breach of trust in releasing the loan to the borrowers without obtaining a first charge.

The decision reached in *Redler* is controversial, and it has been argued that in applying the 'but for' test on these facts the Supreme Court has abolished the distinction between substitutive and reparative compensation.[61] It is an open question whether Australian law will apply *Redler*. Some recent Australian decisions have recognised the distinction between substitutive and reparative compensation,[62] although in all the leading cases the 'but for' test of causation would in fact have been satisfied. It is also established in Australia that common law conceptions of remoteness of damage are inapplicable in equity, so that no question of reasonable foreseeability of loss limits recovery of misapplied trust money.[63]

Negligence in performance

[20.38] Where the trustee's poor performance has caused loss to the trust fund, it might be argued that the trustee has to restore the fund to the value it would have had if the trustee had acted prudently. On this analysis, the trustee's duty is no different from the reinstatement situation. But assessing quantum in this way raises a causation conundrum. Questions of causation and remoteness are irrelevant where trust money has been misapplied. But is the same true where the complaint is that the trustee has performed his duties negligently?

Some commentators favour applying tort principles to cases of negligent loss,[64] although the tort analogy has been rejected by other writers.[65] Most importantly, the theory has been doubted in the High Court. It was stated that 'there must be a real question whether ... any assimilation even in this limited way with the measure of damages in tort'[66] was warranted. The kernel of the arguments against adoption of tort principles appears to be the concern that, if a trustee is only required to act carefully, he will not be demonstrating the loyalty required of a fiduciary.

---

61 R Lee, 'Substitutive Compensation for Breaches of Trust: An Irrelevant Fairy Tale?' (2015) 9(1) *Journal of Equity* 94; L Ho and R Lee, 'Reparative Compensation for Deliberate Breaches of Trust' (2014) 130(4) *Law Quarterly Review* 542; J Edelman, 'An English Misturning with Equitable Compensation' in S Degeling and J Varuhas eds, *Equitable Compensation and Disgorgement of Profit* (Hart Publishing 2017) 91.

62 See n 59.

63 *Re Dawson (deceased)* [1966] 2 NSWR 211; *Sourcebook* 4.3.3a, p 74.

64 P Birks, 'The Content of Fiduciary Obligation' (2002) 16(1) *Trust Law International* 34, 50; C Nugee, 'Suing for Losses to a Pension Scheme – Some Issues' (2001) 15(2) *Trust Law International* 83; R Chambers, 'Liability' in P Birks and A Pretto-Sakmann (eds), *Breach of Trust* (Hart Publishing, 2002) 1; S Elliott and J Edelman, 'Target Holdings Considered in Australia' (2003) 119(4) *Law Quarterly Review* 545; *Bank of New Zealand v New Zealand Guardian Trust Co Ltd* [1999] 1 NZLR 664, 681.

65 J Getzler, 'Equitable Compensation and the Regulation of Fiduciary Relationships' in P Birks and F Rose (eds), *Restitution and Equity: Volume 1 Resulting Trusts and Equitable Compensation* (Mansfield Press, 2000) 235, 255.

66 *Youyang Pty Ltd v Minter Ellison Morris Fletcher* (2003) 212 CLR 484, 500. It has been pointed out that *Youyang* was argued as a case on reparative compensation: see *Agricultural Land Management Ltd v Jackson (No 2)* (2014) 48 WAR 1, [354] (Edelman J).

The fear that a negligent trustee is being allowed to be disloyal is, however, largely misplaced. The better view appears to be that a trustee is not disloyal in a fiduciary sense merely because he was negligent. Disloyalty and poor performance are different things, and poor performance can be cured by orders that acknowledge the trustee could have done better.[67] It is probably sufficient that breaches of a duty of care be remedied by reference to what a reasonable trustee would have achieved. The trustee should not be the insurer of the trust fund against all possible losses. Once it is admitted that liability is not absolute, it can be accepted that concepts like remoteness and foreseeability are appropriate in calculating quantum. Strict 'but for' analysis of causation for loss is inappropriate for negligent breaches of trust. It should be sufficient that the trustee is judged by the standard a reasonable trustee would have achieved. The trust fund will then be restored to the state in which it would have been, had the trustee been acting carefully. This may not necessarily mean it will be restored in full.

Compensation for breach of the conflicts rule

A trustee's conflict of duty and interest or duty and duty may result in a loss to the trust fund. How should quantum for the loss be assessed? The breach will constitute a breach of fiduciary duty, but the compensation payable will depend on the precise nature and consequences of the trustee's breach. If the conflict causes the trustee to misapply trust money, the trustee comes under a strict duty to make restitution.[68] On the other hand, if the conflict results in the trustee not giving impartial advice to the beneficiary, with the result that the beneficiary's reliance on the advice causes financial loss, the beneficiary is entitled to reparative compensation.[69] If the analogy with liability in tort for negligent misrepresentation is followed (see [20.38]), compensation in the latter case should be limited to recovery of reasonably foreseeable loss, but in practice Australian law has not applied the tort analogy. Compensation will be ordered for all loss caused by the breach, except possibly where the beneficiary could have taken reasonable steps to mitigate her loss once the breach had been discovered.[70] The principles applied in each case are those applicable to fiduciaries who are not trustees. They are discussed in chapter 4. [20.39]

Statutory provisions

At the beginning of this century, a raft of statutory provisions was introduced in every Australian jurisdiction,[71] the general aim of which was to limit recovery against wrongdoers to losses those wrongdoers in fact caused. The statutes replace the principle of *joint and several liability* with *proportionate liability*. Previously, where two or more defendants caused [20.40]

67 For example, recovery in *Re Mulligan (deceased)* [1998] 1 NZLR 481.

68 *Re Dawson (deceased)* [1966] 2 NSWR 211; *Sourcebook* 4.3.3a, p 74.

69 Cf *Commonwealth Bank of Australia v Smith* (1991) 42 FCR 390; *Sourcebook* 10.5.2c, p 273.

70 *Commonwealth Bank of Australia v Smith* (1991) 42 FCR 390.

71 *Competition and Consumer Act 2010* (Cth) pt VIA; *Australian Securities and Investments Commission Act 2001* (Cth) s 12GF(1); *Corporations Act 2001* (Cth) ss 1041L–1041S; *Civil Law (Wrongs) Act 2002* (ACT) ch 7A; *Civil Liability Act 2002* (NSW) s 35; *Proportionate Liability Act 2005* (NT) s 9; *Civil Liability Act 2003* (Qld) s 31; *Law Reform (Contributory Negligence and Apportionment of Liability) Act 2001* (SA) s 8; *Civil Liability Act 2002* (Tas) pt 9A; *Wrongs Act 1958* (Vic) pt IVAA; *Civil Liability Act 2002* (WA) pt 1F.

the plaintiff's loss, the plaintiff could recover against one of them (usually the wealthiest) and leave it to the defendants to sort out contribution among themselves. Proportionate liability limits each defendant's damages to the losses caused by their own actions.

The proportionate liability legislation only applies to claims arising from the trustees' failure to take care, and for engaging in misleading or deceptive conduct.[72] It therefore does not apply to claims of loss of trust property which are not based on failure to take care. Moreover, the legislation does not apply to intentional or fraudulent wrongdoing. But where the negligent acts of two or more trustees have caused loss to the trust, it will no longer be sufficient for the beneficiaries to claim full compensation from the wealthiest trustee; each trustee will be liable for his or her share of the loss. It will also be relevant to claims brought by a beneficiary against a trustee and an accessory where there has been a failure to take care, or where there has been deceptive or misleading conduct causing loss to the beneficiary. For example, where a beneficiary has incurred financial loss as a result of being induced to purchase an interest in an investment trust by a misrepresentation made by one of the directors of the trustee company, liability will be apportioned between the trustee company and the director who made the misrepresentation.[73]

[20.41] In cases to which the proportionate liability legislation does not apply, a co-trustee who has been held liable for breach of trust can claim a contribution from her co-trustees. In equity, a passive trustee was held to be just as responsible for a breach of trust as an active trustee.[74] It has also been held that a fraudulent trustee must indemnify non- fraudulent co-trustees,[75] and that a solicitor co-trustee must indemnify co-trustees where the breach was caused by the trustees' reliance on the solicitor's advice.[76] In Victoria, these principles must be read subject to legislation which confers power on the court to order a trustee to make a 'just and equitable' contribution to compensation ordered against a co-trustee, although the equity decisions will no doubt influence the exercise of statutory discretion.[77]

Non-monetary remedies for breach of trust

[20.42] Breach of trust can occur without the trust suffering a loss. Such a breach calls for a non-compensatory remedy. As trusts are creatures of equity any equitable remedy is potentially available. For example, injunctions can be obtained against a trustee to prevent a breach

72 *Australian Consumer Law*, s 18. Liability for misleading and deceptive conduct may be relevant to beneficiaries who purchase their beneficial interest in an investment trust from a corporate trustee. See generally A Gurr, 'Accessory Liability and Contribution, Release and Apportionment' (2010) 34(2) *Melbourne University Law Review* 481. Cf *George v Webb* [2011] NSWSC 1608.

73 A director of a trustee company that commits a breach of trust is liable for having knowingly assisted the breach: *Australian Securities Commission v AS Nominees Ltd* (1995) 62 FCR 504, 523 (Finn J). It is assumed in the text example that the co-directors do not satisfy the knowledge requirement for the purpose of being held liable for 'knowing assistance': see chapter 11.

74 *Bahin v Hughes* (1886) 31 Ch D 390.

75 *Baynard v Woolley* (1855) 20 Beav 583; 52 ER 729.

76 *Lockhart v Reilly* (1856) 25 LJ Ch 697; *Head v Gould* [1898] 2 Ch 250.

77 *Wrongs Act 1958* (Vic) s 24(2). Section 23A includes liability for breach of trust within the statutory contribution scheme. Cf *Wrongs Act 1954* (Tas) s 2, where the definition of 'wrongful act' does not include a breach of trust for the purpose of obtaining statutory contribution.

of trust occurring in the first place. In *Fox v Fox*,[78] a testator left his estate to be divided among his three children. His daughter's share was to be calculated by reference to her marriage settlement. Her two brothers obtained an injunction to stop the trustees dividing the estate in accordance with their incorrect interpretation of the provision. Similarly, courts are frequently called on to make declarations concerning trusts.[79]

A beneficiary may also wish to seek removal of the trustee. Trustees can be removed whether or not there has been a breach of trust.[80] A trust instrument may allow for removal of a trustee; for example, by an 'appointor' nominated by the settlor in the trust instrument as the person who can appoint or remove a trustee. A court can also remove a trustee in the exercise of either its equitable jurisdiction or a statutory jurisdiction. Trustee legislation in all jurisdictions authorises a court to replace a trustee, among other circumstances, when the trustee is unfit to act.[81] Breach of trust does not automatically mean that the trustee should be removed. The breach might be trivial or easily fixed without a loss having been incurred. The court exercises an inherent jurisdiction to remove a trustee when that is in the best interests of the trust. The primary concern of the court is not that a breach of trust has occurred, but that the trust property is at risk or that the trustee cannot be relied upon to perform the trust properly. [20.43]

In *Miller v Cameron*, Dixon J said:

> The jurisdiction to remove a trustee is exercised with a view to the interests of the beneficiaries, to the security of the trust property and to an efficient and satisfactory execution of the trusts and a faithful and sound exercise of the powers conferred upon the trustee. ... [T]he Court forms a judgment based upon considerations, possibly large in number and varied in character, which combine to show that the welfare of the beneficiaries is opposed to his continued occupation of the office.[82]

Trustees have been removed for breaches such as denying the existence of the trust,[83] failing to act impartially between beneficiaries,[84] failing to maintain accounts, failing to understand the trustee's duties and obligations[85] and being in unauthorised positions of conflict of interest.[86] The bankruptcy or insolvency of a trustee does not automatically result in removal at general law. Under the superannuation legislation, however, insolvents cannot act as trustees.[87] [20.44]

78 (1870) LR 11 Eq 142.

79 See, eg, *Re Philips New Zealand Ltd* [1997] 1 NZLR 93.

80 *Blenkinsop v Blenkinsop Nominees Pty Ltd as Trustee for the Blenkinsop Family Trust* [2015] WASC 463, [99]–[104] (conflict and distrust of members of family who constituted boards of two trustee companies justified replacement of trustee companies).

81 ACT s 70; NSW s 70; NT s 27; Qld s 80; SA s 36 ('if it desirable (a) in the interests of the persons (whether identified or not) who are to benefit from the trust, or (b) to advance the purposes of the trust)'; Tas s 32; Vic s 48; WA s 77. A court can remove a trustee in the exercise of its equitable jurisdiction even though no application for removal has been made under a statutory provision: *Piper v Fraser* [2020] SASC 239, [144]–[152].

82 (1936) 54 CLR 572, 580–1; *Sourcebook* 20.5a, p 515.

83 *Waterhouse v Waterhouse* (1998) 46 NSWLR 449.

84 *Re Whitehouse* [1982] Qd R 196.

85 *Mansour v Mansour* (2009) 24 VLR 498.

86 *Monty Financial Services Ltd v Delmo* [1996] 1 VR 65. Cf *Re Connock* [2021] VSC 64 where the conflict of interest was held not to justify removal.

87 *Superannuation Industry (Supervision) Act 1993* (Cth) s 120.

[20.45] Removal of a trustee does not necessarily result in replacement by a new trustee, particularly if sufficient trustees, unaffected by the ground of removal, remain to administer the trust. But if the appointment of a new trustee is required, the following considerations have been held to be relevant to the selection of the replacement:

(1) The wishes of the persons by whom the trust was created, if expressed or implicit in the trust instrument;

(2) A trustee should not be appointed with a view to promoting the interests of some of the beneficiaries in opposition to either to the wishes of the settlor or the interests of other beneficiaries;

(3) Regard should be had to whether the appointment would promote or impede the execution of the trust. In this respect, the court may wish to ascertain the acceptability of the proposed trustee to the beneficiaries.[88]

[20.46] Rescission[89] is available to set aside contracts entered into by trustees in breach of the self-dealing rule, at the suit of the beneficiary. Although all equitable remedies are discretionary, in this case the remedy is rarely denied unless a good faith purchaser has obtained an interest in the subject-matter of the contract.

Standing to sue

[20.47] The appropriate party to commence a suit against a trustee in breach will depend on what kind of trust is involved, what is alleged and what remedy is sought. Charitable trusts (which have no individual objects or beneficiaries) must be enforced by the Attorney-General.[90] Private express trusts can be enforced by a beneficiary, a co-trustee, or a subsequent trustee.[91] If the beneficiaries are seeking replacement of a trustee, they are the appropriate persons to commence action. If the trust has been fully completed, and yet the beneficiaries allege an outstanding breach, they may sue directly.[92] If, however, the trust is a continuing trust, it is usual for action against a defaulting trustee to be taken by his co-trustees, or by new trustees who have replaced him. Indeed, one of the duties of a trustee is to sue another trustee in breach, if that is necessary to 'get in' trust assets.[93] In *Young v Murphy*,[94] it was held that new trustees were able to sue the trustees they had replaced, and that it was not necessary for the beneficiaries to be joined as parties.

In Queensland and Western Australia, the principles developed in equity have been replaced by legislation permitting 'any person who has, directly or indirectly, an interest, whether vested or contingent, in any trust property, or who has a right of due administration in respect of any trust', and who is aggrieved by 'any act, omission or decision of a trustee or other person in the exercise of any power' to apply to the court for a review of the act,

88 *Hancock v Rinehart* (2015) 106 ACSE 207, [120]–[124] (Brereton J).
89 See chapter 5.
90 See [16.2].
91 *Young v Murphy* [1996] 1 VR 279.
92 See, eg, *Youyang Pty Ltd v Minter Ellison Morris Fletcher* (2003) 212 CLR 484.
93 See [17.10].
94 [1996] 1 VR 279.

omission or decision in question.[95] A court will construe the provision broadly in assessing whether an applicant has standing to sue for breach of trust.[96]

Claims brought against third parties – for example, for the restitution of trust property – should be brought by the trustee.[97] The beneficiary has the right to compel the trustee to take action, but a beneficiary who sues the third party must join the trustee as co-defendant, assuming that the trustee refuses to initiate the claim.[98] The joinder enables the court to determine whether the trustee acted in breach of trust by failing to recover the property from the third party in the same proceedings that recovers the property for the trust. [20.48]

It is not necessary for the beneficiaries to be joined to the trustee's claim against a third party unless it is considered, as a practical matter, that the trustee will not adequately represent the beneficiaries' interests.[99] If the beneficiaries have different interests in the outcome of the dispute, they may all have to be joined as parties; alternatively, where the dispute concerns a trust with numerous beneficiaries such as a superannuation trust, representative beneficiaries may be joined to the claim.[100]

WHAT'S ONLINE?

Available at www.cambridge.org/highereducation/isbn/9781009232388/resources:

- Recommended further readings
- Discussion topics

95 Qld s 8; WA s 94.

96 *Re Whitehouse* [1982] Qd R 196, 203–204 (Macrossan J). The provision does not, however, authorise the court to substitute its own discretion for that of the trustee: *Tierney v King* [1983] 2 Qd R 580, 583.

97 If the claim is brought in tort for conversion of trust property, the claim is based on the trustee's possessory title, not the beneficiary's equitable interest: *MCC Proceeds Inc v Lehman Bros* [1998] 4 All ER 657.

98 *Vandepitte v Preferred Accident Insurance Corp of New York* [1933] AC 70 (the joinder of a trustee as co-defendant is sometimes termed 'the *Vandepitte* procedure'); *Trident General Insurance Co Ltd v McNiece Brothers Pty Ltd* (1988) 165 CLR 107, [11] (Deane J); *Ramage v Waclaw* (1988) 12 NSWLR 84.

99 *Nicholson Street Pty Ltd v Letten* [2016] VSCA 157.

100 *Hughes v NM Super Pty Ltd* (1993) 29 NSWLR 653, 656; *Australian Special Opportunity Fund LP v Equity Trustees Wealth Services Ltd* (2015) 323 ALR 570, [156] (Bathurst CJ).

21

TRACING

Introduction

Tracing is not a remedy.[1] It is the process of identifying a new asset as the substitute for the old.[2] Its relevance to equity and trusts can be illustrated by the following example. Suppose a trustee misappropriates $10 000 and pays it into his personal account, which had previously been $20 000 in credit. He later withdraws $25 000 to buy a car. Tracing enables the beneficiaries to identify how the chose in action representing the trust money came to be substituted by a car. The tracing rules also determine how much of the beneficiaries' money remains in the trustee's bank account and how much is represented by an interest in the car. What is traced is not the trust property. The beneficiaries' equitable title to the money will be lost once the car has been bought. It is the value of the beneficiaries' property in the hand of a recipient that is traced.[3] [21.1]

Tracing is distinguishable from *following* and *claiming*. [21.2]

Following is the process of following the same asset as it moves from hand to hand.[4] So, if a trustee misappropriates a painting which is held on trust and gives it to his son, the beneficiaries can *follow* the painting; but if the son sells the painting the beneficiaries can *trace* the proceeds of sale, which are the substitute for the painting. In some cases, the beneficiaries can both follow the original property and trace the substitute for the original property. Following and tracing are alternative processes, although both can arise from the same initial dealing with property. If X's car is taken by Y, who then sells it to Z for $10 000, X cannot claim both the car from Z and the proceeds of sale from Y. Double recovery is not permitted.

In *Creak v James Moore & Sons Pty Ltd*,[5] Watson stole iron from the plaintiff, his employer. Watson's accomplice sold the iron to the defendant and deposited the proceeds in Watson's bank account. Watson was subsequently arrested, and the police withdrew the money from the bank account and paid it to the plaintiff. The plaintiff brought a claim against the defendant for conversion of the iron. A majority of the High Court dismissed the claim. It was held that the plaintiff cannot recover both the iron and the proceeds of sale of the iron since to do so would allow him to recover twice as much as he had lost.

Claiming refers to the process of *recovering* property, or the substitute for that property, from its recipient. When trust property has been misappropriated by the trustee and transferred to a third party the beneficiaries can bring a personal claim (for example, a 'knowing receipt' claim under the first limb of *Barnes v Addy*) or a proprietary claim (such as a proprietary constructive trust over the trust property or its substitute).[6] Both can be claimed if no double recovery is involved. Suppose a trustee misappropriates $10 000 of trust money and gives it to his daughter. She buys a painting with the money which depreciates in value to $8000. Leaving aside personal claims against the trustee, the beneficiaries can

1 See generally Lionel Smith, *The Law of Tracing* (Clarendon, 1997).
2 *Foskett v McKeown* [2001] 1 AC 102, 127 (Lord Millett); *Sourcebook* 21.1a, p 519.
3 Cf generally the arguments made by Pauline Ridge in 'Tracing and Associated Claims in Australian Law' (2020) 14 *Journal of Equity* 32.
4 Ibid.
5 (1912) 15 CLR 426; *Sourcebook* 21.2a, p 523.
6 See chapters 9 and 23.

make a proprietary claim to the painting. They can also bring a personal claim against the daughter, if she has knowledge of the breach of trust, in 'knowing receipt'.[7] This claim will allow the beneficiaries to recover the $2000 deficiency in the trust fund caused by the fall in value of the painting.

This chapter focuses on proprietary tracing claims.

Tracing and claiming at common law and in equity

[21.3] The right to recover specific property at common law is limited. The common law developed an action for the specific recovery of land. Possession of chattels is protected through the actions of detinue, conversion and trespass, but these claims usually only result in an award of damages. Specific restitution of a chattel can only be ordered in detinue.[8] Recovery of property by the exercise of self-help[9] and restoration of property to its true owner in the course of interpleader proceedings[10] is also possible. But these isolated examples of specific recovery fall well short of providing a general remedy for the recovery of property.[11]

[21.4] Equity developed more sophisticated methods for tracing a plaintiff's property, as well as more effective remedies for its recovery.

(a) Equity developed special rules for identifying the plaintiff's property when it has been mixed with other property; for instance, when her money has been mixed in a bank account with other money.[12]

(b) Equitable proprietary remedies are more flexible and effective than the limited recovery allowed at common law. Resulting and constructive trusts[13] restore specific property to claimants when the criteria for the award of these remedies are satisfied. Alternatively, an equitable lien can be imposed over the defendant's property as security for the return of money to the claimant. For example, if D has wrongly mixed P's money with his own in his bank account and buys a car with all the money in the account, an equitable lien will be imposed over the car to secure repayment to P of the money owed to her. If D fails to repay P from his other resources, the car will be sold and P's claim will be satisfied from the proceeds of sale.[14] A constructive or resulting trust entitles the claimant to a share (and possibly

7 See [11.6].

8 The order is usually only made where a plaintiff is unable to purchase a market substitute with a damages award: *Whiteley Ltd v Hilt* [1918] 2 KB 808.

9 *Taylor v Plumer* (1815) 3 M & S 562; 105 ER 721.

10 *Trustee of the Property of FC Jones & Sons v Jones* [1997] Ch 159.

11 For treatment of how tracing is dealt with under the *Personal Property Securities Act 2009* (Cth) see Anthony Duggan, *Australian Personal Property Securities Law* (LexisNexis Butterworths, 3rd ed, 2021) 11.16–11.37.

12 Cf the common law 'first in, first out' rule of *Clayton's Case* (1816) 1 Mer 572; 35 ER 781 with the equitable rules which evolved from *Re Hallett's Estate* (1880) 13 Ch D 696; *Sourcebook* 21.3a, p 526. See [21.8]–[21.27].

13 See chapters 22 and 23. The express trust also entitles adult beneficiaries to claim property, where the requirements of *Saunders v Vautier* (1841) 4 Beav 115; 49 ER 282 are met. See [13.3].

14 *Scott v Scott* (1963) 109 CLR 649; *Sourcebook* 21.7a, p 544.

all) of the property over which the trust has been imposed. The equitable lien, on the other hand, operates as a court-imposed mortgage, entitling the claimant to apply to the court for sale of the property if her claim is not satisfied.

But there are limitations to equity's reach. A proprietary claim cannot be brought against a good faith purchaser for value without notice. Furthermore, proprietary claims can only be made to identifiable property. If the plaintiff's property has been dissipated the plaintiff will only be entitled to personal relief. [21.5]

Since tracing simply refers to the identification of the value of the plaintiff's property in property to which the defendant has title, there should be no difference between tracing at common law and in equity. As Lord Millett observed in *Foskett v McKeown*,[15] one set of tracing rules is sufficient since there is no reason to identify property differently at law and in equity. It is at the claiming stage that the difference between the jurisdictions assumes significance since proprietary remedies are almost exclusively the preserve of equity. [21.6]

A fiduciary requirement?

Older case law linked the ability to trace in equity with the existence of a fiduciary relationship.[16] The authority for the fiduciary requirement was slight and courts have been gradually moving away from it. In *Foskett v McKeown*,[17] Lord Millett suggested that the existence of a fiduciary relationship might be relevant to framing the plaintiff's claim. For example, a beneficiary's right to trace trust money into the hands of a recipient will be based on the trustee's breach of trust; but fiduciary obligations should not otherwise be a precondition to tracing in equity. [21.7]

More recently, it has been said that the ability to trace depends upon identifying a 'proprietary base.'[18] Traditionally, this was satisfied where the plaintiff was a beneficiary under a trust. However, it is not necessary for that proprietary base to be a pre-existing equitable interest. In *Grimaldi*, the Full Federal Court explained that tracing is available where company property is misappropriated by a director, even though the money was not held on trust. Instead, if the recipient of the property has knowledge of the misappropriation and becomes a constructive trustee, this provides the proprietary base.[19] Equitable tracing rules have been used successfully to support claims at common law and in equity to recover stolen money on the basis that the thief becomes a trustee of the stolen funds and a volunteer comes under an obligation to account for stolen money once she is aware of the claim.[20]

15 [2001] 1 AC 102, 128–9. The New South Wales Court of Appeal has specifically allowed equitable tracing rules to identify property in order to make a common law claim in *Heperu Pty Ltd v Belle* (2009) 76 NSWLR 230 and *Fistar v Riverwood Legion and Community Club Ltd* (2016) 91 NSWLR 732 (although the claim failed as the recipient was not a volunteer).

16 *Agip (Africa) Ltd v Jackson* [1991] Ch 547, 566.

17 [2001] 1 AC 102, 128.

18 *Grimaldi v Chameleon Mining NL (No 2)* (2012) 200 FCR 296, 417.

19 (2012) 200 FCR 296, 417–18.

20 For common law claims see *Silversea Cruises Australia Pty Ltd v Abellanoza* [2019] NSWCA 306 and *Heperu Pty Ltd v Belle* (2009) 76 NSWLR 230. For equitable claims see *Sze Tu v Lowe* (2014) 89 NSWLR 317; *Helou v Nguyen* [2014] NSWSC 22; *Lawrie v Hwang* [2012] QSC 422; *Alesco Corporation Ltd v Te Maari* [2015] NSWSC 469.

The fiduciary requirement is, strictly speaking, a prerequisite, not to tracing, but to claiming an equitable remedy. What the plaintiff must prove is that she had *equitable title* in the property the value of which she has traced into property owned by the defendant. Where the claim is made at common law, only common law money remedies should be awarded.

The equitable tracing rules

Mixing money in a bank account

[21.8] Equity has developed rules (sometimes confusingly termed 'irrebuttable presumptions') to determine when a claimant can trace the value of her property into other property to which the defendant has title. The rules apply to the mixing of any kind of property, but the cases are mostly concerned with the mixing of money in bank accounts and it is convenient to consider this scenario. Except where stated otherwise, it should be assumed that the rules apply to all forms of property. We will use breach of trust as an example, even though we have just seen that a fiduciary relationship is not a precondition to tracing in equity.

[21.9] Three variables are relevant to determining the applicable tracing rule:

(1) The identity of the party mixing the claimant's money with other money. Most cases concern a wrongdoer, such as a trustee acting in breach of trust, mixing the claimant's money with his own; but rules have also been developed to cover the situation of a recipient of money from the wrongdoer who mixes the claimant's money.

(2) The title to the money mixed. The wrongdoer may mix his own money with that of the claimant, or he may mix money belonging to two or more claimants. He may of course also do both, mixing his own money with that of several claimants.

(3) The history of the mixed fund after mixing. The important question here will be whether, by the time the tracing claim is made, the fund has increased or decreased in value, or has remained the same.

Scenario 1(a):
A trustee mixes trust money with his own in his bank account and subsequently spends some of the money in the account.

[21.10] Equity allows the beneficiary to trace her money into the mixed fund or into any property purchased from the mixed fund, or both. The key to understanding the tracing rules is to recognise that equity goes to great lengths to preserve the interests of a beneficiary claiming an equitable interest in money paid into a mixed fund as against the interest of the trustee or other title-holder of the fund. Equity's instincts on behalf of equitable interest holders are terrierlike.

[21.11] If there are sufficient funds in the trustee's account, the court can order that the trust money be repaid directly to the trust. Such orders are made not only in the case of trust funds but also in other cases of mixing of fungible property, such as oil or raw materials, which can be separated from the mass composed of the plaintiff's and defendant's property.[21] Where trust property has been combined with the trustee's own property to constitute a new asset which has not appreciated in value, the trust will be entitled to an equitable lien over the asset to secure repayment of the value of its property.[22]

If there are insufficient funds to pay both the trust and the trustee (or his creditors if he is bankrupt), there is an 'irrebuttable presumption' that the trustee has preserved trust money and spent his own money first. In *Re Hallett's Estate*,[23] a solicitor was entrusted with the custody of some Russian bonds by a client. He sold them, together with some bonds held on trust for his own family, and banked the proceeds. He died insolvent, having spent money in the account. The Court of Appeal held that the solicitor must be taken to have spent his own money first and that the remaining money could be traced by the client. The client was entitled to an equitable lien over the account to secure repayment of the proceeds of the bonds. The solicitor's other creditors were not entitled to repayment until the client's claim had been satisfied. [21.12]

In *Re Hallett's Estate*, Jessel MR justified the application of the rule by stating that the solicitor must be presumed to have acted honestly in spending his own money rather than dishonestly by spending the claimant's money.[24] The 'presumption' will often be a fiction, since fiduciaries who mix beneficiary money without authority are usually far from honest. A preferable basis of the right to trace is that it would be unconscionable of the title holder of the mixed fund to deny the plaintiff an equitable title to the mixed fund.[25] [21.13]

Re Hallett's Estate was approved by the High Court in *Brady v Stapleton*[26] where 32 280 shares in a company were fraudulently transferred by Coward to Brady, who already held 1300 shares in the same company. Brady then transferred 17 000 shares to Mrs Coward, who also had knowledge of the fraud, leaving Brady with 16 580 shares. Coward was later made bankrupt. Dixon and Fullagar JJ held that Brady must be presumed to have transferred his own 1300 shares first among the 17 000 shares which he had transferred to Mrs Coward. She was entitled to those shares. All the other shares vested in Coward's trustee in bankruptcy. *Brady v Stapleton* is a decision on following assets, not tracing into substitutes, but the High Court assumed that tracing principles applied to the transfer of the shares. [21.14]

Scenario 1(b):
The trustee mixes trust money with his own in his bank account, and later purchases property with some of the money in the account before exhausting the money remaining in the account.

In *Re Oatway*,[27] a solicitor paid £3000 from an estate of which he was trustee into his own bank account. He withdrew £2137 for the purchase of shares, and later dissipated all [21.15]

21 *Foskett v McKeown* [2001] 1 AC 102.
22 *Re Hallett's Estate* (1880) 13 Ch D 696; *Brady v Stapleton* (1952) 88 CLR 322.
23 (1880) 13 Ch D 696.
24 Ibid 708 (Jessel MR).
25 *Re Walter J Schmidt & Co*, 298 F 314, 316 (1923) (Learned Hand J); *Re French Caledonia Travel* (2003) 59 NSWLR 361, [153]; *Sourcebook* 21.4a, p 530.
26 (1952) 88 CLR 322.
27 [1903] 2 Ch 356; *Sourcebook* 21.3b, p 528.

the money remaining in the account. It was argued that the solicitor must be presumed to have spent his own money first on the shares. Joyce J, however, held that the estate's money was preserved in the shares he had bought, and that he had dissipated his own money. The decision was not based on any 'presumed intention' of the solicitor, but on the policy of preserving trust assets through substitutions of property.

Scenario 1(c):
The trustee mixes trust money with his own in a bank account, and makes payments in and out of that account.

[21.16] The rules stated above are subject to the application of the 'lowest intermediate balance' rule. The rule provides that the trust cannot claim more than the lowest intermediate balance credited to the trustee's bank account between the mixing of the trust money in the account and the bringing of the tracing claim.

[21.17] Suppose D pays $1000 of money belonging to P into D's account, which was previously $1000 in credit. D later spends $1500 from the account on a holiday. After the holiday, D pays $500 into the account, being a payment for work he has done. P can only trace, and obtain a proprietary remedy over, $500 in the account. This is the lowest amount to the credit of the account between the payment of P's money into the account and P bringing her tracing claim. P cannot claim a proprietary remedy over the $500 which D later paid into the account. That later payment was never P's money and so cannot be made subject to a proprietary claim.

[21.18] The lowest intermediate balance rule can operate harshly to deprive claimants of full recovery. If D's bank account is overdrawn at any time after the mixing occurred, it will prevent P from obtaining a proprietary remedy.[28] (This is often referred to as the 'nil balance rule'.) But the rule is a logical consequence of the basis of tracing property. P cannot trace because she cannot identify the later $500 payment as hers. P can still obtain a personal remedy against D for the full amount misappropriated although the personal remedy will provide scant comfort if D is bankrupt.

[21.19] In *Lofts v MacDonald*,[29] a builder entered into a contract with the plaintiffs to build them a house. The plaintiffs handed him two cheques totalling $1600 to be held in a trust account until the work had been completed. The builder paid the cheques into his current account. The builder's account was later reduced to $8.42, but further deposits were made, taking the balance in the account to $2824.50. The plaintiffs sought an equitable lien over the account for $1600, but Campbell J awarded them a lien for $8.42, being the lowest amount in the account standing to the credit of the builder.

[21.20] The rule is subject to an exception. P can claim any money D has paid into the account, after it has been reduced to its lowest intermediate balance, if D paid the money into the account with the intention of benefiting P. The claim to the replenished account is not, however, based on tracing. It is made to 'new money', which never previously belonged to P.

28 See, eg, *Carr v Council of the Law Society of New South Wales* [2020] NSWCA 276, [31] (White JA).
29 (1974) 3 ALR 404.

In permitting P to claim this money, the court gives effect to D's intentions, assuming that the transfer satisfies the legal or equitable requirements for perfecting the gift. If D is bankrupt, P cannot claim this later payment if it constitutes a preference of P over D's other creditors under the *Bankruptcy Act 1966* (Cth).[30]

Scenario 2:
The trustee mixes the money of more than one beneficiary in a bank account and spends some of the money in the account.

Suppose D, a trustee, mixes money belonging to beneficiaries A, B and C in his bank account into which D has also paid $1000 of his own money. D later spends half the money in the account on a holiday. Applying *Re Hallett*, D will be taken to have spent his own $1000 first. But how should the loss be shared among A, B and C? [21.21]

Equity's original approach was to apply the rule in *Clayton's Case*[31] to determine the entitlements of multiple claimants.[32] The rule applies the 'first in, first out' principle to determine title to money in bank accounts. The first payment into a continuing bank account will be appropriated to the first payment out of the account. So, if D pays $1000 of A's money into his account, $1000 of B's money, and finally $1000 of C's money, and later withdraws and spends $1500 from the account, the rule in *Clayton's Case* treats A's $1000 and $500 of B's money as having been spent. B will be entitled to $500 remaining in the account and C will be entitled to $1000.

The rule was also applied to purchases of property from mixed money paid into bank accounts. If, on the same facts, D withdraws $1500 from the account to buy a painting and spends the rest of the money in the account, A and B will be entitled to an equitable lien over the painting to secure repayment of $1000 and $500 respectively.[33]

The application of the rule in *Clayton's Case* has been criticised as being formulaic and capricious. In the first example, there is no good reason why A should be unable to recover any of her money and why C should recover all her money. Similarly, in the second example, there is no good reason why A and B, but not C, should be entitled to a lien over the painting D purchased. The ability of each claimant to recover her money, or to claim an interest in property acquired from a mixed fund, depends on the accident of the order in which money was paid into a bank account.[34]

The rule in *Clayton's Case* has not been applied in Australia to cases where there are insufficient funds to repay multiple beneficiaries.[35] Two main alternative approaches exist. [21.22]

30 *Bankruptcy Act 1966* (Cth) s 121. See F & L [17.245].
31 (1816) 1 Mer 572; 35 ER 781.
32 *Re Stenning* [1895] 2 Ch 433.
33 See [21.22] for discussion of whether A and B will be entitled to share in any appreciation in the value of the painting.
34 The rule in *Clayton's Case* does not apply if there is evidence that the fund was intended to be administered as a common fund for all contributors: *Barlow Clowes International Ltd v Vaughan* [1992] 4 All ER 22. The principle of rateable distribution will determine entitlements to the fund.
35 *Caron v Jahani (No 2)* (2020) 102 NSWLR 537; *Keefe v Law Society of New South Wales* (1998) 44 NSWLR 451; *Re French Caledonia Travel* (2003) 59 NSWLR 361.

One, which has been regarded as the preferred solution,[36] is the 'pari passu' approach. Using the pari passu approach, the beneficiaries will share rateably in the money remaining in the account. So, in scenario 1, A, B and C will each be entitled to $500. In scenario 2, A, B and C will each be rateably entitled to an equitable interest in the painting to secure realisation of a one-third interest out of the proceeds of sale when it is sold. In addition, D is personally liable to compensate each beneficiary for the $500 which cannot be realised by tracing, although the personal remedy of equitable compensation will be worth little if D is bankrupt. The pari passu approach has the attraction of treating all beneficiaries equally, even though, in reality, where there were many transactions on the account, the money that was deposited earliest is most likely to have been withdrawn as a matter of fact. In *Caron v Jahani (No 2)*, Bell P stated: 'the pari passu approach tends to favour earlier investors over later investors because it turns a blind eye to the fact that withdrawals from the fund over time will have proportionately reduced the quantum of deposits made prior to the withdrawals'.[37]

[21.23] The other approach is the 'lowest intermediate balance' or 'rolling charge approach'. This approach was adopted in *Caron v Jahani (No 2)*.[38] In the decision, Bell P in the New South Wales Court of Appeal extensively discussed the law on tracing into a mixed fund containing money of multiple beneficiaries and declined to order a rateable distribution on the facts of the case. The case dealt with a Ponzi scheme run by companies in the Courtenay House group, in which members of the public had invested. The companies were hopelessly insolvent. Beneficiary claims totalled over $57 million but there was only $21 million in the bank account when freezing orders were made on 21 April 2017. Nine investors had deposited additional funds on the day the account was frozen or in the next few days. At first instance, a rateable distribution was ordered.[39] In the appeal, the post-21 April investors sought orders which enabled distribution of their investments to them, on the basis of tracing.[40] Bell P, giving the leading judgment, emphasised that the pari passu approach is a default method of distribution where tracing is impossible or impractical.[41] Further, if it is possible for a beneficiary to trace their entitlement, the Court should permit that.[42] On the facts of the case, it was possible for the post-21 April claimants to trace their own contributions into the bank account as the freezing order meant that their money had not been withdrawn from the account. The liquidators were ordered to distribute their entitlements to them and distribute the rest on a rateable basis.

The effect of the decision is that the 21 April investors are in a much better position than the earlier investors, for whom a tracing exercise is unlikely to be possible due to the number of transactions on the bank account. While the decision does respect tracing principles, the 21 April investors seem to have been lucky by virtue of being in the right place, at the right time.

36 *Australian Securities and Investments Commission v Nelson* (2003) 44 ACSR 719, 723.
37 *Caron v Jahani (No 2)* (2020) 102 NSWLR 537, 541 [13].
38 Ibid.
39 *Re Courtenay House Capital Trading Group Pty Ltd (in liq)* (2019) 139 ACSR 469. In related proceedings, it was also held that $29 million held in a separate account which had not been mixed with the Westpac funds was held solely for investors who had participated in the 'Brexit Special' investment: *Re Courtenay House Capital Trading Group Pty Ltd (in liq)* (2018) 125 ACSR 149.
40 With a deduction for a withdrawal of $60 000 made on 21 April.
41 (2020) 102 NSWLR 537, 563. See also 569.
42 Ibid 571.

The *Caron* decision has been distinguished on the facts in subsequent cases, where funds have been so mixed that rateable distribution was the only practical method of distribution.[43]

Scenario 3:
The trustee mixes the beneficiary's money with his own in his bank, withdraws some of the money and invests it successfully.

The beneficiary will be entitled to the proportion of the investment which represents her contribution to the making of the investment. In *Scott v Scott*,[44] the trustee of a deceased estate applied £1014 from the trust estate, together with his own money, in the purchase of a house for £1700. The trustee later repaid the £1014 to the trust. After his death, the beneficiaries sued his estate for breach of trust. The house was at that time worth £5450. The High Court awarded the beneficiaries an account of profits assessed at 1014/1700 of the value of the house secured by an equitable lien over the house. To allow the trustee to keep the entire appreciated value of the house would be to allow him to profit from his own wrong.[45] [21.24]

The beneficiaries in *Scott v Scott* only claimed an account of profits, but obiter dicta indicated that the beneficiaries would, upon application, have been entitled to the benefit of a constructive trust over the property – the equitable interest representing the share the trust money had made to the appreciated value of the house.[46] In *Foskett v McKeown*,[47] the House of Lords imposed a constructive trust over the proceeds of a life insurance policy which the trustee, in breach of trust, had purchased partly with the beneficiaries' money. The trustee had misappropriated trust money to pay two of five premiums for a life insurance policy, the other premiums being paid from his own money. The policy was taken out for the benefit of his children. After the trustee committed suicide, the children were entitled to a payment of approximately £1 million under the policy. A majority of the House of Lords held that the trust beneficiaries were entitled to the benefit of a constructive trust over the insurance payment amounting to £400 000. This sum represented the two-fifths of the insurance premiums which had been purchased with trust money.

The account of profits secured by an equitable lien awarded in *Scott v Scott* entitles the beneficiaries to the profit assessed by the court at the date of judgment. In contrast, the constructive trust imposed in *Foskett v McKeown* entitles the beneficiaries to a proportionate share of the trust property. If the beneficiary considers that the property in which trust money has been invested in breach of trust is likely to increase in value after the date of judgment, she will be entitled to the benefit of that appreciation under a constructive trust. Conversely, the beneficiaries will bear the risk of any depreciation of the property after the constructive trust has been imposed.

43 *Kelly v Loo* (2021) 390 ALR 669; *Re Direct FX Trading Pty Ltd* [2020] NSWSC 1338.
44 (1963) 109 CLR 649.
45 A proportionate charge was granted in *Krnjulac v Lincu* [2015] NSWCA 367.
46 (1963) 109 CLR 649, 664.
47 [2001] 1 AC 102.

Scenario 4:
The trustee pays the beneficiary's money to an honest volunteer who mixes the money with his own in his bank account.

[21.25] This scenario considers only payments of money to honest volunteers. If the recipient of the money is dishonest, the beneficiaries can trace the trust money into the recipient's bank account on the same basis that they can trace into the trustee's account in scenario 1. Conversely, if the recipient is a good faith purchaser for value without notice of the initial breach of trust, the beneficiaries cannot trace the money since good faith purchase is an absolute bar to tracing in equity. The beneficiaries can, however, trace the property transferred by the purchaser to the trustee in exchange for the trust money.

[21.26] The leading case on scenario 4 is the decision of the English Court of Appeal in *Re Diplock*.[48] Caleb Diplock left his residuary estate 'for such charitable or benevolent object or objects' as his executors in their absolute discretion thought fit. The provision was void because it allowed the executors to distribute money to objects which were not exclusively charitable.[49] But before the provision had been declared void, the executors had distributed a large part of the estate to 139 charities. The testator's next of kin sought to recover money from the recipient charities.

[21.27] The charities in receipt of Diplock money had used it in various ways. Some had mixed it in their bank accounts or used it to purchase or improve property.

(a) *Improvements and alterations to the recipients' property*. Some of the Diplock money had been spent on improving and altering the charities' buildings; for example, money had been spent by a hospital on improving a children's ward. The Court of Appeal held that the money could not be traced into the improvements because the alterations did not necessarily add to the value of the property altered. They might in fact lower its value: 'the money will have disappeared leaving no monetary trace behind'.[50] The aim of a tracing exercise is to trace the value of the plaintiff's property into property to which the defendant holds title; tracing ceases if no value can be identified.[51]

(b) *Payment of unsecured debts*. A charity had used Diplock money to pay off an unsecured debt. The Court of Appeal held that the money could not be traced after the debt had been extinguished.[52] The Court's decision on this point has been challenged.[53] It is true that the money cannot be traced into the hands of the creditor

48 [1948] Ch 465, on appeal to the House of Lords, *Ministry of Health v Simpson* [1951] AC 251. Tim Akkouh and Sarah Worthington, 'Re Diplock' in C and P Mitchell (eds), *Landmark Cases in the Law of Restitution* (Hart Publishing, 2006) 285. In addition to proprietary tracing claims, the next of kin brought personal claims against the charities. See the online resources.

49 *Chichester Diocesan Fund v Simpson* [1944] AC 341. See [16.37].

50 *Re Diplock* [1948] Ch 465, 539; *Sourcebook* 21.6a, p 538.

51 For the argument that the Court of Appeal intuitively applied the change of position defence to the improvements see Elise Bant, *The Change of Position Defence* (Hart Publishing, 2009) 200–1.

52 *Re Diplock* [1948] Ch 465, 549.

53 Lionel Smith, 'Tracing into the Payment of a Debt' (1995) 54(2) *Cambridge Law Journal* 290.

whose debt has been paid; as a good faith purchaser for value without notice, the creditor has a defence to the tracing claim. But where the debt was contracted by the debtor in purchasing an asset it has been suggested that the claimant should be entitled to trace into, and have an equitable lien imposed over, the asset. This form of tracing is known as 'backward tracing' since it enables the claimant to trace into property acquired by the defendant before he received the claimant's money.[54] There is no direct authority for backward tracing in Australian law.[55]

(c) *Payment of secured debts*. A hospital had used Diplock money to pay off a mortgage over its property. The Court of Appeal held that the next of kin could not trace their money into payment of a secured debt since payment of the debt meant that the next of kin's money could no longer be identified.[56] Later decisions have rejected the reasoning of *Re Diplock* on this point.[57] They establish that where the claimant's money has been applied in the discharge of a mortgage, the claimant will be subrogated to the claims of the mortgagee against the mortgagor. In other words, the claimant will 'stand in the shoes' of the mortgagee and is entitled to enforce the mortgagee's remedies against the mortgagor.[58]

(d) *Mixing in the recipients' bank accounts*. Some of the charities had mixed Diplock money with their own in their bank accounts. The Court of Appeal applied the rule in *Clayton's Case*[59] to determine title both to money in the accounts and to property purchased with mixed money. In one case, the application of the rule resulted in the finding that the Diplock money could no longer be traced. In another, it resulted in the finding that Diplock money had been used, with money belonging to the charity, in the purchase of securities. The next of kin were entitled to share the securities rateably with the charity.

It is now accepted that the rule in *Clayton's Case* should not determine the outcome of tracing inquiries since the results of applying the rule are often arbitrary. It is more likely that the principle of rateable distribution will be applied, so that the claimant and the charity will share rateably both money in the mixed account and property purchased from the mixed fund. Rateable distribution may yield to other methods of division if it would be inequitable on the facts of the case.[60]

54 *Bishopsgate Investment Management Ltd v Homan* [1995] Ch 211, 216–17 (Dillon LJ).

55 See the discussion in *Conlan v Connolly* [2011] WASC 160, [911]–[961]; Matthew Conaglen, 'Difficulties with Tracing Backwards' (2011) 127(3) *Law Quarterly Review* 432. In *Federal Republic of Brazil v Durant International Corporation* [2016] AC 97, the Privy Council allowed backwards tracing but said at 313 that the plaintiff must 'establish a co-ordination between the depletion of the trust fund and the acquisition of the asset which is the subject of the tracing claim, looking at the whole transaction, such as to warrant the court attributing the value of the interest acquired to the misuse of the trust fund'.

56 *Re Diplock* [1948] Ch 465, 549.

57 *Boscawen v Bajwa* [1996] 1 WLR 328; *Gertsch v Atsas* (1999) 10 BPR 18,431; *Heperu Pty Ltd v Belle* (2009) 76 NSWLR 230; *Alesco Corporation Ltd v Te Maari* [2015] NSWSC 469.

58 The claimant will not precisely 'stand in the shoes' of the mortgagee, since the original mortgage will have been discharged by the application of the claimant's money. But the mortgagee's rights will be revived for the benefit of the claimant: *Boscawen v Bajwa* [1996] 1 WLR 328, 339, 341 (Millett LJ).

59 See [21.21].

60 See [21.22] and *Re French Caledonia Travel* (2003) 59 NSWLR 361.

(e) *Money invested in securities*. One charity had invested Diplock money in government securities. It had previously purchased some of the same securities with its own money, and later both bought and sold securities. The Court of Appeal rejected the contention that the rule in *Clayton's Case* applied to the purchase of the securities and ordered a rateable apportionment between the next of kin and the charity.[61]

(f) *Used up in general operations*. Some charities had used the money in their general operations. This was dissipated and could no longer be traced.

Defences to equitable tracing claims

[21.28] A claim to a proprietary remedy based on equitable tracing principles will be defeated if one of the following defences is established:

(1) The plaintiff's property is untraceable. In a claim to property based on tracing, the plaintiff must prove that the value of her property can be identified in property to which the defendant holds title. In *Re Diplock*, the next of kin could not prove that the Diplock money, which had been applied to pay for improvements to a hospital ward, had contributed value to the ward. We have also seen that money is untraceable if it has been dissipated or applied to discharge a secured or unsecured debt. Arguably, however, the application of money to discharge a debt should not prevent tracing into an asset in respect of which the debt was contracted.[62]

(2) The recipient is a good faith purchaser for value without notice of the fact that the claimant is entitled in equity to the money. Good faith purchase defeats a tracing claim brought against a recipient of money from the trustee. The claimant can, however, trace and claim property received by the trustee from the recipient as part of the good faith exchange. For example, if a trustee misappropriates $20 000 of trust money and buys a car with the money from a seller who is ignorant of the misappropriation, the money cannot be recovered from the seller who is a good faith purchaser, but the beneficiaries can trace the trust money into the car the trustee has purchased.

(3) Change of position.[63] The change of position defence applies where the recipient of property has in good faith irreversibly changed his position, relying on the validity of the receipt. Unlike the defence of good faith purchase, change of position can protect donees who have, in good faith, applied the beneficiary's money in circumstances in which it would be inequitable to allow tracing. The defence has been applied to tracing claims. In *Gertsch v Atsas*,[64] the defendant

61 [1948] Ch 465, 555–6.

62 See [21.27].

63 Bant (n 51); WMC Gummow, '*Moses v Macferlan*: 250 Years On' (2010) 84(11) *Australian Law Journal* 756.

64 (1999) 10 BPR 18,431.

received $100 000 under the will of a murder victim. The will had been forged by the victim's solicitor. The defendant used the money to discharge a mortgage over her home. She then gave up her job and undertook part-time tertiary study. It was held that the change of position defeated the claim of the victim's next of kin to trace all but $13 750 of the legacy the defendant had received. The application of the money to discharge the mortgage did not defeat the tracing claim; but the defendant had changed her position in the honest belief that she was entitled to the legacy by giving up her job and becoming a part-time student.

(4) Registration as proprietor of Torrens land. On general principles, if a volunteer purchases property with traceable proceeds, the tracing claim will subsist against the volunteer if she still holds the substitute asset, regardless of its type. While different remedies may have been granted over severable assets as opposed to single assets, the tracing issue has not traditionally been problematic. Recent decisions in New South Wales now draw a distinction based on the nature of property acquired by the volunteer. In *Sze Tu v Lowe*[65] and *Fistar v Riverwood Legion and Community Club Ltd*,[66] the New South Wales Court of Appeal has accepted that if a volunteer has become registered as proprietor of Torrens land without fraud, the volunteer's indefeasibility of title is a defence to an equitable tracing claim.[67] In Queensland, where volunteers are expressly granted indefeasible title by statute,[68] the position of volunteers is likely to be similar. Western Australian decisions also take the view that a volunteer obtains an indefeasible title,[69] and the New South Wales authority may be persuasive. However, the Victorian position has long been that a volunteer does not obtain the benefit of indefeasibility.[70] This is also the position in South Australia.[71] Despite this, the Victorian Court of Appeal in *Zekry v Zekry*[72] stated that a volunteer has the benefit of indefeasibility, without considering any of the Victorian case law.[73] Furthermore, while it may be consistent with Torrens orthodoxy that a volunteer obtains indefeasible title, it means that some volunteers who hold traceable proceeds will be protected from proprietary claims while others will not. The variances between jurisdictions and the possible development of personal restitutionary claims may create substantial doctrinal differences between jurisdictions in the future.

65 (2014) 89 NSWLR 317.

66 (2016) 91 NSWLR 732.

67 However, the Court extensively discussed and endorsed the proposition that the volunteer will be liable in money had and received for value retained. As the recipient was not a volunteer, she was not liable.

68 *Land Title Act 1994* (Qld) s 180.

69 *Conlan v Registrar of Titles* (2001) 24 WAR 299; *Gadsdon v Gadsdon* [2003] WASC 48.

70 *Rasmussen v Rasmussen* [1995] 1 VR 613. McMillan J regarded this as the accepted Victorian position in *Imam Ali Islamic Centre v Imam Ali Islamic Centre Inc* [2018] VSC 413.

71 *Peck v Peck* [2010] SASC 258.

72 [2020] VSCA 336.

73 The High Court case of *Farah Constructions Pty Ltd v Say-Dee Pty Ltd* (2007) 230 CLR 89 was cited without discussion.

WHAT'S ONLINE?

Available at www.cambridge.org/highereducation/isbn/9781009232388/resources:

- Recommended further readings
- Further commentary
- Discussion topics
- Practice problem

PART H

RESULTING AND CONSTRUCTIVE TRUSTS

22

RESULTING TRUSTS

Introduction

Resulting trusts arise where property is disposed of in circumstances in which a provider of property does not intend to benefit the recipient.[1] The recipient holds the property on trust for the provider. The property is said to 'result back' to the provider. This does not mean that the equitable interest in the property returns to the provider. What happens is that when the legal title to the property vests in the recipient a new equitable interest is created in favour of the provider.[2] [22.1]

Resulting trusts differ from express trusts in that an express trust gives effect to the settlor's *positive* intention to benefit another by way of trust, whereas a resulting trust gives effect to the provider's *negative* intention – an intention *not* to benefit the recipient. The resulting trust resembles a constructive trust in that it arises by operation of law but differs in that its imposition may be negatived by evidence of the provider's actual intention. [22.2]

Resulting trusts are said to be either 'presumed' or 'automatic'.[3] *Presumed* resulting trusts can be rebutted by evidence that the provider of the property intended to benefit the recipient or to create an express trust in favour of a third party. There are two types of presumed resulting trust. [22.3]

(1) A *purchase money* resulting trust. If P purchases property in the name of D equity presumes that D holds the property on resulting trust for P.

(2) A *voluntary transfer* resulting trust. If P voluntarily transfers property to D, equity presumes that D holds the property on resulting trust for P. Legislation consequential on the repeal of the *Statute of Uses 1535* by State and Territory legislation abolished the application of the voluntary transfer resulting trust to general law land but, except arguably in New South Wales, the presumption still applies to voluntary transfers of land registered with a Torrens title.[4]

What is 'presumed' in these cases is that P declares a trust in her favour when she vests title to the property in D.[5] The presumption can be rebutted by proof that no trust was declared,

1 *Anderson v McPherson (No 2)* [2012] WASC 19, [103] (Edelman J); *Sourcebook* 22.2a, p 553; F & L [21.000]; Robert Chambers, *Resulting Trusts* (Clarendon, 1997) 1–5.

2 *DKLR Holding Co (No 2) Pty Ltd v Commissioner of Stamp Duties (NSW)* (1982) 149 CLR 431, 463 (Aickin J); *Anderson v McPherson (No 2)* [2012] WASC 19, [91] (Edelman J).

3 *Re Vandervell's Trusts (No 2)* [1974] Ch 269, 289 (Megarry J).

4 *Conveyancing Act 1919* (NSW) s 44; *Law of Property Act 2000* (NT) s 7; *Property Law Act 1974* (Qld) s 7; *Property Law Act 1958* (Vic) s 19A(3). See *House v Caffyn* [1922] VLR 67 (Cussen J). The New South Wales provision is worded differently from the equivalent provision in other jurisdictions. Moreover, the definition of 'conveyance' in s 7(1) of the *Conveyancing Act 1919* (NSW) includes a transfer of land under the Torrens system. For different views on the application of the presumption of resulting trust to Torrens land in New South Wales cf *Ryan v Hopkinson* (1990) 14 Fam LR 151 (favouring application of the presumption) with *Newcastle City Council v Kern Land Pty Ltd* (1997) 47 NSWLR 273 (rejecting its application). Even if the presumption of resulting trust is inapplicable, the evidence may show that a transferee of Torrens title land holds the land on trust for the transferor: *Voukidis v C & O Voukidis Pty Ltd (in liq)* [2018] VSC 267, [303].

5 *Anderson v McPherson (No 2)* [2012] WASC 19, [106]; *Sourcebook* 22.3.1a, p 556; W Swadling 'Explaining Resulting Trusts' (2008) 124(1) *Law Quarterly Review* 72; Robert Chambers, 'Is There a Presumption of Resulting Trust?' in Charles Mitchell (ed), *Constructive and Resulting Trusts* (Hart Publishing, 2010) 267.

and that P intended to give or sell the property to D. In the case of property dealings made within certain family relationships, such as where a husband vests title in his wife or a parent gives property to a child, the presumption of resulting trust is not applied. Instead, the presumption is that the provider of the property intended to advance (or make a gift of) the property to the recipient. The presumption of advancement is described at [22.9]–[22.14].

[22.4] *Automatic* resulting trusts arise upon failure of an express trust. The trustee holds the property on resulting trust for the settlor. Failure occurs not only if an express trust fails to comply with legal requirements, such as the rules relating to certainty of objects[6] or the perpetuity rule,[7] but also where the reason for creating the trust no longer exists; for example, where a family trust was constituted in contemplation of a marriage between the intended beneficiaries who afterwards break off their engagement.[8]

Although the resulting trust is 'automatic', in the sense that it cannot be rebutted, it will still be necessary for the court to determine whether the express trust has in fact failed. If the trust instrument expressly or by implication provides for the destination of the trust property in the event of the failure of an interest under the trust, effect will be given to that provision. Even an automatic resulting trust depends in the final analysis on the ascertainment of the settlor's intentions.[9]

There are other situations where an automatic resulting trust might arise. These are cases where the intention of the provider of property has been vitiated or where there is a complete absence of intention to make a disposition, such as where a contract or gift is voidable for misrepresentation, unconscionability or other recognised vitiating factor.[10] If P elects to set aside the transaction, D will hold the property on trust for P (assuming P can identify the property and that P's claim is not defeated by an equitable bar).[11] It has also been suggested that a recipient of stolen money from the thief holds the money, or its traceable product, on resulting trust for the victim of the theft.[12]

In most cases, the trust imposed on the subject-matter of vitiated transactions has been described as constructive.[13] But the practical effect of the trust is that the property is restored to the original owner either because she did not intend to benefit the recipient in the circumstances which have occurred or, in the case of stolen money, because the victim did not intend to make any disposition of the property. There is therefore a sound conceptual argument for classifying the trust in these cases as resulting rather than constructive.

6 See [14.35].
7 See [15.34].
8 *Essery v Cowlard* (1884) 26 Ch D 191. See also *Re the Trusts of the Abbott Fund* [1900] 2 Ch 326; *Sourcebook* 22.4a, p 574 (death of beneficiaries of express trust); *Air Jamaica Ltd v Charlton* [1999] 1 WLR 1399; *Sourcebook* 22.4b, p 575 (surplus in discontinued superannuation trust fund).
9 This is the basis of the rule in *Lassence v Tierney* (1849) 1 Mac & G 551; 41 ER 1379, which provides that where trusts are engrafted onto an absolute disposition of property, and the trusts fail, the absolute gift takes effect and there is no resulting trust.
10 *Reid v Reid* (Supreme Court of New South Wales, Bryson J, 30 Nov 1998). See [5.2].
11 See chapter 6.
12 *Evans v European Bank Ltd* (2004) 61 NSWLR 75, 101 (Spigelman CJ).
13 See [7.14].

Why does equity recognise resulting trusts?

The resulting trust is the most puzzling of the three main categories of trust. The express trust is an established equitable structure for managing wealth. The constructive trust provides equitable machinery for preventing injustice caused by unconscionable conduct. But it is harder to identify the purpose of resulting trusts. Purchase money and voluntary transfer resulting trusts are counterintuitive: most non-lawyers would expect that when A voluntarily vests title to property in B, or purchases property and places title in the name of B, A intended to make a gift of the property to B. [22.5]

It has been suggested that equity is suspicious of gifts and declines to give effect to a gift unless a clear donative intention has been established.[14] The presumption of resulting trust was perhaps based on this suspicion; it presumes that a recipient of property who has not paid for it is not intended to be the absolute owner. However, while the doctrine of resulting trusts can in principle apply to any type of property[15] the doctrine is not in practice applied to small gifts. The legal analysis of your birthday present to a friend is that you intend to make a gift to your friend, not that your friend has rebutted the presumption of resulting trust which would otherwise apply to this voluntary transfer. Equitable suspicion is only aroused by a significant transfer of wealth in circumstances in which the transfer is unexpected.

Another supposed justification is that the resulting trust reflects the intentions of the parties, or at least reflects what they would have intended had they addressed their minds to the circumstances which have occurred.[16] On this analysis, the resulting trust is a 'gap-filling' device, performing much the same kinds of function that the implied term does in contract law. Some applications of the resulting trust (such as the resulting trust in favour of the settlor arising on failure of an express trust) can be rationalised as equitable implied terms. But it is hard to see how the voluntary transfer resulting trust can be analysed in these terms.

In the final analysis, the resulting trust can only be explained in terms of the history of its development. Its origins can be traced to attempts made by landowners in medieval England to avoid the payment of feudal incidents (taxes)[17] and to control the inheritance of their land. A landowner would convey his land during his lifetime to two or more friends (feoffees to uses, in the Norman-French language of the day) while remaining in occupation. Having taken legal title to the land, the feoffees agreed to carry out the landowner's instructions as to how the land was to be held. For example, the feoffees might have been instructed to pay the income from the land to the landowner's eldest son, and to convey the land to him when he attained 21 years of age. The eldest son was the beneficiary ('cestui que trust') of the trust ('use'). The conveyance ensured that when the landowner died, feudal death taxes were not payable since at the time of his death legal title was vested in the feoffees, not the landowner. [22.6]

14 R Chambers (n 1) 16. For criticism of this justification, see Swadling (n 5).
15 See F & L [21.100] for a discussion of the application of resulting trust principles to personal property.
16 Jacobs [1201].
17 The feudal incidents were privileges exercisable by the Crown or a superior landowner. They included the Crown's right of wardship of the landowner's heir and to marry off his children. But, in practice, the privileges were monetarised and regarded as fiscal impositions by landowners. See AWB Simpson, *An Introduction to the History of the Land Law* (Oxford, 1961) 166–7.

An obvious risk was that the landowner might have misjudged the honesty of the feoffees; unscrupulous feoffees might try to keep the land for themselves instead of carrying out the landowner's instructions. The Chancellor eliminated the risk by treating the feoffees as trustees who were obliged to carry out the landowner's wishes. From the landowner's perspective, the most vulnerable period in the arrangement occurred after he had transferred his land to the feoffees, but before he had given them instructions as to how the land was to be held. The Chancellor solved the problem by compelling the feoffees to hold the land on trust for the landowner during this period. An equitable interest was created in favour of the landowner upon the voluntary conveyance of the land to the feoffees.

[22.7] Once the resulting trust arising upon voluntary conveyance had been recognised, other applications of the resulting trust were developed by analogy. It was noticed, for example, that there was little, if any, difference in practice between P buying land in her own name and later voluntarily conveying it to D, and P buying land and immediately vesting legal title in D.[18] The purchase money resulting trust was the outcome of this analogical reasoning.

[22.8] The history of the resulting trust is not a substitute for a convincing contemporary justification for its existence.[19] Nevertheless, the presumption of resulting trust, together with the presumption of advancement, are said to be an 'entrenched landmark'[20] in the law, and some conveyancing practice rests on settled assumptions as to the applicability of the presumptions. There is probably no wholly convincing theoretical justification for the resulting trust: it is an example of how law (including equity) is the product of experience, not logic.[21]

The presumption of advancement

[22.9] In some cases, equity presumes that a disposition of property is intended to take effect as a gift, or advancement, to the recipient. If a husband buys property in the name of his wife,[22] or if a parent buys a property in the name of a child, the purchaser is presumed to have intended to make a gift. The presumption also applies to voluntary transfers made by husbands to wives and by parents to children. The presumption of advancement identifies the circumstances in which the presumption of resulting trust does not apply. Like the presumption of resulting trust, it can be rebutted; for example, by the husband or parent proving that no advancement was intended. If the presumption of advancement is rebutted,

18 The analogy between the resulting trust by voluntary transfer and the purchase money resulting trust was explicitly identified by Eyre LCB in *Dyer v Dyer* (1788) 2 Cox 92, 93; 30 ER 42, 43.

19 In *Calverley v Green* (1984) 155 CLR 242, 267, Murphy J, dissenting, declared that the presumptions of resulting trust and advancement were outmoded, and that equitable title to land should follow the registered title, in the absence of evidence that a separate equitable title had been intended. The majority of the High Court, however, accepted that the presumptions were entrenched landmarks in conveyancing practice.

20 *Nelson v Nelson* (1995) 184 CLR 538, 548 (Deane and Gummow JJ).

21 OW Holmes, 'The Path of the Law' (1897) 10(8) *Harvard Law Review* 457, 465. For the argument that resulting trusts are a response to unjust enrichment see R Chambers (n 1) Part II, and [22.27]–[22.30].

22 *Xiao Hui Ying v Perpetual Trustees Victoria Ltd* [2015] VSCA 124. The presumption has also been applied to a purchase in the name of a fiancée: *Moat v Moat* [1948] 2 All ER 486; *Wirth v Wirth* (1956) 98 CLR 228, 238 (Dixon J). The presumption does not apply to a transfer of property made by a wife to her husband: *March v March* (1945) 62 WN (NSW) 111.

the recipient holds title to the property on resulting trust for the provider unless the evidence establishes that the provider intended to create some other legal relationship, such as an express trust of the property in favour of a third party.[23]

The idea conveyed by the word 'advancement', particularly as applied to advances of capital made by parents to children, is that of setting up the child in life, as opposed to making a mere casual payment.[24] 'Advancement' in equity means more than a gift; it is financial provision made by a person obliged to provide for another which is intended to advance the station in life of that other. In *Murless v Franklin*,[25] Lord Eldon LC stated that in cases of advancement, the transferor of property was 'under a natural obligation to provide for the transferee'. [22.10]

An alternative explanation is that the presumption of advancement reflects the intentions of the parties as to the legal effect of their disposition of property. In *Wirth v Wirth*,[26] Dixon CJ stated that the justification for the presumption is to be found 'in the greater prima facie probability of a beneficial interest being intended in the situations to which the presumption has been applied'. The likelihood that a gift is intended in these cases may be correct, but it is based on an unproven hypothesis that a provider of property wants to benefit the recipient. Moreover, the same hypothesis could well extend to other cases where the presumption of resulting trust currently applies, such as a disposition of property made by one de facto partner to the other.

Criticism of the presumption in Australia has focused on its application to particular relationships, rather than on whether advancement remains appropriate to contemporary social conditions. Recent decisions have identified three issues: [22.11]

(1) Should the presumption of advancement continue to apply to dispositions made by husbands in favour of their wives? A wife's voluntary transfer of her property to her husband attracts the application of the opposite presumption of resulting trust. It might therefore be considered discriminatory for a husband's voluntary transfer of property to his wife to be a presumptive advancement. There is, however, little practical difference in the application of the two presumptions to matrimonial property, particularly where both spouses have contributed to the acquisition of the property. Only slight evidence is needed to rebut the presumptions. The High Court held in *Trustees of the Property of Cummins v Cummins*[27] that, where the contributions to the purchase of the family home are unequal, equity will readily assume that the spouses intended to share the property equally. The position is

23 Cf *Anderson v McPherson (No 2)* [2012] WASC 19, [133]–[138], Edelman J suggesting that the presumption of advancement is not really a presumption at all. See also J Glister, 'Is There a Presumption of Advancement?' (2011) 33(1) *Sydney Law Review* 39. In *Bloch v Bloch* (1981) 180 CLR 390; *Sourcebook* 22.3.2e, p 571, the presumption was rebutted by a finding of resulting trust (Wilson J at 397) or, alternatively, an express trust of land not required to be in writing by reason of the principle that equity does not permit a statute to be used as a cloak for fraud (Brennan J at 402).

24 PE Nygh and PJ Butt, *Butterworths Australian Legal Dictionary* (Butterworths, 1997) 32.

25 (1818) 1 Swan 13; 36 ER 278. See also *Scott v Pauly* (1917) 24 CLR 274, 282 (Isaacs J).

26 (1956) 98 CLR 228, 237.

27 (2006) 227 CLR 278; *Sourcebook* 22.3.2d, p 569. In *Cummins*, title to the property was taken in the names of *both* spouses as joint tenants. It is unclear whether there is an assumption of equal sharing of beneficial title where title has been registered in the name of one spouse: *Commissioner of Taxation v Bosanac (No 7)* (2021) 390 ALR 74, reversed on its facts [2021] FCAFC 158.

obviously different where the property is wholly paid for by one spouse but title is taken solely in the name of the other. The explanation of the latter arrangement is that the purchaser intended to make a gift of the property, even where the wife is the purchaser and the presumption of resulting trust would otherwise apply.[28]

(2) In *Calverley v Green*,[29] Gibbs CJ suggested in obiter dicta that the presumption of advancement should apply to transfers made by a partner in a de facto relationship where the relationship is permanent and the partners hold themselves out to be married. The dictum is unlikely to be applied, particularly now that legislation confers wide-ranging powers on the Family Court to reallocate the property of former de facto partners on relationship breakdown and upon bankruptcy.[30]

(3) Should a transfer of substantial property by an elderly parent to an adult child attract the presumption of advancement? The parent is no longer legally obliged to support the child and may be in greater need of the property than the child. The application of the presumption might, however, be justified if the parent is still under a moral obligation to support the adult child; for example, where the child suffers from a disability or serious medical condition. In *Brown v Brown*,[31] the New South Wales Court of Appeal held that the presumption applied to dispositions of property made by a mother to adult children, although the majority held on very slight evidence that the presumption had been rebutted. The decision was approved by the High Court in *Nelson v Nelson*,[32] where a mother financed the purchase of homes for her adult children. She was held to have rebutted the presumption of advancement which would otherwise have applied to the purchase of property in their names.[33]

[22.12] If advancement carries its traditional meaning of advancing the station in life of the child, there will still be many cases today where a parent wants to advance the interests of an adult child. It would be wrong to assume that adult children are not in need of advancement; for example, many parents help their adult children to buy their first house. Nevertheless, circumstances such as the age and health of the parent and the financial and personal circumstances of the child in the final analysis play the critical role in determining the ease with which the presumption will be rebutted.

[22.13] The applicability of the presumption is determined as *at the time of the transfer*.[34] A parent's transfer of capital to a child made when the parent was aged 50 and in good health

28 *Pettitt v Pettitt* [1970] AC 777, 815 (Lord Upjohn).

29 (1984) 155 CLR 242, 250–1.

30 *Family Law Act 1975* (Cth) pt VIII.

31 (1993) 31 NSWLR 582.

32 (1995) 184 CLR 538; *Sourcebook* 2.2c, p 21.

33 Cf *Pecore v Pecore* [2007] SCC 17 where a majority of the Supreme Court of Canada held that the relationship of parent and adult child was not one of advancement, although on the facts the presumption of resulting trust was rebutted.

34 *Charles Marshall Pty Ltd v Grimsley* (1956) 95 CLR 353; *Shephard v Cartwright* [1955] AC 431; *Trustees of the Property of Cummins v Cummins* (2006) 227 CLR 278, [65]. While post-transfer *statements of intention* by the transferor, not being admissions against interest, are inadmissible in evidence, *Cummins* makes clear that post-transfer *conduct* relating to the property which shed light on the transferor's intention at the time of transfer are admissible.

to a 22-year-old child will not cease to be an advancement simply because 30 years later the parent is in greater need of the money while the child has, in the meantime, accrued substantial wealth.

Application of the presumptions to family property

The presumptions of resulting trust and advancement were once most commonly applied to determine equitable title to the home of former spouses and de facto partners. Family law legislation, conferring on the Family Court a discretionary jurisdiction to reallocate property entitlements on divorce or on termination of a de facto relationship, or where an equitable claim to family property is made in the course of bankruptcy proceedings, has diminished the relevance of the presumptions in this area. They still have a role to play, however, where the relationship has been terminated by death, and to other family relationships such as property disputes between parents and children. The equitable principles apply to all forms of property – not only the home, but also chattels and money in bank accounts. [22.14]

It is impossible to apply the voluntary transfer and purchase money resulting trusts to the purchase of a family home without some practical adaptation of equitable principle. The adaptation is necessary for three reasons: [22.15]

(1) Modern financing of family home purchases has meant a reconceptualisation of what is meant by 'purchase'. The early authorities on resulting trusts usually concerned the purchase of property by direct capital payments. Modern home purchase, however, typically takes the form of purchase on mortgage terms from banks and other institutional lenders. Precise identification of a 'purchaser' of property can be more difficult when it is the financial institution which pays the purchase price to the vendor, and the substantial question is to determine the legal responsibility for repaying the financial institution.[35]

(2) Many aspects of family property-holding rest on tacit assumptions shared by the spouses or partners of which hard evidence, required by a court of law, is deficient. Few couples discuss the beneficial title to the home they have bought, as distinct from the registered title. To the extent that they give the matter any consideration at all, they will generally assume that the equitable title follows the registered title. Only in the absence of an express agreement governing the equitable title, which in any case should be in writing if it is to be enforceable,[36] can the court infer an agreement between the couple from their conduct as to how the equitable title is to be shared. A court cannot go further and impute to the parties an agreement which, as reasonable people, they ought to have made as to the division of beneficial

35 In addition to the purchase price, the incidental expenses of buying property, such as legal costs, stamp duty and registration fees, are relevant to quantifying beneficial title under a resulting trust: *Zhang v Metcalf* [2020] NSWCA 228, [49]. The purchase price is defined in terms of what 'is the cost to the purchasers rather than the benefit to the vendor': *Currie v Hamilton* [1984] 1 NSWLR 687, 691 (McLelland J).

36 See [15.5].

title. The presumptions of resulting trust and advancement can be rebutted by evidence of agreements and understandings actually reached between the parties as to how the equitable title to the home is to be shared. But courts must not make agreements for partners which they have not made for themselves.[37]

(3) The law of resulting trusts rewards financial contributions towards the acquisition of property; it does not value non-financial contributions. The award of equitable interests has traditionally been based on 'the solid tug of money'.[38] This defect has largely been overcome by developments in the law of constructive trusts, which have accorded greater recognition in recent years to the non-financial 'homemaker' contributions made by one partner.[39] Family law legislation has also largely overcome the 'materialism' of the law of resulting trusts.[40] Nevertheless, in cases where there is no statutory discretion to reallocate property, and the criteria for the award of a constructive trust have not been met, the doctrine of resulting trusts does not permit a court to examine the 'whole context' of the family relationship.

[22.16] The leading authority on the application of resulting trust principles to the family home is the High Court decision of *Calverley v Green*.[41] A de facto couple purchased a house in their joint names. The purchase price was $27000, of which the defendant paid $9000 as a deposit, with the balance raised by a mortgage. The defendant told the plaintiff that the finance company required the mortgage to be in their joint names, and at his suggestion they became jointly and severally liable under the loan agreement to make the repayments. The defendant made all the mortgage repayments. The couple split up after living together for 10 years, and the plaintiff claimed a share in the home.

The High Court held that the application of resulting trust principles entitled the plaintiff to a one-third share in the home. In reaching this conclusion, the Court ruled that:

(a) The defendant was entitled to a one-third interest in the home under a purchase money resulting trust by virtue of his payment of a deposit amounting to one-third of the purchase price.

(b) The parties were entitled to an equal beneficial interest in the home by virtue of their *joint liability* to repay the mortgage. Equitable title is not determined by *actual repayments* to the lender of mortgage instalments, since these only discharge the contract of loan entered into with the lender. In the words of Mason and Brennan JJ: 'The payment of instalments under the mortgage was not a payment of the purchase price but a payment towards securing the release of the charge which the parties created over the property purchased.'[42]

---

37 *Allen v Snyder* [1977] 2 NSWLR 685.
38 *Hofman v Hofman* [1965] NZLR 795, 800 (Woodhouse J).
39 See chapter 23.
40 *Family Law Act 1975* (Cth) s 75.
41 (1984) 155 CLR 242; *Sourcebook* 22.3.1b, p 558, and 22.3.2c, p 566.
42 *Calverley v Green* (1984) 155 CLR 242, 257–8. Complications can occur in cases, not concerned with family property, where multiple purchasers acquire interests in land at different times: *Staatz v Berry (No 3)* (2019) 138 ACSR 231 (purchase of land to establish a commune known as the 'Bhula Bhula community'). Constructive trust principles based on a 'failed joint endeavour' provide more flexible solutions to these cases than resulting trust doctrine.

(c) The plaintiff had to account to the defendant for the mortgage instalments in excess of 50%, which he had paid. The right to an account is a personal, not a proprietary, equitable right. A payer who discharges more than her due share of mortgage payments under a mortgage (or other joint loan contract) has a *personal* right to contribution from the party whose share she has paid, but she does not obtain a *proprietary* interest under a resulting trust.

The principal significance of *Calverley* is that it defines 'purchase', for the purpose of imposing a purchase money resulting trust, to include not only a direct cash purchase of the home but also taking out a mortgage to buy a home. Actual repayments of the mortgage instalments, on the other hand, discharge the debt owed to the bank or other lender but do not constitute purchase of the home.

There was no suggestion in *Calverley* that the parties had reached any agreement or understanding which might have modified the division of equitable title based on financial contributions. The circumstances in which equitable title can be modified by factors other than financial contributions were crucial in the later High Court decision of *Trustees of the Property of Cummins v Cummins*.[43] A married couple bought their family home jointly: the wife contributing 76% of the purchase price and the husband the remaining 24%. The husband was a barrister who failed to lodge income tax returns for 45 years. He was made bankrupt on the application of the Tax Office. His wife claimed a 76% interest in the matrimonial home on his bankruptcy, based on her contributions to the purchase price, which would have left the remaining 24% interest to be claimed by the Tax Office. The High Court held that the presumption of resulting trust based on the payment of contributions was rebutted on the facts of the case. Each spouse held a 50% equitable interest in the home, and the husband's half share was payable to the Tax Office. [22.17]

In reaching this conclusion, the High Court emphasised the following facts:

(1) The parties were married. The High Court left open whether the same result would have been reached if they were de facto partners.[44]

(2) The home was the family home. The equitable interests would have reflected their actual financial contributions if they had purchased an investment property.[45]

(3) Title had been taken as joint tenants. Joint tenants notionally hold property as one person in law. On the other hand, taking registered title as tenants in common, meaning that the spouses hold the property in undivided shares, is evidence that the parties intend the equitable title to reflect their actual financial contributions.[46]

43 (2006) 227 CLR 278.
44 Ibid [70].
45 Cf *Bloch v Bloch* (1981) 180 CLR 390; *Buffrey v Buffrey* (2006) 12 BPR 23,619. It is unclear whether the reasoning in *Cummins* is applicable where registered title to the home is taken in the name of only one spouse: *Commissioner of Taxation v Bosanac (No 7)* (2021) 390 ALR 74, reversed on its facts [2021] FCAFC 158.
46 (2006) 227 CLR 278, 303.

An important reason identified in *Cummins* for favouring the equal sharing of the beneficial interest is that, within close personal relationships, the division of financial contributions to the purchase price of the home can be arbitrary. For example, if a married couple arranges for one of them to pay for the home while the other pays for the maintenance and education of the children, it would be inequitable to deprive the latter of a share of the beneficial interest in the home.

[22.18] When spouses purchase investment properties, equity does not presume that the parties intend to share the property equally. If they buy the property in joint names, both contributing to the purchase, the wife's contributions will entitle her to an equitable interest, assessed on resulting trust principles and based on the proportion of the purchase price she pays. But the husband's contributions to the purchase price will presumptively constitute an advancement to the wife. If the husband's contribution to the purchase price exceeds 50%, it will be rebuttably presumed that he intended to confer equality of interest on his wife.[47] So if H and W buy Blackacre, an investment property, in joint names, H contributing 60% of the purchase price and W contributing 40%, W is entitled to a 40% interest in the property by the application of resulting trust doctrine. H will be presumed to have intended to advance 10% of his contribution, thereby bringing W's equitable interest to 50%. In this example, the beneficial title to the property reflects the joint registered title.

The presumption of advancement was rebutted in *Buffrey v Buffrey*.[48] The husband received compensation as a result of a workplace accident. He decided to buy an investment property and paid most of the purchase price out of his compensation, the balance being paid by a small bank mortgage of which he and his wife were co-mortgagors. Title was registered in their joint names. The wife was accused by her former employer of embezzlement of a large sum of money. The employer obtained an interlocutory order preventing dealings with the property, with a view to having the property sold off to satisfy any judgment for fraud obtained against the wife. The trial judge found that the husband had paid 87% of the purchase price of the property, and the wife 13% by virtue of her liability under the joint mortgage. The wife held a 13% interest under a purchase money resulting trust. The employer argued that the husband had advanced 37% of his interest to his wife, with the result that both spouses were entitled to 50% interests in the property. Palmer J held that the presumption of advancement had been rebutted on the evidence. The husband did not intend his wife to have an interest in the property equal to his. He had bought the property as a superannuation investment because he was no longer employed and could not make superannuation contributions out of his earnings. Once the presumption of advancement had been rebutted, he was entitled to an 87% share in the property under a purchase money resulting trust.

[22.19] Even if the presumption of resulting trust, based on the initial financial contributions to the acquisition of property, is not rebutted, quantifying the equitable interests of the parties can be affected by financial or non-financial contributions made subsequent to the acquisition. Changes in the quantum of interest may occur as a result of the application of proprietary estoppel[49] or the *Baumgartner* constructive trust to the

47 *Buffrey v Buffrey* (2006) 12 BPR 23,619, [14].

48 Ibid.

49 [8.6]–[8.12].

changing circumstances of a family relationship.[50] A holistic approach, taking account of both resulting trust and constructive trust principles, must be applied to quantifying beneficial interests in property.

Voluntary transfers of property

Our discussion has so far assumed that identical principles apply to purchase money resulting trusts and voluntary transfer resulting trusts. The principles ought to be the same, since A buying property and arranging for the vendor to place title in the name of B is no different in substance from A buying property and taking title in his name before conveying the property to B. The former gives rise to a purchase money resulting trust while the latter is an example of a resulting trust arising on a voluntary conveyance, but both are mechanisms for vesting legal title to the property in the name of its intended legal owner. The only difference between the two is that A is an intermediate legal owner in the case of a voluntary transfer resulting trust, whereas A takes no legal title to the property under a purchase money resulting trust. [22.20]

A difference between purchase money and voluntary transfer resulting trusts of land exists in some States by virtue of provisions of the property legislation repealing the *Statute of Uses 1535*. The general effect of the legislation is to provide that no use or trust of land is recognised simply because the conveyance of property is voluntary. Most versions of the legislation apply only to voluntary conveyances of land, and not to voluntary transfers of other types of property. A complication is that it has not been enacted in all States and Territories. Even in jurisdictions in which it has been enacted, the wording is not uniform.[51] [22.21]

Resulting trusts arising on failure of an express trust

Suppose an express trust fails because the class of beneficiaries does not comply with the rules for certainty of objects,[52] or because the trust infringes the rule against perpetuities.[53] Who is entitled to the property settled on the terms of the invalid trust? Equity's answer is that the trustees will hold the property on resulting trust for the settlor. If the settlor has died, the property will be held on trust for any beneficiary nominated in his will to take the property or, if he has not executed a will, for the person(s) entitled on his intestacy. A beneficiary of a resulting trust who is of full capacity can require the resulting trustees to transfer the property to her in accordance with the rule in *Saunders v Vautier*.[54] [22.22]

50 *Baumgartner v Baumgartner* (1987) 164 CLR 137. See [23.15]–[23.30]; *Hansen v Noble* (2021) 20 BPR 41,181 (application of both resulting trust and constructive trust principles to a dispute between mother and daughter).

51 See n 4, noting that, with the possible exception of New South Wales, the legislation does not apply to voluntary transfers of land subject to Torrens title. The statutory provisions are discussed in detail in F & L [21.090].

52 See [14.35].

53 See [15.34].

54 (1841) 4 Beav 115; 49 ER 282. See [13.3].

[22.23] One fairly common type of functional trust failure occurs where property settled on express trust has not been, and cannot be, fully disposed of under the terms of the trust. Where the unapplied property has been settled on the terms of a charitable trust, and surplus trust moneys remain after the charitable purposes have been carried out, the money will be applied cy-près for the nearest analogous purpose.[55] But if the trust is not charitable, surplus trust moneys will be held on resulting trust for the settlor. In *Re the Trusts of the Abbott Fund*,[56] a sum of money was collected from subscribers for the maintenance of two deaf women. On their death it was held that money remaining in the fund had to be returned to the subscribers under a resulting trust.

[22.24] In *Re the Trusts of the Abbott Fund*, the Court was satisfied, on a reading of the documentation of the subscription appeal, that the donors had not intended their contributions to pass to the estates of the women for whose maintenance the money had been collected. The resulting trust arose because the donors did not intend to benefit the estates of the women on their death. As we have already noticed, the resulting trust responds to the *absence of intention* to benefit the recipient of property. The trust money will not be held on resulting trust if the trust instrument specifies the destination of surplus funds when the trust purpose has been fulfilled, or where an alternative to a resulting trust can be implied from the circumstances surrounding the creation of the express trust.[57]

[22.25] Where the surplus arises on the termination of a superannuation trust, the destination of any surplus funds will usually be determined by the *Superannuation Industry (Supervision) Act 1993* (Cth).[58] If the trust is not regulated by the Act, the surplus will be returned to contributors, applying resulting trust principles. In *Air Jamaica Ltd v Charlton*,[59] the Privy Council held that on the termination of the trust the surplus was to be divided pro rata between the members of the superannuation fund and the estates of deceased members in proportion to their contributions, regardless of the benefits received by each member and the dates when they made their contributions.

[22.26] The problem of determining the destination of surplus funds often occurs on the dissolution of an unincorporated association such as a sports club. The entitlement, if any, of members of the association to any surplus funds on the dissolution of the association will usually be found in the governing rules of the association which operate as contracts between the members. There is, in this case, no room for resulting trust principles to apply. If the rules are silent on the matter, the surplus will be divided equally among members who are alive at the date of dissolution[60] unless they have received all the benefits to which

55 See [16.39]–[16.43].

56 [1900] 2 Ch 326.

57 *Re Osoba* [1978] 1 WLR 791.

58 *Superannuation Industry (Supervision) Act 1993* (Cth) s 117.

59 [1999] 1 WLR 1399. Cf *Rees v Dominion Insurance Co of Australia Ltd (in liq)* (1981) 6 ACLR 71, where contributors were held to have made their contributions 'out and out', with no expectation of having them returned, so that when the fund was terminated the surplus passed to the Crown as ownerless goods.

60 *Re Bucks Constabulary Fund (No 2)* [1979] 1 WLR 936. Cf *Re West Sussex Constabulary's Widows, Children and Benevolent (1930) Fund Trusts* [1971] Ch 1, where it was held that fund income derived from members' subscriptions passed to the Crown as ownerless goods although donations and legacies made by non-members to the association were held on resulting trust.

they were entitled. In that eventuality the surplus will constitute ownerless property (*bona vacantia*) and pass to the Crown.[61]

Resulting trusts arising in other cases of failure of basis: the *Quistclose* trust

Does a resulting trust arise whenever money is paid for a purpose which the payer wants carried out, and which is not carried out, even if the payee is not an express trustee? Suppose, for example, I give $1000 to the organiser of a local group which is campaigning to have a new railway line constructed to my home suburb. The organiser is not a trustee and the purpose of the appeal may not create an enforceable trust under trusts law.[62] Soon afterwards, the government agrees to construct the railway and the local campaign group is dissolved. I am entitled to recover my unused donation in a common law action for money had and received (in substance a personal claim for unjust enrichment) on the ground of total failure of consideration.[63] Can I instead claim the benefit of a resulting trust over the payment, or over any property acquired with the payment? The principal advantage of awarding the resulting trust as a remedy for failure of consideration, from my point of view, is that my claim to the return of the money will survive the payee's bankruptcy. The resulting trust entitles me to the return of my money, assuming that it can be identified in the organiser's bank account, in priority to his unsecured creditors. [22.27]

Some writers have argued that if money paid to a trustee for a trust purpose which fails is held on resulting trust for the payer then, logically, money paid to a *non*-trustee for a purpose which fails ought also to be held on resulting trust for the payer.[64] The basis of the payment has failed: the payer did not intend to let the payee keep the money if it could not be applied for the purposes of the campaign. [22.28]

In *Westdeutsche Landesbank Girozentrale v Islington London Borough Council*,[65] the House of Lords held that the resulting trust was not a general proprietary remedy for failure of basis. An automatic resulting trust only arises in cases where property is paid to the trustee of an express trust, and the trust cannot be carried into effect or fails to exhaust the whole beneficial interest. In the *Westdeutsche* case, a bank had paid money to a local council under an 'interest rate swaps' agreement which was void because the council had no authority to enter into the contract. The bank argued that the basis of the payment had failed; it had paid the money to the council wrongly believing that the latter had legal [22.29]

61 *Re Bucks Constabulary Fund (No 2)* [1979] 1 WLR 936, 978.
62 See [16.44].
63 *Roxborough v Rothmans of Pall Mall Australia Ltd* (2001) 208 CLR 516; *Equuscorp Pty Ltd v Haxton* (2012) 246 CLR 498.
64 Chambers (n 1) chapter 6; *Sourcebook* 22.6a, p 582. Cf W Swadling, 'A New Role for Resulting Trusts?' (1996) 16(1) *Legal Studies* 110; *Sourcebook* 22.6b, p 583; Swadling (n 5). The argument assumes that the money is traceable by the application of tracing rules. See chapter 21. In addition, a resulting trust cannot be imposed if the failure of basis occurs after the payee has obtained beneficial title to the property, although a personal restitutionary claim will still be available: *Re Goldcorp Exchange Ltd* [1995] 1 AC 74; Chambers (n 1) 145–6.
65 [1996] AC 669.

authority to enter into the swaps agreement. So, it was argued, the bank was entitled to a resulting trust over the money.[66] A majority of the House of Lords rejected this attempt to establish the resulting trust as a general remedy for restitution of money where the basis of a payment fails.

Lord Browne-Wilkinson predicted that if the resulting trust became a general remedy whenever money was paid for a purpose which failed, '[a] new area of unmanageable risk will be introduced into commercial dealings'.[67] Most lenders who can identify some or all of their money in the hands of a bankrupt borrower could claim the benefit of a resulting trust over the money. The number of creditors who could claim priority on the borrower's bankruptcy would be dramatically increased, and the assets available to unsecured creditors would be correspondingly diminished. The costs incurred by potential lenders in investigating resulting trust entitlements of prior creditors would also be significant.[68]

[22.30] A possible exception to the principle that an automatic resulting trust is not a remedy for failure of basis (except in cases where an express trust has failed) is the *Quistclose* trust.[69] We saw in chapter 14 that if A lends money to B on terms that B is not to become beneficial owner of the money but is to apply the money exclusively for the benefit of persons or purposes specified by A, then B becomes a trustee of the money for A.[70] It is unclear whether the trust is express or resulting. An objection to recognising an express trust of the money is that many such trusts are created for non-charitable purposes which are not recognised by trusts law, as when A lends $50 000 to B solely for the purpose of enabling B to buy computer equipment for his business.[71] In *Twinsectra Ltd v Yardley*,[72] where money had been lent solely for the purpose of enabling the borrower to buy a property, Lord Millett analysed the *Quistclose* trust as an application of the resulting trust.[73] When A lends B money on terms that B is not to become beneficial owner, B holds the money on resulting trust for A with a duty or power (depending on the terms of the loan agreement) to apply the money for the purpose specified by A.

The High Court has approved the principles on which the *Quistclose* trust rests without, however, determining whether the trust is express or resulting.[74] Later case law has

66 The bank's reason for claiming a resulting trust rather than seeking restitution in a personal claim for money had and received for failure of consideration was to obtain an award of compound interest. Such an award can be made against a trustee or other fiduciary who has acted in breach of obligation: *Hungerfords v Walker* (1989) 171 CLR 125; *Sempra Metals v Revenue and Customs Commissioners* [2008] 1 AC 561; *Prudential Assurance Co Ltd v Revenue & Customs Commissioners* [2019] AC 929.

67 [1996] 1 AC 669, 709. See also *Roxborough v Rothmans of Pall Mall Australia Ltd* (1999) 95 FCR 185, [74] (Hill and Lehane JJ).

68 Resulting trusts are not registrable as security interests under the *Personal Property Securities Act 2009* (Cth).

69 *Barclays Bank Ltd v Quistclose Investments Ltd* [1970] AC 567; *Sourcebook* 13.3.1a, p 346.

70 See [14.25].

71 *Re EVTR* [1987] BCLC 646. Cf *Duke Unley Pty Ltd v Corporation of the City of Unley* [2020] SASC 224 (payments made for the purpose of creating a permanent car park, but a *Quistclose* analysis was rejected, one reason being that statute regulated the arrangement).

72 [2002] 2 AC 164.

73 Ibid 185–93.

74 *Australasian Conference Association Ltd v Mainline Constructions Pty Ltd* (1978) 141 CLR 335, 353. Cf *Rambaldi (Trustee) v Commissioner of Taxation* (2017) 107 ATR 1, [27]: '[t]he correctness of the decision in *Quistclose*, and Lord Wilberforce's reasoning in support of that decision have been accepted for almost another 50 years on top of the long history preceding the decision'.

revealed differences of judicial opinion on this question. In *Salvo v New Tel Ltd*,[75] the plaintiffs were investors who provided funds to New Tel Ltd for the purpose of financing its business ventures. New Tel entered into an arrangement to buy Digiplus Investments Ltd. For this purpose, $750 000 of the investors' money was paid into an account owned by New Tel's solicitors. The sale did not go ahead. The New South Wales Court of Appeal held that the money raised by New Tel was held on trust for the investors. Spigelman CJ and Young CJ in Eq classified the trust as express, while Handley JA preferred to characterise it as a resulting trust. The judgments contain some analysis of the authorities and academic literature on the *Quistclose* trust. On the facts of *Salvo v New Tel*, however, it was irrelevant how the trust was classified.[76]

Resulting trusts and illegality

Do the presumptions of resulting trust and advancement apply if A transfers property to B voluntarily (ie without B providing consideration) in order to carry out an illegal purpose? The purpose of vesting legal title to the property in B may have been to minimise liability to tax or to maximise a welfare entitlement. Alternatively, A's aim might be to avoid the property being claimed by creditors, or being made subject to a Family Court order in favour of A's former spouse or de facto partner. [22.31]

Before considering the application of resulting trust principles to A's disposition, it is first necessary to consider whether the disposition is liable to be set aside by the application of 'anti-avoidance' legislation. For example, dispositions of property will be set aside both under the *Bankruptcy Act 1966* (Cth) and under State and Territory legislation if they are made with intent to defraud creditors.[77] Similarly, the Family Court possesses statutory powers to set aside a disposition of property made with the intention of defeating an existing or anticipated court order affecting the property.[78] The equitable 'clean hands' doctrine will also be relevant if a party to an illegal transaction applies for equitable relief.[79] [22.32]

Resulting trust principles are relevant if A has vested legal title to the property in B solely in order to carry out an illegal purpose but B, who has provided no consideration for the transfer, later relies on that title to prevent A from recovering the property. Can A argue that he is the beneficial owner of the property by application of a unrebutted presumption of resulting trust? The answer depends, first, on determining whether the illegal purpose has been carried out. If it has not been carried out, A can rely on the presumption of resulting trust to recover the property. Alternatively, if B is A's wife or child, A can adduce evidence to show that the presumption of advancement was rebutted. A's unfulfilled illegal purpose will not prevent him from proving that he is the beneficial [22.33]

75 [2005] NSWCA 281. See also *Raulfs v Fishy Bite Pty Ltd* [2012] NSWCA 135, [51]–[52] (Campbell JA); *Sourcebook* 13.4.5a, p 359.

76 *Quistclose* trusts can provide some, albeit limited, security protection for investors who cannot obtain full security rights by the imposition of a mortgage or charge. They are not registrable as security interests under the *Personal Property Securities Act 2009* (Cth) s 8(1)(h).

77 See [15.29]–[15.30].

78 *Family Law Act 1975* (Cth) s 106B.

79 See [6.16]–[6.23].

owner of the property. In *Martin v Martin*,[80] a husband registered a recently purchased parcel of land in the name of his wife with what was described as the 'nebulous' intention of avoiding liability to land tax. No liability would in fact have been incurred if he had taken title in his own name. The High Court held that the husband was not precluded from bringing evidence to rebut the presumption of advancement simply because the transfer was motivated by tax avoidance considerations.

[22.34] If the illegal purpose has been carried out, A's claim to the return of the property depends on whether it would be contrary to the policy of the law that has been broken to permit restitution. In *Nelson v Nelson*,[81] a mother placed title to a house she had bought in the name of her children, Elizabeth and Peter. Her reason for taking title in their names was to obtain a government subsidy under the *Defence Service Homes Act 1918* (Cth), enabling her to buy another property. Although she was an 'eligible person' under the Act by reason of her late husband's war service, she was not entitled to the subsidy because she already owned another dwelling. On her application form, the mother nonetheless denied having an interest in another property. This false statement meant that she was criminally liable under the *Crimes Act 1914* (Cth) for making an untrue representation with a view to obtaining a financial benefit. On the basis of her statement, the mother obtained the subsidy to buy her second property. The property placed in the names of her children was later sold. Elizabeth claimed half the proceeds. She argued that her mother should not be allowed to rely on her own illegality to rebut the presumption of advancement which applies when a parent places title to property in the name of her children.

The High Court unanimously held that the mother was not prevented by her illegality from rebutting the presumption of advancement and proving that the children held the proceeds of sale of the property on resulting trust for her. A majority of the High Court held that enforcement of the resulting trust was conditional on repaying the Commonwealth the amount of the subsidy she had received.[82]

[22.35] The judgments in *Nelson v Nelson* drew a distinction between transactions or conduct which are themselves prohibited, whether expressly or impliedly, and those which are not prohibited but are nonetheless illegal because the transactions or conduct are associated with some illegal purpose.[83] In the former case, restitution of property will not be allowed. The facts of *Nelson v Nelson* belonged to the second category. In cases of this kind, the issue

80 (1959) 110 CLR 297. See also *Perpetual Executors & Trustees Association of Australia Ltd v Wright* (1917) 23 CLR 185. The principle also applies if A repents of his illegal purpose before it has been fully carried into effect: *Taylor v Bowers* (1876) 1 QBD 291; *Pralle v Knackstedt* (1994) 11 SR (WA) 196.

81 (1995) 184 CLR 538. See [22.11]. It is doubtful if this case involved any illegality but, in response to submissions, the High Court discussed the principles applicable to unexecuted illegal transactions.

82 Dawson and Toohey JJ dissented on the issue of conditioning relief on repayment of the subsidy, holding that the Court should not interfere with the Commonwealth's discretion to claim repayment. Constructive trust relief conditional on repayment to Centrelink was ordered in *Stephenson v Santos* [2020] NSWCA 262. A court can take other steps to enforce the policy of the legislation; for example, by sending the papers of the case to a prosecuting authority: *Jin v Yang* (2008) 13 BPR 25,523.

83 See also *Equuscorp Pty Ltd v Haxton* (2012) 246 CLR 498, French CJ, Crennan and Kiefel JJ at [23] where the distinction is drawn between (i) express prohibition (ii) implied prohibition, and (iii) a transaction associated with an illegal purpose. In *Stephenson v Santos* [2020] NSWCA 262, [39]–[40] (Leeming JA), a deception practised on Centrelink by a beneficiary under a resulting trust in order to obtain rental assistance was held to fall within category (iii).

will be whether it is contrary to the policy of the relevant statute to allow the plaintiff to recover her property by rebutting the presumption of advancement.

The relevant considerations were summarised by McHugh J:

> Courts should not refuse to enforce legal or equitable rights simply because they arose out of or were associated with an unlawful purpose unless:
>
> (a) the statute discloses an intention that those rights should be unenforceable in all circumstances; or
>
> (b) (i) the sanction of refusing to enforce those rights is not disproportionate to the seriousness of the unlawful conduct;
>
> (ii) the imposition of the sanction is necessary, having regard to the terms of the statute, to protect its objects or policies; and
>
> (iii) the statute does not disclose an intention that the sanctions and remedies contained in the statute are to be the only legal consequences of a breach of the statute or the frustration of its policies.[84]

In *Nelson v Nelson*, provisions of the *Defence Service Homes Act 1918* (Cth) authorised the Commonwealth to recover the amount of the subsidy from an applicant not entitled to receive it. Moreover, the *Crimes Act* imposed sanctions on persons making an untrue representation with a view to obtaining a subsidy. The adequacy of these sanctions meant that there was no justification for refusing to enforce the plaintiff's equitable rights, particularly as the refusal would be disproportionate to the seriousness of her conduct.[85]

WHAT'S ONLINE?

Available at www.cambridge.org/highereducation/isbn/9781009232388/resources:

- Recommended further readings
- Further commentary
- Discussion topics
- Practice problem

84 (1995) 184 CLR 538, 613 (McHugh J).
85 Ibid 617.

23

CONSTRUCTIVE TRUSTS

Introduction

A constructive trust is imposed by operation of law when it would be inequitable, by reference to established equitable principles, for the defendant to deny the obligations of trusteeship.[1] The award of a constructive trust usually involves the court ordering the defendant to hold property to which he has title[2] on trust for the plaintiff. But, in some situations, the constructive trust is awarded as a personal remedy; the defendant is held accountable as if he were a trustee. Someone who knowingly assists a trustee or other fiduciary to commit a breach of duty will be accountable as a constructive trustee.[3] As constructive trustee, he must account to the beneficiary for loss caused by the breach.[4] The constructive trust is an 'as if' trust – the defendant is treated by equity as if he were an express trustee, even though he is not.[5] The trustee legislation of all States and Territories defines the words 'trust' and 'trustee' to include a constructive trust and constructive trustee, unless the context otherwise requires.[6] This means that constructive trustees can exercise the statutory powers contained in the legislation. [23.1]

Whether a constructive trustee is subject to the duties imposed on an express trustee, discussed in chapter 17, is unclear. The answer will depend on the nature of the constructive trust imposed. If the duty of the constructive trustee is to convey immediately the subject-matter of the trust to the plaintiff, the constructive trustee will not be under any ongoing management obligations.[7] Although the constructive trust is a remedy for breach of fiduciary duty it does not follow that a constructive trustee is a fiduciary. A fiduciary is someone who voluntarily undertakes to protect the interests of another in a particular matter (see [10.2]). Constructive trusteeship, in contrast, is not voluntarily assumed but is an obligation imposed by judicial decision or by the automatic application of equitable doctrine. Indeed, a constructive trustee is usually the last person a beneficiary would want to act as a fiduciary in her best interests. [23.2]

A distinction is drawn in many of the cases between an 'institutional' and a 'remedial' constructive trust. A difficulty in applying the distinction is that judges and writers often fail to define what they mean by the terms 'institutional' and 'remedial'. In general terms, an institutional constructive trust arises by operation of law from the date of the circumstances which give rise to it: the court's role is simply to declare that a trust has arisen at that date. A 'remedial' constructive trust, on the other hand, is a judicial remedy giving rise to an [23.3]

1 Cf *Parsons v McBain* (2001) 109 FCR 120, [10], citing AW Scott, *Law of Trusts* (Little Brown & Co, 4th ed, 1994) §462.4; *Sourcebook* 23.2, note 5, p 600. For a detailed work on constructive trusts, see Ying Liew *Rationalising Constructive Trusts* (Hart Publishing, 2017).

2 The defendant's title need not be sole, but can be held under a joint tenancy or tenancy in common. An equitable interest can be the subject-matter of an express trust but it is unsettled whether an equitable interest can be held on constructive trust. Equity can prevent unconscientious conduct by the equitable interest-holder without imposing a constructive trust.

3 See [11.17].

4 *Giumelli v Giumelli* (1999) 196 CLR 101, 112 [4]; *Sourcebook* 23.4a, p 610.

5 *McNab v Graham* (2017) 53 VR 311, 340.

6 ACT s 4; NSW s 5; NT s 82; Qld s 5; SA s 4; Tas s 4; Vic s 1; WA s 6.

7 Cf Charles Mitchell and Stephen Watterson, 'Remedies for Knowing Receipt' in C Mitchell ed, *Constructive and Resulting Trusts* (Hart Publishing, 2010) 115 with William Swadling, 'The Fiction of the Constructive Trust' (2011) 64(1) *Current Legal Problems* 399.

enforceable equitable obligation. The extent to which it operates retrospectively to the prejudice of third parties lies at the discretion of the court.[8] Some constructive trusts have been judicially identified as being institutional in character. They include the 'common intention' constructive trust[9] and the constructive trust imposed over stolen money.[10] Conversely, the *Baumgartner* constructive trust and constructive trust relief awarded in estoppel cases are generally regarded as remedial constructive trusts.[11]

The significance of the distinction lies in the more liberal discretion available to the court in determining whether a remedial constructive trust should be awarded. The discretion relates both to the choice of remedy and the fashioning of equitable relief once the remedy has been awarded. The court must first determine whether the successful plaintiff should be awarded a trust over the property claimed (in other words, an ownership interest), as opposed to an equitable lien (which secures the payment of a monetary order over the land) or, most simply, a personal remedy, such as equitable compensation or an account of profits.[12] If the court decides to impose a constructive trust, a further consideration, relating to the fashioning of equitable relief, is to determine the date from which the trust takes effect.[13]

The constructive trust compared with other trusts

Express trust

[23.4] The essential difference between an express trust and a constructive trust is that an express trust is created by the act of a settlor, who manifests an intention to create a trust, whereas a constructive trust is imposed by operation of law.[14] Intention is not irrelevant to the imposition of a constructive trust (indeed, one type of constructive trust is termed a 'common intention' constructive trust) but the source of the obligations imposed on the trustee is the court order, not the intention or expectations of a settlor.

8 *Westdeutsche Landesbank Girozentrale v Islington London Borough Council* [1996] AC 669, 714 (Lord Browne-Wilkinson). The judgment of Deane J in *Muschinski v Dodds* (1985) 160 CLR 583; *Sourcebook* 23.3a, p 601, contains the classic exposition of the institutional/remedial distinction in Australian equity. See also P O'Connor, 'Happy Partners or Strange Bedfellows: The Blending of Remedial and Institutional Features in the Evolving Constructive Trust' (1996) 20(3) *Melbourne University Law Review* 735.

9 *Parsons v McBain* (2001) 109 FCR 120. See [23.10].

10 *Wambo Coal Pty Ltd v Ariff* (2007) 63 ACSR 429, [40]. See [23.41].

11 *Baumgartner v Baumgartner* (1987) 164 CLR 137; *Sourcebook* 23.3b, p 606; see [23.15]; *Giumelli v Giumelli* (1999) 196 CLR 101. However, see *McNab v Graham* (2017) 53 VR 311 discussed at [23.34].

12 *Bathurst City Council v PWC Properties Pty Ltd* (1998) 195 CLR 566; *John Alexander's Clubs Pty Ltd v White City Tennis Club Ltd* (2010) 241 CLR 1. For a non-exhaustive list of some of the factors relevant to the exercise of the discretion, see *Grimaldi v Chameleon Mining NL (No 2)* (2012) 200 FCR 296, [509]–[510].

13 *Muschinski v Dodds* (1985) 160 CLR 583.

14 Many constructive trusts are created by court order, but an order is not essential to the creation of the trust. The execution of contracts for the sale of land, for example, often assumes the existence of the constructive trust without a court order being obtained. See [23.58].

Resulting trust

A resulting trust arises when a provider of property does not intend the recipient to obtain beneficial title to the property; the trust arises upon proof of the provider's *absence of intention* to benefit the recipient.[15] But the intention of a provider of property does not, without more, establish the existence of a constructive trust. The trust arises because it would be unconscientious for the legal owner of the property to assert full beneficial title. Intentions may be relevant to determining whether the legal owner acted unconscionably, but the crucial question is whether the criteria for the imposition of a constructive trust are satisfied, so that it would be unconscientious for the legal owner to deny the plaintiff equitable relief. [23.5]

Categories and principles

Constructive trusts achieve a variety of remedial aims. They include the enforcement of a plaintiff's reasonable expectations, the protection of reliance expenditure, the reversal of unjust enrichment, the prevention of gain by the commission of wrongdoing and the perfection of legally incomplete transactions.[16] The aims reflect the specific criteria for the award of each type of constructive trust. [23.6]

In *Muschinski v Dodds*, Deane J stated that the constructive trust is not 'a medium for the indulgence of idiosyncratic notions of fairness and justice'.[17] A constructive trust will not be imposed simply because to do so would be fair or just to the plaintiff. This means that a plaintiff must bring her claim within a recognised category of constructive trusteeship. For example, where a defendant is a fiduciary who has obtained property for himself while under a duty to obtain it for the plaintiff, the plaintiff will be entitled to the benefit of a constructive trust over the property or its traceable proceeds. This is because the misappropriation of property by fiduciaries is a recognised category of constructive trusteeship. The Australian law of constructive trusts is category-based, although this does not mean that the categories are closed or that the existing categories are incapable of further refinement. The principal categories are examined in the remainder of this chapter.

Constructive trusts and unjust enrichment

It is sometimes suggested that the categories of constructive trusteeship rest on broad principles which have replaced the specific categories of constructive trusteeship. In the USA, for example, the first *Restatement of Restitution* provided that the constructive trust is a remedy for unjust enrichment.[18] But Australian law has never accepted unjust enrichment as the basis of the law of constructive trusts. There may be cases where the practical effect of imposing a constructive trust is to restore to a plaintiff property of which she has been unjustly deprived by the defendant. For instance, the recipient of a mistaken payment can [23.7]

15 See [22.1].
16 G Elias, *Explaining Constructive Trusts* (Clarendon, 1990).
17 (1985) 160 CLR 583, 615.
18 American Law Institute, *Restatement of the Law, Restitution* (1936) §160.

be ordered to hold the payment on constructive trust for the payer. The trust operates here as a restitutionary remedy. But most applications of the constructive trust have nothing to do with reversal of unjust enrichment.[19]

[23.8] There are cases in which a common law action for money had and received, enabling a plaintiff to obtain restitution of money where the defendant has been unjustly enriched by its receipt, will be available as an alternative to a claim to a constructive trust. For example, instead of claiming a constructive trust over stolen money,[20] the plaintiff may be able to bring a common law claim for money had and received.[21] The advantage of the common law claim is that liability is strict: the plaintiff does not have to establish any fault or wrongdoing on the part of the defendant, although the latter will defeat the claim if he establishes that he changed his position in good faith in reliance on the validity of the receipt. The principal disadvantage of the common law claim is that, being personal and not proprietary, a successful claimant will be an unsecured creditor in the defendant's insolvency.

Constructive trusts and unconscionability

[23.9] Another suggested basis of the constructive trust is the prevention of unconscionable, or unconscientious, conduct. Equity, it is said, imposes a constructive trust where it would be unconscionable for a legal owner of property to deny the plaintiff an equitable interest. This proposition is correct at a high level of generality. Moreover, the *Baumgartner* constructive trust, discussed at [23.15], is imposed in order to prevent unconscionable conduct. But 'unconscionability' in this context has a reasonably settled meaning: it applies where a plaintiff's reasonable expectation of acquiring an interest in property would otherwise be defeated by the defendant's conduct. Moreover, proof of unconscionable conduct is not required outside the *Baumgartner* category. A defendant may have behaved improperly in obtaining a personal benefit (such as the fiduciary who deliberately diverts a business opportunity to himself which only the beneficiary is entitled to exploit), but the plaintiff can nonetheless establish her claim to a constructive trust without proving the defendant's moral turpitude. Even a well-intentioned fiduciary can be held accountable as a constructive trustee.[22]

The 'common intention' constructive trust and family property disputes

[23.10] The first type of constructive trust we consider is commonly but inelegantly described as the 'common intention' constructive trust. The criteria for its imposition were explained by

19 Constructive trusts *prevent* unjust enrichment, but that does not bring them within the law of unjust enrichment, which is concerned with the restitution, or giving up, of enrichment which the defendant has unjustly obtained at the expense of the plaintiff: J Edelman and E Bant, *Unjust Enrichment* (Hart Publishing, 2nd ed, 2016) 31–3.

20 See [23.41].

21 *Fistar v Riverwood Legion and Community Club Ltd* (2016) 91 NSWLR 732. The common law claim was based on *Heperu Pty Ltd v Belle* (2009) 76 NSWLR 230. An unjust enrichment claim at common law, based on want of authority, may also be available as an alternative to a 'knowing receipt' constructive trust claim: *Great Investments Ltd v Warner* (2016) 243 FCR 516, [56]–[69].

22 Cf *Boardman v Phipps* [1967] 2 AC 46; *Sourcebook* 10.5.2a, p 268. See [10.45].

Glass JA in *Allen v Snyder*.[23] The plaintiff and defendant lived together as de facto partners for 13 years in the plaintiff's house. When the relationship broke down, the defendant resisted the plaintiff's attempt to evict her from the house by claiming that she was entitled to an equitable interest in the property under a constructive trust. There was no evidence that the defendant had made a financial contribution to the purchase or improvement of the property, although she had paid for some of the furniture. In dismissing her claim, Glass JA identified two criteria for the imposition of a constructive trust:

(1) A common intention or understanding that the claimant will acquire an interest in the property; and

(2) It would be a fraud for the legal owner to deny the interest.[24]

The New South Wales Court of Appeal held that neither requirement was satisfied. In the later case of *Green v Green*,[25] the second element was refined and the question is whether the claimant had acted to her detriment in reliance on the understanding.

In *Allen v Snyder*, Glass JA stated that the relevant intention to acquire an equitable interest must be either express or inferred from the conduct of the parties.[26] Couples rarely make express agreements about how the beneficial title to the home should be shared.[27] The issue in most cases is whether the court can infer an intention, on the part of the plaintiff and the legal owner, that the former will be entitled to an equitable interest in the home. The inference is easily drawn where the plaintiff has contributed to the purchase price of the property (although in that case she will anyway be entitled to an interest under a resulting trust) or has paid for, or made, significant improvements to the property, and there is no evidence that a gift of the contributions was being made.[28] But few other situations give rise to a genuine inference that the plaintiff was entitled to an equitable interest. In some cases, the court finds that the parties intended the plaintiff to acquire an equitable interest because she deserved to be awarded the interest.[29] But the reasoning adopted in these cases does not involve inferring, or deducing, the parties' intentions from the facts. What the court is really doing is imputing an intention to the parties which they never had. The constructive trust awarded in these cases is not really a common intention constructive trust at all. [23.11]

The other requirement of a common intention constructive trust is detriment. In *Green v Green*,[30] the defendant persuaded the plaintiff to leave her parents in Bangkok and live with him in Sydney. He left her after they had two children. The defendant told the plaintiff that [23.12]

23 [1977] 2 NSWLR 685; *Sourcebook* 23.2a, p 591.
24 [1977] 2 NSWLR 685.
25 (1989) 17 NSWLR 343.
26 Ibid 690–1.
27 The agreement would have to be in writing in order to satisfy statutory writing formalities; for example, ss 53(1)(a) or (c) of the *Property Law Act 1958* (Vic) as a 'creation' of an interest in land or potentially a 'disposition' of an existing equitable interest. See [9.36]. A claimant who has acted to her detriment in reliance on an oral agreement can rely on the principle that equity will not permit a statute to be used as a cloak for fraud: *Last v Rosenfeld* [1972] 2 NSWLR 923; *Sourcebook* 15.4a, p 394. See [15.12].
28 The agreement or common intention can arise after the property has been acquired: *Rasmussen v Rasmussen* [1995] 1 VR 613, 616; *Smilevska v Smilevska (No 2)* [2016] NSWSC 397, [165].
29 *Falconer v Falconer* [1970] 3 All ER 449; *Hazell v Hazell* [1972] 1 All ER 923; *Stack v Dowden* [2007] 2 AC 432, 459 (Baroness Hale).
30 (1989) 17 NSWLR 343.

one of the two houses he owned was hers. After the defendant's death, the plaintiff claimed an interest in the house. A majority of the New South Wales Court of Appeal held that her de facto husband held the registered title to the house on constructive trust for both of them as joint tenants. On his death she was entitled to the full beneficial interest in the house by operation of the doctrine of survivorship.

The defendant's statement 'This is your house; I bought it for you' established the necessary intention to give her a half share in one of the defendant's houses. The plaintiff had not incurred any financial detriment in paying for either of the houses or in making improvements to them. Nevertheless, it was held that leaving her family in Bangkok and coming to live with the defendant constituted 'detriment' for the purposes of establishing the criteria for a constructive trust. It is implicit in the majority decision that significant changes in the plaintiff's life induced by the defendant's promise amounted to detriment.

[23.13] A common intention constructive trust takes effect from the date when the plaintiff has acted to her detriment in reliance on the common intention, and not from the date of the court's judgment. In *Parsons v McBain*,[31] the wives of two brothers whose transport business had failed were awarded interests under a common intention constructive trust over their husbands' homes against the trustee in bankruptcy. The Full Federal Court held that their equitable interests under the trust took effect when they had made financial contributions to their husbands' properties, and not from the later date of the Court's declaration of trust. The practical effect of this holding was that the equitable interests had priority over the interests of their husbands' creditors upon the husbands' later bankruptcy.

[23.14] It is sometimes suggested that the 'common intention' constructive trust has been replaced by the unconscionability constructive trust, described in the next section. This is incorrect. The basis for these trusts is intention, while such an intention is not required for the unconscionability constructive trust. However, there may be legitimate doubts concerning the continued operation of the common intention constructive trust as distinct from the constructive trust granted as a remedy for proprietary estoppel.[32] Despite this, it is clear that courts still enforce common intention constructive trusts.[33] While changes to the *Family Law Act 1975* (Cth) and to State and Territory de facto marriage legislation have resulted in constructive trusts becoming less relevant to the resolution of spousal and de facto property disputes,[34] they continue to apply to other family property disputes; for example between parents and children,[35] or between siblings,[36] as well as to informal

31 (2001) 109 FCR 120.

32 See the discussion by Leeming JA in *Bijkerk Investments Pty Ltd v Bikic* [2020] NSWSC 1336.

33 *Rasmussen v Rasmussen* [1995] 1 VR 613; *Parsons v McBain* (2001) 109 FCR 120; *Jin v Yang* (2008) 13 BPR 25,523; *Australian Building Technical Solutions Pty Ltd v Boumelhem* (2009) 2 ASTLR 336; *Gabini v Gabini* [2014] FamCAFC 18; *Stavrianakos v Western Australia* [2016] WASC 64; *Dimitrijevic v Dimitrijevic* [2014] NSWSC 863; *Nathan v Williams* [2020] QCA 138.

34 See [23.29] for a summary of the legislation. *Silvia (trustee) v Williams* [2018] FCAFC 194 is a comparatively rare example of the common intention constructive trust involving spousal property. The husband and wife were still married, and the wife was bankrupt. Title to the family home was held in her husband's name only. Her trustee in bankruptcy sought an order that the wife had an interest in the home pursuant to a common intention constructive trust.

35 *Gabini v Gabini* [2014] FamCAFC 18; *Curran v Western Australia (No 2)* (2012) 226 A Crim R 374.

36 For example, in *Khalif v Khalif* [2020] Fam CA 39, a wife sought a declaration that her husband's brother held part of the property on a common intention trust for her husband.

commercial agreements where an expectation is created that title to property will be shared and the plaintiff has relied on the expectation to her detriment.[37]

The *Baumgartner* constructive trust

In *Muschinski v Dodds*[38] and *Baumgartner v Baumgartner*,[39] the High Court developed a new type of constructive trust founded on equity's traditional concern with the prevention of unconscionable conduct. It resembles the common intention constructive trust in that it enforces the reasonable expectations of a claimant whose contributions to a joint endeavour, whether made in cash or in kind, have created an expectation that she will obtain an interest in property. It differs, however, from the common intention constructive trust in that the expectation of an interest need not be based *only* on an actual or inferred shared understanding, between the claimant and the title-holder, that the contributions made by the former will entitle her to a property interest. The parties' intentions are important, and will often be decisive, but the overall relationship of the parties, including expectations raised by the conduct of one or both of them, will also be taken into account in determining whether the claimant is entitled to an equitable interest. [23.15]

The holistic examination of the relationship between the parties can be criticised on the ground that it involves a potentially limitless inquiry into everything the parties said and did. In practice, the focus of the inquiry is narrow, being limited to the parties' financial and non-financial contributions. Moreover, in contrast to the common intention constructive trust, the *Baumgartner* constructive trust does not require the court to infer the intentions of the parties from the contributions they have made to the relationship. [23.16]

In *Muschinski v Dodds*, de facto partners bought a cottage as tenants in common with the intention of developing it as an arts and crafts centre while living in a prefabricated house on another part of the property. The plaintiff paid the greater part of the purchase price for the land on the understanding that the defendant would fund the development of the arts and crafts centre. The project failed when the couple failed to obtain planning permission for the centre. Soon afterwards, they split up and the plaintiff claimed that she was entitled to a beneficial interest under a constructive trust of more than the 50% of the property to which she was anyway entitled as a legal tenant in common. [23.17]

A majority of the High Court, Brennan and Dawson JJ dissenting, upheld the plaintiff's claim. Mason and Deane JJ imposed a constructive trust to repay to each party their contributions to purchasing and developing the land, and then to divide the proceeds of sale equally between the parties. Since the plaintiff had made the major contribution to the project (about ten-elevenths of the total cost) she was entitled to the greater part of the proceeds of sale. The constructive trust took effect from the date of the High Court's judgment.

Gibbs CJ would not have imposed a constructive trust. The plaintiff and defendant were joint and severally liable as co-debtors to repay debts incurred on the project. Since the plaintiff had paid more than her share of the joint debt, Gibbs CJ held that she was entitled to a restitutionary right of contribution from the defendant for the amount in excess of her

37 *Nathan v Williams* [2020] QCA 138.
38 (1985) 160 CLR 583.
39 (1987) 164 CLR 137.

share that she had paid. The amount to which she was entitled should be secured by a charge over the property.[40]

Deane J, drawing on common law and equitable principles governing the distribution of assets on the dissolution of a partnership or joint venture, and on frustration of a contract, identified three criteria for the imposition of a constructive trust:

(1) The failure of a joint venture or endeavour;

(2) The plaintiff must not be to blame for the failure; and

(3) The plaintiff must have contributed money or other property which would not otherwise have been enjoyed by the defendant.[41]

The joint venture here was both commercial and personal. The personal relationship had not survived the collapse of the business venture to develop the arts and crafts centre. Since the plaintiff had paid most of the financial contributions and was not responsible for the collapse of the business venture it would, in the opinion of Deane J, be unconscionable to deny her an interest under a constructive trust.

[23.18] Deane J's judgment in *Muschinski v Dodds* has shaped the modern development of the law of constructive trusts in Australia. It expounds a principled basis for imposing constructive trusts in cases of relationship breakdown without having to rest the imposition on evidentially dubious findings as to couples' intentions when buying property. In most cases, they will have given no thought to the legal consequences of failure of their relationship or business. But although it demonstrates equity's adaptability to changing social conditions, the judgment is problematic.

[23.19] Deane J's criteria are not easy to apply to the varied circumstances of relationship breakdown. In *Muschinski v Dodds*, the relationship was both commercial and personal. The collapse of the project to create an arts and crafts centre easily fitted the description of a failure of a joint venture. But not all relationships can be characterised as 'failures of a joint venture' without depriving that term of sensible legal meaning. Partnerships and joint ventures are well-understood commercial concepts. But they are not legal terms employed in family contexts and Deane J did not explain how they might be applied to facts other than those of *Muschinski v Dodds*.

[23.20] The requirement that the failure of joint venture must have occurred without blame attributable to the plaintiff has also proved difficult to apply. In commercial disputes, notions of fault and blame are usually applied to tortfeasors and deliberate contract-breakers. But modern family law has largely dispensed with the notion of fault, and it is no longer the role of Family Law Courts to determine each party's share of responsibility for a relationship breakdown.[42] In practice, Deane J's requirement of 'absence of attributable blame' is only applied where one party is seriously at fault.[43]

40 The trial judge had rejected the plaintiff's claim to an interest under a resulting trust, on the ground that the plaintiff had intended the money she had paid to buy the property to be a gift to the defendant, thereby rebutting the presumption of resulting trust: (1985) 160 CLR 583, 589.

41 Ibid 618.

42 *Family Law Act 1975* (Cth) s 48 (the only ground of divorce is the irretrievable breakdown of marriage evidenced by a year's separation). Conduct is not taken into account in maintenance proceedings and proceedings to alter property interests except insofar as the justice of the case requires it to be taken into account under s 75(2)(o).

43 *Kriezis v Kriezis* [2004] NSWSC 167; *Australian Building Technical Solutions Pty Ltd v Boumelhem* (2009) 2 ASTLR 336, [91]–[99], where it is suggested that blame is part of the overall inquiry into unconscionability.

In spite of these difficulties, Deane J's criteria have been considered in numerous subsequent decisions[44] and were applied, albeit with a stronger emphasis on unconscionability, in the later High Court decision of *Baumgartner v Baumgartner*.[45] The *Baumgartner* parties lived in a de facto relationship – first in a unit owned by the defendant and later in a house built on the defendant's land. The defendant had purchased the land with the assistance of a mortgage. Mortgage instalments and other costs were paid from a pooled account into which both parties had paid their earnings, the defendant contributing 55% of the money in the account while the plaintiff contributed the remaining 45%. The plaintiff did not pay any money into the pooled account in the months in which she had and was caring for their child. After leaving the defendant, the plaintiff claimed a share in the home under a constructive trust. [23.21]

The High Court held that the plaintiff was entitled to a 45% share in the home under a constructive trust. The joint judgment of Mason CJ, Wilson and Deane JJ identified 'the foundation for the imposition of a constructive trust' in this kind of case as being the principle that 'a refusal to recognise the existence of the equitable interest amounts to unconscionable conduct … [T]he trust is imposed as a remedy to circumvent the unconscionable conduct'.[46]

The focus of inquiry in *Baumgartner* was upon the direct and indirect contributions made by the plaintiff to the acquisition of property.[47] In substance, the constructive trust enforced the plaintiff's reasonable expectation of acquiring an interest, having regard to the contributions she made to the property.

Assessing contributions

Contributions to the acquisition of property can be financial, non-financial (so-called 'homemaker contributions') or both. In *Baumgartner*, the High Court took both types of contribution into account in quantifying the plaintiff's interest. The plaintiff had made financial contributions to the purchase of the house by paying her earnings into the pooled bank account from which the mortgage instalments and other housing costs were paid. But her non-financial contributions were also recognised since the High Court credited her with the amount she would have earned during the months in which she was precluded from earning by reason of having and caring for a child.[48] The maxim 'equity is equality' can be used as a starting point for quantifying equitable title under a constructive trust, but it is easily displaced, as it was in *Baumgartner*, by evidence that the parties contributed unequally to the purchase or improvement of property. [23.22]

While this type of constructive trust had its genesis in the breakdown of de facto relationships, the jurisdiction has not remained confined to this context. The relationship [23.23]

44 For example, *Henderson v Miles (No 2)* (2005) 12 BPR 23,579; *Cetojevic v Cetojevic* [2007] NSWCA 33; *Cooper v Lees* (2009) 3 ASTLR 558; *Australian Building Technical Solutions Pty Ltd v Boumelhem* (2009) 2 ASTLR 336; *Willis v Western Australia (No 3)* (2010) 4 ASTLR 359.

45 (1987) 164 CLR 137.

46 Ibid 147.

47 Where the plaintiff's claim is based on her contributions to the purchase of property, it may entitle her to either an interest under a constructive trust or a purchase money resulting trust. As *Baumgartner* illustrates, 'contribution' is defined more broadly for the purposes of imposing a constructive trust than under the law of resulting trusts. See [22.16].

48 (1987) 164 CLR 137, 150 (Mason CJ, Wilson and Deane JJ), 157 (Gaudron J).

may be familial or commercial.[49] While non-financial contributions such as childcare and homemaker contributions are relevant in the domestic context,[50] financial contributions are more likely to have been made in the other contexts in which this trust appears.[51]

Equitable adjustments

[23.24] In addition to quantifying the parties' respective equitable interests, a court may also make equitable adjustments in favour of either party to reflect the benefit of occupying the property enjoyed by one party. Adjustments can also be made to reflect payments made by one party which discharge the obligations of the other. The adjustments do not affect the parties' proprietary interests in the home. They entitle the party in whose favour the adjustments are made to the personal remedy of equitable compensation for the loss of the right to occupy the home, or for the costs incurred in paying off the other party's debts. The compensation order may be secured by an equitable lien over the property, so that upon its sale (assuming that the defendant has not paid the plaintiff by that date) the compensation will be realised out of the proceeds of sale. In *Baumgartner*, the High Court made a number of equitable adjustments; for example, to compensate the defendant for mortgage instalments he had discharged for both parties.[52]

Is the *Baumgartner* constructive trust an institution or a remedy?

[23.25] A constructive trust which takes effect from the date of the court's judgment will be classified as remedial since most judicial remedies take effect from that date.[53] The constructive trust imposed in *Muschinski v Dodds* was held by Deane J to take effect from the date of judgment 'lest the legitimate claims of third parties be adversely affected'.[54]

[23.26] The dating of a *Baumgartner* constructive trust is a matter for judicial discretion. In *Baumgartner*, the question of timing of the imposition of the trust was not discussed by the High Court, presumably because no third parties would be affected by its imposition. The timing issue is critical where a mortgage or other security is taken over the disputed property after the plaintiff has made the contributions entitling her to an equitable interest. If the trust takes effect from the date when the contributions are made, the beneficiary will be entitled

49 See, eg, *Hansen v Noble* (2021) 20 BPR 41,181 (mother and daughter); *Re Rowan* [2019] FCA 1871 (an investment joint venture between friends); *Stewart v Owen* (2020) 60 VR 341 (a joint venture for investment); *Clementi v Rossi* [2019] VSC 725 (resulting trust and a failed family joint venture between parents and children); and *Zekry v Zekry* [2020] VSCA 336 (based on a joint venture between a son and his parents).

50 The quantification of a homemaker's equitable interest is a matter on which neither *Muschinski v Dodds* nor *Baumgartner* provides much guidance. Relevant factors include the longevity of the relationship, the extent to which the parties shared responsibility for bringing up children, and the extent to which the partner's earning capacity was enhanced by the homemaker's contributions: *Black v Black* (1991) 15 Fam LR 109, 117 (Clarke JA), cited in *Read v Nicholls* [2004] VSC 66, [61].

51 *Parij v Parij* (1997) 72 SASR 153, 163 (Debelle J).

52 (1987) 164 CLR 137, 150–1.

53 See the online resources.

54 (1985) 160 CLR 583, 623.

to priority over a later equitable mortgagee unless the beneficiary's conduct estops her from asserting priority,[55] or unless the mortgage is registered under title registration legislation and the beneficiary cannot bring her interest within one of the statutory exceptions to the mortgagee's indefeasible title.[56]

A plaintiff may prefer to claim the benefit of a common intention constructive trust rather than a *Baumgartner* constructive trust for priority reasons. The common intention constructive trust is institutional, taking effect when the plaintiff acts to her detriment in reliance on the common intention or understanding.[57] The beneficiary will be entitled to priority over later mortgagees unless she loses priority for the reasons explained in the previous paragraph. If a *Baumgartner* constructive trust is imposed, however, the possibility that it might take effect only at the date of judgment creates a real risk that the plaintiff's equitable interest will be subordinated to a mortgage created between the date of the plaintiff's contributions and the date of judgment. [23.27]

Despite the language of 'constructive trust', the remedy frequently imposed is not a constructive trust, in the sense of being an equitable interest in the defendant's property. Often the court orders the return of the party's contributions, secured by a lien over the property.[58] [23.28]

The impact of family law legislation on constructive trusts

The application of constructive trust principles to disputes between former spouses and de facto partners is now of little significance following the enactment of wide-ranging legislation empowering Family Law Courts to reallocate property rights on relationship breakdown. Section 79 of the *Family Law Act 1975* (Cth) confers jurisdiction on a Family Law Court[59] to alter spouses' property interests, having regard to criteria laid down in s 79(4) of the Act. The jurisdiction is exercisable not only upon divorce, but also where one of the spouses is bankrupt; in the latter case, the court can alter interests vested in the bankrupt spouse's trustee in bankruptcy. [23.29]

Where a de facto relationship, whether heterosexual or same-sex, has broken down after 1 March 2009, a Family Law Court has jurisdiction to alter the property interests of the former de facto partners in accordance with criteria laid down in s 90SM of the *Family Law Act 1975* (Cth). Again, the jurisdiction is exercisable not only upon breakdown of the relationship but also where a de facto partner is bankrupt. Some States have additional legislation permitting courts to make orders regarding property where parties have been in a domestic partnership.[60] The Family Court's jurisdiction to alter the property interests of de facto partners, as well as those held by a trustee in bankruptcy of a de facto partner, does

55 *Shropshire Union Railways & Canal Co v The Queen* (1875) LR 7 HL 496, 566 (Lord Cairns).

56 BJ Edgeworth et al (eds), *Sackville & Neave: Australian Property Law* (LexisNexis Butterworths, 10th ed, 2016) 470–504.

57 *Parsons v McBain* (2001) 109 FCR 120. See [23.13].

58 *Behman v Behman* [2015] NSWSC 1787; *Austin v Hornby* (2011) 16 BPR 30,623; *Henderson v Miles (No 2)* (2005) 12 BPR 23,579; *Taylor v Streicher* [2007] NSWSC 1006.

59 A Family Law Court is, for this purpose, the Family Law Court of Australia, the Federal Magistrates Court, and the Supreme Court of the Northern Territory.

60 *Domestic Relationships Act 1994* (ACT); *Property (Relationships) Act 1984* (NSW); *Domestic Partners Property Act 1996* (SA); *Relationships Act 2003* (Tas); *Relationships Act 2008* (Vic).

not apply to couples ordinarily resident in Western Australia unless they have also been ordinarily resident in a State or Territory to which the de facto provisions of the *Family Law Act* apply for a duration of at least one-third of their relationship, or where they have made a substantial financial or non-financial contribution to the relationship in a State or Territory to which the Act applies. In Western Australia, the Family Court of Western Australia has jurisdiction under the *Family Court Act 1997* (WA). The statute does not empower a court to alter property interests on the bankruptcy of a de facto partner, and the application of constructive trust principles on bankruptcy remains relevant in that State.

[23.30] Although constructive trust principles are therefore largely irrelevant to the determination of spousal and de facto property disputes, in most Australian jurisdictions the law of common intention and *Baumgartner* constructive trusts is now often used in other contexts. They are relevant in two main classes of case:

(1) Family property disputes between family members other than spouses and former de facto partners; for example, between parent and child or between siblings.[61] Spouses of the children may also have a claim.[62] Quasi-domestic disputes may also arise. For example, in *Staatz v Berry (No 3)*,[63] a number of people made financial contributions to the purchase price of a property. They were involved in a joint venture for the property to be a commune where they could all live. The commune failed.

(2) Commercial property disputes. Although the principles governing common intention and *Baumgartner* constructive trusts were developed in the context of family property litigation, the criteria for their application are of general application, and they extend to disputes involving property acquired for commercial purposes. The *Baumgartner* constructive trust has been imposed over the subject-matter of commercial joint ventures.[64] For example, in *Carson v Wood*,[65] a *Baumgartner* constructive trust was imposed over trademarks which the defendant had failed to transfer to a newly formed company in which both the plaintiff and the defendant held equal interests. The practical effect of the court order was to entitle the plaintiff to a half-share in the trademarks.

The constructive trust as a remedy for proprietary estoppel

[23.31] The requirements for a valid estoppel are set out in chapter 8. Relief in proprietary estoppel can be personal or proprietary. A personal remedy was awarded in *Giumelli*

61 *Peterson v Hottes* [2012] QCA 292; *Tamer v Official Trustee in Bankruptcy* [2016] NSWSC 680; *Stavrianakos v Western Australia* [2016] WASC 64; *Marlow v Boyd* [2012] QSC 331. See cases in n 35, 36 and 49.

62 See, eg, *Nolan v Nolan* [2015] QCA 199. Note also that, in some jurisdictions, property claims can be made under statute on the breakdown of a close personal or caring relationship. See S Barkehall Thomas 'Care-givers and property claims: an underutilized statutory jurisdiction' (2018) 27(1) *Australian Property Law Journal* 42.

63 (2019) 138 ACSR 231.

64 See also *Stewart v Owen* [2020] VSC 175.

65 (1994) 34 NSWLR 9.

v Giumelli,[66] where a son was promised by his parents that a block of land would be conveyed to him if he worked for their orchard business. The High Court held that the work done by the son entitled him to the benefit of an estoppel. The relief awarded was equitable compensation, assessed as the value of the block and enforced by a charge over the land. The reasons for denying the plaintiff a proprietary constructive trust included the fact that a partnership action between the parties was still pending in which the proprietary rights of the parties would be clarified, and the fact that other members of the family worked on, and had claims to, the land.

In *Sidhu v Van Dyke*,[67] the High Court indicated that the usual remedy for proprietary estoppel will be the value of the expected interest. A proprietary constructive trust will be imposed over the subject-matter of the estoppel claim if the remedy is not disproportionate to the detriment the plaintiff has incurred in relying on the representation made by the defendant, and if there are no discretionary factors which make the proprietary remedy inappropriate on the facts. In *Thorner v Major*,[68] the plaintiff worked on a cousin's farm without pay for nearly 20 years. He was induced, by various oblique remarks his cousin made, to believe that the farm would be his on his cousin's death. The cousin died without executing a valid will. The House of Lords held that the plaintiff was entitled to the farm because the cousin had created an expectation that he would receive the farm on the cousin's death. In view of the plaintiff's unpaid work on the farm over many years, the appropriate order was to direct that the cousin's personal representatives hold the farm on constructive trust for the plaintiff. By contrast, in *Sidhu*, compensation was awarded.[69] A proprietary award would have affected a third party – the promisor's wife who was part owner of the property. [23.32]

The essential criterion in awarding constructive trust relief is the relief not be disproportionate to the detriment incurred by the plaintiff.[70] There is no justification in awarding the plaintiff a constructive trust over the defendant's entire property when the detriment incurred is very slight, even if the defendant has represented that the property will be the plaintiff's in these circumstances. Equity has many alternatives to the constructive trust and can fashion relief to meet the circumstances of the case. Alternatives include awarding the plaintiff an irrevocable licence to occupy the defendant's property;[71] an equitable lien to secure repayment of the plaintiff's expenditure on the property;[72] and a conveyance to the plaintiff deferred until the plaintiff's discharge from bankruptcy so as not to entitle the plaintiff's creditors to the property.[73] [23.33]

66 (1999) 196 CLR 101.

67 (2014) 251 CLR 505.

68 [2009] 1 WLR 776.

69 (2014) 251 CLR 505. The nature of the remedy was not in dispute on appeal to the High Court.

70 The High Court has said that before a constructive trust is imposed, the Court should decide whether there is an appropriate remedy which falls short of imposition of a trust: see *Giumelli v Giumelli* (1999) 196 CLR 101, 104.

71 *Plimmer v Mayor of Wellington* (1884) 9 App Cas 699; *Milling v Hardie* [2014] NSWCA 163. A licence coupled with a grant of a profit à prendre has also been awarded: *Silovi Pty Ltd v Barbaro* (1988) 13 NSWLR 466.

72 *Unity Joint Stock Mutual Banking Association v King* (1858) 25 Beav 72; 53 ER 563; *Morris v Morris* [1982] 1 NSWLR 61.

73 *O'Brien v Sheahan* [2002] FCA 1292.

[23.34] In *Giumelli v Giumelli*, a majority of the High Court said: 'A constructive trust of this nature is a remedial response to the claim to equitable intervention made out by the plaintiff.'[74] It is clear that the Court has remedial choice. However, in *McNab v Graham*, the Victorian Court of Appeal treated the constructive trust as a remedy for estoppel as institutional. The Court stated that while a constructive trust will not necessarily be awarded, once it has been determined that the constructive trust is an appropriate remedy on the facts, it arises from the date of the behaviour which led to the reliance. This reasoning separates out the discretion as to choice of remedy from the actual decision to impose a constructive trust.

Tate JA stated:

> While it is for a court to determine whether to declare a constructive trust, the date the trust comes into existence is the date from which the equitable interest, the interest in land, arises. That date is, as mentioned, when the conduct occurs that gives rise to the trust; the date when the detrimental reliance renders it unconscionable to depart from the promise.[75]

Further, in relation to the distinction between institutional and remedial constructive trusts, Tate JA suggested: 'It may be that the distinction is not apposite, or not useful, in the context of proprietary estoppel.'[76] It remains to be seen if this approach will have any influence in the area.

The criteria for the award of a constructive trust in estoppel are substantially identical to the requirements of a common intention constructive trust. The two forms of constructive trust relief could sensibly be amalgamated.[77] Nevertheless, as a practical matter, relief in estoppel is more flexible than the proportionate share constructive trust relief awarded in common intention constructive trust cases.

Constructive trusts imposed for breach of fiduciary obligation

[23.35] A fiduciary[78] who has committed a breach of obligation, such as placing himself in a position of conflict between his personal interest and the duty he owes his beneficiary, will be ordered to hold property obtained as a result of the breach on constructive trust for the beneficiary in whose interests he should have been acting. The basic requirements for imposing a constructive trust in this situation are:

(a) a breach of fiduciary obligation; and

(b) the identification of specific property, title to which the fiduciary has obtained by committing the breach.

---

74 (1999) 196 CLR 101, 112.

75 Santamaria JA and Keogh AJA agreeing: (2017) 53 VR 311, 344.

76 Ibid 350.

77 For discussions of possible differences, see *Henderson v Miles (No 2)* (2005) 12 BPR 23,579, [20]–[21]; *Thorner v Major* [2009] 1 WLR 776, 784 (Lord Scott).

78 See chapter 10.

If the fiduciary no longer has the property – for example, because he has spent money for which he should have accounted to the beneficiary – he remains personally accountable for the money.[79] Recipients of property from fiduciaries, and those who assist a fiduciary to commit a breach of duty, are also accountable as constructive trustees.[80]

The standard situations in which a constructive trust is imposed over property obtained by a fiduciary acting in breach of obligation are: [23.36]

(a) Where the fiduciary misappropriates property belonging to the beneficiary. A fiduciary who steals property from the beneficiary will, apart from any applicable criminal penalties, be ordered to hold the property or its proceeds on constructive trust for his victim.[81]

(b) Where the fiduciary has obtained property for himself, or has diverted to himself a business opportunity, which he was under an obligation to obtain for his beneficiary.[82] The property in these cases was never beneficially owned by the beneficiary. Moreover, business opportunities do not constitute property. Nevertheless, the fiduciary must hold the property, and the product of any business opportunity, on constructive trust for the beneficiary.[83]

A breach of fiduciary duty which does not fit into either of these categories occurs when a fiduciary takes a bribe paid by a third party to induce the fiduciary to act in the third party's interests. The fiduciary is personally accountable to the principal for the value of the bribe. The personal remedy will be of limited value to the principal, however, if the fiduciary is bankrupt, or if the principal wants to trace the bribe into specific property acquired with the bribe and to claim a share of that property.[84] In *Lister & Co v Stubbs*,[85] the English Court of Appeal held that the fiduciary was liable to account to the principal for the amount of the bribe received, but was not a constructive trustee. The defendant was an employee of the plaintiff company who purchased supplies for the company. The defendant received commissions from a third party, of which the plaintiff was unaware, in return for arranging for the company to buy the third party's goods. The bribe money was invested and the plaintiff, seeking to trace the bribe into the investments, applied for an interlocutory injunction to prevent the defendant from disposing of the investments. The application was rejected. Even though the defendant was accountable for the bribe money to the plaintiff, the latter was not the equitable owner of the bribe. Critics of *Lister & Co v Stubbs* have argued that it is inconsistent for equity to hold an honest fiduciary, such as Boardman in *Boardman v Phipps*,[86] liable to a constructive trust but not to impose a constructive trust over the proceeds of a bribe received by a dishonest fiduciary. [23.37]

79 *Re Dawson (deceased)* [1966] 2 NSWR 211; *Youyang Pty Ltd v Minter Ellison Morris Fletcher* (2003) 212 CLR 484.

80 See chapter 11.

81 *Black v S Freedman & Co* (1910) 12 CLR 105.

82 *Keech v Sandford* (1726) Sel Cas T King 61; 25 ER 223; *Boardman v Phipps* [1967] 2 AC 46; *Chan v Zacharia* (1984) 154 CLR 178; *Timber Engineering Co Ltd v Anderson* [1980] 2 NSWLR 488.

83 For an instructive example, see the orders made in *Timber Engineering Co Ltd v Anderson* [1980] 2 NSWLR 488.

84 See chapter 21.

85 (1890) 45 Ch D 1; *Sourcebook* 23.5.2a, p 616.

86 [1967] 2 AC 46; *Sourcebook* 10.5.2a, p 268.

[23.38] *Lister & Co v Stubbs* was not followed by the Privy Council in *Attorney-General for Hong Kong v Reid*.[87] Reid, who was employed by the Hong Kong government as Acting Director of Public Prosecutions, was bribed not to pursue certain investigations. He invested the bribe money in New Zealand properties. The Privy Council awarded the Hong Kong Government the benefit of a constructive trust over the New Zealand properties. The maxim that 'equity considers as done that which ought to be done' was invoked: since, in the opinion of the Privy Council, the bribe ought to belong to the Hong Kong Government, the constructive trust ensured that it did belong to the government. In holding Reid liable as a constructive trustee, the Privy Council made explicit reference to the policy of deterring bribery by public officials, it being 'an evil practice which threatens the foundations of any civilised society'.[88]

In spite of its intuitive appeal to commercial morality, the reasoning of the Privy Council decision has been criticised.[89] The mechanical application of the maxim 'equity considers as done that which ought to be done' conceals the policy reasons for imposing the constructive trust. Moreover, while a constructive trust will be no more effective against a solvent fiduciary who has taken a bribe than an account of profits, the practical effect of the trust on the distribution of an insolvent fiduciary's property will be to remove property acquired with the bribe from the pool of assets available to the fiduciary's unsecured creditors. Lord Templeman, who delivered the opinion of the Privy Council, stated that the unsecured creditors ought to be in no better position than the fiduciary himself.[90] But there is no special reason why the claim of the principal to the property purchased with the bribe should be preferred to that of innocent unsecured creditors of the fiduciary.[91]

[23.39] The United Kingdom Supreme Court confirmed in *FHR European Ventures LLP v Cedar Capital Partners LLC*[92] that a constructive trust for the benefit of the principal will be imposed over a bribe received by a fiduciary, as well as over any property acquired with the bribe. In *FHR European Ventures*, an agent negotiating the purchase of shares in a hotel company was paid a secret commission by the vendor of the shares. The Supreme Court imposed a constructive trust over the commission for the benefit of the purchaser. Lord Neuberger, delivering the judgment of the Court, rejected the application of the maxim 'equity considers as done that which ought to be done' but justified the award of the trust on pragmatic grounds, including the tendency of courts in other common law jurisdictions to award a constructive trust in this situation.[93]

[23.40] In Australia, the imposition of a constructive trust over a bribe taken by a fiduciary was considered by the Full Federal Court in *Grimaldi v Chameleon Mining NL (No 2)*.[94]

87 [1994] 1 AC 324; *Sourcebook* 23.5.2b, p 618.

88 [1994] 1 AC 324, 330.

89 Roy Goode, 'Proprietary Restitutionary Claims' in WR Cornish et al (eds), *Restitution Past, Present & Future: Essays in Honour of Gareth Jones* (Hart Publishing, 1998) ch 5; Peter Birks, 'Profits in the Property of Wrongdoing' (1994) 24(1) *University of Western Australia Law Review* 8. The reasoning in *Reid* was expressly rejected in *Sinclair Investments (UK) Ltd v Versailles Trade Finance Ltd* [2011] EWCA Civ 347.

90 [1994] 1 AC 324, 331; *Sourcebook* 23.5.2b, p 618.

91 Birks (n 89). The result in *Reid* was approved by the United Kingdom Supreme Court in *FHR European Ventures LLP v Cedar Capital Partners LLC* [2015] AC 250; *Sourcebook* 23.5.2d, p 621, overruling *Sinclair Investments (UK) Ltd v Versailles Trade Finance Ltd* [2011] EWCA Civ 347.

92 [2015] AC 250; *Sourcebook* 23.5.2d, p 621.

93 *FHR European Ventures LLP v Cedar Capital Partners LLC* [2015] AC 250, [45] (Lord Neuberger).

94 (2012) 200 FCR 296; *Sourcebook* 23.5.2c, p 619. The High Court approved *Lister & Co v Stubbs* (1890) 45 Ch D 1 briefly in obiter dicta in *Ardlethan Options Ltd v Easdown* (1915) 20 CLR 285

Grimaldi, who with co-defendants was a de facto director of the plaintiff company, applied company money towards the acquisition of mining tenements which were exploited profitably. In return for his involvement in the transaction, Grimaldi was paid a 'spotter's fee', consisting of shares and options in another company which ultimately acquired the tenements. The spotter's fee was not a bribe but an undisclosed personal interest. The Full Federal Court held that the unsold shares and options were held on constructive trust for the plaintiff. The Court stated in obiter that a bribe could be captured by a constructive trust. However, the constructive trust was not a remedy to be imposed if there were other remedies capable of doing full justice on the facts of the case. It was suggested that:

> where a bribed fiduciary, having profitably invested the bribe, is then bankrupted and, apart from the investment, is hopelessly insolvent ... a lien on that property may well be sufficient to achieve 'practical justice' in the circumstances. This said, a constructive trust is likely to be awarded as of course where the bribe still exists in its original, or in a traceable, form, and no third party issue arises.[95]

Unlike the constructive trust awarded by the United Kingdom Supreme Court in *FHR European Ventures LLP v Cedar Capital Partners LLC*, which is an institutional constructive trust automatically imposed over the bribe and its invested proceeds, the constructive trust recognised by the Full Federal Court is discretionary and remedial. The award of an equitable lien, as an alternative to the constructive trust, in the example above secures to the principal the amount of the bribe, but the fiduciary's unsecured creditors will be entitled to any profits generated by a successful investment of the bribe, and to the appreciated value of property purchased with the bribe. The preference for the equitable lien in this case is consistent with the principle expressed by the High Court that 'before the court imposes the constructive trust as a remedy, it should first decide whether, having regard to the issues in the litigation, there are other means available to quell the controversy'.[96] Where an equitable lien is imposed over the defendant's land to secure to the plaintiff payment of a judgment debt, the practical effect of the order is to entitle the plaintiff to apply for sale of the land, and payment from the proceeds of the amount owing to him, unless the defendant instead pays the plaintiff the debt from his own resources.

The constructive trust imposed over stolen money and its proceeds

A fiduciary who steals the beneficiary's money is accountable to the beneficiary for the [23.41]
amount stolen as well as for any profit made by successfully investing the money. Equity goes further, however, by imposing a constructive trust over money stolen by a non-

before the recognition in Australia of the remedial constructive trust. See also J Campbell, 'When and Why a Bribe Is Held on a Constructive Trust: The Method of Reasoning Towards an Equitable Remedy' (2015) 39(3) *Australian Bar Review* 320.

95 *Grimaldi v Chameleon Mining NL (No 2)* (2012) 200 FCR 296, [583].

96 *Bathurst City Council v PWC Properties Pty Ltd* (1998) 195 CLR 566, [42]. See also *John Alexander's Clubs Pty Ltd v White City Tennis Club Ltd* (2010) 241 CLR 1, [126]–[129].

fiduciary. In *Black v S Freedman & Co*,[97] an employee stole money and placed it in his wife's bank account. The High Court held that the employee was a constructive trustee of the stolen money and that the trust bound his wife who was a volunteer. The employee was a fiduciary, and the case could have been decided on ordinary fiduciary principles,[98] but O'Connor J stated the principle more broadly: 'where money has been stolen it is trust money in the hands of the thief'.[99] The precise nature of the trust is still unsettled.[100]

[23.42] The juridical basis of the 'stolen money' trust has been much analysed.[101] Since a thief obtains no title to stolen property, it is arguable that the victim of a theft has no need to invoke constructive trusteeship in order to recover her property. The constructive trust over stolen money serves, however, two functions. First, the common law has no action which enables stolen personal property to be specifically recovered. Except in rare cases where specific restitution is ordered in a claim for detinue[102], the victim will only be entitled to damages at common law. The constructive trust over stolen money can be viewed as an example of equity filling an obvious gap in the common law protection of personal property.

Secondly, the constructive trust provides the only proprietary remedy available to recover the proceeds of stolen property.[103] Here also, the only common law relief available is personal, being a claim in conversion, in the case of a chattel, and an action for money had and received, in the case of money.

The constructive trust as a restitutionary remedy for unjust enrichment

[23.43] The stolen money constructive trust discussed in the previous section is in substance, though not in name, a restitutionary remedy for unjust enrichment.[104] The thief, and any

97 (1910) 12 CLR 105; *Sourcebook* 23.6a, p 624. For discussion of an alternative claim in the action for money had and received see *Fistar v Riverwood Legion and Community Club Ltd* (2016) 91 NSWLR 732, discussed at [23.8] (n 21) above.

98 See chapter 10.

99 (1910) 12 CLR 105, 110; *Jones v Southall & Bourke Pty Ltd* [2004] FCA 539.

100 The full Federal Court in *Grimaldi v Chameleon Mining NL (No 2)* (2012) 200 FCR 296, [255] seemed to regard the trust as remedial, but in *Sze Tu v Lowe* (2014) 89 NSWLR 317 the New South Wales Court of Appeal treated it as institutional. See also *Wambo Coal Pty Ltd v Ariff* (2007) 63 ACSR 429, [40].

101 S Barkehall Thomas, 'Thieves as Trustees: The Enduring Legacy of *Black v Freedman*' (2009) 3(1) *Journal of Equity* 52; John Tarrant, 'Thieves as Trustees: In Defence of the Theft Principle' (2009) 3(2) *Journal of Equity* 170; Robert Chambers, 'Trust and Theft' in E Bant and M Harding (eds), *Exploring Private Law* (Cambridge University Press, 2010) 223.

102 Specific restitution of a chattel may be ordered in the tort of detinue: see, eg, *Civil Procedure Act 2005* (NSW) s 93. Delivery up of a chattel can be ordered in equity: *Doulton Potteries Ltd v Bronte* [1971] 1 NSWLR 25. Where delivery up is sought in support of a legal right to possession of the chattel common law damages must be inadequate: *McKeown v Cavalier Yachts Pty Ltd* (1988) 13 NSWLR 303, 312, where a yacht was held to be unique, justifying an order of delivery up rather than damages for detinue.

103 *Evans v European Bank Ltd* (2004) 61 NSWLR 75, [112]–[113]. Spigelman CJ treated the trust as resulting.

104 Alternatively, it can be analysed as an example of restitution for wrongs – the wrong being the theft of the money. See James Edelman and Elise Bant, *Unjust Enrichment* (Hart Publishing, 2nd ed, 2016) 19–21, 29–33 for the distinction between restitution for unjust enrichment and restitution for wrongs.

recipient of the stolen property from the thief, has been unjustly enriched at the expense of the victim. Once the thief has paid the victim's money into his bank account, the bank obtains title to the money although the thief is contractually entitled to payment of an equivalent amount by the bank, assuming that the bank has no knowledge of the theft.[105] The thief is enriched by acquiring rights against his bank by virtue of the deposit of the stolen money in the bank. The constructive trust is the restitutionary remedy which restores these rights to the victim of the theft, and is enforceable not only against the thief but any subsequent recipient of those rights who is not a good faith purchaser for value without notice of the victim's rights.

Constructive trusts fulfil many objectives other than the reversal of unjust enrichment. [23.44] Nevertheless, there are specific applications of the constructive trust which, like the stolen money trust, reverse unjust enrichment. Logically, these cases belong to the law of resulting trusts since the property results back, by virtue of the trust, to the party entitled to the property. Most authorities, however, assume that the trust is constructive.

It is convenient to distinguish between cases of non-contractual transfers of property and contractual transfers of property.

Non-contractual transfers of property

A simple example of a non-contractual transfer of property giving rise to a restitutionary [23.45] constructive trust to reverse unjust enrichment is a mistaken payment. Suppose that P pays D \$100 by mistake. P will have a personal claim in unjust enrichment against D to recover the payment.[106] The claim will be worthless if D is bankrupt and numerous creditors are claiming his few assets. But if P can identify the \$100 in D's bank account by application of the tracing rules,[107] a constructive trust can be imposed over the money or its traceable proceeds for the benefit of P. The elements of the proprietary unjust enrichment claim are:

(a) D's enrichment (the \$100);

(b) The enrichment must be at the expense of P;

(c) The enrichment must be unjust. An enrichment will be unjust if P can identify a legally recognised 'unjust factor'. In this example, mistake is the 'unjust factor'. Courts do not apply generalised notions of justice and injustice; and

(d) P's payment must be traceably identifiable.

A classic, if controversial, authority on the imposition of a constructive trust over a [23.46] mistaken payment is *Chase Manhattan Bank NA v Israel-British Bank (London) Ltd.*[108] The plaintiff bank intended to pay US\$2 million to the credit of a customer of the defendant bank. By mistake, a double payment was made. Before the overpayment could be recovered, the defendant bank went into liquidation. It was held that the defendant held the overpayment on constructive trust for the plaintiff, assuming that the money could be traced.

105 *Joachimson v Swiss Bank Corporation* [1921] 3 KB 110.
106 The cause of action will be an action for money had and received.
107 See chapter 21.
108 [1981] Ch 105; *Sourcebook* 23.7a, p 630.

[23.47] The decision in *Chase Manhattan* has been criticised on the ground that it gives unjustified protection to unjust enrichment claimants when many other creditors in bankruptcy, such as tort victims, cannot claim the benefit of a constructive trust. In *Westdeutsche Landesbank Girozentrale v Islington London Borough Council*,[109] Lord Browne-Wilkinson suggested that the right to proprietary restitution arose when the recipient's conscience was bound. On this analysis, the constructive trust will only be imposed when the recipient learns of the mistake or should have learned of it.

[23.48] The suggestion has been adopted in Australia. In *Wambo Coal Pty Ltd v Ariff*,[110] the plaintiff made payments to Singleton Earthmoving by mistake. Before the payments could be recovered, Singleton went into liquidation. The defendant was appointed administrator of the company and the payments were made over to his administration account. White J held that the plaintiff was entitled to a constructive trust over the mistaken payment as soon as the defendant became aware that it was the plaintiff's money.[111] It was said to be an 'unwarranted windfall' for Singleton's creditors to claim the mistaken payment.[112] Whether a plaintiff's proprietary rights ought to depend on the defendant's knowledge – a matter outside the plaintiff's control – may be doubted. In response, however, it can be argued that a plaintiff's equitable property rights typically depend on the defendant's knowledge insofar as a purchaser of property subject to such rights will not be bound if he does not have notice of them.

[23.49] Constructive trusts based on unjust enrichment are not limited to cases of mistaken payments. It has been held, for example, that property transferred under undue influence[113] or procured by unconscionable conduct[114] will be held on constructive trust for the transferor. Although the decisions were reached by reference to the equitable doctrines of undue influence and unconscionable conduct,[115] the constructive trusts imposed in these cases reversed enrichment which the law recognises as unjust.

Contractual transfers of property

[23.50] In chapter 5, we saw that a contract will be voidable in equity on a number of grounds such as undue influence, unconscionability, and breach of fiduciary duty. The contract will be valid until the plaintiff elects to avoid it. Once the election has been made, the parties will be restored to their pre-contractual position. If property has been transferred under the voidable contract, the recipient will hold the property or its traceable proceeds on constructive trust for the transferor. The constructive trust is a restitutionary remedy for unjust enrichment. The constructive trust awarded where property has been transferred pursuant to a voidable contract differs from the constructive trust awarded where no contract was entered into in

109 [1996] AC 669, 715; *Sourcebook* 23.7, note 2, p 630.

110 (2007) 63 ACSR 429; *Sourcebook* 23.7b, p 631.

111 For this purpose, knowledge of the mistake was defined in terms of the fourth point on the *Baden* scale of knowledge; ie knowing of circumstances which would indicate a mistake to an honest and reasonable person. See [11.9].

112 (2007) 63 ACSR 429, [43].

113 *McCulloch v Fern* [2001] NSWSC 406.

114 *Louth v Diprose* (1992) 175 CLR 621; *McCulloch v Fern* [2001] NSWSC 406.

115 See chapter 7.

that it arises, not immediately on receipt of the property (as in *Chase Manhattan*), or when the recipient learns of the mistake (as in *Wambo*), but when an election has been made to rescind the contract. The election requirement is discussed at [5.10].

The doctrine of mutual wills

Suppose that A and B[116] enter into a contract providing for the distribution of their property after their deaths. The contract provides that each leaves his or her property to the survivor, and that on the death of the survivor their property[117] is to pass to C.[118] Prior to the death of either party, the arrangement is a matter for contract law. Either can withdraw from the arrangement by agreement or by one giving notice of withdrawal to the other which is accepted.[119] If the will of A, the first to die, has been altered otherwise than by revocation on marriage, B can sue A's estate for breach of contract.[120] Contract law, however, will be inapplicable if A dies leaving the property to B in accordance with the terms of the mutual wills, but B leaves the property in his will to someone other than C. A's estate can sue B's estate for breach of contract, but A will be unable to prove compensable loss, and C, who has suffered loss of the expected benefit under the terms of the mutual wills, cannot sue because he is a third party to the contract. It is nonetheless unconscionable for B to break his promise to A when A has relied on that promise in drafting her will. Equity prevents an unconscionable departure from the agreed scheme of mutual wills by compelling B to hold the property subject to the scheme on constructive trust for C.[121] [23.51]

The leading authority on mutual wills is the High Court decision in *Birmingham v Renfrew*.[122] A wife bequeathed her residuary estate to her husband, if he should survive her, the husband promising that on his death he would leave their property to four of her relatives. The husband executed a will in similar terms. At the wife's death her property passed, in accordance with her will, to her husband. The husband, however, executed a new will leaving all his property, including the property bequeathed by his wife, to his sisters. It was proved that the couple had agreed to execute mutual wills. The High Court held that, on receiving the wife's property under her will, the husband was bound by a constructive trust obliging him to leave his estate, including the property received under his wife's will, to the wife's relatives specified in the original mutual wills. In the words of Dixon J: '[T]he equitable obligation to fulfil the contract attaches to the property the subject of the contract and converts the party into a trustee for the objects to be benefited'.[123] [23.52]

116 Mutual wills are usually executed by married couples, but the doctrine is not limited to marriage.

117 Mutual wills usually make provision for the ultimate destination of *both* parties' property, but they can provide that only the property of the *first* party to die is governed by the terms of the mutual will: *Re Green* [1951] Ch 148.

118 C is usually a child, or children, of the marriage.

119 *Stone v Hoskins* [1905] P 194.

120 *Robinson v Ommanney* (1883) 23 Ch D 285.

121 R Croucher, 'Mutual Wills: Contemporary Reflections on an Old Doctrine' (2005) 29(2) *Melbourne University Law Review* 390.

122 (1937) 57 CLR 666; *Sourcebook* 23.8a, p 634. For a modern re-examination of the principles see *Flocas v Carlson* (2015) 15 ASTLR 192, [178]–[192].

123 (1937) 57 CLR 666, 687–8.

[23.53] This constructive trust is unusual in that the trustee is free to enjoy and dispose of the property received under the first will, as well as his own property, as if he were absolute owner. Dixon J analysed the situation at the wife's death as 'a floating obligation suspended, so to speak, during the lifetime of the survivor' which, on his death, crystallises into a trust.[124] The trustee has a limited power to dispose of the trust property, but he cannot make 'gifts and settlements, *inter vivos* … calculated to defeat the intention of the compact'.[125] The content of the 'floating obligation', including the limits of the survivor's power to dispose of trust property, will be determined by the express and implied terms of the contract between the parties.[126]

[23.54] A constructive trust enforceable under the doctrine of mutual wills is not bound by the writing requirements of the *Wills Act* or, if the subject matter of the constructive trust is land, by the *Statute of Frauds* requirement that no interest in land can be created or disposed of except by writing signed by the party creating or disposing of the interest.[127] This does not mean, however, that statutory formalities are wholly irrelevant to the creation of a mutual wills arrangement. If the subject-matter of the arrangement includes land, the writing requirements applicable to such a contract must be satisfied unless an exception to the requirements, such as the doctrine of part performance, applies.[128] Moreover, the mutual wills themselves must comply with the statutory formalities for the creation of a valid will. Once the mutual wills arrangement has been established, however, the constructive trust is fastened onto the property subject to the mutual scheme at A's death in order to prevent unconscionable conduct by B. The operation of the trust is at this point independent of the statutory formalities governing the disposition of interests in property.

Constructive trusts imposed over property transferred under specifically enforceable contracts

[23.55] Suppose V agrees to sell land to P. The contract will be specifically enforceable unless a bar to specific performance, such as delay or hardship, applies.[129] V has been said to hold the land on constructive trust for P.[130] But the purchaser's interest is 'better understood as an equitable right to performance commensurate with the terms of the contract'[131] of sale.

124 Ibid 689.
125 Ibid.
126 *Flocas v Carlson* (2015) 15 ASTLR 192, [192].
127 *Property Law Act 1958* (Vic) s 53(1)(a). See [9.36].
128 *Horton v Jones* (1935) 53 CLR 475; *Flocas v Carlson* (2015) 15 ASTLR 192, [191].
129 See chapters 3 and 6. Specific performance will not be obtainable if a transfer cannot be made without the consent of a third party, such as a government minister, and the consent has not been obtained: *McWilliam v McWilliam's Wines Pty Ltd* (1964) 114 CLR 656, 660–1.
130 *Lysaght v Edwards* (1876) 2 Ch D 499, 506 (Jessel MR).
131 *Westpac Banking Corporation v Queensland* [2016] FCA 269, [13] (Edelman J), summarising *Chang v Registrar of Titles* (1976) 137 CLR 177, 184 (Mason J); *Sourcebook* 23.9a, p 637.

The nature of P's equitable protection will depend on the terms of the contract and the obligations performed under it.[132] Where there are rights outstanding on both sides, the relationship between the parties will be governed by the terms of the contract. V is entitled to payment of the purchase price and, if title is transferred without the price being paid in full, can enforce an equitable lien over the land to secure payment. The purchaser's interest in the performance of the contract is protected by the principles governing equitable relief from forfeiture which preserves the purchaser's right to specific performance in the event of V's unconscientious exercise of a contractual right to terminate the contract.[133] Upon payment of the purchase price under an unconditional contract of sale P obtains an equitable interest in the land. The usual, though not necessary explanation, of the equitable interest is that V holds the land on constructive trust for P.[134] Precisely when P obtains an equitable interest will depend on the terms of the contract and the extent to which P has performed her obligations under the contract, the most important being to pay the purchase price.[135]

The practical consequences of imposing the constructive trust include the following.[136] [23.56] V, as trustee, must exercise due care to preserve and maintain the land pending completion. V must account to P for any rents or profits received, or which ought to have been received, between the agreed date of completion and the actual date of completion. Moreover, if V, in breach of contract, sells the land to a third party he must account to P for the proceeds of sale.[137] On the other hand, risk, for example of damage by fire, passes to P under the contract against which P should insure in order to protect her equitable interest.[138]

The constructive trust can also be significant where property other than land is [23.57] transferred under a specifically enforceable contract. This includes a contract for the sale of an equitable interest under an express trust. For example, if T holds property on express trust for B, an assignment of B's equitable interest to X must be in writing in order to satisfy *Statute of Frauds* writing requirements.[139] But if B enters into a specifically enforceable contract to sell her equitable interest to X for valuable consideration, she will hold the interest on constructive trust for X. The writing requirements of the *Statute of Frauds* do not apply to constructive trusts, so the oral contract has been held to be sufficient to vest title to the equitable interest in X. This application of the constructive trust can enable tax payable on written instruments which convey an interest in property, such as stamp duty, to be avoided.[140]

132 *Tanwar Enterprises Pty Ltd v Cauchi* (2003) 217 CLR 315; *Sourcebook* 23.9b, p 640; *Golden Mile Property Investments Pty Ltd (in liq) v Cudgegong Australia Pty Ltd* (2015) 89 NSWLR 237, [98]–[103] (Emmett JA).

133 See chapter 7.

134 *Golden Mile Property Investments Pty Ltd (in liq) v Cudgegong Australia Pty Ltd* (2015) 89 NSWLR 237, [102] (Emmett JA).

135 *Chang v Registrar of Titles* (1976) 137 CLR 177.

136 *Golden Mile Investments Pty Ltd (in liq) v Cudgegong* (2015) 89 NSWLR 237, [104] (Emmett JA).

137 *Lake v Bayliss* [1974] 2 All ER 1114; *Bunny Industries Ltd v FSW Enterprises Pty Ltd* [1982] Qd R 712.

138 *Rayner v Preston* (1881) 18 Ch D 1.

139 See [9.36].

140 *Halloran v Minister Administering National Parks and Wildlife Act 1974* (2006) 229 CLR 545. Statutory anti-avoidance provisions may in practice prevent the circumvention of writing requirements.

The principle of *Holroyd v Marshall* and assignments of future property

[23.58] A commercially significant application of the vendor–purchaser constructive trust concerns a contract to assign future property. Suppose that R, a retailer, needs money to expand her business or to overcome cashflow problems. R may negotiate finance from a financier, F, in return for assigning to F her right to payment of debts owed to her by present and future customers. The rules for assigning present debts are explained in chapter 9. In the case of future debts, F will be entitled, after providing the finance to R, to enforce future debts as and when they become due to R. The equitable analysis is that R holds the right to enforce future debts ('future property') on constructive trust for F. The debts must be identifiable as the subject-matter of the contract to assign. In practical terms F becomes the equitable owner of the debts once she has provided valuable consideration under the contract to assign future property.

[23.59] The principles for assigning future property in equity were laid down by Lord Westbury in *Holroyd v Marshall*.[141] Lord Westbury laid special emphasis on the specific enforceability of the contract to assign future property as justifying the imposition of the constructive trust on the assignor. In the later decision of *Tailby v Official Receiver*,[142] however, the House of Lords stated that the assignment was enforceable in equity once the consideration had been paid by the assignee, applying the maxim that equity considers as done that which ought to be done. This was also the basis on which the High Court enforced a contract to assign future property in *Palette Shoes Pty Ltd v Krohn*.[143]

[23.60] The principles established in *Holroyd v Marshall* and later cases for assigning future property provide the legal basis of debt factoring, whereby a trader assigns to a financier ('factor') present and future debts owed to the trader in return for cash, or provides them as security for a loan. Where the assignment in substance secures payment or performance of an obligation, the enforceability of the assignment is now governed by the *Personal Property Securities Act 2009* (Cth). The principal significance of the Act is that it replaces equitable priority rules with statutory priority rules based principally but not exclusively on registration of security interests.[144]

WHAT'S ONLINE?

Available at www.cambridge.org/highereducation/isbn/9781009232388/resources:

- Recommended further readings
- Further commentary
- Discussion topics
- Practice problem

141 (1862) 10 HLC 191; 11 ER 999; *Sourcebook* 9.3c, p 218.
142 (1888) 13 App Cas 523; *Sourcebook* 9.3c, note 1, p 219.
143 (1937) 58 CLR 1.
144 *Personal Property Securities Act 2009* (Cth) s 12(2)(j) (assignments included within definition of security interest); s 18(2) includes after-acquired property, the assignment taking effect under s 19(2) by virtue of statutory attachment, not equitable principle. See generally Anthony Duggan, *Australian Personal Property Securities Law* (LexisNexis Butterworths, 3rd ed, 2021).

PART

TERMINATING AND VARYING TRUSTS

24

TERMINATION AND VARIATION OF TRUSTS

Introduction

The duration of all express trusts except charitable trusts is limited by the application of the rule against perpetuities.[1] As explained in chapter 15, the rule does not impose a fixed time limit on the duration of a trust. In most cases, it imposes a limit (nowadays usually 80 years) beyond a which an interest arising under the trust cannot vest.[2] In South Australia, the perpetuity rule has been abolished but a court may, upon application, vary the terms of a trust which has lasted more than 80 years so that the remaining interests vest immediately.[3] [24.1]

There are no limits on the duration of a charitable trust beyond the practical limitation of the availability of trust money to be applied for the charity's objects. If the original objects of the charity become impossible or impracticable to achieve a cy-près scheme will be approved, enabling the trust property to be applied for objects which are as close as possible to the original objects.[4] [24.2]

A well-drafted trust instrument will include a vesting date, within the perpetuity period, on which the trust will come to an end and trust property which has not previously been distributed will vest in specified beneficiaries. In the case of a discretionary trust, where the trustees have not previously exercised their power to advance capital or pay income to objects of the trust, the beneficiaries taking the trust property on the vesting date are often described as the 'default beneficiaries': they take the trust property in default of a prior exercise of discretion by the trustees. If the settlor fails to make provision for the distribution of the trust property by inclusion of a vesting date, the trust will fail upon expiry of the perpetuity period and the property will pass on resulting trust to the settlor or to the settlor's next-of-kin.[5] A discretionary trust will often identify a narrow class of 'specified beneficiaries' who will become entitled to the trust property on the vesting date, together with a wider class of 'general beneficiaries', including the 'specified beneficiaries', who will be objects of the trustees' exercise of discretion until the trust is terminated on the vesting date.[6] Charities can be included among the classes of specified or general beneficiaries. [24.3]

Termination of trusts

The rule in *Saunders v Vautier*

In Anglo-Australian law, a trust may be brought to an end prior to the vesting date described in the previous section by the application of the so-called rule in *Saunders v Vautier*.[7] The rule enables an adult beneficiary to claim her share of the trust property before the vesting [24.4]

1 See [15.34].
2 The rule against indestructible trusts apples a period of 21 years to a non-charitable purpose trust. See [15.37].
3 *Law of Property Act 1936* (SA) ss 61–2. Section 62(2) also empowers a court to vary the terms of a disposition where interests in property cannot, or are unlikely to, vest within 80 years of the date of the disposition.
4 See [16.39].
5 See [22.22].
6 See the terms of the trust in *Mandie v Memart Nominees Pty Ltd* (2020) 62 VR 528, [12]–[38].
7 (1841) 49 ER 282; *Sourcebook* 24.2a, p 646.

date is reached, as well as before any date stipulated in the trust instrument for receiving the share.

[24.5] The following is a formulation of the principle of *Saunders v Vautier*: If all the beneficiaries, being of full legal capacity, have between them an absolute, vested and indefeasible interest in the capital and income of the trust property, they may terminate the trust and require the trustees to transfer the property to them, or to a third party at their direction.

In *Saunders v Vautier*, a testamentary trust directed the trustees to hold certain stock on trust for the testator's nephew, and to transfer the stock, together with the accumulated interest and dividends, to the nephew upon attaining the age of 25. When he was 21 (at that time, the age of majority), the nephew petitioned for termination of the trust and for the trust fund to be transferred to him. It was held that, being an adult and solely entitled under the trust, he was entitled to the trust fund even though he had not attained the age of 25 specified by the testator.

[24.6] Although often described as a 'rule' the principle of *Saunders v Vautier* is not, strictly speaking, a rule at all (in the sense of conferring a duty on trustees) but a power enabling qualified adult beneficiaries to bring the trust to an end and vest the trust property in themselves.[8] The trustees are under a corresponding liability to have the office of trusteeship terminated by the exercise of the power by the beneficiaries.[9] The exercise of the power cannot be excluded or limited by a contrary provision in the trust instrument. Vautier's power to terminate the trust and claim for himself the trust property upon attaining the age of majority prevailed over the explicit provision in the trust instrument entitling him to the property only upon attaining 25.[10]

[24.7] The exercise of the power is subject to some legal and practical limitations.

(1) The beneficiaries must have legal capacity. If the beneficiaries unanimously agree to terminate the trust, one of the beneficiaries being a minor, the trust cannot be terminated by application of the principle of *Saunders v Vautier*. In jurisdictions that have enacted variation of trusts legislation,[11] an application on behalf of the minor can be made to approve an arrangement which revokes the trust.

(2) The beneficiaries must be unanimous if they want to bring the trust to an end. A trust cannot be terminated by a majority vote of the beneficiaries. The distinction between fixed and discretionary trusts, however, is relevant to the application of this requirement since an adult beneficiary of a fixed trust can claim her interest under the trust, over the objections of the other beneficiaries, even if the trust is not to be terminated.

8 *CPT Custodian Pty Ltd v Commissioner of State Revenue* (2005) 224 CLR 98, 119 [44]; *Beck v Henley* [2014] NSWCA 201, [33] (Leeming JA).

9 W Hohfeld, *Fundamental Legal Conceptions As Applied In Legal Reasoning* (Lawbook Exchange, 2000) 50–1.

10 In *Saunders v Vautier*, the purported limitation on the beneficiary's power to terminate the trust was testamentary. Query whether the power is exercisable where the relationship between trustee and beneficiary is contractual, a term of the contract being the exclusion of *Saunders v Vautier*. A relevant consideration may be whether the beneficiary's obligations under the contract have been fully performed. Cf discussion of *CPT Custodian Pty Ltd v Commissioner of State Revenue* at [24.8].

11 See [24.20].

(a) Suppose a trust creates fixed interests; for example, a trust of the money held in the settlor's bank account to be held for A and B in equal shares. A, having legal capacity, can claim her share of the trust money even if B objects to the termination of the trust. In *Beck v Henley,*[12] two voting shares in a private company were held on trust for a brother and sister. The brother invoked the principle of *Saunders v Vautier* to claim one of the shares. The New South Wales Court of Appeal held that he was entitled, over the objections of his sister, to have the share transferred to him.

(b) The application of *Saunders v Vautier* to enable an adult beneficiary of a fixed trust to take her share of the trust property depends on whether the property is specifically severable, in the sense of being readily divisible between the beneficiaries. The test 'is governed by practical considerations and, in particular, by considerations of convenience of division and of the risk of prejudice to other beneficiaries'.[13] In *Beck v Henley*, the sister could not show that permitting her brother to claim his voting share would have prejudiced her interests. There was no premium attaching to the two shares as a parcel, as opposed to the shares individually.[14] Similarly, there will generally be no problem applying *Saunders v Vautier* where beneficiaries hold fixed interest entitlements to money held in a bank account. On the other hand, a beneficiary will usually not be permitted to invoke *Saunders v Vautier* and claim her share of the trust property where the subject-matter consists of a plot of land. This is because the sale of an undivided share of land rarely fetches the proportion of the proceeds of sale that would be realised by the sale of the whole plot.[15]

(c) Where property is held on the terms of a discretionary trust – for example, on trust for such of A, B, C, D and E as the trustees shall select – the trust can be terminated if all the beneficiaries have full legal capacity and unanimously agree to bring the trust to an end. A, B, C, D and E are absolutely entitled to the beneficial interest in the property.[16]

(d) It should not be assumed from this example that all discretionary trusts can be brought to an end by invoking the *Saunders v Vautier* principle. A trust that is valid only because it satisfies the criterion certainty test laid down in *McPhail v Doulton*[17] – for example, a trust for 'such of my employees, and their dependants and relatives as my trustees shall select' – cannot be terminated by this method. This is because there is no point in time when all the beneficiaries, whose unanimous

12 (2014) 11 ASTLR 457; *Sourcebook* 24.3b, p 650.

13 *Manfred v Maddrell* (1950) 51 SR (NSW) 95, 97 (Sugerman J).

14 (2014) 11 ASTLR 457, [64] (Leeming JA). In some cases, a beneficiary cannot invoke *Saunders v Vautier* because the evidence shows that the value per share of the trust's holding of shares in a company is higher than the value of an individual share: *Lloyds Bank v Duker* [1987] 1 WLR 1324, distinguished in *Beck v Henley* (2014) 11 ASTLR 457, [63] (Leeming JA).

15 *Beck v Henley* (2014) 11 ASTLR 457, [38] (Leeming JA), citing *Re Marshall* [1914] 1 Ch 192, 199. Leeming JA left open at [38] the question whether the proposition in the text is universally applicable.

16 *Re Smith* [1928] Ch 915; *Sir Moses Montefiore Jewish Home v Howell & Co (No 7) Pty Ltd* [1984] 2 NSWLR 406, 411 (Kearney J).

17 [1971] AC 424; *Sourcebook* 14.4b, p 382.

consent to termination is required, can be identified. The criterion certainty test determines the validity of a discretionary trust. But it may well be impossible to draw up a list of all the beneficiaries of a trust validated by application of the test. This is because membership of the class of beneficiaries constantly changes. If a list of all the beneficiaries cannot be made when the application for termination is made, the trust cannot be terminated by a unanimous decision of the beneficiaries in accordance with the principle of *Saunders v Vautier*.

(3) The beneficiaries must, between them, be entitled to the entire beneficial interest in the trust property. This is generally expressed by stating that the beneficiaries must have an absolute, vested and indefeasible right to the capital and income of the trust property. Where a trust instrument creates successive interests in property; for example, where a trust is created 'for A for life, remainder for B' both A and B have vested interests, A's being in possession and B's in reversion. Between them, A and B are absolutely entitled to the trust property and, provided they have legal capacity, they can terminate the trust. A contingent beneficiary cannot invoke *Saunders v Vautier* unless the consent of both the contingent beneficiary, as well of all potential beneficiaries in whom title to the property will vest if the contingency is not met, has been obtained.[18] A trust of $100 000 'for A provided that she enrols in a law degree, but if she fails to do so by the age of twenty-one, then to B absolutely', can be terminated by A and B once they attain 18 since they hold the entire beneficial interest in the property between them.[19]

[24.8] The trustee, as well as the beneficiaries, can have a right to the trust property which will prevent the adult beneficiaries from claiming the property for themselves. A trustee has a proprietary right of indemnity from the trust fund to reimburse expenditure incurred for the benefit of the trust.[20] In *CPT Custodian Pty Ltd v Commissioner of State Revenue*,[21] a trustee of a unit trust was entitled to reimbursement of its costs, charges and expenses from the trust fund. The beneficial interest in the fund was divided into units, each unit conferring an equal interest in all the property for the time being held by the trustee. No unit conferred an interest in any discrete part of the trust fund. The Commissioner argued that all the unit holders held the beneficial interest in the land collectively. This would mean that they could terminate the trust and, subject to reimbursing the trustee's costs, divide the land among themselves. They therefore held rights in the land that attracted land tax. The High Court rejected the argument, holding that the unit-holders did not have the right to terminate the trust because the trustee had an unsatisfied right of

18 In *Saunders v Vautier*, it was argued that Vautier's interest was contingent on attaining the age of 25 but it was held, on the construction of the trust instrument, that Vautier's interest was vested, enjoyment being postponed until he attained 25 years of age.

19 *Cox v Archer* (1964) 110 CLR 1, [8]. Cf *Arnott v Kiss* [2014] NSWSC 1385 ('to such of my grandchildren who survive me and attain their respective age of 45 years and in equal shares') where *Saunders v Vautier* was inapplicable because, in the event of the death of all the grandchildren before the age of 45, the testator's son, who opposed the termination of the trust, would become entitled to the trust property.

20 *Carter Holt Harvey Woodproducts Australia Pty Ltd v Commonwealth* (2019) 268 CLR 524; see chapter 19.

21 (2005) 224 CLR 98, *Sourcebook* 24.3a, p 647.

indemnity from the trust fund for its expenses. Until that right had been satisfied, it could not be said that the beneficiaries were entitled to the entire beneficial interest in the trust permitting them to exercise their rights under *Saunders v Vautier*.

Critique of *Saunders v Vautier*

The principle of *Saunders v Vautier* is firmly established in Australian equity, and drafters of family trusts keep in mind the possibility that adult beneficiaries may decide to terminate the trust before the vesting date specified in the trust instrument. But it is a controversial doctrine because it allows the express wishes of the settlor to be overridden. This is illustrated by the facts of *Saunders v Vautier*. [24.9]

United States jurisdictions have rejected *Saunders v Vautier* in favour of what is known as the 'Claflin' doctrine,[22] whereby a trust cannot be terminated, even with the consent of all beneficiaries, prior to the vesting date where continuance of the trust is necessary to carry out a material purpose of the settlor. *Saunders v Vautier* and the Claflin doctrine are based on diametrically opposing conceptions of autonomy in trusts law. *Saunders v Vautier* accords primacy to a holder of a beneficial interest in property who, if of full legal capacity and subject to any public policy constraints, is entitled to dispose of her interest as she pleases. The Claflin doctrine enforces the autonomy of the settlor whose intention in creating the trust should be respected unless there is some public policy objection to enforcing that intention. [24.10]

There is a lively academic literature debating the merits of these competing approaches to terminating trusts.[23] A criticism often directed at the *Saunders v Vautier* principle is that its application is easily evaded by ingenious drafting.[24] This can be achieved, for example, by the inclusion of a general charitable purpose as an object of a discretionary trust.[25]

Variation of trusts

Saunders v Vautier confers a power on qualified beneficiaries to terminate a trust, but it does not permit the beneficiaries to direct the trustees how to perform their duties or to exercise their discretions under an ongoing trust. The beneficiaries cannot, for example, direct the trustees how to invest the trust fund.[26] A trust can only be varied if all the beneficiaries are adult and agree to terminate the trust and reconstitute it on the terms of a varied trust. Adoption of this procedure, which will temporarily vest the legal interest in the trust property in the beneficiaries of the first trust until the second trust is constituted, can result [24.11]

22 *Claflin v Claflin*, 149 Mss 19, 20 NE 454 (1889).

23 P Matthews, 'The Comparative Importance of the Rule in Saunders v Vautier' (2006) 122(2) *Law Quarterly Review* 266; JH Langbein, 'Why the Rule in Saunders v Vautier is Wrong' in PG Turner (ed), *Equity and Administration* (Cambridge University Press, 2016) 189; P Matthews, 'Why the Rule in Saunders v Vautier is Wrong: A Commentary' in PG Turner (ed), *Equity and Administration* (Cambridge University Press, 2016) 203.

24 See Langbein (n 23) 191–3.

25 See also the inclusion of contingencies in a trust instrument so that the adult beneficiaries do not have absolute indefeasible title to the trust property between them: *Laycock v Ingram* [2008] VSC 113.

26 *Re Brockbank* [1948] Ch 206.

in the beneficiaries incurring tax liabilities. The procedure cannot, in any event, be adopted if some beneficiaries lack legal capacity or are unborn.

[24.12] Many trust instruments include a provision empowering the trustees (or a third party such as a guardian or protector) to vary the terms of the trust. Such a provision enables the trustees to adapt the terms of the trust to meet changes of circumstances, including changes in relevant tax law. Whether the provision is effective to authorise a proposed variation is a question of construction of its terms in the context of the overall scheme of the trust.[27] As in contract law, an objective approach is applied to construing a variation clause: 'the Settlor's intention is to be found in the wording of the trust deed, as distinct from speculations about what might have been in her mind when the trust was settled'.[28]

[24.13] If a trust instrument does not include a variation clause, or if the clause does not allow the variation of the terms of the trust that the trustees are seeking, an application must be made for judicial approval of the variation. A court of equity does not have an inherent jurisdiction to approve a variation of trusts.[29] The court does have an 'emergency' (or 'salvage') jurisdiction permitting the trustees to authorise an activity which must necessarily be undertaken if the trustees are to act in the best interests of the beneficiaries.[30] But this jurisdiction does not permit the court to approve any variation of the beneficial interests under a trust.

[24.14] In the absence of an inherent equitable jurisdiction, the source of judicial authority to approve variations of trust must be found in statute. All States and Territories have enacted provisions derived from (but not an exact copy of) the English *Trustee Act 1925* s 57 which authorise the court to confer powers on the trustees in the management or administration of the trust property where it is, in the opinion of the Court, expedient to confer the powers.[31] The statutory 'expediency' jurisdiction has assumed special significance in New South Wales, which has not enacted Variation of Trusts provisions. Recent decisions construing s 81 of the *Trustee Act 1925* (NSW) will be examined at [24.16]–[24.19].

[24.15] Queensland, Tasmania, Victoria and Western Australia have enacted provisions based on the English *Variation of Trusts Act 1958*. This Act enables courts to approve a proposed variation of trust on behalf of persons, such as minors and unborn beneficiaries, who are unable to consent for the purposes of the *Saunders v Vautier* principle. The Australian provisions, which differ in detail from both the English version and from each other, are considered at [24.20]–[24.27]. South Australia has enacted a broad discretionary trust variation of trust provision which is not limited to enabling the court to supply the consent of a beneficiary who could not otherwise invoke *Saunders v Vautier*. The provision is considered at [24.28]–[24.29].

27 *Mercanti v Mercanti* (2016) 50 WAR 495.

28 *Re Owies Family Trust* [2020] VSC 716, [84] (Moore J).

29 *Chapman v Chapman* [1954] AC 429.

30 *Re New* [1901] 2 Ch 534. Courts of equity also have an inherent jurisdiction to approve compromises relating to trustees' and beneficiaries' rights but the jurisdiction does not extend to a power to approve compromises on behalf of those, such as unborn beneficiaries, who do not have rights under a trust.

31 ACT s 81; NSW s 81; NT s 50A (not limiting the exercise of the power to cases of expediency but limiting the power to listed dispositions, and not to 'transactions' generally); Qld s 94; SA s 59B; Tas s 47; Vic s 63; WA s 89 (applicable in cases of difficulty or impracticability, as well as expediency). The Queensland and Western Australian provisions add, as an alternative to 'expediency', the criterion that the proposed transaction 'would be in the best interests of the persons, or the majority of persons, beneficially interested under the trust': see *Re Arthur Brady Family Trust* [2015] 2 Qd R 172, [24]–[26].

The expediency jurisdiction

Section 81 of the *Trustee Act 1925* (NSW) provides: [24.16]

Advantageous dealings

(1) Where in the management or administration of any property vested in trustees, any sale, lease, mortgage, surrender, release or disposition, or any purchase, investment, acquisition, expenditure, or transaction, is in the opinion of the Court expedient, but the same cannot be effected by reason of the absence of any power for that purpose vested in the trustees by the instrument, if any, creating the trust, or by law, the Court–

(a) may by order confer upon the trustees, either generally or in any particular instance, the necessary power for the purpose, on such terms, and subject to such provisions and conditions, including adjustment of the respective rights of the beneficiaries, as the Court may think fit, and

(b) may direct in what manner any money authorised to be expended and the costs of any transaction, are to be paid or borne as between capital and income.

...

Section 81 enables a court to confer powers on a trustee, such as the power to sell or lease trust property, which promote the effective management and administration of trust property. The word 'transaction' in s 81(1) has been construed broadly in order to achieve this purpose.[32] But the section cannot be utilised as a general 'variation of trust' provision, entitling a court to approve the conferral of a power on the trustee to alter the beneficial interests under the trust. [24.17]

In *Re Dion's Investments Pty Ltd*,[33] the trustee of a family trust applied for an order under s 81 which would have inserted a provision into the trust deed enabling the trustee to amend the trust instrument as it thought fit. While the New South Wales Court of Appeal approved the conferral of specific and limited powers on the trustee concerning the method of accounting for trust income, which were shown to be tax efficient, the Court refused to grant the trustee a broad discretion to vary the trust, since the alteration of trust terms, including beneficial interests, is not a 'transaction' within s 81. In the words of Barrett JA: [24.18]

> If the power to be given to the trustee is not a specific power with respect to a particular dealing (or dealings of a particular kind) but, rather, a wide discretionary power to alter the terms of the trust as the trustee thinks fit, the case is not within s 81(1).[34]

In *Cisera v Cisera Holdings Pty Ltd*,[35] the Court of Appeal confirmed the correctness of its decision in *Re Dion Investments Pty Ltd*, stating that the ratio of that case was not confined to holding that an order giving the trustee a general power to amend the trust deed fell outside the definition of 'transaction' in s 81. The Court in *Cisera* determined that a proposed amendment of the trust deed which would have extended the vesting date of the trust was not a 'transaction' within s 81. The financial implications of the decision for the trust were [24.19]

32 *Riddle v Riddle* 85 (1952) CLR 202.
33 (2014) 87 NSWLR 753.
34 Ibid [98].
35 (2018) 98 NSWLR 747.

significant since, had the amendment been allowed, the trust would have saved in the order of $3.4 million capital gains tax.[36]

White JA in *Cisera v Cisera Holdings Pty Ltd* stated that s 81:

> cannot be construed so broadly as to provide a substitute for variation of trusts legislation that the United Kingdom and other Australian States introduced following the decision in *Re Chapman*. For whatever reason, or perhaps for no reason except pressure of other Parliamentary business, New South Wales did not adopt the *Variation of Trusts Act 1958* (UK) that substantially broadened the jurisdiction of courts to vary trusts … The number of successful applications in this State for what might be beneficial changes to the terms of the trusts following *Re Dion Investments* indicate that the issue is ripe for Parliamentary consideration.[37]

The *Variation of Trusts Act* jurisdictions

[24.20] Following the House of Lords decision in *Chapman v Chapman*[38] confirming that courts have no inherent jurisdiction to vary a trust, the United Kingdom enacted the *Variation of Trusts Act 1958*. The Act empowers a court to consent to an arrangement to vary or revoke a trust on behalf of beneficiaries who lack capacity to agree to termination by application of *Saunders v Vautier*. The legislation has been adopted in Queensland, Tasmania, Victoria and Western Australia with only minor modifications.

Section 63A of the *Trustee Act 1958* (Vic) provides:

> **Power of Court to vary trusts**
>
> **(1)** Where property, whether real or personal, is held on trusts arising, whether before or after the commencement of this Act, under any will settlement or other disposition, the Court may, if it thinks fit by order approve on behalf of–
>
> **(a)** any person having, directly or indirectly, an interest, whether vested or contingent, under the trusts who by reason of minority or other incapacity is incapable of assenting; or
>
> **(b)** any person (whether ascertained or not) who may become entitled, directly or indirectly, to an interest under the trusts as being at a future date or on the happening of a future event a person of any specified description or a member of any specified class of persons, so however that this paragraph shall not include any person who would be of that description, or a member of that class (as the case may be) if the said date had fallen or the said event had happened at the date of the application to the Court; or

36 Ibid [24] (White JA). See also *Re Application of Country Road Services Pty Ltd (Browne Family Trust)* [2019] NSWSC 779 where an application to allow trustees to pay a trust's income and capital gain in a tax year to another trust was held not to be a dealing in the management and administration of trust property and so fell outside s 81. Parker J observed at [93] that 'the avoidance of tax would nearly always be expedient. But any such expediency does not arise in the administration of the Browne Family Trust'.

37 Ibid [69], [71].

38 [1954] AC 429.

(c) any person unborn; or

(d) any person in respect of any discretionary interest of his under protective trusts where the interest of the principal beneficiary has not failed or determined–

any arrangement (by whomsoever proposed and whether or not there is any other person beneficially interested who is capable of assenting thereto) varying or revoking all or any of the trusts, or enlarging the powers of the trustees or managing or administering any of the property subject to the trusts:

Provided that except by virtue of paragraph (d) of this subsection the Court shall not approve an arrangement on behalf of any person unless the carrying out thereof would be for the benefit of that person.[39]

...

Section 63A does not confer on the court a wide-ranging discretionary power to authorise a proposed variation of trust. The court's function is solely to approve, on behalf of the persons listed in paragraphs (a)–(d), a proposal to vary or revoke a trust if: [24.21]

(1) it is satisfied (except in the case of applications brought in respect of those having discretionary interests under protective trusts) that the proposed variation will be for the benefit of that person, and, if so,

(2) it thinks fit to approve the variation.[40] At this stage, the court considers the overall impact of the variation on the parties to the trust. It will give a 'practical and business-like consideration of the arrangement', assessing the overall balance of benefits and detriments of the proposed variation to all relevant parties, having regard to their bargaining strength.[41] The fact that a variation may turn out to be disadvantageous to an infant or unborn beneficiary in particular circumstances will not necessarily result in the court rejecting the proposal if the risk is one that an adult would be prepared to take, and one that the court is prepared to take in consenting on behalf of the beneficiary.

The Court order does not of itself vary the trust. It simply provides the consent necessary to enable all the beneficiaries to execute a deed varying the trust on the terms approved by the court.[42] The consent of the parties with legal capacity is obtained by invoking their right to terminate the existing trust under *Saunders v Vautier*. [24.22]

39 Equivalent provisions in other States are: Qld s 95; *Variation of Trusts Act 1994* (Tas) s 14 (this provides that the proposed variation must be 'in the interests of each person on behalf of whom the Court may approve the proposed arrangement' and lists specific matters which a court must consider); WA s 90 (s 90(2) provides that the arrangement must not be approved if it is detrimental to the beneficiary). Among matters to be considered are 'the welfare and honour of the family to which he belongs'. See *Palmer v McAllister* (1991) 4 WAR 206, 211–12.

40 In Western Australia, the proposal must meet the (arguably less demanding) standard of not being detrimental to the beneficiary: WA s 90(2).

41 *Re Van Gruisen's Will Trusts* [1964] 1 All ER 843, 844; *George v Kollias* [2007] VSC 46, [41]–[42].

42 *Goulding v James* [1997] 2 All ER 239, 246–8; *George v Kollias* [2007] VSC 46, [43]. Cf the *Variation of Trusts Act 1994* (Tas) s 15 which provides that the court order gives legal effect to the variation. Under s 13(4) of that Act, the written consent to the variation of the parties whose consent is not being sought from the Court must be given prior to the application.

On whose behalf does a court approve a variation?

[24.23] The categories of beneficiary on whose behalf a court may approve a variation of trust are:

(a) a beneficiary who lacks legal capacity, for example because the beneficiary is a minor or is under a severe cognitive disability.

(b) an unascertained beneficiary. The tortuous wording of paragraph (b) attempts to distinguish between two types of unascertained beneficiary. The first is the person who is nowhere in sight. An example of a beneficiary of this kind is a trust 'for X and for any husband X may marry' where X is unmarried at the time of the application to vary the trust. The court can, by virtue of paragraph (b), consent to the proposed variation on behalf of the unascertained husband. The second type of unascertained beneficiary is one who is identifiable but who has not yet satisfied a condition enabling him or her to qualify as a beneficiary under the trust. A possible example is a trust for X and X's next-of-kin, where X has siblings, A, B, and C who may ultimately qualify as next-of-kin. Paragraph (b) is not intended to include this class of unascertained beneficiary since A, B and C are identified and can, if having legal capacity, consent to the proposed variation themselves.

Whether the drafting of paragraph (b) accurately captures this distinction between two types of unascertained beneficiary is debateable. The distinction is made to turn on whether the *only* reason why the beneficiary was not ascertained was that the contingency which the beneficiary had to satisfy had not occurred. In the case of the trust 'for X and any husband X may marry', the court can consent on behalf of X's putative husband because not only has he not married X at the date of the application to vary (the contingency expressed in the trust deed) but also because he may not even be alive at that time. It is in this sense that he is an unascertained beneficiary 'nowhere to be seen'.

(c) an unborn beneficiary. Suppose that a discretionary trust has been created 'for A and B, their children and grandchildren.' At the time of the application to vary the trust, A and B have two children and no grandchildren. Paragraph (c) authorises the court to consent on behalf of unborn children and grandchildren, even if they would not otherwise come within paragraph (b).[43]

(d) an object of a discretionary trust created as part of a protective trust arrangement. A simple example of a protective trust is a trust 'for A until A becomes bankrupt when the trust income shall be payable to such of A, B, C and D as the trustees shall consider fit.'[44]

The meaning of 'benefit'

[24.24] In all cases except applications under s 63A(1)(d) (discretionary interests under protective trusts), the court must be satisfied that the proposed arrangement is for the benefit of the person on whose behalf the court's approval is sought (or, in Western Australia, that it is not

43 *WE Pickering Nominees Pty Ltd v Pickering* [2016] VSCA 273.

44 See [15.27].

detrimental to the beneficiary).[45] Benefits, for this purpose, can be financial or non-financial. It is well established in the authorities that a court can approve a proposed variation on the ground that it confers a tax benefit on the beneficiary. In *Thomas Hare Investments Ltd v Hare*,[46] where approval was given to a variation which deferred liability to capital gains tax, it was stated:

> Is this court to hesitate to exercise the power by reason of the fact that one of the incidents of the exercise of the power will be a reduction in the amount of tax which would otherwise be payable to the Crown … It seems to me that it would be absolutely wrong that this court, if it has power to resettle these funds, should be deterred from exercising that power on some ground of public policy of this kind. The proposed variation will preserve for the benefit of the beneficiaries some of the funds which would otherwise be paid away in tax; and I cannot see that the express power given to the court … ought to be abandoned for that consideration.[47]

Non-financial considerations can also constitute a 'benefit' justifying judicial approval of an arrangement. In *Re Remnant's Settlement Trusts*,[48] a testator created a trust for the children of his two daughters, stipulating that any child who, on the death of the mother, should be 'practising Roman Catholicism' (defined to include being married to a Roman Catholic) should forfeit any interest under the trust. One of the daughters had become a Roman Catholic, and it was likely that her children would forfeit their interests. Assuming that the forfeiture clause was valid, this would result in a financial gain to the children of the Protestant daughter. Both daughters wanted to prevent the forfeiture, and they applied for a variation of the trust which would have deleted the forfeiture clause. The principal issue was whether the deletion of the forfeiture clause conferred a benefit on the Protestant children. Pennycuick J, approving the variation, took into account two non-financial considerations. First, the forfeiture clause operated as a deterrent to the Protestant children in the selection of spouses. Secondly, the clause represented a possible source of family dissension. [24.25]

Re Remnant's Settlement Trusts has been criticised on the ground that the decision: [24.26]

> extend[s] the notion of benefit much further than can fairly be justified. However much one may despise a forfeiture provision based on a form of religious discrimination, it is going an exceedingly long way to conclude that the elimination of such a provision is for the 'benefit' of one who stands to gain substantial property if it is permitted to operate according to its terms. It has not hitherto been regarded as a function of equity to require its wards to surrender their tangible prospects of advancement in this world in return for the hope of the less tangible rewards of the next.[49]

As *Re Remnant's Settlement Trusts* illustrates, a court must sometimes assess whether an unquantifiable non-financial benefit outweighs a quantifiable financial benefit in assessing

45 WA s 90(2). In Queensland, the 'benefit' requirement does not apply to trusts for unascertained persons whose entitlement is dependent on a future event which the court is satisfied is unlikely to occur: s 95(1A)(a).

46 (2012) 34 VR 656.

47 Ibid [35], citing *Thomson v Thomson & Whitmee* (1954) P 384, 393–4.

48 [1970] 1 Ch 560.

49 *Re Christmas' Settlement Trusts* [1986] 1 Qd R 372, 376–7 (McPherson J). See also *George v Kollias* [2007] VSC 46, [45].

whether a proposed variation is overall beneficial to the beneficiary on whose behalf the court is acting. The evaluation process is inevitably imprecise and can be controversial. In *Re Weston's Settlement*,[50] an application by the settlor to move a family trust from England to the tax haven of the island of Jersey was rejected by the Court of Appeal on the ground that the variation would not constitute a 'benefit' to the settlor's children. Lord Denning considered that the tax advantages of the proposal were outweighed by the disruption to the children's upbringing that the shift in the trust's location would cause:

> I do not believe it is for the benefit of children to be uprooted from England and transported to another country simply to avoid tax … Children are like trees: they grow stronger with firm roots.[51]

Variation or resettlement?

[24.27] There is no provision in s 63A, or in equivalent provisions in other States, requiring the court to take into account the settlor's wishes, if ascertainable, in deciding whether to approve a variation. The opposition of the settlor is not a reason for withholding approval.[52] Nevertheless, courts have drawn a distinction between a variation of a trust and the resettlement of trust property in considering applications. While a variation of a trust is permissible, a proposed resettlement of trust property which alters the basis on which the settlor established the trust will not be approved. It has been said that there is a line to be drawn 'between what is a variation and what, on the other hand, is a completely new settlement'.[53] A proposed variation which alters the beneficial interests under the trust may well be rejected on the ground that is a resettlement. Similarly, a trust of a damages award established for children cannot be varied by postponing the date of payment beyond the age of majority because such a variation, if approved, removes the rationale for creating the trust; namely, to utilise the damages award to meet health and educational costs incurred in childhood.[54]

Section 59C of the *Trustee Act 1936* (SA)

[24.28] The South Australian variation of trusts provision set out in s 59C of the *Trustee Act 1936* differs from the versions enacted in other States in several important respects. First, it is a general provision authorising the court to approve applications to vary or revoke trusts. The court's function is not limited to approving a variation on behalf of beneficiaries who cannot consent on their own behalf. The court must consider the proposed variation in its entirety, having regard to 'the spirit of the trust'.[55] Secondly, the court must be satisfied 'that the application is not substantially motivated by a desire to avoid or reduce the incidence of tax'. Many successful applications brought in England and in the Australian *Variation of Trusts Act* jurisdictions, which were primarily intended to minimise tax liability, would have failed if they had been brought under s 59C.

50 [1969] 1 Ch 234.
51 Ibid 245.
52 *Goulding v James* [1997] 2 All ER 239. Cf *Re Remnant's Settlement Trusts* [1970] Ch 560.
53 *Re Holt's Settlement* [1969] 1 Ch 100, 118 (Megarry J).
54 *Allen v Distillers Co (Biochemicals) Ltd* [1974] QB 384. The proposed arrangement was nonetheless approved in the exercise of the court's inherent jurisdiction to approve compromises.
55 *Trustee Act 1936* (SA) s 59C(3)(d). See *Sourcebook* 24.4c, p 658 for complete extract.

The s 59C jurisdiction has attracted trusts to South Australia despite the absence of a statutory power to approve tax-driven variations. In *Clarke v Ebdon*,[56] for example, an application to vary the trust deed of the Fairfax Foundation, which publishes Fairfax newspapers, was approved under this provision. One of the variations accepted by the Court was to change the governing law of the trust from New South Wales to South Australia. A benefit to the trust accruing from this change was that the trust did not have to comply with the rule against perpetuities because South Australia has abolished the rule.[57] [24.29]

Critique

The discussion of trust variation in the preceding paragraphs serves to emphasise the diversity of State and Territory legislation on the topic. At one extreme, New South Wales has, despite judicial pleas, not enacted legislation empowering the court to vary a trust. Other statutory jurisdictions, such as the 'expediency' jurisdiction, are too limited in scope to remedy the deficiency. At the other extreme, South Australia has enacted wide-ranging variation legislation, providing an incentive to trusts elsewhere in Australia to relocate the law of the trust to that State.[58] Legislation and case law have also taken different approaches to approving variations which have tax minimisation as their primary motivation. [24.30]

States and Territories have adopted uniform laws on trustee investment.[59] One advantage of uniformity is that it discourages 'forum shopping', which in this context means relocating the trust to the jurisdiction which will most readily approve variations in the trust instrument designed to meet the changing financial and social circumstances of the beneficiaries. But a uniform trust variation law will only be enacted if agreement can be reached on questions such as the desirability of empowering judges to authorise variations which minimise a trust's liability to tax, or which allow the rule against perpetuities to be abrogated. These are not dry, doctrinal questions; they raise fundamental considerations relating to the distribution of wealth in Australian society. But in the absence of agreement trustees are likely to continue engaging in 'forum shopping' by applying for a variation in the jurisdiction which is considered to be most receptive to their application. [24.31]

WHAT'S ONLINE?

Available at www.cambridge.org/highereducation/isbn/9781009232388/resources:

- Recommended further readings
- Discussion topics
- Practice problem

56 [2020] SASC 67.

57 Ibid [88]–[90]. At [115] it was noted that there was no jurisdictional requirement that there be any connection between the trust and South Australia although the Court has a discretion to decline to entertain an application if the connection with South Australia is too tenuous. In the event, the Court identified at [116] a substantial connection.

58 In addition to *Clarke v Ebdon* [2020] SASC 67, discussed at [24.29], see also *Sakeld v Sakeld (No 2)* [2000] SASC 296; *Retail Employees Superannuation Pty Ltd v Pain* [2016] SASC 121. Foreign trusts can be varied under variation of trusts legislation provided that the domestic court's jurisdiction requirements are satisfied: *Re Paget's Settlement* [1965] 1 WLR 1046.

59 See chapter 18.

INDEX